Study Guide

to accompany

Economics: Principles and Policy

Twelfth Edition

William J. Baumol
New York University and Princeton University

Alan S. Blinder
Princeton University

Prepared by

Kenneth Slaysman
York College of Pennsylvania

Australia • Brazil • Mexico • Singapore • United Kingdom • United States

ISBN-13: 978-1-111-96992-9
ISBN-10: 1-111-96992-2

Cengage
20 Channel Center Street
Boston, MA 02210
USA

Cengage is a leading provider of customized learning solutions with office locations around the globe, including Singapore, the United Kingdom, Australia, Mexico, Brazil, and Japan. Locate your local office at: **international.cengage.com/region**.

Cengage products are represented in Canada by Nelson Education, Ltd.

To learn more about Cengage platforms and services, register or access your online learning solution, or purchase materials for your course, visit **www.cengage.com**.

Printed at CLDPC, USA, 11-18

TABLE OF CONTENTS

PREFACE

INTRODUCTION

This study guide is designed to be used with *Economics: Principles and Policy*, Twelfth Edition, by William J. Baumol and Alan S. Blinder. This guide is not a substitute for the basic textbook; rather, experience has shown that conscientious use of a supplement such as this guide can lead to greater learning and understanding of the course material. It might also improve your grade.

The chapters in this book parallel those in *Economics: Principles and Policy*, Twelfth Edition. Each chapter in the study guide is a review of the material covered in the textbook chapters. You should first read and study each chapter in the textbook and then use the corresponding chapter in this book. "Use" is the correct verb, as chapters in this book are designed for your active participation.

The material with which you will be working is organized into the following elements.

LEARNING OBJECTIVES

Each chapter starts with a set of behavioral learning objectives. These objectives indicate the things you should be able to do upon completing each chapter.

IMPORTANT TERMS AND CONCEPTS

As one of the learning objectives for each chapter states, you should be able to define, understand, and use correctly the terms and concepts that are listed in this section. They parallel the important terms and concepts listed at the end of the text chapter. Being able to define these terms is likely to be important for your grade. But to really understand what they mean, rather than to temporarily memorize their definition, is even better. The ultimate test of your understanding will be your ability to use correctly the terms and concepts in real life situations.

CHAPTER REVIEW

Each chapter review is a summary discussion of the major points for that chapter. The reviews are designed to be used actively. Frequently, you will need to supply the appropriate missing term or to choose between pairs of alternate words. Some of the missing terms are quite specific and can be found in the list of important terms and concepts. At other times, the answers are less clear-cut, as the following hypothetical example illustrates: "If people expect inflation at higher rates than before, nominal interest rates are likely to _____." Any of the following would be correct answers: increase, rise, go up. In cases like this, do not get concerned if the answer you choose is different from the one in the back of the book.

IMPORTANT TERMS AND CONCEPTS QUIZ

Each chapter contains a quiz to help you review important terms and concepts. Match each term with the most appropriate definition.

BASIC EXERCISES

Most chapters have one or more exercises that are designed for you to use as a check on your understanding of a basic principle discussed in the chapter. Many of the exercises use simple arithmetic or geometry. While getting the correct answers is one measure of understanding, do not mistake the arithmetic manipulations for the economic content of the problems. A hand calculator or spreadsheet program may make the arithmetic less burdensome.

SELF-TEST FOR UNDERSTANDING

Each chapter has a set of multiple choice and true-false questions for you to use as a further check on your understanding. It is important to know not only the correct answers but also why the other alternatives are wrong. Answers for the Self-Tests are in the back of this guide.

APPENDIX

A number of chapters in the text contain an appendix, which generally is designed to supplement the chapter content with material that is either a bit more difficult or offers further exposition of a particular economic concept. In some cases, the review material for the appendix parallels that for the chapter, including learning objectives, important terms and concepts, and so forth. On other cases, the appendix material is reviewed here in the form of an additional exercise designed to illustrate the material discussed in the appendix.

SUPPLEMENTARY EXERCISE

Many chapters end with a supplementary exercise, which may be either an additional mathematical exercise or some suggestions that allow you to use what you have learned in real-world situations. Some exercises use more advanced mathematics. Since many of these exercises review Basic Exercise material, they illustrate how economists use mathematics and are included for students with an appropriate background in mathematics. The mathematics are a means to an end and not an end in themselves. It is most important to understand the economic principles that underlie the Basic Exercise, something that does not depend upon advanced mathematics.

ECONOMICS IN ACTION

Most chapters include a brief example, often from recent newspapers or magazines. Each example has been chosen to show how economic concepts and ideas can help one understand real world problems and issues.

ECONOMICS ONLINE

Many chapters include one or more World Wide Web addresses that you can use to access current information or for additional information.

There is also a homepage for the textbook:

http://www.cengage.com/economics/baumol

STUDY QUESTIONS

Each chapter ends with a short list of study questions. Working with friends on these questions is a useful way to review chapter material and should help on examinations.

Being introduced to economics for the first time should be exciting and fun. For many, it is likely to be hard work, but hard work does not have to be dull and uninteresting. Do not look for a pat set of answers with universal applicability. Economics does not offer answers but rather a way of looking at the world and thinking systematically about issues. As the English economist John Maynard Keynes said:

> The theory of economics does not furnish a body of settled conclusions immediately applicable to policy. It is a method rather than a doctrine, an apparatus of the mind, a technique of thinking, which helps its possessor to draw correct conclusions.

What Is Economics?

Important Terms and Concepts

Opportunity cost

Theory

Economic model

Abstraction

Correlation

Learning Objectives

After completing this chapter, you should be able to:

- describe each of the ten *Ideas for Beyond the Final Exam.*

- explain the role of abstraction, or simplification, in economic theory.

- explain the role of theory as a guide to understanding real-world phenomena.

- explain why correlation need not imply causation.

- understand what is meant by an economic model.

- explain why imperfect information and value judgments will always mean that economics cannot provide definitive answers to all social problems.

CHAPTER REVIEW

Chapter 1 has two objectives: It introduces the types of problems that concern economists, offering a set of important *Ideas for Beyond the Final Exam,* and it discusses the methods of economic analysis, in particular the role of theory in economics.

Problems discussed in the first part of the chapter have been chosen to illustrate basic economic issues to be remembered beyond the final exam. You should not only read this material now, but also reexamine the list at the end of the course. Understanding the economic principles that underlie these basic issues is the real final examination in economics.

The methods of economic inquiry are best described as "eclectic," meaning they are drawn from many sources according to their usefulness to the subject matter. Economists borrow from other social sciences to theorize about human behavior: They borrow from mathematics to express theories concisely and from statistics to make inferences from real-world data about hypotheses suggested by economic theory.

Economists are interested in understanding human behavior not only for its own sake, but also for the policy implications of this knowledge. How can we know what to expect from changes resulting from public policy or business decisions unless we understand how markets work and why people behave the way they do? Consider the ideas discussed in the first part of this chapter. Each derives from economic theory. As you will learn, each idea also offers insight into actual experience and is an important guide to evaluating future changes.

As in other scientific disciplines, theory in economics is an abstraction, or simplification, of innumerable complex relationships in the real world. When thinking about some aspects of behavior, for example, a family's spending decisions or why the price of oil fluctuates so much, economists will develop a model that attempts to explain the behavior under examination. Elements of the model derive from economic theory. Economists study the model to see what hypotheses, or predictions, it suggests. These can then be checked against real-world data. An economist's model will typically be built not with hammer and nails, but with pencil, paper, and computers. The appropriate degree of abstraction for an economic model is determined, to a large extent, by the problem at hand and is not something that can be specified in advance for all problems.

Economists believe they can make an important contribution to resolving many important social issues. It is hoped that by the time you finish this course, you will agree with this belief. At the same time, you should realize that economics offers a way of posing and looking at questions rather than a comprehensive set of predetermined answers to all questions. Economists will always have differences of opinion on final policy recommen-
(1) dations because of incomplete _____ and different _____ judgments.

IMPORTANT TERMS AND CONCEPTS QUIZ

Choose the best definition for each of the following terms.

1. _____ Opportunity cost
2. _____ Abstraction
3. _____ Theory
4. _____ Correlation
5. _____ Economic model

a. Ignoring many details to focus on essential parts of a problem
b. Two variables change simultaneously, whether or not a causal relationship exists
c. Effects on third parties that are not part of an economic transaction
d. Deliberate simplification of relationships to explain how those relationships work
e. Value of the next best alternative
f. Simplified version of some aspect of the economy

BASIC EXERCISES

Each statement or vignette below illustrates one of the 10 important Ideas for Beyond the Final Exam. Which statement goes with which idea?

_____ 1. Opportunity cost is the correct measure of cost.

_____ 2. Attempts to fight market forces often backfire or have unintended consequences.

_____ 3. Nations can gain from trade by exploiting their comparative advantage.

_____ 4. Both parties gain in a voluntary exchange.

_____ 5. Good decisions typically require marginal analysis.

_____ 6. The adverse impact of externalities can often be repaired by market methods.

_____ 7. There is a trade-off between efficiency and equality. Many policies that promote one damage the other.

_____ 8. The government's tools to even out booms and busts are imperfect.

_____ 9. In the short run, policy makers face a trade-off between inflation and unemployment.

_____ 10. In the long run, productivity is almost the only thing that matters for a society's material well-being.

A. In June 2008, Northwest Airlines offered a last-minute roundtrip cybersaver fare between Los Angeles and New York City for $274. This fare required travelers to fly on Saturday and return the following Monday or Tuesday. At the same time, a regular unrestricted fare was more than $1,422, and the ten-day, advance purchase Saturday stay-over fare was around $315. Economists would argue that, properly counted, Northwest was more than covering costs on the $274 passengers.

3

B. "We trade because we can get more of the goods and services we value by devoting our energies to what we can do well and using the proceeds to purchase what others are good at making (or doing)." I.M. Destler, "Trade Policy at a Crossroads," *Brookings Review,* Winter 1999.

C. In New York, individuals who need a passport at the last minute have to pay a $35 fee for rush service and often spend most of a day waiting in line. Others pay up to $150 extra for someone else to stand in line for them. "If six hours of your time is worth more than $150, you're going to be prepared to use one of these services," said George Brokaw, a New York investment banker. "Speeding Up a Passport," *The New York Times,* June 6, 1999.

D. Commenting on the economy in July 1998, Alan Greenspan, Chairman of the Board of Governors of the Federal Reserve System, said, ". . . the extent to which strong growth and high labor force utilization have been joined with low inflation over an extended period is . . . exceptional . . . With labor markets very tight and domestic final demand retaining considerable momentum, the risks of a pickup in inflation remain significant . . . [T]he impending constraint from domestic labor markets could bind more abruptly than it has to date, intensifying inflation pressures." Testimony of Alan Greenspan, Chairman of the Federal Reserve Board of Governors Before the Committee on Banking, Housing, and Urban Affairs, U.S. Senate, July 21, 1998.

E. Third–graders Jennifer and Jolene trade sandwiches at lunch because each prefers what the other's mother fixed.

F. Robert Arnold and Robert Dennis argue that the impact of the growth in labor productivity since the beginning of this century has been astounding. Not only has output per worker increased more than sevenfold, but "the typical workday and typical workweek shrank . . . the share of family income required to meet the bare necessities was cut in half . . . and goods that were once considered luxuries came within reach of the middle class." "Perspectives on productivity growth," *Business Economics,* April 1, 1999.

G. A study of 16 American cities found that advertised rents for vacant units were higher in cities with rent control than cities without rent control. In cities without rent control, advertised rents are distributed almost evenly above and below median rents as measured by the U.S. Bureau of the Census. In cities with rent control, "most available units are priced well above the median. In other words, inhabitants in cities without rent control have a far easier time finding moderately priced rental units than do inhabitants in rent-controlled cities." William Tucker, "Rent control drives out affordable housing," *USA Today* (Magazine), July 1998.

H. "There is great comprehension today that ambitious redistribution policies will reduce either economic efficiency or economic growth, or both, because of undesired behavioral adjustment of work, savings, investment, and entrepreneurship." Assar Lindbeck, "How Can Economic Policy Strike a Balance Between Economic Efficiency and Income Equality," in *Income Inequality: Issues and Policy Options,* a symposium sponsored by the Federal Reserve Bank of Kansas City, August 27–28, 1998.

I. Under the EPA's Acid Rain Program, fossil fuel–fired power plants are allotted SO_2 (sulphur dioxide) emission allowances that allow them to emit one ton of SO_2. Utilities with surplus allowances may sell them to utilities whose emissions levels exceed their allowances.

J. "If we knew precisely where we were, understood precisely the relationship between our instruments and macroeconomic performance, had a single objective, and could instantly affect the variable or variables associated with our target(s), implementing [monetary] policy would be easy... It is precisely

4

because none of these preconditions hold that monetary policy is so difficult and principles are needed to guide its implementation." Remarks by former Federal Reserve Governor Laurence H. Meyer. The Alan R. Holmes Lecture, Middlebury College, Middlebury, Vermont, March 16, 1998.

SELF-TESTS FOR UNDERSTANDING

TEST A

Circle the most appropriate answer.

1. Economists define opportunity cost as
   a. the money price of goods and services.
   b. the lowest price you can bargain for.
   c. the value of the next best alternative.
   d. retail prices including sales taxes.

2. Most economists believe that attempts to set prices by decree
   a. will work best in the long run.
   b. are likely to create significant new problems.
   c. are the only way to establish fair prices.
   d. have a history of practical effectiveness.

3. With respect to international trade,
   a. a country can gain only if its neighbors lose.
   b. countries should try to be self-sufficient of all goods.
   c. only those countries with the highest productivity levels will gain.
   d. a country can gain by producing those goods in which it has a comparative advantage and then trading for those things in which other countries have a comparative advantage.

4. Most economists believe that exchange
   a. is likely to be mutually advantageous to both parties when it is voluntary.
   b. only takes place when one side can extract a profit from the other.
   c. usually makes both parties worse off.
   d. is best when strictly regulated by the government.

5. Marginal analysis is concerned with the study of
   a. buying stocks and bonds on credit.
   b. those groups that operate on the fringes of the market economy.
   c. changes, such as the increase in cost when output increases.
   d. an engineer's fudge factor for possible errors.

6. When the actions of some economic agents impose cost on others, for example, the polluting smoke of a factory or power plant,
   a. market mechanisms may exist that can help remedy the situation.
   b. the only answer is government regulation.
   c. there is very little one can do; such is the price of progress.
   d. it is always best to close down the offending action.

7. Economic analysis suggests that
    a. policies that promote the highest rate of economic growth unambiguously improve the distribution of income.
    b. policies to increase equality may reduce output.
    c. incentives for work and savings have almost no impact on people's behavior.
    d. there is no trade-off between the size of the economic pie and how the pie is divided.

8. Monetary and fiscal policy
    a. can eliminate booms and busts if used appropriately.
    b. have no power to influence the economy.
    c. are too complicated to be of practical use.
    d. are powerful but imperfect tools to limit the swings of the business cycle.

9. Most economists believe that policies to reduce inflation
    a. have never been successful.
    b. will never be adopted in democracies.
    c. normally require a higher rate of unemployment.
    d. have an immediate and lasting impact.

10. Small differences in the productivity growth rate
    a. make little difference, even over periods as long as a century.
    b. can compound into significant differences.
    c. can be safely ignored by citizens and politicians.
    d. will lead only to small differences in the standard of living between countries.

TEST B

Circle T or F for true or false.

T   F   1. Economic models are no good unless they include all of the details that characterize the real world.

T   F   2. Material in this text will reveal the true answer to many important social problems.

T   F   3. Economic theory deliberately simplifies relationships to concentrate on their essential casual elements.

T   F   4. Economists' policy prescriptions differ because of incomplete information and different value judgments.

T   F   5. Theory and practical policy have nothing to do with each other.

T   F   6. If two variables are correlated, we can be certain that one causes the other.

T   F   7. The best economic models all use the same degree of abstraction.

T   F   8. An economist tests a hypothesis when she deliberately simplifies the nature of relationships in order to explain cause and effect.

T   F   9. The dollars one must pay is the best measure of the cost of any decision.

T   F 10. We would all be better off if the government regulated more markets.

T   F 11. The most productive economies would be better off if they did not trade with other nations and tried to produce everything they need by themselves.

T F 12. In any transaction, one party must always gain at the expense of the other.

T F 13. No business should ever sell its output at a price that does not cover its full cost.

T F 14. Because pollution problems are often seen as a market shortcoming, market methods cannot help correct the problem.

T F 15. There is no trade-off between policies that increase output and those that equalize income.

T F 16. The government has all the tools it needs to keep the economy out of recessions.

T F 17. Policies to lower unemployment usually reduce the rate of inflation at the same time.

T F 18. Over the long run, it makes little difference whether productivity grows at 1 percent or 2 percent per year.

| APPENDIX | *Using Graphs*

Important Terms and Concepts

Variable	Slope of a straight (or curved) line	*Y*-intercept	45-degree line
Origin (of a graph)		Ray through the origin, or ray	Production indifference map
	Tangent to a curve		

Learning Objectives

After completing this chapter, you should be able to:

- interpret various graphs.

- use a two-variable graph to determine what combinations of variables go together.

- compute the slope of a straight line and explain what it measures.

- explain how to compute the slope of a curved line.

- explain how a 45-degree line can divide a graph into two regions, one in which the *Y* variable exceeds the *X* variable, and another in which the *X* variable exceeds the *Y* variable.

- construct two-variable and three-variable graphs.

- use a three-variable graph to determine what combinations of the *X* and *Y* variables are consistent with the same value for the *Z* variable.

APPENDIX REVIEW

Economists like to draw pictures, primarily *graphs*. Your textbook and this study guide will make extensive use of graphs. There is nothing very difficult about graphs, but understanding them from the beginning will help you avoid mistakes later on.

All the graphs we will use start with two straight lines, one on the bottom and one on the left side. These edges of the graph will usually have labels to indicate what is being measured in both the vertical and

(1) horizontal directions. The line on the bottom is called the [horizontal/vertical] axis, and the line running up the side is called the _____ axis. The point at which the two lines meet is called the _____. The variable measured along the horizontal axis is often called the *X* variable, whereas the term *Y* variable is often used to refer to the variable measured along the vertical axis.

Figure 1-1 is a two-variable diagram plotting expenditures on alcoholic beverages and ministers' salaries. Does this graph imply that wealthier clergymen drink more, or does it suggest that more drinking in general is increasing the demand for, and hence the salaries of, clergymen? Most likely neither interpretation is correct; just because you can plot two variables does not mean that one caused the other.

Many two-variable diagrams encountered in introductory economics use straight lines, primarily for simplicity. An important characteristic of a straight line is its *slope*, measured by comparing differences between

(2) two points. To calculate the slope of a straight line, divide the [horizontal/vertical] change by the corresponding _____ change as you move to the right along the line. The change between any two points can be used to compute the slope because the slope of a straight line is _____. If the straight line shows that both the horizontal and vertical variables increase together, then the line is said to have a [positive/negative] slope; that is, as we move to the right, the line slopes [up/down]. If one variable decreases as the other variable increases, the line is said to have a _____ slope. A line with a zero slope shows _____ change in the *Y* variable as the *X* variable changes.

Figure 1-1

Ministers' Salaries and Expenditures on Alcohol

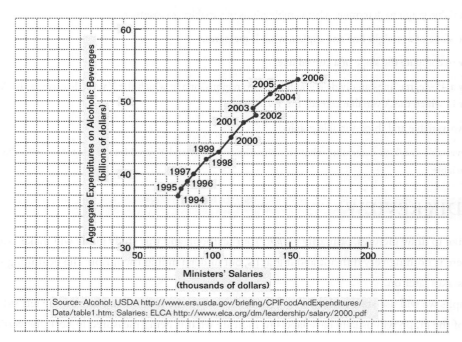

Source: Alcohol: USDA http://www.ers.usda.gov/briefing/CPIFoodAndExpenditures/ Data/table1.htm; Salaries: ELCA http://www.elca.org/dm/leardership/salary/2000.pdf

8

A special type of straight line passes through the origin of a graph. This is called a _____ through the (3) origin. Its slope is measured the same as the slope of any other straight line. A special type of ray is one that connects all points where the vertical and horizontal variables are equal. If the vertical and horizontal variables are measured in the same units, then this line has a slope of +1 and is called the _____ line.

Like straight lines, curved lines also have slopes, but the slope of a curved line is not constant. We measure the slope of a curved line at any point by the slope of the one straight line that just touches, or is _____ to, the line at that point. (4)

A special type of graph is used by economists as well as cartographers. Such a graph can represent three dimensions on a diagram with only two axes by the use of _____ lines. A traditional application (5) of such a graph in economics is a diagram that measures inputs along the horizontal and vertical axes and then uses contour lines to show what different combinations of inputs can be used to produce the same amount of output. This graph is called a _____ _____ map.

IMPORTANT TERMS AND CONCEPTS QUIZ

Choose the best definition for each of the following terms.

1. _____ Variable
2. _____ Origin
3. _____ Slope
4. _____ Tangent to a curve
5. _____ Y-intercept
6. _____ Ray
7. _____ 45-degree line
8. _____ Production indifference map

a. Graph of how a variable changes over time
b. Straight line, touching a curve at a point without cutting the curve
c. Straight line emanating from the origin
d. Object whose magnitude is measured by a number
e. Straight line through the origin with a slope of +1
f. Point at which a straight line cuts the vertical axis
g. Ratio of vertical change to corresponding horizontal change
h. Point where both axes meet and where both variables are zero
i. A graph showing different combinations of two inputs necessary to produce a given level of output

BASIC EXERCISES

READING GRAPHS

These exercises are designed to give you practice working with two-variable diagrams.

1. **UNDERSTANDING A DEMAND CURVE** *Figure 1-2*

   Demand Curve

   The demand curve in **Figure 1-2** represents the demand for new Ph.D. economists.

   a. What quantity would colleges and universities demand if they have to pay a salary of $70,000? _____

   b. What does the graph indicate would happen to the quantity demanded if salaries fall to $50,000? The quantity demanded would [increase/decrease] to _____.

   c. If salaries were $60,000 the quantity demanded would be _____.

   d. What is the slope of the demand curve? _____

   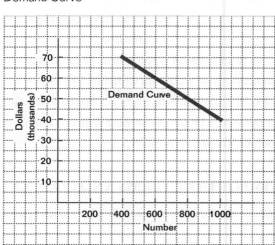

   e. Explain how the slope of the demand curve provides information about the change in the number of new Ph.D. economists demanded as salary changes.

2. **UNDERSTANDING A 45-DEGREE LINE** 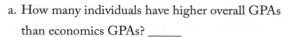 *Figure 1-3*

   45-Degree Line

   Figure 1-3 shows data on grade point averages (GPA) for Valerie and her friends. Overall averages are measured along the horizontal axis while GPAs for courses in economics are measured along the vertical axis. Figure 1-3 also includes a 45-degree line.

   a. How many individuals have higher overall GPAs than economics GPAs? _____

   b. How many individuals do better in economics courses than in their other courses? _____

   c. If all of Valerie's friends had their best grades in economics courses, all of the points in Figure 1-3 would lie [above/below] the 45-degree line.

   d. If all of the points in Figure 1-3 were below the 45-degree line, we could conclude that Valerie and her friends did better in [economics/non-economics] courses.

10

SELF-TESTS FOR UNDERSTANDING

TEST A

Circle the most appropriate answer.

1. The vertical line on the left side of a two-variable diagram is called the
   a. ray through the origin.
   b. vertical axis.
   c. *X* axis.
   d. slope of the graph.

2. A two-variable diagram
   a. can only be drawn when one variable causes another.
   b. is a useful way to show how two variables change simultaneously.
   c. is a useful way of summarizing the influence of all factors that affect the *Y* variable.
   d. can only be used when relationships between variables can be represented by straight lines.

3. The origin of a two-variable graph is
   a. found in the lower right corner of a graph.
   b. the same as the *Y*-intercept.
   c. the intersection of the vertical and horizontal axes where both variables are equal to zero.
   d. found by following the slope to the point where it equals zero.

4. The slope of a straight line is found by dividing the
   a. *Y* variable by the *X* variable.
   b. vertical axis by the horizontal axis.
   c. largest value of the *Y* variable by the smallest value of the *X* variable.
   d. vertical change by the corresponding horizontal change.

5. The slope of a straight line
   a. is the same at all points along the line.
   b. increases moving to the right.
   c. will be zero when the *X* variable equals zero.
   d. is always positive.

6. If a straight line has a positive slope, then we know that
   a. it runs uphill, moving to the right.
   b. the slope of the line will be greater than that of a 45-degree line.
   c. it must also have a positive *Y*-intercept.
   d. it will reach its maximum value when its slope is zero.

11

Figure 1-4

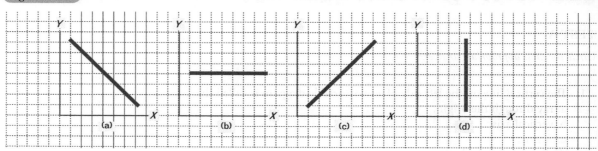

7. Referring to parts (a), (b), (c), and (d) of **Figure 1-4,** determine which line has a(n)

    a. positive slope _____

    b. negative slope _____

    c. zero slope _____

    d. infinite slope _____

Figure 1-5

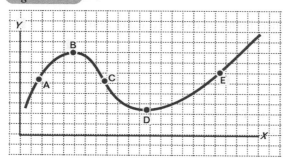

8. Referring to **Figure 1-5,** determine at which point(s) the curved line has a(n)

    a.   positive slope _____ _____ _____

    b.   negative slope _____ _____ _____

    c.   zero slope   _____ _____ _____

    d.   infinite slope _____ _____ _____

9. If when $X = 5$, $Y = 16$ and when $X = 8$, $Y = 10$, then the
    a. line connecting X and Y has a positive slope.
    b. line connecting X and Y is a ray through the origin.
    c. slope of the line connecting X and Y is +6.
    d. slope of the line connecting X and Y is –2.

10. The slope of a curved line is
    a. the same at all points on the line.
    b. found by dividing the Y variable by the X variable.
    c. found by determining the slope of a straight line tangent to the curved line at the point of interest.
    d. always positive.

11. If a curved line is in the shape of a hill, then the point of zero slope will occur at the
    a. origin of the line.
    b. highest point of the line.
    c. Y-intercept of the line.
    d. point where a ray from the origin intercepts the line.

12. The Y-intercept is
    a. the same as the origin of a graph.
    b. the point where a line cuts the Y axis.
    c. usually equal to the X-intercept.
    d. equal to the reciprocal of the slope of a straight line.

13. If the Y-intercept of a straight line is equal to zero, then this line is called
    a. the opportunity cost of a graph.
    b. a ray through the origin.
    c. the 45-degree line.
    d. the X axis.

14. A ray is
    a. any straight line with a slope of +1.
    b. any line, straight or curved, that passes through the origin of a graph.
    c. a straight line with a positive Y-intercept.
    d. a straight line that passes through the origin.

15. If the X and Y variables are measured in the same units, a 45-degree line will
    a. have a positive Y-intercept.
    b. have a negative slope.
    c. show all points where X and Y are equal.
    d. be steeper than the Y axis.

16. If X and Y are measured in the same units, and we consider a point that lies below a 45-degree line, then we know that for the X and Y combination associated with this point,
    a. the X variable is greater than the Y variable.
    b. a line from the origin through this point will be a ray with a slope greater than +1.
    c. the Y variable is greater than the X variable.
    d. the slope of the point is less than 1.

Figure 1-6

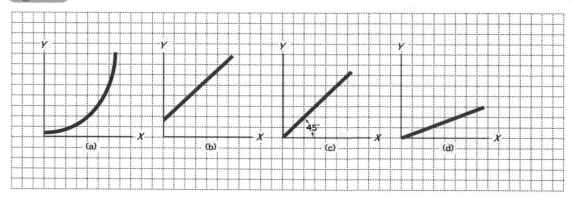

17. Referring to parts (a), (b), (c), and (d) of **Figure 1-6**, which part(s) show a ray through the origin?
    a. (b)
    b. (a) and (c)
    c. (a) and (d)
    d. (c) and (d)

18. If in part (d) of Figure 1-6, the Y variable changes by 2 units when the X variable changes by 5 units, then the slope of the line is
    a. (2/5) = 0.4.
    b. (5/2) = 2.5.
    c. (2 + 5) = 7.
    d. Insufficient information is available to compute.

19. If two straight lines have the same slope, then they
    a. must also have the same Y-intercept.
    b. will show the same change in Y for similar changes in X.
    c. will both pass through the origin.
    d. are said to be complements.

20. A contour map
    a. is always better than a two-variable diagram.
    b. is a way of collapsing three variables into a two-variable diagram.
    c. shows how the Y variable changes when the X variable is held constant.
    d. is only of relevance to cartographers.

TEST B

Circle T or F for true or false.

T F 1. The line along the bottom of a two-variable graph is called the vertical axis.

T F 2. The slope of a line measures the value of the Y variable when the X variable is equal to zero.

T F 3. The slope of a straight line is the same at all points on the line.

14

T   F   4. A negative slope means that the *Y* variable decreases when the *X* variable increases.

T   F   5. The slope of a curved line cannot be measured.

T   F   6. A straight line that has a *Y*-intercept of zero is also called a ray through the origin.

T   F   7. All rays through the origin have the same slope.

T   F   8. If *X* and *Y* are measured in the same units, then a 45-degree line is a ray through the origin with a slope of +1.

T   F   9. If *X* and *Y* are measured in the same units, then any point above a 45-degree line is a point at which the *Y* variable is greater than the *X* variable.

T   F   10. A contour map is a way to show the relationship between two variables in three dimensions.

SUPPLEMENTARY EXERCISE

The following suggested readings offer an excellent introduction to the ideas and lives of economists past and present:

1. *The Worldly Philosophers: The Lives, Times & Ideas of the Great Economic Thinkers,* 7th ed., by Robert L. Heilbroner (Touchstone Books, 1999).

2. *Lives of the Laureates,* 4th edition, edited by William Breit and Barry Hirsch (MIT Press, 2004). This is a collection of recollections by 18 winners of the Nobel Prize in Economics.

ECONOMICS IN ACTION

PLAY BALL

Are baseball players overpaid? Does it make sense to pay someone more than $10 million to play what is, after all, just a game? Does it seem like baseball salaries have gotten out of hand? Even after adjusting for inflation, Babe Ruth's highest salary is estimated to have been slightly more than $700,000. Why are players today paid so much, and does it make economic sense?

Writing in *Scientific American,* Paul Wallich and Elizabeth Corcoran explain the difference in salaries using the concepts of opportunity cost and marginal analysis, ideas used extensively by economists. Under the reserve clause, in effect from 1903 until the mid-1970s, a baseball player who did not like his contract had little choice other than retiring from baseball. Players were not free to bargain with other teams. After the introduction of free agency, baseball players could sell their services to the team with the best offer.

Gerald Scully, in his book *The Business of Major League Baseball,* used statistical techniques to see how hitting and pitching help determine a team's winning percentage and how a team's revenue relates to its record and the size of the market in which it plays. He then estimated how adding a particular player might add to a team's performance and hence its revenue.

Using data from the late 1980s, Scully found that the performance of selected superstars increased team revenues by $2 million to $3 million, numbers consistent with the highest salaries at the time. Using data from the late 1960s, he estimates that superstars increased team revenues by $600,000 to $1 million and noted that the highest salaries were only $100,000 to $125,000.

1. How would marginal analysis help a team determine how much it should offer a free agent?

2. How does the concept of opportunity cost help explain baseball salaries? What was the opportunity cost of a baseball player's time under the reserve clause? How did free agency change the opportunity cost for a player deciding whether to stay with a team or move to a new team?

Sources: Paul Wallich and Elizabeth Corcoran, "The MBAs of Summer," *Scientific American* (June 1992): p. 120. Gerald W. Scully, *The Business of Major League Baseball* (Chicago: University of Chicago Press, 1989).

STUDY QUESTIONS

1. Explain the relationships among theories, models, and hypotheses.

2. Why are theories necessary for understanding the causal links between economic variables? Why can't the facts speak for themselves?

3. Many trace the establishment of economics as a formal field of study to the publication of Adam Smith's *Wealth of Nations* in 1776. Why, after more than 200 years, do so many questions remain?

ECONOMICS ONLINE

Find out about the current and former Nobel Prize winners in Economics at this site maintained by the Nobel Prize committee. There are easy links to the Nobel Prize in Economics from this site:

> http://nobelprize.org

The Minneapolis Federal Reserve Bank regularly publishes interviews with economists in its quarterly publication, *The Region*. The December 1994 interview is with Alan Blinder. You can read these interviews online at:

> http://minneapolisfed.org/pubs/region/int.cfm

The Economy: Myth and Reality

2

Important Terms and Concepts

Factors of production, or Inputs	Gross domestic product (GDP)	Closed economy	Progressive tax
		Recession	Mixed economy
Outputs	Open economy	Transfer payments	

Learning Objectives

After completing this chapter, you should be able to:

- explain the difference between inputs and outputs.

- explain why total output of the American economy is larger than that of other nations.

- explain the difference between a closed and an open economy.

- describe the broad changes in American work experience: Who goes to work outside the home? What sorts of jobs do they hold? What sorts of goods and services do they produce?

- describe who gets what proportion of national income.

- describe the central role of business firms.

- describe the role of government in the American economy.

CHAPTER REVIEW

This chapter offers an introduction to and overview of the American economy. The money value of total output of the American economy is usually measured by something called gross

(1) _____ _____ or _____ for short. American GDP is so large because of the size of the work force and the _____ of American workers. Other countries, for example China and India, have larger populations, but the productivity of their workers does not compare with that of American workers.

Why is the American economy so productive? It is useful to view an economic system as a social mecha-

(2) nism that organizes [inputs/outputs] to produce _____. Many believe that the productivity of the American economy is a reflection of business competition fostered by the extensive use of _____ markets and _____ enterprise.

No economy is self-sufficient. All economies trade with each other, although their reliance on trade varies. The average of exports and imports as a percentage of GDP is often used as a measure of the degree to which

(3) an economy can be called _____ or _____. Compared to other industrialized countries, the United States would look like a(n) [closed/open] economy. Both exports and imports have increased substantially since World War II and are now about 14 percent of American GDP.

The term *real GDP* is used to refer to measures of GDP that have been corrected for inflation. Although the time series graph of real GDP for the United States shows significant growth since World War II, it has not been continual growth. There have been periods when total output declined. These periods are called

(4) _____. How the government should respond during or in anticipation of a period of recession continues to spark controversy.

(5) Organizing inputs, also called _____ of production, is a central issue that any economy must address. For the most part, output in the United States is produced by private firms that compete in free markets. Most economists believe that having to meet the competition is an important reason why the American economy is so productive. Inputs include labor, capital (e.g., machinery and buildings), and natural resources. It is the revenue from selling output that creates income for these factors of production.

In the United States, the largest share of income accrues to which factor of production?

(6) _____. The income earned by those who put up the money to buy buildings and machinery comes in the form of interest and profits. Profits account for about _____ cents of each sales dollar. Most Americans work in [manufacturing/service] industries.

The discussion in the text lists five roles for government:

1) To enforce the rules of business and society, including property rights

2) To regulate business

3) To provide certain goods and services, e.g., national defense

18

4) To raise taxes to finance its operations

5) To redistribute income.

The size of government in the United States relative to GDP is [small/large] compared to most other (7) industrialized countries. This comparison and any others listed do not say whether particular actions are best done by the government or by the private economy. Are there legitimate unmet needs that should be addressed by government, or is government already too big? Much of the material in subsequent chapters is designed to help you understand what markets do well and what they do poorly. It is hoped that a better understanding of the insights from economic analysis will help you decide where you would draw the line between markets and government.

IMPORTANT TERMS AND CONCEPTS QUIZ

Choose the best definition for each of the following terms.

1. _____ Factors of production or Inputs

2. _____ Outputs

3. _____ Gross domestic product (GDP)

4. _____ Open economy

5. _____ Closed economy

6. _____ Recession

7. _____ Transfer payments

8. _____ Progressive tax

9. _____ Mixed economy

a. Money value of final goods and services produced in a year

b. Economy with public influence over the workings of free markets

c. A sustained increase in the average level of prices

d. Money that individuals receive from the government as grants

e. Economy in which exports and imports are small relative to GDP

f. International trade is a large proportion of GDP

g. A period when real GDP declines

h. Labor, machinery, buildings, and natural resources used in production

i. Goods and services desired by consumers

j. The proportion of income paid as taxes increase as income increases

BASIC EXERCISES

THE MORE THINGS CHANGE, THE MORE THEY ARE THE SAME—OR NOT?

Chapter 2 is a quick introduction to the structure of the American economy. These questions ask you to consider how some things may have changed since 1960.

1. What do Americans buy? Complete the missing columns in **Table 2-1** to see how consumption spending has changed. Do these changes surprise you? What do you think explains them? You can find more detail about consumption spending at http://www.bea.doc.gov/National/Index.htm.

Table 2-1

Composition of Consumption Spending

	1960 Spending ($ billions)	Proportion	2010 Spending ($ billions)	Proportion
Durables[a]	45.6	_____	1,089.4	_____
Non-Durables[b]	131.4	_____	2,336.3	_____
Services[c]	154.8	_____	6,923.4	_____
Total	331.8		10,349.1	

[a] e.g., automobiles, furniture
[b] e.g., food, clothing, gasoline
[c] e.g., housing, medical care, entertainment, education

2. How has the spending of the federal government changed? Complete the missing columns in **Table 2-2** to see. Do these changes surprise you? What do you think explains them?

Table 2-2

Composition of Federal Government Spending

	1960[a] Spending ($ billions)	Proportion	2010[a] Spending ($ billions)	Proportion
National Defense	42.9	_____	668.0	_____
Health	2.5	_____	884.4	_____
Income Security	21.7	_____	1,168.6	_____
Interest	8.4	_____	254.0	_____
All Other	11.3	_____	482.5	_____
Total	86.8		3,457.5	

[a] Fiscal Year

3. Who is going to work outside the home now? The labor force participation rate is an important measure of labor markets. It is computed by looking at the number of people working or looking for work as a proportion of total population. This measure excludes those who are retired and those who are not looking for paid work. **Figure 2-1** shows labor force participation by men and women of various ages in 1950. Complete the missing column in **Table 2-3** to compute labor force participation rates for 2010 and then plot your results in Figure 2-1 to see how labor force participation has changed since 1950. Are you surprised by the differences for men and women? Do the changes over time surprise you? What do you think explains these differences?

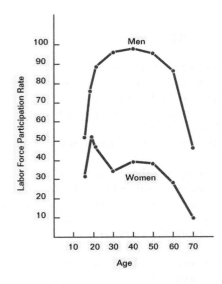

Figure 2-1

Labor Force Participation Rate: 1950 and 2007

Table 2-3

Labor Force Participation: 2010

Age	Men Labor Force[a] (Numbers in thousands)	Men Population (Numbers in thousands)	Men Participation Rate[b]	Women Labor Force[a] (Numbers in thousands)	Women Population (Numbers in thousands)	Women Participation Rate[b]
16–17	4,990	4,540	_____	1,011	4,403	_____
18–19	2,002	4,038	_____	1,904	3,919	_____
20–24	7,864	10,550	_____	7,164	10,497	_____
25–34	18,352	20,465	_____	15,263	20,438	_____
35–44	18,199	19,807	_____	15,247	20,283	_____
45–54	18,856	21,713	_____	17,104	22,284	_____
55–64	12,103	17,291	_____	11,194	18,594	_____
65 & over	3,701	16,769	_____	3,017	21,937	_____

[a]Labor Force = people working plus those looking for work
[b]Labor Force Participation Rate = Labor Force/Population

Source: Bureau of Labor Statistics, *Current Population Survey,* April 2011, http://www.bls.gov/data

21

SELF-TESTS FOR UNDERSTANDING

TEST A

Circle the most appropriate answer.

1. Which of the following helps to explain why the output of the American economy is as high as it is? (There may be more than one correct answer to this question.)
   a. The size of the labor force
   b. The amount of money provided by the government
   c. Business regulation
   d. The productivity of American workers

2. Total output of the U.S. economy
   a. is slightly less than that of Japan.
   b. is comparable to that of other industrialized countries.
   c. exceeds that of other national economies.
   d. is among the lowest for industrialized countries.

3. Many economists believe that the success of the American economy reflects, in part, our reliance on (There may be more than one correct answer.)
   a. regulation.
   b. private enterprise.
   c. free markets.
   d. nationalization.

4. Gross domestic product measures
   a. consumer spending.
   b. the vulgarity of many consumer goods.
   c. unpaid economic activity that takes place inside households.
   d. the money value of all the goods and services produced in an economy in a year.

5. American reliance on foreign trade—exports and imports—is _____ most other industrialized countries.
   a. less than
   b. about the same as
   c. greater than

6. Since 1950, the proportion of women employed in the market place has
   a. declined.
   b. shown little change.
   c. increased considerably.

7. Since the mid-1970s, the proportion of the labor force accounted for by teenagers has
   a. declined.
   b. stayed about the same.
   c. increased.

22

8. Compared to high school graduates, college graduates earn about
   a. the same.
   b. 25 percent more.
   c. 50 percent more.
   d. 67 percent more.

9. The term *recession* refers to
   a. a period of inflation.
   b. a period of above-average economic growth.
   c. reductions in government spending designed to reduce the deficit.
   d. a period when real GDP declines.

10. When referring to inputs, the term *capital* refers to
    a. money business firms need to borrow.
    b. the importance of a firm's head office.
    c. machines and buildings used to produce output.
    d. all of a firm's factors of production.

11. Which of the following would not be classified as an input?
    a. A farmer's time to grow wheat
    b. The farmer's tractor
    c. The farmer's land
    d. The bread that is made from the wheat

12. The majority of American workers work for
    a. manufacturing companies.
    b. the federal government.
    c. state and local governments.
    d. firms that produce a variety of services, including retail and wholesale trade.

13. When businesses pay for factors of production, which of the following gets the largest share of income?
    a. Profits
    b. Labor
    c. Interest
    d. The government (taxes)

14. In the United States there are about
    a. 250,000 business firms or one for every 1,200 people.
    b. 1.5 million business firms or one for every 200 people.
    c. 5 million business firms or one for every 60 people.
    d. 27.5 million business firms or one for every 11 people.

15. When Americans buy goods produced abroad, _____ increase.
    a. exports
    b. taxes
    c. transfer payments
    d. imports

16. When Americans are able to sell goods to foreigners, this adds to
    a. exports.
    b. taxes.
    c. transfer payments.
    d. imports.

17. Consumer spending accounts for _____ of American GDP.
    a. about 33 percent
    b. about 50 percent
    c. about 70 percent
    d. about 90 percent

18. The largest share of federal government spending is for
    a. national defense.
    b. interest.
    c. health.
    d. income security.

19. For the most part, the United States has chosen to let markets determine distribution of before-tax incomes, and then use taxes and _____ to reduce income inequalities.
    a. tariffs
    b. inflation
    c. transfer payments
    d. government production

20. Compared to other industrialized countries, taxes as a percent of GDP in the United States are
    a. among the lowest.
    b. about the same as most other industrialized countries.
    c. among the highest.

TEST B

Circle T or F for true or false.

T   F   1. An economic system is a social mechanism that organizes inputs to produce outputs.

T   F   2. Since World War II, American real GDP has increased every year without interruption.

T   F   3. The American economy is a more open economy than other industrialized economies.

T   F   4. The American economy relies on free markets and private enterprise to a greater extent than most other industrialized economies.

T   F   5. During a recession, unemployment usually increases.

T   F   6. Government production accounts for more than one-half of American GDP.

T   F   7. Interest on the national debt is now the largest category of federal government spending.

T   F   8. Women hold more than one-half of the jobs outside the home.

T   F   9. Most American workers still produce goods rather than services.

T   F 10. Labor gets most of the income generated in the United States.

ECONOMICS IN ACTION

THE PROPER ROLE FOR GOVERNMENT

How far should the government go when regulating business? If the government is to provide some goods and services, what principles determine which goods and services? How far should the government go in redistributing income?

Noted economist Milton Friedman consistently argued for a limited role for government. In a widely publicized Public Broadcasting Service series, Friedman and his wife Rose advocated four principles as tests of the appropriate business of government. National defense, domestic police and justice, the provision of goods and services in the limited cases where markets do not work well, and protection for citizens who cannot protect themselves (e.g., children) define the Friedmans' four principles. These principles, especially the third, could be seen as justifying a wide range of government action. The Friedmans are as concerned with government failures as with market failures. They note that once started, government initiatives are rarely stopped. In their view, the burden of proof should be on the proponents of government action.

The Friedmans argued that government should be organized to maximize individual "freedom to choose as individuals, as families, as members of voluntary groups." They endorsed the view of Adam Smith that as long as individuals do not violate the laws of justice, they should be free to pursue their own interests and that competitive markets rather than government regulation are usually the most effective forms of social organization. "We can shape our institutions. Physical and human characteristics limit the alternatives available to us. But none prevents us, if we will, from building a society that relies primarily on voluntary cooperation to organize both economic and other activity, a society that preserves and expands human freedom, that keeps government in its place, keeping it our servant and not letting it become our master."[1]

The equally renowned John Kenneth Galbraith, on the other hand, argued that increasing affluence led to an imbalance between private and public goods. Goods and services that are marketable to individuals allow private producers to accumulate the financial resources that give them control of labor, capital, and raw materials. Sophisticated advertising creates and sustains demand for private goods, generating more income and profits. This affluence of the private sector is in marked contrast to the poverty of the public sector. Galbraith argues that society needs a balance between private and public goods but that the pernicious effects of advertising that creates the demand that sustains the production of private goods gives rise to a serious imbalance. One result is an increasing demand for private goods and services to protect individuals from the poverty of public goods and services, such as elaborate alarm systems and private guards to counteract the lack of police.

How much increase in public spending is necessary to redress the balance? Galbraith will only say that the distance is considerable. "When we arrive, the opulence of our private consumption will no longer be in contrast with the poverty of our schools, the unloveliness and congestion of our cities, our inability to get to work without a struggle, and the social disorder that is associated with imbalance . . . the precise point of balance will

---

[1]Milton and Rose Friedman, *Free to Choose: A Personal Statement,* Harcourt Brace Jovanovich, 1980.

never be defined. This will be of comfort only to those who believe that any failure of definition can be made to score decisively against the larger idea."[2]

1. How would you define the proper role of government? Where would you draw the line between those activities best left to individual initiative and markets and those that are the appropriate business of government?

STUDY QUESTIONS

1. What is the difference between inputs and outputs? Is steel an input or an output? What about the steel used to build factories compared to the steel used in home appliances?

2. How can output of the American economy be greater than that of countries like China and India with larger populations?

3. What does the historical record show regarding the growth in real GDP and real GDP per capita in the United States?

4. What is meant by a closed or an open economy? How would you characterize the United States?

5. In the United States, who works outside the home for wages and salary and what types of jobs do they hold?

6. How is income in the United States distributed among factors of production?

7. How does the role of government in the American economy compare with that of other industrialized countries?

8. What is meant by the term "mixed economy"?

ECONOMICS ONLINE

The *Statistical Abstract of the United States* is a good place to begin a statistical profile of the United States.

http://www.census.gov/compendia/statab/.

It is often useful to compare the United States to other countries. Information about the major industrialized countries can be found from the homepage for the Organization for Economic Cooperation and Development (OECD).

http://www.oecd.org

The *CIA World Factbook* is a useful summary of information about many countries. It is available online.

http://www.odci.gov/cia/publications/factbook

---

[2]John Kenneth Galbraith, *The Affluent Society*, Houghton Mifflin, 1958.

The Fundamental Economic Problem: Scarcity and Choice

3

Important Terms and Concepts

Resources	Outputs	Principle of increasing costs	Division of labor
Opportunity cost	Inputs	Efficiency	Comparative advantage
Optimal decision	Production possibilities frontier	Allocation of resources	Market system

Learning Objectives

After completing this chapter, you should be able to:

- explain why the true cost of any decision is its opportunity cost.

- explain the link between market prices and opportunity costs.

- explain why the scarcity of goods and services (outputs) must be attributed to a scarcity of resources (inputs) used in production processes.

- draw a production possibilities frontier for a firm or for the economy.

- explain how the production possibilities frontier contains information about the opportunity cost of changing output combinations.

- explain why specialized resources mean that a firm's or an economy's production possibilities frontier is likely to bow outward.

- explain how the shape of the production possibilities frontier illustrates the principle of increasing costs.

- explain why production efficiency requires that an economy produce on, rather than inside, its production possibilities frontier.

- describe the three coordination tasks that every economy must confront.

- explain why specialization and division of labor are likely to require the use of markets.

- describe how the allocation of tasks by the principle of comparative advantage increases the total output of all parties.

- explain how both parties gain from voluntary exchange even if no new goods are produced.

- describe how a market economy solves the three coordination tasks.

CHAPTER REVIEW

"YOU CAN'T ALWAYS GET WHAT YOU WANT"—MICK JAGGER

Even rock stars whose income and wealth are beyond comprehension understand that scarcity and the resulting necessity to make choices are fundamental concerns of economics.[1] This chapter is an introduction to these issues.

(1)   The importance of *choice* starts with the fact that virtually all resources are _____. Most people's desires exceed their incomes, and, thus, everyone makes buying choices all the time. Similarly, firms, educational institutions, and government agencies make choices between what kinds of outputs to produce and what combination of inputs to use.

What is a good way to make choices? The obvious answer is to consider the alternatives. Economists call
(2) these forgone alternatives the _____ _____ of a decision. Imagine it is the night before the first midterm in Introductory Economics, which will cover Chapters 1–6, and here you are only on Chapter 3. A friend suggests a night at the movies and even offers to buy your ticket so "it won't cost you anything." Do you agree? What will you be giving up?

At first, the idea of choices for the economy may sound strange. It may be easiest to imagine such choices being made by bureaucrats in a centrally planned economy. Even though there is no central planning bureau for the U.S. economy, it is useful to think of opportunities available to the American economy. The opportunities selected result from the combined spending and production decisions of all citizens, firms, and governmental units, decisions coordinated by our reliance on markets.

The *production possibilities frontier* is a useful diagram for representing the choices available to a firm or an
(3) economy. The frontier will tend to slope downward to the right because resources are [scarce/specialized]. The frontier will tend to bow out because most resources are _____. Opportunity cost is the best measure of the true cost of any decision. For a single firm or an economy as a whole, with choices represented by a production possibilities frontier, the opportunity cost of changing the composition of output can be measured by the _____ of the production possibilities frontier.

As an economy produces more and more of one good, say automobiles, the opportunity cost of fur-
(4) ther increases is likely to [increase/decrease]. This change in opportunity cost illustrates the principle of _____ cost and is a result of the fact that most resources are [scarce/specialized].

For given amounts of all but one good, the production possibilities frontier for an economy measures the maximum amount of the remaining good that can be produced. Thus, the production possibilities frontier defines maximum outputs or efficient production. Note that all points on the production possibilities frontier represent efficiency in production. There is, of course, no guarantee that the economy will operate on its frontier.
(5) If there is unemployment, then the economy is operating [on/inside] the frontier. If a firm or economy operates inside its production possibilities frontier, it is said to be _____; that is, with the same

---

[1]Before he was a rock star, Mick Jagger studied economics at the London School of Economics.

resources the firm or the economy could have produced more of some commodities. Assigning inputs to the wrong or inappropriate tasks because market prices are sending the wrong signals or discrimination that limits opportunities for individuals will also result in production inefficiency. Assigning tasks according to the principle of comparative advantage helps to achieve economic efficiency.

All economies must answer three questions:
1. How can we use resources efficiently to operate on the production possibilities frontier?
2. What combinations of output shall we produce: that is, where on the frontier shall we produce?
3. To whom shall we distribute what is produced?

The American economy answers these questions through the use of markets and prices. If markets are functioning well, then money prices [will/will not] be a reliable guide to opportunity costs. Problems arise when   (6)
markets do not function well and when items do not have explicit price tags.

IMPORTANT TERMS AND CONCEPTS QUIZ

Choose the best definition for each of the following terms.

1. _____ Resources
2. _____ Opportunity cost
3. _____ Optimal decision
4. _____ Outputs
5. _____ Inputs
6. _____ Production possibilities frontier
7. _____ Principle of increasing costs
8. _____ Efficiency
9. _____ Allocation of resources
10. _____ Division of labor
11. _____ Comparative advantage
12. _____ Market system

a. Resources used to produce goods and services
b. System in which allocation decisions are made in accordance with centralized direction
c. Breaking tasks into smaller jobs
d. Ability to produce goods less inefficiently than other producers
e. Decision on how to divide scarce resources among different uses
f. Instruments used to create the goods and services people desire
g. Graph of combinations of goods that can be produced with available inputs and existing technology
h. Goods and services that firms produce
i. System in which decisions on resource allocation come from independent decisions of consumers and producers
j. Absence of waste
k. Forgone value of the next best alternative
l. Tendency for the opportunity cost of an additional unit of output to rise as production increases
m. A decision that best serves the decision maker's objectives

BASIC EXERCISES

Figure 3-1 shows the production possibilities frontier (PPF) for the economy of Adirondack, which produces bread and computers.

Figure 3-1

Production Possibilities Frontier

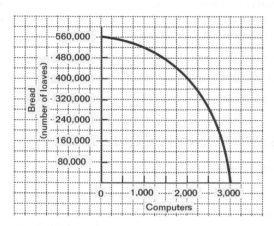

1. If all resources are devoted to the production of bread, Adirondack can produce _____ loaves of bread. In order to produce 1,000 computers, the opportunity cost in terms of bread is _____ loaves. To produce another 1,000 computers, the opportunity cost [rises/falls] to _____ loaves. As long as the PPF continues to curve downward, the opportunity costs of increased computer output will [continue to rise/start to fall]. These changes are the result, not of scarce resources per se, but of _____ resources. (You might try drawing a PPF on the assumption that all resources are equally productive in the production of both outputs. Can you convince yourself that it should be a straight line?)

2. Find the output combination of 2,500 computers and 320,000 loaves on **Figure 3-1.** Label this point A. Is it an attainable combination for Adirondack? Label the output combination 1,500 computers and 400,000 loaves as point B. Is this combination attainable? Finally, label the output combination 1,000 computers and 520,000 loaves as point C. Is this combination attainable? We can conclude that the attainable output combinations for Adirondack are [on/inside/outside] the production possibilities frontier. Among the obtainable output combinations, efficient points of production are located [on/inside/outside] the production possibilities frontier.

3. An output combination is inefficient if it is possible to produce more of one or both goods. Which, if any, of the output combinations identified in question 2 is an inefficient combination? _____ Show that this point is inefficient by shading in all attainable points indicating more of one or both goods.

4. Consider point C in question 2, 1,000 computers and 520,000 loaves of bread, and point D, 2,000 computers and 400,000 loaves of bread. Which point is best for Adirondack and why?

SELF-TESTS FOR UNDERSTANDING

TEST A

Circle the most appropriate answer.

1. Economists define opportunity cost as the
   a. dollar price of goods and services.
   b. hidden cost imposed by inflation.
   c. value of the next best alternative use that is not chosen.
   d. time spent shopping.

2. The position of an economy's production possibilities frontier is determined by all but which one of the following?
   a. the size of the labor force
   b. labor skills and training
   c. the amount of consumption goods the economy can produce
   d. current technology

3. A firm's production possibilities frontier shows
   a. the best combination of output for a firm to produce.
   b. its plans for increasing production over time.
   c. the architectural drawings of its most productive plant.
   d. the different combinations of goods it can produce with available resources and technology.

4. An efficient economy utilizes all available resources and produces the _____ output its technology permits.
   a. minimum amount of
   b. best combination of
   c. one combination of
   d. maximum amount of

5. The fact that resources are scarce implies that the production possibilities frontier will
   a. have a negative slope.
   b. be a straight line.
   c. shift out over time.
   d. bow out from the origin.

6. Which of the following statements implies that production possibilities frontiers are likely to be curved rather than straight lines?
   a. Ultimately all resources are scarce.
   b. Most resources are more productive in certain uses than in others.
   c. Unemployment is a more serious problem for some social groups than for others.
   d. Economists are notoriously poor at drawing straight lines.

7. The set of attainable points for a firm that produces two goods is given by
   a. all points on the production possibilities frontier.
   b. all points inside the production possibilities frontier.
   c. all points on or inside the production possibilities frontier.
   d. none of the above.

8. If an economy is operating efficiently, it will be producing
   a. inside its production possibilities frontier.
   b. on its production possibilities frontier.
   c. outside its production possibilities frontier.
   d. the maximum amount of necessities and the minimum amount of luxuries.

9. The principle of increasing cost is consistent with a _____ production possibilities frontier.
   a. straight-line
   b. bowed-in
   c. shifting
   d. bowed-out

10. The inability of the economy to produce as much as everyone would like is ultimately a reflection of
    a. a lack of money in the economy.
    b. congressional gridlock.
    c. the inability of a market economy to perform the necessary coordination tasks.
    d. a limited amount of productive resources.

11. When, in Figure 3-1, the production of bread is increased from 280,000 loaves to 400,000 loaves, the opportunity cost in terms of reduced output of computers is
    a. 0.
    b. 500.
    c. 2,000.
    d. 2,500.

12. When the output of bread increases by another 120,000 loaves to 520,000, the opportunity cost in terms of reduced output of computers is
    a. 0.
    b. 500.
    c. 1,000.
    d. 2,000.

13. Comparing answers to questions 11 and 12, we can conclude that the production possibilities frontier for Adirondack
    a. is a straight line.
    b. shows a decline in the opportunity cost of more bread.
    c. illustrates the principle of increasing cost.
    d. has a positive slope.

14. Consider a production possibilities frontier showing alternative combinations of corn and computers that can be produced in Cimonoce, a small island in the South Pacific. The opportunity cost of more computers can be measured by the
    a. slope of the production possibilities frontier.
    b. *X*-intercept of the production possibilities frontier.
    c. *Y*-intercept of the production possibilities frontier.
    d. area under the production possibilities frontier.

15. Which of the following implies a shift in the production possiblities frontier for a shoe firm?
    a. raising prices by 10 percent
    b. borrowing money to hire more workers and buying more machines
    c. changing the composition output toward more women's shoes and fewer men's shoes
    d. expanding the advertising budget

16. Which of the following would not shift an economy's production possibilities frontier?
    a. a doubling of the labor force
    b. a doubling of the number of machines
    c. a doubling of the money supply
    d. more advanced technology

17. An optimal decision is one that
    a. will win a majority if put to a vote.
    b. is supported unanimously.
    c. best serves the objectives of the decision maker.
    d. is supported by *The New York Times*.

18. If exchange is voluntary,
    a. there can be mutual gain even if no new goods are produced.
    b. one party will always get the better of the other.
    c. there can be mutual gain only if new goods are produced as a result of the trade.
    d. there can be mutual gain only if the government regulates retail trade.

19. All but which one of the following are examples of waste and inefficiency?
    a. Employment discrimination against women and people of color
    b. Operating on an economy's production possibilities frontier
    c. High levels of unemployment
    d. Quotas that limit the educational opportunities of particular ethnic groups

20. The three coordination tasks that all economies must perform can
    a. only be done by a central planning bureau.
    b. only be done by markets.
    c. only be done inefficiently.
    d. be done by planning bureaus or markets.

TEST B

Circle T or F for true or false.

T F 1. There can never be any real scarcity of manufactured goods because we can always produce more.

T F 2. Market prices are always the best measure of opportunity cost.

T F 3. The principle of increasing costs is a reflection of the fact that most productive resources tend to be best at producing a limited number of things.

T F 4. Markets are incapable of solving the three coordination tasks that all economies must address.

T F 5. Because they have the power to tax, governments do not need to make choices.

T F 6. The existence of specialized resources means that a firm's production possibilities frontier will be a straight line.

T F 7. The existence of widespread unemployment means that an economy is operating inside its production possibilities frontier.

T F 8. An economy using its resources efficiently is operating on its production possibilities frontier.

T F 9. Because they are nonprofit organizations, colleges and universities do not have to make choices.

T F 10. A sudden increase in the number of dollar bills will shift the economy's production possibilities frontier.

SUPPLEMENTARY EXERCISES

1. **THE COST OF COLLEGE**

   Those of you paying your way through college may not need to be reminded that the opportunity cost of lost wages is an important part of the cost of education. You can estimate the cost of your education as follows: Estimate what you could earn if instead of attending classes and studying, you used those hours to work. Add in the direct outlays on tuition, books, and any differential living expenses incurred because you go to school. (Why only differential and not your total living expenses?)

2. **PRODUCTION POSSIBILITIES FRONTIER**

   Consider an economy with a production possibilities frontier between cars (C) and tanks (T) given by

   $$C = 6L^5K^5 - 0.3T^2$$

   where L is the size of the labor force (50,000 people) and K is the number of machines, also 50,000.
   a. What is the maximum number of cars that can be produced? Call this number of cars C^*. The maximum number of tanks? Call this number of tanks T^*.
   b. Draw the PPF graph for this economy.
   c. Is this frontier consistent with the principle of increasing costs?

34

d. Is the output combination $(1/2C^*, 1/2T^*)$ attainable? Is the output combination $(1/2C^*, 1/2T^*)$ efficient? Why or why not?

e. What is the opportunity cost of more tanks when 10 tanks are produced? 50 tanks? 200 tanks?

f. Find a mathematical expression for the opportunity cost of tanks in terms of cars. Is this mathematical expression consistent with the principle of increasing cost?

ECONOMICS IN ACTION

FREE THEATER?

In the summer of 2001, New York City's Public Theater presented Chekhov's *Seagull* at the Delacorte Theater in Central Park. The director was Mike Nichols, and the production starred Meryl Streep, Kevin Kline, and Marcia Gay Harden. The tickets were free, or were they?

Tickets were given away each day at 1 p.m. on a first-come, first-served basis. As Joyce Purnick reported, arriving at 6 a.m. and waiting seven hours would not necessarily get you a ticket. The day she reported on, the first person in line arrived at 12:30 a.m., more than twelve hours before the tickets were distributed. Ms. Purnick concluded that "[t]he scene . . . strongly suggested that free tickets were for the retired, the unemployed, and the vacationing only."

If you were not up for spending the night in Central Park, you could call Peter London. Mr. London would hire students and underemployed actors to stand in line for you. He charged up to $200 for this service.

When there were objections, Mr. London responded that he was not doing anything illegal. "Only unemployed people should see this? I don't see this as being fair," he said.

Were the tickets free? How do you value your time? Would you pay $200 for someone to stand in line for you? Would you be willing to stand in line for someone else for $200? Who was likely to use Mr. London's service: those who felt the opportunity cost of their time was high or low? Who was likely to be interested in working for Mr. London? What is fair?

Source: Joyce Purnick, "Free Theater, but the Lines Unspeakable," *The New York Times,* July 30, 2001.

STUDY QUESTIONS

1. How do markets help an economy address the three coordination tasks of deciding "how," "what," and "to whom"?

2. What do economists mean by opportunity cost and why do they say it is the true measure of the cost of any decision?

3. Explain when market prices are likely to be a good measure of opportunity cost and when they are not.

4. What are the factors that determine the location of a country's production possibilities frontier?

5. What is the difference between resources being scarce and resources being specialized? What are the implications of scarcity and specialization for the production possibilities frontier?

6. How do specialization and the division of labor enhance economic efficiency? Why do they require a system of exchange?

7. What is the difference between attainable points of production and efficient points of production? (It may be easiest to illustrate your answer using a diagram of a production possibilities frontier. Be sure that you can define and identify those points that are attainable and those points that are efficient.)

8. What is meant by the principle of comparative advantage? What does it imply for individuals and economies?

Supply and Demand: An Initial Look

4

Important Terms and Concepts

Invisible hand	Shift in a demand curve	Supply-demand diagram	Law of supply and demand
Quantity demanded	Quantity supplied	Shortage	Price ceiling
Demand schedule	Supply schedule	Surplus	Price floor
Demand curve	Supply curve	Equilibrium	

Learning Objectives

After completing this chapter, you should be able to:

- explain why the quantity demanded and the quantity supplied are not fixed numbers but rather depend upon a number of factors including price.

- draw a demand curve, given appropriate information from a demand schedule of possible prices and the associated quantity demanded.

- draw a supply curve, given appropriate information from a supply schedule of possible prices and the associated quantity supplied.

- explain why demand curves usually slope downward and supply curves usually slope upward.

- determine the equilibrium price and quantity, given a demand curve and a supply curve.

- explain what forces tend to move market prices and quantities toward their equilibrium values.

- list major factors that will affect the quantity demanded by shifting the demand curve.

- list major factors that will affect the quantity supplied by shifting the supply curve.

- distinguish between a shift in and a movement along either the demand or supply curve.

- analyze the impact on prices and quantities of shifts in the demand curve, supply curve, or both.

- explain why sellers are unlikely to be able to pass on the full increase in excise or sales taxes.

- distinguish between price ceilings and price floors.

- explain the likely consequences of government interference with market-determined prices.

CHAPTER REVIEW

Along with scarcity and the need for choice, demand and supply analysis is a fundamental idea that pervades all of economics. After studying this chapter, look back at the Ideas for Beyond the Final Exam in Chapter 1 and see how many concern the "law" of supply and demand.

Economists use a demand curve as a summary of the factors influencing people's demand for different commodities. A demand curve shows how, during a specified period, the quantity demanded of some good changes

(1) as the _____ of that good changes, holding all other determinants of demand constant. A demand curve usually has a (<u>negative/positive</u>) slope, indicating that as the price of a good declines, people will demand (<u>more/less</u>) of it. A particular quantity demanded is represented by a point on the demand curve. The change in the quantity demanded as price changes is a (<u>shift in/movement along</u>) the demand curve. Quantity demanded is also influenced by other factors, such as consumer incomes and tastes, population, and the prices of related goods. Changes in any of these factors will result in a (<u>shift in/movement along</u>) the demand curve.

Economists use a supply curve to summarize the factors influencing producers' decisions. Like the demand

(2) curve, the supply curve is a relationship between quantity and _____. Supply curves usually have a (<u>negative/positive</u>) slope, indicating that at higher prices producers will be willing to supply (<u>more/less</u>) of the good in question. Like quantity demanded, quantity supplied is also influenced by factors other than price. The size of the industry, the state of technology, the prices of inputs, and the price of related outputs are important determinants. Changes in any of these factors will change the quantity supplied and can be represented by a (<u>shift in/movement along</u>) the supply curve.

Demand and supply curves are hypothetical constructs that answer what-if questions. For example, the supply curve answers the question, "What quantity of milk would be supplied if its price were $10 a gallon?" At this point it is not fair to ask whether anyone would buy milk at that price. Information about the quantity

(3) demanded is given by the _____ curve, which answers the question, "What quantity would be demanded if its price were $10 a gallon?" The viability of a price of $10 will be determined when we consider both curves simultaneously.

Figure 4-1 shows a demand and supply curve for stereo sets. The market outcome will be a price of

(4) $_____ and a quantity of _____. If the price is $400, then the quantity demanded will be (<u>less/more</u>) than the quantity supplied. In particular, from Figure 4-1 we can see that at a price of $400, producers would supply _____ sets while consumers would demand _____ sets. This imbalance is a (<u>shortage/surplus</u>) and will lead to a(n) (<u>increase/reduction</u>) in price as inventories start piling up and suppliers compete for sales. If, instead, the price of stereo sets is only $200, there will be a (<u>shortage/surplus</u>) as the quantity (<u>demanded/supplied</u>) exceeds the quantity _____. Price is apt to (<u>decrease/increase</u>) as consumers scramble for a limited number of stereos at what appear to be bargain prices.

These forces working to raise or lower prices will continue until price and quantity settle down at values

(5) given by the _____ of the demand and supply curves. At this point, barring outside

38

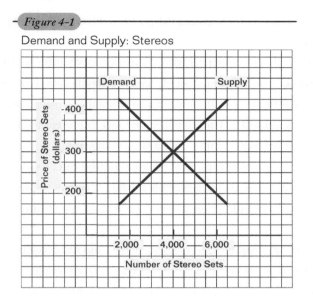

Figure 4-1

Demand and Supply: Stereos

changes that would shift either curve, there will be no further tendency for change. Market-determined price and quantity are then said to be in _____. This price and quantity combination is the only one in which consumers demand exactly what producers supply. There are no frustrated consumers or producers. However, equilibrium price and quantity will change if anything happens to shift either the demand or supply curves. The Basic Exercise in this chapter asks you to examine a number of shifts in demand and supply curves.

Often factors affect demand but not supply, and vice versa. For example, changes in consumer incomes and tastes will shift the (<u>demand/supply</u>) curve but not the _____ curve. Following a (6) shift in the demand curve, price must change to reestablish equilibrium. The change in price will lead to a (<u>shift in/movement along</u>) the supply curve until equilibrium is reestablished at the intersection of the new demand curve and the original supply curve.[1] Similarly, a change in technology or the price of inputs will shift the _____ curve but not the _____ curve. Equilibrium will be reestablished as the price change induced by the shift in the supply curve leads to a movement along the _____ curve to the new intersection.

In many cases governments intervene in the market mechanism in an attempt to control prices. Some price controls dictate a particular price; other controls set maximum or minimum prices. A price ceiling is a (<u>maximum/minimum</u>) legal price, typically below the market-determined equilibrium price. Examples of price (7) ceilings include rent controls and usury laws. A price floor sets a(n) _____ legal price. To

---

[1] If following an increase in consumer income the increase in price were sufficiently large to induce an increase in the size of the industry, the supply curve would shift. However, such a change would take some time. The analysis here focuses on immediate or short-run impacts. Questions of long-run industry equilibrium are addressed in Chapters 8, 9, and 10.

39

be effective, the price floor would have to be (above/below) the market equilibrium price. Price floors are often used in agricultural programs.

In general, economists argue that interferences with the market mechanism are likely to have a number of undesirable features. Price controls will almost surely lead to a misallocation of resources, as it is unlikely legislated prices will equal opportunity cost. If there are a large number of suppliers, price controls will be (8) (hard/easy) to monitor and evasion will be hard to police. In order to prevent the breakdown of price controls, governments quite likely find it necessary to introduce a large number of _____

_____. The enforcement of price controls can provide opportunities for favoritism and corruption. If all of this is not enough, price controls are almost certain to produce groups with a monetary stake in preserving controls. Another form of inefficiency involves the use of time and resources to evade effective controls.

(9) Price ceilings have a history of persistent (shortages/surpluses) and the development of black markets. Prices in the illegal market are likely to be greater than those that would have prevailed in a free market, with substantial income going to those whose only business is circumventing the controls. Over a longer period of time, new investment is likely to (decrease/increase) as controlled prices reduce the profitability of investment in the industry.

Firms try to get around effective price floors by offering nonprice inducements for consumers to buy from them rather than from someone else. (Remember that effective price floors result in excess supply.) These nonprice inducements are apt to be less preferred by consumers than would a general reduction in prices. Price (10) floors will also result in inefficiencies as high-cost firms are protected from failing by artificially (high/low) prices.

40

IMPORTANT TERMS AND CONCEPTS QUIZ

Choose the best definition for each of the following terms.

1. _____ Invisible hand

2. _____ Quantity demanded

3. _____ Demand schedule

4. _____ Demand curve

5. _____ Shift in a demand curve

6. _____ Quantity supplied

7. _____ Supply schedule

8. _____ Supply curve

9. _____ Supply-demand diagram

10. _____ Shortage

11. _____ Surplus

12. _____ Equilibrium

13. _____ Law of supply and demand

14. _____ Price ceiling

15. _____ Price floor

a. Observation that in a free market, price tends to a level where quantity supplied equals quantity demanded

b. Legal minimum price that may be charged

c. Graph depicting how quantity demanded changes as price changes

d. Change in price causing a change in quantity supplied or demanded

e. Number of units consumers want to buy at a given price

f. Individual actions to pursue self-interest in a market system promote societal well-being

g. Table depicting how the quantity demanded changes as price changes

h. Situation in which there are no inherent forces producing change

i. Table depicting how quantity supplied changes as price changes

j. Legal maximum price that may be charged

k. Number of units producers want to sell at a given price

l. Table depicting the changes in both quantity demanded and quantity supplied as price changes

m. Change in a variable other than price that affects quantity demanded

n. Excess of quantity supplied over quantity demanded

o. Graph depicting the changes in both quantity supplied and quantity demanded as price changes

p. Excess of quantity demanded over quantity supplied

q. Graph depicting how quantity supplied changes as price changes

BASIC EXERCISES

These exercises ask you to analyze the impact of changes in factors that affect demand and supply.

1. a. Table 4-1 has data on the quantity of candy bars that would be demanded and supplied at various prices. Use the data to draw the demand curve and the supply curve for candy bars in Figure 4-2.

    b. From the information given in Table 4-1 and represented in Figure 4-2, the equilibrium price is _____ cents and the equilibrium quantity is _____ million candy bars.

Table 4-1

Demand and Supply Schedules for Candy Bars

Quantity Demanded	Price per Bar	Quantity Supplied
1,200	55	1,050
1,100	60	1,100
900	70	1,200
800	75	1,250
700	80	1,300

Figure 4-2

Demand and Supply: Candy Bars

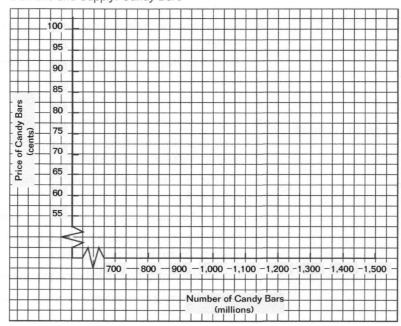

c. Now assume that increases in income and population mean the demand curve has shifted. Assume the shift is such that, at each price, the quantity demanded has increased by 300 candy bars. Draw the new demand curve. At the new equilibrium, price has (<u>increased/decreased</u>) to _____ cents, and quantity has (<u>increased/decreased</u>) to _____ million candy bars. Note that the change in the equilibrium quantity is (<u>less/more</u>) than the shift in the demand curve. Can you explain why?

d. Next assume that Congress imposes a tax of 15 cents on every candy bar sold. As sellers must now pay the government 15 cents for each candy bar sold, the tax can be modeled as a 15 cent upward shift in the supply curve. This tax-induced shift in the supply curve will (increase/decrease) the equilibrium price and _____ the equilibrium quantity. Draw this new supply curve in Figure 4-2. Using the demand curve you drew in part c, the new equilibrium price following the imposition of the candy tax will be _____ cents and the equilibrium quantity will be _____ million candy bars. Compared to the equilibrium price you identified in part c, the increase in the market price of candy bars is (less than/equal to/more than) the new tax.

2. Figure 4-3 shows the demand and supply of chicken. Use Figure 4-3 while you fill in Table 4-2 to trace the effects of various events on the equilibrium price and quantity.

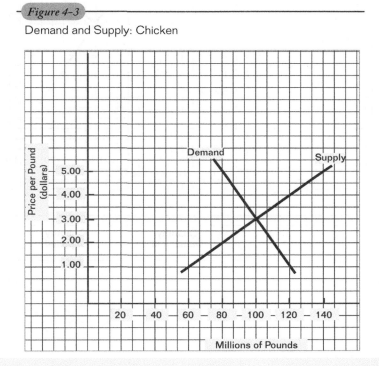

Figure 4-3

Demand and Supply: Chicken

Event	Which curve shifts?	Is the direction left or right?	Does the equilibrium price rise or fall?	Does the equilibrium quantity rise or fall?
a. A sharp increase in the price of beef leads many consumers to switch from beef to chicken.				
b. A bumper grain crop cuts the cost of chicken feed in half.				
c. Extraordinarily cold weather destroys a significant number of chickens.				
d. A sudden interest in Eastern religions converts many chicken eaters to vegetarians.				

Table 4-2

43

3. Figure 4-4 shows the demand and supply of DVDs. Complete Table 4-3 to examine the impact of alternative price ceilings and price floors on the quantity demanded and the quantity supplied. What conclusion can you draw about when ceilings and floors will affect market outcomes?

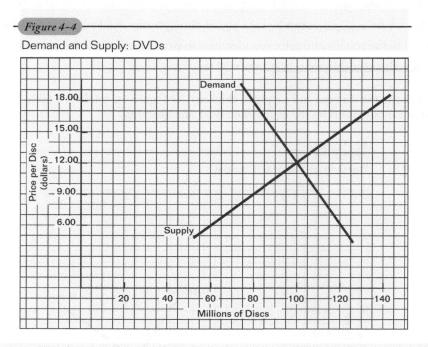

Figure 4-4

Demand and Supply: DVDs

Table 4-3

	Quantity Demanded	Quantity Supplied	Shortage or Surplus
a. Price ceiling = $18			
b. Price ceiling = $9			
c. Price floor = $15			
d. Price floor = $6			

SELF-TESTS FOR UNDERSTANDING

TEST A

Circle the most appropriate answer.

1. A demand curve is a graph showing how the quantity demanded changes when _____ changes.
   a. consumer income
   b. population
   c. price
   d. the price of closely related goods

2. The slope of a demand curve is usually _____, indicating that as price declines the quantity demanded increases.
   a. negative
   b. positive
   c. infinite
   d. zero

3. Quantity demanded is likely to depend upon all but which one of the following?
   a. consumer tastes
   b. consumer income
   c. price
   d. the size of the industry producing the good in question

4. A supply curve is a graphical representation of information in a(n)
   a. demand schedule.
   b. equilibrium.
   c. supply schedule.
   d. balance sheet.

5. If price decreases, the quantity supplied usually
   a. increases.
   b. is unchanged.
   c. decreases.
   d. goes to zero.

6. The entire supply curve is likely to shift when all but which one of the following change?
   a. the size of the industry
   b. price
   c. the price of important inputs
   d. technology that reduces production costs

7. There will likely be a movement along a fixed supply curve if which one of the following changes?
   a. price
   b. technology that reduces production costs
   c. the price of important inputs
   d. the size of the industry

8. There will be a movement along a fixed demand curve when which one of the following changes?
   a. price
   b. population
   c. consumer incomes
   d. consumer preferences

9. Graphically, the equilibrium price and quantity in a free market will be given by the
   a. *Y*-axis intercept of the demand curve.
   b. *X*-axis intercept of the supply curve.
   c. point of maximum vertical difference between the demand and supply curves.
   d. intersection of the demand and supply curves.

10. When the demand curve shifts to the right, which of the following is likely to occur?
    a. Equilibrium price rises and equilibrium quantity declines.
    b. Both equilibrium price and quantity rise.
    c. Equilibrium price declines and equilibrium quantity rises.
    d. Both equilibrium price and quantity decline.

11. If equilibrium price and quantity both decrease, it is likely that the
    a. supply curve has shifted to the right.
    b. demand curve has shifted to the right.
    c. demand curve has shifted to the left.
    d. supply curve has shifted to the left.

12. A shift in the demand curve for sailboats resulting from a general increase in incomes will lead to
    a. higher prices.
    b. lower prices.
    c. a shift in the supply curve.
    d. lower output.

13. Which of the following is likely to result in a shift in the supply curve for dresses? (There may be more than one correct answer.)
    a. an increase in consumer incomes
    b. an increase in tariffs that forces manufacturers to import cotton cloth at higher prices
    c. an increase in dress prices
    d. higher prices for skirts, pants, and blouses

14. From an initial equilibrium, which of the following changes will lead to a shift in the supply curve for Chevrolets?
    a. import restrictions on Japanese cars
    b. new environmental protection measures that raise the cost of producing steel
    c. a decrease in the price of Fords
    d. increases in the price of gasoline

15. If the price of oil (a close substitute for coal) increases, then the
    a. supply curve for coal will shift to the right.
    b. demand curve for coal will shift to the right.
    c. equilibrium price and quantity of coal will not change.
    d. quantity of coal demanded will decline.

16. If the price of shoes is initially above the equilibrium value, which of the following is likely to occur?
    a. Stores' inventories will decrease as consumers buy more shoes than shoe companies produce.
    b. The demand curve for shoes will shift in response to higher prices.
    c. Shoe stores and companies will reduce prices in order to increase sales, leading to a lower equilibrium price.
    d. Equilibrium will be reestablished at the original price as the supply curve shifts to the left.

17. A new tax on backpacks that shifts the supply curve should increase the market price of backpacks
    a. not at all.
    b. by less than the increase in the tax.
    c. by an amount equal to the increase in the tax.
    d. by more than the increase in the tax.

18. Binding price floors are likely to
    a. lead to a reduction in the volume of transactions, as we move along the demand curve, above the equilibrium price to the higher price floor.
    b. result in increased sales as suppliers react to higher prices.
    c. lead to shortages.
    d. be effective only if they are set at levels below the market equilibrium level.

19. Effective price ceilings are likely to
    a. result in surpluses.
    b. increase the volume of transactions as we move along the demand curve.
    c. increase production as producers respond to higher consumer demand at the low ceiling price.
    d. result in the development of black markets.

20. A surplus results when
    a. the quantity demanded exceeds the quantity supplied.
    b. the quantity supplied exceeds the quantity demanded.
    c. the demand curve shifts to the right.
    d. effective price ceilings are imposed.

TEST B

Circle T or F for true or false.

T   F   1. The Law of Supply and Demand was passed by Congress in 1776.

T   F   2. The demand curve for hamburgers is a graph showing the quantity of hamburgers that would be demanded during a specified period at each possible price.

Γ   F   3. The slope of the supply curve indicates the increase in price necessary to get producers to increase output.

T   F   4. An increase in consumer income will shift both the supply and demand curves.

T   F   5. Both demand and supply curves usually have positive slopes.

T   F   6. If at a particular price the quantity supplied exceeds the quantity demanded, then price is likely to fall as suppliers compete for sales.

T   F   7. Equilibrium price and quantity are determined by the intersection of the demand and supply curves.

T   F   8. Because equilibrium is defined as a situation with no inherent forces producing change, the equilibrium price and quantity will not change following an increase in consumer income.

T   F   9. A change in the price of important inputs will change the quantity supplied but will not shift the supply curve.

T   F 10. Increases in commodity specific taxes typically lead to equal increases in market prices.

T   F 11. When binding, price ceilings are likely to result in the development of black markets.

T   F 12. Price controls, whether floors or ceilings, likely will increase the volume of transactions from what it would be without controls.

T   F 13. An effective price ceiling is normally accompanied by shortages.

T   F 14. An effective price floor is also normally accompanied by shortages.

T   F 15. An increase in both the market price and quantity of beef following an increase in consumer incomes proves that demand curves do not always have a negative slope.

SUPPLEMENTARY EXERCISE

Imagine that the demand curve for tomatoes can be represented as:

$$Q = 1,000 - 250P.$$

The supply curve is a bit trickier. Farmers must make planting decisions on what they anticipate prices to be. Once they have made these decisions, there is little room for increases or decreases in the quantity supplied. Except for disastrously low prices, it will almost certainly pay for a farmer to harvest and market his tomatoes. Assuming that farmers forecast price on the basis of the price last period, we can represent the supply curve for tomatoes as:

$$Q = 200 + 150P_{-1},$$

where P_{-1}, refers to price in the previous period. Initial equilibrium price and quantity of tomatoes are $2 and 500, respectively. Verify that at this price the quantity supplied is equal to the quantity demanded. (Equilibrium implies the same price in each period.)

Now assume that an increase in income has shifted the demand curve to:

$$Q = 1,400 - 250P.$$

Starting with the initial equilibrium price, trace the evolution of price and quantity over time. Do prices and quantities seem to be approaching some sort of equilibrium? If so, what? You might try programming this example on a computer or simulating it with a spreadsheet program. What happens if the slope of the demand and/or supply curve changes?

Ask your instructor about cobweb models. Do you think looking at last period's price is a good way to forecast prices?

ECONOMICS IN ACTION

HEY, BUDDY ...

Scalping tickets—selling tickets at whatever the market will bear rather than at face value—is illegal in a number of states, including New York City. In 1992 the high demand for tickets to a retrospective exhibition of Henri Matisse at the Museum of Modern Art prompted renewed interest in the economic effects of scalping. Admission to the exhibition was by special ticket. By the time the exhibit opened, all advance sale tickets had been sold. A limited number of tickets were available each day. Art lovers had to wait in line for up to two hours early in the morning to purchase these tickets at $12.50 each. Tickets also were available without the wait at $20 to $50 from scalpers who evaded the police.

The Monet retrospective exhibit at the Art Institute in Chicago in 1995 attracted such interest that scalpers were reported to be getting $100 for tickets with a face value of $10. Scalpers also do a lively business at the Super Bowl, the Final Four of the NCAA basketball playoffs, and other major sporting and entertainment events.

Why don't museums, the National Football League, and the NCAA simply raise the price of tickets? Some argue that these organizations, along with other businesses, are concerned with "goodwill." Even if higher profits could be earned from higher ticket prices, it might come by sacrificing profits over the long run as goodwill is replaced by ill will and a growing lack of consumer interest.

Some economists view scalpers as providing a service to those who have not planned ahead or do not wish to stand in line. They point out that other businesses, such as airlines, charge a hefty price for last-minute purchases.

It is often argued that scalping should be illegal, as it makes events unaffordable for the average person. Others wonder whether the average person ever gets tickets to such events and, if she does, whether she might not prefer the option of selling her tickets at a handsome profit.

The following two-tier price system has been proposed by some economists. First, a limited number of tickets would be sold at lower prices to those willing to stand in line or enter a lottery. Then the remaining tickets would be sold at whatever price the market will bear.

In fall 2001, the producers of the hit Broadway show "The Producers" announced just such a plan. Their top ticket price had been $100, and it was rumored that scalpers were getting up to $1,000 a ticket. The producers announced a plan under which 50 seats for each performance would be available at $480 a piece.

1. Who is harmed when scalping is illegal? Who would be harmed if scalping were legal?

2. Would you expect legalizing scalping to affect the price of tickets from scalpers? Why?

3. Evaluate the pros and cons of the two-tier price system.

Source: "Tickets: Supply Meets Demand on Sidewalk," *The New York Times*, December 26, 1992; "For the Asking, a $480 Seat," *The New York Times*, October 26, 2001.

STUDY QUESTIONS

1. Why do economists argue that neither quantity demanded nor quantity supplied is likely to be a fixed number?

2. What adjustment mechanisms are likely to ensure that free-market prices move toward their equilibrium values given by the intersection of the demand and supply curves?

3. What important factors help to determine the quantity demanded? The quantity supplied?

4. Why are changes in all of the supply determinants, except price, said to shift the entire supply curve while changes in price are said to give rise to a movement along a fixed supply curve?

5. How do factors that shift the supply curve give rise to movements along a given demand curve?

6. Why do economists expect that an increase in a tax on a specific commodity will not lead to an equal increase in market prices?

7. If price cannot adjust, say due to an effective price ceiling, what factors will likely allocate the quantity supplied among consumers?

8. Consider the demand for a necessity (for example, food), and the demand for a luxury (for example, home hot tubs). For which good would you expect the quantity demanded to show a greater response to changes in price? Why? For which good would you expect the demand curve to be steeper? Why? For which good would you expect the demand curve to show a greater shift in response to changes in consumer income? Why?

Consumer Choice: Individual and Market Demand

5

Important Terms and Concepts

Total monetary utility

Marginal utility

The "law" of diminishing marginal utility

Marginal analysis

Consumer's surplus

Inferior good

Market demand curve

The "law" of demand

Learning Objectives

After completing this chapter, you should be able to:

- distinguish between total and marginal utility.

- explain how the law of diminishing marginal utility can be used to derive an optimal purchase rule.

- explain how the optimal purchase rule can be used to derive a demand curve.

- understand the true cost of any purchase—the opportunity cost.

- explain the role of marginal utility as a guide to maximizing consumer surplus.

- explain the difference between inferior and normal goods.

- derive a market demand curve given information on individual demand curves.

- explain why a market demand curve can have a negative slope even if individual demand curves do not.

- describe the "law" of demand and exceptions to this law.

- understand the limits of rational decision making.

CHAPTER REVIEW

This chapter discusses economic models of consumer choice. These models are what lie behind the negatively sloped demand curves we encountered in Chapter 4. The appendix to the chapter discusses indifference curve analysis, which is a more sophisticated treatment of the same material. This chapter is also an introduction to *marginal analysis,* an extremely powerful tool of economic analysis.

Economists derive implications for individual demand curves by starting with assumptions about individual behavior. One relatively innocent assumption should be sufficient. It concerns consumer preferences and is called the "law" of diminishing marginal utility. Perhaps we should first start with utility.

The term utility refers to the benefits people derive from consuming goods and services. Actual utility is unique to each one of us and thus is unmeasurable. To get around the measurement problem, we will use the term total utility to refer to the maximum amount a consumer will pay for a given quantity of the commodity. (It should be obvious that this amount will differ from person to person. For an individual consumer, total utility will be influenced by her income and preferences.) Rather than focusing on total utility, however, economists have found it useful to pay attention to the additional amount of money that a consumer would pay for

(1) one more unit of the commodity, or _____ utility, measured in money terms. (Marginal utility (will/will not) also be influenced by a person's income and preferences.) The law of diminishing marginal utility is a hypothesis about consumer preferences. It says that additional units of any commodity normally provide less and less satisfaction. As a result, the additional amount a consumer would pay for an additional unit of some commodity will (increase/decrease) the more units he is already consuming. Note that total utility will (decrease/increase) as long as marginal utility is positive, even if marginal utility itself is decreasing.

The law of diminishing marginal utility can be used as a guide to optimal commodity purchases. Optimal purchases are those that maximize the difference between total utility and total expenditures on a commodity.

(2) This difference is called _____ surplus.[1] Our optimal purchase rule says that an individual consumer should buy additional units of a commodity as long as the marginal utility of the additional units exceeds the _____ of the commodity. If marginal utility exceeds price, the addition to total utility from consuming one more unit will be (greater/less) than the addition to total spending, and consumer's surplus will (increase/decrease).

This notion of optimal purchases and purchasing more as long as marginal utility is greater than price is all well and good for a single commodity, but couldn't a consumer run out of income before she has considered optimal purchases of all goods and services? When one looks at demand curves commodity by commodity, this seems a real possibility. But remember, income and preferences influence utility and demand. Total utility measures what people are willing to pay, given their preferences, their income, and the prices of other goods, not

---

[1]There is a geometric interpretation of consumer's surplus. As the demand curve is the curve of marginal utility, the area under the demand curve equals total utility. If a consumer can buy as much as he wants at market prices, total expenditures are price times the quantity purchased. The difference between total utility and total expenditure is consumer surplus and can be represented as the area under the demand curve and above the horizontal line drawn at the market price. For a straight-line demand curve, consumer surplus is a triangle. This triangle is analogous to the shaded bars of Figure 5-3 in the text.

what they desire. As Mick Jagger and the Rolling Stones said, "You can't always get what you want." The appendix to this chapter shows geometrically how total income constrains the demand for individual commodities.

With our optimal purchase rule, it is easy to derive an individual demand curve. A demand curve shows the quantity demanded at different prices, holding all other things constant. (Look back at Chapter 4 if necessary.) To derive an individual demand curve, we confront our consumer with different prices and see how the quantity demanded changes. Our optimal purchase rule tells us that he will purchase more units as long as the marginal utility is (<u>greater/less</u>) than the price of the unit. He will stop when the two are equal. If we now lower the price, (3) we know that he will again try to equate price and (<u>marginal/total</u>) utility, which he does by considering buying (<u>more/less</u>). Thus, as price goes down the quantity demanded tends to go (<u>down/up</u>), and this individual demand curve has a (<u>positive/negative</u>) slope. In fact, an individual's demand curve will be the same as her curve of (<u>marginal/total</u>) utility.

Income also affects an individual's demand for various commodities. We saw in Chapter 4 that a change in income will mean a (<u>shift in/movement along</u>) the demand curve. In terms of the concepts of this chapter, a (4) change in income will influence how much a person would spend to buy various commodities; that is, a change in income will influence total and marginal _____. Following a change in income, we could again conduct our demand curve experiment, and it would not be surprising if the resulting demand curve had shifted. An increase in income will typically mean an increase in the demand for most commodities, but occasionally the demand for some commodity decreases following an increase in income. Commodities whose demand decreases when income increases are called _____ goods. For example, if potatoes were an inferior good, then increased income would lead our consumer to demand (<u>fewer/more</u>) potatoes.

Individual demand curves are a critical building block to market demand curves. If people determine their own demands without regard to others' purchases, then we can derive the market demand curve by the (<u>horizontal/vertical</u>) summation of individual demand curves. For each price we simply add up the individual (5) quantities demanded. If individual demand curves each have a negative slope, the market demand curve must have a(n) _____ slope. Even if individual demand curves are vertical, that is, individuals purchase only a fixed quantity, the market demand curve is still likely to have a negative slope as long as lower prices attract new consumers and higher prices drive some consumers away.

IMPORTANT TERMS AND CONCEPTS QUIZ

Choose the best definition for each of the following terms.

1. _____ Total utility
2. _____ Marginal utility
3. _____ The "law" of diminishing marginal utility
4. _____ Marginal analysis
5. _____ Consumer's surplus
6. _____ Inferior good
7. _____ Market demand curve
8. _____ The "law" of demand

a. Horizontal summation of individual demand curves
b. Difference between total utility and total expenditures for a given quantity of some commodity
c. Observation that additional units of a given commodity generally have decreasing value for a consumer
d. Maximum amount of money a consumer will give in exchange for a quantity of some commodity
e. Maximum amount of money a consumer will pay for an additional unit of some commodity
f. Quantity demanded increases when consumer real income rises
g. Quantity demanded declines when consumer real income rises
h. Method for calculating choices that best promote the decision maker's objective
i. Observation that a lower price generally increases the amount of a commodity that people in a market are willing to buy

BASIC EXERCISES

These exercises review how we use the law of diminishing marginal utility to derive a negatively sloped demand curve.

1. **Table 5-1** presents data on Dolores' evaluation of different quantities of dresses.

Table 5-1

Dresses	Total Utility	Marginal Utility
1	$110	$ _____
2	$210	$ _____
3	$290	$ _____
4	$360	$ _____
5	$410	$ _____
6	$440	$ _____
7	$460	$ _____

a. Use these data to compute the marginal utility of each dress.
b. The optimal purchase rule says to buy more dresses as long as the marginal utility of the next dress exceeds the price of the dress. According to this rule, how many dresses should Dolores buy if they cost

   $90 each? _____ $60 each? _____ $40 each? _____
c. The text defines total utility as the maximum amount Dolores would pay for various quantities of dresses. The difference between what she would be willing to pay and what she has to pay is called _____ surplus.

Table 5-2

Dresses	Price = $90 Total Expenditure	Difference* (Consumer's Surplus)	Price = $60 Total Expenditure	Difference* (Consumer's Surplus)	Price = $40 Total Expenditure	Difference* (Consumer's Surplus)
1	$90	_____	$60	_____	$40	_____
2	180	_____	120	_____	80	_____
3	270	_____	180	_____	120	_____
4	360	_____	240	_____	160	_____
5	450	_____	300	_____	200	_____
6	540	_____	360	_____	240	_____
7	630	_____	420	_____	280	_____

*Differences between total utility and total expenditures

d. Now, fill in columns 3, 5, and 7 of **Table 5-2** to compute Dolores' consumer's surplus at each price. What quantity maximizes consumer's surplus when price equals

$90? _____ $60? _____ $40? _____

How do these quantities compare to your answers to (b)?

e. Use the information in Table 5-1 to plot Dolores' demand curve for dresses in **Figure 5-1**. Is your demand curve consistent with your answers to questions b and c? (It should be.)

Figure 5-1

Demand for Dresses

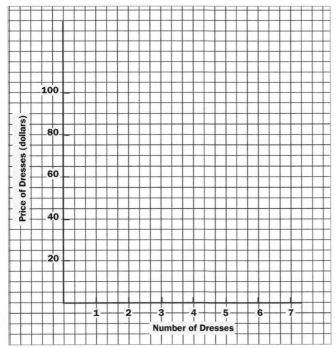

55

2. Consider the following information about Joel's total utility for sweaters:

Number of Sweaters	Total Utility
1	$100
2	$190
3	$27
4	$330
5	$380
6	$410
7	$435
8	$455

a. What marginal utility is associated with the purchase of the third sweater? _____

b. What is Joel's consumer's surplus if he purchases three sweaters at $45 apiece? _____

c. What would happen to Joel's consumer's surplus if he purchased a fourth sweater at $45?

_____

d. How many sweaters should Joel buy when they cost $45 apiece? _____

e. What is Joel's consumer's surplus at the optimal number of sweater purchases? _____

f. If sweaters go on sale and their price drops to $27.50, how many sweaters do you expect Joel to buy?
Why? _____

SELF-TESTS FOR UNDERSTANDING

TEST A

Circle the most appropriate answer.

1. The total utility of any commodity bundle
   a. should be the same for all individuals.
   b. is defined as the maximum amount a consumer will spend for the bundle.
   c. will equal expenditures on the commodity in question.
   d. is not likely to change even if a consumer's income changes.

2. Total utility will increase
   a. as long as marginal utility is positive.
   b. only if marginal utility is greater than price.
   c. if the good in question is not an inferior good.
   d. if consumer surplus is positive.

3. The law of diminishing marginal utility
   a. implies that total utility declines as a consumer buys more of any good.
   b. is an important psychological premise that helps explain why demand curves may have a positive slope.
   c. must hold for every commodity and every individual.
   d. says that increments to total utility usually decrease as an individual consumes more of a commodity.

4. Rick is willing to spend up to $400 for one ski trip this winter and up to $500 for two trips. The marginal utility of the second trip to Rick is
    a. $100.
    b. $200.
    c. $300.
    d. $500.

5. The optimal purchase rule says that consumers should maximize
    a. total utility.
    b. the difference between total utility and consumer surplus.
    c. marginal utility.
    d. the difference between total utility and total expenditures on the good in question.

6. The optimal purchase rule says that to maximize the difference between total utility, measured in money terms, and total expenditures, a consumer should purchase additional units
    a. as long as total utility is increasing.
    b. until marginal utility equals zero.
    c. as long as marginal utility exceeds price.
    d. until marginal utility equals total utility.

7. Consumer surplus refers to the
    a. money a consumer has left over at the end of the month.
    b. accumulation of garbage that could be, but is not, recycled.
    c. difference between total expenditures and what a consumer would have been willing to pay for the same purchases.
    d. the pleasure a consumer takes when he finds an especially good deal.

8. Consumer surplus will increase as long as the marginal utility of each additional purchase is
    a. positive.
    b. increasing.
    c. greater than total utility.
    d. greater than the price of the commodity.

9. If consumers act to maximize consumer surplus, price will be closely related to
    a. total utility.
    b. average utility.
    c. marginal utility.
    d. consumer surplus.

10. On a demand curve diagram, consumer surplus is equal to the
    a. Y-axis intercept of the demand curve.
    b. the market price.
    c. the areas between the demand curve and the horizontal line indicating the market price.
    d. the slope of the demand curve.

11. The law of diminishing marginal utility implies that individual demand curves will typically
    a. have a negative slope.
    b. show no response to a change in price.
    c. slope up and to the right.
    d. have a positive slope.

12. A downward-sloping demand curve means that the quantity demanded will
    a. not change when price changes.
    b. increase when price falls.
    c. increase when price rises.
    d. increase when income increases.

13. Scarcity raises _____ utility but lowers _____.
    a. total; price
    b. marginal; price
    c. marginal; total utility
    d. total; marginal utility

14. The diamond–water paradox indicates that
    a. contrary to economists' assumptions, consumers are really irrational.
    b. price is more closely related to marginal utility than to total utility.
    c. water is an inferior good.
    d. the demand for diamonds is very elastic.

15. The effect of an increase in income on quantity demanded
    a. is always positive.
    b. may be positive or negative.
    c. is positive for necessities and negative for luxuries.
    d. depends on the price elasticity of demand.

16. When economists say that some commodity is an inferior good, they are referring to the impact of a(n)
    a. change in price on the quantity demanded.
    b. increase in the quantity consumed on total utility.
    c. increase in the quantity consumed on marginal utility.
    d. change in income on the quantity demanded.

17. The term *inferior good* refers to goods
    a. made with substandard materials.
    b. that economists dislike.
    c. for which the quantity demanded declines when real income increases.
    d. advertised in the *National Enquirer*.

18. The opportunity cost of a purchase _____ its money cost.
    a. is always less than
    b. is always equal to
    c. is always greater than
    d. may be greater or less than

58

19. Market demand curves can be constructed by
    a. the vertical summation of individual demand curves.
    b. varying the number of people in the market.
    c. charging different people different prices and observing their behavior.
    d. the horizontal summation of individual demand curves.

20. A market demand curve will have a negative slope (there may be more than one correct answer)
    a. if all individual demand curves are downward sloping.
    b. only if the good in question is an inferior good.
    c. even if individual demands are not affected by price, but a lower price attracts new buyers.
    d. if a higher price increases the quantity demanded.

TEST B

Circle T or F for true or false.

T F 1. The term *marginal utility* refers to the amount of dollars that consumers will pay for a particular commodity bundle.

T F 2. If the law of diminishing marginal utility holds for pizza, then the demand curve for pizza should have a negative slope.

T F 3. If a consumer is interested in maximizing the difference between total utility and expenditures, it is optimal to consume more of a commodity as long as the marginal utility of additional units exceeds the market price.

T F 4. Consumer surplus is defined as the difference between price and marginal utility.

T F 5. Maximizing the difference between total utility and total expenditures is the same as maximizing consumer surplus.

T F 6. The term *inferior good* refers to those commodities that economists do not like.

T F 7. If the quantity of ramen demanded decreases when income increases, we can conclude that ramen is an inferior good.

T F 8. If a consumer is rational, he will never buy an inferior good.

T F 9. The opportunity cost of making a purchase is always equal to the money cost of the good being bought.

T F 10. A market demand curve can have a negative slope only if all individual demand curves have a negative slope.

| APPENDIX | *Indifference Curve Analysis*

Important Terms and Concepts

Budget line

Indifference curve

Marginal rate of substitution

Slope of an indifference curve (marginal rate of substitution)

Slope of a budget line

Learning Objectives

After completing this appendix, you should be able to:

- draw a budget line, given data on prices and money income.

- explain the logic behind the four properties of indifference curves:

   (1) higher is better,

   (2) they never intersect,

   (3) they have a negative slope, and

   (4) they are bowed in toward the origin.

- determine optimal commodity bundle(s) for a consumer, given a budget line and a set of indifference curves.

- explain why, if indifference curves are smooth and bowed in to the origin, the optimal commodity bundle is the one for which the marginal rate of substitution equals the ratio of commodity prices.

- use indifference curve analysis to derive a demand curve, that is, show the change in the quantity demanded of a good as its price changes.

- use indifference curve analysis to analyze the impact on commodity demands of a change in income.

APPENDIX REVIEW

Indifference curve analysis is a more rigorous treatment of the material covered in Chapter 5. As the appendix shows, we can study consumer choices by confronting a consumer's desires or preferences, indicated by indifference curves, and with a consumer's opportunities, indicated by a budget line. This approach clearly shows how total purchases are constrained by income.

   The budget line represents all possible combinations of commodities that a consumer can buy, given his

(1) income. The arithmetic of a budget line for two commodities shows that it is a (straight/curved) line with a (positive/negative) slope. An increase in money income will change the (intercept/slope) of the budget line. A change in the price of either commodity will mean a change in the _____ of the budget line. The

60

slope of the budget line is equal to the ratio of the prices of the two commodities. (The price of the commodity measured along the horizontal axis goes on top.)[2]

The budget line indicates all the different ways a consumer could spend her income. In order to figure out what consumption bundle is best for her, we must examine her own personal preferences. Economists use the concept of _____ curves to summarize an individual's preferences. These curves are de-   (2)
rived from a person's ranking of alternative commodity bundles. For two commodities, a single indifference curve is a line connecting all possible combinations (bundles) of the two commodities between which our consumer is _____. From the assumption that more is better, we can deduce (1) that higher indifference curves (are/are not) preferred to lower indifference curves, (2) that indifference curves (never/often) intersect, and (3) that indifference curves will have a (positive/negative) slope.

Indifference curves are usually assumed to be curved lines that are bowed (in/out). The slope of an indiffer-   (3)
ence curve indicates the terms of trade between commodities about which our consumer is indifferent. For a given reduction in one commodity the slope tells us how much (more/less) of the other commodity is necessary to keep our consumer as well-off as before. The slope of the indifference curve is also known as the marginal rate of _____. If indifference curves are bowed in, or convex to the origin, the marginal rate of substitution (increases/decreases) as we move from left to right along a given indifference curve. This change in the marginal rate of substitution is a psychological premise similar to our earlier assumption about declining marginal utility, and it is what makes the indifference curves convex to the origin.[3]

We can now determine optimal consumer choices. The optimal choice is the commodity bundle that makes our consumer as satisfied as possible, given his opportunities. In this case, opportunities are represented by the _____ line, and the evaluation of alternative commodity bundles is given by the   (4)
_____ curves. The best choice is the commodity bundle that puts our consumer on his (highest/lowest) possible indifference curve. This consumption bundle is indicated by the indifference curve that is just tangent to the _____ _____.

From the definition of the slope of a curved line (Appendix to Chapter 1) we know that at the point of tangency the slope of the associated indifference curve will equal the slope of the budget line. Because the slope of the budget line is given by the ratio of the prices of the two goods, we know that at the optimal decision the slope of the indifference curve, or the marginal rate of substitution, will equal the ratio of prices.

The marginal rate of substitution tells how our consumer *is willing* to trade goods, and the price ratio tells us how she *can* trade goods in the market by buying more of one good and less of the other. If these two trading

---

[2]The equation for the budget line is Income $= P_V Q_V + P_H Q_H$, where V refers to the commodity measured on the vertical axis and H refers to the commodity measured on the horizontal axis. Solve this equation for Q_V and you should get $Q_V = \text{Income}/P_V - (P_H/P_V)Q_H$. Income/$P_V$ is the Y-axis intercept and P_H/P_V is the slope of the budget line. You can use this equation to examine the impact of changes in income and prices on the budget line.
[3]Moving to the left along an indifference curve we see that our consumer is willing to trade fewer and fewer units of the horizontal good for each additional unit of the good measured on the vertical axis. That is, each additional unit of the vertical good is worth less and less to our consumer.

ratios are different, our consumer can make herself better off by changing her purchases. It is only when the two trading ratios are equal that her opportunities for gain have been eliminated.

Once you master the logic and mechanics of indifference curve analysis, you can use it to investigate the impact on demand of changes in price or incomes. A change in either income or prices will shift the (5) _____ _____. It is the resulting change in the optimal commodity bundle that helps trace out a movement along the demand curve in the case of a change in the price of the commodity, or the shift in the demand curve in the case of a change in income or a change in the price of the other commodity.

IMPORTANT TERMS AND CONCEPTS QUIZ

Choose the best definition for each of the following terms.

1. _____ Budget line
2. _____ Indifference curve
3. _____ Slope of an indifference curve (Marginal rate of substitution)
4. _____ Slope of a budget line

a. Maximum amount of one commodity a consumer will give up for an extra unit of another commodity
b. Lines connecting all combinations of commodities on a consumer's utility function
c. Line showing all possible combinations of two commodities a consumer can purchase given prices and the consumer's income
d. Line connecting all combinations of commodities that a consumer finds equally desirable
e. Ratio of commodity prices

BASIC EXERCISES

These problems are designed to review the logic of the rule for optimal consumer choice using indifference curve analysis, which says that a consumer should choose the commodity bundle associated with the point of tangency between the budget line and the highest indifference curve.

1. **Figure 5-2** shows Gloria's set of indifference curves between books and hamburgers.
   a. Gloria has an income of $240 that she will spend on books and hamburgers. Hamburgers cost $3 each and paperback books $12 each. Draw the budget line in Figure 5-2 that constrains Gloria's choices. (You might first compute the maximum number of hamburgers Gloria can buy and then

Figure 5-2

Gloria's Indifference Curve

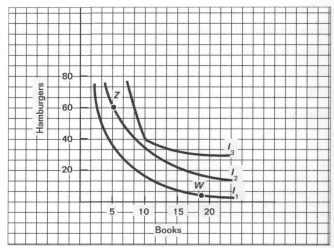

determine the maximum number of books; connect these points on the vertical and horizontal axes with a straight line.)

b. How many hamburgers will Gloria buy? _____ How many books will she buy? _____ In Figure 5-2, label this combination *B* for best choice. (If you drew the budget line correctly, this point should lie on indifference curve I_3.)

c. The combination of 60 hamburgers and 5 books, point *Z*, is obviously not a better choice, as it lies on a lower indifference curve. Assume that Gloria tentatively chooses point *Z* and is considering whether this choice is best. If you put a ruler along indifference curve I_2, you should be able to verify that at point *Z* the marginal rate of substitution of hamburgers for books is 6. This means that Gloria is willing to give up _____ hamburgers in order to be able to buy one more book. However, because books cost only \$12 while hamburgers cost \$3, Gloria has only to give up _____ hamburgers in order to buy one book. This is clearly a good deal for Gloria, and she should reduce her consumption of hamburgers in order to buy more books; that is, she will move down the budget line away from point *Z*.

d. Consider point *W* on indifference curve I_1. Think about the trade-off Gloria would accept as given by the slope of her indifference curve and the trade-off available in the market as given by the slope of the budget line. Explain why Gloria will be better off moving to the left along the budget line away from point *W*.

e. Arguments similar to those in parts c and d indicate that for smooth indifference curves as in Figure 5-2, the optimal consumer choice cannot involve a commodity bundle for which the marginal rate of substitution differs from the ratio of market prices. The conclusion is that the optimal decision must be the commodity bundle for which the marginal rate of substitution

_____.

2. **Figure 5-3** assumes that Sharon spends all of her income on pizza and baseball tickets. The budget line P_1B_1 reflects Sharon's initial income and market prices for pizza and baseball tickets. Her preferences are shown by the curved indifference curves. Initially, Sharon chooses to consume at point *X*.

a. Change in income: Where will Sharon consume following a change in income that shifts the budget line to P_2B_2? _____ Is either good an inferior good? How do you know?

b. Change in price: Where will Sharon consume following a reduction in the price of pizzas that shifts the budget line from P_1B_1 to P_3B_1? _____

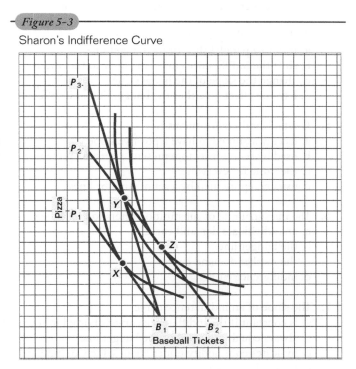

Figure 5-3

Sharon's Indifference Curve

63

SELF-TESTS FOR UNDERSTANDING

TEST A

Circle the most appropriate answer.

1. The budget line
   a. determines an individual's optimal consumption bundle.
   b. will not shift at all if prices of both commodities increase and income is unchanged.
   c. determines an individual's possible consumption bundles.
   d. is a straight line whose slope is given by the rate of inflation.

2. The slope of the budget line
   a. is equal to the marginal rate of substitution.
   b. depends upon a consumer's income.
   c. is determined by commodity prices.
   d. should be positive.

3. Following a change in income,
   a. a consumer's indifference curves will shift.
   b. the slope of the budget line will increase.
   c. individual commodity demand curves will not shift.
   d. the budget line will shift in a parallel fashion.

4. A change in the price of one good will
   a. lead to a parallel shift of the budget line.
   b. shift the indifference curves in closer to the origin.
   c. change the slope of the budget line.
   d. have no effect on either the budget line or indifference curves.

5. A set of indifference curves is
   a. usually assumed to have a positive slope.
   b. used by economists to represent a person's preferences among different commodity bundles.
   c. the same for everyone.
   d. usually represented by a set of straight lines.

6. The marginal rate of substitution refers to the slope of
   a. an individual's demand curve.
   b. the budget line.
   c. the market demand curve.
   d. indifference curves.

7. The slope of an indifference curve
   a. is constant if the indifference curve is bowed in toward the origin.
   b. always equals the slope of the budget line.
   c. indicates commodity trades about which an individual would be indifferent.
   d. is usually positive.

8. The assumption that more is preferred to less is sufficient to prove all but which one of the following?
    a. Indifference curves never intersect.
    b. Indifference curves bow in toward the origin.
    c. Higher indifference curves are preferred to lower ones.
    d. Indifference curves have a negative slope.

9. If, when choosing between beer and pretzels, a consumer is always willing to trade one beer for one bag of pretzels, the resulting indifference curve will
    a. still bow in toward the origin.
    b. be a straight line.
    c. bow out away from the origin.

10. On an indifference curve diagram, optimal purchases are given by
    a. the point where the budget line intersects the Y axis.
    b. the intersection of a ray from the origin and the budget line.
    c. the highest indifference curve that is attainable given the budget line.
    d. any indifference curve that crosses the budget line.

11. The optimal purchases from question 10 occurs where
    a. the quantity of all commodities is equal.
    b. all goods are inferior goods.
    c. demand curves begin to slope up.
    d. the highest indifference curve is tangent to the budget line.

12. If an indifference curve is tangent to the budget line, then the marginal rate of substitution is
    a. less than the ratio of prices.
    b. just equal to the ratio of prices.
    c. greater than the ratio of prices.
    d. zero.

13. On an indifference curve diagram, an increase in the price of one commodity will
    a. cause the resulting budget line to lie inside the original budget line.
    b. lead a consumer to choose a new commodity bundle, but one that is on the same indifference curve.
    c. shift consumer preferences.
    d. have no effect on the demand for either commodity.

TEST B

Circle T or F for true or false.

T   F   1. The budget line is a curved line, convex to the origin.

T   F   2. A change in the price of one commodity will change the slope of the budget line.

T   F   3. A change in income will also change the slope of the budget line.

T   F   4. The assumption that consumers prefer more to less is sufficient to establish that indifference curves will be convex to the origin.

T   F   5. The slope of indifference curves at any point is given by the ratio of commodity prices.

T   F   6. The slope of an indifference curve is also called the marginal rate of substitution.

65

T F 7. Optimal decision making implies that a consumer should never choose a commodity bundle for which the marginal rate of substitution equals the ratio of market prices.

T F 8. Indifference curve analysis shows that consumers should be indifferent about all the commodity bundles along the budget line, e.g., consumers should be indifferent as between points Y and Z in Figure 5-3.

T F 9. Indifference curve analysis shows us that the demand for all goods is interrelated in the sense that changes in the price of one good can affect the demand for other goods.

T F 10. Indifference curve analysis suggests that a doubling of all prices and a doubling of income will not change optimal consumption bundles.

SUPPLEMENTARY EXERCISE

Consider a consumer whose total utility can be represented as

$$U = (F + 12)(C + 20)$$

where F = quantity of food, C = quantity of clothing, and U = the arbitrary level of utility associated with a particular indifference curve. (A different value for U will imply a different indifference curve.)

1. Draw a typical indifference curve. (Try $U = 7,840$.)

2. Can you derive an expression for the demand for food? For clothing? (Try using the equation for the budget line and what you know about optimal consumer choice to derive an equation that expresses F or C as a function of prices and income. The particular form of these demand curves comes from the mathematical specification of the indifference curves. A different specification of the indifference curves would lead to a different demand function.)

3. If food costs $1.50, clothing $3, and income is $300, what combination of food and clothing will maximize utility?

4. Assume the price of food rises to $2. Now what combination of food and clothing maximizes utility?

5. Assume income increases to $330. What happens to the demand for food and clothing? Is either good an inferior good?

ECONOMICS IN ACTION

DRIP, DRIP, DRIP

In spite of periodic wet winters, drought is a consistent threat to residents of Arizona, California, Nevada, and western Colorado. A year or two of below-average rain and snowfall can seriously deplete water reserves. As the effects of a water shortage become progressively more severe, various schemes for water rationing are discussed, but typically these schemes do not involve using prices to ration water. Most water districts set price to cover cost and do not think very much about price as a variable that might limit demand when drought limits supply.

A typical sequence of events will start with a campaign to encourage voluntary reduction in water usage. As drought persists, many areas establish quotas for water usage, usually based on family size, with stiff increases in price for water consumption in excess of the quota. (The dashed line in Figure 5-4 illustrates such a "quota–high price" scheme. The dashed line indicates the total water bill. The price per gallon is given by the slope of the line.)

The "quota–high price" scheme offers a strong incentive to limit water consumption to the basic quota, but there is little monetary incentive to reduce water consumption below the quota. In 1977, when California was in the midst of a significant drought, economist Milton Friedman suggested that rather than impose quotas with high prices for excess consumption, water districts should charge a high price for all water consumption, offering a rebate to consumers with low water consumption. (See *Newsweek,* March 21, 1977.)

The solid line in **Figure 5-4** illustrates a possible "high price–rebate" scheme. To ensure that a water district has enough money to cover its fixed costs, the position and/or slope of the solid line could be adjusted. Parallel shifts of the solid line would affect the maximum rebate and the no-charge point, but not the price of a gallon of water. Shifts in the slope would change the price. For example, pivoting the solid line on point A would change both the price and the maximum rebate, while leaving the cost of the basic water quota unchanged.

Ross and Judy live in San Francisco. During 1976, in response to the growing concern about water conservation, they voluntarily cut their water consumption significantly below the quotas established by other water districts. The San Francisco rationing scheme, not adopted until early 1977, mandated that all San Francisco residents reduce their consumption below 1976 levels by the same percentage. When drought returned to California in the mid-80s, Ross and Judy were heard telling their friends that they were using all the water they could to increase their base use.

Figure 5-4

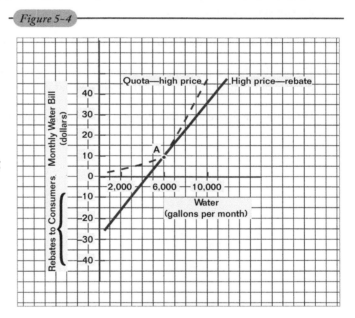

1. What advice would you give to a water district facing a drought? How much reliance should be placed on campaigns for voluntary reductions? How much reliance should be placed on prices? If prices, what sort of scheme would you recommend and why? Do you think price affects people's demand for water? What about businesses, government, and farmers?

STUDY QUESTIONS

1. What is the difference between total and marginal utility?

2. How is it that total utility can increase while marginal utility decreases?

3. Why do economists expect a close relationship between price and *marginal utility* rather than *total utility?*

4. How does the difference between total and marginal utility resolve the diamond–water paradox?

5. What is the logic behind the optimal purchase rule?

6. Why does the law of diminishing marginal utility imply that demand curves are likely to have a negative slope?

7. How do we know that purchasing more of a commodity as long as marginal utility exceeds prices will also maximize consumer surplus?

8. How can there be mutual gain from voluntary trade even when no new goods are produced?

9. Economists have a particular definition of inferior goods that does not refer to the quality of product directly but may be correlated with quality. What is the economist's definition of an inferior good?

10. How can one derive a market demand curve from individual demand curves?

Demand and Elasticity

6

Important Terms and Concepts

(Price) elasticity of demand

Elastic, inelastic, and unit-elastic demand curves

Income elasticity of demand

Complements

Substitutes

Cross elasticity of demand

Optimal decision

Learning Objectives

After completing this chapter, you should be able to:

- compute the price elasticity of demand given data from a demand curve.

- explain why the price elasticity of demand is a better measure of the price sensitivity of demand than the slope of the demand curve.

- explain how the impact of a change in price on total revenue and consumer expenditures depends on the price elasticity of demand.

- describe how various factors affect the elasticity of demand.

- use elasticity in measuring how any one economic variable responds to changes in another.

- compute the cross elasticity of demand given information on the change in the price of good X and the associated change in the quantity of good Y demanded.

- explain how the concept of cross elasticity of demand relates to the concepts of substitutes and complements.

- explain how factors other than price can affect the quantity demanded.

- compute the income elasticity of demand given information on how a change in income changes the quantity demanded.

- understand the time period of the demand curve and economic decision making.

CHAPTER REVIEW

The material in this chapter offers an intensive look at demand curves. Demand curves provide important information for analyzing business decisions, market structures, and public policies.

An important property of demand curves is the responsiveness of demand to a change in price. If a firm raises its price, how big a sales drop is likely? If a firm lowers its price, how large an increase in sales will there be?

To avoid problems with changing units, economists find it useful to measure these changes as percentages. If, for a given change in price, we divide the percentage change in the quantity demanded by the percentage change in the price producing the change in quantity and ignore the negative sign, we have just computed the

(1) price _____ of _____. Remember, this calculation ignores minus signs and uses the *average* price and quantity to compute percentage changes.

It is useful to know the elasticity properties of certain, special types of demand curves. If the demand curve is truly a vertical line, then there is no change in the quantity demanded following any change in price, and the

(2) elasticity of demand is _____. (No demand curve is likely to be vertical for all prices, but it may be for some.) The other extreme is a perfectly horizontal demand curve where a small change in price produces a very large change in the quantity demanded. Such a demand curve implies that if price declines, even just a little, the quantity demanded will be infinite, while if the price rises, even a little, the quantity demanded will fall to zero. In this case, a very small percentage change in price produces a very large percentage change in the quantity demanded, and the price elasticity of demand is, in the limit, _____. The price elasticity of demand along a negatively sloped straight-line demand curve (is constant/changes). One of the Basic Exercises illustrates just this point.

A demand curve with a price elasticity of demand greater than 1.0 is commonly called

(3) _____ while a demand curve with a price elasticity of demand less than 1.0 is called _____. If the price elasticity of demand is exactly 1.0, the demand curve is said to be a(n) _____ _____ demand curve.

Some simple arithmetic, not economics, can show the connection between the price elasticity of demand and the change in total consumer expenditure (or, equivalently, the change in sales revenue) following a change in price. We know that total expenditures or revenues are simply price times quantity, or

$$\text{Consumer expenditures} = \text{Sales revenues} = PQ.$$

A decrease in price will increase quantity as we move along a given demand curve. Whether total revenue increases clearly depends on whether the increase in quantity is big enough to outweigh the decline in price. (Remember the old saying: "We lose a little on each sale but make it up on volume.")

It is mathematics, not economics, that tells us the percentage change in total expenditures or revenue is equal to the sum of the percentage change in price and the percentage change in quantity.[1]

_____

[1]This result is strictly true only for very small changes in P and Q. Total revenue always equals $P \times Q$, but this simple way of calculating the percentage change in total revenue is only true for small changes.

70

$$\begin{array}{ccc} \text{Percentage change} & = & \text{Percentage change} & + & \text{Percentage change} \\ \text{in sales revenues} & & i\ \text{price} & & \text{in quantity} \end{array}$$

Remember that as we move along a given demand curve, a positive change in price will lead to a negative change in quantity, and vice versa.

If the absolute value of the percentage change in quantity is equal to the absolute value of the percentage change in price, then total revenue (<u>will/will not</u>) change following a change in price. In this case, the price elas- (4) ticity of demand is equal to _____.

When the elasticity of demand is greater than 1.0, the absolute value of the percentage change in quantity will be (<u>greater/less</u>) than the percentage change in price. In this case, an increase in price that reduces the (5) quantity demanded will (<u>decrease/increase</u>) total revenue, and a reduction in price that increases the quantity demanded will (<u>decrease/increase</u>) total revenue. Opposite conclusions apply when the price elasticity of demand is less than 1.0. In this case, the percentage change in quantity will be (<u>greater/less</u>) than the percentage change in price. An increase in price that reduces the quantity demanded will (<u>decrease/increase</u>) total revenue, and a reduction in price that increases the quantity demanded will (<u>decrease/increase</u>) total revenue.

The price elasticity of demand refers to the impact on the quantity demanded of a change in a commodity's price. A related elasticity concept compares the change in the quantity demanded of one good with a change in the price of another good. This quotient is called the _____ elasticity of demand. In this case we must (6) keep track of any negative signs.

Some goods, such as knives and forks, cereal and milk, are usually demanded together. Such pairs are called _____ and are likely to have a (<u>positive/negative</u>) cross elasticity of demand. For example a de- (7) cline in the price of milk is likely to (<u>decrease/increase</u>) the demand for cereal. That is, following a decline in the price of milk, the demand curve for cereal will likely shift to the (<u>left/right</u>).

Other goods, such as different brands of toothpaste, are probably close _____ and are likely (8) to have a(n) _____ cross elasticity of demand. What is the likely impact of a change in the price of Crest toothpaste on the demand for Colgate? A decrease in the price of Crest toothpaste would likely (<u>decrease/increase</u>) the demand for Colgate toothpaste. Alternatively, one could say that a decrease in the price of Crest will likely shift the Colgate demand curve to the (<u>left/right</u>).

The price of a commodity is not the only variable influencing demand. Changes in other factors, say, advertising, consumers' income, tastes, and, as we just saw, the price of a close substitute or complement, will mean a (<u>shift in/movement along</u>) a demand curve drawn against price. Finally, remember that a demand curve refers (9) only to a particular period of time.

IMPORTANT TERMS AND CONCEPTS QUIZ

Choose the best definition for each of the following terms.

1. _____ Price elasticity of demand
2. _____ Elastic demand curve
3. _____ Inelastic demand curve
4. _____ Unit-elastic demand curve
5. _____ Income elasticity of demand
6. _____ Complements
7. _____ Substitutes
8. _____ Cross elasticity of demand
9. _____ Optimal decision

a. Ratio of percent change in quantity demanded of one product to the percent change in the price of another
b. A change in price leads to a less than proportionate change in quantity demanded

c. Good for which an increase in price leads to higher demand
d. An increase in price of one good decreases the demand for the other
e. A change in price leads to a more than proportionate change in quantity demanded
f. Ratio of percent change in quantity demanded to percent change in price
g. A change in price accompanied by an equal proportionate change in quantity demanded
h. An increase in the price of one good increases the demand for the other
i. Ratio of percentage change in quantity demanded to percentage change in income
j. Decision that best serves the objectives of the decision maker, whatever those objectives may be

BASIC EXERCISES

These exercises offer practice in calculating and interpreting price elasticities of demand.

1. **The Price Elasticity of Demand**
   a. **Table 6-1** has data on possible prices and the associated demand for schmoos and gizmos. Use these data to plot the demand curves in **Figures 6-1** and **6-2.** Looking at these demand curves, which curve looks more elastic? More inelastic?
   b. Use the data in Table 6-1 to calculate the elasticity of demand for schmoos for a change in price from $60 to $50.[2] It is _____.
   c. Now calculate the elasticity of demand for gizmos for a change in price from $1 to 50 cents. It is _____.
   d. For these changes, which demand curve is more elastic? In fact, if you look closely at the underlying data for both curves—for example, by computing the total revenue—you will see that for both curves the elasticity of demand is _____.

Table 6-1

Demand for Schmoos		Demand for Gizmos	
Price (dollars)	Quantity	Price (dollars)	Quantity
60	200	2.00	2,000
50	240	1.25	3,200
48	250	1.00	4,000
40	300	0.50	8,000

2. **The Price Elasticity of Straight-Line Demand Curves**
   a. Use the data in **Table 6-2** to plot the demand curve for jeans in **Figure 6-3.** It is a (curved/straight) line.

---

[2]Remember to use the average of the two prices or quantities when computing each percentage change. For example, compute the elasticity of demand when the price changes from $60 to $50 as $\left[\frac{40}{220}\right] \div \left[\frac{10}{55}\right]$.

Figure 6-1

Figure 6-2

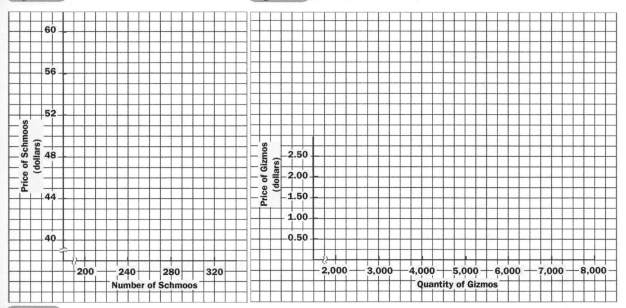

Table 6-2

Price (dollars)	Quantity Demanded	Percentage Change Price	Percentage Change Quantity	Elasticity of Demand	Total Revenue
40	15,000				
36	18,000	_____	_____	_____	_____
32	21,000	_____	_____	_____	_____
28	24,000	_____	_____	_____	_____
24	27,000	_____	_____	_____	_____

b. Using the data in Table 6-2, compute the elasticity of demand for each change in price.[3] What general conclusion can you draw about the elasticity of demand along a straight-line demand curve? The elasticity of demand (increases/decreases) as one moves down and to the right along a straight-line demand curve.

c. Use the same data to compute total revenue for each price-quantity pair in Table 6-2. Compare the change in total revenue to the elasticity of demand. What conclusion can you draw about this relationship?

Figure 6-3

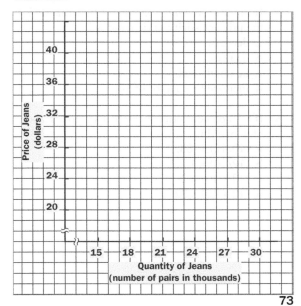

---

[3]Remember to use the average of the two prices or quantities when computing each percentage change. For a change in price from $40 to $36, compute the elasticity of demand as $\left[\dfrac{3,000}{16,500}\right] \div \left[\dfrac{4}{38}\right]$.

73

SELF-TESTS FOR UNDERSTANDING

TEST A

Circle the most appropriate answer.

1. Looking just at the demand curve, the price responsiveness of demand is given by the
   a. Y-intercept.
   b. slope of the demand curve.
   c. slope of a ray from the origin to a point on the demand curve.
   d. product of price times quantity.

2. If when price increases the quantity demanded declines, we know that
   a. the demand curve has a negative slope.
   b. the price elasticity of demand is less than 1.0.
   c. total sales revenue will increase.
   d. total sales revenue will decrease.

3. The price elasticity of demand is defined as the _____ change in the quantity demanded divided by the _____ change in price.
   a. percentage; absolute
   b. absolute; absolute
   c. percentage; percentage
   d. absolute; percentage

4. If the price elasticity of demand is less than 1.0, then for a 10 percent change in price the quantity demanded will change by
   a. less than 10 percent.
   b. exactly 10 percent.
   c. more than 10 percent.
   d. There is not enough information.

5. If the units in which the quantity demanded is measured are changed, say from pounds to ounces, then the price elasticity of demand will
   a. decrease.
   b. increase.
   c. be unaffected.
   d. increase by a factor of 16.

6. If a 10 percent price increase leads to a 12 percent decline in the quantity demanded, the price elasticity of demand is
   a. (10/12) = .83.
   b. (12/10) = 1.2.
   c. (12 − 10) = 2.
   d. (12 + 10) = 22.

74

7. If the elasticity of demand is equal to 1.0, then a change in price leads to
   a. no change in the quantity demanded.
   b. a reduction in total revenue.
   c. a shift in the demand curve.
   d. (ignoring any negative signs) an equal, proportionate change in the quantity demanded.

8. If the elasticity of demand is greater than 1.0, a reduction in price will
   a. decrease total sales revenue.
   b. leave total sales revenue unchanged.
   c. increase total sales revenue.
   d. lead to a reduction in the quantity demanded.

9. Sales revenue will not change following an increase in price if the
   a. price elasticity of demand is equal to 1.0.
   b. demand curve is a straight line.
   c. cross elasticity of demand is positive.
   d. quantity demanded doesn't change.

10. If the demand for apples is inelastic, apple producers could increase total revenue by
    a. decreasing price.
    b. increasing price.
    c. Changing price will not affect total revenue.

11. If a 20 percent decrease in the price of long-distance phone calls leads to a 35 percent increase in the quantity of calls demanded, we can conclude that the demand for phone calls is
    a. elastic.
    b. inelastic.
    c. unit elastic.

12. From the data given above, what would happen to total revenue following a 20 percent decrease in the price of long-distance phone calls? It would
    a. decrease.
    b. increase.
    c. remain the same.

13. Angelita manufactures artificial valves used in open-heart surgery. She is contemplating increasing prices. Total revenue will decrease unless the demand for valves is
    a. elastic.
    b. inelastic.
    c. unit elastic.

14. Goods that are usually used together are said to be
    a. complements.
    b. inelastic.
    c. spin-offs.
    d. substitutes.

15. If goods are substitutes, then the cross elasticity of demand is likely to be
    a. equal to 1.0.
    b. negative.
    c. positive.
    d. zero.

16. The cross elasticity of demand between frozen pizza and home-delivered pizza would be computed as the percentage change in the quantity of frozen pizza demanded divided by the
    a. percentage change in the price of frozen pizza.
    b. percentage change in the quantity of home-delivery pizza demanded.
    c. percentage change in the price of home-delivery pizza.
    d. change in the price of mozzarella cheese.

17. If following an increase in the price of schmoos the quantity demanded of gizmos declined, we would conclude that
    a. the demand for gizmos is inelastic.
    b. gizmos and schmoos are substitutes.
    c. gizmos and schmoos are complements.
    d. schmoos are likely to be a luxury good.

18. If the cross elasticity of demand between two goods is negative, we would conclude that the two goods are
    a. substitutes.
    b. complements.
    c. necessities.
    d. both likely to have inelastic demand curves.

19. If skis and boots are complements, then which one of the following statements is false?
    a. A reduction in the price of skis is likely to increase the sales of boots.
    b. Revenue from ski sales will increase following a reduction in the price of ski boots.
    c. An increase in the price of boots will likely reduce the sales of skis.
    d. The cross elasticity of demand between skis and boots will likely be positive.

20. The income elasticity of demand is measured as the percentage change in
    a. price divided by the percentage change in income.
    b. the quantity demanded divided by the percentage change in income that changes demand.
    c. income divided by the change in demand.
    d. income divided by the percentage change in price.

TEST B

Circle T or F for true or false.

T   F   1. The price elasticity of demand is defined as the change in quantity divided by the change in price.

T   F   2. The elasticity of demand will be the same at all points along a straight-line demand curve.

T   F   3. A vertical demand curve would have a price elasticity of zero.

T   F   4. A demand curve is elastic if, following a decrease in price, the quantity demanded increases.

T   F   5. If demand is inelastic, an increase in price will actually increase the quantity demanded.

76

T   F   6. If the demand for airplane travel is elastic, then a reduction in the price of airline tickets will increase total expenditures on airplane trips.

T   F   7. If two goods are substitutes, then an increase in the price of one good is likely to reduce the demand for the other good.

T   F   8. The cross elasticity of demand between complements is normally negative.

T   F   9. If sales of Whoppers at Burger King increase following an increase in the price of Big Macs at McDonald's, we can conclude that Whoppers and Big Macs are complements.

T   F   10. The price elasticity of demand for Chevrolets is likely to be greater than that for cars as a whole.

T   F   11. A demand curve will shift to the left following an increase in price of a close complement.

T   F   12. An increase in consumer income will shift the demand curve for most goods to the left.

T   F   13. The income elasticity of demand is defined as the percentage change in income divided by the percentage change in price.

T   F   14. Plotting price and quantity for a period of months or years is a good way to estimate a demand curve.

| APPENDIX | *Statistical Analysis of Demand Relationships*

BASIC EXERCISES

Completing these exercises should help underscore the necessity and difficulty of distinguishing between a demand curve and observations on price and quantity that are determined by the intersection of demand and supply curves.

1. Consider the data on the consumption and prices of fresh apples for the period 1994 to 2006 in **Table 6-3.** Plot these data on a piece of graph paper. What does this graph say about the demand for apples? Why?

— *Table 6-3* ————————————————

Year	Quantity (millions of pounds)	Price (dollars per pound)
1990	4,926.7	$0.72
1991	4,618.0	$0.89
1992	4,944.2	$0.89
1993	4,972.2	$0.83
1994	5,126.4	$0.80
1995	5,006.4	$0.83
1996	5,061.9	$0.93
1997	4,961.9	$0.91
1998	5,268.9	$0.94
1999	5,197.2	$0.90
2000	4,958.6	$0.92
2001	4,478.1	$0.87
2002	4,633.7	$0.95

2. Assume that the demand for handheld calculators depends on aggregate consumer income and price as follows:

$$Q_D = -110 + 0.2Y - 5P$$

where

Q_D = quantity demanded (thousands),

Y = consumer income (millions), and

P = price (dollars).

Supply is assumed to be determined as follows:

$$Q_S = 50 + 15P$$

where Q_S = quantity supplied (thousands).

a. Compute the equilibrium price and quantity for 2005, 2006, and 2007, given that consumer income was as follows:

Year	Consumer Income
2005	$3,000
2006	3,100
2007	3,200

Plot these price–quantity pairs for each year on a two-variable diagram. Are these points a good estimate of the demand curve? Why or why not?

b. Assume now that the supply curve for calculators shifts each year in response to technical advances in the production process. To capture these technical advances, we need a new supply curve for each year as follows:

2005　$Q_S = 50 + 15P$

2006　$Q_S = 100 + 15P$

2007　$Q_S = 300 + 15P$

Compute and plot equilibrium price and quantity for each year. (Remember to include the effect of the change in consumer income in the demand curve.) Are these points a good estimate of the demand curve? Why or why not?

ECONOMICS IN ACTION

1. Howard Grant operates a movie theater in New Jersey, just across the Hudson River from New York. He used to show the most recently released movies at a ticket price of $6.50. He was especially discouraged when attendance dropped to 212 people over a full weekend. He then changed the format of his theater to show still current but previously released movies, and he reduced his ticket price to $1. Weekend attendance jumped to 3,782 people. (*The New York Times*, March 20, 1992.)

    a. Using the numbers above, what is the elasticity of demand for movies at Mr. Grant's theater?

    b. What is likely to happen to Mr. Grant's attendance if other theaters adopt his format and lower their prices?

2. In the late spring of 1992, Northwest Airlines offered a promotional fare advertised as parents fly free with children. The program cut fares in half for family travel. American Airlines responded by halving all fares purchased seven days in advance, a move matched by most other airlines. To avoid the anger of passengers who had bought tickets earlier, the airlines agreed that these passengers could reticket at the new, lower fares. Not surprisingly, airlines and travel agents were swamped with calls. At one point, new

bookings were so heavy that some airline executives were reported saying that total sales revenue might not drop "because of the extraordinary high response." (*The New York Times,* June 2, 1992.)

a. What would the price elasticity of demand for air travel have to be if these airline executives were correct?

b. How would we know whether the reduction in ticket prices did double the demand for air travel? Consider the following. In the summer of 1991, June through September, travel on domestic airlines totaled 120 billion passenger miles. In 1992, summer travel totaled 134.5 billion passenger miles. Discuss the relevance of this information for an evaluation of the impact of the reduction in airfares.

3. In December 2001, Leonard Riggio, Chairman of Barnes and Noble, argued that publishers should rethink book pricing. Mr. Riggio was quoted as saying "publishers and retailers would both make more money if books cost less." (*New York Times,* December 16, 2001.) Paul Ingram, a bookstore owner in Iowa City, Iowa, agreed. He was quoted as saying, ". . . they would sell more books and make more money if they lowered the prices."

a. What must be true about the elasticity of demand for books if Mr. Riggio and Mr. Ingram are correct?

STUDY QUESTIONS

1. Why is elasticity measured as the ratio of percentage changes and not just as the ratio of the change in quantity demanded to the change in price?

2. What is the logic behind the statement that the demand for narrowly defined commodities, for example a particular brand of clothing, is more elastic than the demand for broadly defined commodities, that is, all clothing?

3. Which is likely to be larger and why—the price elasticity of demand for luxuries or the price elasticity of demand for necessities?

4. What is meant by the terms "perfectly elastic" and "perfectly inelastic"? What do these demand curves look like and why?

5. How does the elasticity of demand help determine whether a change in price will raise or lower total sales revenue?

6. If a government is interested in increasing revenue, will it want to impose or raise sales taxes on goods with a high or low price elasticity of demand? Why?

7. What is the cross elasticity of demand and how does its numerical value help to determine whether goods are complements or substitutes?

8. Consider the demand for pretzels. Why does the change in the price of a complement, say, beer, or the change in the price of a close substitute, say, potato chips, lead to shifts in the demand curve for pretzels rather than a movement along the curve? What exactly is the nature of the shifts?

Production, Inputs, and Cost: Building Blocks for Supply Analysis

7

Important Terms and Concepts

Short run

Long run

Fixed cost

Variable cost

Total physical product (TPP)

Average physical product (APP)

Marginal physical product (MPP)

Marginal revenue product (MRP)

Economies of scale (increasing returns to scale)

Learning Objectives

After completing this chapter, you should be able to:

- describe the difference between the short run and long run.

- compute the average and marginal physical product for a single input given data on total output at different input levels.

- explain the "law" of diminishing marginal returns.

- compute the marginal revenue product for additional units of some input given information on the marginal physical product of the input and the price of the output.

- explain why a profit-maximizing firm will expand the use of each input until its marginal revenue product equals the price of the input.

- distinguish between diminishing returns following an increase of a single productive input.

- explain the importance of opportunity cost when distinguishing between total cost and total expenditure.

- explain the difference between fixed and variable costs.

- explain why fixed costs, administrative problems of large organizations, and the law of diminishing returns

imply that the short-run average cost curve is usually U-shaped.

- explain how to determine the long-run average cost curve from a set of short-run average cost curves.

- explain how and why the ratio of input prices and the ratio of marginal physical products is relevant to the optimal choice of input combinations.

- explain how total cost—and hence average cost as well as marginal cost—can be computed.

- determine whether a firm's operations show increasing, decreasing, or constant returns to scale, given data on output and on various input combinations.

- explain the relationship between returns to scale and the long-run average cost curve.

- distinguish between diminishing returns to increases of a single productive input and economies of scale when all inputs change.

- explain the difference between analytical and historical cost curves.

CHAPTER REVIEW

In this chapter we will make extensive use of the concept of marginal analysis as a guide to optimal decision making. We will see how marginal analysis can help a firm make optimal decisions about the use of production inputs and how these decisions can be used to derive cost curves. In Chapter 5, we saw how marginal analysis helps to understand optimal consumer decisions. We use it here in an analogous way to understand optimal firm decisions about the use of inputs.

This chapter introduces a potentially bewildering array of curves and concepts—marginal physical product, marginal revenue product, fixed costs, variable costs, long run, and short run. All of these curves and concepts relate to each other and underlie optimal firm decisions. Spending time now to get these relationships clear will save you time in later chapters and the night before the exam.

In deciding whether to use an additional unit of some input, say, hiring more workers, a firm should look at the contribution of the additional workers to both total revenue and total cost. If the increase in revenue (1) exceeds the increase in cost, then profits will (<u>increase/decrease</u>). The increase in revenue comes from producing and selling additional units of output. Economists call the amount of additional output from the use of one more unit of input the marginal (<u>physical/revenue</u>) product of the input. For a firm selling its output at a constant price, the increase in revenue comes from multiplying the additional output by the price at which it can be sold. Economists call this the marginal _____ product.

Consider a small firm that faces fixed market prices for its production inputs. Common sense tells us that a profit-maximizing firm should use additional units of any input if the addition to total revenue exceeds the addition to total cost. Another way of saying the same thing is that the firm should consider using more of an (2) input as long as the marginal (<u>physical/revenue</u>) product exceeds the price of the input. A firm has clearly gone too far if additions to revenue are less than additions to cost. Thus a profit-maximizing firm should expand the use of any factor until the marginal revenue product equals the _____ of the input.

If the price of an input is constant, firms will use more and more units of this input until the marginal revenue product falls to a point where it equals the input price. As a result, firms will usually expand the use of any input past any region of increasing marginal returns and into the region of decreasing returns to the one input.

So far we have talked about the optimal use of only one input. What if production involves trade-offs between more than one input? Our rule holds true for more than one input. The idea is to adjust the use of all inputs until the marginal revenue of each is equal to the price of the input. In symbols, assuming the use of two inputs A and B, we have $MRP_A = P_A$ and $MRP_B = P_B$. A little multiplication and division should show that when the prices of inputs and output are constant, our condition for optimal input use can be rewritten as MPP_A/P_A and MPP_B/P_B.[1]

---

[1]For input A, we can write our condition for optimal input use as MPP_A x $P_{OUTPUT} = P_A$. Dividing both sides of this equality by MPP_A we see that $P_{OUTPUT} = P_A/MPP_A$. Similar results hold for input B. That is, setting MRP_B equal to the price of input B also sets $P_{OUTPUT} = P_B/MPP_B$. Since both fractions are equal to the price of output, they are equal to each other and their reciprocals are also equal, that is if $P_A/MPP_A = P_B/MPP_B$ then $MPP_A/P_A = MPP_B/P_B$, our condition for the optimal input combination.

Either fraction shows how output will change per dollar spent on that input. When the fraction is high, one gets a lot of output per dollar spent. A low fraction means less output per dollar spent. If this ratio were initially high for input B and low for input A, a firm would want to use (<u>less/more</u>) of input B and _____ of input (3) A. Making these adjustments should (<u>increase/reduce</u>) the MPP of input B and _____ the MPP of input A, moving the fractions toward the equality necessary for the optimal input combination.

If the price of an input changes, it is natural to expect the firm's optimal input combination to change. Specifically, it is natural to expect that a profit-maximizing firm will (<u>reduce/increase</u>) the use of any factor (4) whose price has risen. Changing the quantity of one input will typically affect the marginal physical product of other inputs. As a result, a firm will want to rethink its use of all inputs following a change in price of any one input. It is quite likely that following an increase in the price of one input, a profit-maximizing firm will decide to use relatively (<u>less/more</u>) of the more expensive input and relatively _____ of the inputs with un-changed prices.

If all inputs are increased by the same percentage amount, then the percentage increase in output is used to indicate the degree of economies of scale. If output increases by more than the common percentage increase in all inputs, the production function exhibits _____ returns to scale. If output increases by less, (5) there are _____ returns to scale, and if output increases by the same percentage, we would say that returns to scale are _____.

Information about inputs and outputs can be used to construct cost curves for a firm. Over a very short time horizon, previous commitments may limit a firm's ability to adjust all inputs. These commitments often imply that at least one input is predetermined and cannot be adjusted immediately. Imagine a farmer with a five-year lease on a parcel of land and unable to rent additional land. The interval of time over which a firm's fixed com-mitments cannot be adjusted is called the (<u>long/short</u>) run. (6)

When computing the total cost of producing each level of output in the short run we will be interested only in minimum total costs for every level of output. We first use what we know about optimal factor use to deter-mine the most efficient combination of variable inputs. We can then compute minimum total cost. As an ex-ample, assume that production requires two inputs, one of which is fixed in the short run. To compute total cost, the firm must identify what amount of the variable input is necessary to produce different levels of output. Then it can compute total cost for each level of output by multiplying the quantity of the fixed input and the optimal quantity of the variable input by their prices, remembering relevant opportunity costs, and adding the results. After computing total cost, the firm can compute average cost by dividing total cost by the associated level of _____. To compute marginal cost the firm must examine how (<u>average/total</u>) cost changes (7) when output changes.

The period of time over which a firm can adjust all its fixed commitments is called the _____ _____. Long-run cost curves can be derived by either of two equivalent methods. (8) One procedure would first derive short-run cost curves for each possible amount of the fixed input. The long-run cost curve is then determined by joining the _____ segments of the short-run cost curves.

An alternative and equivalent method would treat both factors as variable. One would first use information on the marginal physical product for each input along with input prices to determine the optimal level of both inputs to produce every level of output. Total cost for each output level can then be computed by multiplying optimal input levels by their respective prices and adding the results. Average and marginal cost are then easily computed.

(9)   Since in the long run all factors can be changed, the shape of the long-run average cost curve is related to economies of scale. Constant returns to scale imply that a doubling of output requires twice as much of all inputs. In this case, total costs also double and average cost (<u>falls/is unchanged/rises</u>). Increasing returns to scale mean that twice the output can be produced with (<u>more/less</u>) than twice the inputs and average cost will (<u>fall/rise</u>). With decreasing returns to scale, twice the output requires _____ than twice the inputs and average cost _____.

We've covered a lot of ground and a lot of curves. You may want to take a deep breath before a quick review. One starts with the basic technical information about inputs and output. From this information we can derive total physical product and marginal physical product for a single input. By itself the technical information is not sufficient to determine the minimum cost combination of inputs. Knowing the price of output will let us compute marginal revenue product for each input. Comparing marginal revenue product with input prices will then determine the optimal input quantities. Optimal input quantities, in turn, determine (minimum) total cost for alternative levels of output. Once we know total cost, we can easily compute average and marginal cost. In the short run, there may be fixed costs. In the long run, all inputs, and hence all costs, are variable. In either run, the same optimizing principles apply.

IMPORTANT TERMS AND CONCEPTS QUIZ

Choose the best definition for each of the following terms.

1. _____ Short run
2. _____ Long run
3. _____ Fixed costs
4. _____ Variable costs
5. _____ Total physical product (TPP)
6. _____ Average physical product (APP)
7. _____ Marginal physical product (MPP)
8. _____ Marginal revenue product (MRP)
9. _____ Economies of scale (increasing returns to scale)

a. A graph showing how average cost has changed over time

b. Costs which do not change when output rises or falls

c. Increase in output greater than the proportionate increase in all inputs

d. Period of time long enough for all of a firm's commitments to end

e. Dollar value of output produced by an extra unit of input

f. Graph of output generated by various quantities of one input, holding other inputs fixed

g. Total output divided by total quantity of input

h. Costs that change as the level of production changes

i. Increase in output that results from an additional unit of a given input, holding all other inputs constant

j. Period of time during which none of a firm's commitments will have ended

BASIC EXERCISES

These questions review the concept of optimal input decisions.

Megan and Jamie have invested in Greenacre Farms to grow cornbeans. Since they both work in the city, they will need to hire workers for the farm. **Table 7-1** has data on various input combinations and the resulting output of cornbeans.

1. **Figure 7.1** shows the relationship between total output and labor input for 100 acres of land.

   What is the region of increasing marginal returns? _____

   What is the region of decreasing marginal returns? _____

   What is the region of negative marginal returns? _____

2. Use Figure 7-1 to draw the relationship between total output and labor input, assuming the use of 200 acres of land. Identify the regions of increasing, decreasing, and negative returns.

   Do the same assuming 300 acres of land. How does the output–labor curve, i.e., the curve of total physical product, shift when more land is used?

3. Fill in the middle part of Table 7-1 by computing the marginal physical product of each worker. Check to see that the regions of increasing, diminishing, and negative returns that you identified above correspond to information about the marginal physical product of labor. (The marginal physical product of labor is equal to the slope of the total physical product curve. Check to see that your entries for each row in the middle of Table 7-1 equal the slope of the relevant total product curve in Figure 7-1.)

Table 7-1

Total Output of Cornbeans (thousands of tons)

Number of Workers		1	2	3	4	5	6
Acres	100	1	4	6	7	6	4
of	200	2	6	9.5	12	13	12
Land	300	3	7.5	11	14	16	17

Marginal Physical Product of Labor

		1	2	3	4	5	6
Acres	100	____	____	____	____	____	____
of	200	____	____	____	____	____	____
Land	300	____	____	____	____	____	____

Marginal Revenue Product of Labor

	1	2	3	4	5	6
200 Acres of Land	____	____	____	____	____	____

Figure 7-1

Output of Cornbeans

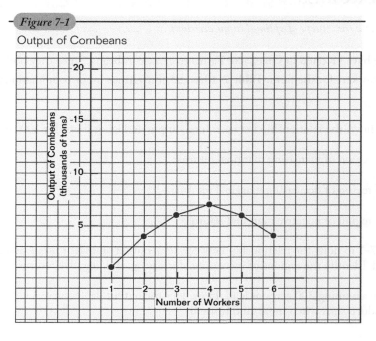

4. Your answers to questions 1, 2, and 3 should confirm that the production of cornbeans eventually shows decreasing returns to labor for all three potential farm sizes. (What about returns to the increased use of land for a fixed amount of labor?)

5. Now consider the following pairs of inputs (acres, workers) and indicate for each whether economies of scale are increasing, decreasing, or constant.

Economies of Scale

   (100, 1) to (200, 2)   _____

   (100, 2) to (200, 4)   _____

   (100, 3) to (200, 6)   _____

   (200, 2) to (300, 3)   _____

   (200, 4) to (300, 6)   _____

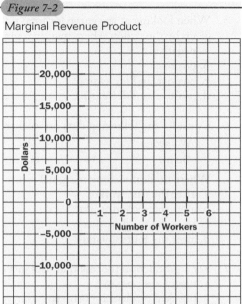

Figure 7-2

6. Assume that cornbeans can be sold for $5 a ton and that Greenacre Farms has 200 acres of land. Calculate the marginal revenue product of labor for 200 acres of land in the bottom part of Table 7-1. Plot the marginal revenue product in **Figure 7-2.** Hired help costs $8,000 for a growing season. Draw a horizontal line in Figure 7-2 at $8,000 to indicate the price of labor. How many workers should Megan and Jamie hire? _____. At the level of labor input you just determined, what is the difference between the proceeds from selling cornbeans (output) and labor costs? _____ (Check to see that your labor input choice maximizes this difference by considering the use of one more or one fewer worker.)

SELF-TESTS FOR UNDERSTANDING

TEST A

Circle the most appropriate answer.

1. A graph of total physical product shows how output changes as
   a. all inputs are increased simultaneously.
   b. the firm adopts new technologies.
   c. the scale of production varies.
   d. one input is increased, holding all others constant.

2. For a production process that uses just one input, average physical product is found by
   a. graphing total output against the number of units of input.
   b. computing the change in output for a unit change in input.
   c. dividing total output by the number of units of input.
   d. multiplying the number of units of input by their cost.

3. The "law" of diminishing marginal returns
   a. says that eventually the marginal physical product of any input must become negative.
   b. applies to only a simultaneous increase in all inputs.
   c. can only be true when there are decreasing returns to scale.
   d. refers to what happens to output as only one factor is increased, all other inputs being held constant.

4. Marginal physical product refers to
   a. the increased revenue from employing an additional worker.
   b. the change in total output from a one-unit increase in a variable input.
   c. total output divided by total input.
   d. total output divided by total cost.

5. When looking at the curve for total physical product, the region of diminishing marginal returns is given by the region where marginal physical product is
   a. negative.
   b. positive.
   c. positive and increasing.
   d. positive and decreasing.

6. Consider the following data on workers and output.

Workers	1	2	3	4	5
Output	10	25	35	42	40

   Where do diminishing marginal returns to workers begin to set in?
   a. after the first worker
   b. after the second worker
   c. after the third worker
   d. after the fourth worker

7. For a production process that uses just one input, a firm should expand output as long as marginal
   a. revenue is positive.
   b. physical product is positive.
   c. revenue product is greater than the price of the input.
   d. physical product is greater than average physical product.

8. The rule for optimal input use implies that a firm should use additional units of an input until
   a. average cost equals the price of the input.
   b. marginal physical product is maximized.
   c. marginal revenue product equals the price of the input.
   d. increasing returns to scale are exhausted.

9. A change in fixed costs affects
   a. marginal physical product of the variable input.
   b. average physical product of the variable input.
   c. marginal cost associated with changes in the variable input.
   d. average cost associated with changes in total output.

10. In the short run, decisions to vary the amount of output will affect all but which one of the following?
    a. fixed costs
    b. variable costs
    c. marginal physical product
    d. average costs

11. As output increases, average fixed costs
    a. first decline and then increase.
    b. decrease continuously.
    c. are constant.
    d. increase more or less continuously.

12. As output increases, average total costs typically
    a. first decline and then increase.
    b. decrease continuously.
    c. are constant.
    d. increase more or less continuously.

13. A change in which of the following will not shift the short-run average cost curve?
    a. the price of output
    b. the price of inputs
    c. the quantity of fixed factors
    d. the marginal physical product of variable inputs

14. The term economies of scale refers to
    a. the change over time in average cost as firms grow larger.
    b. the percentage change in the marginal revenue product divided by the percentage change of the associated input.
    c. the increase in output when only one input is increased.
    d. what happens to total output following a simultaneous and equal percentage increase in all inputs.

15. If all inputs are doubled and output more than doubles, one would say that the production relationship
    a. shows decreasing returns to scale.
    b. shows constant returns to scale.
    c. shows increasing returns to scale.
    d. violates the "law" of diminishing returns.

16. In the long run,
    a. inputs are likely to be less substitutable than in the short run.
    b. all firms will exhibit constant returns to scale.
    c. a firm is assumed to be able to make adjustments in all its fixed commitments.
    d. average cost must decline.

17. The optimal choice of input combinations
    a. is a purely technological decision, unaffected by input prices, and better left to engineers than economists.
    b. can be determined by looking at information on the marginal revenue product and price of various inputs.
    c. will always be the same in both the short and long run.
    d. is likely to include more of an input if its price rises and if other input prices are unchanged.

18. Assume that on a small farm with ten workers, the hiring of an eleventh worker actually lowers total output. Which of the following statements is not necessarily true?
    a. The marginal physical product of the last worker is negative.
    b. The marginal revenue product of the last worker is negative.
    c. A profit-maximizing firm would never hire the eleventh worker.
    d. The operations of the farm show decreasing returns to scale.

19. Marginal revenue product (MRP) is equal to
    a. MPP/P_{OUTPUT}.
    b. $MPP \times P_{OUTPUT}$.
    c. P_{OUTPUT}/MPP.
    d. $MPP \times P_{INPUT}$.

20. The ratio of a productive input's marginal physical product (MPP) to its price is a measure of the
    a. marginal cost of expanding output.
    b. average cost of expanding output.
    c. efficiency of production.
    d. increase in output from spending an extra dollar on this input.

TEST B

Circle T or F for true or false.

T F 1. The "law" of diminishing returns says that economies of scale can never be increasing.

T F 2. The marginal physical product of an input refers to the increase in output associated with an additional unit of that input when all other inputs are held constant.

T F 3. The marginal revenue product measures the total revenue that a firm will have at different use levels of a particular input.

T F 4. If a firm's operations show increasing returns to scale from the additional use of all inputs, it violates the "law" of diminishing returns.

T F 5. If a firm's operations show decreasing returns to scale, it is likely that long-run average costs will be increasing.

T F 6. The short run is defined as any time less than six months.

T F 7. The curve of average fixed cost is usually U-shaped.

T F 8. Long-run cost curves will always lie above short-run cost curves.

T F 9. Inputs are likely to be more substitutable in the long run than in the short run.

T F 10. Historical data on costs and output is a good guide to the relevant cost curves for a firm's current decisions.

| APPENDIX | *Production Indifference Curves*

Learning Objectives

After completing this appendix, you should be able to:

- describe how diminishing returns to a single factor help determine the shape of a typical production indifference curve.

- determine what input combination will minimize costs for a given level of output, given information about production indifference curves and input prices.

- explain how a firm's expansion path helps determine (minimum) total cost for every possible output level.

- use a production indifference curve to explain how a change in the price of one productive factor can affect the least cost combination of inputs.

Important Terms and Concepts

Production indifference curve

Budget line

Expansion path

APPENDIX REVIEW

A set of production indifference curves (or isoquants) is a geometrical device that can be used to represent a production function involving two inputs and one output. The horizontal and vertical axes are used to measure quantities of each input. A line connecting all input combinations capable of producing the same amount of output is called the _____ _____ curve. Each separate curve represents a (1) particular output level. Higher curves will mean (<u>more/less</u>) output.

Production indifference curves will have a (<u>negative/positive</u>) slope as a reduction in the use of one in- (2) put must be compensated for by an increase in the use of the other input. Production indifference curves (<u>will/will not</u>) bow in toward the origin. This last property follows from the "law" of _____ _____ returns. Production indifference curves (<u>do/do not</u>) cross.

Production indifference curves tell a firm what alternative combinations of inputs it could use to produce the same amount of output. An optimizing firm should not be indifferent to these alternatives. To determine the least costly combination of inputs, the firm will need to know the price of each input. From this information, the firm can construct a budget line showing combinations of inputs that can be purchased for the same total cost. The budget line is a (<u>curved/straight</u>) line. The slope of the budget line is given by the ratio of input prices. (3) The price of the input measured on the horizontal axis goes on the top of the ratio. The intercept on each axis comes from dividing the total budget by the price of input measured on that axis.

91

(4) To minimize cost for a given level of output, the firm chooses that combination of inputs lying on the (highest/lowest) budget line consistent with the given level of output. For smooth and convex production indifference curves, the least costly input combination is given by the point of tangency between the budget line and the relevant production indifference curve. A change in the price of either input will change the slope of the budget line and result in a new optimal input combination. It is now easy to see that an increase in the price of one input will typically lead firms to use (less/more) of that input and _____ of the input whose price has not changed.

(5) The procedure described in the previous paragraph will determine the optimal input combination to minimize cost for a given output target. Using the same procedure to find the lowest cost input combination for different levels of output defines the firm's _____ path. It also allows us to compute total cost for any level of output. At this point, division and subtraction will allow us to compute average and marginal cost. What level of output maximizes profits is considered in the next chapter.

Is the solution to the question of optimal input combinations in this appendix consistent with the earlier discussion that determined optimal inputs by comparing input prices and marginal revenue products? Yes. Although it may not be immediately obvious, the slope of the production indifference curve equals the ratio of marginal physical products. When we choose the optimal input combination from the point of tangency where the slope of the production indifference curve equals the slope of the budget line, we set the ratio of marginal products equal to the ratio of input prices. In symbols, assuming that our two inputs are A and B, choosing the point of tangency between the production indifference curve and the budget line means that

$$MPP_A/MPP_B = P_A/P_B.$$

Some multiplication and division[2] allows us to rewrite this expression as

$$MPP_A/P_A = MPP_B/P_B,$$

which we have seen is equivalent to our earlier condition for the optimal use of inputs.

IMPORTANT TERMS AND CONCEPTS QUIZ

Choose the best definition for each of the following terms.

1. _____ Production indifference curve
2. _____ Budget line
3. _____ Expansion path

a. Locus of firm's cost-minimizing input levels for different output levels
b. Graph showing how total output varies as one input is increased
c. Graph depicting all combinations of input quantities that yield a given level of output
d. Representation of equally costly input combinations

---

[2]Multiply both sides of the expression by MPP_B and divide each side by P_A.

BASIC EXERCISES

Figure 7-3 shows a production indifference curve for producing 6,000 tons of cornbeans. This curve is derived from data given in Table 7-1.

1. (Read all of this question before answering.) If land can be rented at $65 an acre a year and if labor costs are $8,000 a worker per year, what is the least cost combination for producing 6,000 tons of cornbeans? Restrict your answer to the dots in Figure 7-3 that correspond to data in Table 7-1.

   _____ acres and _____ workers

   If land rents for $125 a year and labor costs $8,000 a worker, what is the least cost input combination for producing 6,000 tons of cornbeans?

   _____ acres and _____ workers

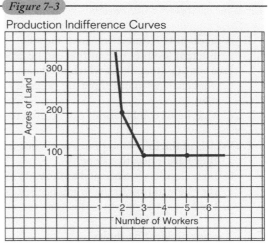

Figure 7-3

Production Indifference Curves

Remember that the ratio of input prices determines the slope of the budget line. For a given set of input prices draw the budget lines that pass through each of the possible input combinations. Remember that for a given set of input prices, these lines should be parallel and the least cost combination is given by the lowest budget line. Can you explain why?

2. From your answer to the previous question, you know that if the cost of using land is relatively low, the least cost input combination will use more land with a smaller number of workers. You also know that if the cost of using land rises enough, an optimizing farmer would be induced to use less land and more workers. What is the rental price of land that just tips the balance away from the input combination of 200 acres and two workers to the combination of 100 acres and three workers?

   $ _____ .

   The answer to this question comes from "rotating" a budget line around the outside of the production indifference curve. For given input prices, find the lowest budget line that just touches the production indifference curve. This point will show the lowest cost input combination. As one input price changes, the slope of the budget line will change and the lowest cost budget line rotates around the outside of the production indifference curve. If the price of land is low, the input combination of 200 acres and two workers will be on the lowest budget line. As the price of land rises, the slope of the budget line becomes flatter, and there will come a point where suddenly the input combination of 100 acres and three workers is on the lowest budget line.

SELF-TESTS FOR UNDERSTANDING

TEST A

Circle the most appropriate answer.

1. A production indifference curve shows
   a. different levels of output that can be produced with a given amount of inputs.
   b. levels of output about which producers should be indifferent.
   c. what changes in one input are necessary to keep the marginal physical product of a second input constant.
   d. what input combinations can be used to produce a given level of output.

2. Which of the following properties is not true of production indifference curves?
   a. They have a negative slope.
   b. Their slope is always equal to the ratio of input prices.
   c. They bow in toward the origin because of the "law" of diminishing returns.
   d. The amount of output is the same for all points on the production indifference curve.

3. A single budget line shows
   a. how total cost varies when the level of output changes.
   b. how production costs vary when the price of inputs changes.
   c. what different combinations of inputs can be purchased with a fixed budget.
   d. how production costs have changed over time.

4. The budget line
   a. has a positive slope.
   b. will shift in a parallel fashion in response to an increase in the price of one input.
   c. is a straight line with a negative slope reflecting relative input prices.
   d. will have a different slope following an equal percentage change in the price of all inputs.

5. The optimal input combination for a given level of output is determined by
   a. the Y-axis intercept of the budget line.
   b. the point where marginal utility is equal to price.
   c. the point of tangency between the lowest budget line and the relevant production indifference curve.
   d. where the relevant production indifference curve intersects the budget line.

6. Using budget lines to determine the optimal input combination for every possible level of output traces out
   a. the total physical product curve.
   b. a firm's expansion path.
   c. marginal revenue product.
   d. a firm's average cost curve.

7. When the price of one input increases, the
   a. budget line will shift out in parallel fashion.
   b. budget line will shift in toward the origin in parallel fashion.
   c. slope of the budget line will change.
   d. production indifference curves will shift.

94

8. If production requires two inputs, labor and capital, and the price of both doubles,
   a. the slope of the budget line will double.
   b. production indifference curves will become steeper.
   c. the marginal physical product of the more expensive input will decline.
   d. the slope of the budget line and the least costly input combination do not change.

9. Which one of the following will not occur after a reduction in the price of one input?
   a. The budget line will shift in such a way that a fixed production budget can now buy more of the cheaper input.
   b. The optimal input combination for a given level of output is likely to involve the use of more of the cheaper input.
   c. The minimum total cost for producing a given level of output will fall.
   d. Each production indifference curve will show a parallel shift.

TEST B

Circle T or F for true or false.

T   F   1. Production indifference curves have a positive slope because higher output usually requires more of both inputs.

T   F   2. Typically, a production indifference curve will bow in at the middle because of the "law" of diminishing returns.

T   F   3. A firm minimizes cost for any level of output by choosing the input combination given by the tangency of the budget line to the production indifference curve.

T   F   4. An increase in the price of either input will make the budget line steeper.

Γ   F   5. If production requires the use of two inputs, x_1 and x_2, a change in the price of x_1 will never affect the optimal use of x_2.

T   F   6. A change in the price of output will change the cost-minimizing input combination for a given level of output.

T   F   7. For given input prices, the tangencies of production indifference curves with alternative budget lines trace out a firm's expansion path.

SUPPLEMENTARY EXERCISES

Assume that the production of widgets (W) requires labor (L) and machines (M) and can be represented by the following expression[3]

$$W = L^{1/2} M^{1/2}.$$

1. Measuring machines on the vertical axis and labor on the horizontal axis, draw a production indifference curve for the production of 500,000 widgets.

---

[3]This particular mathematical representation of a production function is called the Cobb-Douglas production function. Charles Cobb was a mathematician. Paul Douglas was an economist at The University of Chicago, president of the American Economic Association, and United States senator from Illinois from 1948 to 1966. You might enjoy reading the comments by Albert Rees and Paul Samuelson about Douglas and his work in the *Journal of Political Economy*, October 1979, Part 1.

2. L measures labor hours and M measures machine hours. In the long run, both machine and labor hours are variable. If machine hours cost $48 and labor hours cost $12, what is the cost-minimizing number of labor and machine hours to produce 500,000 widgets? (Whether it is profitable to produce 500,000 widgets depends on the price of widgets.)

3. Assume that the firm has 125 machines capable of supplying 250,000 machine hours and that labor hours are the only variable input.
   a. Draw a picture of total output as a function of the number of labor hours.
   b. Use the production function to derive an expression for the marginal physical product of labor conditional on the 250,000 machine hours. Draw a picture of this function. What, if any, is the connection between your pictures of total output and marginal physical product?
   c. Divide your picture of the marginal physical product into regions of increasing, decreasing, and negative marginal returns to labor. (Note: Not all areas need exist.)
   d. If the price of widgets is $50 and the price of labor is $12 per hour, what is the optimal number of labor hours that the firm should use? How many widgets will the firm produce?

4. Graph the expansion path for this production function on the assumption that labor hours cost $12 and machine hours cost $48.

5. Are returns to scale in the production of widgets constant, increasing, or decreasing?

STUDY QUESTIONS

1. What is the difference between diminishing marginal returns and negative marginal returns?

2. Why does the discussion of optimal input use focus on marginal revenue product and not average revenue product?

3. What is the relation between marginal physical product and marginal revenue product?

4. Why is it optimal for a firm to use more of an input as long as marginal revenue product is greater than the price of the input?

5. What is the difference between fixed and variable cost?

6. Why do economists typically use a U-shaped curve to represent an average cost curve?

7. What is the difference between the short run and the long run?

8. If a firm's production function shows increasing returns to scale, what will its long-run average cost curve look like and why?

9. Why isn't a firm's long-run average cost curve found by connecting the minimum points of its short-run average cost curves?

10. Consider a production function that involves the input of two factors. For each factor individually, increases in inputs lead to diminishing returns. However, when both inputs are increased simultaneously, there are increasing returns to scale. Can this be possible? Explain how.

11. If output can be produced with varying quantities of different inputs, how can a firm figure out the cost-minimizing input combination?

12. Is data on how average cost has evolved over time appropriate to analyze the cost implications of different output levels today? Why or why not?

Output, Price, and Profit: The Importance of Marginal Analysis

Important Terms and Concepts

Optimal decision

Total profit

Economic profit

Total revenue (TR)

Average revenue (AR)

Marginal revenue (MR)

Marginal profit

Learning Objectives

After completing this chapter, you should be able to:

- explain why a firm can make a decision about output or price, but not usually about both.

- explain how and why an economist's definition of profit differs from that of an accountant.

- explain why the demand curve is the curve of average revenue.

- calculate total and marginal revenue from data on the demand curve.

- calculate average and marginal cost from data on total cost.

- use data on costs and revenues to compute the level of output that maximizes profits.

- explain why the point of maximum profit should be associated with a point of zero marginal profit.

- explain why comparing marginal revenue and marginal cost is equivalent to looking at marginal profit.

- explain why profit is maximized only when marginal revenue is (approximately) equal to marginal cost.

- explain how selling at a price below average cost can increase profits if price is above marginal cost.

CHAPTER REVIEW

This is the last of four building block chapters that explore what lies behind the demand and supply curves introduced in Chapter 4. As with Chapters 5 and 7, this chapter makes extensive use of marginal analysis, one of the most important tools an economist has. In this chapter, marginal analysis is used to help decide how much output a firm should produce to maximize its profits.

While marginal analysis is a powerful tool for business decision making, it is applicable in many nonbusiness situations as well. For example, how much should the government spend to clean up the environment? Or a related question: To clean up our lakes and rivers, should the government require all industries and towns to reduce their discharges by an equal percentage, or is there a more efficient alternative? As discussed in Chapter 17, marginal analysis can help answer these questions.

You may already have had more experience with marginal analysis than you realize. Have you ever had to pay federal income taxes? If so, you might dig out your records and make two calculations. Your total taxes divided
(1) by your total income would be your (<u>average/marginal</u>) tax rate. Now assume that you had $100 more income. Figure out how much more taxes you would have owed. This increase in taxes divided by the $100 additional income would be your (<u>average/marginal</u>) tax rate.

Your grade point average is another example of the distinction between marginal and average. If you want to raise your overall GPA, what sorts of grades do you need? The grades you earn this semester are the marginal contribution to your overall grade average. Similarly, a baseball player's batting record for a single game is a marginal measure when compared with his season's batting average.[1]

In whatever context, marginal analysis focuses on the effect of changes. For business output decisions, marginal analysis looks at the effect on costs, revenues, and profits as output changes. The change in total
(2) cost from changing output by one unit is called _____ cost. The change in total revenue from producing and selling one more unit is _____ revenue. Marginal profit is the change in total _____ as output expands by one unit. Because profits equal revenue minus costs, marginal profit equals marginal _____ minus marginal _____.

(3)   Economists usually assume that business firms are interested in maximizing (<u>average/marginal/total</u>) profit. This assumption need not be true for all firms, but economists have found that models based on this assumption provide useful insights into actual events. (Remember the discussion in Chapter 1 about the role of abstraction in theory.) Economists are interested in marginal profit, not as an end in itself, but because marginal profit is an extremely useful guide to maximizing total profit.

---

[1]One could take the position that each time at bat, rather than a whole game, is the real marginal measure. On this view, the marginal measure is either 1.000 (a hit) or 0.000 (no hit). Consistent with Rule 4 in the Appendix to this chapter, every hit increases a player's overall batting average and every at-bat without a hit lowers one's overall batting average.

100

It should be common sense that any firm interested in maximizing profit will want to expand output as long as the increase in total revenue exceeds the increase in total costs. If the increase in revenue is less than the increase in cost, the firm has gone too far. Rather than looking at total revenue and total cost, we could just as easily look at the changes in revenue and cost as output changes. An increase in output will add to profits if the increase in revenue is greater than the increase in costs. An economist might make the same point by saying that an increase in output will add to profits if (marginal/average) revenue exceeds (marginal/average) cost. We (1) could also say that an increase in output will add to total profits as long as marginal profits are (positive/zero/negative). Total profits will stop rising when marginal profits fall to _____; that is, when marginal revenue _____ marginal cost.

IMPORTANT TERMS AND CONCEPTS QUIZ

Choose the best definition for each of the following terms.

1. _____ Optimal decision

2. _____ Total profit

3. _____ Economic profit

4. _____ Total revenue

5. _____ Average revenue

6. _____ Marginal revenue

7. _____ Marginal profit

a. Net earnings minus a firm's opportunity cost of capital

b. Total revenue divided by quantity of output

c. Addition to profit from producing an additional unit of output

d. Amount firm must spend to produce a given quantity of output

e. Difference between total revenue and total costs

f. Best outcome for the decision maker

g. Price of output times quantity sold

h. Addition to total revenue when producing one more unit of output

BASIC EXERCISES

1. **Wanda's Widget Company**

   This exercise is designed to review the use of marginal revenue and marginal cost as a guide to maximizing profits.

   a. **Table 8-1** has data on demand for widgets from Wanda's Widget Company as well as data on production costs. Total revenue and total cost are plotted in the top panel of Figure 8-1. Fill in the column on total profits by subtracting total cost from total revenue. Plot the data on total profit in the second panel of **Figure 8-1.** Looking just at your graph of total profit, what output level maximizes total profits?

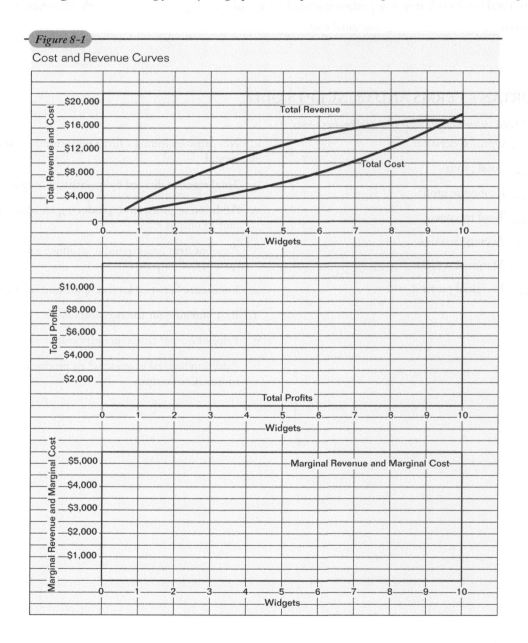

Figure 8-1

Cost and Revenue Curves

Table 8-1

Wanda's Widget Company

Marginal Revenue	Total Revenue	Demand Curve Price (dollars)	Output	Total Cost (dollars)	Marginal Cost	Total Profits
_____	3,500	3,500	1	2,000	_____	_____
_____	6,600	3,300	2	3,000	_____	_____
_____	9,300	3,100	3	4,100	_____	_____
_____	11,600	2,900	4	5,300	_____	_____
_____	13,500	2,700	5	6,900	_____	_____
_____	15,000	2,500	6	8,900	_____	_____
_____	16,100	2,300	7	11,100	_____	_____
_____	16,800	2,100	8	13,400	_____	_____
_____	17,100	1,900	9	15,800	_____	_____
_____	17,000	1,700	10	18,300	_____	_____

b. Complete Table 8-1 by computing marginal cost and marginal revenue. Plot each series in the bottom panel of Figure 8-1. Marginal revenue exceeds marginal cost up to what level of output? _____ Looking just at your graph of marginal cost and marginal revenue, what output level maximizes total profits? Is this the same answer as above?

c. **Figure 8-2** plots the average cost of producing widgets. Use the data on the demand curve from Table 8-1 to plot the curve of average revenue in Figure 8-2. Using the profit-maximizing level of output determined above, find the profit-maximizing price on the demand curve: Draw the rectangle for total revenue and shade it lightly with positively sloped lines. Using the average cost curve, draw the rectangle for total cost and shade it lightly with negatively sloped lines. This rectangle should overlap a part of the rectangle for total revenue. The nonoverlapped part of the total revenue rectangle is a measure of total (cost/profit/revenue). Maximizing total profit maximizes the size of this rectangle. It (does/does not) maximize the difference between average revenue and average cost. It (does/does not) imply that output should increase whenever average revenue, i.e., price, exceeds average cost.

Figure 8-2

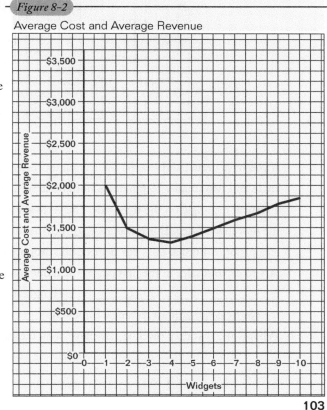

Average Cost and Average Revenue

103

d. (Optional) Assume now that there is an increase in the fixed costs Wanda must pay. Specifically assume that all of the entries in the column for total cost in Table 8-1 are now $3,000 higher. Write out a new version of Table 8-1 to determine the profit-maximizing level of output following the increase in fixed costs. What happens to total profits? Consider Figures 8-1 and 8-2. Explain which curves shift and why.

2. **The Geometry of Marginal Revenue**

a. **Figure 8-3** shows the demand curve for Medalist bicycles. Draw a rectangle for total revenue on the assumption that 55,000 bicycles are sold. Lightly shade this rectangle with horizontal lines. Assume now that 70,000 bicycles are sold rather than 55,000. Draw a rectangle for total revenue at this higher level of sales. Lightly shade this rectangle with vertical lines.

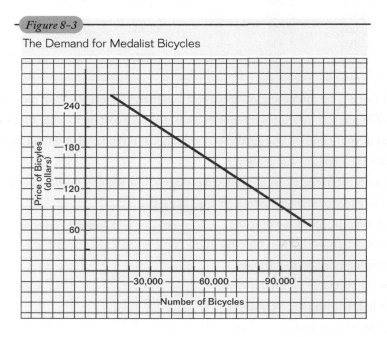

Figure 8-3

The Demand for Medalist Bicycles

If you have drawn and shaded the rectangles correctly, you should have a large, cross-hatched rectangle and two smaller rectangles: a horizontal rectangle on the top of the cross-hatched rectangle and a vertical rectangle on the right side. The vertical rectangle represents revenue from additional sales at the new lower price. This rectangle (is/is not) a complete measure of marginal revenue. It measures the receipts of additional sales but neglects the drop in revenue from the reduction in price that was necessary to expand sales in the first place. The reduction in revenue on previous units is represented by the _____ rectangle. The geometric representation of marginal revenue is the (vertical/horizontal) rectangle minus the _____ rectangle.

b. What is the marginal revenue associated with increasing output from 55,000 to 70,000 bicycles?

SELF-TESTS FOR UNDERSTANDING

TEST A

Circle the most appropriate answer.

1. The logic of the demand curve says that business firms can choose
   a. both the level of output and the level of prices.
   b. the level of output or the level of prices but not both.
   c. to sell whatever quantity they want at whatever price.
   d. only those levels of output where marginal cost equals marginal revenue.

2. The assumption of profit maximization is
   a. likely to be true for all firms.
   b. the same as the assumption of satisficing.
   c. a useful abstraction that gives sharp insights.
   d. the best description of what firms actually do.

3. Total profit is equal to
   a. average revenue minus average cost.
   b. marginal revenue minus marginal cost.
   c. total revenue minus total cost.
   d. zero when marginal cost equals marginal revenue.

4. Marginal profit is
   a. the difference between total revenue and total cost.
   b. only positive at the profit-maximizing output level.
   c. another term for the return on an owner's own time and resources.
   d. the change in profit when output increases by one unit.

5. Marginal cost equals
   a. total cost divided by total output.
   b. the change in total cost associated with an additional unit of output.
   c. the change in average cost.
   d. the slope of the average cost curve.

6. Average cost is found by
   a. dividing total cost by output.
   b. multiplying marginal cost by output.
   c. looking at how total cost changes when output changes.
   d. considering how price changes with quantity along the demand curve.

7. If total costs are increasing then
   a. marginal cost must also be increasing.
   b. marginal cost must be positive.
   c. average cost must be greater than marginal costs.
   d. average cost must be increasing.

8. The demand curve is the curve of
   a. total revenue.
   b. marginal revenue.
   c. variable revenue.
   d. average revenue.

9. Marginal revenue to a firm is
   a. the same as the demand curve for the firm's output.
   b. found by dividing price by output.
   c. found by dividing output by price.
   d. the change in revenue associated with an additional unit of output.

10. When output increases by one unit, marginal revenue will typically be
    a. less than the new lower price.
    b. equal to the new lower price.
    c. greater than the new lower price.

11. Marginal profit equals the difference between
    a. total revenue and total cost.
    b. average revenue and average cost.
    c. marginal revenue and marginal cost.
    d. the demand curve and the marginal cost curve.

12. As long as total revenue is greater than total cost,
    a. marginal profit must be positive.
    b. total profit must be increasing.
    c. total profit will be positive.
    d. marginal revenue will be greater than marginal cost.

13. If marginal revenue is greater than marginal cost, then a firm interested in maximizing profits should probably
    a. reduce output.
    b. expand output.
    c. leave output unchanged.

14. To maximize profits, a firm should produce where
    a. marginal cost is minimized.
    b. average cost is minimized.
    c. marginal revenue equals marginal cost.
    d. marginal revenue is maximized.

15. If a firm has chosen an output level that maximizes profits, then at this level
    a. marginal profits are also maximized.
    b. average cost is minimized.
    c. further increases in output will involve negative marginal profits.
    d. the difference between average revenue and average cost is maximized.

16. Once a firm has determined the output level that maximizes profits, it can determine the profit-maximizing price from
    a. the demand curve.
    b. setting its usual markup on average cost.
    c. adding marginal cost to marginal revenue.
    d. adding marginal cost to average cost.

17. Producing where marginal revenue equals marginal cost is the same as producing where
    a. average cost is minimized.
    b. total profit is maximized.
    c. average cost equals average revenue.
    d. marginal profit is maximized.

18. An economist's definition of profit differs from that of an accountant because
    a. the economist is only interested in marginal cost and marginal revenue.
    b. the economist includes the opportunity cost of owner-supplied inputs in total cost.
    c. accountants cannot maximize.
    d. economists cannot add or subtract correctly.

19. If accounting profits are zero, it is likely that economic profits are
    a. negative.
    b. also zero.
    c. positive.

20. If marginal revenue is less than average cost, a firm
    a. should reduce output; it loses the additional revenue but saves more in cost.
    b. must be losing money.
    c. should consider a temporary shutdown.
    d. can still increase profits if marginal revenue exceeds marginal cost.

TEST B

Circle T or F for true or false.

T   F   1. Business firms can decide both the price and quantity of their output.

T   F   2. Firms always make optimal decisions.

T   F   3. The demand curve for a firm's product is also the firm's marginal revenue curve.

T   F   4. Marginal revenue is simply the price of the last unit sold.

T   F   5. An output decision will generally not maximize profits unless it corresponds to a zero marginal profit.

T   F   6. Marginal profit will be zero when marginal revenue equals marginal cost.

T   F   7. An economist's measure of profit would typically be smaller than an accountant's.

T   F   8. A reduction in fixed costs should lead a firm to increase output.

T   F   9. As long as average revenue exceeds average cost, a firm is making profits and should increase output.

T   F   10. It never pays to sell below average cost.

107

| APPENDIX | *The Relationships Among Total, Average, and Marginal Data*

BASIC EXERCISES

These questions are designed to help review the relationships between total, average, and marginal measures described in the appendix to Chapter 8.

1. **Table 8-2** contains information on Heather's first ten games with the college softball team. The table includes her batting performance for each game, a marginal measure, as well as her season average updated to include the results of each game. Answer the following questions to see if the marginal and average data from Heather's batting record are consistent with the rules in the Appendix to Chapter 8. It may be useful to first plot both the marginal and average data in **Figure 8-4**.

   a. According to Rule 3, the marginal and average records should be equal on the first day of the season. Is this the case?

   b. According to Rule 4, if the marginal data are equal to the average, the average should be unchanged. Check to see if this is always the case.

Table 8-2

Heather's Batting

Game	At-bats	Hits	Daily Batting Average	Season Batting Average
1	4	2	.500	.500
2	4	2	.500	.500
3	4	1	.250	.417
4	3	1	.333	.400
5	4	3	.750	.474
6	3	1	.333	.455
7	6	2	.333	.429
8	3	0	.000	.387
9	4	2	.500	.400
10	5	2	.400	.400

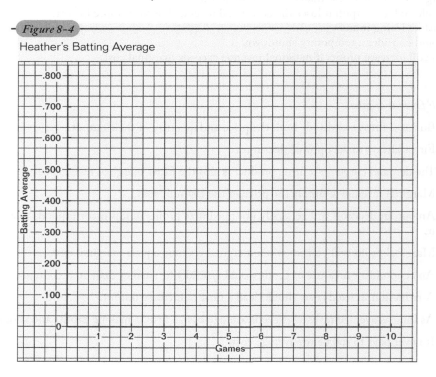

Figure 8-4

Heather's Batting Average

Figure 8-5

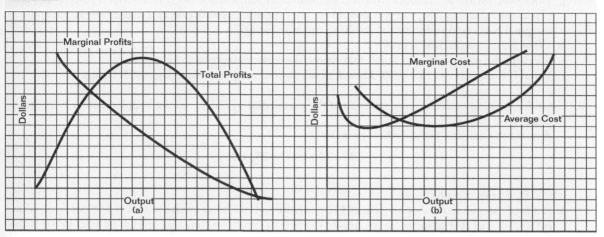

c. According to Rule 4, if the marginal data are less than the average, the average should decline. Check to see if this is always the case.
d. According to Rule 4, if the marginal data are greater than the average, the average should increase. Check to see if this is always the case.

2. Explain what is wrong with both of the illustrations in **Figure 8-5.**
   a. For part (a) of Figure 8-5, assume that the total profit curve is correct and draw an appropriate marginal profit curve.
   b. For part (b) of Figure 8-5, assume that the average cost curve is correct and draw an appropriate marginal cost curve.

SUPPLEMENTARY EXERCISES

MATHEMATICAL EXAMPLES OF PROFIT MAXIMIZATION

1. The demand for Acme stereos is

$$Q = 1,200 - 4P$$

where Q represents output measured in thousands of sets and P represents price. The total cost of producing stereos is given by

$$TC = 16,000 + 120Q - .4Q^2 + .002Q^3.$$

a. What are Acme's fixed costs?
b. What mathematical expression describes average costs? Marginal costs?
c. Plot average cost and marginal cost. Does your marginal cost curve go through the minimum point of your average cost curve?
d. Use the information from the demand curve to derive a mathematical expression for marginal revenue.
e. On the same graph as in c draw the demand curve (the average revenue curve) and the marginal revenue curve.

f. What does your graph suggest about the profit-maximizing level of output?

g. Does your answer in f coincide with a direct mathematical solution for Q when MR = MC? It should. (To answer this question, you will need to set the expressions you derived for marginal revenue and marginal cost equal and solve the resulting equation for Q.)

h. What is Acme's maximum profit?

i. Shade in the portion of your graph that represents maximum profit.

j. What if fixed cost were $20,000? How, if at all, do your answers to b, c, d, g, and h change?

2. Consider the mathematical representation of the production of widgets in the Supplementary Exercise to Chapter 7.

Assume the demand for widgets is given by

$$W = 2,500,000 - 25,000P_W$$

where P_W = price of widgets.

a. If a firm can purchase labor services at $12 per hour and machines can be rented at $48 per hour, what is the marginal cost of increases in output? What is the profit-maximizing level of output? What is the market price of widgets?

b. Assume now that the firm owns 100 machines that supply 200,000 machine hours and that the firm can purchase labor at a cost of $12 per hour. Derive an expression for marginal cost and determine the profit-maximizing level of output on the assumption that the number of machines is fixed at 100. What is the market price of widgets?

3. **Profit Maximization and the Elasticity of Demand**

A profit-maximizing firm will not try to produce so much output that it is operating in the inelastic portion of its demand curve. Why not? What about the firm producing stereos and widgets in problems 1 and 2 above? What is the elasticity of demand at the profit-maximizing point of output?

ECONOMICS IN ACTION

FAIR TRADE, FREE TRADE, AND MARGINAL COST

American trade laws, like those of many other countries, include antidumping provisions. Foreign producers are not supposed to have access to American markets if they sell their output at unfairly low prices. The concern is that a foreign producer might drive American competitors out of business and then be in a position to act as a monopolist, raising prices and restricting output. Such actions are sometimes called ruinous competition.

Complaints about dumping by foreign firms are typically initiated by American producers, not consumers, and investigated by an office of the U.S. government. If a complaint is found to have cause, the government can impose antidumping tariffs on specific foreign manufacturers that are intended to establish prices that reflect "fair value," that is, raise prices to a level sufficient to cover fully allocated costs plus a normal profit. Recent examples involve imports of computer chips and steel.

Fully allocated cost is another term for the average cost of purchased inputs, including labor. Normal profit refers to the opportunity cost of the investment by a firm's owners. (As we have seen, economists include both measures when they talk of average cost.)

1. Are there conditions under which domestic producers would willingly sell output for less than "fair value," that is, less than average cost? (For example, from an initial position of equilibrium, how might a domestic producer respond to a temporary shift of the demand curve to the left during a recession?)

2. How does one distinguish possible ruinous competition from normal market fluctuations and the natural tendency of all producers to exploit opportunities to limit competition? Should foreign producers be prohibited from behavior that domestic producers are likely to engage in on a regular basis?

SOURCE: "Cement Shoes for Venezuela," Peter Passell, *New York Times,* September 25, 1991. "Thriving Steel Industry Needs No Import Curb, Experts Say; Trade: House vote illustrates lure of protectionism. Production last year was second highest in history"; Donald W. Nauss, *Los Angeles Times,* March 22, 1999.

STUDY QUESTIONS

1. Why can't firms sell as much output as they want at whatever price they want?

2. How can it be that expanding output when average revenue is greater than average cost is not guaranteed to increase profits?

3. The condition for profit maximization is stated in terms of marginal revenue and marginal cost. What would happen to total profits if instead a firm produced where average revenue equaled average cost?

4. Why isn't marginal revenue equal to the price of the last unit sold?

5. Why is the demand curve also the curve of average revenue?

6. Why is it better to produce where marginal profit is zero rather than at some point where marginal profit is greater than zero?

7. What are the differences between profits as measured by an economist and profits as measured by an accountant? Which is likely to be larger? Why?

8. Should a firm raise or lower its price following a decrease in fixed costs? Why?

9. How can it be rational for a firm to continue producing if the price it receives is less than the (average) cost of production?

Securities, Business Finance, and the Economy: The Tail that Wags the Dog?

9

Important Terms and Concepts

Corporation	Plowback (retained earnings)	Leverage
Limited liability	Takeover	Mortgage
Common stock	Speculation	Mortgage-backed security
Bond	Random walk	Securities
Inflation	Credit Default Swap	Subprime mortgage
Interest rate	Derivative	

Learning Objectives

After completing this chapter, you should be able to:

- describe the unique characteristics of corporations.

- explain how limited liability limits the risks faced by investors in corporate stock.

- explain why bond prices fall when interest rates go up and vice versa.

- explain the similarities between stocks and bonds.

- explain how the use of stocks or bonds shifts risk between a corporation and financial investors.

- explain the advantages of plowback as a source of funds to a corporation.

- explain why the stock market is of critical importance to the financing of corporations even if new stock is-

sues account for only a small proportion of new funds raised by corporations.

- discuss the importance of regulation of the stock market.

- discuss the advantages and disadvantages of corporate takeovers.

- discuss the role of speculation both in the economy and in the securities markets.

- understand the nature of risk inherent in the stock market.

- explain how leverage contributed to the 2007–2009 financial crisis.

CHAPTER REVIEW

This chapter explores the advantages and disadvantages of corporations as a way of organizing businesses. Special attention is given to the different ways in which corporations raise funds and to the markets on which corporate securities are traded.

A corporation is a firm with the legal status of a fictional individual, owned by a large number of stockholders and run by an elected board of directors and officers. A major advantage of forming a corporation is that stockholders, the legal owners of the business, are not liable for the firm's debts. Having

(1) _____ liability makes it possible for corporations to raise very large sums of money in the pursuit of profits. Although accounting for only about 20 percent of businesses, corporate revenues total more than 70 percent of gross domestic product.

A corporation that raises funds by selling shares of ownership and offering a stake in profits is issuing

(2) (stock/bonds). If a corporation issues securities that promise to pay fixed sums as interest and principal, it is issuing _____. Corporations can also borrow directly from large financial institutions, such as banks or insurance companies. The most common way of raising funds is to directly reinvest part of a corporation's profits. This method of raising funds is called _____. Corporations typically prefer to use plowback to finance corporate investments as it avoids the cost and scrutiny that accompany new issues of stocks and bonds.

Assuming a firm does not become bankrupt, a bond that is held to maturity offers the bondholder a fixed

(3) stream of payments. Investing in stock promises dividend payments and stock prices that (are/are not) known at the time of purchase. The greater uncertainty of dividends and stock prices as compared to bond payments leads many investors to conclude that stocks are (more/less) risky than bonds. From the viewpoint of a firm, (bonds/stocks) are more risky, because a failure to (meet bond payments/pay dividends) can force bankruptcy.

This comparison understates the risk to individual investors of investing in bonds. If a bond must be sold before maturity and interest rates have changed, the market price of the bond will also change. If interest rates have risen, previously issued bonds with low coupon payments will look less attractive unless their price

(4) (rises/falls). Holders of these bonds will suffer a (gain/loss). Conversely, if interest rates have fallen, competition for existing bonds with high coupon payments will (increase/decrease) the price of previously issued bonds.

Stocks and bonds are traded in markets that sometimes have a specific location, such as the New York Stock Exchange, but they are also traded by dealers and brokers who keep track, by telephone or computer, of the lat-

(5) est price changes. New stock issues (are/are not) usually sold through established exchanges. Two important functions served by established exchanges include reducing the _____ of stock ownership by providing a secondary market in existing shares and determining the current price of a company's stock. In the latter role, established exchanges help allocate the economy's resources to those firms that, in the market's judgment, are expected to make the most profitable use of those resources.

Speculators are not much different from most investors who hope to profit from increases in stock prices. From a general perspective, speculation serves two important functions. First, it can help decrease price fluctuations. Buying at low prices in anticipation of being able to sell next year at high prices will, in fact, make prices today (<u>higher/lower</u>) than they otherwise would be and will also make prices next year _____   (6) than they otherwise would be. The second function of speculation is that it can provide _____ for those who want to avoid taking risks. Commodity speculators will agree now on a price to be paid for buying crops next year, thus insuring a farmer against the adverse effects of a decrease in price. Other speculators may agree now on a price at which to sell crops next year to a milling company, thus insuring the miller against the adverse effects of an increase in price.

The behavior of individual stock prices has long fascinated investors. Much time and effort is spent trying to forecast price movements. Some investors look at things like a firm's earnings and its current stock price; others plot recent stock prices and try to discover laws of motion in their graphs. Economists have also studied the changes in individual stock prices. Much of this research supports the conclusion that changes in stock prices are essentially unpredictable; that is, they look like a(n) _____ _____. Such a   (7) result could arise because of essentially random waves of buying and selling as investors try to outguess each other. It could also arise from investors' careful study and analysis of individual companies, study that is so complete that all anticipated events are fully reflected in current stock prices. From this perspective, changes in stock prices can only reflect currently unanticipated events, events that will likely look like random events.

Derivatives are a type of security that have recently become very popular. They can be used to (<u>reduce/eliminate</u>) risk. A particular type of derivative, Credit Default Swaps, played a significant role in the financial crisis of 2007-2009. CDS are bought by investors as _____ to protect their investments.   (8) When the housing market crashed and homeowners began to default on their mortgages, returns on these investments that were _____ from homeowner's mortgage payments, (<u>fell/rose</u>) and the value of these mortgage-related products declined rapidly. Insurers, unprepared for such widespread default (<u>could/could not</u>) cover their CDS contracts and a(n) _____ followed.

Another contributor to the 2007–2009 financial crisis was the extensive use of leverage. Leverage refers to the use of (<u>borrowed/laundered</u>) money for the purchase of risky securities. Leverage (<u>magnifies/minimizes</u>)   (9) both the possible gains and losses from an investment.

IMPORTANT TERMS AND CONCEPTS QUIZ

Choose the best definition for each of the following terms.

1. _____ Corporation
2. _____ Limited liability
3. _____ Common stock
4. _____ Bond
5. _____ Inflation
6. _____ Interest rate
7. _____ Plowback (retained earnings)
8. _____ Takeover
9. _____ Speculation
10. _____ Random walk
11. _____ Credit Defaults Swap
12. _____ Derivative
13. _____ Leverage
14. _____ Mortgage
15. _____ Mortgage-backed security
16. _____ Securities
17. _____ Subprime mortgage

a. A financial instrument that derives its value from some underlying investment(s)
b. Change in variable is completely unpredictable
c. Legal obligation of owners to repay company debts only with money already invested in the firm
d. The use of borrowed money to purchase assets
e. Purchase of risky assets in anticipation of favorable price changes
f. Stocks and bonds
g. Corporation's promise to pay a fixed sum at maturity plus annual interest
h. Portion of a corporation's profits that management returns to shareholders
i. A group of individuals not currently in control of a firm buys enough stock to gain control
j. A financial instrument that functions like an insurance policy that protects a lender
k. Firm owned by stockholders, with the legal status of a fictitious individual
l. A mortgage made to a borrower who may not be able to repay the loan
m. Piece of paper that gives holder a share of ownership in a company
n. Portion of a corporation's profits that management decides to keep and reinvest
o. Amount borrowers are contracted to pay lenders per dollar borrowed
p. A security whose returns to investors come from a pool of mortgages
q. Increase in average price of goods and services
r. A type of loan used to buy a house

BASIC EXERCISE

1. **Bond Prices and Interest Rates**

   The market price of a $1,000 bond paying interest once a year can be calculated by computing the present value of future payments:

   $$\text{Price} = \sum_{t=1}^{N} \frac{INT}{(1+i)^t} + \frac{1000}{(1+i)^N}$$

   where P = market price, i = market interest rate, N = number of years to maturity, and INT = annual interest payment.

It may be easiest to complete the following exercises if you use a spreadsheet program on a computer or a sophisticated hand calculator.

a. Show that if *INT* = $80 and *i* = .08, the market price of this bond will be $1,000 for *N* = 10.

b. Now vary *i*, holding *INT* constant at $80 and *N* constant at 25 years. Note how the price of a bond issued with a coupon payment of $80 changes as market interest rates change. You should find that price is less than $1,000 when *i* is greater than .08 and price is greater than $1,000 when *i* is less than .08.

c. Choose a particular value for *i*, say .06, and calculate the difference in price from the original $1,000 as *N* varies from one year to 25 years. Remember to keep *INT* = 80. You should find that the difference in price is greater as *N* gets larger; that is, longer term bonds show a greater change in price for a given change in interest rates. Can you explain why?

SELF-TESTS FOR UNDERSTANDING

TEST A

Circle the most appropriate answer.

1. Corporations account for _____ percent of businesses in the United States.
   a. about 10
   b. slightly more than 20
   c. just under 50
   d. more than 70

2. Which of the following actions gives you a share of ownership in a company?
   a. buying a bond
   b. buying a share of stock
   c. extending a loan
   d. selling to a speculator

3. The term *limited liability* refers to
   a. the use of limit orders when buying stocks.
   b. the priority bondholders have on corporate assets in case of liquidation or bankruptcy.
   c. the protection stockholders have against the debts and liabilities of a corporation.
   d. stock market rules that limit trading when there are large declines in stock prices.

4. Bonds are often said to be more risky to _____ while stocks are riskier for _____.
   a. investors; firms
   b. firms; investors

5. The returns to investing in stocks include which of the following? (There may be more than one correct answer.)
   a. dividends
   b. interest
   c. repayment of principal
   d. capital gain or loss when sold

117

6. Corporations can raise money in all but which one of the following ways?
   a. issue shares of stock
   b. borrow money in the form of bonds
   c. reinvestment or plowback profits
   d. pay dividends

7. Which of the following is the most important source of new funds for corporations?
   a. new stock issues
   b. corporate bonds
   c. plowback (i.e., retained earnings)
   d. bank loans

8. If held to maturity and with no risk of bankruptcy, bonds offer investors
   a. the prospect of substantial capital gains if company profits increase.
   b. unknown interest payments that will fluctuate with profits.
   c. the opportunity to sell their bond at its original price at any time.
   d. known interest payments.

9. A decrease in interest rates will tend to _____ the price of existing bonds.
   a. increase
   b. lower
   c. have no effect on

10. Jamal purchased a newly issued General Electric bond several years ago with coupon payments offering an interest rate of 10 percent. Since then, market interest rates on similar bonds have fallen to 6 percent. Which of the following is true?
    a. If Jamal sold his bonds today at their current market price, he would have to sell them for less than he paid.
    b. If held to maturity and General Electric does not default, Jamal will earn 6 percent on his original investment.
    c. Anyone purchasing such bonds today at their current market price and holding them to maturity can expect to earn 10 percent on the investment.
    d. The market value of the bonds that Jamal bought will have increased from the price he paid.

11. Five million shares of stock are outstanding in XYZ Corporation. If the price of XYZ stock rises by $1, then
    a. XYZ Corporation will have $5 million more to invest or use to pay higher dividends.
    b. existing shareholders will benefit by $1 a share.
    c. investors who hold XYZ bonds will have suffered a capital loss.
    d. XYZ Corporation will owe federal tax on the increased stock price.

12. All of the following, except which one, contributed to the financial crisis of 2007–2009?
    a. credit default swaps
    b. leverage
    c. subprime mortgages
    d. diversification

13. Which of the following is an example of leverage?
    a. Samantha buys a risky stock for $100, using $20 of her own money and $80 that she borrows.
    b. Edgar spends $100 on a risky stock rather than for groceries for his family.
    c. Raul buys 100 shares of 10 different stocks.
    d. Jean-Pierre exchanges 1,000 euros for $1,460 for his trip to the United States.

14. A derivative is:
    a. a mortgage made to a customer with questionable credit worthiness.
    b. a type of security whose value is determined by the price movements of some underlying investment(s)
    c. the annual payment made to the owners of corporate stock.
    d. the fixed payment made to the owners of corporate bonds.

15. The important economic functions of organized stock exchanges include all but which one of the following?
    a. Offering investors insurance against the risk of changes in stock prices.
    b. Reducing the risk of purchasing stock by offering investors a place to sell their shares should they need the funds for some other purpose.
    c. Helping allocate the economy's resources, since companies with high current stock prices will find it easier to raise additional funds to pursue investment opportunities.

16. If Maxine is to be a successful speculator, she must buy during a period of excess
    a. supply and sell during a period of excess supply.
    b. supply and sell during a period of excess demand.
    c. demand and sell during a period of excess demand.
    d. demand and sell during a period of excess supply.

17. Which of the following are correct? (There may be more than one correct answer.)
    a. Speculators only make prices higher than they otherwise would be.
    b. Speculators offer a form of insurance to those who want to avoid the risk of price fluctuations.
    c. Speculators tend to smooth out extreme price movements.
    d. Speculators serve no useful social function.

18. Advantages to existing stockholders from takeovers can include all but which one of the following?
    a. the elimination of incompetent management
    b. increasing the price of an undervalued company
    c. a greater chance that low earnings will grow to match their potential
    d. the time and effort of top management in responding to the takeover bid

19. To say that stock prices follow a random walk is to say that
    a. stock prices are easily predicted given information about past prices.
    b. the predictions of stock analysts are uniformly better than those of individual investors.
    c. day-to-day changes in stock prices are essentially unpredictable.
    d. over the long run, individual investors will only lose money by buying stocks.

TEST B

Circle T or F for true or false.

T   F   1. Corporations, while constituting a minority of the number of business organizations, are the most important form of organization when measured by total sales revenue.

T   F   2. Limited liability means that investors in corporations cannot lose more than what they invested.

T   F   3. Assuming no bankruptcy, a corporate bond is a riskless investment even if the bond must be sold before maturity.

T   F   4. A diversified portfolio is less risky than investment all of one's money in a single stock.

T   F   5. Buying stock only when it reaches a pre-specified price is an example of limited liability.

T   F   6. Whenever a share of General Motors' stock is sold on the New York Stock Exchange, General Motors gets the proceeds.

T   F   7. A corporation that decides to issue stock will typically offer the shares initially through one of the regional stock exchanges.

T   F   8. Established stock exchanges, such as the New York Stock Exchange, are really just a form of legalized gambling and serve no social function.

T   F   9. The finding that stock prices follow a random walk implies that investing in stock is essentially a gamble.

T   F   10. Profitable speculation involves buying high and selling low.

SUPPLEMENTARY EXERCISES

1. **Portfolio Diversification**

   This exercise is meant to illustrate the principle of diversification. Assume you invested $10,000 on December 31, 2006, and sold your holdings one year later on December 31, 2007. **Tables 9-1 and 9-2** contain data for a number of popular stocks in 2007. Table 9-1 shows the results of dividing your investment among each of the 10 stocks, $1,000 in each. The entries in Table 9-2 assume that your $10,000 was invested in just one company. Column (2) shows the number of shares purchased on December 31, 2006. Column (3) reports stock prices on December 31, 2007.

   a. Column (4) has spaces for the value of your stock holdings on December 31, 2007. Complete this column in both tables by multiplying stock prices on December 31, 2007, by the number of shares bought a year earlier; that is, multiply each entry in column (2) by the corresponding entry in column (3).

   b. Complete column (6) by adding the dividends you received in 2007, column (5), to the value of your stock holdings in column (4). Column (6) shows the total value of your investments, dividends plus the change in stock prices, after one year. Be sure to sum all of the entries in column (6) for Table 9-1.

   c. Each entry in column (6), Table 9-2, shows how you would have done had you invested all of the $10,000 in the stock of just one company. The sum for column (6), Table 9-1, shows the results of a 10-stock portfolio. How do your results illustrate the link between portfolio diversification and risk?

Table 9–1

Portfolio Stock Returns: 2007

Company	Number of Shares if Investing $1,000 12/31/2006	Price per Share on 12/31/2007	Value of Shares on 12/31/2007	Dividends Received During 2007	Value of Stock + Dividend
Apple	46.79	$64.40	_____	$0.00	_____
Best Buy	19.14	$59.42	_____	$8.42	_____
Cisco	41.27	$19.32	_____	$0.00	_____
ExxonMobil	24.39	$51.26	_____	$26.34	_____
FedEx	14.81	$98.49	_____	$4.15	_____
General Electric	32.28	$36.50	_____	$28.41	_____
Home Depot	28.18	$42.74	_____	$9.58	_____
Merck	21.65	$32.14	_____	$32.90	_____
Microsoft	36.54	$26.72	_____	$11.69	_____
Walmart	18.85	$52.82	_____	$9.80	_____
				Total Portfolio:	_____

Table 9–2

Individual Stock Returns: 2007

Company	Number of Shares if Investing $10,000 12/31/2006	Price per Share on 12/31/2007	Value of Shares on 12/31/2007	Dividends Received During 2007	Value of Stock + Dividend
Apple	467.95	$64.40	_____	$0.00	_____
Best Buy	191.42	$59.42	_____	$84.23	_____
Cisco	412.71	$19.32	_____	$0.00	_____
ExxonMobil	243.90	$51.26	_____	$263.41	_____
FedEx	148.15	$98.49	_____	$41.48	_____
General Electric	322.79	$36.50	_____	$284.05	_____
Home Depot	281.77	$42.74	_____	$95.80	_____
Merck	216.45	$32.14	_____	$329.00	_____
Microsoft	365.36	$26.72	_____	$116.92	_____
Walmart	188.50	$52.82	_____	$98.02	_____

ECONOMICS IN ACTION

IF YOU'RE SO SMART, WHY AREN'T YOU RICH?

Can you or your stockbroker consistently beat the market? Many economists would answer no unless you have inside information on which it is illegal to trade. Presumptions about the inability of individuals to beat the market are closely linked to notions of efficient markets and random walks. Formally the hypothesis of efficient markets implies that stock prices reflect all available information about future profitability. For example, should

121

there be new information about increased profits from investing in stock X, the price of stock X should rise immediately as investors and stock managers seek to take advantage of this information. In this way all available information is incorporated into current stock prices.

On this view, stock prices change only as new information becomes available. New information that is easily foreseen would already be incorporated into stock prices. The conclusion is that new information must be unpredictable and changes in the price of individual stocks will tend to look random. Some stocks are riskier than others and need to offer a higher expected return to compensate for the possibility that they may turn out to be a bust. Riskier stocks with above average returns are not a violation of the efficient markets hypothesis, as the risk of such investments is part of currently available information.

Does all this mean that one cannot make money in the stock market? No, one can make money, but once you have decided how much risk you are willing to accept, do not expect that you or your stockbroker can consistently do better than other investors who are willing to accept similar risks. In any given year some investors and investment professionals will do better than others. The efficient markets hypothesis suggests that over a period of years it will be hard for anyone to consistently beat the market.

Some have likened beating the market to guessing whether a fair coin toss will come up heads or tails. Imagine you asked this question of everyone attending a Michigan-Notre Dame football game in Ann Arbor. If half the crowd said heads and half said tails, more than 50,000 people would have predicted the coin toss correctly. After 10 flips about 100 people would still have a perfect record of prediction. Do they know something we don't know? Would you want to bet on their continued ability to predict the flip of a coin?

The discussion of efficient markets has a certain surface plausibility, but how does one test whether markets are in fact efficient? Economists have defined three notions of efficiency—weak, semi-strong, and strong. Weak efficiency requires that information on past prices of stock X is of no use in forecasting future prices. Semi-strong efficiency requires that no publicly available information is helpful, while strong efficiency says that no relevant information, published or not, helps to forecast stock prices. Tests for various forms of efficiency involve elaborate computer estimation and/or simulation of trading rules based on past prices and other information. Remember that any profit from a particular trading rule has to be sufficient to offset the brokerage fees for trading as well as any other costs of implementing the rule.

As computers have become more powerful it has been possible to test for a wider range of trading rules. Situations have been identified where there appear to be small but predictable returns in excess of the market average. One of the best known of these is the so-called "January effect" where portfolios of the shares of small companies have consistently done better in January than the stock market as a whole. What explains such inefficiencies? No one is sure. If the decisions of a sufficient number of investors are determined by mood and feeling rather than hardheaded analysis, it might be possible that inefficiencies could persist with smart traders winning at the expense of others. It may also be that the identification of trading rules that beat the market will work to eliminate their profit potential as they are adopted on a wide-scale basis.

What is an individual investor to do?

Source: Mark Hulbert, "Why Small-Cap Stocks are So Hot in Cold Weather," *The New York Times*, November 18, 2001. You might want to look at the symposium of papers on the stock market and speculative bubbles in the Spring 1990 issue of *The Journal of Economic Perspectives*.

STUDY QUESTIONS

1. The text points out that although only a small percentage of business firms, corporations account for a much larger percentage of business sales and output. This difference arises because the biggest firms are corporations. Why are the biggest firms corporations?

2. Why is most business investment financed by plowback or retained earnings rather than by new stock issues or bonds?

3. What explains the inverse relationship between market interest rates and bond prices?

4. Why is it often said that bonds are riskier than stocks to a corporation but stocks are riskier than bonds for investors?

5. Do derivative securities reduce risk or are they a source of added risk?

6. What is a subprime mortgage and how did they contribute to the financial crisis of 2007–2009?

7. How can an investor use leverage and what risk does the use of leverage create?

8. What is the economic role of the stock market if new stock issues are seldom used to finance business investment?

9. Many people would like to regulate speculators on the belief that they are greedy predators who profit only on the misfortune of others. Why do economists often disagree with this assessment?

10. How can one make money investing in stocks if day-to-day changes in stock prices are unpredictable?

ECONOMICS ONLINE

1. There are now lots of ways to follow stocks, bonds, and mutual funds on the web. Many mutual funds and stock exchanges have their own homepages. Here are some popular sites that contain financial information and give access to these other sites.

   CBS MarketWatch

   http://www.marketwatch.com

   CNN Financial

   http://www.Money.cnn.com

   Bloomberg

   http://www.bloomberg.com

USA Today

http://www.usatoday.com/money

Yahoo

http://dir.yahoo.com/business_and_economy/finance_and_investment

2. The Securities and Exchange Commission regulates trading in stocks and bonds. See what they are up to at their homepage. You might want to investigate EDGAR, the SEC's electronic database of corporate reports.

http://www.sec.gov

The Firm and the Industry under Perfect Competition

10

Important Terms and Concepts

Perfect competition

Price taker

Variable cost

Firm's supply curve

Industry supply curve

Economic profit

Learning Objectives

After completing this chapter, you should be able to:

- describe the conditions that distinguish perfect competition from other market structures.

- explain why the study of perfect competition can be profitable even if few industries satisfy the conditions of perfect competition exactly.

- explain why under perfect competition the firm faces a horizontal demand curve while the industry faces a downward-sloping demand curve.

- explain the relation of price, average revenue, and marginal revenue as seen by individual firms under perfect competition.

- find the profit-maximizing output level for a perfectly competitive firm given information on the firm's marginal cost curve and the market price for its output.

- understand the case of short-term losses and the rules governing shut-down decisions.

- explain why a perfectly competitive firm's short-run supply curve is the portion of its marginal cost curve that is above average variable costs.

- derive a perfectly competitive industry's short-run supply curve given information on the supply curves for individual firms.

- understand how the equilibrium of a perfectly competitive industry in the long run may differ from the short-run equilibrium.

- use the concept of opportunity cost to reconcile economic and accounting profits.

- explain how freedom of entry and exit imply that in the long run firms operating under perfect competition will earn zero economic profit.

- explain why the long-run supply curve for a competitive industry is given by the industry's long-run average cost curve.

- explain how perfect competition implies the efficient production of goods and services.

CHAPTER REVIEW

This chapter uses the concepts developed in earlier chapters to study in more detail the supply decisions of firms. The discussion also adds important material about market structures. The decisions of individual firms depend not only upon their production functions and cost curves, but also upon the type of market structure the firm faces. Different market structures have important implications for demand conditions that firms face. This chapter focuses on the abstraction of the market structure of perfect competition. Later chapters will investigate other market structures—monopolistic competition, oligopoly, and pure monopoly.

Perfect competition is distinguished from other market structures by four conditions:

(1)   a.   (<u>Few/Many</u>) buyers and sellers.

        b.   (<u>Differentiated/Identical</u>) product.

        c.   (<u>Easy/Difficult</u>) entry and exit.

        d.   (<u>Perfect/Imperfect</u>) information.

Conditions a, b, and d imply that the actions of individual buyers and sellers (<u>do/do not</u>) affect the market price for the identical product. Condition c implies that the number of firms can easily expand or contract and leads to the condition that long-run equilibrium will be characterized by (<u>positive/zero/negative</u>) economic profits.

An important first step to analyzing the firm's decisions in a particular market structure is to be careful about what the market structure implies for the firm's demand curve and its marginal revenue. Let us first consider the short-run supply decision of an individual firm under perfect competition. Since the actions of this firm will not affect the market price, the firm can sell as much or as little as it wants at the prevailing market price.

(2) Alternatively, we may say that the firm faces a (<u>horizontal/vertical</u>) demand curve. In Chapter 8 we saw that the demand curve is also the curve of average revenue. If the demand curve is horizontal, then besides being the curve of average revenue it is also the curve of _____ revenue. (Remember the picture of marginal revenue in the Basic Exercise of Chapter 8. If the demand curve is horizontal, there is no horizontal rectangle to subtract.) As we saw in Chapter 8, the firm maximizes profits by producing where MC = MR. Under perfect competition, MR = P, thus under perfect competition the firm should produce where MC = MR = P.

We can now derive the short-run supply curve for the firm by imagining that the firm faces a variety of possible prices and considering what output the firm would supply at each price. These price–output pairs will define the firm's short-run supply curve. For many possible prices, short-run supply will be given by the inter-

(3) section of price and the (<u>average/marginal</u>) cost curve. If price drops below the minimum of the average total cost curve, the MC = P rule maximizes profits by minimizing _____. Even if price is less than average total cost, the firm should continue to produce as long as price exceeds average _____ cost. If the firm decides to produce nothing, it still must cover its fixed costs. As long as price exceeds average variable cost, there will be something left over to help cover these costs. Putting all of this together, we

can conclude that under perfect competition, a firm's short-run supply curve is given by the portion of the

_____ _____ curve above average _____ cost.

The industry short-run supply curve is given by the (horizontal/vertical) summation of individual firm's sup-   (4)
ply curves. Market price, the variable so crucial to individual firms decisions, will be given by the intersection of
the market _____ and _____ curves. In the short run, the number of firms in the
industry is fixed; the short-run industry supply curve will come from the supply decisions of existing firms.

In the long run, existing firms may expand (or contract) and/or there will be more (fewer) firms if the short-
run equilibrium involves economic profits (losses). For example, if general market returns are around 8 percent
and investments in the firm show a return of 6 percent, an economist would conclude that the firm has an
economic (loss/profit) of _____ percent. In this case, by investing elsewhere and earning 8 percent, the firm's   (5)
owners would be (better/worse) off. The 8 percent is the _____ cost of capital to the firm
and it is an important part of costs as counted by the economist. Thus, economists focus on economic profits as
the indicator of entry or exit rather than on accounting profits. The condition of long-run equilibrium that (ac-
counting/economic) profits be zero is consistent with _____ profits equal to general market rates
of return.

As firms expand or contract and enter or leave, the industry short-run supply curve will shift appropriately, price will adjust as we move along the industry demand curve, and industry long-run equilibrium will be
achieved when there are no further incentives for the supply curve to shift from expansion/entry or contraction/
exit of new or existing firms. **Figure 10-1**(a) illustrates a firm in a perfectly competitive industry. Figure 10-1(b)
shows the industry demand and supply. The illustrated firm will be making economic (profits/losses). Shade   (6)
in the appropriate rectangle showing economic profits or losses. There will be an incentive for some firms to
(enter/leave) the industry. As the number of firms in the industry changes, the supply curve in Figure 10-1(b)

Figure 10-1

Competitive Market Equilibrium

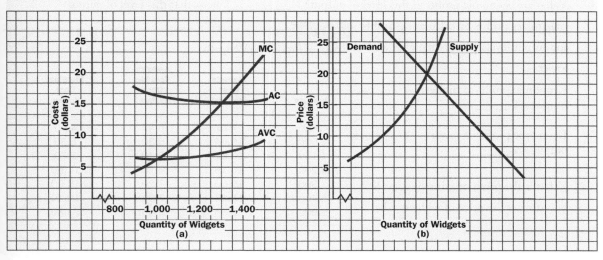

127

will shift to the (right/left) and price will (rise/fall). If the cost curves in Figure 10-1(a) are representative of long-run costs for all current and potential firms in the industry, long-run equilibrium will involve a price of $_____. Note that at all times our representative firm is producing where MC = *P*. But in the long-run equilibrium, MC = *P* = minimum _____ _____ _____ cost. It is this last condition that explains the efficiency of perfectly competitive markets.

IMPORTANT TERMS AND CONCEPTS QUIZ

Choose the best definition for each of the following terms.

1. _____ Perfect competition
2. _____ Price taker
3. _____ Variable cost
4. _____ Firms supply curve
5. _____ Industry supply curve
6. _____ Economic profit

a. The portion of the marginal cost curve that exceeds average variable cost
b. Return to an owner's investment in her firm in excess of the return on alternative investments
c. Single buyer in a market
d. Many small firms selling an identical product
e. Costs that depend upon the quantity of output
f. Agent or firm too small to affect the market price
g. Industry's long-run average cost curve

BASIC EXERCISE

*This exercise is designed to explore the short-run supply curve for a firm under perfect competition. Assume that widgets are produced by perfectly competitive firms. The data in **Table 10-1** are consistent with Figure 10-1 and are for a representative widget firm. Although not listed separately in Table 10-1, producing widgets involves fixed costs of $10,140.*

1. If the price of widgets is $19.10, what is the profit-maximizing level of output? _____

   What are economic profits at this level of output? $ _____ Check that this level of output maximizes profits by calculating profits for output levels 100 units higher and lower.

   Economic profits at higher output = $ _____

   Economic profits at lower output = $ _____

2. What is the profit-maximizing level of output if the price of widgets falls

Table 10-1

Costs of Producing Widgets

Quantity	Average Cost (dollars)	Average Variable Cost (dollars)	Marginal Cost (dollars)
900	17.67	6.40	4.60
1,000	16.44	6.30	6.30
1,100	15.62	6.40	8.60
1,200	15.15	6.70	11.50
1,300	15.00	7.20	15.00
1,400	15.14	7.90	19.10
1,500	15.56	8.80	23.80

128

to $11.50, below all values for average cost? _____ What are economic profits at this level of output? $ _____ Again check that this level of output maximizes profits or minimizes losses by considering output levels 100 units higher, 100 units lower, and no production.

Economic losses at higher output = $ _____

Economic losses at lower output = $ _____

Economic losses at zero output = $ _____

3. If the price of widgets is $6.00, what is the profit-maximizing level of output? Why?

_____

4. What general conclusion can you draw about the short-run supply curve for a firm operating under conditions of perfect competition?

_____

_____

5. Note that in question 1, when the market price was assumed to be $19.10, the profit-maximizing level of output was at a point where price exceeded both average cost and average variable cost. Remembering that under perfect competition a firm can sell as much output as it wants at the given market price, why isn't it profitable for the firm to produce even more when price exceeds average costs?

6. If many firms can produce widgets with the same cost functions, what is the long-run equilibrium price of widgets? $_____ What is the associated level of production for the representative firm?

_____

SELF-TESTS FOR UNDERSTANDING

TEST A

Circle the most appropriate answer.

1. Which of the following is inconsistent with perfect competition?
   a. perfect information about products
   b. one firm producing the total industry output
   c. freedom of entry
   d. freedom of exit

2. If production is limited to a few large firms, the resulting market structure is called
    a. perfect competition.
    b. monopolistic competition.
    c. oligopoly.
    d. pure monopoly.

3. If a firm can sell any amount of output without affecting price, we say that the demand curve for this firm is
    a. horizontal.
    b. inelastic.
    c. equal to the marginal cost curve.
    d. indeterminate.

4. Which one of the following is not true under perfect competition?
    a. The firm's demand curve is horizontal.
    b. The firm's demand curve is also the curve of average revenue.
    c. The firm's demand curve is also the curve of marginal revenue.
    d. The firm's demand curve is inelastic.

5. If a firm's demand curve is horizontal, marginal revenue equals
    a. average cost.
    b. marginal cost.
    c. average revenue.
    d. minimum long-run average cost.

6. If a firm's demand curve is horizontal, the firm should produce
    a. as much output as it can.
    b. more output as long as price exceeds average variable cost.
    c. at the point where marginal cost equals price.
    d. at the minimum of its long-run average cost curve.

7. Under perfect competition, a profit-maximizing firm should shut down when price falls below
    a. average cost.
    b. average variable cost.
    c. marginal cost.
    d. fixed costs.

8. The short-run supply curve for a firm under perfect competition is the portion of the firm's marginal cost curve that is above the
    a. average total cost curve.
    b. average fixed cost curve.
    c. average variable cost curve.
    d. minimum of the marginal cost curve.

9. Under perfect competition, industry supply in the short run is given by
    a. the intersection of market demand and average cost.
    b. the horizontal sum of firm's short-run supply curves.
    c. the horizontal sum of firm's average cost curves.
    d. a fixed markup over average variable cost.

130

10. Which of the following is not a characteristic of long-run equilibrium under perfect competition?
    a. production where P = MC
    b. zero accounting profits
    c. zero economic profits
    d. production where P = minimum average cost

11. Which of the following explains why economic profits in a perfectly competitive industry will equal zero in the long run?
    a. the assumption of perfect information
    b. the elasticity of market demand
    c. the ease of entry and exit by new and existing firms
    d. the existence of fixed costs that must be covered in the long run

12. When economic profits equal zero, we know that accounting profits will
    a. also be zero.
    b. likely understate economic profits.
    c. be at their minimum.
    d. equal the opportunity cost of an owner's investment in her firm.

13. In long-run equilibrium under perfect competition, all but which one of the following are equal to price?
    a. average cost
    b. marginal cost
    c. marginal revenue
    d. fixed cost

14. Under perfect competition, price will equal average cost
    a. in the short run.
    b. in the long run.
    c. in both the short and long run.
    d. never.

15. Under perfect competition, firms will produce where MC = P
    a. in the short run.
    b. in the long run.
    c. in both the short and long run.
    d. never.

16. Under perfect competition, price is determined by the intersection of the industry supply and demand curves
    a. in the short run.
    b. in the long run.
    c. in both the short and long run.
    d. never.

17. Under perfect competition, the industry's long-run supply curve is
    a. horizontal.
    b. its long-run average cost curve.
    c. its long-run average variable cost curve.
    d. its long-run fixed cost curve.

18. Economic profits will be positive as long as price
    a. equals marginal cost.
    b. is greater than average variable cost.
    c. is greater than average fixed cost.
    d. is greater than average cost.

19. Imagine that pencils are produced by firms with U-shaped average costs under conditions of perfect competition. Concern about the quality of education has increased government spending on education and disturbed the original long-run equilibrium by shifting the demand curve for pencils to the right. Which one of the following is not a likely response?
    a. Pencil prices rise initially in response to the increase in demand.
    b. Existing firms are likely to earn positive economic profits in the short run.
    c. Existing firms in the industry expand output to the point where average cost equals the new, higher price.
    d. New firms are likely to enter the industry in response to earnings above the opportunity cost of capital.

20. Widgets are produced by perfectly competitive firms. The demand curve for widgets has a negative slope. A technological innovation dramatically reduces average and marginal costs for current and potential widget manufacturers. All but which one of the following will occur?
    a. The quantity supplied increases in the short run.
    b. The price of widgets declines in the short run.
    c. Economic profits increase in the short run.
    d. Economic profits will be positive in the long run.

TEST B

Circle T or F for true or false.

T F 1. Perfect competition is characterized by many firms producing similar but not identical products.

T F 2. Under perfect competition, firms maximize profits by always producing at the minimum of their average cost.

T F 3. Freedom of entry and exit are really unnecessary for the existence of perfect competition.

T F 4. Under perfect competition a firm is always guaranteed to earn positive economic profits if it produces where MC = *P*.

T F 5. Under perfect competition, the demand curve facing the industry is horizontal.

T F 6. A competitive firm should always expand output as long as price exceeds average cost.

T F 7. The firm's short-run supply curve is given by the portion of its marginal cost curve with a positive slope.

T F 8. In long-run equilibrium, perfectly competitive firms will show positive accounting profits but zero economic profits.

T F 9. If price is less than average cost, a firm is always better off shutting down.

T F 10. Perfect competition is studied because a very large number of markets satisfy the conditions for perfect competition.

SUPPLEMENTARY EXERCISES

Consider a firm with the following total cost curve:

$$TC = 10{,}140 + 0.00001Q_3 - 0.02Q_2 + 16.3Q$$

where Q is output. (This cost curve is consistent with the Basic Exercise.)

1. Derive equations for the firm's
    a. average cost.
    b. average variable cost.
    c. marginal cost.

2. Draw a picture showing these various measures of cost as a function of output.

3. Verify that the marginal cost curve goes through the bottom of the average cost curve and the average variable cost curve.

4. Assume this firm operates in a perfectly competitive market. Derive a mathematical expression for the firm's supply curve.

ECONOMICS IN ACTION

MORE COMPETITIVE MARKETS?

The development of the Internet and the web has had an important impact on many consumers. While a number of the early claims about how the web would change the world were clearly overblown, it is appropriate to ask whether the availability of shopping alternatives on the web will make markets more or less competitive. To date it appears that results paint a somewhat mixed but optimistic picture.

One of the conditions for perfectly competitive markets is that buyers need good information about the quality and characteristics of commodities as well as good information about the prices offered by different sellers. Can the Internet help? Some observers point to price comparison sites on the web and the opportunity for customer comments as ways in which the Internet increases consumer information.

A story in the *Los Angeles Times* describes how Internet auction sites have changed the market for collectibles by creating a pricing mechanism that is available to all participants. Buyers, especially novice buyers, are able to see market prices and do not have to negotiate one-on-one with more experienced sellers. Similarly, uninformed sellers can easily check prices. David Welch, an Illinois dealer in collectibles, noted, "The advantage I had was knowledge. If someone had something for $25 and I knew it was worth $300, my knowledge was what gave me the edge." Now eBay gives sellers more information about whether what they have is really as rare as hen's teeth and thus worth a lot or not.

Florain Zettelmeyer, Fiona Morton, and Jorge Silva-Risso concluded that the anonymity of the Internet can help buyers by making it more difficult for salespeople to identify particular buyers who would be willing to pay

133

more. In particular when looking at prices that consumers pay when buying an automobile, the authors conclude that "the Internet is disproportionately beneficial to those who have personal characteristics that put them at a disadvantage in negotiating."

Others are not so sure that the Internet always promotes privacy. Online sites can keep track of buyers and use this information to charge buyers different prices. At one point Amazon.com was forced to issue an apology and refunds when customers complained about differential prices of DVDs. Amazon said it was testing randomly chosen discounts for their effectiveness while cynics argued that Amazon was "discounting heavily to new visitors while repaying old customers for their loyalty by charging them higher prices."

Other economists who have looked at Internet shopping find that firms have found ways to make price comparisons difficult rather than easy. Shipping and restocking charges are not always clear. Differences in model numbers along with custom-made store brands make direct price comparisons difficult.

1. Have you bought over the Internet or used the Internet to gather product information? Did your experience make you a more informed consumer? On balance, do you think the Internet will improve or reduce the efficiency of markets? Why?

SOURCES: Fiona M. Scott Morton, Florian Zettelmeyer, Jorge Silva-Risso, "Consumer Information and Price Discrimination: Does the Internet Affect the Pricing of New Cars to Women and Minorities?" Yale SOM Working Paper No. ES-15; Haas School, UC Berkeley Marketing Working Paper No. 01-2, December 2001; Marcia Pledger, "Finding the best deals online," *The Cleveland Plain Dealer*, December 11, 2001; David Streitfeld, "Dispenser of Instant Treasures," *Los Angeles Times*, November 22, 2001; Tim Jackson, "INSIDE TRACK: Why Amazon looks to Japan," *The Financial Times* (London), November 7, 2000; Mike Meyers, "Economists: Comparison Shipping on the Web a Mixed Bag," *Minneapolis Star Tribune*, January 27, 2002.

STUDY QUESTIONS

1. What conditions are necessary for perfect competition?

2. Which of these conditions helps to ensure that in the long run economic profits are driven to zero? Explain.

3. How can firms in a perfectly competitive industry face a horizontal demand curve when the demand curve for the industry is sloping downward?

4. Explain the difference between average cost, average variable cost, and marginal cost. Which is relevant for the short-run supply decisions of firms in a perfectly competitive industry? Why?

5. How can it be profitable for a firm to stay in business if price is less than average cost?

6. Often firms think that if they raise their price just a bit they might lose a few customers but make enough from those who remain to increase profits. Why wouldn't a firm in a perfectly competitive industry do the same thing? What about reducing price just a bit in an effort to attract more customers?

7. What is meant by the efficient production of commodities and how is it fostered by market forces under perfect competition?

8. The discussion of equilibrium makes a distinction between the short run and the long run. What is it that is different between the short run and the long run for firms and for an industry of perfectly competitive firms?

9. If long-run equilibrium yields zero economic profits, why do any firms stay in a perfectly competitive industry?

Monopoly

11

Important Terms and Concepts

- Pure monopoly
- Barriers to entry
- Patents
- Natural monopoly
- Monopoly profits
- Price discrimination

Learning Objectives

After completing this chapter, you should be able to:

- define a monopoly and explain why unrestrained pure monopolies are rarely found in practice.

- describe what factors allow a particular monopoly to persist.

- explain why a monopolist cannot determine both price and quantity.

- explain why for a monopolist marginal revenue is less than price.

- calculate a monopolist's profit-maximizing price and output, given information on costs and demand.

- explain why, unlike with a competitive firm, there is no supply curve for a monopolist.

- explain why a monopolist will receive positive economic profits in both the short and long runs.

- explain how a monopoly can give rise to an inefficient allocation of resources.

- describe why a monopolist's demand and cost curves may differ from those of a comparable competitive industry.

- identify specific ways in which monopoly can offset some of its undesirable consequences.

- show how price discrimination can increase a monopolist's profit.

CHAPTER REVIEW

In Chapter 10 we studied the decisions of firms operating in markets characterized as perfect competition, that is, markets with lots of firms competing to produce and sell the same commodity. Chapters 7 and 8 considered optimal firm decisions. This chapter will use the tools we developed in Chapter 8 to examine a pure monopoly, (1) a market with (<u>one</u>/many) firm(s) producing a single good with (<u>no</u>/lots of) close substitutes. Not only is there no competition at the moment, but also the entry and survival of potential competitors is extremely unlikely. The essence of a pure monopoly is one producer without effective competition.

A pure monopoly may arise for one of two broad reasons. If the technology of large-scale production enables one firm to produce enough to satisfy the whole market at lower average costs than a number of smaller firms (2) can, the result is a(n) _____ monopoly. Legal restrictions such as exclusive licensing or patents; advantages the monopolist acquires for himself, such as control of a vital input or technical superiority; or special risks faced by potential entrants who must spend large amounts on factories or advertising before realizing any revenue can also create a pure monopoly. All of these factors would deter potential competitors and are called _____ to _____.

The study of a pure monopoly often starts by assuming that some enterprising entrepreneur is able to monopolize a previously competitive industry. It is also traditional to assume that the monopolist initially faces the previous industry demand curve and operates with the same cost curves.

Under pure competition, individual firms face demand curves that are horizontal; that is, any firm can sell as much as it wants at the market price. A monopolist will face the industry demand curve with a (3) (positive/<u>negative</u>/zero) slope. The monopolist who wants to sell more must (raise/<u>lower</u>) his price. A monopolist who raises his price will find that sales (<u>decrease</u>/do not change/increase).

The monopolist maximizes profit just like any other profit-maximizing firm; that is, the monopolist (4) chooses the output level at which (<u>marginal</u>/average) cost equals (<u>marginal</u>/average) revenue. Now the only trick is to figure out what the relevant cost and revenue curves look like. Marginal cost comes from the monopolist's total costs in exactly the same way that it does for anyone else. The tricky part is marginal revenue. Marginal revenue is the addition to total revenue from producing and selling one more unit. Under perfect competition, the actions of an individual firm have no effect on the market price and marginal revenue equals _____. But with a monopolist, quantity decisions affect price and marginal revenue (is/<u>is not</u>) equal to price.

(5)   Remember from Chapter 8 that the demand curve is the curve of (<u>average</u>/marginal) revenue. From Rule 4 in the Appendix to Chapter 8 we know that when average revenue is declining, marginal revenue will be (<u>less</u>/more) than average revenue. In other words, for the monopolist with a downward-sloping demand curve, the curve of marginal revenue will lie (above/<u>below</u>) the curve of average revenue. (Remember the geometry of marginal revenue in the Basic Exercise to Chapter 8 in the Study Guide.) A similar use of Rule 4 indicates that when average cost is rising, the marginal cost curve will lie _____ the average cost curve.

138

Once we have used the marginal cost and marginal revenue curves to compute the monopolist's profit-maximizing output level, we can use the (<u>demand/supply</u>) curve to figure out what price he should charge. We   (6)
know that since the curve of marginal revenue lies below the demand curve, the monopolist's market price will be (<u>greater/less</u>) than both marginal revenue and marginal cost. We also know that if average cost is rising, average cost will be (<u>greater/less</u>) than marginal cost and hence also (<u>greater/less</u>) than the market price given by the demand curve. Thus, for a profit-maximizing monopolist, operating at a level where average cost is rising, price will be greater than average cost and the monopolist will receive positive economic profits. Since, by definition, the monopolist is the only supplier, new firms (<u>will/will not</u>) arise to compete away these profits. Compared with results under pure competition, the monopolist's profit-maximizing behavior will result in a (<u>higher/lower</u>) price and a (<u>higher/lower</u>) level of output in both the short and long run. (If average costs are not rising, the long-run viability of the monopolist requires that price exceed average cost.)

In Chapter 14 we will see that pure competition leads to an efficient allocation of resources. Efficient resource allocation requires that the marginal utility (MU) of each commodity equal its marginal cost (MC). In Chapter 5 we learned that optimal consumer decisions lead to the result that MU equals price. In Chapter 10 we saw that under perfect competition, optimal firm decisions imply that MC equals _____.   (7)
The upshot is clearly that under pure competition MU equals MC. With a pure monopoly as outlined above—that is, with the same demand and cost curves—we know that while consumers will continue to equate MU and P, the monopolist will equate MC to _____ _____, which is (<u>greater/less</u>) than P. The result is that with a pure monopoly, MU is (<u>greater/less</u>) than MC. Increased quantity of the monopolized commodity would yield marginal benefits, measured by MU, that are (<u>less than/the same as/greater than</u>) marginal costs. In this sense, the monopoly leads to an inefficient allocation of resources.

It is important to note that in the discussion above we assumed that the monopolist faces demand and cost curves that are the same as those of the previously competitive industry. However, several factors could shift these curves following a change in market structure. Advertising might shift demand and cost curves. Savings from centralizing various operations and avoiding duplication might shift the cost curves (<u>up/down</u>).   (8)
Inefficiencies from greater size would have the opposite effect. Particular results will depend upon particular circumstances.

Why do we say there is no supply curve for a monopolist? Remember that the supply curve shows the relationship between each possible market price and the quantity supplied. Under pure competition a firm takes price as given and then decides how much to produce, knowing that its individual quantity decision (<u>will/will not</u>) affect the market price. The firm's supply curve comes from considering its reaction to possible   (9)
prices. But the monopolist (<u>does/does not</u>) take price as given. The monopolist chooses the one quantity that maximizes profits and receives the price given by the point on the demand curve consistent with the quantity. The monopolist is a price (<u>maker/taker</u>).

IMPORTANT TERMS AND CONCEPTS QUIZ

Choose the best definition for the following terms.

1. _____ Pure monopoly
2. _____ Barriers to entry
3. _____ Patents
4. _____ Natural monopoly
5. _____ Monopoly profits
6. _____ Price discrimination

a. Impediments preventing potential rivals from entering an industry
b. Industry in which advantages of large-scale production enable a single firm to supply the market demand at a lower average cost than a number of smaller firms could
c. Industry with a single buyer for the entire market
d. Charging different prices to different customers when the cost of supplying customers is the same
e. Industry with single supplier of a product for which there are no close substitutes
f. Economic profits that persist in the long run
g. Temporary government grants of exclusive production rights to product's inventors

BASIC EXERCISES

These exercises are designed to offer practice in computing the profit-maximizing quantity and price for a monopolist.

1. Mario has a monopoly in the production of widgets. **Table 11-1** contains data on the demand for widgets and the cost of producing them. Use this data to compute Mario's profit-maximizing quantity and the associated price.

   a. One way is to consider columns 2 and 5 of **Table 11-2**. Choose the output level that maximizes the difference. That level of output is _____ widgets.

Table 11-1

Mario's Cost and Revenue

Quantity	Average Revenue (Price)	Average Cost
12	$9,500	$7,068.00
13	9,300	6,957.00
14	9,100	6,894.00
15	8,900	6,869.40
16	8,700	6,876.00

Table 11-2

Marginal Revenue and Cost

(1) Quantity	(2) Total Revenue	(3) Marginal Revenue	(4) Marginal Cost	(5) Total Cost
12	$114,000			$84,816
13	120,900	_____	_____	90,441
14	127,400	_____	_____	96,516
15	133,500	_____	_____	103,041
16	139,200	_____	_____	110,016

b. The second way is to fill in columns 3 and 4 of Table 11-2 by computing marginal revenue and marginal cost. Mario could maximize profits by increasing production as long as marginal _____ exceeds marginal _____ widgets. In this case, Mario maximizes profits by producing _____ widgets.

c. To maximize profits Mario should charge a price of $ _____.

d. What is Mario's profit? _____

It is sometimes argued that monopolists do not have to worry about what consumers are willing to pay, they can charge what they want. Assume that the production of widgets involves significant pollution, and the government has imposed a pollution charge that costs Mario $1,000 a widget. **Table 11-3** contains the original data on demand along with the new average cost data that reflect the $1,000 a widget pollution charge.

e. Use **Table 11-4** to compute the new profit-maximizing output level. Mario's new profit-maximizing output level is _____ and the associated price is $ _____.

f. Note that while the pollution charge is $1,000 a widget, Mario's profit-maximizing price increases by only $_____. Why doesn't Mario simply raise his price by the full $1,000?

g. What is the new level of profits? $_____.

h. (Optional) What would have happened if, instead of a per-unit tax, the government had simply fined Mario $13,000 for polluting and imposed no further charges? Compared with the initial situation and the situation with the per unit tax, what happens to Mario's profit-maximizing level of output, and actual profits with this lump-sum pollution charge?

Table 11-3

Revenue and Cost after the Pollution Tax

Quantity	Average Revenue (Price)	Average Cost
12	$9,500	$8,068.00
13	9,300	7,957.00
14	9,100	7,894.00
15	8,900	7,869.40
16	8,700	7,876.00

Table 11-4

Marginal Revenue, Total Cost, and Marginal Cost after the Pollution Tax

(1) Quantity	(2) Total Revenue	(3) Marginal Revenue	(4) Marginal Cost	(5) Total Cost
12	114,000			_____
13	120,900	_____	_____	_____
14	127,400	_____	_____	_____
15	133,500	_____	_____	_____
16	139,200	_____	_____	_____

Which tax reduces pollution the most? (When answering this question be sure you are working with the correct cost curves. Adjust Table 11-2, remembering that at each output level, total costs will now be $13,000 higher than the entries in column 5.)

2. This exercise illustrates how a monopolist may be able to increase her profits by engaging in price discrimination. **Table 11-5** contains data on the demand for snow tires in Centerville and Middletown. Centerville does not get much snow, and the demand for snow tires is quite elastic. Middletown is smaller, and gets more snow; it should not be surprising that the demand for snow tires in Middletown is less elastic than in Centerville. Snow tires are supplied to both cities by a monopolist who can produce tires with a fixed cost of $2,500,000 and a constant marginal cost of $10 a tire.

a. Assume that the monopolist charges the same price in both towns. Use the data on total demand to compute the monopolist's profit-maximizing level of output and price. First compute total revenue in order to compute marginal revenue per tire by dividing the change in total revenue by the change in output. Then compare marginal revenue to the monopolist's marginal cost of $10 to determine the profit-maximizing level of output.

Price? $ _____

Output? _____

Profits? $ _____

Table 11-5

Demand for Snow Tires

Price	Quantity Demanded Centerville	Middletown	Total Demand	Total Revenue	Marginal Revenue
$48	10,000	40,000	50,000	_____	
45	25,000	43,750	68,750	_____	
42	40,000	47,500	87,500	_____	
39	55,000	51,250	106,250	_____	
36	70,000	55,000	125,000	_____	
33	85,000	58,750	143,750	_____	
30	100,000	62,500	162,500	_____	
27	115,000	66,250	181,250	_____	

b. Assume now that the monopolist is able to charge different prices in the towns; that is, she is a price discriminator. Can the monopolist increase her profits by charging different prices? Complete **Table 11-6** to answer this question.

Profit-maximizing price in Centerville: $ _____

Profit-maximizing price in Middletown: $ _____

Quantity of snow tires in Centerville: _____

142

Table 11-6

Total and Marginal Revenue

| Price | Centerville | | | Middletown | | |
	Total Revenue	Marginal Revenue		Total Revenue	Marginal Revenue	
$48	_____			_____		
45	_____	_____		_____	_____	
42	_____	_____		_____	_____	
39	_____	_____		_____	_____	
36	_____	_____		_____	_____	
33	_____	_____		_____	_____	
30	_____	_____		_____	_____	
27	_____	_____		_____	_____	

Quantity of snow tires in Middletown: _____

Total Profits: $ _____

c. In which town did the monopolist raise the price? In which town did she lower the price? The monopolist should charge a higher price in the town with the lower elasticity of demand. Can you explain why? Is that the case here?

SELF-TESTS FOR UNDERSTANDING

TEST A

Circle the most appropriate answer.

1. Pure monopoly is characterized by
   a. many firms producing slightly different products.
   b. many firms producing slightly different products that are close substitutes.
   c. such a small number of firms that each must figure out how the others will respond to its own actions.
   d. one firm, with no competitors, producing a product with no close substitutes.

2. Which one of the following is not likely to lead to a monopoly?
   a. patents
   b. control of the sole source of an important commodity
   c. a commodity with many close substitutes
   d. significant increasing returns to scale

3. A natural monopoly arises when
    a. natural resources are an important input.
    b. there are significant cost advantages to large-scale production.
    c. the government prohibits entry.
    d. patents protect a firm's technology.

4. Which of the following is not an example of a barrier to entry?
    a. patents that give exclusive rights to production
    b. the existence of large fixed costs before one can begin production
    c. a legal charter that grants its holder the right to be the sole supplier
    d. a simple production process with constant average cost and no fixed costs

5. Which of the following is likely to represent a monopoly?
    a. the largest department store in town
    b. the University of Iowa, which is the largest employer in Iowa City
    c. the local gas and electric company, which operates under an exclusive contract from the city
    d. Amtrak

6. If in order to sell more a firm must reduce the price on all units sold, we can conclude that the firm's demand curve
    a. has a positive slope.
    b. is horizontal.
    c. slopes down and to the right.
    d. is vertical.

7. Under the conditions of question 6, we know that marginal revenue will
    a. be less than average revenue.
    b. equal average revenue.
    c. exceed average revenue.

8. If average costs are increasing, marginal cost will be
    a. less than average cost.
    b. equal to average cost.
    c. greater than average cost.
    d. Insufficient information to determine whether marginal cost will be above or below average cost.

9. A monopolist maximizes profit by producing where
    a. marginal cost equals marginal revenue.
    b. marginal cost equals marginal utility.
    c. average cost equals average revenue.
    d. the difference between average cost and average revenue is greatest.

10. Once a monopolist has determined the profit-maximizing level of output, the price she should charge is given by the curve of
    a. marginal revenue.
    b. marginal cost.
    c. average cost.
    d. average revenue.

11. A monopolist's profits are found by multiplying the quantity produced by the difference between
    a. marginal cost and marginal revenue.
    b. marginal cost and average revenue.
    c. average cost and average revenue.
    d. average cost and marginal revenue.

12. A monopolist's economic profits will
    a. be competed away in the long run.
    b. be driven to the opportunity cost of capital.
    c. persist in the long run.
    d. be limited by usury laws.

13. Because a monopolist is a price maker, it is typically said that he has
    a. an inelastic demand curve.
    b. no demand curve.
    c. no supply curve.
    d. an upward-sloping demand curve.

14. An entrepreneur who monopolizes a previously competitive industry and now faces the same demand curve and produces with the same cost function will typically maximize profits by
    a. forcing consumers to buy more at a higher price.
    b. producing less and charging a higher price.
    c. increasing volume.
    d. lowering both output and price.

15. A price-discriminating monopolist producing in one plant and selling in two markets will operate such that
    a. price is equal in both markets.
    b. profits are equal in both markets.
    c. marginal revenue is equal in both markets.
    d. quantities sold are equal in both markets.

16. A monopolist cannot simply pass on any increase in average cost because
    a. marginal cost exceeds average cost.
    b. the average cost curve often has a positive slope.
    c. the monopolist's demand curve is typically downward sloping.
    d. of concerns about excessive profiteering.

17. An increase in a monopolist's average cost will lead to a(n)
    a. increase in price by the same amount, as the monopolist passes on the price increase.
    b. increase in price only if marginal cost increases.
    c. decrease in price as the monopolist needs to sell more in order to cover increased costs.
    d. increase in price only if the elasticity of demand is less than 1.0.

18. Some argue that because they control the whole market and can thus garner all of the benefits, monopolies are more likely to foster innovations. Statistical evidence
    a. confirms this argument.
    b. suggests exactly the reverse.
    c. lacks a firm conclusion.

19. An increase in a monopolist's fixed cost will
    a. reduce the profit-maximizing level of output.
    b. not affect the profit-maximizing level of output.
    c. increase the profit-maximizing level of output as the monopolist needs to sell more to cover costs.

20. If marginal cost is greater than zero, we know that a monopolist will produce where the elasticity of demand is
    a. greater than 1.0.
    b. equal to 1.0.
    c. less than 1.0.

TEST B

Circle T or F for true or false.

T F 1. A pure monopoly results when only a few firms supply a particular commodity for which there are no close substitutes.

T F 2. Significant increasing returns to scale, which reduce average costs as output expands, may result in a natural monopoly.

T F 3. A pure monopolist can earn positive economic profits only in the long run.

T F 4. An entrepreneur who successfully monopolizes a competitive industry will face a horizontal demand curve just like each of the previous competitive firms.

T F 5. A monopolist maximizes profits by producing at the point at which marginal cost equals marginal revenue.

T F 6. If in a monopolistic industry, demand and cost curves are identical to a comparable competitive industry, and the demand curve slopes downward while the average cost curve slopes upward, then the monopolist's price will always exceed the competitive industry's price, but the monopolist's output will be larger.

T F 7. A monopolist has a greater incentive to advertise than does an individual firm under pure competition.

T F 8. When market price is greater than average cost, a monopolist can always increase profits by producing more.

T F 9. A price-discriminating monopolist would increase profits by charging all consumers the same price.

T F 10. Price discrimination always hurts consumers.

SUPPLEMENTARY EXERCISES

1. The demand curve for the first problem in the Basic Exercise is

$$Q = 59.5 - 0.005P.$$

The total cost curve is

$$TC = 52,416 + 225Q_2.$$

   a. Derive mathematical expressions for total revenue, marginal revenue, average cost, and marginal cost.
   b. Plot the demand, marginal revenue, average cost, and marginal cost curves.
   c. Use your expressions for marginal revenue and marginal cost to solve for the profit-maximizing level of output. Is your answer consistent with your graph in part b and your answer to the Basic Exercise?
   d. What is the impact of the per-unit pollution tax and the fixed-charge pollution tax on your expressions for total, average, and marginal cost? Do differences here help explain the impact of these taxes on the profit-maximizing level of output?

2. Why is (a) the correct answer to question 20 in Test A? (You might want to refer back to Chapter 7.)

ECONOMICS IN ACTION

THE HIGH COST OF NEW DRUGS

In the early 1990s, the debate over health-care reform at the beginning of the Clinton Administration focused attention on the pricing policies of drug companies. This concern has not abated as low-income countries in Africa struggle with the cost of drugs to treat AIDS. The cost of drugs to treat anthrax and the actions of several countries to abridge patent agreements in the face of what looked like national emergencies in the fall of 2001 along with President Bush's successful lobbying of Congress for a prescription drug bill for senior citizens have only intensified concerns about drug prices.

Consider the case of Tacrine, the first drug recommended by an advisory panel of the Food and Drug Administration to treat Alzheimer's disease. Industry observers were expecting Tacrine would cost more than $1,000 a year even though it is not effective for most patients. What explains such high prices for this and other new drugs?

Some point to the high cost of drug research, and the fact that most new ideas are not successful, as justification for the high cost of drugs. Pharmaceutical manufacturers argue that drugs save money, as even expensive drugs are often cheaper than hospitalization or surgery.

Regulating drug prices to allow manufacturers a reasonable rate of return while recognizing the significant research and development costs a company incurs—that is, setting prices on the basis of cost-plus pricing—has been advocated by some. Others are concerned that this approach may only subsidize and encourage wasteful and mediocre research. Sam Peltzman, a professor of economics at the University of Chicago, argues that

147

one should not be surprised by high prices. Patents mean that drug companies enjoy a ten-year monopoly. As Peltzman puts it, "These companies are not charities—they are charging what the market will allow."

Are there other solutions? Peltzman has advocated limiting patent monopolies to five years. Others argue that the concept of managed competition, under which patients are organized into large groups to bargain with drug companies and other health care providers, is necessary for patients to get the best price. Some are less optimistic that patients, even if organized into large groups, will be successful in bargaining with drug companies who hold a monopoly position unless patients are willing to refuse drug treatments that cost too much.

Uwe Reinhardt, a health economist at Princeton University, has advocated a variant on the bargaining approach through the use of a "reference pricing" system, such has been used in Germany. Under this approach, insurers would provide a larger reimbursement for drugs that are truly new, different, and for which its manufacturer agrees to the reference price. Other drugs would be available to consumers, but with a lower reimbursement. Reinhardt has suggested that private insurers and the government set aside 1 percent of their current expenditures on prescription drugs to establish an independent research institute to determine what drugs would qualify for the reference pricing system.

1. How would you determine a fair price for new drugs?

2. What would it take to enforce your concept of fair prices and what side effects are likely to be associated with enforcement?

3. Do you think there should be changes in the terms of patents for new drugs? If so, what and why?

4. What do you think explains the high price of new drugs?

Sources: Elizabeth Rosenthal, "Exploring the Murky World of Drug Prices," *The New York Times,* March 28, 1993; Uwe E. Reinhardt, "How to Lower the Cost of Drugs," *The New York Times,* January 3, 2001; Malcolm Gladwell, "Who's really to blame for the cost of drugs?" *The New Yorker,* October 25, 2004.

STUDY QUESTIONS

1. Why are barriers to entry important for the preservation of a monopolist's monopoly?

2. What is the difference between a price taker and a price maker? Which description is relevant for a monopolist?

3. Why do economists argue that monopoly leads to an inefficient allocation of resources?

4. Who has the greater incentive to advertise and why, a firm in a purely competitive industry or a monopolist?

5. Are there conditions under which society might benefit from a monopoly? Explain.

6. What is meant by the term "price discrimination"?

7. How can a monopolist increase profits by engaging in price discrimination?

8. Will price discrimination always raise prices for customers?

9. Why doesn't a monopolist simply raise her price by the full cost of things like pollution charges?

10. If both monopolists and competitive firms produce where marginal revenue equals marginal cost, why are the results of a competitive industry and a monopolized industry different?

Between Competition and Monopoly

12

Important Terms and Concepts

Monopolistic competition	Price war	Payoff matrix	Zero sum game
Oligopoly	Sales maximization	Dominant strategy	Repeated games
Cartel	Kinked demand curve	Maximin criterion	Credible threat
Price leadership	Sticky price	Nash equilibrium	Perfectly contestable markets

Learning Objectives

After completing this chapter, you should be able to:

- compare the four conditions that define monopolistic competition with those of perfect competition.

- explain why and how the long-run equilibrium of a firm under monopolistic competition differs from that of a firm under pure competition.

- explain why firms under monopolistic competition earn zero profit in the long run even though they face a downward-sloping demand curve.

- explain why monopolistic competitors are said to have excess capacity.

- explain why it is so difficult to make a formal analysis of an oligopolistic market structure.

- describe briefly the alternative approaches to modeling oligopolistic behavior.

- explain why most economists believe it is difficult to maintain the discipline necessary to sustain a cartel.

- use marginal cost and marginal revenue curves to derive the implications for price and quantity of sales maximization as opposed to profit maximization.

- use marginal cost and marginal revenue curves to explain how a kinked demand curve can imply sticky prices.

- analyze a payoff matrix to see if there is a dominant strategy.

- use the maximin criterion to determine the final outcome in a game-theory setting.

- analyze Nash equilibrium, zero-sum games, and repeated games.

- understand how credible threats could be used as entry-blocking strategies.

- explain how the concept of contestable markets means that even in an industry with few firms, no firm will earn long-run profits in excess of the opportunity cost of capital, and inefficient firms will not survive if entry and exit are costless.

- compare different attributes of the four market forms.

CHAPTER REVIEW

Pure competition and pure monopoly are the polar examples of market structure most easily analyzed in textbooks. Actual markets tend more toward *monopolistic competition* and *oligopoly,* which are the subjects of this chapter. It is harder to model firm behavior in these market structures, especially in the case of oligopoly. However, profit maximization remains a dominant objective for most firms and marginal cost and marginal revenue curves still are important tools when analyzing the decisions firms make.

A market structure in which there are numerous participants, freedom of entry and exit, perfect infor-
(1) mation, and product heterogeneity is referred to as _____ competition. Because each seller is able to partially differentiate his product, individual firms will face a demand curve with a (negative/positive/zero) slope. At each point in time, profit-maximizing firms will try to produce at the output level where _____ _____ equals _____. The assumption of freedom of entry and exit implies that in the long run under monopolistic competition firms will earn (negative/positive/zero) economic profit. If existing firms are earning positive economic profits, the (entry/exit) of new firms will shift the demand curve down (and may raise costs) until the demand curve is just tangent to the (average/marginal) cost curve.

A market structure with only a few firms producing a similar or identical product, and in which some firms
(2) are very large, is called a(n) _____. Formal analysis of such market structures is difficult; when considering the decisions of one firm, one must also take into account the possible reactions of competitors. No single model describes all the possible outcomes under oligopoly, and economists have found it useful to consider a number of possible models and outcomes. If firms in an oligopolistic market band together and act like a single profit-maximizing monopolist, the resulting group is called a(n) _____. If most firms look to pricing decisions made by a dominant firm, economists refer to the outcome as one of _____ _____.

Oligopolistic firms tend to be large corporations with professional managers. Some argue that managers are likely to be more interested in maximizing total revenue than in maximizing profits. This outcome is more likely if the compensation of managers depends more upon the size of the firm than upon its profitability. A firm interested in maximizing sales revenue will increase output until marginal revenue equals
(3) _____. Compared with profit maximization, sales maximization will mean a (higher/lower) price and a(n) _____ quantity.

Another traditional element of the analysis of oligopoly is the concept of a kinked demand curve. Such a demand curve comes from assuming that your competitors (<u>will/will not</u>) match any decrease in your price (4) but (<u>will/will not</u>) match any increase in your price. As a result, there is a gap in the (<u>marginal/average</u>) revenue curve, and profit-maximizing prices may not change unless there is a significant shift in the marginal _____ curve.

Game theory has been used productively by a number of economists to study oligopolistic behavior. Game theory involves listing the possible outcomes of your moves and your opponents' countermoves in a(n) _____ matrix and then choosing an appropriate _____. If there is one strategy (5) that always yields the highest return regardless of what your competitors do, that strategy is referred to as a(n) _____ strategy. If firms choose a strategy that protects them against the worst possible outcome, they are choosing a(n) _____ strategy. If firms choose strategies to maximize payoffs assuming competitors stick to their announced strategies, the result is called a(n) _____ equilibrium. If one firm's gain is the other firm's loss, the set of strategic choices are called a(n) _____ - _____ game. In repeated games, _____ becomes important and may lead to higher long-run profits. Threats are likely to be most effective if they are _____.

The concept of perfectly contestable markets suggests that even oligopolists may be limited in their ability to earn monopolistic profits. The crucial condition for perfect contestability is that _____ and (6) _____ are costless and unimpeded. In such a case, competitors would get into and out of the market whenever profits exceeded the _____ _____ of _____. While no market may be perfectly contestable, the extent to which markets are contestable will limit the ability of firms to charge monopolistic prices.

IMPORTANT TERMS AND CONCEPTS QUIZ

Choose the best definition for each of the following terms.

1. _____ Monopolistic competition
2. _____ Oligopoly
3. _____ Cartel
4. _____ Price leadership
5. _____ Price war
6. _____ Sales maximization
7. _____ Kinked demand curve
8. _____ Sticky price
9. _____ Payoff matrix
10. _____ Dominant strategy
11. _____ Maximin criterion
12 _____ Nash equilibrium
13. _____ Zero-sum game
14. _____ Repeated game
15. _____ Credible threat
16. _____ Perfectly contestable markets

a. Group of sellers who join together to control production, sales, and price

b. Listing of outcomes linked to the strategic choices of competitors

c. Selling at a lower price than your competitor without regard to cost

d. Market in which entry and exit are costless and unimpeded

e. Price does not change even if there are changes in cost

f. Threat that would not harm threatener if carried out

g. Many firms selling slightly different products

h. Selecting the strategy that yields the maximum profit, assuming your opponent tries to damage you as much as possible

i. Situation where one firm sets the price and other firms follow

j. Situations that are played out again and again

k. Situation where price declines are matched by competitors while price increases are not

l. Best result when one assumes opponents will stick to their chosen strategy

m. Industry composed of a few large rival firms

n. Expanding output to the point where marginal revenue equals zero

o. Operating independently, players choose strategies that lead to a worse outcome than would be chosen if players could coordinate strategies

p. A single strategy yields the highest payoff regardless of the strategy chosen by your competitor

q. One competitor's gain is the other's loss

BASIC EXERCISES

These problems explore several important issues in the analysis of monopolistic competition and oligopoly.

1. Our discussion of monopolistic competition argued that long-run equilibrium implies the firm's demand curve will be tangent to its average cost curve. We have also argued that profit maximization requires that marginal revenue equal marginal cost (or, alternatively, that firms should expand output as long as marginal revenue exceeds marginal cost). How do we know that marginal revenue equals marginal cost at the quantity given by the tangency between the demand curve and the average cost curve?

Table 12-1

Alice's Restaurant

Quantity	Average Revenue	Average Cost	Total Revenue	Total Cost	Total Profit
600	$19	$21.67	$11,400	$13,000	$-1,602
800	17	17.50	13,600	14,000	-400
1,000	15	15.00	15,000	15,000	0
1,200	13	13.33	15,600	16,000	-396
1,400	11	12.14	15,400	17,000	-1,596

Figure 12-1

Alice's Restaurant: Profit, Cost, and Demand

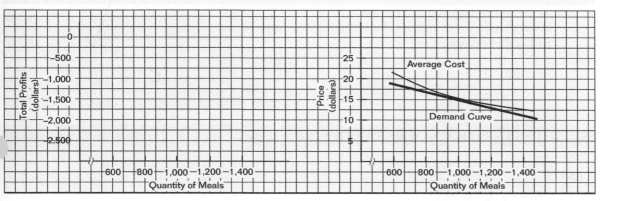

a. **Table 12-1** contains data on weekly costs and revenue for Alice's Restaurant. Average revenue and average cost are plotted in **Figure 12-1.** Note that the demand curve is tangent to the average cost curve. Plot total profits in the left half of Figure 12-1. What output level maximizes profits?

b. Use the data in Table 12-1 to compute marginal revenue and marginal cost in **Table 12-2.** According to Table 12-2, what level of output maximizes profits? Why?

Table 12-2

Alice's Restaurant: Marginal Revenue and Marginal Cost

Quantity	Marginal Revenue	Marginal Cost
800	_____	_____
1,000	_____	_____
1,200	_____	_____
1,400	_____	_____

155

2. **Figure 12-2** shows the kinked demand curve for a profit-maximizing firm that produces TV sets in an oligopolistic situation.

a. What is the profit-maximizing level of output and the corresponding price if TVs can be produced at a marginal cost of $100?

Quantity _____

Price _____

b. Assume that marginal cost increases by 25 percent to $125 per TV. Describe what happens to the profit-maximizing levels of price and quantity following this increase in marginal cost.

c. What increase in marginal cost would be necessary to induce a change in behavior on the part of this oligopolist and why?

d. What decrease in marginal cost would be necessary to induce a change in behavior on the part of this oligopolist and why?

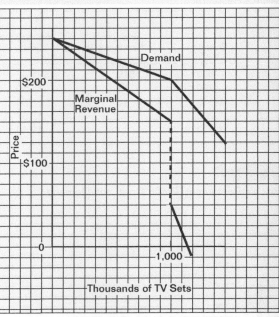

Figure 12-2

Kinked Demand Curve

SELF-TESTS FOR UNDERSTANDING

TEST A

Circle the most appropriate answer.

1. Which of the following is the important difference between perfect and monopolistic competition?
   a. few sellers rather than many
   b. heterogeneous rather than homogeneous product
   c. barriers to entry rather than freedom of entry
   d. long-run positive economic profits rather than zero economic profits

2. Monopolistic competition would be most appropriate when describing which of the following?
   a. collusion between contractors when bidding for government contracts
   b. the production of automobiles in the United States
   c. much retail trade in the United States
   d. the production of wheat

3. Under monopolistic competition the heterogeneity of output implies that
   a. individual firms face downward-sloping demand curves.
   b. both marginal cost and marginal revenue will increase with additional units of output.
   c. individual firms can make positive economic profits even in the long run.
   d. in the long run, individual firms will produce at minimum average cost.

156

4. Free entry and exit under monopolistic competition means that in the long run
   a. firms will earn economic profits.
   b. a firm's demand curve will be tangent to its average cost curve.
   c. a firm will operate where marginal cost exceeds marginal revenue.
   d. only one firm can survive.

5. Under monopolistic competition, firms are likely to produce
   a. to the left of the point of minimum average cost.
   b. at the point of minimum average cost.
   c. to the right of the point of minimum average cost.

6. Which of the following is most likely an example of monopolistic competition?
   a. the airline industry
   b. restaurants in Denver
   c. competition between automobile manufacturers
   d. cable television in Atlanta

7. Which of the following characterizes a firm's short-run equilibrium under monopolistic competition?
   a. production where average cost equals price
   b. production at minimum average cost
   c. production where marginal revenue equals marginal cost
   d. zero economic profits

8. Which of the following does not characterize a firm's long-run equilibrium under monopolistic competition?
   a. production where average cost equals price
   b. production at minimum average cost
   c. production where marginal revenue equals marginal cost
   d. zero economic profits

9. If long-run economic profits are zero, we know that firms are producing where
   a. marginal cost equals average cost.
   b. marginal revenue equals average cost.
   c. marginal cost equals price.
   d. average cost equals price.

10. The situation where a few large firms produce similar products is referred to as
    a. monopolistic competition.
    b. an oligopoly.
    c. contestable markets.
    d. price leadership.

11. Oligopoly may be associated with all but which one of the following?
    a. price leadership
    b. collusive behavior
    c. advertising
    d. lots of firms

12. If oligopolistic firms get together to carve up the market and act like a monopolist, the result is called a
    a. cabal.
    b. contestable market.
    c. cartel.
    d. natural monopoly.

13. A firm interested in maximizing sales revenue will produce at a point where
    a. marginal revenue equals marginal cost.
    b. average cost is minimized.
    c. marginal revenue equals zero.
    d. average revenue equals average cost.

14. A firm that maximizes sales revenues instead of profits will charge
    a. a higher price.
    b. a lower price.
    c. the same price but will advertise more.

15. Game theory may be especially useful in analyzing a firm's behavior under conditions of
    a. pure competition.
    b. monopolistic competition.
    c. oligopoly.
    d. pure monopoly.

16. The term *payoff matrix* refers to
    a. bribes paid by cartels.
    b. the structure of winnings in an office pool on the NCAA basketball championship.
    c. the set of possible outcomes in a game theory situation.
    d. players' shares in the NFL playoffs.

17. The term *kinked demand curve* refers to
    a. economists' inability to draw straight lines.
    b. the demand for X-rated movies.
    c. industries with substantial economies of scale.
    d. a situation where competitors match price decreases but not price increases.

18. If a firm faces a kinked demand curve, the demand curve for price increases will likely
    a. be steeper than for price decreases.
    b. have a positive slope.
    c. be more elastic than for price decreases.
    d. be less elastic than for price decreases.

19. Markets can be perfectly contestable if
    a. products are identical.
    b. entry and exit are free and easy.
    c. only two firms are bidding against each other.
    d. long-run economic profits are zero.

20. All but which one of the following market structures are likely to result in a misallocation of resources?
    a. perfect competition
    b. monopolistic competition
    c. oligopoly
    d. monopoly

TEST B

Circle T or F for true or false.

T F 1. Firms that operate under conditions of oligopoly are likely to engage in lots of advertising.

T F 2. Heterogeneity of output is an important feature of monopolistic competition.

T F 3. Under monopolistic competition, freedom of entry and exit will guarantee that a firm always earns zero economic profit, in both the short run and the long run.

T F 4. For profit-maximizing firms under monopolistic competition, marginal revenue equals marginal cost in the short run but not in the long run.

T F 5. There would be an unambiguous social gain if in a market with monopolistic competition some firms were forced by regulation to stop producing.

T F 6. Oligopoly is characterized by a small number of firms, some very large, producing an identical or similar product.

T F 7. Arrangements such as price leadership and tacit collusion can be important in oligopolistic markets.

T F 8. A firm that maximizes sales revenue will typically charge a higher price than a firm that maximizes profits.

T F 9. An oligopolist facing a kinked demand curve will see a more elastic demand curve for price increases than for price decreases.

T F 10. Perfectly contestable markets are only possible when there are a large number of competing firms.

SUPPLEMENTARY EXERCISES

1. The equations below for demand and total cost underlie the first problem in the Basic Exercises. Use these equations to derive explicit expressions for marginal cost, marginal revenue, and average cost. Now solve for the level of output that maximizes profits. Compare your answer with the results you obtained in the Basic Exercises.

$$Q = 2,500 - 100P \text{ (demand curve)}$$

$$TC = 10,000 + 5Q \text{ (total cost curve)}$$

where Q = total quantity, P = price, and TC = total cost.

2. This problem illustrates the difference between maximizing profits and maximizing sales. Demand and total cost are given by the equations below.

Demand

$$Q = 16{,}000 - 200P$$

Total Cost

$$TC = 0.00000015625Q_3 - 0.003125Q_2 + 40.625Q$$

a. If the firm maximizes profits, what are output, price, and profits?
b. If the firm maximizes sales revenue, what are output, price, and profits?
c. Is it true that maximizing sales revenue involves a higher quantity, lower price, and lower profits?

3. For an interesting discussion of apparent tacit collusion in practice and how academic research along with the resulting publicity changed behavior, see William G. Christie and Paul H. Schultz, "Policy Watch: Did Nasdaq Market Makers Implicitly Collude?" *Journal of Economic Perspectives* (Vol. 9, Number 3) Summer 1995, pp. 199–208. Figure 1 is a dramatic piece of evidence.

ECONOMICS IN ACTION

COMPETITION OR COLLUSION?

What do the latest mergers of telecommunications companies mean—more or less competition?

There was a time when there was no Internet, no cable television and only one telephone company, AT&T, known to many as Ma Bell. The reason there was only one telephone company was the belief that telephone service was a natural monopoly. In many ways AT&T was very successful. It grew to employ more than a million people, and its stock was the epitome of a safe investment for widows and orphans.

People did not own their telephones, AT&T did, and monthly telephone bills included a rental charge for the phone. The AT&T monopoly began to unravel in the 1960s when MCI entered the long-distance market using microwave technology.

The emergence of cell phone networks eliminated the distinction between local and long-distance calls, undermining earlier regulation that attempted to separate the two. Cable companies, originally formed to bring high-quality television service to people's homes, now offer Internet access with high quality Internet phone service, a new emerging technology.

In late 2004 and early 2005, it almost seemed like there was a new telecom merger everyday as first Sprint and Nextel announced plans to merge, SBC bought out AT&T, and Verizon moved to acquire MCI. Will the result be increased competition among a small number of surviving giants or will consumers lose as a small number of companies conspire to act as a monopolist?

Surviving firms argue that mergers are necessary to take advantage of new technologies to improve customer service and competitive positioning. They argue that they are not competing among themselves but compet-

160

ing against cable companies and the Internet. Others are not so sure and expect consumers will be faced with limited choice of costly bundled services many do not want. "Companies always say that the next merger will be the one to unleash competition," according to Mark Cooper, research director for the Consumer Federation of America. "The reality is that these are consolidations. They take alternatives away from consumers."

Steven Pearlstein is more optimistic and argues that "(T)he traditional distinctions between local and long distance, voice and data, Internet and television are increasingly irrelevant." At the same time Pearlstein argues that the big question for regulators is whether to permit emerging companies to retain exclusive control over their own networks or whether they should be required to grant access to competitors to ensure a competitive market.

1. Who was right, Cooper or Pearlstein? What has happened to the price of cell phone service? Have telecom consolidations meant an increase in price or a reduction?

2. Were consumers better off dealing separately with their local phone service, a cell phone provider, a cable company, and an Internet service provider, or have consolidations offered consumers better options at better prices?

Source: Steve Pearlstein, "Calling for Real Competition," *Washington Post,* February 16, 2005. David Lazarus, "Verizon reduces choices," *San Francisco Chronicle,* February 15, 2005.

STUDY QUESTIONS

1. How does monopolistic competition differ from perfect competition?

2. What is meant by the notion that monopolistic competition leads to excess capacity?

3. "As monopolistic competition leads to excess capacity, there will be an unambiguous social gain if government regulation reduces the number of firms and eliminates the excess capacity." Do you agree or disagree? Why?

4. What difference would it make if a firm acts to maximize profits or to maximize sales?

5. As a cartel is assumed to act to maximize profits, why do economists believe that cartels are difficult to establish and tend to self-destruct?

6. How can a kinked demand curve help explain price stickiness in an oligopolistic setting?

7. "Even if there are few firms in a market, the power of these firms to charge high prices will be limited if markets are contestable." Why is free and easy exit as important to contestable markets as free and easy entry?

8. What is the maximin criterion for choosing among strategies in a game theory setting?

9. Why is reputation an important element in repeated games?

161

Limiting Market Power: Regulation and Antitrust

13

Important Terms and Concepts

Economies of scale	Concentration ratios	Regulation
Monopoly power	Herfindal-Hirschman index	Economies of scope
Antitrust policy	Predatory pricing	Cross-subsidization
Concentration of industry	Bundling	Price cap

Learning Objectives

After completing this chapter, you should be able to:

- explain why monopoly power is undesirable.

- analyze how the various antitrust laws help in protecting competition.

  describe how concentration ratios are calculated and how, in the United States, they have changed.

- describe how concentration may or may not be related to market power.

- describe what is meant by predatory pricing and how one might identify it.

- explain how antitrust laws can be used to thwart competition.

- describe the major purposes of regulation.

- discuss arguments for and against bigness per se.

- evaluate the arguments supporting regulation.

- explain why marginal cost pricing may be infeasible in an industry with significant economies of scale.

- explain why allowing a firm to earn profits equal to the opportunity cost of its capital provides little incentive for increased efficiency.

- summarize recent experience under deregulation of several industries.

CHAPTER REVIEW

Economists and others have long argued whether bigness per se is good or bad. Opponents contend that the flow of wealth to firms with significant market power is socially undesirable and should be restrained. Profit-

(1) maximizing monopolists are likely to lead to a misallocation of resources as they produce (<u>less/more</u>) output than is socially desirable, and large firms with significant market power have (<u>less/more</u>) inducement for innovation.

Proponents counter that large firms are necessary for successful innovation. They maintain that many big

(2) firms, because of (<u>increasing/decreasing</u>) returns to scale, can yield benefits to the public as a result of the associated (<u>reduction/increase</u>) in unit cost that accompanies large-scale production. To break up these firms into smaller units would (<u>increase/decrease</u>) costs. The United States has chosen to deal with potential monopolies through the use of regulation and antitrust policy.

ANTITRUST POLICY

Antitrust policy is designed to control the growth of monopolies and prevent undesirable behavior from powerful firms. Reducing your price to destroy your rivals and become a monopolist is

(3) called _____ _____. Economists argue that a price below average cost (<u>is/is not</u>) by itself evidence of predatory pricing. Remember that setting price below average cost may maximize profits by minimizing losses. Only if price is below marginal or average _____ cost might there be evidence of predatory pricing. Even then the courts have held that there must be evidence that such prices were adopted to harm rival firms and that the predatory firm could subsequently raise prices to monopoly levels.

There is no perfect measure of how concentrated an industry is. One widely used gauge looks at the percent of industry output accounted for by the four largest firms. This measure is called a four-firm

(4) _____ ratio. The _____ - _____ index gives greater weight to large firms by squaring and summing the market share of firms. In this century, concentration ratios in the United States have shown (<u>much/little</u>) change.

REGULATION

Regulatory procedures have been adopted for several reasons including:

(5)   A. To regulate the actions of natural monopolies in industries where economies of _____ and economies of _____ mean that free competition between a large number of suppliers (<u>is/is not</u>) sustainable.

B. To ensure service at reasonable prices to isolated areas. It is argued that regulation is necessary so that suppliers can offset (<u>above/below</u>)-cost prices in isolated areas with (<u>above/below</u>)-cost prices elsewhere and thus be protected from competitors who concentrate only on the profitable markets.

Regulation of prices is a very complicated undertaking. Established to prevent abuses of monopoly such as charging prices that are "too high," the regulatory agencies have, in many cases, actually raised prices. In these cases, regulation preserves the shadow of competition only by protecting (<u>high/low</u>)-cost, inefficient firms.   (6)
Economists typically argue for the use of marginal cost as a more appropriate basis for regulated prices.

The application of marginal cost pricing is difficult in an industry with significant economies of scale. In this case, average cost will (<u>decline/increase</u>) as output increases. When average cost declines, marginal cost is   (7)
(<u>greater/less</u>) than average cost and setting price equal to marginal cost will mean (<u>losses/profits</u>).

Sometimes regulation limits overall profitability rather than prices. For example, a firm's rate of return might be limited to 10 percent. While rate of return regulation might seem to limit the ability of firms to exercise monopoly power, it also (<u>enhances/reduces</u>) the incentive for firms to be efficient. In the absence of profit regula-   (8)
tion, successful efforts to reduce costs will be rewarded with higher profits. If profits are regulated, there is less incentive to seek out the most efficient means of production. To solve this problem, some advocate the use of price ceilings that decline over time and leave firms free to earn higher profits through even greater efficiency. Experience with deregulation, especially in airline, transportation, and telephone service, is now close to two decades old, and a number of trends have emerged.

a. Adjusted for inflation, prices have generally declined.

b. Local airline service has not suffered, as was feared, due to the establishment of specialized commuter airlines.

c. New firms have entered previously regulated industries, although not all have survived.

d. Unions in previously regulated industries have been under significant pressure to reduce wages and adjust work rules.

e. Some have argued that product quality has declined while others argue that consumers prefer lower prices.

f. In industries like airlines there is a legitimate concern about safety, but evidence to date shows no adverse impact.

IMPORTANT TERMS AND CONCEPTS QUIZ

Choose the most appropriate definition for each of the following terms.

1. _____ Economies of scale
2. _____ Monopoly power
3. _____ Antitrust policy
4. _____ Concentration of industry
5. _____ Concentration ratios
6. _____ Herfindahl-Hirschman Index
7. _____ Predatory pricing
8. _____ Bundling
9. _____ Regulation
10. _____ Economies of scope
11. _____ Cross-subsidization
12. _____ Price cap

a. Losses on one product balanced by profits on another
b. Discounts to customers who buy a set of products as a group
c. Legal restrictions or controls on business decisions of firms
d. Pricing to destroy rivals
e. Ability of a firm to affect the price of its output for its own benefit
f. Sum of the square of market share for firms within an industry
g. Percentage of an industry's output produced by the largest firms
h. Temporary monopoly for the initial use of an innovation
i. Pre-assigned price ceilings that decline in anticipation of future productivity growth
j. Savings acquired through simultaneous production of different products
k. Policies designed to control growth of monopoly and to prevent powerful firms from engaging in "anti-competitive" practices
l. Savings acquired through increases in quantities produced
m. Share of the total sales or assets of the industry in the hands of its largest firms.

BASIC EXERCISES

1. **Economies of Scale**

   This exercise illustrates the difficulty of marginal cost pricing when average cost declines.

   Imagine that the efficient provision of telephone calls in a medium-sized city involves an initial investment of $100 million financed by borrowing at 6.00 percent and variable cost of 5 cents a phone call. The phone company's annual fixed cost would be $6.0 million (6.00 percent of $100 million).
   a. Use this information about costs to plot marginal cost and average total cost in **Figure 13-1.** (Use the $6.00 million figure for annual fixed cost.)
   b. Assume that regulators set price at 5 cents, the level of marginal cost. What is the firm's profit position if 60 million calls a year are demanded at that price? 90 million? 150 million?
   c. Is setting price equal to marginal cost a viable option in this case? Why or why not?

166

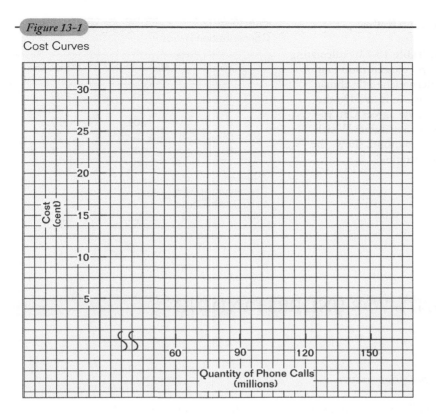

Figure 13-1

Cost Curves

2. **Predatory Pricing**

Michelle owns a company that manufactures Yuk, a gooey substance that drips down the wall in a horrible mess but can be peeled off without damaging paint or wallpaper. While Michelle thought that Yuk would appeal to grade school children, she has found that her strongest market is college students. Michelle is concerned about plans by a rival firm to introduce Splat, a similar product. Yuk can be produced with a fixed cost of $50,000 and a variable cost of 75¢ a pound. Michelle hopes to produce and sell 100,000 pounds of Yuk at an average cost of $1.25 a pound.

a. If average variable cost is taken as an indicator of predatory pricing, how far could Michelle lower her price without fear of losing a court case over possible predatory pricing?

b. As argued in Chapter 7, while it can be "profitable" for firms to continue production even if price is less than average cost, once price has dropped below average variable cost, the firm would be better off shutting down production. The discussion in this chapter suggested that predatory pricing requires a firm to set price below average variable cost. How can it ever be in Michelle's or any company's interest to sell at a price below average variable cost?

167

3. **Concentration Ratios**

Complete **Table 13-1** by calculating the four-firm concentration ratio and the Herfindahl-Hirschman index for each industry. Do the rankings always agree? Can you explain why they differ? Which industry do you think shows the most concentration?

■ *Table 13-1*

Concentration Ratios

Firm	Market Share	Market Share	Market Share
A	50	22.5	75
B	10	22.5	5
C	10	22.5	5
D	10	22.5	5
E	10	5	5
F	10	5	5
Four-Firm Concentration Ratio	_____	_____	_____
Herfindahl-Hirshman Index	_____	_____	_____

SELF-TESTS FOR UNDERSTANDING

TEST A

Circle the most appropriate answer.

1. Antitrust policy seeks to (there may be more than one correct answer)
   a. force firms to set price equal to marginal cost.
   b. prevent the acquisition of monopoly power.
   c. limit the maximum market share of firms to 25 percent.
   d. ban anticompetitive practices.

2. Monopoly power is undesirable because (there may be more than one correct answer)
   a. monopolists face less pressure to innovate than competitive firms.
   b. monopoly prices have adverse impacts on the distribution of wealth.
   c. monopolies will set price equal to marginal cost.
   d. prices charged by monopolists typically result in a misallocation of resources.

3. Antitrust policy should be most concerned with industries where (there may be more than one correct answer)
   a. there are substantial economies of scale.
   b. entry is cheap and easy.
   c. the Herfindahl-Hirschman index is low.
   d. entry requires significant upfront fixed costs.

4. Regulations that limit market power and economic behavior affect industries producing about _____ percent of GDP.
   a. 5
   b. 10
   c. 25
   d. 40

5. Which of the following is an example of economies of scale?
   a. Anna finds her costs increasing as she tries to increase the production of her custom designed clothes.
   b. Jim discovers that a 15 percent reduction in price leads to a 30 percent increase in sales.
   c. Sarah realizes that her firm's expertise and experience in producing specialized medical equipment will be useful in the production of testing equipment for physicists.
   d. Intel is able to reduce unit costs when it doubles production of computer chips.

6. Which of the following is an example of economies of scope?
   a. An increase in circulation for the Daily Planet would involve only printing costs and require no increase in the editorial staff.
   b. Ramona and Ricardo have invested their wealth in a portfolio of stocks, bonds, and real estate.
   c. In an effort to keep production lines busy all year, Arctic Enterprises produces a variety of small-engine home and garden tools in addition to its successful line of snowblowers.
   d. AT&T used profits from long-distance calls to reduce monthly charges for local phone service.

7. Significant economies of scale and economies of scope are examples of a
   a. nationalized industry.
   b. natural monopoly.
   c. regulated industry.
   d. competitive industry.

8. Regulation that sets prices at a level that just covers costs and allows for a fair rate of return
   a. provides a strong incentive for efficiency and innovation.
   b. provides little incentive for efficiency and innovation.

9. The term cross-subsidy refers to
   a. an angry firm that does not receive a subsidy.
   b. higher prices on some products/services that help to cover costs on other products/services.
   c. congressional subsidies for agriculture.
   d. the financing of Christian churches.

10. Regulation has promoted cross-subsidization as a way of
    a. dealing with universal service to isolated, high-cost locations.
    b. protecting the economy.
    c. promoting efficiencies from synergetic business combinations.
    d. addressing the effects of self-destructive competition.

11. If regulators want existing firms to engage in extensive cross-subsidization they
    a. should encourage entry of new firms.
    b. will need to pursue privatization as a long-run strategy.
    c. will need to restrict entry.
    d. prevent firms from taking advantage of economies of scale.

12. Marginal cost pricing is not feasible in industries characterized by
    a. an elastic demand curve.
    b. constant returns to scale.
    c. rising average costs.
    d. significant economies of scale.

13. Concerns about marginal cost pricing in industries with significant economies of scale arises because
    a. demand is typically inelastic.
    b. marginal cost will be below average cost.
    c. fixed costs are likely to be small.
    d. average revenue declines as firms try to sell more.

14. The term price caps refers to
    a. price floors.
    b. price ceilings that decline in anticipation of future efficiencies.
    c. limits on a firm's overall profits.
    d. attempts to control inflationary increases in prices.

15. To serve customers, competitors must sometimes share a common facility, often owned by one of the competitors. This common facility is called a(n)
    a. essential link.
    b. keystone facility.
    c. marginal unit.
    d. bottleneck facility.

16. If a firm lowers its price below average variable cost to drive out rivals, it is said to be engaging in
    a. predatory pricing.
    b. price discrimination.
    c. tying contracts.
    d. tacit collusion.

17. If an industry is composed of ten firms, each the same size, then the four-firm concentration ratio would be
    a. 4.
    b. 10.
    c. 40.
    d. 100.

18. In the case of a pure monopoly the Herfindahl-Hirschman index would be
    a. 100.
    b. 1,000.
    c. 10,000.
    d. 100,000.

19. Deregulation of the airline industry in the United States has
    a. resulted in higher prices for airline tickets.
    b. led to widespread abandonment of service to smaller towns.
    c. depressed profits and wages in the airline industry.
    d. increased the monopoly power of established airlines like Delta and United.

20. Studies of concentration and market power conclude that
    a. any increase in concentration ratios tends to increase prices.
    b. contestable markets are the most susceptible to the exercise of market power.
    c. a strong correlation exists between concentration and the use of market power.
    d. whether increases in concentration will allow firms to exercise more market power depends upon whether other factors favor collusion.

TEST B

Circle T or F for true or false.

T F 1. Regulators are exclusively concerned with getting regulated industries to lower prices.

T F 2. The term economies of scope refers to the reduction in average costs that come from large-scale production.

T F 3. Fair-rate-of-return regulations—that is, price controls that allow firms in an industry to earn profits sufficient to cover the opportunity cost of their capital—offer strong incentives for efficiency and innovation.

T F 4. Setting price equal to marginal cost is not a viable strategy in industries subject to increasing returns to scale.

T F 5. In the absence of regulation, firms required to provide service to isolated communities at high cost might find their more profitable low-cost markets taken over by competitors through a process called cream skimming.

T F 6. If price is less than average cost, this is strong evidence of predatory pricing.

T F 7. Any price discount for buying a bundle of goods and services is strong evidence of anticompetitive behavior.

T F 8. Four-firm concentration ratios show a significant increase in concentration of American business during the last 100 years.

T F 9. Evidence clearly shows that any increase in concentration leads to an increase in market power.

T F 10. Research by economists suggests that only the largest firms can afford to engage in research and development.

SUPPLEMENTARY EXERCISE

The two lists in **Table 13-2** identify the 25 largest industrial firms in the United States in 1929 and 1955, ranked by assets. The list for 1955 comes from the first *Fortune*[1] list of the 500 largest industrial companies. The list for 1929 comes from work by two economists, Norman Collins and Lee Preston.[2]

See if you can list the largest firms today. Then look up the most recent list of the *Fortune* 500. It is usually in the May issue of *Fortune* and can be found on the Web at http://www.fortune.com. Beginning in 1995 the *Fortune* list was modified to include the 500 largest corporations, not just the 500 largest industrial corporations. Of the original 500 industrial firms included in the 1955 list, only 116 appear in the 1995 list. How many of the corporations listed in Table 13-2 are still in the top 25 or even the top 500? How many corporations have slipped in ranking? How many have gained?

In 1955 the companies listed in Table 13-2 had sales that totaled $46.8 billion. Their sales equaled 12 percent of GDP. What are comparable figures today?

Fortune also publishes a list of the 500 largest corporations in the world. How big are the biggest American firms when compared to their international competition?

Table 13-2

Largest Firms

1929	Rank	1955
U.S. Steel	1	Standard Oil (N.J.)
Standard Oil (N.J.)	2	General Motors
General Motors	3	U.S. Steel
Bethlehem Steel	4	Du Pont
Anaconda	5	Mobil Oil
Ford Motor Company	6	Standard Oil (Ind.)
Mobil Oil	7	Gulf Oil
Standard Oil (Ind.)	8	Texaco
Gulf Oil	9	General Electric
Shell Oil	10	Standard Oil (Cal.)
Texaco	11	Bethlehem Steel
Standard Oil (Cal.)	12	Westinghouse
Du Pont	13	Union Carbide
General Electric	14	Sinclair Oil
Armour	15	Phillips Petroleum
Sinclair Oil	16	Western Electric
Allied Chemical	17	Cities Service
International Harvester	18	Shell Oil
Western Electric	19	Chrysler
Union Oil	20	International Harvester
Union Carbide	21	Alcoa
Swift	22	Anaconda
Kennecott Copper	23	American Tobacco
International Paper	24	Republic Steel
Republic Steel	25	Kennecott Copper

ECONOMICS IN ACTION

PREDATORY PRICING

In May 1999 the federal government filed an antitrust suit accusing American Airlines of engaging in predatory pricing. The Justice Department reported, after an 18-month investigation, that company documents titled "Dallas-Ft. Worth Low Cost Carriers Strategy," showed that American had deliberately incurred short-term losses to eliminate three low-cost competitors—Vanguard Airlines, Sun Jet International, and Western Pacific—from the Dallas-Fort Worth airport. The Justice Department suit cited internal memos that said American "would like to 'drive [Vanguard] from the market' and 'get [Western Pacific] out.'"

According to Joel Klein, head of the Justice Department's antitrust division, "American adopted a predatory responsive strategy, saturating the market in which the start-up carriers had begun service with as much new, low-fare service of its own as was necessary to drive out the start-ups." In announcing the suit, the Justice Department released the following data, which they said illustrated how American Airlines implemented a policy of predatory pricing.

	Colorado Springs	Kansas City	Wichita, KA
Average nonstop one-way fare			
Before competition	$158	$113	$110
With competition	$88	$83	$57
Post-competition	$133	$125	$96
Average number of passengers per month			
Before competition	3,723	22,423	4,465
With competition	19,909	31,228	11,246
Post-competition	9,237	23,460	8,540

American, which controls about 70 percent of scheduled seats out of Dallas-Fort Worth, was willing to risk losing money to drive out the three actual competitors and to discourage future potential competitors. According to the Justice Department, American's dominant position at the airport would allow it to earn back any losses by exercising market power.

American Airlines officials rejected the argument that it had engaged in predatory pricing or flooded the market with extra flights. They called the suit sour grapes on the part of airlines that had been unable to compete successfully and said there was nothing illegal about "tough talk." Spokesperson Chris Chiames argued hat American simply matched the competition with regard to price and added flights when the lower prices attracted additional customers. "It would have a chilling effect on the marketplace if companies felt they could not match prices of competitors," said Chiames.

A major issue is whether the new prices were below variable cost. American asserted they were not while the Justice Department argued that they were below American's established measures of acceptable profits and thus predatory.

Seasoned court observers said it would be difficult for the government to win its case, citing a 1986 decision in which the Supreme Court said, "Cutting prices in order to increase business often is the very essence of competition." Mistaken conclusions of predatory pricing "chill the very conduct the antitrust laws are designed to protect."

1. Has the government proven that American priced flights below cost and that American had plausible means for recouping losses? Or is American right and is the lawsuit just a way for competitors to win in court what they could not win in the marketplace?

Sources: Stephen Labaton and Laurence Zuckerman, "Airline is Accused of Illegal Pricing: U.S. Says American Was Trying to Drive Out Competitors," *The New York Times*, May 14, 1999. Laurence Zuckerman, "Airline Suit: 70's Revival in Antitrust," *The New York Times*, May 15, 1999. Anna Wilde Matthews and Scott McCartney, "U.S. Sues American Air in Antitrust Case," *The Wall Street Journal*, May 14, 1999; Keith L. Alexander, "American Airlines Ruling Appealed," *The Washington Post*, January 17, 2002.

STUDY QUESTIONS

1. What is the difference between economies of scale and economies of scope?

2. Why do regulators often work to increase rather than limit prices?

3. Why does the text say that not all big firms have monopoly power?

4. What is meant by the term cross-subsidy?

5. Why aren't prices based on marginal cost a feasible alternative in cases of natural monopolies arising from economies of scale?

6. How do price caps provide an incentive for efficiency?

7. What is your evaluation of the American experience with deregulation?

8. Why regulate at all? Why not let the free market work without regulation?

9. How are concentration ratios measured?

10. Has American business become more or less concentrated over the last 50 years? 100 years?

11. What does the evidence suggest about increasing concentration and the use of market power?

12. Consider antitrust policy that divided the largest firms whenever the four-firm concentration ratio in any industry exceeded 50 percent. Would such a policy be good for the country? Why or why not?

13. Should American antitrust laws include an explicit exclusion for cooperative research and development activities? Why?

14. How effective do you believe American antitrust laws have been?

ECONOMICS ONLINE

The Antitrust Division of the U.S. Department of Justice maintains its own homepage.

http://www.usdoj.gov/atr

Concentration ratios for many industries from the 1997 as well as the 2002 Economic Census are posted at this site. Concentration ratios are calculated for the largest 4, 8, 20, and 50 companies. Information from the 2007 Economic Census is scheduled to be posted during 2009 and 2010.

http://www.census.gov/epcd/www/concentration.html

174

ECONOMICS IN ACTION

In June 2001, the Justice department's case was dismissed by Judge J. Thomas Marten who said, "There is no doubt that American may be a difficult, vigorous, even brutal competitor, but here, it engaged only in bare, but not brass, knuckle competition." In January 2002, the Justice Department appealed.

The government lost its appeal.

The Case for Free Markets: The Price System

14

Important Terms and Concepts

Efficient allocation of resources

Laissez-faire

Input-output analysis

Consumer's surplus

Producer's surplus

Learning Objectives

After completing this chapter, you should be able to:

- explain the difference between an efficient and inefficient allocation of resources.

- explain how competitive markets, in which all producers and consumers respond to common market prices, can allocate resources efficiently.

- describe situations in which price increases may be in society's best interest.

- list the three coordination tasks that must be solved by any system of resource allocation.

- explain input-output analysis and the near impossibility of central planning.

- explain how prices play a critical role in determining both the allocation of resources and the distribution of income.

- explain how competitive markets maximize the sum of consumer's surplus plus producer's surplus.

- use marginal analysis to show how perfect competition achieves optimal output.

- describe the conditions under which an inefficient allocation of resources might be preferred to an efficient allocation.

CHAPTER REVIEW

This chapter discusses how prices work to allocate resources and how they affect the efficiency of the economy. In particular, it is shown that in a competitive economy, the self-serving actions of utility-maximizing individuals and profit-maximizing firms can lead to an efficient allocation of the economy's resources. The complete, rigorous proof of this proposition is usually discussed only in graduate courses in economic theory and involves the use of some fairly advanced mathematics. This chapter offers a simpler introduction to this material.

The efficiency implications of a laissez-faire, competitive economy are important reasons why economists have great respect for the workings of the price system. But the proof of this abstract proposition is not a proof that we should dismantle the government and that all markets should be unregulated. The proposition refers to

(1) the efficiency of a perfectly competitive economy. Many aspects of the American economy (are/are not) consistent with the requirements for a competitive economy. The implications of these real-world imperfections are an important part of Chapters 15 through 21. Also, efficiency is not the only way to judge the workings of an economy. Notions of fairness, or equity, are also important and may at times lead to a preference for less efficient, but fairer, nonmarket procedures.

Sometimes proposals to change prices for efficiency reasons are opposed because of their potentially adverse impact on a particular group. For example, higher taxes on energy to foster conservation and the development of alternative energy sources to reduce our dependence on foreign energy are often opposed because it is believed they will increase the cost of living for poor households. These equity considerations are an important part of any final decision. However, many economists argue that it is preferable to address the issue of income distribution through general taxes or transfers rather than by limiting changes in prices that promote efficiency. For example, changes in income tax credits, personal exemptions, or the standard deduction could be used to provide protection to lower income households while letting higher energy prices provide an incentive for all households, rich and poor, to reduce their use of energy.

(2) All economies must answer three questions. First is the question of output _____: How much of each type of good and service should be produced? Next, there is the question of production _____: How should various productive inputs be allocated among the millions of firms and plants in order to meet the original output decisions? Finally, there is the question of the _____ of goods and services: How are the available goods and services to be divided among consumers? How do we evaluate the job that an economy does in answering these questions? Economists typically use two yardsticks: efficiency and equity. This chapter concentrates on efficiency.

Economic efficiency is an important but relatively abstract concept. If by redistributing the commodities that are produced we can make everyone better off in his or her own estimation, we would say that the initial alloca-

(3) tion of commodities (was/was not) efficient. It is only when there are no more opportunities to make some individuals better off while not worsening the situation of others that economists would characterize the economy as _____.

There are usually many efficient allocations of resources. For example, each point on an economy's production possibilities frontier is (efficient/inefficient) in terms of the production of output. If an economy is operating on (4) this frontier, it is impossible to increase the output of one good without _____ the output of one or more other goods.

Let us consider in more detail how a competitive economy achieves efficiency in the selection of output. (The Supplementary Exercises to this chapter discuss efficiency in production and output distribution.) Efficiency in the selection of output requires that, for the quantity produced, the marginal utility of the last unit to consumers must equal the marginal cost of producers.

Why is this condition necessary for an efficient output selection? Remember that the definition of efficiency refers to consumers' evaluations of their own well-being, an evaluation that economists assume consumers are making when they maximize the difference between total utility and spending. If the marginal utility of some good exceeds the marginal cost of producing more units, then the production of at least one more unit of output will result in a net (increase/decrease) in consumer well-being. Consumers benefit by the increase in their utility (5) while the cost to society of additional production is given by the marginal _____. If marginal utility exceeds marginal cost, the benefit to consumers from increased production will be (greater/less) than the cost to society, and the initial output selection (is/is not) efficient. It is only when marginal utility (exceeds/equals/is less than) marginal cost that there are no more opportunities for net gains.

It is one of the beauties of a competitive economy that utility-maximizing individuals and profit-maximizing firms will, while pursuing their own self-interests, make decisions that result in marginal utility being equal to marginal cost. Our optimal purchase rule of Chapter 5 showed that utility-maximizing consumers will purchase additional units until the marginal utility of the last unit consumed equals the _____ of the (6) commodity. The discussion in Chapter 8 showed that profit-maximizing firms will equate marginal revenue and _____ _____. The discussion in Chapter 10 showed that for a firm under perfect competition, marginal revenue is equal to _____. Thus a profit-maximizing firm under perfect competition, producing where marginal cost equals marginal revenue, will be producing where the marginal cost of the last unit produced equals the _____ of the commodity.

To summarize, utility-maximizing consumers set marginal _____ equal to price, and prof- (7) it-maximizing competitive firms set marginal _____ equal to price. The result is that marginal utility (exceeds/equals/is less than) marginal cost, our condition for efficiency in the selection of output.

Consumer's surplus is the difference between the maximum amount a consumer would be willing to pay for an item and the market price she has to pay. Any consumer who is unwilling to pay the market price does not and receives no consumer surplus. Producer's surplus is the difference between the market price and the lowest price at which a supplier would be willing to supply the item. The virtue of competitive market prices determined by the intersection of the demand and supply curves is that this price and the resulting quantity (maximize/minimize) the sum of consumer's and producer's surplus. (8)

179

A centrally planned economy would attempt to answer the three basic questions of output selection, production planning, and product distribution by direct decree, without the use of prices. Often in these economies, decisions about output selection were made with little attention to individual consumer preferences. More weight was typically given to the planners' preferences for such things as increased production of steel and electricity, although periodic newspaper accounts of a readjustment of production goals in response to consumer unrest and the final collapse of central planning in Eastern Europe and the former Soviet Union showed that even planners cannot forget entirely about consumers.

Once decisions about output levels have been made, a central planner must be sure that productive inputs are allocated to ensure that the production goals can in fact be achieved. One type of analysis that takes account (9) of the interindustry flows of inputs necessary for the production of goods for final use is _____ - _____ analysis. A major limitation of this type of analysis is the enormity and complexity of the required information. It is a major conceptual advantage that the price system in a competitive economy does not require that this information be centralized.

IMPORTANT TERMS AND CONCEPTS QUIZ

Choose the best definition for each of the following terms.

1. _____ Efficient allocation of resources
2. _____ Laissez-faire
3. _____ Input-output analysis
4. _____ Consumer's surplus
5. _____ Producer's surplus

a. Situation in which one person's welfare can be improved without injury to anyone else
b. Technique of simultaneously solving equations that link necessary inputs to output for all industries
c. Situation that takes advantage of every opportunity to make some individuals better off without harming others
d. Difference between what a consumer would pay and must pay
e. Minimal interference with the workings of the free market
f. Difference between what a firm gets from selling at the market price and what it would accept

BASIC EXERCISE

This problem is designed to illustrate the logic of the rule for efficiency in output selection.
Discussion in the chapter indicated that efficiency in the selection of output requires marginal utility to equal marginal cost for all commodities. If not, it is possible, by changing the selection of output, to improve consumers' well-being.

Consider an economy's production of shirts. Assume that at the current level of shirt output, the marginal utility of shirts is $25 and the marginal cost is $15.

1. The production of one more shirt will increase total utility by $ _____. The production of one more shirt will cost society $ _____.

2. In Chapter 5 we saw that utility-maximizing consumers will maximize the difference between total utility and total spending. This difference equals the money value of their well-being. Looking at the change in utility and assuming that the price of shirts is equal to their marginal cost of $15, we can see that the production of one more shirt will increase consumer well-being by $ _____. Efficiency in the production of shirts requires (<u>more/fewer</u>) shirts.

3. What if the marginal utility of an additional shirt is $15 and the marginal cost is $18? Then the production of an additional shirt will (<u>increase/decrease</u>) consumer well-being by $ _____ and efficiency in the production of shirts will call for (<u>more/fewer</u>) shirts.

4. If the marginal cost of additional shirts is constant at $18, then in order that there be no opportunity for a change in the production of shirts to increase consumer well-being, enough shirts should be produced so that the marginal utility of an additional shirt is $ _____.

SELF-TESTS FOR UNDERSTANDING

TEST A

Circle the most appropriate answer.

1. For any economy that uses the price system, which of the following is not necessarily true?
   a. Prices play an important role in shaping the allocation of resources.
   b. Prices play an important role in shaping the distribution of income and wealth.
   c. Prices will reflect consumer preference and income.
   d. Prices of necessities will be low, and prices of luxuries will be high.

2. The price system distributes goods and services on the basis of income and
   a. scarcity.
   b. consumer preferences.
   c. education.
   d. planner preferences.

3. The three basic coordination tasks for resource allocation that economies may solve by markets or planning include all but which one of the following?
   a. the distribution of output among consumers
   b. how much of different goods to produce
   c. the allocation of available resources to the production of different goods
   d. the amount of money that the government will print

4. The use of prices to allocate goods among consumers means that
   a. all consumers will be able to buy an equal share of all outputs.
   b. the resulting allocation must necessarily be inefficient.
   c. wealthy consumers will be able to command a greater amount of output.
   d. there must be persistent inflation in order to choke off consumer excess demand.

5. Prices in competitive markets affect all but which one of the following?
    a. the allocation of inputs among competing producers
    b. the allocation of output among consumers
    c. the distribution of income
    d. the location of the production possibilities frontier

6. Consider the production possibilities frontier shown in **Figure 14-1**. Efficiency in production is given by
    a. all of the points inside the frontier.
    b. all of the points on or inside the frontier.
    c. all of the points on the frontier.
    d. the point of equal output of all goods.

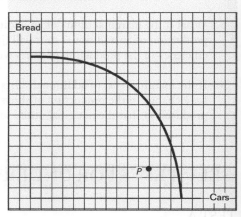

Production Possibilities Frontier

7. Consider production at point *P* in Figure 14-1. If the economy produces at point *P*, one would say that output selection is
    a. efficient.
    b. inefficient.
    c. efficient or inefficient depending upon consumers' preferences.

8. Under conditions of perfect competition, firms will choose to produce the quantity of output such that
    a. MC = AC.
    b. MU = total utility.
    c. MC = *P*.
    d. AC = *P*.

9. In competitive markets consumers will demand particular commodities up to the point where
    a. MU = MC.
    b. MU = *P*.
    c. MC = *P*.
    d. MU = 0.

10. The condition for optimal output selection is
    a. MC = *P*.
    b. MC = MU.
    c. MRP = *P*.
    d. MU = *P*.

11. Competitive markets can meet the criterion for efficiency in production planning
    a. through the use of input-output tables.
    b. only after Congress approves the president's budget proposal.
    c. automatically.
    d. less efficiently than centrally planned economies.

12. If the marginal utility of color television sets is $300 and the marginal cost is $200, then efficiency in output selection requires that the production of color television sets should
    a. increase.
    b. decrease.
    c. neither increase nor decrease.

13. The change in the production of color television sets from question 12 will likely
    a. increase marginal cost and marginal utility.
    b. increase marginal cost and decrease marginal utility.
    c. decrease marginal cost and marginal utility.
    d. decrease marginal cost and increase marginal utility.

14. An efficient allocation of resources
    a. will always be fair.
    b. is the best allocation possible.
    c. means the economy is operating somewhere on its production opportunity frontier.
    d. is always better than an inefficient allocation.

15. Leon does not now own a motorcycle. He would pay up to $2,000 for one. Motorcycles produced by competitive firms in long-run equilibrium, earning zero economic profit, cost $4,000 to produce. Which of the following is false?
    a. Leon is not likely to buy a motorcycle.
    b. Since Leon's marginal utility is less than the marginal cost of production, there would be a social gain if direct government controls reduced the price of motorcycles.
    c. The marginal utility of a motorcycle to someone must be at least $4,000.

16. If resources have been allocated in a way that meets the requirements of economic efficiency, then we know that
    a. output is being produced in accordance with the preferences of the Council of Economic Advisers.
    b. production occurs at a point inside the economy's production possibilities frontier.
    c. there is no reallocation of resources that can make some individuals better off without making others worse off.
    d. the marginal cost of producing every commodity has been minimized.

TEST B

Circle T or F for true or false.

T   F   1. The term laissez-faire refers to an economy with minimal economic regulation by government.

T   F   2. If resources are being allocated efficiently, we know that there is no better allocation possible.

T   F   3. Efficient resource allocation always requires the intervention of a central planner to set prices correctly.

T   F   4. Efficiency in the selection of output requires that the marginal utility of every commodity be equal to its marginal cost.

T   F   5. An unregulated competitive economy is incapable of achieving appropriate efficiency conditions for all commodities.

T   F   6. Input-output analysis is a mathematical tool to aid in the distribution of output among consumers without using the price system.

T   F   7. Charging higher prices on public transportation during rush hours can be an example of using the price system to increase efficiency.

T   F   8. Considerations of fairness may sometimes lead a society to prefer an inefficient allocation to an efficient one.

T   F   9. Efficiency in the distribution of goods implies that everyone will get an equal share of all goods.

T   F   10. Competitive markets promote efficiency in output selection because both firms and consumers respond to the same price.

SUPPLEMENTARY EXERCISES

The first two exercises illustrate the implications of the rules for efficiency in the allocation of output among consumers and in the allocation of productive inputs.

1. **Efficiency in the Distribution of Output Among Consumers**

    The rule for efficiency in the distribution of output among consumers is that for every commodity every consumer must have the same marginal utility. If not, it would be possible to redistribute output among consumers in a way that makes at least one person better off without harming anyone else.

    Imagine that Todd and Nicole both consume steaks and pizzas. The initial allocation of steak and pizza has resulted in the following marginal utilities:

	Marginal Utility	
	Todd	Nicole
Steaks	$ 9.00	$ 6.00
Pizza	4.00	4.00

   a. Is the condition for efficiency in the distribution of output satisfied? _____ If not, there should be some, possibly many, reallocations of output that will increase either Todd's or Nicole's total utility (or both) without reducing total utility for the other.

   b. Imagine that Nicole gives Todd one steak in exchange for two pizzas. On net, considering the full effects of the trade, what is the change in Todd's utility? (increase/decrease) $ _____ Nicole's utility? (increase/decrease) $ _____ An implication of the utility changes of the reallocation is that the initial allocation was (efficient/inefficient).

   c. How do competitive markets work to ensure that uncoordinated individual demands will satisfy the condition for efficiency in the distribution of output among consumers?

2. **Efficiency in Production Planning**

    The rule for efficiency in Production Planning says that if two inputs, labor and land, are both used to produce two outputs, then inputs should be assigned to each output until the ratio of marginal

184

physical product for two inputs is the same in all uses. If not, it will be possible to reallocate resources and increase the production of at least one commodity without decreasing the production of other commodities.

a. We know from Chapter 8 that this condition will be automatically satisfied under perfect competition for profit-maximizing firms that buy inputs at given prices. Perhaps less clear is that if this condition is not satisfied, then it would be possible to reallocate inputs among firms and produce more total output— with the same quantity of inputs. Consider the following table showing the initial marginal physical products of land and labor in the production of corn and tomatoes. Note that the ratio of marginal physical products in the production of corn (120/40) is less than the ratio in the production of tomatoes (1,200/200).

Marginal Physical Product of Labor and Land in the Production of Corn and Tomatoes

	Corn (bushels)	Tomatoes (pounds)
Labor (person)	120	1,200
Land (acre)	40	200

Consider the reallocation of one worker from corn production to tomato production. As a result of this reallocation of labor, the production of corn will fall by _____ bushels and the production of tomatoes will rise by _____ pounds. Now consider moving four acres of land from tomato production to corn production. As a result of the reallocation of land, the production of corn will rise by _____ bushels and the production of tomatoes will fall by _____ pounds. Counting the reallocation of both land and labor, the production of corn changes by _____ bushels and the production of tomatoes changes by _____ pounds.

b. How do competitive markets work to ensure that the uncoordinated decisions of firms satisfy the condition for efficiency in the allocation of productive inputs?

Efficiency in the selection of inputs helps to achieve efficiency in the choice of outputs. We have seen that efficiency in the selection of outputs requires that MU = MC. In competitive markets, MU = MC because utility-maximizing individuals see to it that MU = P. The discussion below shows how efficiency in the selection of inputs helps to ensure that competitive firms produce where MC = P.

We saw in Chapter 6 that our rule for optimal use of inputs could also be expressed in terms of marginal revenue product. Using symbols, our optimal input rule says

$$P_Q \times MPP_X = P_X$$

where P_Q is the product price, P_X is the input price, and MPP_X is the marginal physical product of input X in the production of Q. If we divide both sides of the equation by MPP_X we get

$$P_Q = P_X/MPP_X$$

Note that P_X/MPP_X is the marginal cost of producing more output by using more of input X. If we buy one more unit of input X, we spend P_X and get MPP_X more units of output at a cost of P_X/MPP_X per unit of additional output. A profit-maximizing firm will use the optimal input rule for all its inputs. Thus, the marginal cost of an output expansion by the use of any single input, of the many that a firm may use, will be equal to the marginal cost from the additional use of any other input.

3. You can look up information about the most recent input-output table for the U.S. economy on the Web at http://www.bea.gov/industry/io_annual.htm. The most detailed input-output tables, the

185

benchmark tables are organized with information for almost 500 industries. These tables are available for 1982, 1987, 1992, and 1997 to 2002.

There are several input-output tables. One table indicates which industries use which commodities. Another table indicates which industries produce which commodities. The table of direct requirements shows what direct inputs are necessary per unit of output of each industry. The table of direct and indirect requirements solves all the input-output relationships and shows how the output of every industry must adjust in order to increase the output of any one industry. It is this table that takes into account such indirect requirements as increased electricity to make more steel in order to increase the output of cars.

a. How many separate pieces of information do these input-output tables contain? How long do you think it would take you to solve all the interrelationships and produce a table of direct and indirect requirements without the help of a computer?

b. Which industries produce mainly for final uses and which produce mainly intermediate outputs, that is, inputs for other industries?

c. You can find input-output information on the web as far back as the 1982 benchmark tables. Pick one or two favorite industries and see how total and direct requirements from the most recent input-output table have changed over time.

d. If you are a planner concerned with the year 2012, how would you determine what input-output requirements are relevant?

ECONOMICS IN ACTION

HI-HO, HI-HO, IT'S OFF TO WORK WE GO

It's not only bridges that get congested. On Sunday morning, additional cars do not seem to interfere with the traffic flow on most urban highway systems, but on Monday morning or Friday afternoon each additional driver adds to congestion, makes every other driver's commute take longer, and seems to turn many highways into linear parking lots.

The highway and road systems of most large cities seem to be a clear case of too many vehicles and too few roads. Yet building more roads seems only to increase the traffic without solving the problem. Economist Kenneth A. Small, writing in *The Brookings Review,* talks of a reservoir of potential drivers, deterred from driving by existing congestion, who quickly fill up new roads as they are completed. Small is skeptical that policies such as campaigns to promote ride-sharing, mass transit, staggered work hours, or high-occupancy-vehicle lanes will have more than a temporary impact on urban congestion. Are there market mechanisms that would improve the situation? Small believes there are, specifically congestion pricing— "charging motorists a very high premium for using the most popular roads during peak hours."

Small argues that congestion pricing provides an incentive for drivers to consider alternative routes, alternative times, and/or alternative means of transportation. The other policies listed above focus on only a subset of travelers while providing no incentive for the vast majority of drivers to change their behavior. While no one likes paying tolls, not many of us like being stuck in traffic, either.

To be successful, Small argues that congestion pricing must impose tolls that vary widely by time of day and are sufficiently high at peak demand to have a measurable impact. Although not its primary purpose, Small believes congestion pricing also would improve air quality by reducing both the volume of traffic and the higher emissions associated with congestion.

Small is concerned that congestion prices might be a burden for lower income families and argues that a portion of the revenues collected should be used in ways that benefit low-income households. He proposed using one-third for reimbursements to travelers through an employee commuting allowance and fuel tax reduction; another third for reductions of the portion of sales and property taxes that subsidize highways and transportation; and the remaining third for improvements to transportation services, including mass transit and critical highway projects.

1. What is your evaluation of Small's proposal?

2. The Orange County Express Lanes described in this chapter of the text are a form of congestion pricing. Why do you think there are not more examples?

3. Would you be willing to pay $1 to save thirty minutes in traffic? Would you be willing to pay $6.75?

Source: Kenneth A. Small, "Urban Traffic Congestion: A New Approach to the Gordian Knot, " *Brookings Review,* Spring 1993, pp. 6–11.

STUDY QUESTIONS

1. What are the three coordination tasks that must be solved by any system of resource allocation?

2. Why is the determination of efficient allocations a largely technical exercise with many potential solutions rather than a method for determining the best allocation for the economy?

3. Why isn't point P in Figure 14-1 an example of efficiency in output selection? Starting at point P, show what other possible points of production dominate point P in terms of efficiency considerations. Is there only one such point or a set of points? If a set, how can there be more than one?

4. Is it ever possible that society would be better off with higher rather than lower prices? Explain.

5. Should an economy always prefer an efficient allocation to an inefficient allocation? Explain.

6. How can a price system (market mechanism) hope to solve the large number of coordination decisions that are included in the mathematics of an input-output table for the entire economy?

187

The Shortcomings of Free Markets

15

Important Terms and Concepts

Production possibilities frontier

Resource misallocation

Beneficial Externality

Detrimental Externality

Marginal social cost (MSC)

Marginal private cost (MPC)

Marginal social benefit (MSB)

Marginal private benefit (MPB)

Public good

Private good

Depletability

Excludability

Rent seeking

Moral hazard

Principals

Agents

Stocks options

Cost disease of the personal services

Learning Objectives

After completing this chapter, you should be able to:

- list the major shortcomings of free markets.

- explain why detrimental externalities mean that marginal private costs will understate marginal social costs.

- explain why beneficial externalities mean that marginal private benefits will understate marginal social benefits.

- explain why the existence of externalities, whether beneficial or detrimental, will result in an inefficient allocation of resources.

- describe the important characteristics of public goods.

- explain why these characteristics mean that private profit-maximizing firms will not supply public goods.

- explain why some people believe that free markets are unlikely to result in an appropriate allocation of resources between the present and the future.

- explain when individuals or firms will engage in rent-seeking behavior.

- explain why insurance companies worry about moral hazard.

- explain why information might be asymmetric as between principals and agents, and why stock options have often been ineffective.

- explain how uneven productivity growth results in the cost disease of personal services.

CHAPTER REVIEW

This chapter lists seven issues often seen as shortcomings of unregulated markets. Some have been discussed in previous chapters, and several others will receive a more complete treatment in later chapters. The discussion here focuses on four of the seven: externalities, public goods, the trade-off between present and future consumption, and the cost disease of personal services.

Chapter 3 introduced the concept of an economy's *production possibilities frontier*. We saw that the slope of the frontier measured how much the output of one commodity must decrease in order to increase the production of another commodity. In other words, the slope of the production possibilities frontier measures the

(1) _____ cost of increasing the output of any one commodity.

Chapter 14 explained how a market economy can lead to an *efficient allocation of resources*, one where marginal utilities and marginal costs are equal. If the marginal utility of the last unit of some good is not equal to the marginal cost of producing that last unit, the result is a *misallocation of resources*. The virtue of competitive

(2) markets is that firms maximize profits by producing where price equals _____ _____ and individuals maximize by consuming where price equals _____ _____. Thus, our condition for an efficient allocation is automatically satisfied. An economy that satisfies all of the assumptions necessary for perfect competition will automatically result in an efficient allocation of resources. The economy will operate (on/inside) the production possibilities frontier.

For reasons mentioned at the beginning of the chapter the wrong prices may get established, leading to an inefficient allocation of resources. For example, if price is greater than marginal cost, the economy will tend to

(3) produce too (much/little) of a good to maximize consumer benefits. There may be a case for government intervention to help establish prices that will lead to an efficient allocation.

EXTERNALITIES

Many economic activities impose incidental burdens or benefits on other individuals for which there is

(4) no compensation. These sorts of activities are said to involve _____. If an activity, such as pollution, harms others and there is no compensation, we say that there are _____ externalities. If an activity benefits others who do not pay for the benefits they receive, we say that there are _____ externalities.

Externalities imply that many activities are likely to have private benefits and costs that are different from

(5) social benefits and costs. In the case of detrimental externalities, social costs will be (higher/lower) than private costs, while in the case of beneficial externalities, social benefits will be _____ than private benefits.

(6) Private, profit-maximizing firms will base their production decisions on (private/social) costs. When externalities are important the result will be an (efficient/inefficient) use of resources. In the case of detrimental externalities, too (much/little) of the commodity in question will be produced. In the case of beneficial

190

externalities, unregulated markets are likely to produce (<u>less/more</u>) output than is socially desirable. Schemes for taxes and subsidies are in principle capable of adjusting private costs and benefits to more adequately reflect social costs and benefits.

PUBLIC GOODS

Most goods provided by private, profit-maximizing firms have two primary characteristics. The first is that the more of a good you use, the less there is for someone else. This characteristic is called _____. The second is that you must pay for goods in order to use them. This charac- (7) teristic is called _____. Goods that have neither of these characteristics are called _____ goods. Things like national defense, police protection, beautiful parks, and clean streets are examples of such goods.

   Once public goods are provided to one individual, their benefits are available to all and cannot easily be restricted to just a few people. It is (<u>difficult/easy</u>) to exclude nonpayers. As a result, it is difficult to get indi- (8) viduals to pay for the goods they can enjoy for free when someone else is paying for them. This is sometimes referred to as the free- _____ problem.

   Besides the problem of lack of excludability, one person's use of public goods, such as enjoying a park, does not usually deplete the supply for others. In technical language, the marginal cost of serving additional users is _____. This contrasts with private goods, where providing additional units of output requires addi- (9) tional resources and entails a positive marginal cost. An efficient allocation of resources requires that price equal marginal social cost. The clear implication is that from an efficiency standpoint, public goods should be priced at _____. One should not be surprised if profit-maximizing firms fail to provide public goods.

PRESENT AND FUTURE CONSUMPTION

The productive use of resources is time specific. Loafing today will not make tomorrow twice as long. A machine that is idle one week does not mean that twice as many machine hours will be available the next week. While the use of resources is time specific, the consumption of output is not. Output can be saved, either directly by adding to inventories in warehouses or indirectly by building plants and machines that increase future production possibilities. Thus, an economy does have the ability to transfer consumption through time by acts of saving and investment.

   The rate of interest is an important determinant of how much investment will take place. A number of observers have questioned whether the private economy will result in interest rates and investment spending that are socially optimal. In the real world, monetary and fiscal policies can be used to manipulate interest rates and will influence investment in ways that may not correspond to the best plans for the future. Some observers, such as the English economist A. G. Pigou, have argued that people are simply shortsighted when it comes to saving for the future.

Individual investment projects often entail great risk for the individual investors but little risk for society.

(10) Bankruptcy may wipe out an investor's financial investment, but it (<u>does/does not</u>) destroy buildings and machines. These capital goods will still be around for others to use. It has been argued that the high individual risk will result in a level of investment that is (<u>less/more</u>) than socially optimal.

(11) Many decisions, such as damming a canyon, are essentially _____, and there is concern that in these cases decisions in unregulated markets may not adequately represent the interests of future generations. These arguments suggest that even competitive markets may result in inappropriate decisions about savings and investments.

COST DISEASE OF PERSONAL SERVICES

Many services—doctor visits, education, police protection—require significant labor input and offer

(12) (<u>limited/substantial</u>) opportunities for increases in labor productivity. By contrast, increasing mechanization and technological innovations have resulted in substantial increases in labor productivity in the production of many commodities. Increased labor productivity has led to higher wages for workers in these industries. Since workers can move among occupations, the wages of teachers, nurses, and police, for example, have had to increase to remain competitive with job opportunities in other industries. In manufacturing industries, increased labor productivity helps offset the cost pressures from higher wages. In many service industries, limited opportunities exist for increases in labor productivity to help contain cost pressures. The result is that many personal services have become more expensive over time because of the uneven pattern of increases in labor productivity. Increases in productivity always make an economy better off in the sense that it can now produce more of all goods, including personal services. But at the same time, society will find that lagging productivity in service industries means that the cost of these services has increased. Concerns about controlling costs may be misdirected if the major problem is the natural market response to differential productivity growth.

IMPORTANT TERMS AND CONCEPTS QUIZ

Choose the best definition for each of the following terms.

1. _____ Production possibilities frontier
2. _____ Resource misallocation
3. _____ Externalities
4. _____ Marginal social cost
5. _____ Marginal private cost
6. _____ Marginal social benefit
7. _____ Marginal private benefit
8. _____ Public good
9. _____ Private good
10. _____ Depletability
11. _____ Excludability
12. _____ Rent seeking
13. _____ Moral hazard
14. _____ Principals
15. _____ Agents
16. _____ Stock options
17. _____ Cost disease of personal services

a. Tendency of clients who have the lowest risks to be the most likely insurance customers
b. Results of activities that provide incidental harm or benefit to others
c. Tendency for the real cost of services to increase because of difficulty of increasing productivity
d. Portion of marginal benefit that accrues to those who engage in activity
e. Total marginal benefit, marginal private benefit plus benefits to others
f. Commodity or service whose benefits are not depleted by an additional user and for which it is difficult to exclude people from enjoying its benefits
g. Unproductive activity in pursuit of profit
h. Utility of a change in output differs from its opportunity cost
i. Parties to a transaction know different things about the item to be exchanged
j. Marginal private cost plus costs imposed on others
k. Commodity or service whose benefits are depleted by an additional user and for which people are excluded from its benefits unless they pay
l. The ability to keep someone who does not pay from enjoying a commodity
m. Tendency of insurance to discourage risk-avoiding behavior
n. Portion of marginal cost paid by those who engage in the activity
o. Those to whom decision-making authority is delegated
p. Commodity is used up when consumed
q. Curve that shows the maximum quantities of outputs it is possible to produce with the available resources and technology
r. Decision makers who delegate their power to others
s. Option to buy stock at predetermined price

BASIC EXERCISES

This exercise is designed to illustrate the cost disease of personal services.

Table 15-1 has spaces to compute the costs of producing both widgets and police services; both are assumed to be produced with only labor input. (Wages for police officers and for workers in the widget factory are assumed to be equal, as individuals can choose between these occupations.)

Table 15-1

Costs of Producing 240,000 Widgets

	(1)	(2)	(3)
Widgets per worker	1,920	2,000	3,000
Number of workers[a]	125	____	____
Annual earnings per worker	$21,120	$22,000	$33,000
Total labor costs (total cost)	____	____	____
Cost per widget	____	____	____

Costs of Producing 200,000 Hours of Police Services

	(1)	(2)	(3)
Hours per police officer	2,000	2,000	2,000
Number of police officers[b]	100	____	____
Annual earnings per police officer	$21,120	$22,000	$33,000
Total labor cost (total cost)	____	____	____
Cost per hour of police services	____	____	____

[a]240,000 ÷ widgets per worker
[b]200,000 ÷ hours per police officer

1. Fill in the missing spaces in the first column to determine the cost per widget of producing 240,000 widgets and the cost per hour of 200,000 hours of police services.

2. The first entry in the second column assumes that labor productivity in the production of widgets has risen by 4.17 percent. The earnings of widget workers and police officers are assumed to increase by the same percentage as productivity. Now fill in the rest of the second column. What has happened to the average cost of producing one widget? What about the cost of producing one hour of police services?

3. The first entry in column 3 assumes that the growth in average labor productivity continues for another ten years. Again, the growth in earnings is assumed to match the growth in productivity. Fill in the rest of column 3. What is the increase in the cost of producing one widget? _____. What about the cost of one hour of police services? _____.

4. One way to hold the line on police costs is to refuse to increase salaries for police officers. Another way is to reduce the number of police officers. What are the long-run implications of both these policies?

SELF-TESTS FOR UNDERSTANDING

TEST A

Circle the most appropriate answer.

1. The condition for efficient resource allocation is
   a. MC = MR.
   b. *P* = Average Revenue.
   c. MU = MC.
   d. MU = Price.

2. Which of the following is a clear indicator of a misallocation of resources?
   a. Barney and Michelle, who subscribe to *Gourmet* magazine, despair over the increasing number of fast-food outlets.
   b. In the long run, farmer Fran makes zero economic profit.
   c. After careful study, economists have concluded that the economy of Arcadia is operating at a point inside its production possibilities frontier.
   d. The latest census survey indicates that the top 10 percent of the income distribution has an average income that is more than fifteen times that of the bottom 10 percent.

3. The term *externalities* is used by economists to describe
   a. economic decisions by foreign governments.
   b. occupants of extraterrestrial spaceships.
   c. all economic activity that takes place outside the classroom.
   d. activities that impose costs or benefits on third parties.

4. Economists expect profit-maximizing competitive firms to expand production as long as price exceeds
   a. marginal social cost.
   b. marginal utility.
   c. marginal private cost.
   d. average cost.

5. Which of the following is an externality?
   a. imperfect information
   b. your pride in the new home entertainment system you just purchased at a bargain price
   c. natural monopolies, such as the local electric utility
   d. the new road built for the NASA tracking station that has substantially reduced transportation costs for local farmers

6. A detrimental externality arises when
    a. the actions of a firm provide unintended benefits for third parties.
    b. having bought insurance, Jason figures he doesn't need to buy as sturdy a bike lock.
    c. a firm's managers cannot be closely monitored by stockholders.
    d. the actions of a firm impose costs on families living near the firm's plants.

7. In the presence of detrimental externalities, marginal private cost is usually
    a. less than marginal social cost.
    b. equal to marginal social cost.
    c. greater than marginal social cost.

8. Economists argue that if the production of paper is associated with detrimental externalities, a free market will likely
    a. produce less paper than is socially desirable.
    b. produce the socially optimal quantity of paper in spite of the detrimental externality.
    c. produce more paper than is socially desirable.

9. If the production of gizmos involves beneficial externalities, then it is likely that
    a. a free market will produce too many gizmos.
    b. marginal private benefits are less than marginal social benefits.
    c. a tax on the production of gizmos will lead to a more efficient allocation.
    d. the use of gizmos does not involve depletion.

10. Economists define public goods as
    a. all things the government spends money on.
    b. economic activities that impose costs or benefits on third parties.
    c. goods and services that many people can enjoy at the same time and from which it is difficult to exclude potential customers who do not want to pay.
    d. goods and services that should receive public subsidy such as improved health care and better housing for poor families.

11. Economists expect that profit-maximizing firms in competitive markets will produce _____ public goods.
    a. too few
    b. too many
    c. about the right quantity
    d. no

12. For a pure public good, the marginal cost of serving an additional user is equal to
    a. $1,000.
    b. $100.
    c. $10.
    d. $0.

13. Which of the following does not have the characteristics of a public good?
    a. clean rivers
    b. visits to the doctor
    c. police and fire protection
    d. unscrambled radio and television signals

14. The "free-rider" problem refers to
    a. the difficulty of stopping kids from sneaking onto the local merry-go-round.
    b. using subsidies to encourage the production of goods with beneficial externalities.
    c. the difficulty of getting people to voluntarily contribute to pay for public goods.
    d. increasing problems with hitchhikers on the interstate highways.

15. Which of the following is an argument that free markets may result in an inappropriate amount of saving and investment? (There may be more than one correct answer.)
    a. Investment projects are often riskier to individuals than to the community.
    b. Government policy may manipulate interest rates for reasons of short-term macroeconomic policy.
    c. Due to "defective telescopic faculties," people do not give enough consideration to the future.
    d. Many decisions concerning natural resources are made without enough consideration given to their irreversible consequences.

16. Which of the following explains the cost disease of personal services?
    a. the supply effects of price controls, such as rent control
    b. the existence of monopoly elements in the economy
    c. detrimental externalities
    d. the uneven prospects for improved labor productivity in different sectors of the economy

17. Which of the following is *not* likely to suffer from the cost disease of personal services?
    a. individual piano lessons
    b. the production of television sets
    c. colleges and universities that strive to maintain an unchanged student-faculty ratio
    d. orchestras and symphonies

18. Which of the following is an example of rent seeking?
    a. the efforts of lobbyists to get Congress to restrict the import of foreign steel
    b. Cleon's efforts to find an inexpensive apartment before school starts
    c. the hours Juan and Ramona spend working in their own restaurant
    d. the time and effort Julie spends studying to be a doctor

19. As used by economists, the term *moral hazard* refers to the
    a. temptations of large cities on impressionable teenagers.
    b. state of much television programming.
    c. tendency of insurance to make people less concerned about risky behavior.
    d. dangers of sexually transmitted diseases among single men and women.

20. Decisions by company managers that make their own lives more comfortable at the cost of reducing stockholder profits are examples of
    a. moral hazards.
    b. principal-agent problems.
    c. detrimental externalities.
    d. public goods.

197

TEST B

Circle T or F for true or false.

T   F   1. An unregulated market economy would never have business cycles.

T   F   2. Externalities, whether beneficial or detrimental, imply that marginal social cost is always less than marginal private cost.

T   F   3. An activity that causes damage to someone else and for which there is no compensation is said to involve a detrimental externality.

T   F   4. A beneficial externality is likely to result in marginal private benefits exceeding marginal social benefits.

T   F   5. Economists define public goods as anything for which the government spends money.

T   F   6. The fact that it is difficult to restrict the use of public goods to those who are willing to pay is the problem of depletability.

T   F   7. The provision of public goods is complicated by the "free-rider" problem.

T   F   8. The fact that public goods are not depleted by use implies that the marginal cost of providing the goods to one more consumer is zero.

T   F   9. The interest rate plays an important role in the allocation of resources between the present and the future because it affects the profitability of investment projects.

T   F 10. Many investment projects will entail less risk for the individual investor than for the community as a whole.

SUPPLEMENTARY EXERCISES

1. Consider the economy of Beethovia, which produces two goods: widgets and music recitals. Widgets are manufactured with capital and labor according to the following production function:

$$W = 60L^{1/2}K^{1/2},$$

where L = number of workers producing widgets and K = number of machines. Music recitals are labor intensive and produced according to the following production function:

$$M = 50 \times L.$$

There are 40,000 workers in Beethovia, meaning that the sum of labor allocated to the production of widgets and recitals cannot exceed 40,000, and initially there are 22,500 machines, or $K = 22,500$.

a. Draw the production possibilities frontier for Beethovia showing the trade-off between the production of widgets and recitals. (It is probably easiest to arbitrarily fix the number of recitals, calculate how many workers it will take to produce that many recitals, and then calculate the maximum production of widgets with the remaining labor and all the machines.)

b. Competitive markets have initially resulted in 39,601 widget workers and 399 musicians. At this allocation, what is the marginal product and average product of labor in the production of widgets? In the production of recitals?

198

   c. Assume that saving and investment by the people of Beethovia increase the number of machines to 28,900. At the initial allocation of labor, but with the new number of machines, what is the marginal and average product of labor in the production of widgets? What has happened to the productivity of workers in the production of recitals?

   d. What has happened to the opportunity cost of music recitals; that is, what is the new slope of the production possibilities frontier at the allocation of workers specified in question b? To answer this question, either draw a new production possibilities frontier or derive a mathematical expression for the slope of the frontier.

   e. If you have answered question d correctly, you should have determined that the cost of recitals has increased. Recitals suffer from the cost disease of personal services. At the same time, how can you show that the increase in productivity has made Beethovia unambiguously richer?

2. Go to the library or bookstore and get a copy of *Encounters with the Archdruid* (New York: Farrar, Straus and Giroux, 1971) by John McPhee. The book reports on three encounters between David Brower, who was president of the Sierra Club, and other individuals who wanted to dam the Colorado River, build a copper mine in the Cascades, and develop Hilton Head Island. Many think that McPhee's description of the raft trip down the Colorado River with Brower and Floyd Dominy, who was head of the Bureau of Reclamation, is especially good.

   a. Whose position do you favor?

   b. Is Brower always right? Is he ever right?

ECONOMICS IN ACTION

STANDARDS OR TAXES?

In 1975, after the significant increase in international oil prices, the Energy Policy and Conservation Act mandated minimum corporate average fuel economy (CAFE) standards for new passenger cars sold in the United States. Originally established at 18.5 miles per gallon (mpg) for 1978, the CAFE standards are now 27.5 mpg for cars and 20.7 mpg for light trucks, a category that includes sport utility vehicles. Under the original policy, CAFE standards were to increase still further to reduce American dependency on foreign oil and to help reduce carbon dioxide emissions. Since the mid-1990s, Congress has frozen CAFE standards.

   Following the terrorist attacks of September 11, 2001, there has been renewed interest in limiting America's dependence on imported oil. In late November 2001, Robert F. Kennedy, Jr., a lawyer for the Natural Resources Defense Council, argued for CAFE standards of 40 miles per gallon by 2012 and 55 miles per gallon by 2020. Kennedy argued that even modest increases in gas mileage would limit the need to import oil and had the potential to save more oil than could be found in the Arctic National Wildlife Refuge.

   Columnist Virginia Postrel disagrees with Kennedy's approach. Citing work by economists Pietro S. Nivola and Robert W. Crandall, Postrel argues that increased gas taxes would be a more efficient means of reducing consumption. CAFE standards affect only new cars, which account for only a small proportion of total cars and miles driven. If higher CAFE standards increase the price of new cars, they may induce people to hold on to older, less fuel-efficient cars. By lowering the marginal cost of driving, higher CAFE standards might also in-

199

crease the number of miles driven by new car owners. In contrast, a fuel tax has opposite effects. It provides an incentive to get rid of older, less efficient cars for newer cars while increasing the marginal cost of driving for all drivers. If one is worried about the impact of higher gasoline taxes on low-income families, one could couple an increase in gas taxes with a reduction in income or payroll taxes targeted at low-income families.

It has been argued that CAFE standards were originally preferred by legislators because their cost is hidden in the price of new cars while an increased gasoline tax is quite visible. Postrel argues that increased CAFE standards might well come with exceptions that may have unintended consequences. She points out that the original standards had an exception for light trucks that was meant to reduce the cost of work vehicles, an exception that contributed to the proliferation of sport utility vehicles.

1. Which would you favor to reduce oil consumption, higher CAFE standards, higher gasoline taxes, or higher taxes on all uses of petroleum? Which do you think would be more effective? Which do you think is fairer? Why?

2. Do you think that reducing oil consumption should be a national priority?

Sources: Robert F. Kennedy, Jr., "Better Gas Mileage, Greater Security, *The New York Times,* November 24, 2001; Virginia Postrel, "Setting fuel-efficiency targets for vehicle fleets makes little sense," *The New York Times,* December 6, 2001.

STUDY QUESTIONS

1. Why do economists argue that externalities, whether beneficial or detrimental, are likely to lead to a misallocation of resources?

2. Why does a free market tend to overproduce goods with detrimental externalities?

3. Why does a free market tend to underproduce goods with beneficial externalities?

4. How can the price system help correct the problems of externalities?

5. What are the distinguishing characteristics of a public good as compared with a private good?

6. Why can't we leave the provision of public goods to profit-maximizing firms?

7. Do you believe that unregulated private markets will save too little or too much? Why?

8. Colleges and universities are often urged to hold tuition increases under the inflation rate. What does the concept of the cost disease of personal services suggest would happen if such a policy were followed for the next ten years?

9. What is rent-seeking behavior and why do people engage in it?

10. Is direct government regulation the appropriate response to all market failures?

The Market's Prime Achievement: Innovation and Growth

16

Important Terms and Concepts

Externality	GDP	Research and development (R&D)	Process innovation
Per capita income	Invention	High-tech	Basic research
Productivity	Innovation	Ratchet	Applied research
Industrial revolution	Entrepreneur	Product innovation	Technology trading
Capitalism			Cross licensing

Learning Objectives

After completing this chapter, you should be able to:

- explain why market economies have a stronger record of innovation than other forms of economic organization.

- explain the importance of innovation for economic growth.

- explain the role of innovative entrepreneurs in free-market innovation.

- understand why no firm in a high-tech industry can afford to fall behind its rivals in an innovation arms race.

- explain Schumpeter's Model and the initial entrepreneur's "monopolistic" earnings.

- explain how the concepts of marginal cost and marginal revenue can help a firm determine how much to spend on research and development.

- explain the difference between process and product innovation.

- analyze the impact of process innovations on price and output.

- explain the difference between basic and applied research.

- describe some of the arrangements firms might use to control the risk associated with specific R&D projects.

- evaluate the arguments about whether free economies invest enough in R&D.

CHAPTER REVIEW

This chapter reviews some of the microeconomic forces behind the process of innovation. Up to the Industrial Revolution, economic growth as we know it today hardly existed. Many products and processes at the beginning of the eighteenth century would have been familiar to Roman citizens. The past 200 years have seen a dramatic change. Labor at the beginning of the twenty-first century is much more productive than at the beginning of the nineteenth century. What explains this dramatic increase in labor productivity, and why have capitalist economies been so successful at it?

Major factors responsible for the growth in labor productivity include increased education and experience of the labor force, investment in plant and equipment, and the almost continuous development and introduction (1) of new products and production processes or _____. Today it seems that competition between firms in innovation is as important as price competition.

It is helpful to distinguish between invention and innovation. Research that focuses on fundamental scien- (2) tific ideas or entirely new products is an example of _____ while _____ refers to the entire process that prepares new ideas for practical use and marketing. Individuals who organize firms to exploit new products or production technologies are called _____. Breakthrough innovations come disproportionately from (small entrepreneurial/large) firms. At the same time one should not underestimate the cumulative impact of numerous incremental improvements to a wide range of consumer and industrial products.

Research and development activities are organized expenditures by firms to develop new products and processes. That is, rather than leaving innovation to chance, firms make clear decisions to invest in innovation. R&D budgets are like other business decisions and can be analyzed using the tools and concepts we have developed in earlier chapters. As with other business decisions, firms should expand R&D expenditures as long as (3) the expected marginal returns are greater than the marginal _____. While some individual innovations have been wildly profitable, the returns to innovation as a whole do not appear to offer abovenormal profits, a result that should not be surprising under conditions of free _____.

Why is innovation such an important part of capitalist economies? Why has innovation become such an important part of competition? Some have suggested that the kinked revenue model is an important part of the explanation. If a firm does not keep up with the competition in terms of the attractiveness of its products or the efficiency of its production processes, it will lose out. As a result, a firm that spends less on R&D runs the risk of not keeping up. There is little incentive to spend more than the average, as your competitors will only match your efforts. However, when someone's efforts have made an important difference, competitors need to increase their R&D spending to keep up. This process that works to sustain R&D spending is called a (4) _____.

Innovations have important impacts for the economy as a whole. Many innovations enlarge the range of choices for consumers and producers; that is, they create cumulative change. Many innovations have characteristics of public goods in that repeated use of an innovation neither uses it up nor requires that the act of innovation be repeated.

Do firms spend enough on innovation? Those who are concerned that firms spend too little point out that most innovations have beneficial _____, that is new and enhanced products and production pro-   (5) cesses offer significant benefits to lots of people in terms of better commodities and lower prices. As a result, the social benefits to innovation may exceed the private returns and profit-maximizing firms may stop short of a social optimum. The _____ system is an attempt to overcome this problem as its provides exclusive monopoly or licensing rights for a period of time. Competitive pressures to match the innovative efforts of competitors also works to increase spending on innovations. Licensing and technology trading are ways that firms try to capture the external benefits of their investments in R&D.

Individual R&D projects can be quite risky. Not all new products make it to market. Large firms can begin to reduce the risk of R&D by sponsoring numerous projects. Firms can also enter into arrangements to share the innovations of other firms through technology _____ and cross   (6) _____ of patents.

Do consumers benefit from innovation? Product innovations mean new or enhanced products but at what cost? Process innovations that lower the marginal cost of production should mean an unambiguous gain for consumers through (<u>higher/lower</u>) output and _____ prices.   (7)

203

IMPORTANT TERMS AND CONCEPTS QUIZ

Choose the best definition for each of the following terms.

1. _____ Externality
2. _____ Per capita income
3. _____ Productivity
4. _____ Industrial Revolution
5. _____ Capitalism
6. _____ GDP
7. _____ Invention
8. _____ Innovation
9. _____ Entrepreneur
10. _____ Research and development (R&D)
11. _____ High-Tech
12. _____ Ratchet
13. _____ Product innovation
14. _____ Process innovation
15. _____ Basic research
16. _____ Applied research
17. _____ Technology trading
18. _____ Cross licensing

a. Process of introducing new products or methods of production
b. Research on scientific knowledge and general principles
c. Total production divided by total hours of labor input
d. Individual who organizes a new firm
e. Research on specific products or processes
f. Agreements to share patents in return for money or access to other patents
g. Average income per person
h. Introduction of new products or major modification to existing products
i. Production processes controlled by private firms with minimal government control
j. Innovation that changes the way a commodity is produced
k. Growth in economic output
l. Organized efforts to invent new and improve existing products and processes
m. Shared use of technological innovations among firms
n. Total domestic production in a year
o. Permits increases but prevents decreases
p. New technologies that spurred economic growth in England toward the end of the 18th century
q. Firms and industries that use cutting edge technologies
r. Activity that creates uncompensated benefits or damages for third parties
s. Creation of new products and processes or the discovery of ideas that underlie them

204

BASIC EXERCISE

DOES IT REALLY MATTER?

Why all the fuss about innovation? Can a 1 percent difference in the rate of economic growth make all that much difference?

1. Complete **Table 16-1** to see if the rate of economic growth will make any difference for your great-grandchildren.

   Table 16-1

   The Impact of Differences in Economic Growth on GDP per Capita

Year	Growth Rate of GDP Per Capita 0%	0.5%	1.0%	1.5%	2.0%
2000	$31,000	$31,000	$31,000	$31,000	$31,000
2100	_____	_____	_____	_____	_____

2. According to the text, on average the standard of living in the United States increased by slightly more than sevenfold during the twentieth century. Which of the growth rates in Table 16-1 would produce a similar result during the twenty-first century?

SELF-TESTS FOR UNDERSTANDING

TEST A

Circle the most appropriate answer.

1. For the 1500 years before the Industrial Revolution, economic growth in Europe
   a. was actually negative.
   b. was close to zero.
   c. averaged 2.5 percent per year.
   d. resulted in labor that was twenty times more productive than in Roman times.

2. What type of economy has shown the strongest record of innovation and growth?
   a. socialist economies
   b. soviet-style central planning
   c. capitalist economies
   d. feudalism

205

3. According to the text, which two of the following have played especially crucial roles in the ability of capitalist economies to sustain high rates of innovation? (there may be more than one correct answer.)
   a. the encouragement of cartels in key sectors of the economy
   b. the use of innovation as a way of competing with rivals
   c. targeted investments by the government in key sectors of the economy
   d. markets that are free from tight regulation and limiting customs

4. Which of the following does not help to explain the record of innovation and growth in capitalist economies?
   a. enforceability of contracts
   b. development of the patent system
   c. competitive pressures for innovation
   d. royal prerogatives that give the king or emperor the rights to new innovations

5. Entrepreneurs are involved with which of the following? (there may be more than one correct answer.)
   a. The organization of new business.
   b. The exploitation of new production techniques
   c. The marketing of new products
   d. Risk taking

6. Breakthrough innovations
   a. are the focus of R&D efforts of large firms.
   b. come disproportionately from small, entrepreneurial firms.
   c. focus on user friendliness.
   d. involve small improvements to existing products.

7. Firms should expand spending on R&D as long as
   a. the marginal revenue from expected innovations exceeds marginal cost.
   b. the average revenue from all of a firm's innovations exceeds average cost.
   c. the results are patentable.
   d. it is on applied rather than basic research.

8. Consider a software company that spends $200 million to develop a new computer program that can be reproduced at $5 a copy. Setting price equal to the marginal cost of additional copies will
   a. guarantee positive profits.
   b. necessarily increase shareholder value.
   c. mean the company will never recover its R&D costs.
   d. be the same as setting marginal cost equal to marginal revenue.

9. Under conditions of free entry, one would expect that the returns to innovation as a whole would be
   a. very high.
   b. equal to market average rates of return.
   c. zero.
   d. negative.

10. Which of the following observations would you associate with the term ratchet?
    a. An arrangement that forces down technological spending.
    b. A serious shortcoming of free-enterprise economies.
    c. It explains why R&D spending is expected to reduce over a period of time.
    d. An arrangement that permits increases but prevents decreases.

11. Which is an example of a process innovation?
    a. A university researcher identifies the electrical properties of a new synthetic material.
    b. A chemist for DuPont discovers a new fabric.
    c. A partnership between a history and a computer science student results in a new computer-based action game set in sixteenth century Japan.
    d. An engineer for Ford finds an application, of existing technology, that when applied to rust proofing car bodies saves $150 per car.

12. Which is an example of a product innovation?
    a. Post-it notes
    b. a government grant to a researcher who is studying polymer chemistry
    c. Boeing reorganizes its production line to enhance worker productivity
    d. Einstein's theory of relativity

13. Which is an example of a basic research?
    a. new methods for making stronger sheets of glass for large windows
    b. new designs from Ralph Lauren
    c. the development of an artificial kidney
    d. the discovery of DNA

14. Which of the following is most likely to support basic research?
    a. the National Association of Manufacturers
    b. Microsoft
    c. the federal government
    d. Ford Motor Company

15. The term technology trading
    a. refers to the venture capitalists who specialize in funding high-tech startup companies.
    b. refers to the export and import of high-tech capital goods.
    c. was coined by the stockbroker who first sold shares of IBM.
    d. is a way that firms can try and manage the risk of research and development.

16. Which of the following is an example of technology trading?
    a. Eli Whitney left England for America with the plans for the cotton gin in his head.
    b. Two companies agree to share innovations.
    c. Jane is employed to reverse engineer the latest innovation from her firm's major competitors.
    d. The federal government supports basic research in university laboratories.

207

17. The kinked revenue model helps to explain
    a. the returns to innovation.
    b. product innovations rather than process innovations.
    c. why firms tend to match R&D spending of their competitors.
    d. why profit-maximizing firms are likely to favor applied research over basic research.

18. An innovation that improves an existing product would be an example of (there may be more than one correct answer)
    a. basic research.
    b. product innovation.
    c. process innovation.
    d. applied research.

19. In the United States, R&D spending is
    a. about 28 percent of GDP.
    b. about 2.8 percent of GDP.
    c. about 0.28 percent of GDP.
    d. only conducted by the federal government.

20. A process innovation that leads to a downward shift in a monopolist's marginal cost curve should
    a. lower price and lower output.
    b. lower price and increase output.
    c. increase price and increase output.
    d. increase price and lower output.

TEST B

Circle T or F for true or false.

T   F   1. Labor today is not much more productive than it was 200 years ago.

T   F   2. There is little reason to expect that capitalist economies will be more successful at innovation than centrally planned economies.

T   F   3. Innovation is a major source of economic growth.

T   F   4. The R&D efforts of large firms are often focused on improvements to existing products and process.

T   F   5. The kinked revenue model of innovation works like a ratchet to sustain the level of R&D spending.

T   F   6. Firms can reduce the risk associated with R&D efforts by engaging in technology trading.

T   F   7. The development of a new or improved production process is an example of basic, not applied, research.

T   F   8. Profit-maximizing firms are likely to devote more resources to applied research than basic research.

T   F   9. The externality problem is likely more severe for basic rather than applied research.

T   F 10. Process innovations should lower price and increase output, even for monopolists.

ECONOMICS IN ACTION

CREATIVE DESTRUCTION[1]

Was the boom-bust cycle of many dot-com companies at the turn of the century a unique event? Are the problems of large fixed costs and low variable costs unique to the Internet and software industry? Are the concepts of process and product innovation new?

Economist Hal Varian would answer all questions with a decisive no. Writing in *The New York Times,* Varian described the evolution of the automobile industry in the United States. During the first decade of the twentieth century, there were more than 240 startup companies in the automobile industry. Henry Ford developed a dominating position as he focused on process innovation. As Varian explains, "Ford experimented relentlessly with mass-production techniques. He built big and reaped the cost advantages from economies of scale and vertical integration . . . By 1923, Ford was producing nearly half the automobiles sold in America."

But Ford's dominant position was vulnerable to product innovation championed by Alfred Sloan of General Motors who introduced annual model changes. Ford, who is reported to have said that the American public could have a car in any color it wanted as long as it was black, found it difficult to compete against Sloan's innovation.

Varian argues that companies like Dell Computer have been able to emulate Ford's focus on lowering costs through process innovation, but he wonders if this makes them vulnerable to product innovation from future competitors.

Railroads showed a similar boom-bust cycle. Here the underlying dynamic was the importance of large-scale networks that entailed significant fixed costs but operated with low marginal costs. Railroad companies made significant fixed investments in track and rolling stock in the 1880s only to face fierce competition in the 1890s as the marginal cost of operating on tracks already laid with rolling stock that was already purchased was relative low. The result was that the investment boom of the 1880s was followed by widespread bankruptcies in the 1890s.

1. It is easy to identify the winners after the dust has settled, but how does one identify the winners in advance? One might argue that the experience of the railroads, the automobile industry and dot-com companies have involved a fair amount of overinvestment. Is this wasteful investment that should be controlled by the government or is this an essential element of the dynamic nature of capitalism?

Source: Hal R. Varian, "Economic Scene: The technology sector's rise and fall is a tale as American as the Model T," *The New York Times,* December 14, 2000.

---

[1]Economist Joseph Schumpeter first described the process of innovation and competition as "creative destruction." Schumpeter argued that it is an essential element of the vitality of capitalism.

209

STUDY QUESTIONS

1. Why do capitalist economies have a better record of innovation that planned economies?

2. What is the difference between basic and applied research? Which is more likely to be done by profit-maximizing firms? Why?

3. What is the difference between process and product innovation? Are these examples of basic or applied research?

4. Why don't software companies set prices equal to the marginal cost of reproducing their software programs?

5. What is meant by the kinked revenue model of spending on innovation?

6. How can firms control the risk associated with specific R&D projects?

7. What is meant by the public good aspect of innovations?

8. Does the American economy spend enough on research and development?

9. Should the government spend money on research and development? If so, should it favor basic or applied research? Why?

Externalities, the Environment, and Natural Resources

17

Important Terms and Concepts

Externality

Direct controls

Pollution charges (taxes on emissions)

Emissions permits

Learning Objectives

After completing this chapter, you should be able to:

- analyze environmental problems faced by planned and market economies.

- explain why, in most cases, it is impossible to reduce pollution to zero.

- explain why unrestricted competitive markets are likely to result in a socially unacceptable level of pollution.

- explain why it is unlikely that profit-maximizing private firms can be expected to clean up the environment.

- describe the three major approaches to limiting pollution.

- compare the advantages and disadvantages of using taxes and permits to control pollution.

- explain why the price of depletable resources should be expected to rise year by year.

- explain how and why actual prices of depletable resources have behaved differently.

- describe the three virtues of rising prices for scarce resources.

- explain why known reserves for many resources have not tended to fall over time.

CHAPTER REVIEW

This chapter explores the economics of environmental protection and resource conservation, with emphasis on the strengths and weaknesses of a market economy in dealing with both issues.

ENVIRONMENTAL PROTECTION

Pollution is one example where unregulated markets will fail to achieve an efficient allocation of resources. Typically, pollution imposes little or no cost on the polluter, yet it imposes costs on others. In the language of

(1) economists, pollution is an example of a detrimental _____. Pollution happens because individuals, firms, and government agencies use the air, land, and waterways as free dumping grounds for their waste. Economists believe that if there is a high cost to using these public resources, then the volume of pollution will (<u>increase/decrease</u>) because people will be more careful about producing wastes and/or they will choose less costly alternatives for waste disposal. One way to make the use of public resources costly is to impose (<u>taxes/subsidies</u>) in direct proportion to the volume of pollution emitted. This is an example of using the price system to clean up the environment.

(2) Many government policies have relied on volunteerism and direct _____. Economists are skeptical of relying on voluntary cooperation as a long-range solution. Cleaning up the environment is costly, and firms that voluntarily incur these costs are likely to be undersold by less public-spirited competitors. A government ruling that mandates an equal percentage reduction in pollution activity by all polluters is an example of a direct control. Economists argue that since the costs of reducing pollution are apt to vary among polluters, an equal percentage reduction by all polluters is likely to be (<u>efficient/inefficient</u>) compared with other alternatives, such as emissions taxes. Differential reductions in pollution will be (<u>less/more</u>) efficient, as it is likely to cost less for some firms to reduce pollution.

(3) Faced with an emissions tax, firms will reduce pollution until the (<u>marginal/average</u>) cost of further reductions exceeds the tax. Firms that continue to pollute pay the tax; other firms will pay for pollution-control devices. All firms will choose the least costly alternative. The sale or auction of emission permits also generates a market price that firms must pay if they pollute. One advantage of emission permits is that by controlling the number of permits, there may be greater control over the final volume of pollution.

While economists have a strong preference for market-based approaches to reducing pollution, there may be cases where one needs to rely on voluntarism or direct control. For example, when conditions have changed suddenly and action must be taken quickly, there may not be time to implement a program of pollution taxes or emission permits. If monitoring pollution is not possible or prohibitively expensive, direct controls may be a preferable alternative, and society may prefer to ban especially dangerous activities.

RESOURCE CONSERVATION

Some resources, such as trees and fish, are called renewable resources. As long as breeding stocks are not destroyed, these resources will replenish themselves. The rest of this chapter concentrates on nonrenewable or depletable resources such as minerals and oil. In this case there is no reproduction, although there may be recycling.

Many observers have voiced concern that the world is running out of natural resources. They allege that soon the quantity of resources supplied will not be able to keep up with the quantity of resources demanded and that the result will be massive shortages and chaos. Yet, in a free market we know that the quantity demanded (<u>can/can never</u>) exceed the quantity supplied, because demand and supply will always be brought into equilibrium by adjustments in _____. This fundamental mechanism of free markets, first discussed in Chapter 4, is as applicable to the supply and demand of scarce resources as it is to any other commodity. (4)

Over time one might expect the price of depletable resources to increase year by year as the most accessible and inexpensive sources of supply are used up first. That is, the prices of depletable resources should show a rising trend.[1] Economic analysis suggests that the trend in price is a better indicator of depletion than estimates of reserves, which are of necessity based on current extraction technology and exploration. The discovery of new resource reserves or new methods of manufacturing that economize on the use of resources, technological progress that reduces the cost of extraction, and government attempts at price controls can all affect the price of depletable resources.

Data on known reserves, rather than declining as implied in the literal interpretation of a nonrenewable resource, have typically shown increases during the past 50 years. These increases in reserves reflect the workings of the price system as the incentive from higher prices has induced new exploration and made the use of high-cost deposits profitable. It is important to remember that pressure for higher prices is what equates demand and supply, avoids chaos, and facilitates the adjustment to alternative technologies.

Many economists see increasing prices for depletable resources as an important virtue of free markets. Increasing prices help to deal with the problem of declining reserves in three important ways:

a. Increasing prices (<u>encourage/discourage</u>) consumption and waste and provide a(n) (<u>disincentive/incentive</u>) for conservation on the part of consumers. (5)

b. Increasing prices (<u>encourage/discourage</u>) more efficient use of scarce resources in the production of commodities.

c. Increasing prices provide a(n) (<u>disincentive/incentive</u>) for technological innovation and the use of substitutes as well as (<u>encouraging/discouraging</u>) additional exploration and the exploitation of high-cost sources of supply.

---

[1]Economist Harold Hotelling suggested that even if extraction costs are constant, the price of a depletable resource of known finite supply should increase at a rate equal to the rate of interest. This increase is necessary so that investments in the depletable resource offer a competitive rate of return.

IMPORTANT TERMS AND CONCEPTS QUIZ

Choose the most appropriate definition for each of the following terms.

1. _____ Externality
2. _____ Direct controls
3. _____ Pollution charges
4. _____ Emissions permit

a. Monetary penalties used to make polluting financially unattractive

b. Fees paid to polluting firms in exchange for reductions in pollution

c. Result of activities that affect other people, without corresponding compensation

d. Authorization to pollute up to a specified level

e. Legal limits on pollution emissions or performance specifications for polluting activities

BASIC EXERCISES

POLLUTION TAXES

This exercise examines the implications of alternative pollution taxes.

Assume that plastic trash bags are produced in a market that is best characterized as one of perfect competition. Manufacturers have long used local rivers as convenient dumping grounds for their industrial wastes. **Figure 17-1** plots the average cost of producing trash bags. These data are applicable for each firm.

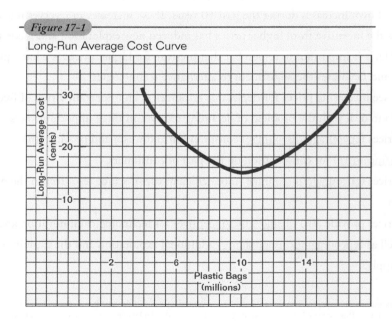

Figure 17-1

Long-Run Average Cost Curve

(y-axis: Long-Run Average Cost (cents); x-axis: Plastic Bags (millions))

1. a. In the absence of pollution-control measures, what is the long-run equilibrium price of plastic bags? $_____. What is the long-run equilibrium level of output for each firm? $_____ million. (To answer this question you may want to review the material in Chapter 10 about long-run equilibrium under perfect competition.)

   b. The amount of pollution discharge is directly proportional to the number of bags produced. Assume that the government imposes a pollution charge of 5 cents per bag. Draw in the new average cost curve on Figure 17-1. In the long run, will there be an increase, a decrease, or no change in each of the following as a result of the pollution charge? (Assume for now that there is no pollution-control technology, that each firm must pay the tax, and that the demand for plastic bags declines as price rises.)

      Industry output   _____

      Price   _____

      Number of firms in the industry _____

      Average cost curve for each firm _____

      Output level of each firm   _____

      Total pollution   _____

   c. Assume that pollution-control equipment becomes available. This equipment will eliminate 75 percent of pollution at an average cost of 4 cents per bag. Explain why no firm will adopt the pollution-control equipment if the pollution charge is unchanged at 5 cents a bag. (Assume that the cost of the control equipment is all variable cost at 4 cents per bag and that there is no fixed-cost component.)

   d. Assume now that the tax is shifted to the volume of emissions, not to the number of bags produced, and that it is equivalent to 5 cents a bag if no pollution-control equipment is installed. Will any firm purchase the pollution-control equipment?

   e. With the emissions tax at a rate equivalent to 5 cents per bag, to what rate must the cost of pollution control decline before firms will use it? If the cost of pollution control is constant at 4 cents, to what rate must the tax increase to induce firms to install the pollution-control equipment?

   f. Assume now that the costs of reducing pollution are not identical for all firms. For simplicity, assume that there are two types of firms, low-cost pollution-control firms and high-cost pollution-control firms. The low-cost firms can eliminate pollution at costs lower than the emissions tax but the high-cost firms cannot. What is the result of imposing an emissions tax? What will happen to total industry output? Will any firms leave the industry? If so, which ones, the high-cost or the low-cost firms? Why?

Year	Real GDP (Billions of $2000)	Energy Consumption (quadrillion BTUs)	Energy Consumption per $1,000 GDP (thousands of BTUs)	Year	Real GDP (Billions of $2000)	Energy Consumption (quadrillion BTUs)	Energy Consumption per $1,000 GDP (thousands of BTUs)
1970	3,771.9	67.8	_____	1990	7,112.5	84.7	_____
1971	3,898.6	69.3	_____	1991	7,100.5	84.6	_____
1972	4,105.0	72.7	_____	1992	7,336.6	86.0	_____
1973	4,341.5	75.7	_____	1993	7,532.7	87.6	_____
1974	4,319.6	74.0	_____	1994	7,835.5	89.3	_____
1975	4,311.2	72.0	_____	1995	8,031.7	91.2	_____
1976	4,540.9	76.0	_____	1996	8,328.9	94.2	_____
1977	4,750.5	78.0	_____	1997	8,703.5	94.7	_____
1978	5,015.0	80.0	_____	1998	9,066.9	95.2	_____
1979	5,173.4	80.9	_____	1999	9,470.3	96.8	_____
1980	5,161.7	78.3	_____	2000	9,817.0	98.9	_____
1981	5,291.7	76.3	_____	2001	9,890.7	96.4	_____
1982	5,189.3	73.3	_____	2002	10,048.8	98.0	_____
1983	5,423.8	73.1	_____	2003	10,301.3	98.8	_____
1984	5,813.6	76.7	_____	2004	10,675.8	100.3	_____
1985	6,053.7	76.5	_____	2005	11,003.4	100.6	_____
1986	6,263.6	76.8	_____	2006	11,319.4	99.8	_____
1987	6,475.1	79.2	_____				
1988	6,742.7	82.8	_____				
1989	6,981.4	85.0	_____				

Table 17-1

Source: GDP: Bureau of Economic Analysis, U.S. Department of Commerce http://bea.gov/national/nipaweb/SelectTable.asp?Popular=Y , Table 1.1.6; Energy Annual Energy Review, US Department of Energy, Table 1.5. http://www.eia.doe.gov/emeu/aer/txt/ptb0105.html and Monthly Energy Review http://www.eia doe.gov/overview_hd.html; Prices: Economic Report of the President, 2005, Table B-60 http://www.gpoaccess.gov/eop/tables08.html Accessed: June 15, 2008.

2. a. **Table 17-1** contains data on real output and energy consumption for the U.S. economy. Use these data to compute the use of energy per thousand dollars of GDP.

   b. **Figure 17-2** shows real energy prices, i.e., energy prices divided by the consumer price index. Complete Figure 17-2 by plotting the data on energy consumption per thousand dollars of GDP. Use this graph to discuss the pattern of energy consumption during the last thirty years.

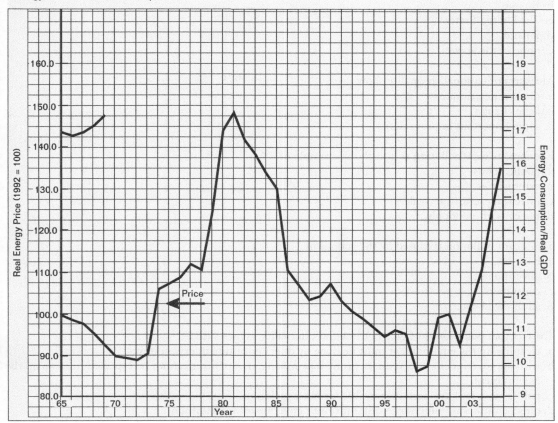

Figure 17-2

Energy Prices and Consumption

SELF-TESTS FOR UNDERSTANDING

TEST A

Circle the most appropriate answer.

1. Which of the following suggests that, except for recycling, all economic activity results in a disposal problem?
   a. OPEC
   b. the law of conservation of energy and matter
   c. emissions permits
   d. externalities

2. Which of the following countries has avoided significant pollution problems?
   a. China
   b. Russia
   c. The United States
   d. Poland
   e. none of the above

3. Measures of national air quality show _____ since 1975.
   a. marked deterioration
   b. little change
   c. some important improvements

4. Economists view pollution as a textbook example of
   a. public goods.
   b. externalities.
   c. increasing returns to scale.
   d. the evils of monopoly.

5. Significant pollution is caused by the actions of
   a. business.
   b. government.
   c. consumers.
   d. all of the above.

6. The fact that pollution is often a detrimental externality suggests that
   a. cleaning up the environment must be done by direct government expenditures.
   b. without government intervention, profit-maximizing private firms cannot be expected to clean up the environment.
   c. public agencies have been responsible for most pollution.
   d. direct controls are superior to other forms of government intervention.

7. Which of the following is not an example of using financial incentives to clean up the environment?
   a. mandated pollution-control equipment so all producers will reduce the emission of industrial pollutants by 50 percent
   b. a graduated tax that increases with the polluting characteristics of each automobile engine
   c. the sale of a limited number of permits to control emissions into Lake Erie
   d. allowing firms to buy and sell emission rights originally assigned under a program of direct controls

8. The use of pollution charges as a means of cleaning up the environment
   a. is the predominant form of pollution control in the United States.
   b. is likely to be more efficient than a system of direct controls.
   c. would be most appropriate in situations calling for sudden action, such as a serious smog condition.
   d. would have exactly the same effects on the volume of pollution as do subsidies for pollution-control equipment.

9. As a strategy to control pollution, voluntarism
   a. is the best long-run strategy.
   b. may be the only practical alternative in cases where surveillance is impractical.
   c. should be the most effective alternative.
   d. has significant efficiency advantages as compared with pollution taxes.

10. Economists typically argue that _____ are likely to be most effective in reducing pollution over the long run.
    a. direct controls
    b. taxes on emissions
    c. voluntary programs
    d. specifications as to allowable equipment and/or procedures

11. Pollution charges are likely to be more efficient than direct controls because
    a. most of the reduction in pollution will be done by those who can implement reductions at low cost.
    b. everyone will be forced to show the same percentage reduction in pollution.
    c. no one likes paying taxes.
    d. pollution is a detrimental externality.

12. Compared with a system of direct controls, pollution charges
    a. are basically a "carrot" approach, relying on everyone's voluntary cooperation.
    b. are likely to lead to an equal percentage reduction in emissions from all pollution sources.
    c. will not reduce pollution, as firms will simply pass on these costs to their consumers with no impact on output levels.
    d. offer an incentive for continually reducing emissions, rather than reducing them just to some mandated level.

13. On free markets, the depletion of a scarce natural resource should lead to
    a. declining prices.
    b. no change in prices.
    c. rising prices.

14. Which one of the following would be expected to reduce the price of a depletable natural resource?
    a. the establishment of an effective producer cartel
    b. the discovery of previously unknown reserves
    c. an increase in the rate of inflation
    d. an increase in GDP

15. The quantity demanded of a scarce resource can exceed the quantity supplied
    a. if there is a sudden surge in demand.
    b. as economic growth increases demand.
    c. if monopolistic suppliers withhold supply.
    d. only if something prevents prices from adjusting.

16. The record of resource prices in the twentieth century shows
    a. a steady trend toward lower real prices for all resources.
    b. little trend in the real price of many resources.
    c. that most have increased year by year.

17. Rising resource prices can be a virtue as they provide an incentive for all but which one of the following?
    a. increased waste
    b. increased use of substitutes
    c. increased conservation
    d. increased innovation

18. Known reserves of a number of natural resources have
    a. declined.
    b. remained roughly constant.
    c. actually increased.

19. Measured relative to total output, i.e., GDP, the use of energy in the United States is now
    a. about as high as it has ever been.
    b. about the same as it has been for the last 20 years.
    c. significantly lower than it was 20 years ago.

20. Effective price ceilings for natural resources would likely
    a. provide an increased incentive for further exploration.
    b. shift the demand curve to the left.
    c. induce consumers to conserve.
    d. lead to resource shortages.

TEST B

Circle T or F for true or false.

T F 1. Pollution has been a serious problem only since World War II.

T F 2. Only capitalist economies suffer from extensive pollution.

T F 3. When considering public policies to limit discharges of wastes into a river basin, an equal percentage reduction by all polluters is likely to be the most economically efficient policy.

T F 4. Pollution charges imposed on monopolist firms will have no effect on the volume of their polluting activity because they will simply pass on the higher costs in the form of higher prices.

T F 5. Efficiency considerations strongly suggest that society should spend enough to reduce all pollution to zero.

T F 6. If left unchecked, the free-market mechanism will cause the demand for natural resources to exceed supply.

T F 7. During the past 100 years, the relative prices of virtually all natural resources have shown dramatic increases.

T F 8. Since 1950 known reserves of most minerals have dropped dramatically.

T   F   9. Rising prices for natural resources provide an incentive for increased exploration and the development of new extraction technology.

T   F   10. Rising prices can help control resource depletion as they induce firms and households to conserve.

SUPPLEMENTARY EXERCISES

POLLUTION AND PRICES

Can a producer simply pass on to its customers any pollution charges it must pay? This numerical example expands upon the problem in the Basic Exercise.

Consider the production of plastic bags, which cause pollution in direct proportion to the volume of production. The demand for bags is given by

$$Q = 2,600 - 40P$$

where Q is measured in millions of bags and P is measured in cents.

1. Assume that plastic bags are produced by a monopolist at a cost of 15 cents a bag; that is,

$$TC = 15 \times Q.$$

   Plot the demand, marginal revenue, average cost, and marginal cost curves on a piece of graph paper. What is the monopolist's profit-maximizing level of output, the associated price, and its profits?

2. The government now imposes a pollution tax equivalent to 5 cents a bag, that is, $TC = 0.20 \times Q$. What happens to output, prices, and profits if the monopolist simply raises the price by 5 cents? Can he do better by charging a different price? If so, what is that price, the associated quantity, and the new level of profits?

3. Assume now that bags are produced by identical small firms under conditions of perfect competition. Each firm produces bags with average cost given by

$$AC = 0.4(Q - 10)^2 + 15.$$

   What is the long-run market equilibrium price and quantity? How many firms are in the industry? How many bags does each firm produce?

4. Again the government imposes a pollution tax equivalent to 5 cents a bag on each producer. What happens in the short run when there are still the same number of bag producers? What about the long run? How many firms will produce how many bags at what price?

ECONOMICS IN ACTION

HEAVY METAL

It seems like we cannot pick up a newspaper without reading about some impending ecological disaster or some resource that is about to disappear. The late economist Julian Simon was an outspoken critic of such doomsday forecasts. He argued that our ancestors faced similar apparent disasters and, with some effort, overcame them. In many cases this involved learning how to use new metals or new sources of energy. According to Simon, the ultimate resource is human ingenuity. He was fond of quoting Henry George: "Both the jayhawk and the man eat chickens, but the more jayhawks, the fewer the chickens, while the more men, the more chickens."

In 1980 Simon issued a challenge to those predicting disaster. He argued that if resources were becoming increasingly scarce, their real price should increase. Simon offered the following $1,000 bet: Pick any resources and any future date. On that date, look to see if resource prices have risen by more or less than inflation. If prices were to rise by more than inflation, Simon would pay. If prices had not risen as fast as inflation, Simon would collect.

Simon's challenge was accepted in October 1980 by Paul Ehrlich, author of *Population Bomb*, along with John Harte and John Holdren. They chose five metals: chrome, copper, nickel, tin, and tungsten. On paper, they spent $200 on each metal, buying 51.28 pounds of chrome, 196.56 pounds of copper, 65.32 pounds of nickel, 229.16 pounds of tin, and 13.64 pounds of tungsten. The bet was to look at the inflation-adjusted price of this market basket of metal in October 1990. If, after adjusting for inflation, the market basket of metal cost more than $1,000, Simon would pay Ehrlich, Harte, and Holdren the difference from $1,000. On the other hand, if the total cost were less than $1,000, Ehrlich, Harte and Holdren owed Simon the difference.

The controversy was renewed in the spring of 1995 when, writing in the *San Francisco Chronicle*, Simon again offered to accept a bet, this time on "any trend pertaining to human welfare." Paul Ehrlich and Stephen Schneider responded by offering a package bet on 15 measures including average global temperature, the concentration of tropospheric ozone, emissions of sulfur dioxide in Asia, and biodiversity. Simon rejected their offer arguing that their measures would have only indirect effects on people. Simon preferred more direct measures such as life expectancy or the trend in deaths from skin cancer.

1. Who do you think won the original bet? What was the magnitude of the payoff?

2. What has happened to the prices of the five metals since 1990? (Remember you will need to correct for inflation as the bet concerned relative prices.)

3. If, today, you could choose either side of the original bet, with the outcome to be determined ten years from now, which would you take and why?

4. What about the most recent set of proposed wagers? What has happened to Ehrlich's and Schneider's preferred measures? What has happened to Simon's preferred measures? Which do you think is a more reasonable measure of trends in human welfare? Which side would you take? (Remember to check your wager against actual results in ten years.)

STUDY QUESTIONS

1. What do economists mean when they say pollution is an externality?

2. Why do unregulated competitive markets tend to produce more pollution than is socially desirable?

3. Would it be a good idea to reduce all pollution to zero? Why?

4. Why do economists argue that emission taxes are a more efficient means of reducing pollution than direct controls?

5. Why do economists argue that price is a better indicator of the scarcity of resources than estimates of reserves?

6. If we are running out of a particular resource, why would economists expect its price to rise?

7. What is the history of resource prices over the twentieth century?

8. Under what circumstances can the quantity demanded of a depletable resource exceed the quantity supplied?

9. What are the three virtues of rising prices for natural resources?

10. Why haven't reserves for many resources been falling over time as use of these resources continues to grow every year?

ECONOMICS ONLINE

Lots of information on energy production, consumption, and prices is available from the U.S. Department of Energy

http://www.eia.doe.gov/emeu

Taxation and Resource Allocation

18

Important Terms and Concepts

Ability-to-pay principle

Average tax rate

Benefits principle of taxation

Burden of a tax

Corporate income tax

Direct taxes

Economic efficiency

Excess burden

Excise tax

Fiscal federalism

Horizontal equity

Incidence of a tax

Indirect taxes

Marginal tax rate

Payroll tax

Personal income tax

Progressive taxes

Property tax

Proportional taxes

Regressive taxes

Social Security system

Tax deductions

Tax exempt

Tax loopholes

Tax shifting

Vertical equity

Learning Objectives

After completing this chapter, you should be able to:

- distinguish between progressive, proportional, and regressive tax systems.

- describe the major taxes levied by the federal government and identify which are direct taxes and which are indirect taxes.

- explain why the payroll tax is regressive.

- explain what issues make the financing of Social Security controversial.

- describe the major taxes levied by state, and local governments.

- explain the concept of fiscal federalism.

- contrast various concepts of fair or equitable taxation.

- explain the concept of efficiency in taxation and the difference between the burden and the excess burden of a tax.

- explain how changes in economic behavior can enable individuals to shift the burden of a tax, that is, explain what is wrong with the flypaper theory of tax incidence.

- explain what factors influence how the burden of a tax will be shared by consumers and suppliers.

- explain how some taxes can lead to efficiency gains, not losses.

CHAPTER REVIEW

This chapter concentrates on taxes: What taxes are collected in America and what economic effects they have. Few people like paying taxes. In fact, many people make adjustments in their behavior to reduce the taxes they must pay. These adjustments are an important part of the economic impact of taxes, an aspect often overlooked in popular discussions.

(1) Taxes are levied by federal, state, and local governments. For the most part, federal taxes tend to be (direct/indirect) taxes, while state and local governments rely more on _____ taxes. The largest revenue raiser for the federal government is the _____ _____ tax. Next in line in terms of revenue raised is the _____ tax. Other important federal taxes include the _____ income tax and excise taxes.

(2) When talking about income tax systems it is important to distinguish between average and marginal tax rates. The fraction of total income paid as income taxes is the (average/marginal) tax rate, while the fraction of each additional dollar of income paid as taxes is the _____ tax rate. If the average tax rate increases with income, the tax system is called _____. If the average tax rate stays constant for all levels of income, the tax system is said to be _____, while if the average tax rate falls as income increases, the result is a(n) _____ tax system. Tax exemptions have been used to influence favored activities, sometimes for broad social purposes and other times in response to effective political lobbying of special interests. Regardless of why they were enacted, tax exemptions typically (do not affect/increase/reduce) the progressivity of the personal income tax.

(3) The Social Security system is financed by (income/payroll) taxes. These taxes are considered (regressive/progressive) because they (do/do not) apply to all sources of income and because, except for taxes to support Medicare, after a certain level of income the marginal tax rate becomes _____. Social Security benefits do not work like private pension funds because benefits are not limited by individual contributions. The Social Security system was able to offer retired people good benefits for two reasons: (a) Real wages and incomes of those currently employed showed substantial growth; and (b) the number of working people was large relative to the number of retired individuals. The slowdown in the growth of real wages, changes in the age structure of the population, and the increasing lifespan of retirees required changes in the earlier approach to Social Security. Adjustments in both taxes and benefits have attempted to solve the problem by accumulating a surplus in the Social Security trust fund to pay future benefits. However, these adjustments (are/are not) sufficient for a permanent solution.

(4) The major state and local taxes, _____ taxes, and _____ taxes, are indirect taxes. State income taxes are also an important source of revenue for many states. In addition to the taxes raised by state governments, there is a system of transfers from the federal to state governments called fiscal _____.

Economists use the dual criteria of equity and efficiency to judge taxes. When talking about the fairness of a tax, we are talking about _____. Various criteria have been advanced to judge the fair- (5) ness of a particular tax. The principle that equally situated individuals should pay equal taxes is referred to as _____ equity. The principle that differentially situated individuals should be taxed in ways that society deems fair is referred to as _____ equity. The ability-to-pay principle is an example of _____ equity. Rather than looking at the income and wealth of families, there is an alternative approach to taxation that says people should pay in proportion to what they get from public services. This principle for taxation is called the _____ principle. User fees, for example using gas taxes for highways or entrance fees for parks, are examples of the _____ principle.

Efficiency is the other criterion that economists use to judge taxes. Almost all taxes cause some inefficiency. The amount of money that would make an individual as well off with a tax as she was without the tax is called the _____ of the tax. Sometimes it just equals the tax payment an individual makes, but more (6) generally it is (greater/less) than an individual's tax payment. The difference between the total burden and tax payments is called the _____ _____. The reason that tax payments typically understate the total burden of a tax is that the existence of the tax will often induce a change in behavior. Measuring only the taxes paid (does/does not) take account of the loss of satisfaction resulting from the induced change in behavior. The excess burden is the measure of the inefficiency of a particular tax. The principle of efficiency in taxation calls for using taxes that raise the same revenue but with the (largest/smallest) excess burden. That is, he principle of efficiency calls for using taxes that induce the smallest changes in behavior.

Often taxes will affect even those people who do not pay them. Imagine that the government imposes a $50 excise tax on bicycles, paid by consumers at the time of purchase. The tax will shift in the supply curve, as illustrated in **Figure 18-1**. Consumers do not care why the price of bicycles has increased; there is no reason for their demand curve to shift. The change in price from the new tax will lead to a movement along the demand curve. Suppliers collect the tax for the government and are concerned with what is left over after taxes in order to pay their suppliers and cover their labor cost and the opportunity cost of their capital. How suppliers will respond to the after-tax price is given by the original supply curve. The price that consumers must pay comes from adding the excise tax onto the original supply curve and is given by the dashed line in Figure 18-1.

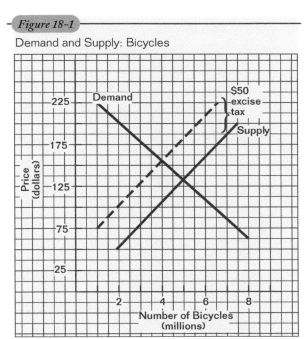

Figure 18-1

Demand and Supply: Bicycles

227

Looking at **Figure 18-1,** we see that compared with the original equilibrium, the new equilibrium involves a
(7) (higher/lower) price to consumers, a (higher/lower) price to suppliers, and a (larger/smaller) quantity of bicycles
produced. It would not be surprising if the change in supply resulted in unemployed bicycle workers, lower
wages for employed bicycle workers, and fewer bicycle firms. None of these workers or firms paid the tax, yet all
were affected by it.

As seen in the bicycle example, when consumers adjust to the new tax, they shift part of the burden onto
others. The question of how the burden of taxes is divided among different groups is the question of tax
(8) _____. At first glance it might appear that the burden of the tax is borne entirely by consumers who pay it at the time of sale. As the bicycle example makes clear, if consumers change their behavior as
a result of the tax, they may succeed in _____ part of the burden of the tax.

The study of tax incidence shows that the incidence of excise or sales taxes depends on the slopes of both
(9) the _____ and _____ curves. Payroll taxes, such as Social Security taxes, are like an
excise tax on labor services. Statistical work suggests that for most workers the supply of labor services is relatively (elastic/inelastic) with respect to wage rates, which in turn suggests that (workers/firms) rather than
_____ bear most of the burden of the payroll tax.

IMPORTANT TERMS AND CONCEPTS QUIZ

Choose the most appropriate definition for each of the following terms.

1. _____ Progressive tax
2. _____ Proportional tax
3. _____ Regressive tax
4. _____ Average tax rate
5. _____ Marginal tax rate
6. _____ Direct taxes
7. _____ Indirect taxes
8. _____ Personal income tax
9. _____ Tax loopholes
10. _____ Tax exempt
11. _____ Tax deductions
12. _____ Payroll tax
13. _____ Corporate income tax
14. _____ Excise tax
15. _____ Social Security system
16. _____ Property tax
17. _____ Fiscal federalism
18. _____ Horizontal equity
19. _____ Vertical equity
20. _____ Ability-to-pay principle
21. _____ Benefits principle of taxation
22. _____ Economic efficiency
23. _____ Burden of a tax
24. _____ Excess burden
25. _____ Incidence of a tax
26. _____ Tax shifting

a. Provision in the tax code that reduces taxes below statutory rates if certain conditions are met
b. Average tax rate increases with income
c. People who derive benefits from a government-provided service should pay the taxes to support it
d. Amount an individual would have to receive to make her as well off with the tax as she was without it
e. Allocation of the burden of a tax to specific groups
f. Tax levied on the assessed values of houses, office buildings, etc.
g. Taxes levied on people
h. Equally situated individuals should be taxed equally
i. Average tax rate falls as income rises
j. Income that is not included in taxable income
k. Sales tax on a specific commodity
l. Situation where economic reactions to a tax mean others bear part of the burden of the tax
m. System of grants from one level of government to the next
n. Ratio of taxes to income
o. Wealthier people should pay higher taxes
p. Average tax rate is the same at all income levels
q. Amount by which the burden of a tax exceeds the tax paid
r. Fraction of each additional dollar of income that is paid in taxes
s. Taxes levied on specific economic activities
t. Differently situated individuals should be taxed differently in a way society deems fair
u. Items that are subtracted before computing taxable income
v. Tax levied on the income of an individual or a family
w. A highly regressive tax levied on the earnings from work
x. Tax levied on the profits of corporations
y. Raises funds from the payroll tax and pays benefits to retirees
z. An economy uses every available opportunity to make someone better off without making anyone else worse off

229

BASIC EXERCISES

This exercise is designed to illustrate how the incidence of an excise tax depends on the elasticity (slope) of the demand and supply curves.

1. **Table 18-1** has data on the demand and supply of running shoes. In **Figure 18-2,** plot the demand curve from column 1 and the supply curve from column 3.

2. Determine the initial equilibrium price and quantity of running shoes.

    Price $ _____

    Quantity _____

3. Now assume that in a fit of pique, non-running legislators impose a fitness tax of $10 on each pair of shoes. Draw the new supply curve by shifting the original supply curve by the magnitude of the excise tax. The new equilibrium price is $ _____ and the new equilibrium quantity is _____.

4. How much more do consumers, who continue to buy running shoes, pay? $ _____. How does this increase in price compare with the excise tax of $10?

5. What is likely to happen to employment, wages, and profits in the running shoe industry?

Table 18-1

Demand for and Supply of Running Shoes

Demand (millions of pairs)		Price (dollars)	Supply (millions of pairs)	
(1)	(2)		(3)	(4)
68	53.0	30	38	48.00
65	52.5	32	40	48.33
62	52.0	34	42	48.67
59	51.5	36	44	49.00
56	51.0	38	46	49.33
53	50.5	40	48	49.67
50	50.0	42	50	50.00
47	49.5	44	52	50.33
44	49.0	46	54	50.67
41	48.5	48	56	51.00
38	48.0	50	58	51.33
35	47.5	52	60	51.67
32	47.0	54	62	52.00

Figure 18-2

Demand for and Supply: Running Shoes

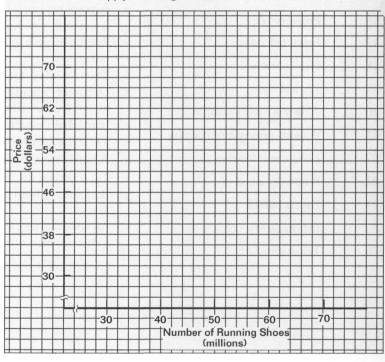

230

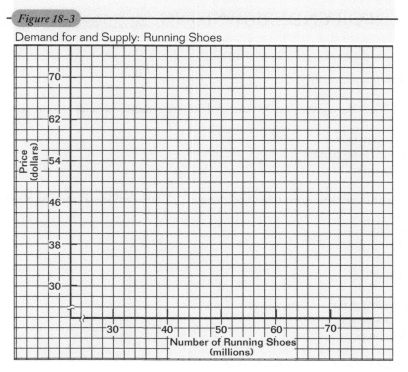

Figure 18-3

Demand for and Supply: Running Shoes

6. On **Figure 18-3,** plot the demand curve from column 2 and supply curve from column 3 of Table 18-1. Comparing Figures 18-2 and 18-3, we have the same supply curve but different demand curves. Both figures should show the same initial equilibrium price and quantity.

7. At the initial equilibrium price and quantity, which demand curve is more elastic? _____. (Review the appropriate material in Chapter 8 if you do not remember how to compute the price elasticity of a demand curve. Remember this distinction when it comes to comparing results.)

8. Now analyze the impact of the imposition of the same excise tax of $10 per pair of running shoes using Figure 18-3. The new equilibrium price is $ _____ and the new equilibrium quantity _____. In which case, Figure 18-2 or Figure 18-3, does the equilibrium price of running shoes rise the most? In which case are the volume of employment and the level of wages likely to fall the least? From this comparison we can conclude that the more inelastic the demand curve, the more the burden of an excise tax will be borne by _____.

9. Use information on demand from either column 1 or 2 and the two supply curves in columns 3 and 4 in Table 18-1 to analyze how the incidence of the tax is affected as the elasticity of supply changes.

SELF-TESTS FOR UNDERSTANDING

TEST A

Circle the most appropriate answer.

1. In the United States during the past 30 years, federal, state, and local taxes as a proportion of GDP have
   a. declined continuously.
   b. fluctuated with little trend.
   c. increased dramatically.

2. For the most part the federal government relies on _____ taxes while state and local governments rely on _____ taxes.
   a. excise; property
   b. sales; income
   c. property; sales
   d. direct; indirect

3. Direct taxes are levied on
   a. specific economic activities.
   b. reproducible property.
   c. people.
   d. the value added at each stage of production.

4. Which of the following are examples of direct taxes? (There may be more than one correct answer.)
   a. excise taxes
   b. income taxes
   c. estate taxes
   d. property taxes

5. Which of the following is an indirect tax?
   a. income taxes
   b. inheritance taxes
   c. head taxes
   d. sales taxes

6. Fiscal federalism refers to
   a. Alexander Hamilton's plan for assuming the debts of the individual states.
   b. federal government control of state and local spending.
   c. grants from one level of government to another.
   d. the balance between taxes paid to the federal government and the value of federal contracts received, measured on a state-by-state basis.

7. If income taxes are progressive, then the average tax rate
   a. decreases as income increases.
   b. is unchanged as income increases.
   c. increases as income increases.

232

8. If income taxes are progressive, then the marginal tax rate will _____ as income increases.
   a. decrease
   b. remain constant
   c. increase
   d. Any of the above are correct.

9. Christopher earned $20,000 last year and paid 10 percent or $2,000 in income taxes. His marginal income tax rate is 15 percent. If his income rises by $10,000 this year to $30,000, his income taxes will go up by
   a. $1,000.
   b. $1,500.
   c. $2,500.
   d. $10,000.

Use the following income tax schedule to answer questions 10 through 12.

Income	Taxes
$20,000	$4,000
$50,000	$10,000
$100,000	$20,000

10. The marginal tax rate
    a. decreases.
    b. is constant.
    c. increases.

11. The average tax rate
    a. decreases.
    b. is constant.
    c. increases.

12. This income tax system is
    a. regressive.
    b. proportional.
    c. progressive.

13. The ability-to-pay principle of taxation is an example of
    a. horizontal equity.
    b. vertical equity.
    c. the benefits principle.
    d. fiscal federalism.

14. If two families are identical in all respects, the principle of horizontal equity says that
    a. both families should pay more income taxes than other families with less income.
    b. both families should pay the same income tax.
    c. both families should have a lower average tax rate than a richer family.
    d. income taxes are, from a social viewpoint, a more appropriate form of taxation than are payroll taxes.

15. Which of the following is an example of the benefits principle of taxation?
    a. excise taxes on expensive jewelry
    b. higher property taxes as a percent of market value for more expensive homes
    c. public support for a new baseball stadium that is financed by a tax on baseball tickets
    d. Social Security taxes

16. The burden of a tax is defined as
    a. revenue raised minus the cost of collection.
    b. the proportion of taxes paid by individuals rather than corporations.
    c. the amount of money that would make a taxpayer as well off as he was before the tax was introduced.
    d. revenue raised plus the cost of collection.

17. The burden of most taxes is _____ the revenue raised.
    a. less than
    b. equal to
    c. greater than

18. The excess burden of a tax is
    a. the cost of collecting the tax.
    b. a measure of the inefficiency of the tax.
    c. best measured by the amount of complaining done by taxpayers.
    d. highest when the tax induces the least change in behavior.

19. A sales tax on which of the following will involve a small excess burden?
    a. a tax on a commodity with a zero price elasticity of demand
    b. a tax on a commodity with a very high elasticity of demand
    c. a tax on a commodity consumed primarily by poor families
    d. a tax on a commodity consumed primarily by rich families

20. The flypaper theory of tax incidence, which says that the burden of a tax is borne by those who pay the tax, is
    a. usually right.
    b. an example of the benefits approach to taxation.
    c. usually wrong.
    d. a measure of the vertical inequity of taxes.

21. Tax loopholes typically introduce new inefficiencies and _____ the progressivity of the income tax.
    a. reduce
    b. have little effect on
    c. increase

TEST B

Circle T or F for true or false.

T F   1. During the past 30 years federal, state, and local taxes have taken an ever-increasing share of the GDP.

T F   2. Federal payroll taxes are a more important source of revenue than the federal corporate income tax.

234

T　F　3. State personal income taxes are an example of a direct, as opposed to indirect, tax.

T　F　4. State taxes are primarily indirect taxes.

T　F　5. The principle of horizontal equity says that equally situated individuals should be taxed equally.

T　F　6. The ability-to-pay principle says that people who derive benefits from a particular public service should pay the taxes to finance it.

T　F　7. The burden of a tax is normally less than the revenue raised by the tax.

T　F　8. If a tax does not induce a change in economic behavior, then there is no excess burden.

T　F　9. The flypaper theory of incidence is correct in regard to Social Security taxes.

T　F　10. The concept of excess burden proves that taxes can never improve efficiency.

SUPPLEMENTARY EXERCISES

1. **How Flat Is the Flat Tax?**

The proposition that a comprehensive income tax with no loopholes would increase efficiency has led some to advocate what is called a flat tax. Most flat tax proposals have a basic exemption after which all income is taxed at the same rate. Proposals differ in the magnitude of the basic exemption, the tax rate to be used after that, whether some forms of income might be excluded from taxation, or whether some deductions would be allowed. (See Economics in Action below for a discussion of this last point.)

　　Consider a flat tax that uses a rate of 20 percent but allows a personal exemption of $5,000 for every individual— man, woman, or child. Taxable income for a family of four would be $20,000 less than their before-tax income. Complete **Table 18-2** to compute the marginal and average tax rates that a

Table 18-2

Marginal and Average Tax Rates for a Family of Four

Before Tax Income	Total Taxes	Average Tax Rate[a]	Marginal Tax Rate[b]
$20,000	_____	_____	
$30,000	_____	_____	_____
$40,000	_____	_____	_____
$50,000	_____	_____	_____
$100,000	_____	_____	_____
$250,000	_____	_____	_____

[a]Average tax rate = (Total taxes) ÷ (Before tax Income)
[b]Marginal tax rate = (Change in taxes) ÷ (Change in income)

family of four would face at different levels of income.

235

2. **Revenue-Maximizing Cigarette Taxes**

In the early 1990s there was considerable discussion of a possible increase in the federal tax on cigarettes. Some saw an increase as a cash cow to finance medical care reform or to help reduce the federal deficit. If interested in maximizing the amount of revenue, one would need to be careful not to raise the tax so high that demand fell so much and tax revenues actually declined.

Writing separately in *The New York Times* in June of 1993, economists Jeffrey Harris and Michael Grossman offered dramatically different estimates of the demand elasticity. Drawing on Canadian experience, Harris suggested that the price elasticity of demand for cigarettes was around 0.25. He estimated that a $2 increase in cigarette taxes would raise an additional $28 billion in revenue each year. Grossman argued that because of the addictive properties of smoking, the response to a change in price would be small in the short run but much larger in the long run.

The following straight-line demand curves are approximations of the Harris estimate and Grossman's long-run demand curve. Both of these demand curves have been constructed to mimic actual price and quantity data for 1992 when 24.9 billion packs of cigarettes were sold in the United States at an average price of $2 a pack that included a tax of $0.24.

Harris: $Q = 30.80 - 2.95\,(P + T)$

Grossman: $Q = 46.72 - 10.91\,(P + T)$

a. Verify that when $P + T = 2$ each demand curve is consistent with the 1992 quantity and price combination.
b. For each estimate of the demand curve and on the assumption that the supply curve for cigarettes is horizontal at a net-of-tax price of $1.76 a pack, i.e., $P = 1.76$, what tax maximizes tax revenues? (If you have access to a spreadsheet program on a computer, you might set up a small example that calculates the quantity demanded and tax revenues at different taxes. Alternatively, after writing down the expression for total tax revenues, you could differentiate the expression to find the value of T that maximizes revenue.)
c. What is the price elasticity of demand for each demand curve? For which estimate of demand, the estimate with the high or low elasticity, is the revenue-maximizing tax highest? Why?
d. Actual tax revenues will depend upon the price elasticity of supply as well as the price elasticity of demand. Question b assumed that the price elasticity of supply was infinite. What would happen to the incidence of any increase in taxes if the price elasticity of supply were zero or somewhere in between?

ECONOMICS IN ACTION

A PERSON'S MORTGAGE IS HER TAX DEDUCTION

While a person's home may or may not be a castle, her mortgage is likely to yield a handsome tax deduction. Under current law, taxpayers may deduct from taxable income mortgage interest on up to $1 million of mortgage debt they have used to acquire and improve first or second homes and interest on up to $100,000 of home-equity loans regardless of the purpose of the loan. No other consumer interest is deductible. Whether it is in an individual's best interest to take the mortgage interest deduction depends upon the magnitude of

236

her mortgage interest and other deductions vis-à-vis the standard deduction. For example, in 2004, a family could itemize deductions or take a standard deduction of $9,500. If a family's deductions, including mortgage interest, totaled less than $9,500, then it made more sense to use the standard deduction. In the mid-1990s, at a time when about 64 percent of households were homeowners and, of these, a bit less than 60 percent had a mortgage, only 28 percent of taxpayers used the mortgage interest deduction. For the others, using the standard deduction rather than itemizing was preferable.

Not surprisingly, higher income taxpayers with larger homes and larger mortgages derive the largest benefit from the mortgage interest deduction. Peter Dreier, a professor of public policy at Occidental College in Los Angeles, estimated that in the mid-1990s, 44 percent of the tax benefits associated with the mortgage interest deduction went to the richest 5 percent of taxpayers. Professor Dreier estimated that the tax savings for these rich taxpayers was about $22 billion annually, an amount that was roughly the same as government spending on subsidized housing for the poor.

The popularity of the mortgage interest deduction is such that a number of prominent flat tax proposals would retain the deduction while attempting to eliminate other deductions and loopholes. For example, in early 1996 Republican candidates for president were divided on this issue. According to a story in *The New York Times* subtitled "Republicans tiptoe around the mortgage deduction," only Malcolm Forbes, Jr. stated publicly that he favored elimination of the mortgage interest deduction as part of implementation of a flat tax. Pat Buchanan wanted to retain it, while Senators Bob Dole and Phil Gramm managed to avoid taking a hard position one way or the other.

What explains the popularity of a mortgage interest deduction when only a minority of taxpayers use the deduction each year and the benefits go disproportionately to rich taxpayers? Counting only those who use the deduction in a single year understates the constituency who supports the deduction. Many homeowners took advantage of the mortgage interest deduction when they first bought their home. Sellers and potential homeowners see the deduction as an important part of a buyer's financial planning. Some argue that public policy should support home ownership and that the mortgage interest deduction does just that. Others argue that one could achieve the same objective with a tax credit rather than a tax deduction and that a tax credit would be fairer.[1] Stricter limits on the magnitude of mortgage interest that could be deducted have also been proposed. States with the highest house prices, for example, California, New York, Connecticut, and New Jersey, would be most affected by such a change.

There is concern that elimination of the mortgage interest deduction would disrupt housing markets causing the price of many homes to decline. Estimates of such effects vary, but most analysts agree that the largest adjustments would occur for the most expensive homes. Should the deduction be eliminated suddenly, the Mortgage Bankers Association projects an increase in mortgage defaults. Economists who argue in favor of elimination of the mortgage interest deduction see it as part of a broader strategy of tax reform. They are concerned that the favorable tax treatment of mortgage interest has distorted investment away from business

---

[1]Assume that two families each pay $1,000 mortgage interest. A tax credit of 20 percent would reduce the taxes of both families by $200. In contrast the value of a deduction depends upon a family's marginal tax rate, which in turn depends upon its income. For example, in 2004 the value of a $1,000 deduction to a family of four earning $35,000 was $100 while the same $1,000 deduction would save $350 for a rich family paying the highest marginal tax rate.

237

capital toward houses, in particular, housing for the rich. One might also note that not all countries allow homeowners to deduct mortgage interest. For example, levels of home ownership are high in Canada and Australia, two countries without mortgage interest deduction.

1. Should anything be done about the mortgage interest deduction? Should it be eliminated? Should stricter limits be adopted? Should it be turned into a tax credit?

2. If a decision were made to eliminate or change the mortgage interest deduction, what would you expect to happen to house prices and the affordability of housing? What provisions, if any, should be made for homeowners who purchased homes believing that the mortgage interest deduction would not be changed?

SOURCE: "The Pitfall in the Flat Tax, Republicans Tiptoe Around the Mortgage Deduction," *The New York Times,* January 12, 1996.

STUDY QUESTIONS

1. Should income taxes be progressive or proportional? Explain your reasoning.

2. Without changing the level of spending, should your state increase income taxes in order to reduce sales taxes or increase sales taxes to reduce income taxes? Why?

3. Why do economists consider the Social Security tax to be regressive?

4. In the final analysis, who pays the Social Security tax, workers or firms?

5. What is fiscal federalism?

6. What is the difference between horizontal and vertical equity?

7. If a progressive income tax meets social concerns about vertical equity, can it also satisfy concerns about horizontal equity? Explain.

8. What is the difference between the benefits principle of taxation and the concept of ability to pay?

9. Why do economists say that the burden of a tax is usually greater than the revenue raised by the tax?

10. Is it true that the more elastic the demand curve, the smaller the amount of any sales tax that consumers will pay? Explain.

11. Should the United States move to a flat tax system?

12. What would you do about Social Security?

ECONOMICS ONLINE

Get your tax forms and find data about the federal tax system from the IRS homepage.

http://www.irs.gov/

Should states use tax incentives as a way to attract businesses? Does the country as a whole benefit from this sort of activity or is this just a way for companies to minimize their taxes by playing off states against each other? Examine these questions at a web site maintained by the Federal Reserve Bank of Minneapolis:

http://minneapolisfed.org/research/studies/econwar

The Congressional Budget Office releases studies on a variety of tax topics on a regular basis. The CBO can be found on the web at http://www.cbo.gov. Studies that might be of special interest include the following:

- Effective Federal Tax Rates: 1979-2001, April 2004

http://www.cbo.gov/showdoc.cfm?index=5324

- Effective Federal Tax Rates Under Current Law, 2001 to 2014, August 2004

http://www.cbo.gov/showdoc.cfm?index=5746

- Recent CBO studies on Social Security are listed at

http://www.cbo.gov/publications/collections/collections.cfm?collect=5

The Tax Policy Center is a joint venture of the Urban Institute and Brookings Institution "to provide independent analyses of current and longer-term tax issues and to communicate its analyses to the public and to policymakers in a timely and accessible manner."

http://www.taxpolicycenter.org

Pricing the Factors of Production

Important Terms and Concepts

Factors of production

Entrepreneurship

Marginal physical product (MPP)

Marginal revenue product (MRP)

Derived demand

Capital

Investment

Interest

Economic rent

Marginal land

Economic profit

Invention

Innovation

Learning Objectives

After completing this chapter, you should be able to:

- explain why the demand curve for a factor of production is the downward-sloping portion of its marginal revenue product curve.

  explain why the demand for inputs is a derived demand.

- distinguish between investment and capital.

- explain how changes in interest rates may affect the profitability of specific investment decisions and hence the demand for funds.

- explain why the supply of funds from savers with fixed savings objectives may not increase when interest rates rise.

- explain who gains, who loses, and why, under an effective usury ceiling.

- distinguish between land rents and economic rents.

- identify inputs that receive economic rent, given supply curves of various slopes.

- explain why the fact that apartment buildings need to be maintained and that they can be reproduced at close to constant cost implies that, in the long run, rent control measures are likely to be self-defeating.

- explain why, in the real world, profits are likely to offer returns in excess of the interest rate.

- explain how the concept of economic rent is relevant to issues concerning the taxation of profits.

CHAPTER REVIEW

This chapter initiates the discussion of input prices by considering what determines the rental price of money, the rental price of land, and the income of entrepreneurs. If this material is combined with the material in the next chapter on wages—the rental price for labor services—and the material in Chapter 17 on the price of natural resources, we have a complete theory of income distribution based on marginal

(1) _____. This chapter and the next build upon our earlier discussion of optimal input use by firms. We saw earlier that the demand for factors of production can be derived from profit-maximizing considerations. A firm should be willing to pay for labor, land, natural resources, and so forth because it can use these factors to produce and sell output. As we have learned, the demand curve for a particular factor of production is derived from the downward-sloping portion of the marginal _____ product curve.

INTEREST

Interest rates adjust to balance the demand for funds by borrowers and the supply of funds from lenders. The

(2) demand curve for funds has a (<u>negative/positive</u>) slope, indicating that at lower interest rates people will want to borrow (<u>less/more</u>). The supply curve of funds is most likely to have a (<u>negative/positive</u>) slope, indicating that a (<u>higher/lower</u>) interest rate is necessary to induce lenders to increase the supply of loans.[1] An effective usury ceiling would impose an interest rate (<u>above/below</u>) the market clearing rate as determined by the intersection of the demand and supply curves.

The demand for funds for business borrowing derives from a consideration of the profitability of investment projects. In earlier chapters we talked about capital and labor as factors of production. Investment projects add to the stock of capital. The profitability of investment projects is another way of referring to the marginal revenue product of more capital. The profitability of investment projects is complicated because most projects require dollar outlays immediately while offering returns in the future. To evaluate the profitability of an investment we need some way of comparing current and future dollars. Economists and business people compare future and present dollars through a process called _____. As explained in the appendix to this chapter, this process relies on interest rate calculations. Higher interest rates will mean that (<u>fewer/more</u>) investment projects will be profitable. Thus higher interest rates will be associated with a (<u>higher/lower</u>) quantity of funds demanded and imply a negatively sloped demand curve for business borrowing.

RENT

When considering the notion of rent, remember that economists use the term in a special way different from

(3) everyday usage. Most of the rent that you may pay for an apartment (<u>is/is not</u>) economic rent. Economic rent refers to the earnings of a factor of production that (<u>equal/exceed</u>) the minimum amount necessary to keep that factor in its current employment.

---

[1]Savers with fixed goals, e.g., saving for a specific purpose, may be able to reduce the amount of money they need to lend if interest rates increase.

242

If the supply curve of some factor, such as land, is really vertical, it means that the factor would be willing to work for as little as nothing. It also means that it is impossible to duplicate this factor at any cost; otherwise, a high enough price would induce an increase in supply, and the supply curve would not be vertical. In the case of a vertical supply curve, (some/all) of the market price would be economic rent. If the supply curve of some fac-   (4) tor is a horizontal line, the market price will reflect exactly what is necessary to induce any supply. In this case an economist would say that the factor receives _____ economic rent.

An upward-sloping supply curve means that higher prices will induce an increase in supply, but there will be some units of supply that would have been present at lower prices. In this case (most/all) units of the factor   (5) will receive some economic rent. In fact, it is only the marginal unit, the unit on the supply curve at the market equilibrium price, that earns no economic rent. The market price is as high as it is to induce this last unit to supply itself. All other units would have been available at a lower price, and thus (part/all) of their earnings are economic rent. Land is a traditional input to use when talking about rent, but remember that land is not the only factor to earn economic rent. Anyone who would stay in a particular job for less pay, because he or she likes the work or the location, or for any other reason, (is/is not) earning some economic rent.

When considering land rentals it is clear that not all land is the same: Some parcels are more productive or better located than others. Economists would expect that land rents, the price for using a piece of land for a period of time, will adjust to reflect these differences. More productive land that produces the same output at lower cost will receive a (higher/lower) land rent. In equilibrium, rents should adjust so that the cost of produc-   (6) ing the same quantity of output, including land rents, will be _____ on all parcels of land. If not, there is a clear incentive to use the land with lower total cost. This incentive to switch parcels increases the rent on the originally low-cost piece of land and decreases rent on the other pieces of land. The process stops only when land rentals have adjusted to again equate total cost.

As with any other productive factor, an increase in the demand for goods produced with land will (decrease/increase) the demand for land. Poor quality land, whose use was unprofitable at lower output prices,   (7) will now become profitable to use. Thus, more land will be used, and land rents will again adjust to equal- ize the costs of production on all parcels. As a result, the rent on previously used, higher quality land will (increase/decrease). An additional part of the response to increased land demand is likely to be (more/less) in- tensive use of existing land.

PROFIT

Profits are a residual item after revenues have been used to pay other costs—labor, material inputs, interest on borrowed funds, rent, and taxes. Profits also represent the return on equity investments in a firm.[2] In a world of perfect certainty, capitalists should expect the profits on their investments to offer a return just equal to the in- terest rate. The rate of interest would be the opportunity cost of their equity investment in the firm. Any higher

---

[2]Equity refers here to the amount of their own money the owners have invested in their company. Specifically, if they dissolved the company and paid off its creditors, the amount left over is their equity.

return would be competed away. Any lower return would lead some funds to be invested elsewhere in the pursuit of returns at least equal to the interest rate. (Remember that in simple competitive markets, economic profits equal zero in long-run equilibrium.)

In the real world, investments are not certain. Many business investments look like uncertain gambles. If entrepreneurs dislike taking risks, then profits will have to offer them the expectation of returns that are (greater/less) than the rate of interest. Profits that are the result of monopoly power would be (greater/less) than the interest rate. Finally, successful innovation will often give an entrepreneur temporary monopoly profits and lead to a rate of profit that is (greater/less) than the interest rate. The effects of taxing profits will depend upon whether profits are mostly economic rents or mostly a necessary return to attract entrepreneurial talent.

IMPORTANT TERMS AND CONCEPTS QUIZ

Choose the best definition for the following terms.

1. _____ Factors of production
2. _____ Entrepreneurship
3. _____ Marginal physical product
4. _____ Marginal revenue product
5. _____ Derived demand
6. _____ Capital
7. _____ Investment
8. _____ Interest
9. _____ Economic rent
10. _____ Marginal land
11. _____ Economic profit
12. _____ Invention
13. _____ Innovation

a. Payment to a factor of production in excess of the minimum amount necessary to keep the factor in its present employment

b. Additional units of a given input add diminishing amounts to total output

c. Starting firms, introducing innovations, and taking the necessary risks in seeking business opportunities

d. Change in sales revenue from selling the marginal physical product of an additional unit of input

e. Flow of resources into the production of new capital

f. Act of generating a new idea

g. Inputs used in the production process

h. Payment for the use of funds

i. Land on the borderline of being used

j. Producer's demand for inputs

k. Act of putting a new idea into practical use

l. Increase in output from a one-unit increase in a given input

m. Stock of plant and equipment from past investment

n. Total revenue minus total cost including the opportunity cost of owner-supplied inputs

BASIC EXERCISES

This exercise is designed to illustrate how differences in land rents reflect differences in productivity.

This summer Darlene can work as a checker at the local grocery store for as many hours as she wants, earning $10 an hour. She also is considering raising flowers for sale on one of two plots of land. The sunny plot has good soil, and Darlene estimates that if she worked 40 hours a week she could earn $500 a week raising flowers on this land. The second plot is marginal land available for free. It would require the use of fertilizer and special mulches to raise the same quantity of flowers. Darlene estimates these extra costs would total $60 a week.

1. Calculate Darlene's economic profit from using the marginal plot of land on the assumption that it is available at zero rent. Do not forget to include the opportunity cost of Darlene's own work as an element of cost.

2. If Darlene's estimate of the increased cost of using the marginal land is typical of other uses, what market rent would you expect to be charged for the use of the sunny plot and why?

3. Explain why the profit that Darlene could earn from using the marginal plot of land limits the rent the owner of the sunny plot will be able to charge.

SELF-TESTS FOR UNDERSTANDING

TEST A

Circle the most appropriate answer.

1. The demand for factors of production is
   a. an applied demand.
   b. insensitive to changes in the price of factors.
   c. best represented as an upward-sloping curve.
   d. a derived demand.

2. Profit-maximizing firms will use more of a productive factor as long as the price of the factor is less than its
   a. marginal revenue product.
   b. marginal cost.
   c. marginal physical product.
   d. average product.

3. The demand curve for productive factors is the downward-sloping portion of the relevant
   a. marginal physical product curve.
   b. marginal cost curve.
   c. marginal revenue product curve.
   d. average cost curve.

245

4. If the price of widgets increases,
    a. we should see a movement along the demand curves for factors producing widgets.
    b. the demand curves for factors producing widgets should shift to the right.
    c. the best guess is that there will be little change in the demand for factors producing widgets.
    d. the demand curves for factors producing widgets should shift to the left.

5. The concept of discounting suggests that when compared with a dollar next year, a dollar today is worth
    a. less.
    b. the same.
    c. more.

6. If interest rates increase, the difference in the value of $100 today compared with $100 next year will
    a. decrease.
    b. be unchanged.
    c. increase.
    d. be impossible to determine.

7. Firms produce output using land, labor, natural resources, entrepreneurship, and
    a. capital.
    b. investment.
    c. interest.
    d. economic rent.

8. Firms undertake _____ to add to the stock of _____.
    a. innovation; invention
    b. discounting; investment
    c. investment; capital
    d. capital; investment

9. Which of the following is an example of investment as opposed to capital?
    a. the fleet of 747s owned by American Airlines
    b. Julia's purchase of 100 shares of Xerox stock
    c. the five apartment buildings owned by Julio
    d. the new warehouse that Kimberly will have built this year

10. Economists expect that land rents will
    a. adjust to equalize total costs of production across different parcels of land.
    b. mean that more productive parcels of land receive higher rents.
    c. result in more intensive use of more productive parcels of land.
    d. all of the above.

11. Parcel of land G can be used to raise corn at a cost of $50,000. The same amount of corn can be raised on parcel P for $75,000. An economist would expect the rent on parcel G to exceed that on parcel P by
    a. $25,000.
    b. $50,000.
    c. $75,000.
    d. $125,000.

12. Marginal land refers to land that
    a. is most productive for growing any given crop.
    b. is on the borderline of being used in productive activity.
    c. earns economic rent.
    d. borders interstate highways in rural areas.

13. The term economic rent refers to
    a. the sales tax portion of consumer purchases.
    b. rent paid by economists for their apartments.
    c. earnings by factors of production greater than necessary to induce supply.
    d. land rents.

14. If the supply curve for some factor of production can be represented as a horizontal line, an economist would say that _____ of the income earned by this factor is economic rent.
    a. none
    b. some
    c. all

15. An input will earn pure economic rent if the supply curve for the input is
    a. horizontal.
    b. upward sloping.
    c. vertical.

16. Which of the following individuals are earning economic rent?
    a. Ruth, who says, "If this job paid any less I'd quit; it wouldn't be worth the hassle."
    b. Sergio, who says, "This job is so interesting I'd work here even for a lot less."
    c. Nick, whose purchase of an apartment building should bring him a return equal to the interest rate.
    d. Sophia, who is expecting a substantial profit from her investment in the manufacture of solar energy panels to compensate her for the risks she is taking.

17. Rent seeking refers to
    a. efforts of college students to find apartments each fall.
    b. the use of productive resources in the pursuit of political opportunities for profits.
    c. attempts to get departments within a company to pay for space they occupy.
    d. a landlord's efforts to collect from deadbeat tenants.

18. In a world of competitive firms with no uncertainty or risk, economists expect that the profit rate will be
    a. less than the rate of interest.
    b. equal to the rate of interest.
    c. higher than the rate of interest.

19. Monopoly power, whether permanent or temporary, means that profits will be
    a. less than the rate of interest.
    b. equal to the rate of interest.
    c. higher than the rate of interest.

20. Higher taxes on profits will have little impact if
    a. profits are mostly economic rent.
    b. profits are equal to nominal interest rates.
    c. profits are growing.
    d. the supply curve for entrepreneurial talent is horizontal.

TEST B

Circle T or F for true or false.

T   F   1. The demand curve for a factor of production is identical to its curve of marginal physical productivity.

T   F   2. Interest rates represent the market price for the use of funds.

T   F   3. Discounting means using the rate of interest to compare future and present dollars.

T   F   4. The factories that the Ford Motor Company uses to produce cars are an example of capital rather than investment.

T   F   5. According to economists, only land earns economic rent.

T   F   6. Inputs available in perfectly elastic supply will earn no economic rent.

T   F   7. The rent on any piece of land should equal the difference between production costs on that piece of land and production costs on the next-best available piece of land.

T   F   8. The law of diminishing returns implies that an increase in the demand for land will actually reduce the rent paid on most parcels of land.

T   F   9. The reason that most rent-control laws have adverse effects in the long run is that the long-run supply of structures, as opposed to land, is likely to be quite elastic.

T   F   10. Economic theory proves that the rate of profits must equal the rate of interest.

| Appendix | *Discounting and Present Value*

Important Terms and Concepts

Discounting

Present value

Learning Objective

After completing the exercises below, you should be able to

• appreciate how discounting or present value calculations can help when considering investment decisions.

IMPORTANT TERMS AND CONCEPTS QUIZ

Choose the best definition for the following term.

1. _____ Present value
   a. The current value of dollars to be received or paid at various dates in the future
   b. Future worth of a sum of money receivable or payable at the present date

BASIC EXERCISES

1. **Discounting and Investment Decision**

   Eric has an opportunity to purchase a machine to make gyros. The machine cost $4,000 and is expected to last two years. After other expenses, Eric expects this investment to return $2,000 next year and $2,500 in two years. Is buying the machine a good investment?

   a. Fill in the column of **Table 19-1** to compute the present value of costs and returns on the assumption that Eric uses his own $4,000 and the interest rate is 10 percent.

   Table 19-1

   Cash Flows from Investing in Eric's Gyro Machine

Time	Item	Amount	Present Value* 5 percent	Present Value* 10 percent
Now	Cost	$4,000	$4,000	$4,000
One year	Return	2,000	_____	_____
Two years	Return	2,500	_____	_____
		Present value of all returns	_____	_____
		Net present value of project	_____	_____

   *Present value = dollars in *n* years ÷ $(1 + i)^n$ = (dollars in the *n*th year) divided by (1 plus the rate of interest multiplied by itself *n* times)

   b. Add up the present value of the returns and compare this sum with the cost of the machine. Which is greater? _____. If the interest rate is 10 percent, should Eric purchase the machine? _____.

c. Assume now that the interest rate is 5 percent. Fill in the relevant column of the table to compute the present value of the returns at an interest rate of 5 percent.

d. Sum the present value of the returns and compare this sum with the cost of the machine. Which is greater? _____. If the interest rate is 5 percent, should Eric purchase the machine? _____.

e. The decision rule discussed in the text, and the one you should have used when answering questions b and d, compares the present value of future returns to the cost of an investment project.[3] If the present value of the returns exceeds the cost, it means that Eric can do better by undertaking the investment than by investing in financial assets that yield the rate of interest we used to discount the future returns. If the present value of the returns is less than the cost, it means that Eric would do better with a financial investment. You can verify that this is the case by filling in the missing parts of **Table 19-2** for interest rates of 5 and 10 percent.

Table 19-2

Can Eric Do as Well by Investing $4,000 at the Rate of Interest?

	Interest Rate	
	5 percent	10 percent
1. Initial deposit	$4,000	$4,000
2. Interest after one year (5 percent and 10 percent of line 1)	_____	_____
3. Balance after one year (line 1 plus line 2)	_____	_____
4. Withdrawal after one year*	$2,000	$2,000
5. New balance (line 3 minus line 4)	_____	_____
6. Interest during second year (5 percent and 10 percent of line 5)	_____	_____
7. Balance after second year (line 5 plus line 6)	_____	_____

Compare line 7 with the $2,500 Eric would have received in the second year if he had bought the gyro machine. Line 7 should be greater (less) if the net present value of the project in Table 17-1 is negative (positive). That is, if the net present value of the project is negative (positive), Eric will do better (worse) by making a financial investment at the given rate of interest.

*This $2,000 matches the return after one year from the gyro investment.

---

f. What if Eric had to borrow the money? Would the same sorts of calculations be sufficient to help you decide whether he should borrow the money? The answer is yes. The reason is that while figuring the present value of the returns, you are accounting for interest payments whether Eric has the money or not. If he does not have the money, he will need to pay a lender. Even if he does have the money he will need to "pay" himself as much as he might have earned in some other investment. That is, he will need to meet the opportunity cost of his own money. Fill in the missing parts of **Table 19-3**, which has been constructed to illustrate just this point.

To summarize:

a. Present value calculations use interest rates to transform dollars in the future into their equivalent today.

b. Comparing the present value of returns and costs is a good way to evaluate investment opportunities.

c. Comparing the present value of returns and costs is a good procedure whether you have to borrow the money or not, assuming that you can borrow or lend at the same rate of interest you are using in your present value calculations.

---

[3]In this example all costs occur "today" and all returns come in the future. Thus one needs to discount the returns and compare them to the cost. If a project will incur costs in future years, then one should compare the present value of all current and future costs with the present value of all future returns.

Table 19-3

What if Eric Had to Borrow the $4,000?

		Interest Rate	
		5 percent	10 percent
1.	Amount borrowed	$4,000	$4,000
2.	Interest due at end of first year	$ 200	$ 400
3.	Cash flow from investment	$2,000	$2,000
4.	Net cash flow after interest payment (line 3 minus line 2)	_____	_____
5.	Interest earned during second year by investing net cash flow (5 percent and 10 percent of line 4)	_____	_____
6.	Cash flow from investment	$2,500	$2,500
7.	Total at end of second year (line 4 plus line 5 plus line 6)	_____	_____
8.	Interest due at end of second year	$ 200	$ 400
9.	Loan repayment	$4,000	$4,000
10.	Net (line 7 minus line 8 and line 9)	_____	_____

The crucial question is whether the gyro investment offers any return after paying back the loan with interest. Any dollars left over are pure profit for Eric since he did not invest any of his own money. It should be true that Eric will have a positive (negative) net if the present value of returns is greater (less) than the present value of costs. Is it?

(The entries on line 10 are dollars in the second year. What is the present value of these dollars? How do these present values compare with the net present values calculated in Table 17-1 above?)

d. If the present value of returns equals the present value of costs, an investment opportunity offers the same return as investing at the rate of interest.

e. If the present value of returns exceeds the present value of costs, an investment opportunity offers a greater return than investing at the rate of interest.

f. If the present value of returns is less than the present value of costs, an investment opportunity offers a worse return than investing at the rate of interest.

2. **When Is $1,000,000 Not $1,000,000?**

On Wednesday, April 14, 1993, Don Calhoun earned $1,000,000 for about five seconds of work. Or did he? After reluctantly accompanying a friend to a basketball game between the Chicago Bulls and Miami Heat, Mr. Calhoun was chosen at random from the audience. Standing at one free-throw line, he was given one shot at the basket at the other end of the court. His baseball-like hurl was all net.

Like most state lotteries, the million dollars that Mr. Calhoun received was not $1,000,000 immediately, rather it was a commitment to pay $50,000 a year for 20 years. What is the cost of Mr. Calhoun's $1,000,000 to the restaurant and soft-drink sponsors of the long free-throw contest (or their insurance company)? Why is it less than $1,000,000?

SUPPLEMENTARY EXERCISES

CAN YOU SHARE IN MONOPOLY PROFITS?

Assume that the major oil companies are able to exercise considerable monopoly power and, as a result, earn substantial monopoly profits on their investments, far in excess of the interest rate. Can you share these profits and earn the same high rate of return by buying oil company stocks?

What determines the price of oil company stocks? An economist would expect the market price to be close to the present value of the future returns from owning the stock, that is, close to the present value of expected future dividends and capital gains. Thus if dividends are high because of huge monopoly profits, the price of the stock will be _____. If huge monopoly profits and the resulting future dividends were known for sure, what rate of return do you think you could earn by buying oil company stocks? Just who does earn those monopoly profits?

ECONOMICS IN ACTION

NICE WORK IF YOU CAN GET IT

A number of observers have charged that compensation for executives of American corporations is excessive. Certainly the compensation received by some individuals has been eye-catching, notably the $650 million that Charles Wang, CEO of Computer Associates, realized in 1999 and the $706 million that Lawrence Ellison, CEO of Oracle, received in 2002. The $236 million that Michael Dell, CEO of Dell Computer, received in 2000 seem puny only by comparison. In the 1980s, direct salary payments were a major part of executive compensation. Since then stock options have become increasingly important and by the late 1990s accounted for over half of executive compensation at large companies.[4] Stock options give an individual the right to purchase stock at a specified price. This price is called the exercise price of the option. If a company does well and its stock price increases, there may be a substantial difference between the stock price and the exercise price. The increasing importance of stock options in executive compensation reflects several factors: legislation authored by U.S. Representative Martin Sabo (D-Minnesota) to limit the ability of corporations to deduct large salary payments from taxable income; criticism that compensation bore little relation to performance; the 1990s stock market boom; and changes in tax laws that tax capital gains at lower rates than salary.

While stock options would seem to link compensation to performance, critics say that in practice compensation and the awarding of options often bear little relation to stock performance. Since executives sit on each other's boards of directors they are hardly the ones to be trusted when it comes to setting each other's compensation. There was much criticism of rising executive compensation in 2001 and 2002, a period when stock prices dropped by an average of 40 percent. *Forbes* magazine reports annually on CEO compensation and grades pay

---

[4]Stock options are not restricted just to top executives. Startup companies often offer stock options to attract employees.

252

against performance. In 2004 Forbes gave the Disney Corporation an F for awarding its CEO, Michael Eisner, compensation that averaged $121 million a year over the previous six years when investors in Disney stock were losing 5 percent a year.

Writing in *The Wall Street Journal* in 1999, Alfred Rappaport, professor emeritus at Northwestern University, Kellogg Graduate School of Management, argued that the structure of stock options is not efficient. Just as a rising tide raises all boats, a rising stock market is likely to result in stock price increases that have nothing to do with the performance or leadership of individual CEOs. Rappaport argues that much of the rise in stock values in the late 1990s was related to declines in interest rates and inflation, factors that bore no relation to the contributions of an individual CEO. Citing a survey by LEK Consulting, Rappaport notes that more than 60 percent of stock options granted from 1993 to 1999 were for below average performance; that is, the increase in the price of stock of these companies was less than the increase in broad market averages. Rappaport argues that the exercise price of stock options should be linked to an index of the stock of a company's competition as is the case for a number of European companies. In this way, options would have value only if the company's stock outperformed its competitors.

SOURCE: Alfred Rappaport, "Stock Options that Don't Reward Laggards," *The Wall Street Journal*, March 30, 1999; "Executive Pay," *The Wall Street Journal*, April 8, 1999; "CEOs and Their Indian Rope Trick," *The Economist*, December 11, 2004.

1. What sorts of incentives and rewards for executive performance are in the best interests of stockholders? of the economy?

2. Should there be limits on executive compensation? If so, what and why? What would be the effect on incentives of different limits?

3. What do you think of Rappaport's idea to link the exercise price of stock options to a relevant stock price index?

STUDY QUESTIONS

1. What does it mean to say that the demand for a factor of production is a derived demand?

2. Why is the demand curve for a factor of production the downward-sloping portion of the factor's curve of marginal revenue product?

3. What is the difference between investment and capital?

4. How does discounting help a firm determine the profitability of investment projects?

5. How is the profitability of investment projects affected when interest rates change?

6. What is the definition of economic rent?

253

7. Why isn't the rent you pay for an apartment economic rent?

8. What is meant by the statement in the text that almost all employees earn some economic rent?

9. What explains differences in rent for different parcels of land?

10. Why doesn't competition work to limit profits to the rate of interest?

11. What is the difference between invention and innovation?

ECONOMICS ONLINE

You can get information on executive compensation online from *Forbes* magazine.

http://www.forbes.com/ceos

The AFL-CIO maintains a web page that tracks executive compensation.

http://www.aflcio.org/corporateamerica/paywatch/

Labor and Entrepreneurship: The Human Inputs

20

Important Terms and Concepts

Investments in human capital

Substitution effect

Income effect

Backward-bending

Human capital theory

Labor union

Monopsony

Bilateral monopoly

Collective bargaining

Innovative entrepreneurship

Marginal revenue product of labor (MRP_l)

Learning Objectives

After completing this chapter, you should be able to:

- explain how the demand for labor is derived from a firm's profit-maximizing decisions about the use of factors of production.

- discuss recent trends in American labor markets.

- describe the impact of labor saving innovations on wages.

- explain how income and substitution effects influence the slope of the supply curve of labor.

- explain how income and substitution effects influence the slope of the supply curve of labor.

- use demand and supply curves to determine the equilibrium wage and employment in a competitive labor market.

- discuss the factors that help explain why wages differ among individuals.

- discuss how human capital theory explains the observed correlation between more education and higher wages.

- distinguish between a monopsonist and a monopolist.

- explain the role of entrepreneurs in guiding critical market activities.

CHAPTER REVIEW

In a competitive market without minimum wages or unions, wages and employment—the price and quantity of labor services—will be determined by the interaction of the demand for and the supply of labor services and can be analyzed with tools that should now be familiar—demand and supply curves.

The supply of labor comes from individual decisions to work. Individual decisions to supply work are simultaneously decisions to forgo leisure. Thus, a decision to supply less labor is simultaneously a decision to demand (1) _____. At higher wages, the same number of working hours will mean a larger income. If leisure is not an inferior good, people are apt to demand (more/less) leisure as their income increases. This suggests that the supply of labor might (increase/decrease) as wages increase. This is called the (income/substitution) effect of higher wages, but it is only part of the story.

Higher wages also increase the opportunity cost of an hour of leisure. As a result we expect that as wages (2) increase the substitution effect will lead people to work (more/less). The ultimate effect of increased wages comes from the sum of the income and substitution effects. Statistical evidence suggests that at low wages the _____ effect predominates and labor supply (increases/decreases) with an increase in wages, while at high wages the two effects tend to (enhance/offset) each other. The response of individuals to a change in wages, the income and substitution effects, helps determine the slope of the labor supply curve. Other factors, such as the size of the available working population and nonmonetary aspects of many jobs, help determine the position of the labor supply curve. The strength of the income and substitution effects is important for an understanding of the historical evidence on real wages and average weekly hours in the United States.

The demand for labor comes from the decisions of firms to use labor as one of many factors of production. Labor services are valuable because they add to output and, businesses hope, to profits. Thus the demand for labor is a derived demand. The discussion in earlier chapters of how a profit-maximizing firm makes optimal decisions about the use of factors of production showed that a firm should use more of any factor as long as the addition to revenue exceeds the addition to cost or, in technical terms, as long as the marginal revenue product (3) of the factor is (greater/less) than the marginal cost of the factor. A firm's demand curve for labor is determined by its curve of marginal (physical/revenue) product. The curve has a (negative/positive) slope because of the law of diminishing marginal returns.

In competitive markets, equilibrium wages and employment are determined by the intersection of the market demand and supply curves, which come from the horizontal summation of firms' demand curves and individuals' supply curves. Any factor that shifts either curve will change equilibrium wages and employment. For example, an increase in the demand for a firm's output or a technological innovation that increases the productivity of (4) labor should shift the (demand/supply) curve and lead to (higher/lower) wages, employment, or both. It is often argued that labor-saving innovations eliminate jobs as the same output can be produced with fewer workers. Yet these innovations also increase the productivity of workers and shift a country's production possibilities frontier.

As long as macroeconomic policy works to match aggregate demand with a country's aggregate supply potential, innovations should, over time, work to increase real wages.

Wages will differ for a number of reasons. Differences in abilities and work effort will affect individual wages. Differing amounts of other factors of production would also be expected to affect the marginal physical product of labor and hence wages. If individual skills are not easily duplicated, as may be the case for star athletes or performers, wages will be high as they contain significant economic rents. If skills are easily duplicated, one would expect that competition in the form of entry would work to keep wages in line with the costs of acquiring skills.

Education and wages are positively correlated—people with more education typically earn higher wages. Human capital theory views these higher wages as the return from investments in human capital—that is, the time, money, and effort spent on schooling and training.

Currently, about 13 percent of American workers belong to unions. Union membership as a proportion of the labor force has been declining since the 1950s. The shift from manufacturing to service industries, deregulation, changing preferences of American workers, and the threat of foreign competition have all been suggested as possible explanations for this decline.

In some labor markets, unions are the only supplier of labor services; that is, they are a (monopolist/monopsonist). As such, they face a trade-off between wages and employment just as a monopoly (5) supplier of widgets faces a trade-off between price and output. Sometimes a union, as a monopolistic supplier of labor, faces a single buyer of labor services. When one buyer constitutes the entire market demand, the buyer is called a(n) _____. Both monopolists and monopsonists realize that their decisions about quantity must at the same time affect price. Monopolists who want to sell more must accept a (higher/lower) price (wage), and monopsonists who want to buy more must pay a(n) _____ price (wage). If a monopsonist faces a monopolist, then the whole market has only _____ participants. The technical term for this situation is _____ monopoly. Each will consider the actions of the other, and, as for oligopoly, the outcome is difficult to predict.

_____ provide guidance to some critical market activities. It is they who organize and es- (6) tablish new firms. They design new enterprises and often use new firms to introduce innovations that play such a critical part in the economic growth. Innovations allow them to earn _____ profit for a short period of time. Generous profit will attract other individuals with entrepreneurial ambitions, who seek to enter the market with competitive and imitative products. This competitive entry first (reduces/increases) and finally brings to an end the temporary excess of price over the competitive level that was initially enjoyed by the entrepreneur.

There are two special features of invention: first, the (fixed/variable) cost characteristic of the required R&D (7) expenditures and many of the other costs entailed in bringing an invention to market successfully and, second, the (public/private) good attribute of invention. Both of these attributes mean that there is a significant portion of the cost of an invention that is totally absent from marginal cost. This has several implications. First, invention cannot be successful financially if the price is set equal to_____ cost. Such a price would not cover any of the R&D cost and the related outlays are entirely absent from the marginal cost of an innovation. So for innovative products, P = MC is a recipe for financial loss and disaster in an innovative firm. Second, this means that, initial monopoly profits may only be the amount of revenue needed to cover those fixed R&D costs and any similar outlays.

IMPORTANT TERMS AND CONCEPTS QUIZ

Choose the most appropriate definition for each of the following terms.

1. _____ Marginal Revenue Product of Labor (MRP_L)

2. _____ Income effect (of higher wages)

3. _____ Substitution effect (of higher wages)

4. _____ Backward-bending supply curve of labor

5. _____ Human capital theory

6. _____ Union

7. _____ Monopsony

8. _____ Bilateral monopoly

9. _____ Collective bargaining

10. _____ Innovative entrepreneurship

a. Reduction in supply of labor as wages increase

b. Market situation in which there is only one producer

c. Viewing education as an investment in a person's earning potential

d. Market composed of a single seller and a single buyer

e. Organization of workers to negotiate with employers over wages and other terms and conditions of employment

f. Impact on demand for increased leisure from higher income when wages increase

g. Market situation in which there is only one buyer

h. Increased opportunity cost of leisure as wages increase

i. Addition to revenue from hiring one more worker to increase output

j. Discussions between labor and management to determine wages and other conditions of employment

k. Someone who introduces a new product, new production process or finds a new market for his products

BASIC EXERCISES

This problem illustrates the determination of wages and employment in both a competitive market and a market monopolized by a labor union.

Tony runs a small company, Bearpaw Boots that manufactures hiking boots. **Table 20-1** shows output per month for different quantities of labor.

258

1. Fill in the third column by using the data in the second column to compute the marginal physical product of each additional worker.

2. Tony can sell boots for $120 a pair. Each boot contains $40 worth of leather, leaving $80 for wages or profits. As Tony has a small firm, the price of boots is unaffected by the quantity that he sells. Fill in the fourth column by computing the marginal revenue products of each worker. Be sure to use the $80 net figure rather than the $120 gross.

3. Tony wants to maximize profits. How many workers should he employ if monthly wages are $2,200?

_____ (You can check to be sure your answer maximizes profits by checking profits when Tony hires one more or one less worker.)

Table 20-1

Employment and Output for Bearpaw Boots

Number of Bootmakers	Total Number of Pairs of Boots per Month	Marginal Physical Product (boots)	Marginal Revenue Product (dollars)
1	60	_____	_____
2	115	_____	_____
3	165	_____	_____
4	210	_____	_____
5	250	_____	_____
6	285	_____	_____
7	315	_____	_____
8	340	_____	_____
9	360	_____	_____
10	375	_____	_____

4. **Figure 20-1** shows the supply of bootmakers for the entire industry.

Assume there are 100 competitive firms just like Tony's. Using your data on the marginal revenue product for a typical firm, plot the market demand for bootmakers. What is the equilibrium market wage and employment? $_____ and _____. At the equilibrium market wage, how many workers should Tony employ? _____ What are Tony's profits? _____ What are Tony's profits? _____.

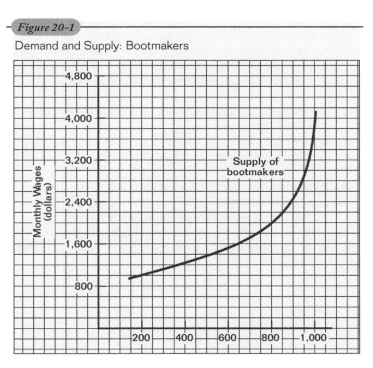

Figure 20-1

Demand and Supply: Bootmakers

5. Assume now that the IAB, the International Association of Bootmakers, has been successful in unionizing bootmakers. In order to evaluate possible alternative goals, the union has asked you to use your knowledge of the industry demand curve to answer the following questions:

   a. If union membership is limited to 400 persons, what is the maximum monthly wage the union can get from employers? $_____

   b. If the union wage is set at $1,400 a month, what is the maximum amount of employment?
      $_____

   c. What wage and employment combination will maximize total wage payments? $_____

SELF-TESTS FOR UNDERSTANDING

TEST A

Circle the most appropriate answer.

1. A change in which of the following will affect the slope of the labor supply curve?
   a. an increase in the working age population
   b. a technological innovation that increases labor productivity
   c. an increase in the price of a competitive firm's output
   d. an increase in the willingness of people to trade higher money incomes for more leisure

2. A change in which of the following will affect the position of the labor supply curve?
   a. an increase in the working age population
   b. a technological innovation that increases labor productivity
   c. an increase in the price of a competitive firm's output
   d. an increase in the willingness of people to work longer hours in return for higher wages

3. The income and substitution effects mean that the supply of labor _____ when wages increase.
   a. will always increase
   b. may rise or fall
   c. will always decline

4. If the supply of labor is backward bending, then
   a. we're probably talking about manual labor.
   b. even higher wages are needed to increase supply.
   c. the income effect is greater than the substitution effect.
   d. the incentive to work more hours when wages are higher is outweighing the income effect of higher wages.

5. Historical data that show a declining workweek along with rising real wages are probably reflecting
   a. minimum wage laws.
   b. the income effect of higher wages.
   c. the substitution effect of higher wages.
   d. the Taft-Hartley Act.

6. The demand for labor is the downward-sloping portion of the _____ curve for labor.
   a. marginal physical product
   b. marginal cost
   c. marginal revenue product
   d. average revenue

7. A change in which of the following will affect the demand for labor by shifting the marginal physical product of labor schedule?
   a. the demand for a firm's output
   b. the amount of other factors of production per worker
   c. the supply of labor
   d. the minimum wage

8. A change in which of the following will affect the demand for labor by shifting the marginal revenue product of labor schedule?
   a. the demand for a firm's output
   b. union militancy
   c. the supply of labor
   d. the minimum wage

9. The dramatic reduction in the proportion of the labor force in agriculture in the past 200 years reflects
   a. a decline in the demand for food.
   b. increased foreign competition.
   c. government policies that have discriminated against agriculture.
   d. the increased productivity of farm workers.

10. The supply curve for schmoos is upward sloping. An increase in the demand for schmoos (the demand curve shifts to the right) will lead to all but which one of the following?
    a. The price of schmoos increases.
    b. The marginal physical product of labor schedule shifts upward.
    c. The marginal revenue product of labor schedule shifts upward.
    d. The demand curve for labor to produce schmoos shifts upward.
    e. Employment and/or wages increase in the schmoo industry.

11. In recent years the income premium for college graduates as compared to high school graduates has
    a. narrowed.
    b. stayed about the same.
    c. increased.
    d. fluctuated with little trend.

12. The theory of human capital says that
    a. individuals can repair their own bodies with artificial parts, just like machines.
    b. soon all work will be done by robots.
    c. individual decisions to seek training and new skills can be modeled in the same way as ordinary investment decisions, involving present costs in the expectation of future returns.
    d. slavery in the United States was doomed because it was uneconomical.

13. Human capital theory explains the correlation between education and wages as the result of
    a. learning in school that enhances productivity.
    b. sorting by social class.
    c. the dual labor market.
    d. the growing influence of white-collar unions.

14. What percent of American workers belong to unions?
    a. 42 percent
    b. 23 percent
    c. 13 percent
    d. 7 percent

15. In contrast with experience in Europe and Japan, unions in America
    a. are much more political.
    b. have resulted in almost twice the level of strike activity found in any other country.
    c. involve a smaller percentage of the labor force than in most countries.
    d. have been less adversarial than unions in Japan.

16. A single union that controls the supply of labor to many small firms is a
    a. socialist.
    b. monopsonist.
    c. oligopolist.
    d. monopolist.

17. If one company is the sole employer of labor, it is called a(n)
    a. arbitrator.
    b. monopolist.
    c. oligopolist.
    d. monopsonist.

18. According to Joseph Schumpeter, an innovative entrepreneur earns
    a. zero economic profit in the short-run.
    b. monopoly profit in the short-run.
    c. excess profit in the long-run.
    d. monopoly profit in the long-run.

19. Which of the following are the attributes of innovation?
    a. Fixed cost and public good
    b. Fixed cost and private good
    c. Variable cost and public good
    d. Variable cost and private good

20. A firm sells a product to one group of customers at a lower price than it sells it to another, even though it costs exactly the same to serve the two groups. The prices that are charged are called
    a. predatory.
    b. dumping.
    c. discriminatory.
    d. bundling.

TEST B

Circle T or F for true or false.

T F 1. Information on the marginal revenue product of labor can be used to derive a firm's demand for labor.

T F 2. The law of diminishing returns implies that the demand curve for labor will have a negative slope.

T F 3. The income effect of higher wages suggests that the supply of labor schedule may have a positively sloped portion.

T F 4. An increase in wages that increases the quantity of labor supplied is represented as a shift in the supply curve.

T F 5. If a labor union has complete control over the supply of a particular type of labor, it is a monopsonist.

T F 6. A market with a single buyer and a single seller is called an oligopoly.

T F 7. In general there is no conflict between union attempts to maximize wages for current union members and attempts to provide employment for the largest possible number of workers.

T F 8. A labor union faces a demand curve that is perfectly elastic.

T F 9. Price of an innovative product will initially be high and then will gradually be driven down by competition.

T F 10. Fixed costs and public good attributes in invention implies that invention will be successful financially if the price is set equal to marginal cost.

SUPPLEMENTARY EXERCISES

1. **Wages and Employment Under Monopsony**

   This problem is designed to show how monopoly elements in labor markets, either a monopsonist firm or a monopolist union, can affect wages and employment.

   Assume that Bearpaw Boots (the subject of the Basic Exercise for the chapter) is located in a small, isolated town in northern Maine and is the sole employer of bootmakers. Tony still sells his boots in a competitive market for a net price of $80. **Table 20-2** (on the next page) contains data on what wages Tony must pay to get various numbers of employees.

a. Use the data in the first two columns of Table 20-2 to plot the supply curve of labor in Figure 20-2. Use the data on the marginal revenue product computed in Table 20-1 to plot the demand curve for labor in Figure 20-2. These curves intersect where wages are $ _____ and the number of employees is

_____ .

b. Will Tony pay the wage determined by the intersection in question a? Remember, Tony is the only employer of bootmakers in town. As he employs additional workers, he must pay a higher wage not only to each new employee but also to all existing employees. Thus the marginal cost of an additional worker is (greater/less) than the wage. Fill in the remaining columns of Table 20-2 to compute Tony's marginal labor costs.

c. Plot the figures on marginal labor costs in **Figure 20-2**.

d. Tony should increase employment as long as the marginal revenue of additional workers exceeds the marginal cost. Using this logic, Tony's profit-maximizing level of employment is _____ workers.

e. While the curve of marginal labor cost is critical for Tony's calculation of the profit-maximizing level of employment, it is the supply curve for labor that tells Tony how much he must offer workers. What is the lowest wage that Tony must offer in order to attract the profit-maximizing number of workers? $ _____

Table 20-2

Supply of Bootmakers in a Small, Isolated Town

Number of Bootmakers	Monthly Wage (dollars)	Total Labor Cost[a] (dollars)	Marginal Labor Cost[b] (dollars)
1	600	_____	_____
2	800	_____	_____
3	1,000	_____	_____
4	1,200	_____	_____
5	1,400	_____	_____
6	1,600	_____	_____
7	1,800	_____	_____
8	2,000	_____	_____
9	2,200	_____	_____
10	2,400	_____	_____

[a] Total Labor Cost = (Number of bootmakers) × (Monthly Wage)

[b] Marginal Labor Cost = change in Total Labor Cost. For example, when employing 2 workers rather than 1, Total Labor Cost changes by $1,000.

Figure 20-2

Demand and Supply: Bootmakers

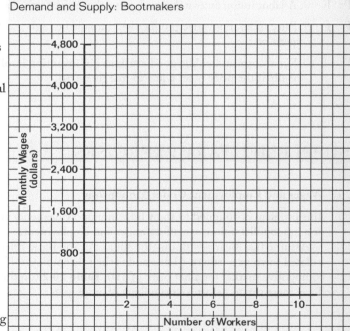

f. What are Tony's profits (net revenue minus total wages)? _____

g. If Tony must pay a minimun wage of $2,200 a month and can hire as many workers as he wants at the minimum wage, what would happen to wages and employment?

h. Would a union necessarily force the minimum wage solution to question g on Tony? Why or why not?

STUDY QUESTIONS

1. Why does the income effect of an increase in wages tend to reduce the supply of labor when wages increase?

2. Why does the substitution effect of an increase in wages tend to increase the supply of labor when wages increase?

3. What explains the demand for labor?

4. Demand and supply analysis seems to suggest that there should be a single wage, yet there is significant variation in the wages individuals receive. What other factors explain the difference in wages among individuals? Which of these factors can be seen as factors affecting the demand and supply curves and which cannot?

5. What is human capital theory and how might it explain differences in wages? How do theories of sorting and dual labor markets differ from human capital theory?

6. Economists often argue that a union can only raise wages by accepting a reduction in employment. When a union faces this sort of trade-off, what might it do to try and increase both employment and wages?

8. Is the introduction of labor-saving technological innovations good or bad for workers? for the economy? Why?

10. What are the implications of fixed-cost and public good attributes in invention?

ECONOMICS ONLINE

The Bureau of Labor Statistics offers a wealth of data and information about labor markets.

http://www.bls.gov

What's up at the AFL-CIO? Find out by checking their homepage.

http://www.aflcio.org

Does it pay to go to college? This web site has historical data on income and educational attainment for men, women, Blacks, Whites, and Hispanics. See for yourself by checking the data in Tables P-16 through P-35.

http://www.census.gov/hhes/income/histinc/incperdet.html

Poverty, Inequality, and Discrimination

Important Terms and Concepts

Poverty line

Absolute concept of poverty

Relative concept of poverty

Economic discrimination

Temporary Assistance to Needy Families (TANF)

Food stamps

Negative income tax (NIT)

Earned Income Tax Credit (EITC)

Affirmative action

Learning Objectives

After completing this chapter, you should be able to:

- discuss some of the facts of poverty and income distribution.

- describe the implications of the use of absolute or relative concepts of poverty.

  describe what factors account for differences in incomes, which of these factors reflect voluntary choices, and why these factors make identifying economic discrimination so difficult.

- explain why the trade-off between equality and efficiency implies that the optimal distribution of income will involve some inequality.

- explain the concept of a negative income tax and how it affects work incentives.

- explain why, if implementing a negative income tax program, policy makers can only choose two of the following three parameters: guaranteed level of income, tax rate, and break-even level of income.

- describe the controversy surrounding programs for affirmative action.

CHAPTER REVIEW

Discussions of poverty in America usually focus on the number of households below the poverty line. In 2009

(1) this dividing line was about $_____ a year for a household of four. It is adjusted every year for changes in prices. Since the yearly adjustment reflects only the change in prices and not general increases in real income, the poverty line is a(n) (<u>absolute/relative</u>) concept of poverty rather than a(n) _____ concept.

U.S. income data show that in 2009, households with incomes above $100,000 were in the top 20 percent of

(2) the income distribution. The top 20 percent of households received _____ percent of income while the bottom 20 percent received _____ percent.

Why do incomes differ? The list of reasons is long and includes differences in abilities, intensity of work, risk taking, wage differentials for unpleasant or hazardous tasks, schooling and training, work experience, inherited wealth, luck, and discrimination. Some of the reasons for differences in incomes represent voluntary choices by individuals to work harder, take more risks, or accept unpleasant work in order to earn higher incomes.

Economic discrimination is defined as a situation in which equivalent factors of production receive

(3) _____ payments for equal contributions to output. Average differences in income between large social groups, such as men and women or blacks and whites, (<u>are/are not</u>) sufficient proof of economic discrimination. These average differences tend to (<u>overstate/understate</u>) the amount of economic discrimination. To accurately measure the impact of possible discrimination, we must first correct for the factors listed above that could create differences in income without implying economic discrimination. Some factors, such as schooling, are tricky. For instance, differences in wages associated with differences in schooling would not imply any discrimination if everyone has had an equal opportunity for the same amount of schooling. But it is unclear whether observed differences in schooling represent voluntary choices or another form of discrimination.

Measures to equalize incomes may adversely affect the work effort of these individuals. In more technical

(4) terms, efforts for greater equality may reduce _____. This important trade-off does not mean that all efforts to increase equality should be abandoned. It does mean that efforts to increase equality have a price and should not be pushed beyond the point where the marginal gains from further equality are worth less than the marginal loss from reduced efficiency. Exactly where this point is reached is the subject of continuing political debate.

The trade-off between equality and efficiency also suggests that in the fight for greater equality one should choose policies with small rather than large effects on efficiency. Economists argue that many welfare programs have been inefficient. One important reason is the relatively large reduction in benefits for each additional dol-

(5) lar of earned income. These high implicit marginal tax rates (<u>increase/decrease</u>) the incentive for increased work effort on the part of welfare recipients who are able to work.

Many economists favor replacing the current welfare system with a negative income tax, that is, a system of direct cash grants tied to income levels and linked to the tax system. These schemes usually start with a minimum guaranteed level of income and a tax rate that specifies the decrease in the cash grant for every dollar increase in income. A low tax rate will retain significant work incentives; however, a low tax rate also means that grants continue until income is quite high. The point where payments from the government stop and payments to the government start is called the

_____ level of income. (6)

A negative income tax with a low marginal tax rate can offer significantly better work incentives to those currently receiving welfare, but there will be (positive/negative) work incentives for those not now on welfare (7) but who become eligible for grants. Experiments with versions of a negative income tax have investigated the size of these negative work incentives and found them to be (large/small). Food Stamps and the Earned Income Tax Credit resemble a negative income tax.

IMPORTANT TERMS AND CONCEPTS QUIZ

Choose the most appropriate definition for each of the following terms.

1. _____ Poverty line
2. _____ Economic discrimination
3. _____ TANF
4. _____ Food stamps
5. _____ Negative income tax
6. _____ Earned Income Tax Credit
7. _____ Affirmative action

a. Amount of income below which a family is considered "poor"
b. Active efforts to recruit and hire members of underrepresented groups
c. Tax credits that are linked to wage or salary income
d. Income share of poorest quartile of income distribution
e. Time limited welfare assistance
f. Income-conditioned cash grants available to all families
g. Equivalent factors of production receive unequal pay for equal contributions to output
h. Stamps that allow families to buy food at subsidized prices

BASIC EXERCISES

This problem illustrates the high marginal tax rates that often result from combining welfare programs. The numbers in this problem do not come from any specific welfare program but illustrate how the combination of separate and well intended programs can produce unintended consequences.

Imagine a welfare system that offers a family of four the following forms of public support.

- Food stamps that offer the family $450 a month or $5,400 a year but require payments equal to 25 percent of income above $500 a month or $6,000 a year.

- Housing subsidy that gives the family an apartment worth $600 a month or $7,200 a year. The family must contribute 30 percent of its net income toward rent. Net income is determined as 80 percent of gross income.

- A TANF grant of $6,000 a year that is reduced by one-third of any family income.

1. Fill in column 7 of **Table 21-1** by computing net income after taxes and after welfare payments for the different levels of earned income.

Table 21-1

Subsidy Programs

(1) Earned Income	(2) Social Security and Income Taxes*	(3) Earned Income Taxed Credit	(4) Food Stamps	(5) Housing Subsidy	(6) TANF Grant	(7) Net Income (1) − (2) + (3) + (4) + (5) + (6)
$ 0	$ 0	$ 0	$5,400	$7,200	$6,000	_____
6,000	372	2,410	5,400	5,760	4,000	_____
9,700	601	3,890	5,075	4,872	2,767	_____
12,700	787	4,204	4,325	4,152	1,767	_____
18,000	1,116	3,510	3,000	2,880	0	_____
18,550	1,150	3,405	2,863	2,748	0	_____
30,000	2,690	993	0	0	0	_____
31,175	2,880	741	0	0	0	_____
35,000	3,500	0	0	0	0	_____

2. Use the data in columns 1 and 7 to plot net income against earned income in **Figure 21-1**. Plot each pair of points and then connect successive pairs with a straight line. What does the graph suggest about work incentives under these programs?

3. Use the data in Table 21-1 to complete **Table 21-2**, computing the implicit marginal tax rates that this family faces as it earns income. What is the relationship between the implicit marginal tax rates you computed in Table 21-2 and the slope of the graph in Figure 21-1? How do these marginal rates compare with the statutory marginal tax rates under the positive portion of federal income taxes, which ranged from 10 percent to 35 percent in 2007? (Note that in 2007 the highest rate applied only to taxable incomes above $349,701. In 2007 the Social Security tax rate of 6.2 percent applied to wage and salary income up to $97,500. The Medicare Hospitalization Insurance rate of 1.45 percent applied to all wage and salary income.)

Figure 21-1

Income Before and After Subsidy Program

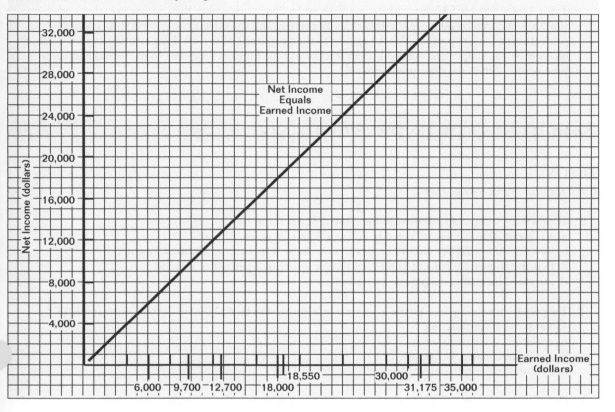

Table 21-2

Income and Implicit Tax Rates after Subsidies

(1) Earned Income	(2) Net Income Column (7) from Table 21-1	(3) Change in Earned Income	(4) Change in Net Income	(5) Implicit Taxes (3) – (4)	(6) Implicit Marginal Tax Rate (5) ÷ (3)
$0	_____				
$6,000	_____	$6,000	_____	_____	_____
$9,700	_____	$3,700	_____	_____	_____
$12,700	_____	$3,000	_____	_____	_____
$18,000	_____	$5,300	_____	_____	_____
$18,550	_____	$550	_____	_____	_____
$30,000	_____	$11,450	_____	_____	_____
$31,175	_____	$1,175	_____	_____	_____
$35,000	_____	$3,825	_____	_____	_____

271

4. One could reduce the implicit marginal tax rate by lowering the rate at which benefits are reduced under any of the programs. To investigate the impact of such reductions, construct a new version of Table 21-1 in which TANF payments are reduced by 25 percent rather than 33 percent, the food stamp subsidy is reduced by 10 percent rather than 25 percent, and the housing subsidy is reduced by 20 percent instead of 30 percent. What happens to the magnitude of the subsidy payments at each level of income? What happens to the break-even level of income for each program? What would happen to total public outlays for these programs?

SELF-TESTS FOR UNDERSTANDING

TEST A

Circle the most appropriate answer.

1. The facts on income distribution in the United States show
   a. a substantial move toward equality during the last 30 years.
   b. that the richest 20 percent of families receive about 80 percent of the total income.
   c. that the poorest 20 percent of families receive less than 2 percent of income.
   d. increased inequality during the past 20 years.

2. The poverty line computed by the government, estimated to be $22,000 in 2009, is an example of
   a. statistical discrimination.
   b. a relative concept of poverty.
   c. an absolute concept of poverty.
   d. economic discrimination.

3. Defining poor people as those who fall in the bottom 20 percent of the income distribution
   a. is an absolute concept of poverty.
   b. is a relative concept of poverty.
   c. means that continued economic growth will eliminate poverty.
   d. implies that all of above all correct.

4. Economic growth is likely to be most effective when poverty is measured as a(n) _____ concept.
   a. aggregate
   b. absolute
   c. proportional
   d. relative

5. Since 1975, the proportion of people below the official poverty line
   a. increased and decreased with little trend.
   b. decreased significantly.
   c. rose substantially.
   d. has stayed constant.

6. If the United States adopted the European definition of poverty of one-half average income, the number of families considered poor would likely
   a. be smaller.
   b. show no change.
   c. increase.

7. Compared with other industrial countries, data on the distribution of income in the United States show
   a. more inequality than most other countries.
   b. about the same degree of inequality.
   c. much more equality.

8. In 2009, the richest 20 percent of families received about _____ percent of total income.
   a. 23
   b. 32
   c. 50
   d. 57

9. In 2009, the poorest 20 percent of families received _____ percent of total income.
   a. less than 2
   b. between 3 and 4
   c. slightly more than 10
   d. 20

10. In 2009, families with an income above _____ were in the top 20 percent of the income distribution.
    a. $57,000
    b. $73,000
    c. $100,000
    d. $108,000

11. Consider a negative income tax scheme with a guaranteed minimum income of $8,000 for a family of four and a tax rate of 50 percent. The break-even level of income would be
    a. $4,000.
    b. $8,000.
    c. $12,000.
    d. $16,000.

12. If the Vincents earn $8,000 in wages, their total income after including the negative income tax would be
    a. $4,000.
    b. $8,000.
    c. $12,000.
    d. $16,000.

13. Reducing the tax rate while retaining the same minimum guarantee will
    a. reduce the break-even level of income.
    b. leave the break-even level of income unchanged.
    c. increase the break-even level of income.
    d. There's too little information to know.

14. If a negative income tax system is to be financed within a given budget, then a reduction in the negative tax rate to increase work incentives
    a. must be offset by a reduction in the minimum guaranteed level of income.
    b. needs no change in the minimum guaranteed level of income.
    c. must be offset by an increase in the minimum guaranteed level of income.

15. Which of the following work like a negative income tax? (There may be more than one correct answer.)
    a. food stamps
    b. Social Security taxes
    c. estate taxes
    d. Earned Income Tax Credit

16. When evaluated as a whole, taxes in the United States
    a. actually increase income inequality.
    b. have little impact on the distribution of income.
    c. make a small contribution toward a more equal distribution of income.
    d. dramatically increase the equality of after-tax income as compared to before-tax income.

17. If two individuals with similar productivity receive different pay for the same work, an economist would call this evidence of
    a. economic discrimination.
    b. poverty.
    c. statistical discrimination.
    d. luck.

18. All but which one of the following could give rise to differences in income without implying discrimination?
    a. schooling
    b. ability
    c. compensating wage differential for night work
    d. intensity of work effort

19. Which of the following would be an example of economic discrimination?
    a. Census data show that, on average, women earn less than men.
    b. Nurses earn less than doctors.
    c. Over the period 1990 to 2000, plumbers and electricians received larger percentage wage increases than did college professors.
    d. A careful study showing that among blacks and whites with identical education, work experience, productivity, and motivation, blacks earn less than whites.

20. The study of economics shows that the optimal amount of income inequality would result in the richest 10 percent of the population receiving
    a. 10 percent of total income.
    b. 25 percent of total income.
    c. 50 percent of total income.
    d. None of the above.

TEST B

Circle T or F for true or false.

T F 1. It is easier for economic growth to eliminate poverty as measured by an absolute standard, but not as measured by a relative standard.

T F 2. U.S. data show no change in poverty since 1960 as measured by the proportion of persons below the poverty line.

T F 3. In the United States, the incidence of poverty is about the same for all social groups, e.g., men – women, black – whites.

T F 4. Including in-kind income, e.g., public housing, health care and food stamps, means that poverty in the United States has been eliminated.

T F 5. In the United States, the 20 percent of families that are poorest receive about 20 percent of total income.

T F 6. The optimal amount of inequality is a poverty rate of 10 percent.

T F 7. The fact that women, white or black, have lower average incomes than white men, is sufficient proof of economic discrimination.

T F 8. In the absence of monopolies, unregulated markets would result in an equal distribution of income.

T F 9. Some differences in income reflect voluntary choices, such as decisions to work more hours or to take early retirement.

T F 10. The federal personal income tax system has substantially reduced the degree of income inequality in the United States.

|Appendix | *The Economic Theory*

The Appendix to Chapter 21 analyzes two forms of economic discrimination, discrimination by employers and discrimination by employees. For which form of economic discrimination can competitive market forces be expected to help minimize discrimination and why? Why would one expect market forces to not be effective in fighting the other form of discrimination?

SUPPLEMENTARY EXERCISES

1. **Table 21-3** reports data from the World Bank on the distribution of income for nine countries. Use **Figure 21-2** to compare the distribution of income by plotting the cumulative proportion of income against the cumulative proportion of population. Note that your line will start in the lower left-hand column of the graph as 0 percent of the population receives 0 percent of the income and it will end at the upper right-hand corner where 100 percent of the population receives 100 percent of the income. Which countries show the greatest equality in the distribution of income? Which show the greatest inequality?

   Note: Each column shows the proportion of total income received by that corresponding percentage of the population. For example, the first column shows the proportion of income received by the poorest 10 percent of the population; the second column shows the proportion of income received by the poorest 20 percent of the population; the last column shows the proportion of income received by the richest 10 percent of the population.

— *Table 21-3* —————————————————————————————————

Data on Income Distribution for Selected Countries

	Year	Lowest 10%	Lowest 20%	Second 20%	Third 20%	Fourth 20%	Highest 20%	Highest 10%
Finland	2000	4.0%	9.6%	14.1%	17.5%	22.1%	36.7%	22.6%
Germany	2000	3.2%	8.5%	13.7%	17.8%	23.1%	36.9%	22.1%
Italy	2000	2.3%	6.5%	12.0%	16.8%	22.8%	42.0%	26.8%
South Korea	1998	2.9%	7.9%	13.6%	18.0%	23.1%	37.5%	22.5%
Mexico	2000	1.0%	3.1%	7.2%	11.7%	19.0%	59.1%	43.1%
Norway	2000	3.9%	9.6%	14.0%	17.2%	22.0%	37.2%	23.4%
Sweden	2000	3.6%	9.1%	14.0%	17.6%	22.7%	36.6%	22.2%
United Kingdom	1999	2.1%	6.1%	11.4%	16.0%	22.5%	44.0%	28.5%
United States	2000	1.9%	5.4%	10.7%	15.7%	22.4%	45.8%	29.9%

Source: World Bank, 2004 World Development Indicators, Table 2.7

The Distribution of Income label: **Distribution of Income**

276

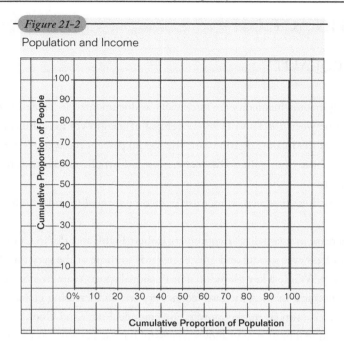

Figure 21-2

Population and Income

2. In 2006 median household income in the United States was $48,200 while mean household income was $59,067. Which measure, the median or the mean, is a better measure of income equality? Why?

3. Following is a suggested list of additional readings on three important topics covered in this chapter.

On the general issue of trade-offs between increased equality and reduced efficiency, read Arthur Okun's *Equality and Efficiency: The Big Trade-off,* published by the Brookings Institution, 1975. This important book is the source of the "leaky bucket" analogy used in the text.

The taxation of estates is a topic where the ratio of political rhetoric to economic analysis is very high. Find out more about estate taxes by reading "Ancestor Worthship: Everything you always wanted to know about estate taxes," *The Milken Institute Review,* Third Quarter 2000, pp. 36-49, by economists William Gale and Joel Slemrod.

Women now account for about 49 percent of the American labor force. Economic issues concerning the role of women in the labor force are examined by Claudia Goldin in *Understanding the Gender Gap: An Economic History of American Women,* Oxford University Press, 1990.

4. Investigate the details of welfare programs in the city or county in which you live. Use this information to construct your own version of Table 21-1.

277

ECONOMICS IN ACTION

INCREASING INEQUALITY

The facts about increasing income inequality are quite clear as documented in Table 21-2 in the text. Economist Edward Wolff notes that between 1983 and 1998, 47 percent of the growth in real income in the United States went to the top 1 percent of the income distribution. The top 20 percent received 89 percent. While changes in other countries may not have been quite so dramatic, most industrialized countries have seen similar trends toward increasing inequality.

What is less clear is why there has been an increase in income inequality and whether anything should be done about it.

What explains the increase in inequality? Economists Robert Frank and Philip Cook argue that in many fields, the economy now offers ever greater and greater rewards to those at the very top. They have termed this the "winner-take-all society." While a key player on a professional sports team or a hot pop star has had the ability to command astronomical salaries, modern technology and an increasing global marketplace now allows those in other fields to exercise similar market power. For example, Frank and Cook argue that the ability to create national and international brands now allows successful business executives to command similar eye-popping compensation.

Increased returns to education have also been cited by many as an important factor helping to explain the increase in income inequality. Economist Marvin Kosters notes that the income advantage for college graduates over high school graduates has doubled since the early 1970s.

Should anything be done about the increase in income inequality? A number of economists would say no. To the extent that the market is rewarding particular skills or education, these economists would be concerned that any attempt to interfere with the market outcome could produce important unintended consequences.

Others are not quite as sure. Economist David Ellwood notes that a host of problems like drug use, teenage pregnancy, and reduced life expectancy are associated with low incomes. Increasing inequality will make these problems worse for those at the bottom of income distribution. Economist James Heckman is quoted in *The New York Times* as saying, "Never has the accident of birth mattered more
. . . this is a case of market failure: children don't get to 'buy' their parents, and so there has to be some kind of intervention to make up for these environmental differences."

1. What do you think explains the trend toward increasing income inequality? What if anything would you advocate to resist or reverse this trend?

Sources: Robert H. Frank, "Talent and the Winner-Take-All Society," *The American Prospect*, Vol 5, Issue 17, March 21, 1994. Alexander Stille, "Grounded by an income gap," *The New York Times*, December 15, 2001.

STUDY QUESTIONS

1. Which is the most meaningful measure of poverty, an absolute standard or a relative standard? Why?

2. If one defines poverty as the poorest 20 percent of the population, then the poor will always be with us. What if one defines poverty as incomes that are less than 50 percent of median income? Under this definition is it necessarily true that the poor will always be with us? If not, what would it take to eliminate poverty?

3. When looking for a measure of average income, one might consider mean income or median income. The Census Bureau reports information on both. What is the difference between the mean and the median as a measure of average tendency? Which do you think is a better measure of average incomes?

4. Differences in income may be related to a number of factors. What factors reflect voluntary choices and what factors might reflect economic discrimination?

5. How does a negative income tax improve work incentives as compared with a system of overlapping poverty programs?

ECONOMICS ONLINE

The United States Census Bureau has a wealth of data available on the web about American income distribution. You can access this data at

http://www.census.gov/hhes/www/income.html

Information on how the Census Bureau measures poverty as well as detailed data on poverty measures is available at

www.census.gov/hhes/www/poverty.html

Emmanuel Saez, Professor of Economics at the University of California, Berkeley, studies income distribution. You can access his data on changes in income distribution in the United States during the twentieth century from his web site at

http://elsa.berkeley.edu/~saez/index.html.

An Introduction to Macroeconomics

Important Terms and Concepts

Aggregation

Aggregate demand curve

Aggregate supply curve

Inflation

Recession

Gross domestic product (GDP)

Nominal GDP

Real GDP

Final goods and services

Intermediate goods

Real GDP per capita

Deflation

Fiscal policy

Stagflation

Monetary policy

Stabilization policy

Learning Objectives

After completing this chapter, you should be able to:

- explain the difference between microeconomics and macroeconomics.

- determine whether particular problems are within the realm of microeconomics or macroeconomics.

- describe the role of economic aggregates in macroeconomics.

- explain how supply-demand analysis can be used to study inflation, recessions, and stabilization policy.

- distinguish between real and nominal GDP.

- explain how GDP is a measure of economic production, not economic well-being.

- characterize, in general terms, the movement in prices and output during the last 130 years.

- use aggregate demand and supply curves to explain how stabilization policy addresses problems of unemployment and inflation.

CHAPTER REVIEW

Economic theory is traditionally split into two parts, microeconomics and macroeconomics. If one studies the

(1) behavior of individual decision-making units, one is studying _____. If one studies the behavior of entire economies, one is studying _____. This chapter is an introduction to macroeconomics.

The American economy is made up of millions of firms, hundreds of millions of individuals, and innumerable different goods and services. Since it would be impossible to list each of these firms, individuals, and commodities, economists have found it useful to use certain overall averages or aggregates. The concept of domestic product is an example. If we concentrate on macroeconomic aggregates, we ignore much of the micro detail; whereas by concentrating on the micro detail, we may miss the big picture. The two forms of analysis are not substitutes; rather, they can be usefully employed together. (Remember the map analogy in Chapter 1 of the text.) It has been argued that only successful macroeconomic policy leads to a situation in which the study of microeconomics is important, and vice versa.

Supply and demand analysis is a fundamental tool of both micro and macro theory. In microeconomics one looks at the supply and demand for individual commodities, while in macroeconomics one studies aggregate supply and aggregate demand. The intersection of the demand and supply curves in microeconomics determines

(2) equilibrium _____ and _____. In macroeconomics the intersection of the aggregate demand and supply curves determines the price level and aggregate output, or the gross

_____ _____.

(3)   A sustained increase in the price level would be called _____, whereas a sustained decrease would be called _____. Because of long-term growth factors, domestic product in the U.S. economy usually increases every year. Periods when real domestic product declines are referred to as _____. With an unchanged aggregate supply curve, an outward (rightward) shift of the aggregate demand curve would lead to (higher/lower) prices and (higher/lower) output. Higher prices would also result if the aggregate supply curve shifted to the (left/right), but, this time, higher prices would be associated with a(n) (increase/decrease) in output. Such a combination of rising prices and declining output is called _____. If both curves shift to the right at the same rate, then it is possible to have increased output without inflation.

(4)   Gross domestic product is defined as the sum of the _____ values of all _____ goods and services produced in the domestic economy and sold on organized markets during a year. Because GDP counts only production in the domestic economy it (excludes/includes) the foreign operations of American firms and _____ the activities of foreign firms and workers operating in the United States. For the most part GDP includes only those newly produced goods and services that are traded in

282

markets. Illegal activities, the underground economy, and unpaid housework (and childcare) are all examples of economic activities that (<u>are/are not</u>) included in GDP.

To measure GDP, economists and national income statisticians use prices to add up the different kinds of output. If one uses today's prices, the result is (<u>nominal/real</u>) GDP. If one values output using prices from some base period, one gets _____ GDP. Which is the better measure of changes in output? (<u>Nominal/Real</u>) GDP. If all prices rise and all outputs are unchanged, (<u>nominal/real</u>) GDP will increase while _____ GDP will not.   (5)

It is important to remember that GDP is a measure of production; it (<u>is/is not</u>) a measure of economic well-being. The economic activity necessary to recover from a natural disaster such as an earthquake or hurricane is likely to (<u>decrease/increase</u>) GDP while _____ people's sense of well-being. Similarly, goods and services used to clean up the environment mean a (<u>larger/smaller</u>) GDP but are likely to reflect a (<u>higher/lower</u>) sense of well-being.   (6)

If you look at a long period of American history, you will see that there have been periods when both output and prices have risen and fallen. The long-term trend for output is (<u>up/down</u>). The overall trend for prices (<u>depends/does not depend</u>) upon the period you are reviewing. Up until World War II, prices rose and fell whereas since 1945, prices seem only to have _____.   (7)

The government would like to keep output growing, thus avoiding recession; at the same time, it would like to keep prices from rising, thus avoiding (<u>inflation/deflation</u>). Attempts to do just this are called _____ policy. The American government has been formally committed to such policies only since the end of World War II. A look at Figures 22-5 and 22-6 in the text suggests that since 1950, stabilization policy has done a good job of avoiding _____ but not of avoiding _____. Chapter 33 discusses why this result is not surprising; that is, why, if one concentrates on maintaining high levels of employment and output, the result is likely to be higher prices.   (8)

IMPORTANT TERMS AND CONCEPTS QUIZ

Choose the best definition for each of the following terms.

1. _____ Microeconomics
2. _____ Macroeconomics
3. _____ Aggregation
4. _____ Aggregate demand curve
5. _____ Aggregate supply curve
6. _____ Inflation
7. _____ Deflation
8. _____ Recession
9. _____ Gross domestic product (GDP)
10. _____ Nominal GDP
11. _____ Real GDP
12. _____ Final goods and services
13. _____ Intermediate goods
14. _____ GDP per capita
15. _____ Stagflation
16. _____ Fiscal policy
17. _____ Monetary policy
18. _____ Stabilization policy

a. Period of expansion in an economy's total output
b. Period of decline in an economy's total output
c. Inflation occurring while the economy is growing slowly or in a recession
d. Gross domestic product calculated at current price levels
e. Actions by the Federal Reserve that affect interest rates and/or the money supply
f. Government programs designed to prevent or shorten recessions and to counteract inflation
g. Products purchased by their ultimate users
h. Study of behavior of an entire economy
i. Combining individual markets into a single, overall market
j. Gross domestic product calculated using prices from some agreed-upon base year
k. Products purchased for resale or for their use in producing other products
l. Sustained decrease in general price level
m. Graph of quantity of domestic product demanded at each possible price level
n. Sum of money values of all final goods and services produced in the domestic economy and sold on organized markets within the year
o. Graph of quantity of domestic product produced at each possible price level
p. Study of individual decision-making units
q. Sustained increase in general price level
r. Output divided by populations
s. The government's plan for spending and taxes

BASIC EXERCISES

These exercises use the aggregate demand–aggregate supply diagram to review a few basic concepts.

1. **Figure 22-1** has four panels. The solid lines indicate the initial situation, and the dashed lines indicate a shift in one or both curves.

   a. Which panel(s) suggest(s) a period, or periods, of inflation? _____

   b. Which panel(s) suggest(s) a period, or periods, of deflation? _____

      (Did prices in the U.S. economy ever decline in the 20th century? If so, when? _____)

   c. Which panel(s) illustrate(s) growth in real output with stable prices? _____

   d. Which panel(s) illustrate(s) stagflation? _____

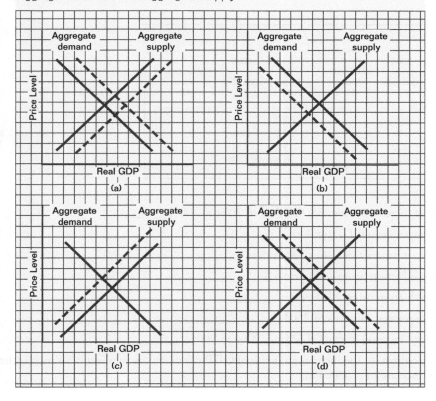

Figure 22-1

Aggregate Demand and Aggregate Supply

2. Stabilization policy involves changes in government policies designed to shorten recessions and stabilize prices. For reasons examined in later chapters, stabilization policies have their initial and primary effect on the aggregate demand curve. For the cases listed below, explain how stabilization policy can reestablish the initial levels of output and prices. Do this by indicating the appropriate shift in the aggregate demand curve. (The exact policies that will achieve these shifts will be described in detail in later chapters.)

   a. Inflation [panel (d)]

   b. Recession [panel (b)]

   c. Consider panel (c), the case of stagnation. If the government is restricted to policies that shift the aggregate demand curve, what will happen to output if the government adopts policies to combat inflation and restore the original price level? What happens to prices if the government is committed to maintaining the original level of output?

3. **Table 22-1** contains data on output and prices in a hypothetical economy that produces only fast food.

   a. Calculate the money value of the production of hamburgers, shakes, and fries by multiplying price and quantity. Sum these results to calculate nominal gross domestic product (GDP) for each year.

Table 22-1

Prices and Quantities

| | | 2004 | | | 2005 | |
	Price (1)	Quantity (2)	Nominal Value (3)	Price (4)	Quantity (5)	Nominal Value (6)
Hamburgers	$2.00	300	_____	$2.80	310	_____
Shakes	1.00	300	_____	1.30	320	_____
Fries	0.75	300	_____	0.90	330	_____
		Nominal GDP	_____		Nominal GDP	_____

   b. What is the percentage increase in nominal GDP from 2004 to 2005? _____

   c. Use 2004 prices to compute real GDP for 2005.

   Value of 2005 hamburger production using 2004 prices _____

   Value of 2005 shake production using 2004 prices _____

   Value of 2005 fries production using 2004 prices _____

   Real GDP for 2005 (expressed in terms of 2004 prices) _____

   d. Calculate the percentage increase in real GDP from 2004 to 2005. _____

   e. How does this figure compare to the increase in nominal GDP calculated in question b? Which is the better measure of the increase in production?

SELF-TESTS FOR UNDERSTANDING

TEST A

Circle the most appropriate answer.

1. Microeconomics is concerned with
   a. economic aggregates.
   b. the actions of individual economic decision-making units.
   c. small people.
   d. small countries.

2. The study of macroeconomics focuses on
   a. the economic actions of large people.
   b. decisions by the largest 500 industrial companies.
   c. the prices and output of all firms in an industry.
   d. the behavior of entire economies.

3. Which of the following is an example of a macroeconomic aggregate?
   a. the national output of Haiti
   b. the total output of General Motors
   c. employment at Wal-Mart
   d. the price of unleaded gas

4. The aggregate demand curve shows
   a. the history of real GDP over the recent past.
   b. alternative levels of domestic output that policymakers might choose.
   c. how the quantity of domestic product demanded changes with changes in the price level.
   d. the demand for goods and services by the federal government.

5. The graph showing how the quantity of output produced by all firms depends upon the price level is called the
   a. aggregate supply curve.
   b. Phillips curve.
   c. production possibilities frontier.
   d. economy's aggregate indifference curve.

6. GDP measures the sum of money values of
   a. all goods sold in the domestic economy during the past year.
   b. all final goods and services produced in the domestic economy during the past year.
   c. attendance at all the worst movies during the past year.
   d. all payments to household domestic help during the past year.

7. GDP is designed to be a measure of
   a. economic activity conducted through organized markets.
   b. national well-being.
   c. all economic activity during the preceding year.
   d. all economic transactions involving cash.

287

8. Using current prices to aggregate all final output in the economy will yield
   a. nominal GDP.
   b. real GDP.
   c. the cost of living.
   d. GDP in constant dollars.

9. Real GDP is computed by valuing output at
   a. manufacturers' costs.
   b. current prices.
   c. prices from an agreed-upon base year.
   d. last year's rate of inflation.

10. Which of the following would not be included in GDP for 2005?
    a. the production of refrigerators in 2005
    b. the government's purchase of paper clips produced in 2005
    c. consumer expenditures on haircuts in 2005
    d. General Motors' expenditures on steel for producing Cadillacs in 2005

11. Which of the following would not be part of GDP for 2005?
    a. Stacey's purchase of a 2005 Chevrolet
    b. Tanya's purchase of the latest iMac
    c. Ramon's expenditures on new furniture for his apartment
    d. Jamal's purchase of a guitar originally used by John Lennon in 1965

12. Which of the following is counted by the GDP statisticians?
    a. Jerita's purchase of Boeing stock from Walter
    b. your spending on tuition and fees for this year
    c. Durwood's winnings from his bookie
    d. the value of Yvonne's volunteer time at her daughter's school

13. Which of the following will be measured as an increase in GDP but need not reflect an increase in economic well-being?
    a. expenditures to clean up a major oil spill in Prince William Sound
    b. the value of the time Roland spends painting his own house
    c. the cost of new medical care that reduces infant mortality
    d. earnings of numbers runners in Chicago

14. In 1990, nominal GDP was $5.803 trillion. In 1991, nominal GDP increased to $5.986 trillion. On the basis of just this information, which of the following statements is true?
    a. Total output of the American economy was greater in 1991 than in 1990.
    b. The whole increase in nominal GDP was the result of inflation.
    c. Actual output increased by 3.15 percent. [(5.986 − 5.803) ÷ 5.803] = .0315
    d. It is impossible to determine what happened to prices and output from data on nominal GDP alone.

15. A recession is likely to occur if
    a. unemployment is falling.
    b. the aggregate supply curve shifts to the right.
    c. the increase in nominal GDP exceeds the increase in real GDP.
    d. the aggregate demand curve shifts to the left.

16. Inflation is defined as a period of
    a. rising nominal GDP.
    b. generally rising prices.
    c. falling real GDP.
    d. falling unemployment.

17. Which of the following conditions will result in stagflation?
    a. The aggregate demand curve shifts to the right.
    b. The aggregate demand curve shifts to the left.
    c. The aggregate supply curve shifts to the right.
    d. The aggregate supply curve shifts to the left.

18. Stabilization policy refers to actions by the government to
    a. keep real GDP from rising.
    b. minimize changes in government regulation.
    c. prevent recessions and fight inflation.
    d. equalize the rate of unemployment and inflation.

19. Successful stabilization policy to reduce inflation would shift
    a. the aggregate supply curve to the left.
    b. the burden of taxes from individuals to corporations.
    c. the aggregate demand curve to the left.
    d. decision making about monetary policy to the Congress.

20. In the period following World War II, the historical record shows
    a. more frequent and severe recessionary dips in real output than before World War II.
    b. an economy that appears to be more inflation prone.
    c. little if any increase in real GDP.
    d. little increase in the price level.

TEST B

Circle T or F for true or false.

T F 1. A study of the economy of Luxembourg would be an example of microeconomics.

T F 2. GDP is an example of a macroeconomic aggregate.

T F 3. An increase in nominal GDP necessarily implies an increase in real GDP.

T F 4. Changes in real GDP are a better measure of changes in national output than changes in nominal GDP.

T F 5. Deflation can occur only as a result of shifts in the aggregate supply curve.

T F 6. On the eve of World War II, national output, or real GDP, was not much greater than at the end of the Civil War.

T F 7. Stagflation refers to the simultaneous occurrence of rising prices and little if any increase in output.

T F 8. A reduction in taxes that is meant to spur consumer spending would be an example of fiscal policy.

T F 9. Federal Reserve's policies designed to increase interest rates would be an example of monetary policy.

T F 10. Stabilization policy refers to attempts by the government to influence both prices and output by shifting the aggregate demand curve.

ECONOMICS IN ACTION

LEADING INDICATORS AND TURNING POINTS

The text describes recessions as a period when real GDP declines. This is also the definition that is used by many media commentators. However, the timing of business cycle expansions and recessions has traditionally been determined by a group of economists associated with the National Bureau of Economic Research (NBER). For a number of reasons, the NBER Business Cycle Dating Committee has concentrated its attention on monthly data. GDP data are only available quarterly, i.e., for three-month periods; data on quarterly GDP is not immediately available as it takes some time to gather all of the relevant data to construct accurate estimates of GDP, and data on GDP are often revised years later. As a result, the NBER committee has traditionally focused on four monthly measures of economic activity: total civilian employment, industrial production, personal income less transfer payments adjusted for inflation, and manufacturing and trade sales adjusted for inflation.

During the summer of 2001 there was much commentary in the press about whether the economic expansion of the 1990s had ended and the United States had slipped into a recession. These concerns were only heightened by the terrorist attacks of September 11.

Using **Figure 22-2**, how would you have dated the end of the expansion and the beginning of the 2001 recession? How would you have dated the end of the recession?

The committee's decision is reported in the answers section of the Study Guide, but make your own determina-

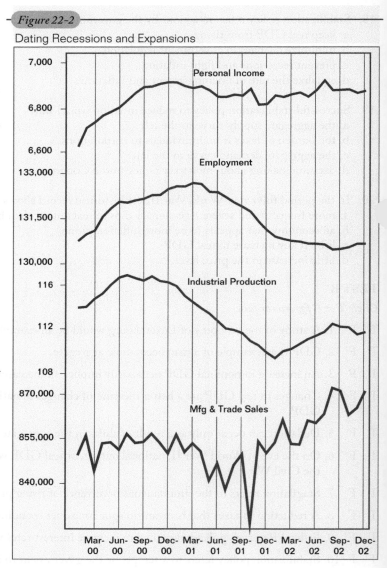

Figure 22-2

Dating Recessions and Expansions

tion before looking at their decision. As should be clear from Figure 22-2, measures of economic activity do not go up and down in lockstep. Your determination, like that of the NBER committee, is likely to require some weighting and averaging of these series.

Economist James Tobin has argued that the traditional approach to dating business cycles is misguided in that it assumes that any increase in economic activity would forestall the beginning of a recession or signal the end of a recession. Tobin notes that in a growing economy, output and employment have to increase simply to keep pace with a growing population and more productive workforce. He prefers growth-oriented dating and definitions of business cycles. Any period where the growth of output and employment failed to match the growth in the potential output would be called a recession or growth-recession.

1. How would you date the end of the 1990s expansion? Why?

2. How would you date the end of the recession? Why?

3. Do you think the definition of recessions should be growth-oriented as advocated by Tobin? Why?

4. Just who are the members of the NBER Business Cycle Dating Committee? Read about them in "Six economists play the dating game," *Fortune*, October 29, 2001.

Information on the timing of business cycles back to 1854 can be found on the NBER web site at http://www.nber.org/cycles/cyclesmain.html.

STUDY QUESTIONS

1. Why is GDP, a measure of domestic production, not a good measure of national well-being?

2. Why does GDP exclude the sales of existing goods and assets such as used college textbooks and existing homes?

3. Why does GDP include only final goods and exclude intermediate goods?

4. Which is the better measure of the change in domestic output, nominal GDP or real GDP? Why?

5. Should measures of GDP include estimates of nonmarket economic activity? Why?

6. How can stabilization policy help to reduce unemployment? Inflation?

7. If stabilization policy has the strongest and most immediate impact on aggregate demand, what are the implications for prices when the government wants to reduce unemployment? What are the implications for unemployment when the government wants to reduce prices?

8. What might account for the differences in the U.S. economy's record of economic growth and inflation after 1950 as compared with the period before World War II?

ECONOMICS ONLINE

You can get current information on a number of economic indicators from the following government web sites:

White House Economic Statistics Briefing Room

http://www.whitehouse.gov/fsbr/esbr.html

Bureau of Economic Analysis (U.S. Department of Commerce)

http://www.bea.gov/

Bureau of Labor Statistics (U.S. Department of Labor)

http://www.bls.gov/eag/eag.us.htm

U.S. Census Economic Briefing Room

http://www.census.gov/cgi-bin/briefroom/BriefRm

Statistical Abstract of the United States

Http://www.census.gov/compendia/statab

Economic Indicators, a monthly publication prepared by the Council of Economic Advisers for the Joint Economic Committee

http://www.gpoaccess.gov/indicators/browse.html

The Goals of Macroeconomic Policy

23

Important Terms and Concepts

Inputs	Production function	Unemployment insurance	Expected rate of inflation
Outputs	Unemployment rate	Purchasing power	Capital gain
Growth policy	Discouraged workers	Real wage rate	
Economic growth	Frictional unemployment	Relative prices	
Labor productivity	Structural unemployment	Redistribution by inflation	
Potential GDP	Cyclical unemployment	Real rate of interest	
Labor force	Full employment	Nominal rate of interest	

Learning Objectives

After completing this chapter, you should be able to:

- summarize arguments in favor of and opposed to higher rates of economic growth.

  explain how potential GDP is estimated and how growth in potential GDP is related to an economy's growth potential.

- explain why growth in labor productivity is the major determinant of the growth in living standards.

- explain how economists use the concept of potential GDP to measure the economic cost of unemployment.

- describe how the Bureau of Labor Statistics measures the number of unemployed and in what ways this number may overestimate or underestimate the unemployment level.

- explain the differences between frictional, structural, and cyclical unemployment.

- summarize the debate over how much unemployment is consistent with full employment.

- explain why unemployment insurance only spreads the financial burden of unemployment that individuals

  would otherwise face, but does not eliminate the economic cost of unemployment.

- distinguish between real and mythical costs of inflation.

- explain how the concept of real wages suggests that inflation has not systematically eroded the purchasing power of wages.

- distinguish between changes in prices that reflect a change in relative prices and changes that reflect general inflation.

- distinguish between real and nominal rates of interest.

- describe how the difference between real and nominal rates of interest is related to expectations about the rate of inflation.

- explain how the taxation of nominal magnitudes can mean that, during a period of inflation, savers and investors will receive a reduced real return after taxes.

- explain why the variability of inflation is important to an understanding of the cost of inflation.

CHAPTER REVIEW

This chapter is an introduction to three important issues at the heart of the formulation of macroeconomic policy: economic growth, unemployment, and inflation.

ECONOMIC GROWTH

The tools of economics cannot help you determine whether an economy should grow faster or slower; they can, however, identify the sources of growth and the consequences of more or less growth. In particular, a number of economists oppose zero economic growth on the grounds that a move in this direction would require extensive government controls and may seriously hamper efforts to eliminate poverty and to protect the environment. Solutions to these last two problems are likely to require more rather than fewer resources. Many feel that it is easier to reach a political agreement to devote resources to problems of poverty and the environment if total output is expanding rather than if it is not growing.

(1) Over long periods of time the major determinant of material well-being or living standards is the growth in labor _____. Growth in labor productivity explains why, on the average, during the last 150 years each generation has been wealthier than its parents. Continued growth in labor productivity will mean that your children and their children will be wealthier than you are.

For a firm producing a single output, measuring labor productivity per hour is a simple matter of dividing output by total labor hours. For the American economy as a whole, labor productivity is measured as real GDP
(2) divided by total labor hours. An increase in labor productivity means that (more/less) output can be produced with the same number of labor hours. If aggregate output were unchanged, an increase in labor productivity would mean (more/less) unemployment. But remember that total output and the unemployment rate are determined by the intersection of the aggregate _____ and aggregate _____ curves. An increase in productivity means that the economy's capacity to produce has increased; that is, the aggregate supply curve has shifted to the (left/right) and there has been a(n) (increase/decrease) in potential GDP. It is macroeconomic policy that helps to determine whether we take advantage of new possibilities.

What makes labor more or less productive? While there are many factors, certainly the intensity of work, the quality of training, the availability of more and better equipment, and the level of technology are important
(3) factors. Sustained growth in labor productivity (is/is not) a relatively new phenomenon, tracing back about (2,000/200) years. The following word equations show why growth in labor productivity is the basic determinant of living standards or output per capita:

We can express total output as the product of labor productivity and total hours worked:

$$\text{Output} = \text{Output}/\text{Total hours worked} \times \text{Total hours worked}$$

If we want to examine output per capita, the following expression will be helpful:

$$\frac{\text{Output}}{\text{Population}} = \frac{\text{Output}}{\text{Hours worked}} \times \frac{\text{Hours worked}}{\text{Employment}} \times \frac{\text{Employment}}{\text{Population}}$$

294

The expression on the left of the equal sign in the second equation is output per capita. The first expression on the right side of the equal sign is labor productivity. The second and third expressions measure the number of hours a typical worker works and the proportion of the population that works. Notice that two of the numerators and denominators on the right-hand side of the equal sign can be canceled, establishing the equality of the expression. If the number of hours per worker does not change and the proportion of the population that works is constant—that is, if the second and third terms on the right-hand side do not change—then the only way that output or GDP per capita can increase is if labor productivity increases. During the 20th century, it was the growth in labor productivity that dominated the other two terms.

UNEMPLOYMENT

Unemployment has two sorts of costs. The personal costs include not only the lost income for individuals out of work, but also the loss of work experience and the psychic costs of involuntary idleness. The economic costs for the nation as a whole can be measured by the output of goods and services that might have been produced by those who are unemployed.

Economists have attempted to measure the economic cost of unemployment by estimating what output would have been at full employment. These figures are estimates of (<u>potential</u>/actual) real GDP. The economic (4) cost of unemployment is the difference between potential real GDP and _____ real GDP.

Unemployment statistics come from a monthly survey by the Bureau of Labor Statistics. People are asked if they have a job. If they answer no, they are asked if they are laid off from a job they expect to return to, are actively looking for work, or are not looking for work. From these answers government statisticians derive estimates of employment, unemployment, and the labor force. These numbers are not above criticism. When unemployment rates are high or rising, some people give up looking for work because they believe that looking for work is not worth the effort. These people are called_____ workers. An increase in the (5) number of people who have given up looking for work means a(n) (<u>increase</u>/decrease) in the amount of statistical unemployment and is an important reason why some observers feel that the official unemployment statistics (<u>understate</u>/overstate) the problem of unemployment. All part-time workers are counted as employed. If part-time work is involuntary and these individuals would prefer full-time work, official unemployment statistics will (<u>understate</u>/overstate) the problem of unemployment. If liberal unemployment compensation induces people to call themselves unemployed even if they have no intention of looking for work then official statistics will (<u>overstate</u>/understate) unemployment.

Some unemployment occurs naturally from the normal workings of labor markets, as people join the labor force and look for their first job, look for better jobs, move to new locations, and so forth. Such unemployment is called _____ unemployment and involves people who are temporarily without a job more or (6) less voluntarily. Full employment would not eliminate this kind of unemployment. Full employment would eliminate unemployment that is due to a decline in the economy's total production; that is, at full employment there would be no _____ unemployment. Unemployment may also occur because people's skills are no longer in demand due to automation or massive changes in production. This type of unemployment is called _____ unemployment.

How do we determine how much unemployment is consistent with full employment or, more succinctly, what is the full employment rate of unemployment? In the early 1960s, President Kennedy argued that the United States should aim for an employment rate of 4 percent. During the 1970s it was argued that the in-

(7) creasing number of young workers in the labor force meant a higher percentage of (cyclical/frictional/structural) unemployment and (decreased/increased) the full employment rate of unemployment. Some argued that more generous unemployment compensation had increased the incentive for people to say they were looking for work when they really were not, a change that would increase the full employment rate of unemployment. Finally, many economists base their estimate of the full employment rate of unemployment on their evaluation of the links between unemployment and inflation. Experience in recent years suggests that the full employment rate of unemployment is (higher/lower) than estimates from the 1970s and 1980s but there is considerable uncertainty about its precise value.

Unemployment insurance can help ease the burden of unemployment for individual families, but it

(8) (can/cannot) protect society against the lost output that the unemployed might have produced. Employing these people in the future does not bring back the hours of employment that have already been missed. Unemployment compensation provides (complete/partial) protection for (all/some) unemployed workers.

INFLATION

There are important and valid reasons why people are concerned about continuing inflation. Nevertheless, quite a few popular arguments against inflation turn out to be based on misunderstandings. Many people worry

(9) that a high rate of inflation reduces their standard of living, or their (real/nominal) income. But the facts show that periods of high inflation are often accompanied by equally large if not larger increases in wages. For many workers, their real standard of living, or the change in their wages adjusted for the change in prices, continues to increase, even during periods of rapid inflation. A worker whose wages double when prices double is able to consume (more/less/the same) goods and services (than/as) before the rise in prices and wages. In this case one would say that real wages (increased/were unchanged/decreased).

(10)   During inflationary periods most prices increase at (the same/different) rates. As a result, goods and services with smaller than average price increases become relatively (more/less) expensive than they were before. Analogously, goods and services with larger than average price increases become relatively _____ expensive. Relative prices change all the time, during both inflationary and noninflationary periods. Changes in relative prices usually reflect shifts in demand and/or supply curves or various forms of government interventions. It is inaccurate to blame inflation for a change in relative prices.

But inflation does have real effects. One important effect is the redistribution of wealth between borrowers and lenders in inflationary periods. If lenders expect higher prices in the future they will demand

296

(<u>higher/lower</u>) interest rates to compensate them for the loss of purchasing power of the future dollars used   (11)
to repay loans. Economists have thus found it useful to distinguish between nominal and real interest rates. If
one looks at interest rates only in terms of the dollars that borrowers pay and lenders receive, one is looking at
_____ interest rates. If one looks at interest rates in terms of the purchasing power the borrower will
pay the lender, one is looking at _____ interest rates. During periods of inflation it is usual for nominal
interest rates to incorporate expectations of inflation. There need be no unexpected redistribution of income
between borrowers and lenders if actual inflation matches the expectations of inflation embodied in nominal
interest rates.

If a change in the rate of inflation is accurately foreseen, and if nominal interest rates are correctly adjusted
to reflect the change in expected inflation, then nominal interest rates (<u>will/will not</u>) change while real inter-   (12)
est rates will (<u>also change/be unchanged</u>). More typically, expectations of inflation are incorrect, in which case
inflation will result in a redistribution of wealth between borrowers and lenders. Who gains and who loses
will depend on whether the adjustment of nominal interest rates is too large or too small. Lenders lose when
the adjustment of nominal interest rates is too (<u>large/small</u>) and borrowers lose when the adjustment is too
_____. The tax treatment of interest payments and capital gains can have a substantial impact on the
real after-tax rate of return. Problems here reflect the fact that the tax system, originally designed for a world of
no inflation, focuses on (<u>nominal/real</u>) interest rates.

Over the long run, small unexpected differences in the rate of inflation can compound to create large differ-
·nces in profits and losses. Since most business investments depend on long-term contracts, this area of economic activity may suffer during periods of high inflation. The difficulty of making long-term contracts is a real
cost of inflation.

Inflation that proceeds at a fairly moderate and steady pace may pose few problems for an economy, but inflation that progresses at high, sometimes accelerating, and often variable rates imposes significant social and
economic costs. There is no simple borderline between the two. In different countries or in different periods of
time, the dividing line will vary considerably.

IMPORTANT TERMS AND CONCEPTS QUIZ

Choose the best definition for each of the following terms.

1. _____ Inputs
2. _____ Outputs
3. _____ Economic growth
4. _____ Growth policy
5. _____ Labor productivity
6. _____ Potential GDP
7. _____ Labor force
8. _____ Production function
9. _____ Unemployment rate
10. _____ Discouraged workers
11. _____ Frictional unemployment
12. _____ Structural unemployment
13. _____ Cyclical unemployment
14. _____ Unemployment insurance
15. _____ Purchasing power
16. _____ Real wage
17. _____ Relative prices
18. _____ Real rate of interest
19. _____ Nominal rate of interest
20. _____ Capital gain

a. Labor, machinery, buildings, and other resources used to produce output
b. Number of people holding or seeking jobs
c. Output per hour of labor input
d. Government transfer payments to eligible workers if unemployed
e. Percentage of labor force unemployed
f. Interest payments, in percentage terms, measured in dollars
g. Total output divided by population
h. Unemployed people who cease looking for work, believing that no jobs are available
i. Unemployment attributable to decline in economy's total production
j. Unemployment due to normal workings of the labor market
k. Government policies to promote economic growth
l. Interest payment, in percentage terms, measured in terms of purchasing power
m. Volume of goods and services that money wage will buy
n. Unemployment due to changes in nature of economy
o. Price of an item in terms of some other item
p. Volume of goods and services that a sum of money will buy
q. Level of real output attainable if all resources were fully employed
r. Increase in total output
s. Difference between an asset's selling price and its original cost
t. Goods and services that firms produce
u. Legal maximum interest rate
v. Relationship between inputs and outputs

BASIC EXERCISES

1. Who Gains and Loses from an Adjustment of Nominal Interest Rates?

This problem is designed to illustrate how the adjustment of nominal interest rates, when it is an accurate reflection of future inflation, can leave the real costs and returns to borrowers and lenders unchanged. For simplicity this problem ignores taxes.

Angela Abbott has a manufacturing firm. After paying other costs she expects a cash flow of $10 million, out of which she must pay the principal and interest on a $5 million loan. If prices are unchanged and if the interest rate is 5 percent, Angela expects a nominal and real profit of $4,750,000. This result is shown in the first column of **Table 23-1.**

Table 23-1

Angela's Cash Flow

	(1)	(2)	(3)	(4)
1. Price level	1.00	1.10	1.10	1.10
2. Sales revenue minus labor and materials costs*	10,000,000	11,000,000	11,000,000	11,000,000
3. Principal repayment	5,000,000	5,000,000	5,000,000	5,000,000
4. Interest rate	0.05	0.05	0.155	0.20
5. Interest payment [(4) × (3)]	250,000	_____	_____	_____
6. Total nominal payment to lender [(3) + (5)]	5,250,000	_____	_____	_____
7. Real payment to lender [(6) ÷ (1)]	5,250,000	_____	_____	_____
8. Nominal profits [(2) − (6)]	4,750,000	_____	_____	_____
9. Real profits [(8) ÷ (1)]	4,750,000	_____	_____	_____

*Inflation of 10 percent is assumed to increase sales revenue, labor costs, and materials costs by 10 percent each. As a result, the difference between sales revenue and labor plus material costs also increases by 10 percent in columns 2, 3, and 4.

The next three columns reflect three possible alternatives. The second column shows the consequences of unexpected inflation of 10 percent. In the third column, nominal interest rates have adjusted in expectation of an inflation of 10 percent, which actually occurs. And in the last column, nominal interest rates reflect the consequences of expecting a higher rate of inflation than actually occurs.

a. Fill in the missing figures in the second column. Compare the real returns to both Angela and her lender with those of the noninflationary situation in column 1. Who gains and who loses when there is unexpected inflation?

b. Fill in the missing figures in the third column. This is the case in which nominal interest rates have adjusted appropriately. (The approximation is to add the rate of inflation, 10 percent, to the rate of interest in the noninflationary situation, 5 percent. The extra 0.5 percent comes from a more complex and complete adjustment.) Compare the real returns in rows 7 and 9 with the comparable figures in column 1. Who gains and who loses now?

c. Fill in the missing figures in column 4, where interest rates have adjusted in anticipation of a rate of inflation higher than the rate that actually occurs. Who gains and who loses when inflation turns out to be less than expected?

2. When Were High Interest Rates Really Low?

Let R = nominal interest rate,
π = actual rate of inflation, and
r = real rate of interest.

Economists expect expectations of inflation to influence nominal interest rates. When borrowers repay lenders, the real interest rate that borrowers pay and lenders receive will depend upon the actual rate of inflation. One can measure real interest rates after the fact as $r = R - \pi$. Consider the data in **Table 23-2**. Column 1 shows data on nominal interest rates on one-year government securities issued in December of each year from 1975 through 2003. Column 2 shows the rate of inflation over the same period, December to December, as measured by the consumer price index. (For example, the rate of

Table 23-2

Nominal and Real Interest Rates

	Nominal Interest Rate on 1-Year Government Securities (December)	Rate of Inflation (December to December)	Real Interest Rate
1975	6.60%	4.9%	_____ %
1976	4.89%	6.7%	_____ %
1977	6.96%	9.0%	_____ %
1978	10.30%	13.3%	_____ %
1979	11.98%	12.5%	_____ %
1980	14.88%	8.9%	_____ %
1981	12.85%	3.8%	_____ %
1982	8.91%	3.8%	_____ %
1983	10.11%	3.9%	_____ %
1984	9.33%	3.8%	_____ %
1985	7.67%	1.1%	_____ %
1986	5.87%	4.4%	_____ %
1987	7.17%	4.4%	_____ %
1988	8.99%	4.6%	_____ %
1989	7.72%	6.1%	_____ %
1990	7.05%	3.1%	_____ %
1991	4.38%	2.9%	_____ %
1992	3.71%	2.7%	_____ %
1993	3.61%	2.7%	_____ %
1994	7.14%	2.5%	_____ %
1995	5.31%	3.3 %	_____ %
1996	5.47%	1.7%	_____ %
1997	5.53%	1.6%	_____ %
1998	4.52%	2.7%	_____ %
1999	5.84%	3.4%	_____ %
2000	5.60%	1.6%	_____ %
2001	2.22%	2.4%	_____ %
2002	1.45%	1.9%	_____ %
2003	1.31%	3.3%	_____ %

SOURCES: Federal Reserve, Bureau of Labor Statistics.

300

inflation reported for 1975 is from December 1975 to December 1976, the same period for which a holder of the government security earned interest.)

a. Complete column 3 by subtracting the rate of inflation from the nominal rate of interest to compute the real rate of interest.

b. The nominal interest rates from column 1 are plotted in **Figure 23-1**. Plot the real interest rates you calculated in column 3 in Figure 23-1.

Figure 23-1

Nominal and Real Interest Rates

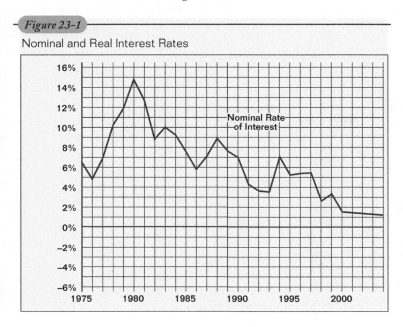

c. Were actual real rates ever negative? If so, how can this be?

d. When were interest rates highest? Is the answer different depending upon whether one is looking at nominal or real interest rates? Which do you think is the best measure of when interest rates were highest?

This exercise has made use of data on actual inflation to calculate after-the-fact real interest rates. Remember that when individuals decide to borrow or lend they typically know the nominal interest rate they will receive or have to pay, but they cannot know what the real interest rate will turn out to be, as that will depend upon future inflation. Thus decisions to borrow and lend will be strongly influenced by expectations of inflation and the corresponding expectations for real interest rates.

301

3. When Was Gasoline Most Expensive?

Table 23-3 has data on the average retail price of a gallon of unleaded gasoline since 1976. Use the data on the CPI for each year to adjust the price of gasoline to see when gasoline was most expensive relative to the price of other goods as measured by the CPI. As explained in the Appendix to Chapter 23, for each year you will need to divide the price of gasoline by the CPI and then multiply by 100.

While 2003 and 2004 show some of the highest nominal prices, when was the relative price of gasoline highest? Was it 2003 or 2004?

Table 23-3

Price of Gasoline

Year	Retail Price of Unleaded gasoline	CPI (82-84 = 100)	Price of gasoline adjusted for inflation
1976	$ 0.61	56.9	$ _____
1977	0.66	60.6	_____
1978	0.67	65.2	_____
1979	0.90	72.6	_____
1980	1.25	82.4	_____
1981	1.38	90.9	_____
1982	1.30	96.5	_____
1983	1.24	99.6	_____
1984	1.21	103.9	_____
1985	1.20	107.6	_____
1986	0.93	109.6	_____
1987	0.95	113.6	_____
1988	0.95	118.3	_____
1989	1.02	124.0	_____
1990	1.16	130.7	_____
1991	1.14	136.2	_____
1992	1.13	140.3	_____
1993	1.11	144.5	_____
1994	1.11	148.2	_____
1995	1.15	152.4	_____
1996	1.23	156.9	_____
1997	1.23	160.5	_____
1998	1.06	163.0	_____
1999	1.17	166.6	_____
2000	1.51	172.2	_____
2001	1.46	177.1	_____
2002	1.36	179.9	_____
2003	1.59	184.0	_____
2004	1.88	188.9	_____

Source: Bureau of Labor Statistics

SELF-TESTS FOR UNDERSTANDING

TEST A

Circle the most appropriate answer.

1. Labor productivity is defined as
   a. output per capita.
   b. GDP divided by population.
   c. the growth in output per worker.
   d. output per hour of labor input.

2. A country's standard of living is usually measured as
   a. GDP per capita.
   b. output per worker.
   c. the growth in GDP.
   d. output per unit of labor input.

3. Which of the following would not explain differences in labor productivity between countries?
   a. the amount of capital per worker
   b. the level of technology
   c. the size of the labor force
   d. the amount of training received by workers

4. The production function tells us how much the economy can produce using all but which one of the following?
   a. labor
   b. capital
   c. outputs
   d. the state of technology

5. Indicate which examples go with which concepts.
   a. an older, unemployed telephone operator replaced by new, computerized switching machines
   b. an unemployed college senior looking for her first job
   c. a former construction worker who has given up looking for work because he believes no one is hiring
   d. an unemployed retail clerk who was laid off because of declining sales associated with a general business recession

   frictional unemployment _____

   structural unemployment _____

   cyclical unemployment _____

   discouraged worker _____

6. Which of the following factors implies that official statistics may understate the magnitude of the problem of unemployment? (There may be more than one correct answer.)
   a. discouraged workers
   b. the loss of expected overtime work
   c. generous unemployment benefits
   d. involuntary part-time work

7. Which of the following people are eligible for unemployment compensation?
   a. a mechanic for Ford Motor Company laid off because of declining auto sales
   b. a housewife seeking paid work after six years spent at home with two small children
   c. a college senior looking for his first job
   d. an engineer who quits to find a better job

8. Which one of the following groups experiences the highest rate of unemployment?
   a. married men
   b. college graduates
   c. teenage workers
   d. adult nonwhite workers

9. The measure of output that the economy could produce with the full employment of all people and factories is called
   a. real GDP.
   b. potential GDP.
   c. nominal GDP.
   d. expected GDP.

10. The difference between potential GDP and actual GDP is a reflection of
    a. frictional unemployment.
    b. cyclical unemployment.
    c. usury laws.
    d. nominal interest rates.

11. The growth of GDP can be expressed as the sum of which of the following?
    a. the growth rate of the labor input
    b. the rate of inflation
    c. the real rate of interest
    d. the growth rate of labor productivity

12. Unemployment insurance
    a. eliminates the cost of unemployment to the economy as a whole.
    b. means that no unemployed worker need suffer a decline in his or her standard of living.
    c. helps to protect insured individuals by spreading the cost.
    d. must be paid back by the unemployed once they find a new job.

13. The real rate of interest relevant for a lender about to lend money is measured as the
    a. nominal interest rate divided by the rate of inflation.
    b. nominal interest rate minus the expected rate of inflation.
    c. rate of inflation minus the nominal interest rate.
    d. the increase in nominal GDP divided by the rate of increase in prices.

14. A nominal interest rate of 10 percent and inflationary expectations of 4 percent imply a real interest rate of _____ percent.
    a. 4
    b. 6
    c. 10
    d. 14

15. If suddenly everyone expects a higher rate of inflation, economists would expect nominal interest rates to
    a. fall.
    b. stay unchanged.
    c. rise.

16. If inflation is unexpected, there is apt to be a redistribution of wealth from
    a. borrowers to lenders.
    b. lenders to borrowers.
    c. rich to poor.
    d. poor to rich.

17. With overall inflation at 5 percent, if the price of jeans increases by 7 percent and the price of calculators declines by 3 percent, we would say that the relative price of
    a. jeans and calculators has increased.
    b. jeans has increased and the relative price of calculators has decreased.
    c. jeans and calculators has decreased.
    d. jeans has decreased and the relative price of calculators has increased.

18. Assume that in a world without inflation, interest rates are 4 percent and 25 percent of interest income must be paid to the government in taxes. (That is, the after-tax real return to lenders is 3 percent.) Assume now that inflation is expected to be and turns out to be 4 percent. Assume further that nominal interest rates increase to 8 percent in line with expectations of inflation at 4 percent. With taxes based on nominal income, what is the after-tax real return when nominal interest rates increase to 8 percent?
    a. less than 3 percent
    b. unchanged at 3 percent
    c. more than 3 percent

19. If your wages go up by 10 percent when prices go up by 7 percent, the increase in your real wage is about _____ percent.
    a. 3
    b. 7
    c. 10
    d. 17

305

20. The historical evidence suggests that in periods with high rates of inflation, nominal wages
    a. increase at about the same rate as before.
    b. increase at much lower rates than inflation.
    c. also increase at high rates.
    d. remain unchanged.

TEST B

Circle T or F for true or false.

T   F   1. Long term, it makes little difference whether productivity grows at 1 percent per year or at 3 percent per year.

T   F   2. If the growth in real GDP is less than the growth in potential GDP, there will be an increase in unemployment.

T   F   3. In periods of high unemployment, the only people whose incomes are reduced are those who are out of work.

T   F   4. The official unemployment statistics are adjusted to include those people with part-time jobs who are looking for full-time work.

T   F   5. Unemployment insurance protects society against lost output from unemployment.

T   F   6. Potential GDP is an estimate of the maximum possible output our economy could produce under conditions similar to wartime.

T   F   7. Most economists agree that full employment should be defined as an unemployment rate of zero.

T   F   8. Inflation does not redistribute wealth between borrowers and lenders because nominal interest rates are automatically adjusted to reflect actual inflation.

T   F   9. The historical record shows that low inflation will always lead to high inflation.

T   F 10. Predictable inflation is likely to impose less cost than unpredictable inflation.

| Appendix | *How Statisticians Measure Inflation*

Learning Objectives

After completing this appendix, you should be able to:

• construct a price index from data on prices and the composition of the market basket in the base year.

• use a price index to compute real measures of economic activity by deflating the corresponding nominal measures.

• use a price index to compute the rate of inflation from one period to the next.

• explain how the market baskets differ for the Consumer Price Index and the GDP deflator.

Important Terms and Concepts

Index number	Consumer Price Index	GDP deflator
Index number problem	Deflating	

306

IMPORTANT TERMS AND CONCEPTS QUIZ

Choose the best definition for each of the following terms.

1. _____ Index number

2. _____ Index number problem

3. _____ Consumer Price Index

4. _____ Deflating

5. _____ GDP deflator

a. Dividing a nominal magnitude by a price index to express the magnitude in constant purchasing power

b. Magnitude of some variable relative to its magnitude in the base period

c. Price index obtained by dividing nominal GDP by real GDP

d. Measure of price level based on the spending of urban households

e. Average change in consumer prices

f. Differences between consumption patterns of actual families and the market basket used for a price index

BASIC EXERCISES

The following exercise should help you review the material on price indexes presented in the appendix to Chapter 23.

Table 23-4 presents data on expenditures and prices for a hypothetical family that buys only food and clothing. We see that in 2004 this family spent $5,000 on food at $2 per unit of food, and $10,000 on clothing at $25 per unit. Note that between 2004 and 2005, dollar expenditures by this family increased by 15.65 percent, rising from $15,000 to $17,348. Is this family able to consume 15.65 percent more of everything? Clearly not, since prices have risen. How much inflation has there been on average? What is the increase in real income for this family? These are the sorts of questions that a good price index can help you answer.

1. Use the data in Table 23-4 to construct a family price index (FPI) using 2004 as the base year.

Table 23-4

Prices and Expenditures

Year	Food Price	Food Expenditures	Clothing Price	Clothing Expenditures	Total Expenditures
2004	$2.00	$5,000	$25.00	$10,000	$15,000
2005	$2.36	$5,900	$26.50	$11,448	$17,348

a. Divide expenditures by price to find the quantities of each good purchased in 2004. This is the base-period market basket.

Quantity of food _____

Quantity of clothing _____

b. Use 2005 prices to find out how much the base-period market basket would cost in 2005.

2005 cost of 2004 market basket _____

c. Divide the 2005 cost of the base-period market basket by the 2004 cost of the same market basket and multiply by 100 to compute the value of the FPI for 2005.

FPI for 2005 _____

d. Convince yourself that if you repeat steps b and c using 2004 prices you will get an answer of 100 for the value of the FPI for 2004.

e. Estimate inflation by computing the percentage change in your price index from 2004 to 2005.

Inflation between 2004 and 2005 _____

f. Divide total dollar expenditures in 2005 by the 2005 FPI and multiply by 100 to deflate 2005 nominal expenditures.

Real expenditures in 2005 (2004 prices) _____

Percentage change in real expenditures 2004 to 2005 _____

Remember the following points about price indexes:
- Most price indexes, like the Consumer Price Index, are computed by pricing a standard market basket of goods in subsequent periods.
- A price index can be used to measure inflation and to deflate nominal values to adjust for inflation.
- Different price indexes, such as the Consumer Price Index and the GDP deflator, will show slightly different measures of inflation because they use different market baskets.

2. (Optional) Compute a new FPI using 2005 as the base period rather than 2004. Now the value of your price index for 2005 will be 100 and the price index for 2004 will be something less than 100. Does this index give the same measure of inflation as the index with 2004 as the base period? Do not be surprised if it does not. Can you explain why they differ?

SUPPLEMENTARY EXERCISES

1. **Table 23-5** contains data on consumer prices for seven countries. Try to answer each of the following questions or explain why the information in Table 23-5 is insufficient to answer the question.
   a. In 1970, which country had the lowest prices?
   b. In 2004, which country had the highest prices?
   c. During the period 1970 to 2004, which country experienced the most inflation as measured by the percentage change in the consumer price index? Which country experienced the least inflation?

Table 23-5

Consumer Prices (1982-84 = 100)

	Canada	France	Germany	Italy	Japan	United Kingdom	United States
1970	35.1	28.8	52.8	17.1	38.5	21.8	38.8
1980	76.1	72.3	86.7	63.2	90.9	78.5	82.4
1990	135.5	133.0	112.2	159.6	111.4	148.2	130.7
2000	164.9	157.6	142.6	231.9	121.0	200.1	172.2
2004	181.0	170.3	150.8	256.3	118.7	219.4	188.9

SOURCE: *Economic Report of the President, 2000 and 2005,* Table B-108.

2. How Much Difference Can Small Differences Really Make?

The text argues that although the differences in the growth rate of GDP per capita over the period 1870 to 1979 for the United States, Japan, and the United Kingdom seem quite small when compounded over 100-plus years, the differences can be quite large. Can such small differences really make much of a difference?

Fill in the last column in **Table 23-6** to find out. It compares the experience of three countries, all assumed to start with the same level of GDP per capita.

Table 23-6

The Cumulative Impact of Small Differences in Growth Rates

Country	Annual growth rate of GDP per capita	Initial level GDP per capita	GDP per capita after 109 years
A	1.8%	10,000	_____
B	2.3%	10,000	_____
C	3.0%	10,000	_____

3. How Accurate Are Consumer Expectations of Inflation?

You can check for yourself. The Federal Reserve Bank of St. Louis posts data on inflation expectations from the University of Michigan survey of consumers. Try comparing this data to the actual change in consumer prices that you can compute using data on the CPI from the same web site.

Data on inflation expectations are found under the "Business/Fiscal" heading at

http://research.stlouisfed.org/fred2

It may be easiest to use the search option. Search for "University of Michigan Inflation Expectations." Data on the CPI is found at the same web site under the heading "Consumer Price Indexes." You will need to compute the actual rate of inflation from the data on the CPI.

ECONOMICS IN ACTION

HOW TO MEASURE INFLATION

Does the Consumer Price Index (CPI) overstate inflation? If so, by how much? In the late 1990s these questions were of more than academic interest. They became an important part of discussions about how to balance the federal budget. A number of federal programs, most notably Social Security payments and income tax brackets, are adjusted annually in step with increases in the CPI. If the CPI overstates inflation, these adjustments have been too generous in the sense that federal government spending would be larger and revenues would be smaller than they should be to account for inflation. If inflation has been overstated, then the apparent stagnation in real wages that one finds when using the CPI to adjust nominal wages has given a misleading picture of real income.

In 1995, while looking for ways to eliminate the deficit, the Senate Finance Committee asked a panel of prominent economists, headed by Michael Boskin, an economist at Stanford University and former Chairman of the Council of Economic Advisers, to study this issue and make a recommendation to the Committee.

The panel issued its final report in December 1996. It concluded that the CPI has overstated inflation by about 1.1 percent per year for four reasons: Substitution bias—as the CPI prices a fixed market basket, it ignores the response of consumers to change their market basket in favor of goods and services with smaller price increases; outlet bias—CPI sampling procedures have tended to ignore the shift of consumers to large discount stores like Wal-Mart and Costco; quality bias—CPI procedures are not always able to identify when an increase in price reflects improved quality; new product bias—because the CPI market basket is changed so infrequently, it often misses the large declines in price that usually accompany the introduction of new products.

In late 2001, the Bureau of Labor Statistics (BLS) announced that it will adjust the consumer market basket every two years instead of every six to eight years. It also announced that it will adjust its sample of stores more frequently.

Others are not so sure that the Boskin Commission's criticisms were all on target. These critics question BLS procedures to measure quality changes and are also skeptical of how the Boskin Commission proposed to handle new products. A more fundamental difference has to do with the role of price index like the CPI. The Boskin Commission argued in favor of a consumer price index that measures the cost of living. Critics acknowledge that, while in principle quality improvements reduce the cost of maintaining the previous standard of living, a real focus on the cost of living should include many other factors that may have increased the cost of living, e.g., increase in congestion, environment degradation, and commodities where quality has decreased rather than increase.

1. Do you think that the CPI has overstated inflation? If so by how much?

2. What would you recommend that the Bureau of Labor Statistics do?

Sources: The Boskin Committee Report is available online at http://www.ssa.gov/history/reports/boskinrpt.html. For a contrary view see Dean Baker, "The Inflated Case Against the CPI," *The American Prospect*, December 1, 1996. Baker's article is available online at http://www.prospect.org/print/V7/24/baker-d.html. See also Jolie Solomon, "An economic speedometer gets an overhaul," *The New York Times*, December 23, 2001; Jeff Madrick, "A new study questions how much anyone really knows about the real rate of inflation in the U.S.," *The New York Times*, December 27, 2001.

STUDY QUESTIONS

1. What is the difference between measures of labor productivity and output per capita?

2. Why is the growth of labor productivity so important for the growth in standards of living?

3. What factors are important for growth in labor productivity?

4. Is it possible for the growth in a country's standard of living to exceed the growth in labor productivity? If so, how, and is it likely that such a difference could be sustained over a long period of time?

310

5. Why doesn't unemployment insurance eliminate the cost of unemployment for the economy as a whole?

6. Do you believe the official rate of unemployment overstates or understates the seriousness of unemployment? Why?

7. Which concepts of unemployment—frictional, structural, and cyclical—are relevant when considering the full-employment rate of unemployment? Why?

8. What rate of unemployment is an appropriate target for macroeconomic policy?

9. When does an increase in the price of textbooks reflect a change in relative prices and when does it reflect inflation?

10. During a period of inflation, which is likely to be higher, nominal or real interest rates? Why?

11. Will inflation always redistribute income from lenders to borrowers?

12. Do you agree or disagree with the argument that the taxation of interest and capital gains should be based on real returns rather than nominal returns? Why?

13. Which is likely to have more adverse effects, steady or variable inflation? Why?

ECONOMICS ONLINE

The Bureau of Labor Statistics keeps tabs on employment, unemployment, and consumer prices. You can access current and historical data online at the following web sites:

Employment: http://www.bls.gov/bls/employment.htm

Consumer prices: http://www.bls.gov/cpi

Economic Growth: Theory and Policy

24

Important Terms and Concepts

Human capital	Property rights	Cost disease of the personal services
Convergence hypothesis	On-the-job training	Development assistance
Capital	Invention	Foreign direct investment
Investment	Innovation	Multinational corporations
Capital formation	Research and development (R&D)	

Learning Objectives

After completing this chapter, you should be able to:

- Explain why growth policies concentrate on efforts to increase

  ○ the rate of capital formation

  ○ the rate of improvement in workforce quality

  ○ the rate of technical progress.

- Describe policies that are meant to address each of these three pillars of economic growth.

- Explain why countries with initial low levels of productivity might be expected to see higher growth in productivity than countries with high levels of productivity.

- Describe the convergence hypothesis and explain whether all countries are participating.

- Describe American productivity growth experience and evaluate the arguments that have been advanced to explain this experience.

- Describe the cost disease of personal services and explain why the production of manufacturing goods would not be expected to suffer the same problem.

- Describe the growth experience of low-income countries and explain why it often differs from that of high-income countries.

CHAPTER REVIEW

Macroeconomic policymakers have two major tasks. One task focuses on the long run and is concerned with
(1) the rate of growth of potential GDP. This task is called _____ policy. The other task is concerned with keeping the economy close to its potential and is called _____ policy. This chapter is concerned with the first task.

We saw in the last chapter that the growth in labor productivity is the major factor in determining the growth in output per capita or standards of living in the long run. As such it should not be surprising that growth policy focuses on the growth in labor productivity. The three pillars of productivity growth are the rate
(2) at which an economy adds to its stock of factories, machines, and software through _____; the rate at which technology improves through _____ and _____; and the rate at which the quality of the workforce or the stock of _____ capital improves. While the level of output depends upon the size of the capital stock, the current state of technology, and the quality of the work force, the growth in output depends upon the growth in these same factors.

Comparing the growth experience across countries suggests that many countries with low levels of productivity are able to grow more quickly than countries that start with higher levels of productivity. This dif-
(3) ferential experience has been called the _____ hypothesis and arises because low productivity countries are able to learn from high productivity countries. It is the high productivity countries that need to (imitate/innovate) while the low productivity countries can _____. While a number of countries have been able to grow in this fashion, not all countries belong to the "convergence club." Political instability and weak property _____ often plague those that do not.

A country that wants to improve its growth prospects will want to focus policy actions on the three pillars of productivity growth. That is, it will want to adopt and promote policies that support capital formation, improvements in the quality of the work force, and invention and innovation. Policies that support capital formation
(4) are likely to include (high/low) real-interest rates, growth-oriented tax policies, and levels of aggregate demand close to potential output so that demand presses against productive capacity. The success of these policies is enhanced when there is a strong rule of law with secure property rights. It is also important to remember that higher levels of investments (are/are not) costless. For a country operating on its production possibilities frontier the opportunity cost of more investment will be a(n) (decrease/increase) in the output of consumption goods.

Policies that support improvements in the quality of the work force are those that support education and on-the-job training. Data on the earnings of college graduates suggest that in the United States the returns on higher education are quite substantial. Policies to support invention and innovation are likely to include government support for research and development through tax policy, public/private partnerships, and direct support of basic research.

314

It is not always possible to neatly assign growth policies to one of the three pillars. For example, policies that support scientific, technical, and business education are likely to be an important part of policies to enhance research and development. Policies that support invention and innovation will also support high levels of capital formation as firms seek to take advantage of new opportunities.

The record of productivity growth in the United States over the last half century shows some marked differences. For 25 years, from 1948 to 1973, productivity grew at about 2.9 percent per year. Productivity growth then slowed dramatically and averaged only 1.4 percent per year for the next 22 years. Experience from 1995 until the beginning of the recession in 2001 has been more optimistic with productivity growth averaging 3.0 percent per year.

Exactly why productivity growth slowed down so dramatically in the 1970s is not fully understood. Possible explanations include lagging investment, higher energy prices, a decline in work force quality, and a slowdown in the pace of innovation, although not all of these explanations seem as compelling on close examination. The growth in productivity since 1995 seems more closely related to advances in information technology and a surge in _____ spending.   (5)

It is important to remember that not all sectors of the economy participate equally in the process of economic growth. In particular, much of the growth in labor productivity is concentrated in parts of the economy that produce (<u>goods/services</u>) rather than _____. In parts of the economy where labor input and   (6) direct personal contact are important, e.g., medical care, education, the arts, police protection, it is harder to find ways to increase productivity that do not degrade the quality of services. While one person using a synthesizer might try playing a Beethoven quartet, many are likely to conclude that it is not the same as four string players.

Because labor is mobile across sectors of the economy, wages and salaries in personal service sectors of the economy need to keep pace with other sectors of the economy where high rates of growth in productivity can support wage increases without implying price increases. The result is higher relative prices for the personal service sectors of the economy, a phenomenon known as the _____ _____ of personal   (7) services.

Growth policies in developing countries will also focus on the three pillars of growth but are likely to be more difficult to implement. Low levels of income make it harder to find the resources for investment in capital, education, and technology. Rich countries can help by providing development assistance. Technology may be imported by encouraging multinational corporations to make direct investments, but there is often resistance to such actions. Adverse geographical conditions and government corruption are additional challenges facing many developing countries.

IMPORTANT TERMS AND CONCEPTS QUIZ

Choose the most appropriate definition for each of the following terms.

1. _____ Human capital
2. _____ Convergence hypothesis
3. _____ Capital
4. _____ Investment (or capital formation)
5. _____ Property rights
6. _____ On-the-job training
7. _____ Invention
8. _____ Innovation
9. _____ Research and development (R&D)
10. _____ Cost disease of the personal services
11. _____ Development assistance
12. _____ Foreign direct investment
13. _____ Multinational corporation

a. Low productivity countries experience higher growth in productivity
b. Stock of factories, office buildings, and machines
c. Purchase or construction of real business assets in a foreign country
d. Discovering new products or new production methods
e. Devoting resources to the production of new plants, more equipment, and software
f. Reduced output of consumption goods when output of investment goods increases
g. Grants and low interest loans to developing countries
h. Amount of education and training embodied in a nation's labor force
i. Increasing relative prices for services that require direct personal contact
j. Business or government activity that is purposely designed to stimulate invention and innovation
k. Laws and conventions that assign ownership rights
l. Skills workers acquire while working
m. Putting new ideas into practice
n. Corporation that operates in many countries

BASIC EXERCISES

1. This exercise illustrates the difference between the level of labor productivity and the growth of labor productivity. In particular, we will see whether a decline in the growth of labor productivity results in a decline in the level of productivity. Assume that labor productivity is originally $12 per hour, and that it grows at an annual rate of 2.9 percent for 25 years, and 1.4 percent for the next 22 years.

   a. What is labor productivity at the end of the first 25 years? $ _____

   b. What is labor productivity at the end of the next 22 years? $ _____

   c. Did the decline in the rate of growth of productivity lead to a decline in the level of productivity?

2. Can small differences in growth rates make all that much difference for productivity? Assume that we can index American productivity in 2000 at a value of 100. Fill in the blanks below to show what our productivity index would show in 2050 and 2100 at different rates of growth.

Growth Rate of Productivity	Productivity Index 2050	Productivity Index 2100
1.4 percent	_____	_____
2.5 percent	_____	_____
3.0 percent	_____	_____

SELF-TESTS FOR UNDERSTANDING

TEST A

Circle the most appropriate answer.

1. Stabilization policy is concerned with
   a. an economy's growth prospects.
   b. maintaining competitive conditions in industries that might otherwise become monopolized.
   c. seeing that an economy is plagued by neither high unemployment nor high inflation.
   d. maintaining stable exchange rates vis-à-vis other currencies.

2. Growth policy is concerned with
   a. an economy's growth prospects.
   b. maintaining competitive conditions in industries that might otherwise become monopolized.
   c. seeing that an economy is plagued by neither high unemployment nor high inflation.
   d. maintaining stable exchange rates vis-à-vis other currencies.

3. The growth in potential GDP is equal to the sum of which of the following?
   a. growth in population
   b. growth in labor hours
   c. growth in labor productivity
   d. growth in capital stock

4. The three pillars of productivity growth include which of the following?
   a. growth in the capital stock
   b. growth in technology
   c. growth in unemployment
   d. growth in human capital

5. Increases in which of the following would not be expected to increase labor productivity?
   a. capital stock
   b. technology
   c. labor force
   d. human capital

317

6. If the growth in labor productivity declines from 3 percent per year to 1.5 percent per year, then
   a. labor productivity will continue to increase although at a slower rate than before.
   b. standards of living will increase only if there is an expansion in average hours per worker.
   c. labor will become less productive over time.
   d. the result will be a declining standard of living.

7. The convergence hypothesis suggests that the growth of labor productivity in the most advanced country
   a. will exceed that of all other countries.
   b. will be less than that of many other countries.
   c. must decline.

8. A major factor leading to the convergence of growth rates across countries is probably the
   a. use of the dollar as the international currency of commerce.
   b. increased levels of GDP devoted to military spending in many countries.
   c. adoption of the euro.
   d. quick pace by which new technologies are spread among countries.

9. The essence of the convergence hypothesis can be summarized by noting that countries with the most advanced technology must _____ while less advanced countries can _____.
   a. import; export
   b. invest; save
   c. innovate; imitate
   d. educate; train

10. A low productivity country that is part of the convergence club will find that the growth in its productivity
    a. lags behind that of more advanced countries.
    b. is about the same as that of more advanced countries.
    c. is greater than that of more advanced countries.

11. Capital formation is another term for
    a. innovation.
    b. investment expenditures.
    c. invention.
    d. capital gains.

12. Which of the following is not conducive to a high level of investment expenditures?
    a. high real interest rates
    b. expectations of rapid economic growth
    c. new technologies that have created new markets
    d. political stability and clearly defined property rights

13. A country's stock of human capital can be increased by which of the following? (There may be more than one correct answer.)
    a. high real interest rates
    b. on-the-job training
    c. higher high school graduation rates
    d. lower taxes on capital gains

318

14. Since 1980 the income of college graduates has grown _____ the income of high school graduates.
    a. more slowly than
    b. about the same as
    c. much faster than

15. Which of the following is not a policy tool to stimulate research and development?
    a. reductions in taxes when businesses spend money on R&D
    b. monetary policy
    c. public/private research collaborations like the human genome project
    d. direct government expenditures through agencies like the National Science Foundation

16. When compared to the previous 25 years, the growth in productivity over the period 1973 to 1995 was
    a. lower.
    b. about the same.
    c. higher.

17. When compared to the previous 22 years, the growth in productivity over the period 1995 to 2009 was
    a. lower.
    b. about the same.
    c. higher.

18. When trying to understand the recent increase in the growth of productivity, most analysts cite which two of the following factors?
    a. high levels of private investment spending
    b. advances in information technology
    c. increasing energy prices
    d. declining high school graduation rates

19. Which of the following is least likely to suffer from the cost disease of personal services?
    a. manufacturing
    b. health care
    c. education
    d. the arts

20. The cost disease of personal services reflects which of the following? (There may be more than one correct answer.)
    a. Increases in labor productivity will lead to an increase in real wages.
    b. Increases in labor productivity are likely to be slow where personal contact is an important part of quality of service provided.
    c. In the long run, real wages in different occupations need to rise at similar rates if different occupations are to continue to be attractive to young people.

319

TEST B

Circle T or F for true or false.

T   F   1. Productivity growth in the United States is higher than in most other industrialized countries.

T   F   2. Since 1970 the growth in productivity in the United States has been about three times as high as it was right after World War II.

T   F   3. A decline in the rate of growth of American labor productivity means a decline in the productivity of American workers.

T   F   4. Increased investment spending leading to more capital formation is likely to increase the rate of economic growth.

T   F   5. The growth in potential GDP is equal to the growth rate in hours worked plus the growth rate of labor productivity.

T   F   6. In recent years workers with a college degree have earned more than 40 percent more than workers with just a high school degree.

T   F   7. All countries are now participating in the process of convergence of labor productivity.

T   F   8. According to the convergence hypothesis, low productivity countries will experience lower rates of growth of labor productivity than high productivity countries.

T   F   9. Investment is more likely when firms have excess capacity than when sales mean that firms must operate at full capacity.

T   F   10. Labor productivity in services industries should grow more rapidly than in the manufacturing sector of the economy.

SUPPLEMENTARY EXERCISE

Assume that growth policies were successful in raising income per capita in China to equal that of the United States. Because of the initial higher level of incomes in the United States, $37,800 vs. $5,000, it would take a number of years for Chinese incomes to reach parity with those in the United States. When answering the questions below assume that the growth rate of income per capita in the United States is 2 percent per year.

How fast would income per capita in China have to grow to match that of the United States in 50 years? In 100 years?

Income per capita in China has been growing at close to 8 percent per year. If it continued to grow at this rate, how long would it take to match that of the United States if income per capita in the United States continues to grow at 2 percent per year?

What does the convergence hypothesis say about China's ability to sustain a higher rate of economic growth as its income approaches that of the United States?

ECONOMICS IN ACTION

HOW TO IMPROVE WORLD ECONOMIC GROWTH

While there is widespread agreement about the importance of increasing economic growth in developing countries, there is as yet no agreement about what are the best ways to achieve this aim or even where to begin. The latter disagreement reflects in part the significant number of challenges that low-income countries face.

In September 2000, the United Nations adopted eight aggressive goals for worldwide economic development. Called the Millennium Development Goals, they include

- Eradicate extreme poverty and hunger by reducing by half the proportion of people living on less than a dollar a day and reducing by half the proportion of people who suffer from hunger

- Ensure that all boys and girls complete a full course of primary schooling

- Eliminate gender disparity in primary and secondary education preferably by 2005, and at all levels by 2015

- Reduce by two-thirds the mortality rate among children under five

- Reduce by three-quarters the maternal mortality ratio

- Combat HIV/AIDS, malaria, and other diseases by halting and beginning to reverse the spread of HIV/AIDS, the incidence of malaria, and other major diseases

- Ensure environmental sustainability

- Develop a global partnership for development.

Regardless of one's ranking of these goals, there is less agreement on what steps will be most effective to achieve them. Some, like economist Jeffrey Sachs, Director of the Earth Institute at Columbia University, argue for massive infusions of foreign aid from developed countries. Sachs estimates that achieving the Millennium goals will require an investment of $150 billion a year of development assistance.

How does $150 billion compare to current aid flows? In 2007 aid flows from developed countries were $103 billion, about 0. 28 percent of the GDP of donor countries. Sachs notes that development aid of $150 billion would raise contributions to a little more than 0.50 percent of GDP, still short of the goal of 0.70 percent endorsed by donor countries in 2002.

Before arguing for massive increases in foreign aid, some economists and others point to the importance of free trade, low taxes, deregulation, privatization, and the critical nature of the rule of law and reductions in government corruption. In March 2005, the Commission for Africa, sponsored by the British government, issued a document, "Our Common Interest" that called for a "radical change in the way donors behave and deliver assistance" to African nations. The report argued that corruption and misgovernment in Africa have been an impediment to economic growth, but goes on to argue for increased foreign aid and adjustments to trade policies in developing countries that have been a significant obstacle to African export growth.

The Copenhagen Consensus, a project organized by Bjorn Lomborg, head of the Environment Assessment Institute in Denmark, pulled together a panel of distinguished economists in May 2004 to evaluate a number of proposals to increase economic development, especially in low-income countries. The development challenges reviewed by the panel included civil conflicts, climate change, communicable diseases, education, financial stability, governance, hunger and malnutrition, migration, trade reform, and water and sanitation.

At the top of the panel's list for action was controlling HIV/AIDS, followed by fighting malnutrition. Third on their list was reducing trade barriers and eliminating agricultural subsidies. Using cost-benefit analysis the panel did not support proposals to mitigate climate change and implement the Kyoto protocol on greenhouse-gas emissions. Although subsequently some members of the panel argued that they were evaluating the specific proposal they had been asked to review and not the importance of the issues per se.

How much progress has been made in increasing GDP per capita in developing countries? How much progress has been made with regard to the specific UN Millennium Development Goals? How important is foreign aid to achieving these goals? How would you evaluate the importance of the issues reviewed by the Copenhagen Consensus?

Sources: "Spend $150 billion Per Year to Cure World Poverty," Daphne Eviatar, *New York Times*, November 7, 2004; "Putting the world to rights—Copenhagen Consensus," *The Economist*, June 5, 2004; "The Debate over Global Warming is getting rancorous," *The Economist*, February 5, 2005. David White, "Top-Level call for radical change in Africa aid," *Financial Times* (London), March 11, 2005.

You might be interested in the following web sites:

• UN Millennium Goals: http://www.un.org/millenniumgoals

• This website tracks 48 indicators to measure progress towards the Millennium Development goals: http://millennium-indicators.un.org/unsd/mi/mi_goals.asp

• The Copenhagen Consensus: http://www.copenhagenconsensus.com

• The Earth Institute: http://www.earthinstitute.columbia.edu

STUDY QUESTIONS

1. Why is labor productivity so much higher in some countries than others?

2. What are the three pillars of increased productivity?

3. If a country wants to increase its capital stock, what policies might it follow?

4. If a country wants to increase the quality of its work force, what policies might it follow?

5. If a country wants to improve its technology, what policies might it follow?

6. How are a country's options in regard to increasing productivity different depending upon whether the country is a high or low productivity country?

322

7. What explains the apparent convergence of labor productivity and standards of living among the world's leading industrial countries?

8. What does the convergence hypothesis suggest about the growth of labor productivity in the United States compared to that of other industrialized countries?

9. What do you think explains the American experience with productivity growth over the last half-century?

10. What is the cost disease of personal services?

11. Do you think that the United States should pursue policies that work to increase the rate of American economic growth? Why or why not?

12. Why are successful growth policies so difficult to achieve in many developing countries?

ECONOMICS ONLINE

The World Bank works with developing countries to help them improve their growth prospects. The Bank tracks data for developing and developed countries. Data is available by country and topic at the following web site.

http://www.worldbank.org/data

For example, to compare data on schooling in different countries, click on Data by Topic and then on Education.

Aggregate Demand and the Powerful Consumer

25

Important Terms and Concepts

Aggregate demand

Consumer expenditure (C)

Investment spending (I)

Government purchases (G)

Net exports ($X - IM$)

$C + I + G + (X - IM)$

National income

Disposable income (DI)

Circular flow diagram

Transfer payments

Scatter diagram

Consumption function

Marginal propensity to consume (MPC)

Movement along the consumption function

Money fixed assets

Permanent tax change

Personal saving rate

Shifts of consumption function

Temporary tax change

Learning Objectives

After completing this chapter, you should be able to:

- distinguish between spending, output, and income.

- describe what spending categories make up aggregate demand.

- distinguish between investment spending as a part of aggregate demand and as financial investment.

- explain why, except for some technical complications, national product and national income are necessarily equal.

- explain how disposable income differs from national income.

- derive a consumption function given data on consumption and disposable income.

- compute the marginal propensity to consume at various levels of income.

- explain why the marginal propensity to consume is equal to the slope of the consumption function.

- distinguish between factors that result in a *movement along* the consumption function and factors that result in a *shift* of the function.

- explain why consumption spending is affected by a change in the level of prices even if real income is unchanged.

- describe why permanent and temporary changes in taxes of the same magnitude would be expected to have different impacts on consumption spending.

- explain why investment spending is so volatile.

- describe how income and prices, both domestic and foreign, affect the demand for imports and exports.

- explain how a change in the exchange rate will affect net exports.

CHAPTER REVIEW

This chapter introduces two key concepts that economists use when discussing the determination of an economy's output: aggregate demand and the consumption function. These concepts will be fundamental to the material in later chapters.

The total amount that all consumers, business firms, government agencies, and foreigners are willing to spend on goods and services produced by the domestic economy is called aggregate

(1) _____. Economists typically divide this sum into four components: consumption expenditures, investment spending, government purchases, and net exports. Food, clothing, movies, and haircuts are examples of (<u>consumption/investment/government</u>) expenditures. New factories, office buildings, machinery, and houses would be examples of _____ spending. Red tape, filing cabinets, and the services of bureaucrats are examples of _____ purchases. American wheat and tractors sold abroad are examples of (<u>exports/imports</u>), and American purchases of French wines, Canadian paper, and Mexican oil are examples of _____. The difference between exports and imports is called _____ _____. Economists use national income accounts to keep track of these components of demand. The appendix to this chapter provides an introduction to these accounts.

There is a close analogy between the demand for a single product and aggregate demand. As seen in the study of consumer demand in microeconomics, economists argue that demand should be seen as a schedule showing how the quantity demanded depends upon a number of factors, including price. In later chapters we will see that aggregate demand is also a schedule showing how the demand by everyone for newly produced goods and services is affected by a variety of factors, including the overall level of prices or, for short, the price level.

Two other concepts that are closely related to aggregate demand are national product and national income.

(2) National product is simply the output of the economy. National income is the (<u>before/after</u>)-tax income of all the individuals in the economy. Disposable income is the income of individuals after _____ have been paid and any _____ payments from the government have been counted. The circular flow diagram shows that national product and national income are two ways of measuring the same thing: Producing goods and selling them results in income for the owners and employees of firms.

Economists use the concept of a consumption function to organize the determinants of consumption expenditures. Specifically, the consumption function is the relation between aggregate real consumption expen-

(3) ditures and aggregate real (<u>disposable/national</u>) income, holding all other determinants of consumer spending constant. Higher disposable income leads to (<u>more/less</u>) consumption spending. A change in disposable income leads to a (<u>shift in/movement along</u>) the consumption function. A change in one of the other factors that affect consumer spending, such as wealth, the price level, real interest rates, or expectations of future income, leads to a(n) _____ _____ the consumption function.

An increase in the price level affects consumption spending and is an important reason why aggregate demand, _____ + _____ + _____ + _____ – _____, is a schedule. If prices are higher, we expect   (4)
(more/less) consumption spending. Consumption spending changes because the value of many consumer assets is fixed in money terms, and an increase in the price level will (increase/decrease) the purchasing power of these assets. It is important to remember that higher prices will lead to lower real consumption expenditures even if real disposable income is constant. Consider a situation where prices double. If income doubles, there is no change in the purchasing power of consumers' income, but there is a loss to consumers from the decline in the purchasing power of their money fixed assets. It is this latter decline that leads to a shift in the consumption function in response to a change in the price level.

A change in income taxes changes disposable income, and the consumption function tells us how a change in disposable income will affect consumption spending. For example, a reduction in income taxes would (increase/decrease) disposable income. After computing the change in disposable income, one could   (5)
estimate the initial impact on consumption spending by multiplying the change in disposable income by the marginal propensity to consume. A permanent increase in taxes would be expected to have a (larger/smaller) effect on consumption expenditures than a temporary tax increase of the same magnitude because the permanent increase changes consumers' long-run income prospects by (more/less) than the temporary increase. The same argument works in reverse and implies that temporary tax changes have a (larger/smaller) impact on consumption expenditures than do permanent tax changes. One must also remember that while it may be easy to calculate the movement along the consumption function from a change in taxes, other factors influencing consumption are likely to be changing at the same time, making it difficult to predict the final change in consumption spending.

We have seen the important role that income plays as a determinant of consumption expenditures. There is no such central factor influencing investment expenditures. Instead, investment expenditures are influenced by a variety of factors, including interest rates, taxes, technical change, the strength of the economy, and business confidence. If any of these factors change, investment spending is likely to change.

Net exports are the difference between exports and imports. Exports reflect foreign demand for American production and imports come from American demand for foreign goods and services. It should not be surprising that both are influenced by income and prices. The tricky part is keeping straight whose income influences which demand, and how changes in American and foreign prices influence net exports.

IMPORTANT TERMS AND CONCEPTS QUIZ

Choose the best definition for each of the following terms.

1. _____ Aggregate demand
2. _____ Consumer expenditure (*C*)
3. _____ Investment spending (*I*)
4. _____ Government purchases (*G*)
5. _____ Net exports (*X – IM*)
6. _____ National income
7. _____ Disposable income (*DI*)
8. _____ Transfer payments
9. _____ Consumption function
10. _____ Marginal propensity to consume
11. _____ Movement along the consumption function
12. _____ Shift of the consumption function
13. _____ Money fixed asset
14. _____ Personal saving rate

a. Relation between aggregate real consumption expenditures and aggregate real disposable income
b. Income of individuals after taxes and transfer payments
c. Purchases of newly produced goods and services by all levels of government
d. Total amount spent by consumers on newly produced goods and services
e. Change in consumption due to a change in disposable income
f. Gross national product divided by price level
g. Total amount consumers, firms, government agencies, and foreigners are willing to spend on final goods and services
h. Total spending by firms on new plants and equipment plus spending by consumers on new homes
i. Change in consumption divided by change in disposable income
j. Asset whose value is fixed in terms of dollars
k. Exports minus imports
l. Total before-tax earnings of all individuals in economy
m. Change in consumption due to a change in any factor affecting consumption other than disposable income
n. Government grants to individuals
o. Ratio of saving to disposable income

BASIC EXERCISES

Note that the first three problems are based on income and consumption data for individual families rather than aggregate income and consumption. Along with the fourth problem, they will give you practice using and understanding the MPC.

1. **Table 25-1** reports some data on disposable income and consumption.
   a. For each change in disposable income, compute the marginal propensity to consume by dividing the change in _____ by the change in _____.
   b. The average propensity to consume is defined as the ratio of consumption expenditures to disposable income or APC = *C* ÷ *DI*. For example, when disposable income is $20,000, the average propensity to

328

Table 25-1

Disposable Income and Consumption Spending

Disposable Income	Change in Disposable Income	Marginal Propensity to Consume	Change in Consumption Expenditures	Consumption Expenditures	Average Propensity to Consume
$20,000				$18,000	_____
$40,000	$20,000	_____	$15,000	$33,000	_____
$60,000	$20,000	_____	$15,000	$48,000	_____
$80,000	$20,000	_____	$15,000	$63,000	_____
$100,000	$20,000	_____	$15,000	$78,000	_____

Figure 25-1

Consumption Function

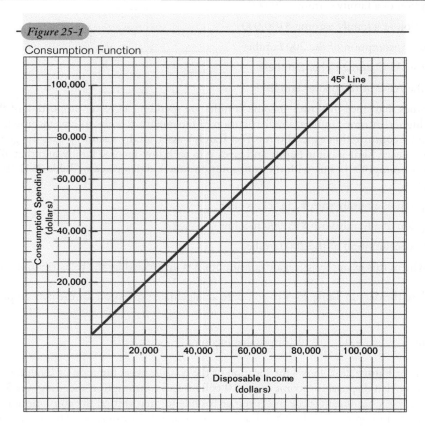

consume is 0.90 = $18,000 ÷ $20,000. Use the data on disposable income and consumption to fill in the column for the APC.

c. Are the average and marginal propensities equal? Do the differences surprise you? Can you explain them? Perhaps steps d through f will help.

d. Use the graph of **Figure 25-1** to draw the consumption function consistent with the data in Table 25-1. (Locate each income-consumption data pair and then draw a line connecting the points.)

e. The MPC is represented by what part of your graph?

329

f. The APC can be represented by the slope of a ray from the origin to a point on the consumption function. Remember the slope of any straight line, including a ray, is the vertical change over the horizontal change. When measured from the origin, the vertical change of a ray to a point on the consumption function is C and the horizontal change is DI. Thus the slope of the ray, $(C \div DI)$, is the APC. Draw rays to represent the APC for incomes of $20,000 and $100,000. How does the slope of your rays change as income increases? Is this change consistent with changes in the APC you calculated in step c?

2. Imagine an economy made up of 100 families each earning $20,000, and 100 families each earning $100,000. Each family consumes according to the consumption function described in Table 25-1.
   a. Fill in the following:

   Consumption of a family earning $20,000   _____

   Consumption of a family earning $100,000   _____

   Aggregate consumption of the 200 families   _____

   b. What is the APC of the richer families? _____

   What is the APC of the poorer families?   _____

   c. Randy argues that since the lower-income families are spending a greater proportion of their income than the higher-income families, a redistribution of income from high- to low-income families will increase total consumption expenditures. Test Randy's assertion by assuming that the government takes $5,000 from each high-income family and gives it to each low-income family, and that all families adjust their consumption in line with the consumption function described in Table 25-1. Then fill in the following:

   Consumption of a family with $25,000 income _____

   Consumption of a family with $95,000 income _____

   Aggregate consumption of the 200 families _____

   d. Explain why in this example aggregate consumption is unaffected by the redistribution of income.

3. (Optional) Use the data in Table 25-1 to compute an algebraic expression for the consumption function.

   Consumption = _____ + 0. _____ 3 (disposable income)

4. The lower line in **Figure 25-2** shows the location of the consumption function of Baulmovia in 2004. In 2004, Baulmovian disposable income was $6.0 trillion and consumption spending was $5.5 trillion. In 2005, there was a significant surge in consumer confidence that shifted the consumption function to the higher line in Figure 25-2. In 2005, Baulmovian disposable income was $6.5 trillion and consumption spending was $6.05 trillion.

   Consider an estimate of MPC that is calculated by looking at the change in consumption spending and the change in disposable income from 2004 to 2005.

   a. Change in C _____ change in DI _____ MPC _____

   b. How does this estimate of MPC compare to the slope of either consumption function? Explain any differences.

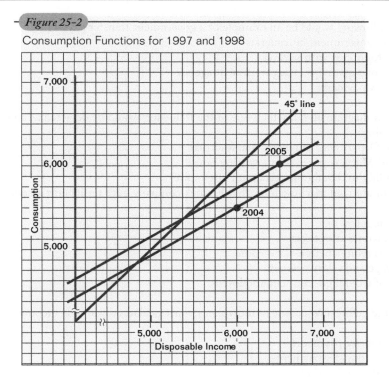

Figure 25-2

Consumption Functions for 1997 and 1998

SELF-TESTS FOR UNDERSTANDING

TEST A

Circle the most appropriate answer.

1. Which of the following is not a part of aggregate demand?
   a. consumption expenditures
   b. national income
   c. net exports
   d. investment expenditures

2. When thinking about aggregate demand, economists use the term investment to refer to all except which one of the following?
   a. the newly built house that Roberta just bought
   b. the stock in General Electric that Ralph bought with his summer earnings
   c. the new factory that is being built on the edge of town
   d. the new machinery that Sherry bought to start her own company

331

3. Which of the following would be an example of a government transfer payment?
   a. wages paid to government bureaucrats
   b. a tax refund for excess withholding
   c. the purchase of paper clips by a government agency
   d. Social Security payments

4. In a circular flow diagram all but which one of the following would be depicted as an injection into the stream of spending?
   a. the Defense Department purchases a new airplane
   b. Michelle and Mathew purchase an existing house
   c. Alice's spending to rebuild her restaurant after a fire
   d. the new computerized machine tools that Elaine's company buys for its new assembly line

5. National income refers to
   a. consumers' income after taxes.
   b. the sum of everyone's before-tax income.
   c. employee wage and salary payments.
   d. the income of federal government employees.

6. Starting with the before-tax income of individuals, one calculates disposable income by
   a. adding taxes.
   b. subtracting transfer payments.
   c. adding taxes to transfer payments.
   d. subtracting taxes and adding transfer payments.

7. A graphical representation of how consumption spending varies with changes in disposable income is called the
   a. aggregate demand curve.
   b. income-expenditure schedule.
   c. consumption function.
   d. Phillips curve.

8. A change in which one of the following would be associated with a movement along the consumption function?
   a. current disposable income
   b. wealth
   c. the price level
   d. expected future income

9. A change in all but which one of the following would be associated with a shift in the consumption function?
   a. wealth
   b. interest rates
   c. current disposable income
   d. the price level

10. MPC refers to the
    a. *Y*-axis intercept of the consumption function.
    b. slope of the consumption function.
    c. ratio of consumption spending to income.
    d. slope of a ray from the origin to a point on the consumption function.

11. If MPC is 0.7, then a $100 billion change in disposable income will be associated with what change in consumption spending?
    a. $20 billion
    b. $30 billion
    c. $70 billion
    d. $100 billion

12. If a $100 billion increase in disposable income results in a $75 billion increase in consumption spending, then MPC is
    a. 0.25.
    b. 0.50.
    c. 0.75.
    d. 1.0.

13. If consumption spending declines by $45 billion when disposable income declines by $50 billion, what is MPC?
    a. 0.9
    b. 0.1
    c. −0.1
    d. −0.9

14. If an increase in prices is matched by an increase in incomes such that there is no change in real disposable income, then
    a. there should be no effect on consumption spending.
    b. the increase in prices will lead to a movement along the consumption function.
    c. one should expect MPC to decline.
    d. the impact of the change in prices on the purchasing power of money fixed assets should lead to a shift in the consumption function.

15. If MPC is 0.8, a $100 billion change in the wealth of consumers will lead to a(n)
    a. $100 billion change in consumption spending.
    b. $80 billion change in consumption spending.
    c. movement along the consumption function.
    d. shift in the entire consumption function.

16. An increase in real interest rates
    a. always leads to a decrease in consumption spending as it provides an increased incentive for greater saving.
    b. can be modeled as a movement along the consumption function.
    c. always leads to an increase in consumption spending as the higher interest rate allows savers to reach fixed objectives with smaller savings.
    d. does not appear to have influenced consumption spending very much one way or the other.

333

17. Which type of tax change would be expected to have the largest impact on consumption spending?
    a. a one-time tax rebate
    b. a one-time tax surcharge
    c. a permanent reduction in tax rates
    d. a reduction in tax withholding "to get money into the hands of consumers" that is enacted with no change in taxes due at the end of the year

18. Investment spending as measured in the national income accounts
    a. is a fairly constant proportion of GDP.
    b. includes all transactions on the New York Stock Exchange.
    c. is quite volatile as it is influenced by business confidence.
    d. is high correlated with disposable income.

19. An increase in foreign income should lead to a(n)
    a. increase in exports.
    b. decrease in exports.
    c. decrease in imports.
    d. increase in imports.

20. An increase in American prices should lead to a(n)
    a. decrease in imports.
    b. decrease in net exports.
    c. increase in exports.
    d. increase in net exports.

TEST B

Circle T or F for true or false.

T F 1. Aggregate demand is the aggregate of individual household consumption decisions.

T F 2. The consumption function reflects the close relationship between consumption spending and national output.

T F 3. Disposable income equals national income minus taxes.

T F 4. A change in consumption divided by the change in disposable income that produced the change in consumption is called the marginal propensity to consume.

T F 5. An increase in the level of prices is likely to reduce consumption expenditures.

T F 6. The effect of a change in the level of prices on consumption would be viewed graphically as a shift in the consumption function.

T F 7. By increasing household wealth, a big increase in the stock market is likely to lead to a movement along the consumption function.

T F 8. The magnitude of the impact of a change in taxes on consumption expenditures is likely to depend on whether consumers view the change in taxes as permanent or temporary.

T F 9. A temporary decrease in taxes is likely to have a smaller impact on consumption than will a permanent decrease.

T F 10. The demand for exports is likely to be influenced by foreign income while the demand for imports is influenced by domestic income.

334

| Appendix | *National Income Accounting*

Learning Objectives

After completing this appendix, you should be able to:

- describe the three alternative ways of measuring GDP and explain why, except for bookkeeping or statistical errors, they give the same answer.

- explain how the national income accounts treats production that is not sold on markets.

- explain why national income accounting treats government purchases of goods and services differently from government transfer payments.

- explain the difference in theory and practice between the following macro measurements: GDP, NNP, and national income.

Important Terms and Concepts

National income accounting

Gross domestic product (GDP)

Gross private domestic investment

National income

Net national product (NNP)

Depreciation

Gross national product

APPENDIX REVIEW

Although included in an appendix, this material on national income accounting deserves special treatment. When working through this material, do not lose sight of the forest for the trees. The forest is composed of broad income concepts, such as gross domestic product (GDP) and national income, what each of these concepts measures and how they relate to one another. This appendix is an introduction to the forest rather than to each individual tree.

The national income accounts measure economic activity: the production of goods and services and the incomes that are generated as a result. Accurate measurement of production and income is an important prerequisite to attempts to understand and control the economy. National income accounts are centered around measurement of gross domestic product (GDP). Consumption (C), investment (I), government purchases of goods and services (G), and net exports ($X - IM$) are the individual components of GDP. National income is an alternative measure of total economic activity.

GDP is defined as the sum of the money values of all _____ goods and services that are   (1)
(produced/sold) during a specified period of time, usually one year. Economists use money values or market prices to add up the very different types of output that make up GDP. Some production—government output and inventories—require special treatment as they are not sold on markets.

335

The emphasis on final goods and services is important because it avoids double counting of intermediate goods. (The need to avoid double counting is also the key to why the three alternative ways of measuring GDP are conceptually equivalent.) It is important to remember that GDP is a statement of production, not sales. It is only production that creates new goods available for consumption or investment. Thus GDP, as a measure of production, is the appropriate measure of how much new consumption or investment our economy can enjoy.

There are three ways to measure GDP. Perhaps the simplest way to measure GDP is to add up the purchases of newly produced final goods and services by private individuals and firms—for consumption and investment—by the government and by foreigners. For the United States in 2004, this sum of $C + I + G + (X - IM)$ was estimated to be about $10.7 trillion.

(2)   Net exports are (<u>imports/exports</u>) minus _____. We add exports to $C + I + G$ because, even though bought by foreigners, exports are American products and GDP is a measure of total production in the United States. We subtract imports because C and I and G include spending on imports, and we want a measure that reflects only those goods and services (<u>purchased/produced</u>) in the United States.

All of a firm's sales receipts eventually end up as income for someone, directly in the case of workers, creditors, and firm owners, and indirectly in the case of payments to suppliers, who in turn use this money to pay their workers, creditors, and so forth. Thus, instead of measuring GDP as purchases of final goods and services, we could equivalently add up all incomes earned in the production of goods and services. This sum of factor in-

(3) comes plus indirect business taxes is also called national _____ and is the second way to measure GDP.

National Income is conceptually similar to GDP but differs from U.S. national income accounts because of several items: A) Conceptually national income and net national product (NNP) should be equal but as each is estimated separately there is often a small statistical discrepancy. B) The difference between net national product

(4) and gross national product is _____, which refers to the portion of current total production that is used to replace those parts of the capital stock that have deteriorated as a result of current production. If GNP were all one edible good, we could eat NNP while maintaining our productive capacity. Eating GNP would reduce our productive capacity as we would not be replacing worn-out plants and machines. C) National income and hence gross national product measures the income of American nationals whether they are in the United States or not and excludes the income of foreign nationals working in the United States. Adjusting for income that Americans receive from business activities abroad and for income that foreigners receive for business activities in the United States gives us gross domestic product, i.e., it measures the production of final goods and services within the borders of the United States.

To measure GDP as the money value of final goods and services, one would start by collecting sales data for final goods. The second way of measuring GDP, total factor incomes, would start with the collection of income data from firms and individuals. The third way of measuring GDP looks at the difference between a firm's sales receipts and its purchases from other firms. This difference, also called a firm's _____

(5) _____, is the amount of money a firm has to pay the factors of production that it has employed,

336

including the profits firm owners pay themselves. Thus, the sum of total value added in the economy is the third way to measure GDP.

IMPORTANT TERMS AND CONCEPTS QUIZ

Choose the best definition for each of the following terms.

1. _____ National income accounting
2. _____ Depreciation
3. _____ Value added

a. Bookkeeping and measurement system for national economic data
b. Value of an economy's capital used up during a year
c. Revenue from sale of product minus amount paid for goods and services purchased from other firms
d. Loss on value of business assets from inflation

BASIC EXERCISES

These problems are designed to give you practice in understanding alternative ways of measuring GDP.

1. Consider the following two-firm economy. Firm A is a mining company that does not make purchases from firm B. Firm A sells all its output to firm B, which uses the output of Firm A to make goods that it sells to consumers.

	Firm A	Firm B
Total sales	$500	$1,700
Wages	400	800
Profits	100	400
Purchases from other firms	0	500

a. What are the total sales for the economy? $ _____
b. What is the total value of sales for final uses? $ _____
c. What is the total of all factor incomes? $ _____
d. What is value added for firm A? $ _____
e. What is value added for firm B? $ _____
f. What is the total value added of both firms? $ _____
g. What is GDP? $ _____
h. What is national income? $ _____

2. **Table 25-2** (on page 338) contains information on a three-firm economy. Firm A sells only to other firms. Firm B has both an industrial and a household division. Firm C sells only to final consumers. Note also that production by firm *C* was greater than sales, thus the entry showing the addition to inventories. Simple addition shows that the sum of factor incomes, in this case wages and profits, is

equal to $4,700. Answer the following questions to see if the two other ways of measuring GDP give the same answer. The tricky part of this question is the treatment of production that has not been sold, but added to inventories. You may want to review the discussion of inventories in the appendix before answering the following questions.

Table 25-2

	Firm A	Firm B	Firm C
Total Sales	$1,000	$2,500	$3,000
Sales to firm B	$400		
Sales to firm C	$600	$1,000	
Sales to consumers		$1,500	$3,000
Change in inventories			$200
Wages	$750	$1,800	$1,200
Profits	$250	$300	$400

a. Calculate value added for each firm and the sum of value added for all firms.

Value Added, firm A _____

Value Added, firm B _____

Value Added, firm C _____

Sum _____

b. GDP is defined as the production of newly produced final goods and services. It is typically calculated by summing sales of newly produced final goods and services. Sales to consumers are an important part of final sales but they only total $4,500. What is missing to get to GDP of $4,700?

SELF-TESTS FOR UNDERSTANDING

TEST A

Circle the most appropriate answer.

1. GDP is
   a. the sum of all sales in the economy.
   b. the sum of all purchases in the economy.
   c. the sum of money value of all newly produced final goods and services produced during a year.
   d. equal to $C + I + G + X + IM$.

2. Conceptually, GDP can be measured by all but which one of the following?
   a. Add up all factor payments by firms in the economy.
   b. Add up all purchases of final goods and services, $C + I + G + (X - IM)$.
   c. Add up total sales of all firms in the economy.
   d. Add up value added for all firms in the economy.

3. When measuring GDP, money values are for the most part determined by
   a. the cost of production.
   b. market prices.
   c. estimates prepared by national income accountants who work for the U.S. Commerce Department.
   d. banks and Eastern money interests.

4. Which of the following is not valued at market prices when computing GDP?
   a. imports
   b. investment
   c. government output
   d. exports

5. Which of the following would add to this year's GDP?
   a. Nick purchases a new copy of the Baumol/Blinder textbook for this course.
   b. Ashley purchases a used copy of the Baumol/Blinder textbook for this course.
   c. Susan purchases 100 shares of GM stock.
   d. Steve sells his three-year-old car.

6. Which of the following transactions represents the sale of a final good as opposed to sale of an intermediate good?
   a. Holly sells peaches from her farm to the Good Food Packing and Canning Company.
   b. Good Food sells a load of canned peaches to Smith Brothers Distributors.
   c. Smith Brothers sells the load of canned peaches to Irving's Supermarket.
   d. You buy a can of peaches at Irving's.

7. Which of the following events results in an addition to gross private domestic investment?
   a. Managers of the Good Earth, a newly formed food co-op, buy a used refrigerator case for their store.
   b. Sony's office in Tokyo buys a new IBM computer.
   c. The U.S. Air Force purchases a new plane for the president.
   d. Southwest Airlines purchases 20 new planes so it can expand its service.

8. Gross private domestic investment includes all but which one of the following?
   a. the new home purchased by Kimberly and Jason
   b. Ryan's purchase of a used fax machine for his new business
   c. the increase in the inventory of newly produced but unsold cars
   d. the construction of a new plant to manufacture microchips for Intel

9. When measuring GDP, government purchases include all but which one of the following?
   a. salaries paid to members of Congress
   b. newly produced red tape purchased by government agencies
   c. Social Security payments to older Americans
   d. concrete for new highway construction

10. If net exports are negative it means that
    a. the national income accountant made a mistake.
    b. depreciation is greater than net exports.
    c. Americans are consuming too many foreign goods.
    d. imports exceed exports.

11. Which accounts for the largest proportion of national income?
    a. profits
    b. employee compensation
    c. rents
    d. interest

12. In the national income accounts, transfer payments are
    a. subtracted from national income in the calculation of disposable income.
    b. included in *G*, government purchases of goods and services.
    c. added to wages when computing national income.
    d. not a direct component of GDP, and are reflected in GDP only when they influence consumption spending.

13. Which of the following adds to consumption spending as measured by the national income accountants?
    a. Howard buys a used CD at Play It Again Sam.
    b. Rachel builds a new store to house her business.
    c. Tyrone buys three new suits when he gets a job as a marketing representative.
    d. Hilary sells the computer she bought when she first came to campus four years ago.

14. Which of the following is not part of the difference between GDP and national income?
    a. depreciation
    b. income earned by foreigners working in the United States
    c. profits
    d. income earned by Americans from foreign business activities

15. Depreciation explains the difference between
    a. GNP and NNP.
    b. NNP and National Income.
    c. GDP and National Income.
    d. savings and investment.

16. Value added by a single firm is measured as total sales revenue
    a. minus factor payments.
    b. plus indirect business taxes.
    c. plus depreciation.
    d. minus the purchase of intermediate goods.

17. Additions to inventory
    a. add to next year's GDP when the goods are actually sold.
    b. are simply ignored when calculating GDP.
    c. add to current GDP.
    d. are priced at zero since they have not been sold.

18. When measuring GDP, government outputs are
    a. appropriately valued at zero.
    b. valued by estimates of their market prices.
    c. valued at the cost of inputs needed to produce them.
    d. added to transfer payments to measure *G* in $C + I + G + X - IM$.

TEST B

Circle T or F for true or false.

T   F   1. GDP is designed to be a measure of economic well-being, not a measure of economic production.

T   F   2. If you measured GDP by adding up total sales in the economy, you would be double or triple counting many intermediate goods.

T   F   3. Production that is not sold but is instead added to inventories is not counted in GDP.

T   F   4. If GM started its own steel company rather than continuing to buy steel from independent steel companies, GDP would be lower because intrafirm transfers are not part of GDP but all interfirm sales are.

T   F   5. Since the output of government agencies is not sold on markets, it is not included in GDP.

T   F   6. Value added is the difference between what a firm sells its output for and the cost of its own purchases from other firms.

T   F   7. The difference between GDP and national income is net exports.

T   F   8. Adding up value added for all firms will underestimate GDP as it ignores the production of intermediate goods.

T   F   9. Corporate profits are the largest component of national income.

T   F   10. The sum of value added for all firms in the economy is equal to the sum of all factor incomes—wages, interest, rents, and profits.

SUPPLEMENTARY EXERCISES

1. Consider the following nonlinear, consumption function.

$$C = 120DI^{1/2}$$

Restricting yourself to positive values for disposable income, graph this function. What happens to MPC as income increases? Can you find an explicit expression for MPC as a function of income? (Knowledge of simple calculus will be helpful.) Use this new consumption function to re-answer Basic Exercise question 2 about income redistribution. Does your answer change? If so, why?

ECONOMICS IN ACTION

DO AMERICANS SAVE ENOUGH?

Do Americans save too little? It would certainly seem so. From 1960 to 1989, household savings as measured in the national income accounts averaged 9 percent of disposable income. Savings have declined continuously since then, averaging only 1 percent of disposable income in 2004.

While Americans have always saved less than individuals in other industrialized countries, the decline in savings has come at a time when there is increasing concern about the ability of Americans to provide for their

341

own retirement and concerns about future growth rates for the economy as a whole. It also occurred at a time when there were increasing tax incentives to increase savings. Indeed by 2004 economists Elizabeth Bell, Adam Carasso, and C. Eugene Steuerle estimated that government spending on tax incentives to increase savings were greater than savings themselves. It appeared that rather than increasing savings, there were substantial portfolio adjustments in search of tax advantages.

As we have seen, savings, investment, and economic growth are closely related. Higher levels of investment are likely to mean higher levels of economic growth. If a country is to invest more, it seems obvious that it must consume less, that is, it must save more. Savings levels as low as 1 percent seem only to spell disaster for the future.

Some were less concerned and argued that the decline in household savings during the 1990s was hardly surprising and only part of the story. Families with significant holdings of stock saw substantial increases in their wealth even without increased saving. Economic theory has always recognized that an increase in wealth is likely to lead to an increase in consumption spending at the expense of a reduction in savings.

Economists Dean Maki and Michael Palumbo looked at stock holdings and savings behavior. They found the decline in household savings was concentrated among the wealthiest families who had the largest holdings of stock and other assets with significant price appreciation over the 1990s.

The decline in personal savings did not lead to a decline in private investment as a proportion of GDP. How can this be? First, a fair amount of U.S. national savings is done by businesses rather than households, and business savings showed no decline over the 1990s. Second, national savings is also influenced by the state of the government's budget. Government budgets, especially that of the federal government, showed a significant move to surplus over the 1990s, adding to rather than subtracting from national savings, although since 2000 increasing federal government deficits have meant that on net government savings now subtracts from national savings. Finally, a country can sustain or increase the level of private investment even in the facing of declining domestic savings if it is willing to borrow from other countries. This is exactly what the United States did over the 1990s as the trade deficit, the excess of imports over exports, increased as a proportion of GDP.

Those who are concerned about savings are also concerned about whether the gains in the stock market represent permanent increases in wealth or transitory gains from unrealistic stock price increases. They also point out that while a country can sustain levels of investment by foreign borrowing, increasing international indebtedness may only be planting the seeds for future trouble.

1. Who is right, those concerned that America is saving too little or those who say that traditional ways of looking at this issue are inappropriate?

2. Should we be concerned about increased international borrowing?

3. Should Americans save more? If so, what policy measures would you endorse to encourage savings?

4. Why do you think that savings-linked tax advantages have not increased aggregate personal savings?

Sources: David Leonhardt, "A Blasphemy Spreads: Debts are O.K.," *New York Times,* January 19, 2002. Edmund L. Andrews, "Savings: Lots of Talk But Few Dollars," *New York Times,* March 13, 2005.

STUDY QUESTIONS

1. What are the four major components of GDP? (Why are imports subtracted when everything else is added?)

2. What is the difference between national income and disposable income?

3. How is MPC different from the proportion of disposable income that is spent on consumption?

4. MPC can be represented by what part of the consumption function?

5. Why does a change in the price level or in expected future incomes lead to a shift in the consumption function rather than a movement along the function?

6. If planning a reduction in income taxes to increase consumption spending by $200 billion, what difference would it make if MPC were 0.75 or 0.90? Would you expect any differences if the reduction in taxes were to be permanent or temporary? Why?

7. What are the different ways one can measure GDP?

8. Economists often use national income or GDP interchangeably as a measure of the level of aggregate economic activity. What is the difference between national income and GDP?

9. Why is investment spending so volatile? Does the volatility of investment mean that policy changes by the government have no impact on investment?

10. "Exports will change with changes in foreign but not domestic income. They will also change if foreign or domestic prices change." How can it be that exports respond to domestic prices but not domestic income?

11. How do imports respond to changes in domestic income, foreign income, domestic prices, and foreign prices?

ECONOMICS ONLINE

Check here for the most recent estimates of GDP: http://www.bea.gov/

The Economic Report of the President is issued every year in February. The Report includes extensive tables with historical data on macroeconomic activity including Gross Domestic Product and its components. Use the following URL to access copies of the Economic Report of the President and its statistical tables back to 1995.

http://www.gpoaccess.gov/eop/download.html

Demand-Side Equilibrium: Unemployment or Inflation?

26

Important Terms and Concepts

Equilibrium

Expenditure schedule

Induced investment

$Y = C + I + G + (X - IM)$

Income-expenditure (or 45° line) diagram

Aggregate demand curve

Full-employment level of GDP (potential GDP)

Recessionary gap

Inflationary gap

Coordination of saving and investment

Coordination failure

Multiplier

Induced increase in consumption

Autonomous increase in consumption

Learning Objectives

After completing this chapter, you should be able to:

• draw an expenditure schedule, given information about consumption spending, investment spending, government purchases, and net exports.

  determine the equilibrium level of income on the demand side and explain why the level of income tends toward its equilibrium value.

• describe how a change in the price level affects the expenditure schedule and the equilibrium level of income on the demand side.

• describe how the impact of a change in prices on the expenditure schedule can be used to derive the aggregate demand curve.

• explain why equilibrium GDP can be above or below the full-employment level of GDP.

• explain why any autonomous increases in expenditures will have a multiplier effect on GDP.

• explain why the multiplier expression, $1/(1 - MPC)$, is oversimplified.

• explain the difference between an autonomous and an induced increase in consumption expenditures.

• explain how and why economic booms and recessions tend to be transmitted across national boundaries.

• describe how any change in autonomous spending leads to a shift in the aggregate demand curve.

CHAPTER REVIEW

This chapter is an introduction to explicit models of income determination. The model discussed in this chapter is relatively simple and is not meant to be taken literally. Do not be put off by the simplicity of the model or its lack of realism. Careful study now will pay future dividends in terms of easier understanding of later chapters, in which the implications of more complicated models are described.

The central focus of this chapter is on the concept of the equilibrium level of income and output. (You may want to review the material in Chapter 25 on the equality of national income and national output.) The models discussed in this chapter show us how spending decisions are reconciled with production decisions of firms to determine the equilibrium level of GDP on the demand side.

When considering the determination of the equilibrium level of GDP, it is important to distinguish between output and income on the one hand and total spending on the other. If total spending exceeds current production, firms will find that their inventories are decreasing. They are then likely to take steps to (decrease/

(1) increase) production and output. Analogously, if total spending is less than current output, firms are likely to find their inventories _____, and they are likely to take steps to _____ production.

The concept of equilibrium refers to a situation in which producers and consumers are satisfied with things the way they are and see no reason to change their behavior. Thus the equilibrium level of GDP must be a level of GDP at which firms have no reason to increase or decrease output; that is, at the equilibrium level of GDP,

(2) total spending will be (less than/equal to/greater than) output. The determination of the equilibrium level of output thus reduces to

   A. describing how total spending changes as output (and income) changes, and

   B. finding the one level of output (and income) at which total spending equals output. In the simplified model discussed in this chapter, there are four components to total spending: consumption, investment, government purchases, and net exports.

The income-expenditure diagram is a useful tool for analyzing the determination of the equilibrium level of

(3) output. Output (and income) is measured along the (horizontal/vertical) axis, and spending is measured on the _____ axis. To find the equilibrium level of output (and income) we need to know how total spending changes as output (and income) change, and we need to know where total spending equals output. The relationship between total spending, $C + I + G + (X - IM)$, and income is given by the expenditure schedule. The 45° line shows all possible points of equilibrium as it is the line where the vertical distance, i.e., spending, is equal to the horizontal distance, i.e., output and income.

The one place where actual spending as shown by the expenditure schedule is equal to output is given by

(4) the _____ of the expenditure schedule and the 45° line. This is the equilibrium level of output

because it is the only level of output where total spending is equal to output. At any other level of output, total spending will not be equal to output. You should be sure that you understand why the economy tends to move to the equilibrium level of output rather than getting stuck at a level of income and output where total spending is either larger or smaller than output. Consider what happens to business inventories when spending is greater or less than output. Do not get confused between this tendency to move to the equilibrium level of output on the income-expenditure diagram and the real possibility that the economy can end up at a point away from full employment.

Any particular expenditure schedule relates total spending to income for a given level of prices. If prices change, total spending will change, even for the same level of real income. In particular, a higher price level is apt to mean (less/more) consumption spending because of the decline in the purchasing power of the   (5)
money assets of consumers. A change in the price level will also affect net exports. Specifically, higher prices (increase/reduce) exports and _____ imports as domestically produced goods are (less/more) price competitive vis-à-vis foreign goods. These changes in consumption spending and net exports will lead to a (downward/upward) shift in the expenditure schedule and a new equilibrium of income that is (higher/lower) than before. In the opposite case, a lower price level would (decrease/increase) consumption spending and _____ net exports. The result will be a (higher/lower) equilibrium level of income.

The relationship between the price level and the equilibrium level of income given by the income-expenditure diagram is called the aggregate demand curve. The aggregate demand curve is derived from the income-expenditure diagram and, from the viewpoint of demand, shows how the equilibrium level of income changes when the _____ _____ changes. The qualifier "from the viewpoint of demand" is important.   (6)
Complete determination of the equilibrium level of income/output and the equilibrium price level comes from the interaction of the aggregate demand and aggregate supply curves.

At this point we are considering only the demand side of the economy. Nothing that has been said so far implies that, with regard to demand, the equilibrium level of output must equal the full-employment level of output. It may be larger or it may be smaller. It all depends upon the strength of aggregate demand. In particular, if savings plans at full employment are greater than investment plans, spending will be (less/more) than full   (7)
employment output and equilibrium on the demand side will result in a(n) _____ gap. The importance of savings and investment plans in determining equilibrium means that recessions and inflation can be seen as failures of coordination. If the equilibrium level of output exceeds the full-employment level of output, the difference is called a(n) _____ gap.

What happens to the equilibrium level of income if demand changes? From the perspective of the income-expenditure diagram, the change in the equilibrium level of GDP will be a multiple of the original change in spending. In particular, our analysis will be concerned with parallel shifts in the expenditure schedule that are represented graphically as a change in the vertical axis intercept of the expenditure schedule. A parallel shift in the expenditure schedule shows the same change in spending at all levels of income and is thus a change in

347

(8) (<u>autonomous/induced</u>) spending. Spending that changes when income changes, such as the response of consumption spending to a change in income, is called a(n) _____ change.

Multiplier analysis shows that the equilibrium level of GDP changes by a multiple of the change in autonomous spending, which is where we get the term "multiplier." The basic reason for this multiplier result is relatively simple: Increased spending by one sector of the economy means increased sales receipts for other sectors of the economy. Higher sales receipts will show up in bigger paychecks or profits or both—in short, higher incomes. These higher incomes will then induce more consumer spending, which in turn will result in still higher incomes and more consumption spending by others, and so on and so on.

What determines the value of the multiplier? There are several alternative, but equally valid, ways of answering this question. In the text, the value of the multiplier is determined by summing the increments to spending and income that follow from the original autonomous change in spending. When consumption is the only in-

(9) duced spending, the oversimplified multiplier expression turns out to be 1/(1 − _____).

Here is an alternative derivation of the same result. We know that in equilibrium national output, or income, will equal total spending:

$$Y = C + I + G + (X - IM).$$

Now assume that there is an autonomous increase in investment spending that induces subsequent increases in consumption spending. At the new equilibrium, we know that the change in the equilibrium level of national output must equal the change in total spending. If net exports and government purchases do not change, the change in total spending will have two parts. One is the autonomous change in investment spending and the other is the induced change in consumption spending. We know that

Change in equilibrium level of income	=	Autonomous change in investment spending	+	Induced change in consumption spending

It is possible to represent this symbolically. Let ΔY represent the change in the equilibrium level of income and ΔI represent the autonomous change in investment spending. What about the induced change in consumption spending? The discussion of the consumption function in Chapter 25 told us that consumption spending

(10) will change as disposable _____ changes. Further, with the use of the concept of the marginal propensity to consume, we can represent the change in consumption spending as the product of the change in disposable income multiplied by the _____. When taxes do not vary with income, $\Delta DI = \Delta Y$ and we can represent the change in consumption as $\Delta Y \times \text{MPC}$. If we substitute all these symbols for the words above, we see that

$$\Delta Y = \Delta I + (\Delta Y \times \text{MPC}).$$

We can now solve this equation for the change in income by moving all terms in ΔY to the left-hand side of the equation:

$$\Delta Y - (\Delta Y \times \text{MPC}) = \Delta I.$$

348

If we factor out the ΔY we can rewrite the expression as

$$\Delta Y(1 - MPC) = \Delta I.$$

We can now solve for ΔY by dividing both sides of the equation by $(1 - MPC)$.

$$\Delta Y = \Delta I [1 / (1 - MPC)].$$

Note that ΔI is the initial change in autonomous spending and $1/(1 - MPC)$ is the multiplier. The change in the equilibrium level of income is found by multiplying these two terms. That is

$$
\begin{array}{ccc}
\text{Change in equilibrium} & & \text{Autonomous change in} \\
\text{level of income} & = & \text{investment spending}
\end{array}
\quad \times \quad \text{Multiplier}
$$

Although our derivation was different, the multiplier expression we just identified, $1/(1 - MPC)$, is the same as the one in the text and is subject to the same limitations.[1] That is, this expression is oversimplified. There are four important reasons why real-world multipliers will be (smaller/larger) than our formula. These reasons are   (11) related to the effects of _____, international _____, _____ taxes, and the _____ system.

The simplified multiplier expression we derived above is applicable when analyzing a shift in the expenditure schedule in the 45° line diagram. As such, this expression assumes that prices (do/do not) change. To complete   (12) our analysis on the demand side, we need to see how our multiplier analysis affects the aggregate demand curve. The multiplier analysis we have done by using the income-expenditure diagram shows us that if prices are constant, the equilibrium level of income will change following any change in autonomous spending. This result is true at all price levels and implies that a vertical shift in the expenditure schedule following a change in autonomous spending leads to a (movement along/shift in) the aggregate demand curve. In fact, it leads to a (horizontal/vertical) shift in the aggregate demand curve. The magnitude of the shift can be computed with the help of the multiplier, as shown in Figure 26-12 in the text.

---

[1] A more general expression for the multiplier is $1/(1 - \text{slope of the expenditure schedule})$. The multiplier is based on summing the rounds of spending induced by an autonomous increase in spending. In the model of this chapter only consumption spending changes as income changes. Appendix B examines what happens when imports vary with income. We will see then that the slope of the expenditure schedule is flatter and the multiplier is smaller.

IMPORTANT TERMS AND CONCEPTS QUIZ

Choose the best definition for each of the following terms.

1. _____ Equilibrium level of GDP
2. _____ Expenditure schedule
3. _____ Induced investment
4. _____ Income-expenditure diagram
5. _____ Aggregate demand curve
6. _____ Recessionary gap
7. _____ Inflationary gap
8. _____ Potential GDP
9. _____ Coordination failure
10. _____ Multiplier
11. _____ Induced increase in consumption
12. _____ Autonomous increase in consumption

a. Graph of quantity of national product demanded at each possible price level
b. Line showing relationship between GDP and total spending
c. Full-employment level of GDP
d. Increase in consumer spending not due to an increase in income
e. When equilibrium GDP exceeds full-employment GDP
f. Level of output where aggregate demand equals total production
g. Investment spending that changes with changes in GDP
h. Ratio of change in equilibrium GDP to change in autonomous spending that causes GDP to change
i. When full-employment GDP exceeds equilibrium GDP
j. Two-variable graph that allows plotting of total real expenditures against real income
k. Savings plans at full employment differ from investment plans at full employment
l. Increase in consumer spending due to an increase in disposable income
m. Table or graph showing how saving depends on consumption

BASIC EXERCISES

These exercises are designed to give you practice with the income-expenditure diagram and deriving the aggregate demand curve.

1. **Equilibrium Level of Income**

   This exercise shows you how the expenditure schedule is derived and how it helps to determine the equilibrium level of income. For this exercise it is assumed that prices are constant with the price level having a value of 100.

   a. Use the data on consumption spending in **Table 26-1** to show how consumption spending varies with income in **Figure 26-1**.
   b. Add investment spending to the line drawn in Figure 26-1 to show how consumption plus investment spending varies with income.
   c. Now draw the expenditure schedule by adding G and (X – IM) to the line drawn in step b.
   d. Next, draw a line representing all the points where total spending and income could be equal. (This is the 45° line. Do you know why?)
   e. The 45° line represents all the points that could be the equilibrium level of income. Now circle the one point that is the equilibrium level of income. What is the equilibrium level of income on your graph?

350

Table 26-1

Data for Expenditure Schedule

Y	Tx	DI	C	I	G	X	IM	Total Spending C + I + G + X – IM
9,500	1,800	7,700	6,500	1,500	1,750	1,200	1,350	_____
9,750	1,800	7,950	6,700	1,500	1,750	1,200	1,350	_____
10,000	1,800	8,200	6,900	1,500	1,750	1,200	1,350	_____
10,250	1,800	8,450	7,100	1,500	1,750	1,200	1,350	_____
10,500	1,800	8,700	7,300	1,500	1,750	1,200	1,350	_____
10,750	1,800	8,950	7,500	1,500	1,750	1,200	1,350	_____
11,000	1,800	9,200	7,700	1,500	1,750	1,200	1,350	_____

Figure 26-1

Expenditure Schedule

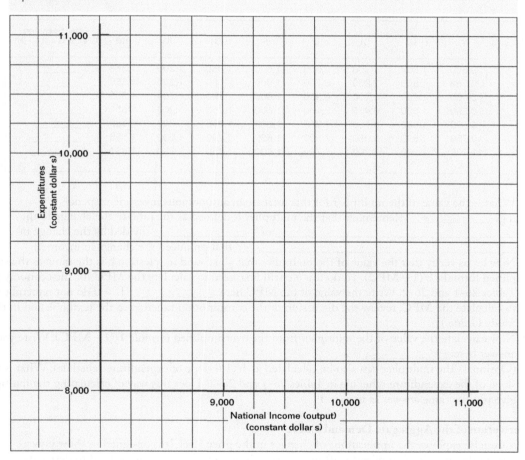

f. Check your answer by filling in the Total Spending column in Table 26-1 to see where total spending equals income. You should get the same answer from Table 26-1 as you do from the graph.

g. Why isn't the equilibrium level of output $9,750 billion? If for some reason national output and income started out at $9,750 billion, what forces would tend to move the economy toward the equilibrium you determined in questions e and f?

h. Using the data in Table 26-1 and assuming that the full-employment level of output income is $10,250 billion, is there an inflationary or recessionary gap? How large is the gap? If the full-employment level of income were $9,800 billion, how large would the inflationary or recessionary gap be?

2. **The Multiplier**

a. Assume now that an increase in business confidence leads to an increased level of investment spending of $1,600 billion at all levels of national income. Complete **Table 26-2** and draw the new expenditure schedule in Figure 26-1 to see what happens to the equilibrium level of income and consumption spending at the new equilibrium level of income.

Table 26-2

Data for Expenditure Schedule Following Increase in Investment Spending

Y	Tx	DI	C	I	G	X	IM	Total Spending C + I + G + X − IM
9,500	1,800	7,700	6,500	1,600	1,750	1,200	1,350	_____
9,750	1,800	7,950	6,700	1,600	1,750	1,200	1,350	_____
10,000	1,800	8,200	6,900	1,600	1,750	1,200	1,350	_____
10,250	1,800	8,450	7,100	1,600	1,750	1,200	1,350	_____
10,500	1,800	8,700	7,300	1,600	1,750	1,200	1,350	_____
10,750	1,800	8,950	7,500	1,600	1,750	1,200	1,350	_____
11,000	1,800	9,200	7,700	1,600	1,750	1,200	1,350	_____

b. What is the value of the multiplier for this increase in autonomous investment spending? _____ (Remember that the multiplier is defined as the ratio of the change in the _____ _____ of _____ divided by the change in _____ _____ that produced the change in income.)

c. Now let us verify that the value of the multiplier that you found in question b is the same as the simplified formula $1/(1 - MPC)$. To do this we will first need to calculate the MPC for the economy in Tables 26-1 and 26-2. Write the value of the MPC here: _____. (If you do not remember how to calculate the MPC, review the discussion of the consumption function in the textbook and in this Study Guide.)

d. Now calculate the value of the multiplier from the oversimplified formula $1/(1 - MPC)$. Write your answer here: _____.

e. (Optional) The multiplier can also be calculated as $1/(1 - \text{slope of expenditure schedule})$. What is the slope of the expenditure schedule in Tables 26-1 and 26-2? Does this way of calculating the multiplier give you the same answer as in part d?

3. **Derivation of the Aggregate Demand Curve**

This exercise explores the implications of changes in the price level. It is designed to show how a change in the price level implies a shift in the expenditure schedule and can be used to derive the aggregate demand curve.

a. The data in Table 26-1 assumed that prices were constant with the price level at a value of 100. Mark the point in **Figure 26-2** that shows the price level of 100 and the equilibrium level of income you found when answering questions e and f of Exercise 1.

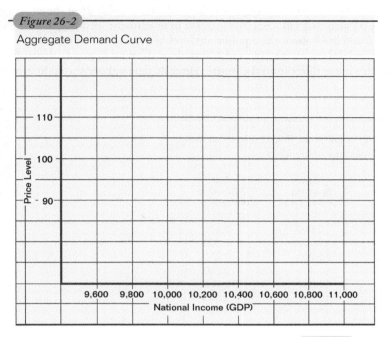

Figure 26-2

Aggregate Demand Curve

b. Economic research has determined that if prices rose to 110, consumption spending and net exports would decline by a total of $100 billion at every level of real income. **Table 26-3** shows the relevant information. Each entry in the column for a price level of 110 should be 100 less than the values you calculated for total spending in question 1.f. What is the new equilibrium level of income on the income-expenditure diagram with this higher price level? Mark the point in Figure 26-2 that shows the price level of 110 and this new equilibrium level of income.

Table 26-3

Total Spending at Different Price Levels

Real Income (Output)	Total Spending (Price Level = 90)	Total Spending (Price level = 110)
9,500	9,700	9,500
9,750	9,900	9,700
10,000	10,100	9,900
10,250	10,300	10,100
10,500	10,500	10,300
10,750	10,700	10,500
11,000	10,900	10,700

c. This same research determined that if prices fell to 90, consumption spending and net exports would increase over amounts shown in Table 26-1 by a total of $100 billion at every level of real income. What is the new equilibrium level of income on the income-expenditure diagram for this lower price level? Mark the point in Figure 26-2 that shows the price level of 90 and this new equilibrium level of income.

d. The points you have marked in Figure 26-2 help to trace what curve?

e. Connect these points to verify that your curve has a (<u>negative/positive</u>) slope.

4. The Multiplier and the Aggregate Demand Curve

Question 2 asked you to consider the impact of an increase in investment spending. We saw then that an increase in investment spending shifts the expenditure schedule and leads to a new equilibrium on the income-expenditure diagram. What about the aggregate demand curve? **Table 26-4** shows the impact of the price level on total spending following the increase in investment spending. Use this information from Tables 26-2 and 26-4 about the equilibrium level of income on the income expenditure diagram when the price level equals 90, 100, and 110 to draw the new aggregate demand curve in Figure 26-2. How does this curve differ from the initial aggregate demand curve you drew in question 3?

Table 26-4

Total Spending at Different Price Levels Following Increase in Investment Spending

Real Income (Output)	Total Spending (Price Level = 90)	Total Spending (Price level = 110)
9,500	9,800	9,600
9,750	10,000	9,800
10,000	10,200	10,000
10,250	10,400	10,200
10,500	10,600	10,400
10,750	10,800	10,600
11,000	11,000	10,800

SELF-TESTS FOR UNDERSTANDING

TEST A

Circle the most appropriate answer.

1. Of production, income, and spending, _____ and _____ are always equal while _____ equals the other two only in equilibrium.
   a. spending and income; production
   b. production and spending; income
   c. income and production; spending

2. The expenditure schedule is a relationship between
   a. the equilibrium level of national income and prices.
   b. consumption spending and national income.
   c. total spending and national income.
   d. consumption spending and prices.

3. The expenditure schedule is derived by showing how which of the following vary with income? (There may be more than one correct answer.)
   a. *C*—consumption
   b. *DI*—disposable income
   c. *G*—government purchases
   d. *I*—investment spending
   e. *IM*—imports
   f. *T*—taxes
   g. *X*—exports

4. If investment spending were now higher at all levels of income, the expenditure schedule would
   a. shift down.
   b. show no change.
   c. shift up.

5. Induced investment means the expenditure schedule
   a. is flatter than before.
   b. shifts up.
   c. shifts down.
   d. is steeper than before.

6. In the income-expenditure diagram, the equilibrium level of output is given by the intersection of the expenditure schedule and the
   a. consumption function.
   b. aggregate demand curve.
   c. 45° line.
   d. level of full-employment output.

7. When total spending is less than output,
   a. inventories are likely to be increasing.
   b. inventories are likely to be decreasing.
   c. there will be a shift in the expenditure schedule.
   d. firms are likely to raise prices.

8. When total spending is equal to output,
   a. the resulting level of output is called the full-employment level of output.
   b. the level of income is given by the intersection of the expenditure schedule and the 45° line.
   c. there is never an inflationary gap.
   d. the expenditure schedule and the aggregate demand curve coincide.

9. At the equilibrium level of income which one of the following is not necessarily true?
   a. The expenditure schedule will intersect the 45° line.
   b. There will be no unexpected changes in business inventories.
   c. There will be no unemployment.
   d. The equilibrium level of output and the price level will together determine one point on the aggregate demand curve.

10. If, at the full-employment level of income, consumers' savings plans are equal to firms' investment plans, then
    a. the equilibrium level of income will be equal to the full-employment level of income.
    b. there will be an inflationary gap.
    c. firms will find their inventories increasing.
    d. the economy will be producing less than potential output.

11. There is a recessionary gap when the equilibrium level of income is
    a. less than potential GDP.
    b. equal to the full-employment level of GDP.
    c. greater than potential GDP.

12. A lower price level will _____ the equilibrium level of income on the income-expenditure diagram.
    a. decrease
    b. not affect
    c. increase

13. The aggregate demand curve is a relationship between the price level and
    a. consumption spending.
    b. the equilibrium level of income on the income-expenditure diagram.
    c. full-employment GDP.
    d. the interest rate.

14. A lower price level will lead to which of the following? (There may be more than one correct answer.)
    a. an increase in exports
    b. a shift in the consumption function
    c. a shift in the expenditure schedule
    d. a shift in the aggregate demand curve

15. The multiplier is defined as the ratio of the change in
    a. autonomous spending divided by the change in consumption expenditures.
    b. the equilibrium level of income divided by the increase in consumption spending.
    c. the equilibrium level of income divided by the change in autonomous spending that produced the change in income.
    d. consumption spending divided by the change in autonomous spending.

16. The multiplier shows that
    a. any increase in induced spending will be a multiple of the increase in income.
    b. an autonomous increase in spending will increase income by a multiple of the increase in autonomous spending.
    c. to influence income, any change in autonomous spending must be a multiple of the induced changes in spending.
    d. an induced change in spending will lead to a multiple increase in income.

17. The oversimplified multiplier formula is
    a. $1/MPC$.
    b. $1/(MPC - 1)$
    c. $MPC(1 - MPC)$
    d. $1/(1 - MPC)$

18. The secret behind the multiplier is
    a. the government's printing press.
    b. understanding that an autonomous increase in investment spending leads to an autonomous increase in consumption spending.
    c. understanding that any increase in autonomous spending induces additional increases in spending as income increases.
    d. the gnomes of Zurich.

19. Actual multipliers will be less than theoretical multipliers because of which of the following? (There may be more than one correct answer.)
    a. inflation
    b. accounting practices
    c. international trade
    d. the government deficit
    e. income taxes
    f. price controls
    g. the financial system

20. An autonomous change in spending can be modeled as a(n)
    a. horizontal shift in the expenditure schedule.
    b. tilt in the slope of the expenditure schedule.
    c. vertical shift in the expenditure schedule.
    d. increase in MPC.

21. If MPC were 0.6 and prices did not change, the multiplier would be
    a. $1/0.6 = 1.67$.
    b. 0.6.
    c. $1/(1 - 0.6) = 2.5$.
    d. $1/(1 + 0.6) = 0.63$.

22. The textbook multiplier would be largest if MPC were
    a. 0.73.
    b. 0.89.
    c. 0.45.
    d. 0.67.

23. The multiplier is useful in calculating the
    a. slope of the consumption function.
    b. horizontal shift in the aggregate demand curve following an increase in autonomous spending.
    c. vertical shift of the expenditure schedule following a change in autonomous spending.
    d. shift of the consumption function following an increase in autonomous spending.

24. The multiplier response following a decrease in investment spending would have what impact on the aggregate demand curve?
    a. horizontal shift to the left
    b. no impact
    c. horizontal shift to the right

357

TEST B

Circle T or F for true or false.

T   F   1. The expenditure schedule refers to a relationship between total spending and the level of output (and income).

T   F   2. The equilibrium level of GDP never equals the full-employment level of GDP.

T   F   3. If total spending exceeds national output, the resulting decrease in inventories should lead firms to reduce the level of output and production.

T   F   4. The intersection of the expenditure schedule and the 45° line determines one point on the aggregate demand curve.

T   F   5. The term recessionary gap refers to a situation in which the equilibrium level of GDP is less than the full-employment level of GDP.

T   F   6. Because consumers usually invest their savings at financial institutions, there can be no difference between desired savings and desired investment for the economy.

T   F   7. The aggregate demand curve refers to a relationship between the price level and the equilibrium level of income as determined on the income-expenditure diagram.

T   F   8. An increase in the level of prices will lead to a movement along the expenditure schedule.

T   F   9. The multiplier is defined as the ratio of a change in autonomous spending divided by the resulting change in the equilibrium level of income.

T   F   10. Multiplier responses mean that the equilibrium level of national income is likely to change by less than any change in autonomous spending.

T   F   11. Multiplier increases illustrated on the income-expenditure diagram are based on the assumption that prices do not change.

T   F   12. Actual multiplier responses to changes in autonomous spending are likely to be less than that suggested by the formula $1/(1 - MPC)$.

T   F   13. If income increases because of an autonomous increase in investment spending, the resulting increase in consumption spending is called an induced increase.

T   F   14. The impact of a shift in the aggregate demand curve on prices and real output will depend upon the slope of the aggregate supply curve.

| Appendix A | *The Simple Algebra of Income Determination*

BASIC EXERCISES

This exercise is meant to illustrate the material in the Appendix to Chapter 26.

If we are willing to use algebra we can use equations rather than graphs or tables to determine the equilibrium level of output. If we have done all our work accurately, we should get the same answer regardless of whether we use graphs, tables, or algebra.

The following equations are consistent with the numbers in Table 26-1:

(1)	C	$=$	$340 + 0.8\,DI$
(2)	DI	$=$	$Y - T$
(3)	T	$=$	$1{,}800$
(4)	I	$=$	$1{,}500$
(5)	G	$=$	$1{,}750$
(6)	X	$=$	$1{,}200$
(7)	IM	$=$	$1{,}350$
(8)	Y	$=$	$C + I + G + (X - IM)$

1. Equation 1 is the consumption function. It shows how consumption spending changes with changes in disposable income. To derive the expenditure schedule we need to figure out how spending changes with changes in national income. Start by substituting equations 2 and 3 for disposable income and taxes into equation 1 to see how C varies with Y.

   (9) $\qquad\qquad C = \underline{\hspace{1.5cm}} + \underline{\hspace{1.5cm}} Y.$

2. Now use equation 9, along with equations 4, 5, 6, and 7, to show how total spending varies with Y.

   (10) $\qquad C + I + G + (X - IM) = \underline{\hspace{1.5cm}} + \underline{\hspace{1.5cm}} Y.$

3. Equation 10 is the expenditure schedule. Equation 8 is the 45° line. To find the one level of income where spending equals output (and income), substitute the right-hand side of equation 10 for the right-hand side of equation 8 and solve for the equilibrium level of Y.

   $$Y = \underline{\hspace{1.5cm}}$$

   Substituting the right-hand side of equation 10 for the right-hand side of equation 8 is the algebraic way of finding the intersection of these two lines.

4. Now assume that investment increases by 100 to 1,600, that is equation 4 changes to $I = 1600$. Repeat steps 2 and 3 to solve for the new equilibrium level of income. What is the change in the equilibrium level of income? What is the value of the multiplier?

| Appendix B | *The Multiplier with Variable Imports*

The following questions are meant to illustrate the major point of Appendix B: When the demand for imports increases with domestic GDP, the multiplier will be smaller.

1. **Table 26-5** is similar to Table 26-1 except that imports increase with income. Compute total spending to verify that the equilibrium level of income in Table 26-5 is the same as in Table 26-1.

Table 26-5

Expenditure Schedule Data with Variable Imports

Y	Tx	DI	C	I	G	X	IM	Total Spending C + I + G + X − IM
9,500	1,800	7,700	6,500	1,500	1,750	1,200	1,325	_____
9,750	1,800	7,950	6,700	1,500	1,750	1,200	1,338	_____
10,000	1,800	8,200	6,900	1,500	1,750	1,200	1,350	_____
10,250	1,800	8,450	7,100	1,500	1,750	1,200	1,363	_____
10,500	1,800	8,700	7,300	1,500	1,750	1,200	1,375	_____
10,750	1,800	8,950	7,500	1,500	1,750	1,200	1,388	_____
11,000	1,800	9,200	7,700	1,500	1,750	1,200	1,400	_____

2. **Table 26-6** is based on the assumption that investment spending has increased by $125. The new equilibrium level of income is _____.

Table 26-6

Expenditure Schedule Data with Variable Imports Following Increase in Investment Spending

Y	Tx	DI	C	I	G	X	IM	Total Spending C + I + G + X − IM
9,500	1,800	7,700	6,500	1,625	1,750	1,200	1,325	_____
9,750	1,800	7,950	6,700	1,625	1,750	1,200	1,338	_____
10,000	1,800	8,200	6,900	1,625	1,750	1,200	1,350	_____
10,250	1,800	8,450	7,100	1,625	1,750	1,200	1,363	_____
10,500	1,800	8,700	7,300	1,625	1,750	1,200	1,375	_____
10,750	1,800	8,950	7,500	1,625	1,750	1,200	1,388	_____
11,000	1,800	9,200	7,700	1,625	1,750	1,200	1,400	_____

3. We calculate the multiplier as before: the change in the equilibrium level of income divided by the change that changed income. Now the multiplier is _____.

4. Explain any difference between this multiplier and the one you calculated in question 2 of the Basic Exercises.

SUPPLEMENTARY EXERCISES

1. Use all of the equations in Appendix A but assume that consumption depends upon income with a one-period lag. That is

$$C = 300 + 0.8DI\,(-1)$$

a. Confirm that the equilibrium level of income is 10,000. That is, if income last period was 10,000, then total spending, $C = I + G + (X - IM)$, will equal 10,000 this period.

b. Now assume that investment spending increases by 100 to 1,600. Assuming that consumption responds with the one-period lag, simulate your model to investigate how the change in investment spending affects this economy over time. Does the level of income appear to converge to a new equilibrium value? What is that value? What is the multiplier for the change in investment spending? How does the multiplier from your simulation compare to the oversimplified formula of $1/(1 - MPC)$?

c. Investigate the impact of increases and decreases in net exports. Investigate the impact of a change in government purchases. Investigate the impact of autonomous changes in consumption spending, that is, a change in the constant term of the consumption function.

d. What happens if the MPC changes? You will need first to determine the initial equilibrium level of income for given levels of investment spending, net exports, and autonomous consumption spending. Then simulate your model to see how the change in the MPC affects the multiplier.

ECONOMICS IN ACTION

AUTONOMOUS AND INDUCED CHANGES IN CONSUMPTION SPENDING

The multiplier shows how an autonomous increase in spending, through its impact on income, induces additional spending. The final result is that the equilibrium level of income increases by more than, or by a multiple of, the original autonomous change. We have also seen the close link between disposable income and consumption spending. Indeed, the induced changes in consumption spending are a critical part of the multiplier process.

Can changes in consumption spending ever initiate multiplier changes or are they only a part of a process that must be initiated by some other element of spending? To answer this question one must distinguish between factors that shift the consumption function and factors that lead to a movement along the consumption function. As a particular example, let's consider material from the 2004 Report of the Council of Economic Advisers.

Early each year, the President's Council of Economic Advisers issues its annual report. The council's report is published along with the Economic Report of the President. The volume's statistical appendix reports numerous data series that measure the macroeconomic performance of the economy. The council's report itself includes commentary on recent developments, a forecast for the upcoming year, and a detailed study of two or three topics of interest. The report is a mixture of politics and economic analysis as it is, in part, a brief for the policies of the president.

The February 2004 Report included the following comments about consumption spending during 2003.

Consumer spending increased briskly in 2003…

The pickup in spending growth in the second half of the year corresponded to an increase in the rate of growth of household income…Other factors also likely contributed to the strengthening of consumer spending over the course of 2003. The robust performance of equity markets and solid gains in home prices bolstered wealth… Consumer sentiment was depressed early in the year by the prospect of war with Iraq. Sentiment jumped in April and May following the successful resolution of major combat operations and then was little changed until November, when it picked up noticeably. By the end of the year, household sentiment was somewhat higher than it had been at the end of 2002 and much higher than it was just prior to the war with Iraq… [P]ersonal saving was likely depressed by the boost to consumption from low interest rates both directly through the availability of low-interest-rate loans on durable goods and indirectly through the funds made available by cash-out mortgage refinancings.

The report cites several factors as helping to explain consumer spending: household income, consumer wealth and increased consumer confidence over the year, increases in house prices, lower interest rates and associated mortgage refinancing.

1. Which of these factors reflects a movement along an unchanged consumption function and which reflects a shift in the consumption function? Which would initiate a multiplier process and which would be part of the multiplier response to an autonomous change in spending?

2. What does the most recent Report say about autonomous and induced elements of consumption spending and other categories of spending?

SOURCE: *Economic Report of the President,* February 2004 (Washington, D.C.: United States Government Printing Office), p. 84–89.

STUDY QUESTIONS

1. The expenditure schedule shows how total spending changes with domestic income. What categories of spending does the expenditure schedule need to include?

2. What would happen to the expenditure schedule if the marginal propensity to consume were larger or smaller? Why?

3. What would happen to the expenditure schedule if there were a change in any of the following: investment spending, government purchases of goods and services, exports, or imports?

4. What would happen to the expenditure schedule if investment spending or imports increased as national income increases?

5. According to the text, equilibrium occurs at the intersection of the expenditure schedule and the 45° line. Why there? What prevents points to the left or right of the intersection from also being points of equilibrium?

6. Why do we say the expenditure schedule is drawn for a given level of prices?

7. What happens to the expenditure schedule if prices increase or if they decrease?

8. Plotting different price levels and the corresponding equilibrium level of income from the income-expenditure diagram results in what curve?

9. Looking just at the expenditure schedule, how can you represent a change in autonomous spending? A change in induced spending?

10. How can it be that a change in autonomous spending results in an even larger change in the equilibrium level of income?

11. What happens to the value of the multiplier if the MPC is larger? Smaller? Why?

12. What are the four shortcomings of the multiplier formula $1/(1 - MPC)$?

13. Do these shortcomings mean that the formula overstates or understates the likely value of the multiplier?

14. What is the mechanism by which a recession in Europe may lead to a decline in output in the United States?

15. What is the relation between the multiplier analysis on the income-expenditure diagram following an autonomous change in spending and the resulting shift of the aggregate demand curve?

Bringing in the Supply-Side: Unemployment and Inflation?

27

Important Terms and Concepts

Aggregate supply curve

Productivity

Equilibrium of real GDP and the price level

Recessionary gap

Inflationary gap

Self-correcting mechanism

Stagflation

Inflation and the multiplier

Learning Objectives

After completing this chapter, you should be able to:

- describe how the aggregate supply curve is derived from an analysis of business costs and why it slopes upward.

- distinguish between factors that will lead to a movement along or a shift in the aggregate supply curve.

- use the aggregate demand/aggregate supply graph to determine the equilibrium price level and the equilibrium level of real GDP.

- use the aggregate demand/aggregate supply graph to analyze how factors that shift either the aggregate demand curve or the aggregate supply curve will affect the equilibrium level of prices and output.

- use the aggregate demand curve/aggregate supply graph to explain what kinds of shifts in the aggregate demand curve and the aggregate supply curve can give rise to a period of stagnation.

- explain how an inflationary gap will self-destruct.

- explain how a recessionary gap will self-destruct.

- use the aggregate demand/aggregate supply diagram to show

  ○ demand-side inflation tends to be associated with a booming economy.

  ○ supply-side inflation tends to be associated with a slowing economy.

  ○ how favorable supply-side shocks enable an economy to have high employment and low inflation at the same time.

  ○ how increases in prices reduce the value of the multiplier.

CHAPTER REVIEW

In Chapter 4 we first learned that for individual commodities, equilibrium price and quantity are determined by the intersection of the relevant demand and supply curves. The same logic holds when analyzing the economy as a whole. The level of prices and aggregate output is determined by the intersection of the aggregate demand and aggregate supply curves. We have also learned how the aggregate demand curve can be derived from analyzing how changes in the price level affect the spending decisions that underlie the expenditure schedule. In this chapter we will derive the aggregate supply curve and show how the price level and aggregate output are determined.

The aggregate supply curve is a schedule, showing for each possible price level, the total quantity of goods and services that all businesses are willing to supply during a specified period of time, holding all other factors influencing aggregate supply constant. You should note that the same logic applies here as to discussions of the supply decisions of individual firms. Businesses will adjust supply in pursuit of profits.

If prices rise while production costs per unit of output remain unchanged, we expect firms to

(1) (increase/decrease) output. If prices stayed higher and production costs did not increase at all, would there be any limit to the increase in profits firms could derive from increases in output? Even if the prices of inputs do not increase, microeconomic analysis suggests that production costs will rise as firms try to expand output, putting a limit on the profitable increase in output. (Remember that in the short run, the supply curve for an individual firm is the upward-sloping portion of the firm's marginal cost curve.) The increase in output induced by an increase in the price level is a (movement along/shift in) the aggregate supply curve. Any change in production costs in the face of an otherwise unchanged price level—for example, an increase in energy prices imposed by a foreign supplier or an increase in money wages—will also affect profits and will lead to an adjustment in the quantity of goods and services that businesses are willing to supply. This time, however, the change in supply is a(n) _____ _____ the aggregate supply curve. The aggregate supply curve would also shift following a change in productivity or in the available supplies of labor or capital. For example, as investment increases the stock of capital, the aggregate supply curve will shift to the (left/right).

Now, having derived both the aggregate demand curve and the aggregate supply curve, we are in a position to use both to determine the final equilibrium level of prices and aggregate output, or GDP. See **Figure 27-1** for example, where the equilibrium price level of 100 and the equilibrium level of GDP of $10,000 billion are

(2) given by the (intersection/slope) of the aggregate demand and supply curves. A higher price level, say, 110, implies (a) a lower quantity of aggregate demand as consumers respond to the loss of purchasing power of their money assets and net exports (increase/decrease) following the increase in domestic prices, and (b) a larger quantity of aggregate supply as firms respond to higher prices. Clearly, more supply and less demand cannot be a point of equilibrium, since firms would experience continual (increases/decreases) in inventories. The result is likely to be reduced output and price reductions that move the economy back toward equilibrium. Similarly, a lower price level, such as 90, would induce analogous, although opposite, reactions.

366

Figure 27-1

Aggregate Demand and Aggregate Supply

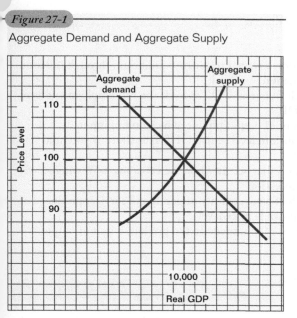

Figure 27-2

Aggregate Demand and Aggregate Supply

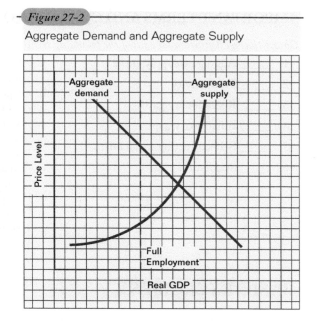

Nothing in the analysis so far guarantees that the intersection of the aggregate demand and aggregate supply curves will be at the level of output corresponding to full employment. If the final equilibrium level of output is different from the full-employment level of output, the result is either a recessionary gap or an inflationary gap. Consider **Figure 27-2,** which shows a(n) _____ gap. As unemployment falls below (3) frictional levels and material inputs become scarce, higher input prices will shift the aggregate supply curve (inward/outward) leading to a (movement along/shift in) the aggregate demand curve, (higher/lower) prices, (higher/lower) output, and the eventual elimination of the inflationary gap. Note that the simultaneous increase in prices and wages does not prove that increasing wages cause inflation. Both are best seen as a symptom of the original inflationary gap.

If the aggregate demand and aggregate supply curves intersect to the left of the full-employment level of output, there will be a(n) _____ gap. The rigidity of wages and other input prices in the (4) face of unemployment means that while a recessionary gap will eventually self-destruct, the process may be slow and painful.

Stagflation refers to the simultaneous occurrence of increasing prices and increasing unemployment. The previous analysis suggests that stagflation is a natural result of the self-destruction of a(n) (inflationary/recessionary) (5) gap. Stagflation can also occur as a result of adverse shifts in the aggregate _____ curve. Favorable shifts in the aggregate supply curve will result in (falling/rising) prices and _____ GDP.

IMPORTANT TERMS AND CONCEPTS QUIZ

Choose the best definition for each of the following terms.

1. _____ Aggregate supply curve

2. _____ Productivity

3. _____ Recessionary gap

4. _____ Inflationary gap

5. _____ Self-correcting mechanism

6. _____ Stagflation

a. Economy's way of restoring equilibrium through inflation or deflation

b. Equilibrium real GDP exceeds the full-employment level of GDP

c. Amount of output produced by a unit of input

d. Equilibrium level of real GDP falls short of potential GDP

e. Inflation that occurs while the economy is growing slowly or in recession

f. Graph of total quantity of goods and services produced at each possible price level

g. Amount of input required to produce a unit of output

BASIC EXERCISES

This exercise first reviews the derivation of the aggregate demand curve and then uses both the aggregate demand and aggregate supply curves to determine the equilibrium level of income.

1. **Figure 27-3** shows an income-expenditure diagram in the top half and a price level–aggregate output diagram in the bottom half. The middle expenditure schedule in the top half duplicates the original situation described in Basic Exercise 1 of the previous chapter and assumes that the price level with this expenditure schedule is 100. The dashed line extending into the bottom figure shows how this output level, together with its associated price level, can be plotted in the lower diagram. It is one point on the aggregate demand curve.

   a. A decrease in the price level to 90 would increase consumption spending because a reduction in prices (decreases/increases) the purchasing power of consumer money assets and _____ net exports. These changes shift the expenditure schedule up. The new expenditure schedule, for a price level of 90, is shown in the top half of Figure 27-3. What is the equilibrium level of income in the income-expenditure diagram for a price level of 90?

   b. Plot the combination of prices and output from part a in the lower diagram. This is a second point on the aggregate demand curve.

   c. A price level of 110 would depress consumer spending and net exports, shifting both the consumption function and the expenditure schedule. Use the expenditure schedule for a price level of 110 to plot a third point on the aggregate demand curve.

   d. Draw the aggregate demand curve by connecting the three points now plotted in the lower diagram.

   e. Using the aggregate demand curve you have just derived and the aggregate supply curve that is already drawn, what is the equilibrium level of prices and real GDP?

   f. If the level of full-employment output were $10 trillion, would there be an inflationary gap or recessionary gap? How, if at all, might such a gap self-destruct and where would the price level and real GDP end up?

   g. If the level of full-employment output were $10.125 trillion, would there be an inflationary gap or recessionary gap? How, if at all, might such a gap self-destruct and where would the price level and real GDP end up?

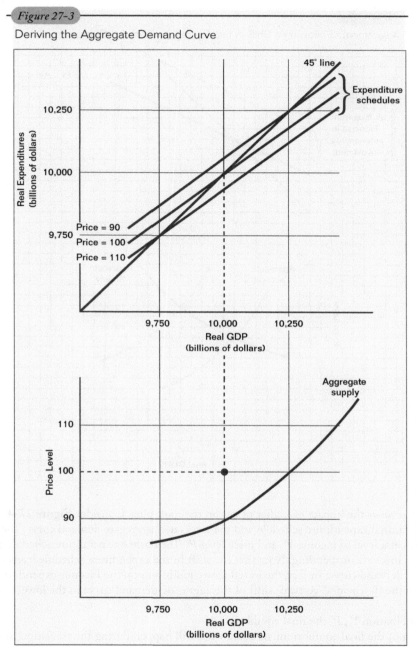

Figure 27-3

Deriving the Aggregate Demand Curve

h. If the level of full-employment output were $10.250 trillion, would there be an inflationary or recessionary gap? How, if at all, might such a gap self-destruct and where would the price level and real GDP end up?

369

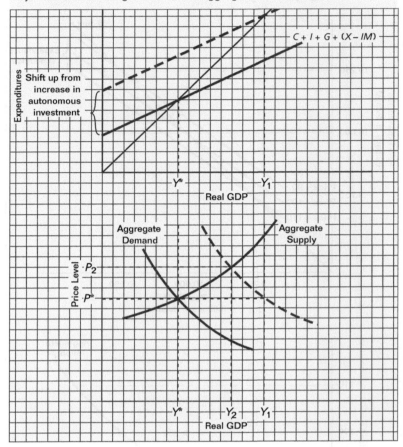

Figure 27-4

Adjustments Following a Shift in the Aggregate Demand Curve

2. This exercise reviews the impact of higher prices on the multiplier. Consider **Figure 27-4.** The heavy lines show an initial expenditure schedule and the associated aggregate demand curve. The initial equilibrium is at a level of income Y^*, and price level P^*. The dashed expenditure schedule comes from an increase in investment spending. Note that the shift in the expenditure schedule leads to a shift in the aggregate demand curve. In fact, the initial new equilibrium on the income-expenditure diagram, Y_1, is equal to the (horizontal/vertical) shift of the aggregate demand curve in the lower half of the diagram.

a. Is the combination Y_1, P^* the final equilibrium?

b. If Y_1, P^* is not the final equilibrium, describe what will happen during the transition to the final equilibrium.

3. In **Table 27-1,** fill in the blanks as indicated to analyze the response to each change. In the first two columns use S or M for "shift in" or "movement along." In the last two columns use + or −.

Table 27-1

Adjustments to External Shocks

	Aggregate Demand Curve	Aggregate Supply Curve	Equilibrium Real GDP	Equilibrium Price Level
A reduction in business investment spending				
An increase in the price of many basic commodities used as inputs in the production of final goods and services				
An increase in the demand for exports caused by an economic boom abroad				
An increase in labor productivity due to a technological breakthrough				
A reduction in consumer spending due to a fall in the stock market				
A large increase in energy prices				

SELF-TESTS FOR UNDERSTANDING

TEST A

Circle the most appropriate answer.

1. The aggregate supply curve
   a. slopes down to the right.
   b. has a positive slope.
   c. slopes up to the left.
   d. has a negative slope.

2. The slope of the aggregate supply curve reflects the fact that
   a. inflation reduces the value of the oversimplified multiplier.
   b. the costs of important inputs, such as labor, are relatively fixed in the short run.
   c. the marginal propensity to consume is less than 1.0.
   d. recessionary gaps take a long time to self-destruct.

3. The aggregate supply curve will shift following changes in all but which of the following?
   a. the price level
   b. wage rates
   c. technology and productivity
   d. available supplies of factories and machines

371

4. Which of the following will shift the aggregate supply curve outward?
   a. lower prices
   b. higher wages
   c. higher energy prices
   d. improvements in technology that increase labor productivity

5. The price level and the equilibrium level of real GDP
   a. are determined by the intersection of the aggregate demand and aggregate supply curves.
   b. will always occur at full employment.
   c. can be found in the income-expenditure diagram.
   d. do not change unless the aggregate demand curve shifts.

6. A change in the price level
   a. will lead to a shift in the aggregate supply curve.
   b. will lead to a shift in the aggregate demand curve.
   c. reflects a shift in the aggregate demand curve and/or aggregate supply curve.
   d. will always lead to stagnation.

7. A higher price level will lead to which of the following? (There may be more than one correct answer.)
   a. a reduction in the purchasing power of consumers' money fixed assets
   b. a downward shift in the consumption function
   c. an increase in imports
   d. a decrease in exports
   e. a downward shift in the expenditure schedule

8. An inflationary gap occurs
   a. when the equilibrium level of GDP exceeds potential GDP.
   b. whenever there is an upward shift in the expenditure schedule.
   c. whenever aggregate supply exceeds aggregate demand.
   d. during periods of high unemployment.

9. From an initial position of full employment, which one of the following will not lead to a recessionary gap?
   a. a shift in the aggregate supply curve in response to an increase in energy prices
   b. a reduction in investment spending due to a decline in business confidences
   c. a reduction in consumer spending due to an adverse shift in consumer expectations
   d. an increase in exports that follows a business expansion in Europe

10. Which of the following is not associated with the elimination of an inflationary gap?
    a. rising prices
    b. falling output
    c. increased employment
    d. rising wages

11. Which of the following is most likely to lead to an inflationary gap?
    a. an increase in government purchases of goods and services to fight a recession
    b. an increase in exports that occurs when unemployment rates are high
    c. a significant reduction in energy prices
    d. any increase in spending that shifts the aggregate demand curve to the right when GDP is at or beyond potential GDP

372

12. In the face of a recessionary gap, the economy's self-correcting mechanism reflects the effects of
    a. weak labor markets.
    b. trade deficits.
    c. government deficits.
    d. an MPC that is less than 1.0.

13. Which of the following is most likely to lead to stagflation?
    a. a reduction in investment spending due to a decline in business confidence
    b. an increase in exports that occurs when unemployment rates are high
    c. a significant increase in energy prices
    d. a technological breakthrough that lowers production costs

14. Which of the following lead(s) to an increase in net exports? (There may be more than one correct answer.)
    a. decrease in exports
    b. decrease in imports
    c. increase in imports
    d. increase in exports

15. From an initial position of equilibrium, exports increase by $100 billion as Europe experiences a business boom. This change will lead to which of the following? (There may be more than one correct answer.)
    a. an increase in net exports
    b. an upward shift of the expenditure schedule
    c. a shift to the right in the aggregate supply curve
    d. a shift to the right in the aggregate demand curve

16. At the new equilibrium following the increase in exports, U.S. GDP will be _____ and the U.S. price level will be _____.
    a. higher; lower
    b. lower; lower
    c. higher; higher
    d. lower; higher

17. The economy will experience increases in output with little inflation whenever
    a. the aggregate supply curve shifts to the left.
    b. the aggregate demand curve shifts to the right.
    c. both the aggregate demand and supply curves shift to the right in a similar fashion.
    d. the expenditure schedule becomes steeper.

18. Year-to-year changes in GDP and prices are probably best seen as the result of
    a. shifts in the aggregate demand curve that move the economy along an unchanged aggregate supply curve.
    b. shifts in the aggregate supply curve that move the economy along an unchanged aggregate demand curve.
    c. shifts in both the aggregate demand and aggregate supply curves.

373

19. Prices rise following an increase in autonomous spending whenever the
    a. marginal propensity to consume is less than 1.0.
    b. multiplier is greater than 1.0.
    c. aggregate demand curve has a negative slope.
    d. aggregate supply curve has a positive slope.

20. The aggregate demand curve–aggregate supply curve diagram shows that the multiplier will be smaller than suggested by the original shift of the expenditure schedule whenever the
    a. aggregate demand curve slopes down and to the right.
    b. aggregate demand curve slopes up and to the right.
    c. aggregate supply curve slopes up and to the right.
    d. MPC is less than 1.0.

TEST B

Circle T or F for true or false.

T   F   1. The aggregate supply curve shows for each possible price the total quantity of goods and services that the nation's businesses are willing to supply.

T   F   2. The aggregate supply curve slopes upward because businesses will expand output as long as higher prices make expansion profitable.

T   F   3. An increase in the capital stock from business investment will shift the aggregate supply curve to the right.

T   F   4. The impact of unemployment on wages and prices is part of the process by which recessionary gaps self-destruct.

T   F   5. If the aggregate supply curve shifts to the left, the result will be stagnation.

T   F   6. The economy's self-correcting mechanisms ensure that the aggregate demand and aggregate supply curves will always intersect at potential output.

T   F   7. If the aggregate demand and supply curves intersect to the left of the full employment level of output there will be a recessionary gap.

T   F   8. A period of excessive aggregate demand is likely to be followed by a period of stagnation as the inflationary gap self-destructs.

T   F   9. During the elimination of an inflationary gap, the real cause of inflation is excessive wage demands on the part of labor.

T   F   10. Analysis of the aggregate supply curve shows that the multiplier derived from the income-expenditure diagram typically understates the final change in output.

374

SUPPLEMENTARY EXERCISE

The following equations are consistent with Basic Exercise 1.

$T = 1,800$

$DI = Y - T$

$C = 790 + 0.8DI - 4.5P$

$I = 1,500$

$G = 1,800$

$X - IM = -150 - 0.5P$

$C + I + G + (X - IM) = Y$ (45° line)

Aggregate supply curve: $Y = 7,750 + 25P$

T = taxes

DI = disposable income

C = consumption expenditures

I = investment expenditures

G = government purchases

X = exports

IM = imports

Y = GDP

P = price level

1. Use the consumption function along with the level of investment spending, government purchases, and net exports to determine an expression for the expenditure schedule. (Don't forget to substitute for disposable income and note that this expression will involve the variable P. Remember a single Expenditure Schedule assumes that the price level does not change. When P changes, the Expenditure Schedule will shift.)

2. Use the expenditure schedule and the equation for the 45° line to determine an expression for the aggregate demand curve.

3. Now use both the aggregate demand curve and the aggregate supply curve to determine the equilibrium level of prices and GDP.

4. Resolve the system on the assumption that investment expenditures decrease to 1,450.

ECONOMICS IN ACTION

HOW VARIABLE IS THE AGGREGATE SUPPLY CURVE?

What explains fluctuations in GDP—shifts in the aggregate demand curve or shifts in the aggregate supply curve? Keynesian analysis focuses on shifts in aggregate demand as the major source of fluctuations in output. In this view, the aggregate supply curve shifts out year by year more or less regularly and deviations from potential or full-employment output are largely the result of shifts in the aggregate demand curve that are greater or less than the shift in the aggregate supply curve. In recent years an alternative view has argued that the growth of potential output and the associated shifts in the aggregate supply curve may be less regular and more variable than had been suspected.

What difference does it make whether potential output grows smoothly or fluctuates from year to year? Estimates of potential output and the difference of actual output from potential are an important determinant of changes in fiscal and monetary policy. For example, when the economy is operating below potential, expansionary policies that increase aggregate demand can increase output and employment. If the aggregate supply curve is relatively flat, the increase in output may have little impact on prices. The magnitude of changes in fiscal and monetary policy to increase aggregate demand will be influenced by estimates of the shortfall from potential output.

But if GDP is low in part because of an adverse shift in the aggregate supply curve, then expansionary policy that ignores the decrease in potential output could turn out to be too expansionary, push the economy above potential, and create unwanted inflationary pressures. On the other hand, if GDP increased above traditional estimates of potential output because of a favorable shift in the aggregate supply curve, stabilization policy that tried to reduce aggregate demand because of a concern about possible inflationary pressures would unnecessarily increase unemployment.

Why is it so difficult to figure out how the aggregate supply curve is shifting? As economists John Boschen and Leonard Mills point out, potential GDP is not directly observable. Neither is the aggregate demand curve or the aggregate supply curve. The levels of output and prices that we observe give us information about where these curves intersect, but by themselves do not identify one curve or the other. In order to identify the aggregate supply curve one needs to use economic theory and make appropriate assumptions about factors that affect aggregate supply, just as we have done with regard to factors that affect aggregate demand. These theories of the aggregate supply curve are then tested by comparing implications of the models with data from the real world. Models of the aggregate supply curve are still relatively new and estimates of the importance of supply-side factors in explaining fluctuations in output cover a wide range. A number of these estimates suggest that a one-third of the variation in output might be attributed to variability in the growth of potential GDP while others range as high as 50 to 70 percent.

1. What are the implications for stabilization policy if fluctuations in the aggregate supply curve account for 10 percent or 50 percent of the fluctuations in output?

SOURCES: John Boschen and Leonard Mills, "Monetary Policy with a New View of Potential GNP," *Business Review*, Federal Reserve Bank of Philadelphia (July/August 1990), pp. 3-10; and Satyajit Chatterjee, "Productivity Growth and the American Business Cycle," *Business Review*, Federal Reserve Bank of Philadelphia (September/October 1995), pp. 13–22.

STUDY QUESTIONS

1. Why is the aggregate supply curve drawn sloping upward to the right?

2. What factors influence the position of the aggregate supply curve?

3. What market forces move the economy to the equilibrium level of output and prices given by the intersection of the aggregate demand curve and aggregate supply curve?

4. Evaluate the following statement: "All periods of inflation are caused by excessive demands for high wages on the part of labor."

5. What is the process by which an inflationary gap self-destructs?

6. Is an adverse supply shock likely to give rise to an inflationary gap or a recessionary gap? Why?

7. What are some of the reasons the economy's self-correcting mechanisms might work slowly in the face of a recessionary gap?

8. What is meant by stagnation and when is it likely to occur?

9. How do considerations of aggregate supply affect the value of the multiplier?

10. How might shifts in the aggregate supply curve help to explain the experience of the later 1990s when inflation and unemployment declined at the same time?

Managing Aggregate Demand: Fiscal Policy

28

Important Terms and Concepts

Fiscal policy

Automatic stabilizers

Learning Objectives

After completing this chapter, you should be able to:

- describe the process by which a change in government purchases of goods and services will lead to a shift in the expenditure schedule and the aggregate demand curve.

- describe the process by which a change in taxes will lead to a shift in the expenditure schedule and the aggregate demand curve.

- explain why income taxes reduce the value of the multiplier.

- explain why the multiplier for a change in income taxes will be less than the multiplier for a change in government purchases of goods and services.

- explain how automatic stabilizers help to reduce fluctuations in GDP when there are changes in autonomous spending.

- explain why economists treat government transfer payments like negative taxes, not like government purchases of goods and services.

- describe the process by which a change in government transfer payments will lead to a shift in the aggregate demand curve.

- explain why active stabilization policy need not imply that government must get bigger and bigger.

- use the aggregate demand and supply diagram to show how supply-side tax cuts hope to reduce the impact on prices associated with stabilization policy to eliminate a recessionary gap.

- describe the kernel of truth in supply-side economics.

- discuss the reservations that most economists have in regard to supply-side economics.

CHAPTER REVIEW

The models of income determination in earlier chapters included a rather passive government. This chapter uses a more realistic model of taxes and provides a framework for considering how and when the government

(1) should vary spending and taxes. The government's plans for spending and taxes are called (fiscal/monetary) policy. The only trick is to understand how government spending and taxes affect the curves we have already derived, that is, how government spending and taxes affect the expenditure schedule, the aggregate demand curve, and the aggregate supply curve. After this, the analysis proceeds exactly as before: For a given price level, the equilibrium level of income on the income-expenditure diagram is determined by the intersection of the (consumption/expenditure) schedule and the 45° line. A change in prices will affect consumption spending and net exports. The different price levels and the associated equilibrium levels of income on the income-expenditure diagram can be combined to form the aggregate _____ curve. This curve together with the aggregate _____ curve will determine the final equilibrium for income and prices. A change in the government's fiscal policy will shift one or more of the curves and lead to new equilibrium values for income and prices.

There are three important ways government fiscal policy influences total spending in the economy:

A. The government purchases goods and services.

B. The government collects *taxes,* reducing the spending power of households and firms. Particular taxes may affect incentives for working, saving, investing, or spending.

C. The government gives *transfer payments* to some individuals, e.g., Social Security payments, thereby increasing their disposable income.

Government purchases of goods and services are a direct addition to total spending in the economy; that is,

(2) they shift the expenditure schedule (up/down) by the full amount of the purchases. Thus, if government spending increased by $1, the expenditure schedule would shift up by $_____. (An increase in autonomous consumption spending, investment spending or net exports of $1 would also shift the expenditure schedule up by $_____.) Thus, changes in government spending shift the expenditure schedule in exactly the same way as other changes in autonomous spending and should have similar multiplier effects.

(3) Government taxes (are/are not) a direct component of spending on currently produced goods and services. Personal income taxes affect consumption spending through their impact on disposable income. Following a decrease in personal income taxes, consumers' disposable income will be (higher/lower). The initial effect on consumption spending will depend in part on whether consumers view the tax change as permanent or temporary. The largest impact will come from a (permanent/temporary) tax cut. The change in consumption spending following the reduction in taxes will be determined by the marginal propensity to consume, which

380

is (<u>less than/equal to/greater than</u>) 1.0. Thus, changes in personal income taxes affect spending, but indirectly through their effect on consumption expenditures. A change in corporate income taxes will change corporate profits after taxes, and is likely to affect _____ expenditures.

The third important function of the government that affects total spending is the magnitude of government transfer payments. These payments, like taxes, are not a direct element of total spending on goods and services. Also, like personal taxes, they affect total spending because they affect people's disposable _____ (4) and thus their _____ spending. Remember that taxes are earned but not received while transfers are received but not earned. Thus in the models we will be working with, disposable income is equal to GDP (<u>minus/plus</u>) taxes (<u>minus/plus</u>) transfers, and transfers can be thought of as negative taxes. An important feature of income taxes (and some transfer payments) is that they vary with GDP. Taxes go (<u>down/up</u>) and transfer payments go _____ as GDP goes up.

We have seen that the multiplier process arises because any autonomous increase in spending means higher income for those who supply the newly demanded goods. These higher incomes will lead to more consumption spending, and so on, and so on. This process continues to take place, but it is important to remember that each round of spending produces an increase in income *before* taxes. With income taxes some of the increase in before-tax income goes to pay taxes, and after-tax income (or disposable income) will increase by (<u>more/less</u>) than it would in an economy with fixed taxes. Thus, each induced round of consumption spending will be (5) (<u>smaller/larger</u>) than before.

To summarize, in an economy with income taxes and transfer payments that vary with income, each round in the multiplier process will be smaller than before, and thus the multiplier effect on income, from any increase in autonomous spending, will be (<u>smaller/larger</u>) than before. The impact of income taxes on the multiplier is (6) another important reason why our earlier formula for the multiplier, 1/(1 − MPC), was oversimplified.

We can see these same results graphically on the income-expenditure diagram. Up to now we have assumed that taxes did not vary with income. A $1 change in GDP meant a $1 increase in disposable income and led to an increase in consumption spending given by the MPC. Since in these models consumption spending was the only type of spending that changed when GDP changed, the slope of the expenditure schedule was equal to the _____. Now when we consider the impact of income taxes, we see that a $1 increase in GDP (7) leads to a(n) (<u>smaller/equal/larger</u>) increase in disposable income and a(n) _____ increase in consumption spending than before. The result is a (<u>flatter/steeper</u>) expenditure schedule.

As we saw earlier, the multiplier can be derived from the slope of the expenditure schedule. The slope of the expenditure schedule can be written as

$$\text{Slope of the Expenditure Schedule} = \frac{\Delta C}{\Delta GDP} + \frac{\Delta I}{\Delta GDP} + \frac{\Delta G}{\Delta GDP} + \frac{\Delta X}{\Delta GDP} + \frac{\Delta IM}{\Delta GDP}$$

Earlier we had assumed that all terms except $\frac{\Delta C}{\Delta GDP}$, were zero. Let us look more closely at $\frac{\Delta C}{\Delta GDP}$, which we can rewrite as

$$\frac{\Delta C}{\Delta GDP} = \left(\frac{\Delta C}{\Delta D}\right) \times \left(\frac{\Delta D}{\Delta GDP}\right)$$

The first term on the right-hand side of the equal sign is the marginal propensity to consume. If taxes do not vary with income, the second term will equal 1.0. An income tax means the second term is

(8) (greater than/equal to/less than) 1.0 and the slope of the expenditure schedule is less than the marginal propensity to consume.[1]

We have now added government purchases of goods and services, taxes, and transfers to our model of income determination. Taken together, these variables are an important determinant of the equilibrium level of income. Changes in these variables, just like the changes in autonomous spending we considered in earlier chapters, will have multiplier effects on the equilibrium level of GDP. The deliberate manipulation of fiscal policy variables may help the government achieve its desired objectives for GDP and prices. Manipulation of government fiscal policy variables for GDP objectives is an example of stabilization policy. For example, if the government

(9) wants to increase GDP, it can decide to (increase/decrease) government purchases of goods and services, _____ personal taxes, _____ corporate taxes, or _____ transfer payments to individuals.

One of the reasons it is so difficult to agree on fiscal policy is that there are so many choices, all of which could have the same impact on national income, but very different impacts on other issues, such as the size of the public versus private sector, the burden of taxes between individuals and corporations, the composition of output between consumption and investment spending, and the amount of income redistribution through transfers to low-income families.

One might believe that if we could decide upon the amounts of government purchases, taxes, and transfers, effective fiscal policy would be simply a technical matter of choosing the right numbers so that the expenditure schedule would intersect the 45° line, and the aggregate demand curve would intersect the aggregate supply curve at full employment. In actuality, uncertainties about (a) private components of aggregate demand, (b) the precise size of the multiplier, (c) exactly what level of GDP is associated with full employment, (d) the time it takes for changes in fiscal policy to affect spending, and (e) the vagaries of the political process all mean that fiscal policy will continue to be subject to much political give and take. One hopes that appropriate economic analysis will contribute to a more informed level of debate.

---

[1]This analysis also helps us see how induced spending affects the slope of the expenditure schedule. For example, if investment spending increases when GDP increases, then $\Delta I/\Delta GDP$ will be greater than zero and the expenditure schedule will be steeper. If imports increase with increases in GDP, then $\Delta IM/\Delta GDP$ will be greater than zero and the slope of the expenditure schedule will be flatter.

382

Changes in government spending or tax rates shift the aggregate demand curve, directly in the case of government purchases and indirectly through impacts on private spending in the case of taxes and transfer payments. Any shift in the aggregate demand curve, including shifts from changes in fiscal policy, affects both prices and output as we move along the aggregate _____ curve. Thus, expansionary fiscal policy,   (10) designed to increase GDP, is also likely to (increase/decrease) prices. Supply-side fiscal policies attempt to minimize the impact on prices through changes that shift the aggregate supply curve at the same time that they shift the aggregate demand curve.

Since 1980, there has been much attention given to supply-side tax cuts. Most economists have a number of reservations about the exaggerated claims of ardent supporters of supply-side tax cuts: Specific effects will depend on exactly which taxes are reduced; increases in aggregate supply are likely to take some time, while effects on aggregate demand will be much quicker. By themselves supply-side tax cuts are likely to lead to increased income inequality and to bigger, not smaller, government budget deficits. Do not let these serious objections to exaggerated claims blind you to the kernel of truth in supply-side economics: Marginal tax rates are important for decisions by individuals and firms. In particular situations, reductions in marginal tax rates can improve economic incentives.

IMPORTANT TERMS AND CONCEPTS QUIZ

Choose the best definition for each of the following terms.

1. _____ Fiscal policy
2. _____ Automatic stabilizers
3. _____ Government transfer payments
4. _____ Supply-side tax cuts

a. All income is taxed at a single rate
b. Money the government gives to individuals in the form of outright grants
c. The government's plan for spending and taxes
d. Tax policy designed to shift the aggregate supply curve to the right
e. Features of the economy that reduce its sensitivity to shifts in demand

BASIC EXERCISES

This exercise is designed to show how changes in government purchases and taxes will have multiplier effects on the equilibrium level of income and how these multipliers can be used to help determine appropriate fiscal policy. To simplify the numerical calculations, the exercise focuses on the shift in the expenditure schedule, holding prices constant. That is, we will consider how changes in fiscal policy shift the aggregate demand curve.

Table 28-1 has data on GDP, taxes, disposable income, consumption, investment, government spending, exports, and imports. This table is similar to Table 28-1 except that here taxes vary with income while in Table 28-1 they did not.

Table 28-1

Constant Prices

Income (Output) Y	Taxes T	Disposable Income DI	Consumption Spending C	Investment Spending I	Government Purchases G	Exports X	Imports IM	Total Spending $C + I + G + (X - IM)$
9,500	1,675	7,825	6,600	1,500	1,750	1,200	1,350	_____
9,750	1,738	8,013	6,750	1,500	1,750	1,200	1,350	_____
10,000	1,800	8,200	6,900	1,500	1,750	1,200	1,350	_____
10,250	1,863	8,388	7,050	1,500	1,750	1,200	1,350	_____
10,500	1,925	8,575	7,200	1,500	1,750	1,200	1,350	_____
10,750	1,988	8,763	7,350	1,500	1,750	1,200	1,350	_____
11,000	2,050	8,950	7,500	1,500	1,750	1,200	1,350	_____

1. Complete the column for total spending to determine the equilibrium level of GDP $ _____

2. Assume now that government purchases decrease by $200 to $1550 as shown in **Table 28-2.** Following the decrease in government purchases, the new equilibrium level of income is
$ _____.

Table 28-2

Constant Prices

Income (Output) Y	Taxes T	Disposable Income DI	Consumption Spending C	Investment Spending I	Government Purchases G	Exports X	Imports IM	Total Spending $C + I + G + (X - IM)$
9,500	1,675	7,825	6,600	1,500	1,550	1,200	1,350	_____
9,750	1,738	8,013	6,750	1,500	1,550	1,200	1,350	_____
10,000	1,800	8,200	6,900	1,500	1,550	1,200	1,350	_____
10,250	1,863	8,388	7,050	1,500	1,550	1,200	1,350	_____
10,500	1,925	8,575	7,200	1,500	1,550	1,200	1,350	_____
10,750	1,988	8,763	7,350	1,500	1,550	1,200	1,350	_____
11,000	2,050	8,950	7,500	1,500	1,550	1,200	1,350	_____

3. The multiplier for this decrease in government purchases is _____. (This multiplier can be computed by dividing the change in the equilibrium level of income by the change in government purchases.) How does the value for the multiplier compare with the value for the multiplier in Basic Exercise of Chapter 26? The only difference here is that taxes are assumed to vary with income. In particular the marginal propensity to consume is the same in Tables 28-1, 28-2, and Tables 26-1 and 26-2.

4. Now let us use the multipliers computed in question 3 to figure out what changes in government purchases would be necessary to raise the equilibrium level of income from its initial value given in question 1 to its full-employment level of $10,750.

   The necessary increase in government purchases is $_____.

   (You can answer this question by figuring out what appropriate change in government purchases when multiplied by the relevant multiplier will equal the desired change in income.) Alternatively one could have lowered taxes to stimulate demand. How would you choose between using changes in government purchases of goods and services and changes in taxes when you want to use fiscal policy to influence aggregate demand?

5. What is the new equilibrium level of income if, from the initial equilibrium given in question 1, investment expenditures rather than government purchases fall by $200? (Now investment spending will be $1,700 while government purchases stay at $1,800. Create a new version of Table 28-1 if necessary.) What can one say about multipliers for autonomous changes in public versus private purchases of goods and services?

SELF-TESTS FOR UNDERSTANDING

TEST A

Circle the most appropriate answer.

1. Fiscal policy involves decisions about all but which one of the following?
   a. income tax rates
   b. the magnitude of transfer payments
   c. interest rates
   d. government purchases of goods and services

2. The impact of transfer payments on disposable income suggests that an increase in transfer payments will have the same effect as a(n)
   a. increase in taxes.
   b. increase in government purchases of goods and services.
   c. decrease in government purchases of goods and services.
   d. decrease in taxes.

385

3. A simultaneous reduction in income taxes and transfer payments of $15 billion will leave aggregate disposable income
   a. lower than before the change.
   b. unchanged.
   c. higher than before the change.

4. An increase in government purchases will
   a. shift the expenditure schedule down.
   b. leave the expenditure schedule unchanged.
   c. shift the expenditure schedule up.

5. A decrease in taxes will
   a. shift the expenditure schedule down.
   b. leave the expenditure schedule unchanged.
   c. shift the expenditure schedule up.

6. An increase in transfer payments will
   a. shift the expenditure schedule down.
   b. leave the expenditure schedule unchanged.
   c. shift the expenditure schedule up.

7. Income taxes mean that the difference between GDP and disposable income will _____ as GDP increases.
   a. decrease
   b. stay the same
   c. increase

8. When taxes, transfers, investment spending, net exports, and government purchases do not vary with GDP, the slope of the expenditure schedule will be
   a. less than the MPC.
   b. equal to the MPC.
   c. greater than the MPC.

9. If a system of fixed taxes and transfers is replaced with taxes and transfers that vary with income, the slope of the expenditure schedule will be
   a. less than before.
   b. unchanged.
   c. greater than before.

10. The initial impact of a change in income taxes is on _____ and _____.
    a. imports; exports
    b. disposable income; investment
    c. investment; consumption
    d. disposable income; consumption

11. Equal reductions in government purchases and taxes are likely to
    a. shift the expenditure schedule down.
    b. leave the expenditure schedule unchanged.
    c. shift the expenditure schedule up.

12. If the basic expenditure multiplier is 2.0 and if the government wishes to decrease the level of GDP by $80 billion, what decrease in government purchases of goods and services would do the job?
    a. $20 billion
    b. $40 billion
    c. $80 billion
    d. $160 billion

13. Instead of decreasing government purchases, the same objectives, in terms of reducing GDP, could also be achieved by
    a. reducing government transfer payments.
    b. reducing taxes.
    c. increasing both taxes and government transfer payments by equal amounts.
    d. reducing both taxes and government transfer payments by equal amounts.

14. Which of the following would help eliminate a recessionary gap?
    a. decrease in taxes
    b. decrease in transfer payments
    c. decrease in government purchases
    d. increase in tax rates

15. A 10 percent reduction in income tax rates would
    a. lower the value of the basic expenditure multiplier.
    b. not affect the value of the basic expenditure multiplier.
    c. raise the value of the basic expenditure multiplier.

16. An increase in tax rates will lead to all but which one of the following?
    a. a decrease in the value of the multiplier
    b. a movement along the aggregate demand curve
    c. a reduction in the equilibrium level of GDP
    d. a shift of the expenditure schedule

17. Which of the following is not an example of an automatic stabilizer?
    a. unemployment compensation
    b. the corporate income tax
    c. a special program to build more highways enacted to help combat a recession
    d. personal income taxes

18. Political conservatives could still argue for active stabilization policy as long as the government agreed to _____ during periods of boom and _____ during recessions.
    a. increase taxes; increase government spending
    b. increase government spending; lower taxes
    c. lower government spending; lower taxes
    d. lower taxes; increase government spending

387

19. Supply-side tax cuts are designed to increase output without raising prices by shifting the
    a. expenditure schedule.
    b. aggregate demand curve.
    c. aggregate supply curve.
    d. 45° line.

20. Critics of supply-side tax cuts would agree with all but which one of the following?
    a. Supply-side tax cuts are likely to increase inequality in the distribution of income.
    b. Supply-side tax cuts will substantially reduce the rate of inflation.
    c. Supply-side tax cuts are likely to mean bigger deficits for the federal government.
    d. Supply-side tax cuts will have a larger initial impact on aggregate demand than on aggregate supply.

TEST B

Circle T or F for true or false.

T   F   1. An increase in income tax rates will increase the multiplier.

T   F   2. When taxes increase with increases in income, a $1 change in GDP will mean a smaller change in disposable income.

T   F   3. Income taxation reduces the value of the multiplier for changes in government purchases but does not affect the multiplier for changes in investment.

T   F   4. Since taxes are not a direct component of aggregate demand, changes in taxes do not have multiplier effects on income.

T   F   5. Changes in government purchases of goods and services and in government transfer payments to individuals are both changes in government spending and thus have the same multiplier effects on the equilibrium level of income.

T   F   6. Reducing tax rates would help to eliminate an inflationary gap.

T   F   7. Active stabilization policy implies that the government must get bigger and bigger.

T   F   8. Automatic stabilizers reduce the sensitivity of the economy to shifts in aggregate demand.

T   F   9. Only the aggregate supply curve will shift following a supply-side tax cut that increases investment spending by firms.

T   F 10. There is general agreement among economists that supply-side tax cuts will increase output with little impact on prices.

| Appendix A | *Graphical Treatment of Taxes and Fiscal Policy*

BASIC EXERCISES

The following problem is meant to illustrate the material in Appendix A. Table 28-3 is the same as Table 28-2 except that taxes are lower at each possible level of income.

Table 28-3

Constant Prices

Income (Output) Y	Taxes T	Disposable Income DI	Consumption Spending C	Investment Spending I	Government Purchases G	Exports X	Imports IM	Total Spending $C+I+G+(X-IM)$
9,500	1,425	8,075	6,800	1,500	1,550	1,200	1,350	_____
9,750	1,488	8,263	6,950	1,500	1,550	1,200	1,350	_____
10,000	1,550	8,450	7,100	1,500	1,550	1,200	1,350	_____
10,250	1,613	8,638	7,250	1,500	1,550	1,200	1,350	_____
10,500	1,675	8,825	7,400	1,500	1,550	1,200	1,350	_____
10,750	1,738	9,013	7,550	1,500	1,550	1,200	1,350	_____
11,000	1,800	9,200	7,700	1,500	1,550	1,200	1,350	_____

1. A comparison of consumption spending in Tables 28-2 and **28-3** when $Y = 9,500$ shows the initial impact on consumption spending when taxes are reduced. Taxes decreased by $250, disposable income increased by $250, and consumption spending increased by _____. The increase in consumption spending should equal the MPC times the increase in disposable income. Does it?

2. What is the new equilibrium level of income following the reduction in taxes? _____

3. Was the reduction in taxes analyzed in questions 1 and 2 self-financing? That is, was the increase in GDP stimulated by the reduction in taxes large enough so that on balance there was no decrease in government tax revenues? (Be sure to compare tax receipts at the equilibrium level of income in Table 28-2 with tax receipts at the equilibrium in Table 28-3.)

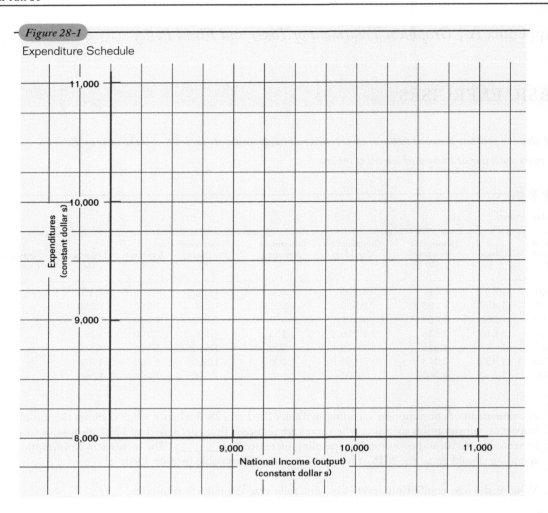

Figure 28-1

Expenditure Schedule

4. Use **Figure 28-1** to show the impact of variable taxes on the slope of the expenditure schedule and thus on the value of the multiplier. Start by plotting the expenditure schedule from Table 28-1. Label this expenditure schedule "Fixed Taxes." Now plot the expenditure schedule from Table 28-1. Label this expenditure schedule "Variable Taxes." Which expenditure schedule is steeper? Now assume that investment spending increases by 200. Carefully draw new expenditure schedules that are 200 higher than before. Be sure you do not change the slope of each expenditure schedule. What happens to the equilibrium level of income following the shift of the Fixed Taxes expenditure schedule? What happens to the equilibrium level of income following the shift of the Variable Taxes expenditure schedule? Explain the differences.

| Appendix B | *Algebraic Treatment of Fiscal Policy and Aggregate Demand*

BASIC EXERCISES

This exercise is meant to illustrate the material in the Appendix to Chapter 28. Just as in other chapters, we can use equations rather than graphs or tables to determine the equilibrium level of output and relevant multipliers. If we have done our work accurately, we should get the same answer regardless of whether we use graphs, tables, or algebra.

The following equations underlie the numerical example in the Basic Exercise.

$C = 340 + 0.8DI$

$T = -700 + 0.25Y$

$DI = Y - T$

$Y = C + I + G + (X - IM)$

1. What is the equilibrium level of income if investment spending is $1,500 billion, net exports are −$150 billion, and government purchases are $1,750 billion? Be sure that $C + I + G + (X - IM) = Y$.

2. Assume that both across-the-board taxes and government purchases decline by $50 billion so that government purchases are $1,700 billion and the tax equation is

$$T = -750 + 0.25Y.$$

Is the equilibrium level of income unchanged following the balanced reduction in the size of the government? Why? What about the government deficit $(G - T)$?

3. Calculate the multiplier for each of the following:
   - change in investment spending
   - change in government purchases
   - change in exports
   - change in fixed taxes (that is, change in intercept of tax equation)

4. Explore the implications for fixed and variable taxes by replacing the equation for *T* with $T = 1,800$. Now there are only fixed taxes. First calculate the equilibrium level of income when $G = 1,750$. Then consider the simultaneous reductions in G and T described in question 2. Now consider the various multipliers in question 3. How, if at all, do answers differ when there are only fixed taxes?

SUPPLEMENTARY EXERCISES

1. In his analysis of the impact of the 1964 tax cut, which reduced taxes on a permanent basis, Arthur Okun estimated that the MPC was 0.95.[2] At the same time, Okun estimated that the basic expenditure multiplier, applicable for any increase in autonomous spending, was only 2.73, not 20, which comes from the oversimplified formula of 1/(1 − MPC). How can such a large MPC be consistent with such a small multiplier?

2. The 1964 reduction in personal taxes was about $10 billion. Okun estimated that this tax reduction raised GDP by $25.9 billion. The ratio of the change in GDP to the change in taxes was only 2.59, not 2.73, the value of the basic expenditure multiplier. How can you account for this discrepancy?

    (*Hint:* In his analysis, Okun assumed prices did not change, so price effects on consumption expenditures are not part of the answer. You should think about whether the basic expenditure multiplier—the multiplier for a shift in the expenditure schedule—is the appropriate multiplier to apply directly to the change in taxes.)

3. What is it like to advise the president of the United States about economic policy? Martin S. Feldstein was chairman of the Council of Economic Advisers during the Reagan administration. You might enjoy reading his observations on the workings of the council and serving as chairman of the council in "The Council of Economic Advisers and Economic Advising in the United States" (*The Economic Journal,* September 1992, pp. 1223–1234).

ECONOMICS IN ACTION

GROWTH AND TAXES

What is the relation between taxes and economic growth? Do high taxes impede growth and would countries be unambiguously better off if they lowered taxes?

For some, the answers to these questions are obviously yes. Reporting in *The New York Times*, Anna Bernasek suggests that the evidence for this viewpoint is cloudy at best. While taxes may affect individual behavior, Bernasek argues that "there is surprisingly little evidence that tax rates are an important factor in determining the nation's economic prosperity." She quotes economists William Easterly and Sergio Rebelo who in 1993 concluded, "the evidence that tax rates matter for growth is disturbingly fragile."

More recently economist Joel Slemrod and Jon Bakija looked at the relationship between marginal tax rates and productivity. They found that over the period 1950 to 2002, periods with the highest growth in productivity were also periods with the highest tax rates. In addition, high tax countries tend to be the most affluent.

While no economist would suggest that these findings are a license to increase taxes without limit, Bernasek suggests that the findings of Easterly, Rebelo, Slemrod, and Bakija "call into question why, if taxes are so bad for growth, their effect doesn't show up more prominently." All of this is not to suggest that some behaviors are not

---

[2]Arthur M. Okun, "Measuring the Impact of the 1964 Tax Cut," in W. W. Heller, ed., *Perspectives on Economic Growth* (New York: Vintage Books, 1968), pp. 25-49.

392

influenced by tax rates. For example, changes in investment tax policy appear to influence the timing of business investment in order to maximize tax advantages. However tax advantages for personal saving appears to have had little impact on aggregate household savings.

Economist Peter Lindert would not be surprised by Bernasek's report. In a recent book, *Growing Public*, he explores the links between high taxes, high levels of social spending, and economic growth. Lindert argues that some forms of social spending, e.g., spending on education, can improve economic growth and nations with high levels of taxes and spending are often careful to choose efficient tax schemes that minimize adverse impacts. In many European countries this has meant high sin taxes—taxes on smoking and drinking—and relatively lighter taxes on capital that could easily move from one country to another should tax rates get too high.

Bernasek worries that a belief in lowering tax rates to spur economic growth could result in spiraling deficits and pressures to reduce important public investments in areas like infrastructure, education, and basic research.

1. What do you think is the relationship between tax rates and growth rates? What evidence supports and contradicts your position? If a country wanted to support a high level of social spending, what forms of taxation would be the most efficient and do the least damage to growth prospects?

Sources: Anna Bernasek, "Economic View: Do Taxes Thwart Growth? Prove It?," *The New York Times*, April 3, 2005. Peter Lindert, *Growing Public*, (Cambridge University Press: 2004).

STUDY QUESTIONS

1. How does the multiplier for a change in government spending compare to the multipliers in earlier chapters for changes in investment spending, net exports, and the autonomous component of consumption spending?

2. Why do income taxes reduce the value of the multiplier?

3. What is meant by the term *automatic stabilizers*? In what sense are they automatic? In what sense do they stabilize the economy?

4. If you were charged with recommending changes in government purchases, taxes, and transfers to shift the aggregate demand curve to the right, what sorts of changes in each of these elements of fiscal policy would do the job?

5. How would you choose between the alternatives you proposed when answering question 4?

6. Why is designing fiscal policy to achieve full employment subject to such intense political debate rather than being a technical exercise best left to economists?

7. "Active stabilization policy—the deliberate use of fiscal policy to avoid recessions and inflation—must inevitably lead to bigger and bigger government." Do you agree or disagree? Why?

8. What are some examples of supply-side tax cuts? Explain how and why each of your examples is expected to affect the aggregate supply curve.

9. If supply-side tax cuts could increase the equilibrium level of output without increasing prices, they would be a superior instrument for short-run stabilization policy. Are supply-side tax cuts likely to work in this way? Why or why not? If not, what are supply-side tax cuts good for?

10. What would be necessary if tax cuts were to be self-financing? How likely are these conditions to be met in practice?

ECONOMICS ONLINE

Reports of the Congressional Budget Office analyzing the president's budget proposals, summarizing the economic and budget outlook, and reporting on special studies are published on a regular basis. They are available online at

http://www.cbo.gov

Money and the Banking System

Important Terms and Concepts

Run on a bank

Barter

Money

Medium of exchange

Unit of account

Store of value

Commodity money

Fiat money

M1

M2

Near moneys

Liquidity

Fractional reserve banking

Deposit insurance

Moral hazard

Federal Deposit Insurance Corporation (FDIC)

Required reserves

Asset

Liability

Balance sheet

Net worth

Deposit creation

Excess reserves

Money Multiplier

Systemic Risk

Systemically Important ("Too Big to Fail")

Learning Objectives

After completing this chapter, you should be able to:

- explain the advantages of using money over barter.

- distinguish between various functions of money. Which are unique to money? Which are shared with other assets?

- list the desirable features of objects serving as money.

- distinguish between commodity money and fiat money.

- explain the differences between Ml and M2 as measures of money.

- describe the historical origins of fractional reserve banking and explain why the industry is so heavily regulated today.

- explain how the banking system as a whole can create deposits, given an initial injection of bank reserves.

- use the required reserve fraction to derive the oversimplified deposit creation multiplier.

- explain why the deposit creation multiplier, based on the required reserve fraction, is oversimplified.

CHAPTER REVIEW

Whether the love of money is the root of all evil or not, there is no argument that money has an important influence on the way our economy operates. The right amount of money can help to keep employment up and prices stable. Too much money may lead to excessive inflation; too little money may lead to excessive unemployment. This chapter is an introduction to money. What is it? Where did it come from? What role do banks play in the creation of money? The next chapter discusses how the government regulates the amount of money in the economy, and the chapter after that discusses the influence of money on economic activity.

It is possible that a society could be organized without money. If everyone were self-sufficient there would, by definition, be no trading between individuals and no need for money. If people concentrated their productive activities on what they did best and traded with each other to get goods they did not produce themselves, they might be able to get along without money. Direct trading of goods for goods, or goods for services, is called

(1) _____. For it to be successful there must be a double coincidence of wants. As societies become more complicated and people become ever more specialized, it is clear that barter becomes (less difficult/more difficult).

When a society uses a standard object for exchanging goods and services, a seller will provide goods or services to a buyer and receive the standard object as payment. The efficiency of such a system should be obvious. You no longer have to find someone who not only has what you want but also wants what you have.

(2) Anyone who has what you want will now do. Economists would call the standard object _____. If the object serving as money has intrinsic value in nonmonetary uses, such as gold or jewelry, it is called _____ money. When objects serve as money it is useful that they be divisible, of uniform quality, durable, storable at little or no cost, and compact. Many commodity monies fail on one or more of these criteria. Today money has little intrinsic value and is called _____ money. Such money has value because everyone believes that everyone else will exchange goods and services for it. The bedrock for this foundation of faith is that the government will stand behind the money and limit its production.

When it comes to measuring the quantity of money, exactly where one draws the line is a bit unclear. We have defined money as a standard object used for exchanging goods and services. On this count, the sum of all coins and currency outside of banks plus the wide variety of checking accounts at banks and credit unions surely

(3) belongs in any measure of money. The measure that focuses on these items is known as _____. If one also includes savings accounts (because funds in savings accounts can easily be transferred into checking accounts), money market deposit accounts, and money market mutual funds, one is measuring _____.

Consider the data on elements of M1 and M2 for June 2004.

Currency (including traveler's checks)	$925.0 billion
Checkable deposits	943.0 billion
Savings deposits, including money market deposit accounts	6,278.6 billion
Money market mutual funds	707.2 billion[1]

---

[1]H.6 Statistical Release, Board of Governors of the Federal Reserve System, H.6 Money Stock Measures, http://www.federalreserve.gov/releases/h6/hist/. Accessed April 6, 2005.

How big is

M1? $ _____ billion (4)

M2? $ _____ billion

Given the importance of bank deposits in all measures of money, it is important to understand how the banking system can create money. Banks subject to deposit reserve requirements must hold reserves that are at least as great as some stated percentage of their deposits. Reserves can be either cash in a bank's vaults or money that the bank has on deposit at its local Federal Reserve Bank. We will learn more about the Federal Reserve System in the next chapter. The stated percentage is the required reserve ratio. Thus, only some of the money used to open or to add to a bank deposit must be kept by the bank to meet reserve requirements. The rest can be used to make loans in the search for more profits. This system is known as fractional reserve banking.

The multiple creation of deposits is the counterpart to bank (lending/borrowing). Assume that banks are (5) subject to a 10 percent reserve requirement. Following a new deposit of $1,000, the maximum amount of the new deposit that this bank could lend out and still meet the reserve requirement is $_____. As the proceeds of the loan are deposited in other banks, new deposits will be created. For the banking system as a whole, the maximum amount of loans that can be made, and thus the maximum amount of deposits that can be created following an increase in bank reserves, is limited by the _____ _____ _____. The precise sequence of the multiple deposit creation process is illustrated in the Basic Exercise for this chapter.

Mathematical formulas have been devised to determine the maximum increase in deposits that can be created by the banking system following an increase in bank reserves:

Maximum increase in deposits = Initial increase in bank reserves × (1/_____ _____) (6)

The deposit creation formula is oversimplified for two reasons:

A. The formula assumes that the entire proceeds of each loan will eventually be re-deposited in the banking system. If some of the proceeds of a loan do not get redeposited, then the deposit creation multiplier will be (larger/smaller). (7)

B. The formula also assumes that every bank makes as large a loan as possible; that is, each bank is assumed to make no changes in its holdings of _____ reserves. If banks increase their holdings of such reserves, then the money creation formula would be (larger/smaller).

The discussion of the deposit creation multiplier showed how deposits can be created following an increase in bank reserves. The emphasis was on how a change in reserves leads to a change in deposits. One should not be surprised to learn that *total* deposits in all banks are similarly limited by *total* reserves. The cash deposit discussed in the text results in an increase in total reserves of the banking system. However, most increases in reserves at one bank are offset by a decrease in reserves at some other bank, with no change in reserves of the banking system as a whole. Consider Derek, who takes money out of his account at Bank A. Derek uses the money to buy a home computer, and the dealer deposits this money in her bank, Bank B. While Bank B

397

experiences an increase in reserves, Bank A shows a decrease. The process of multiple deposit creation initiated (8) at Bank B is offset by a process of multiple deposit _____ starting with Bank A. On net there is (some/no) increase in reserves and deposits for the banking system as a whole. The important factor for expanding deposits is new reserves available to the banking system. We will learn in the next chapter how the Federal Reserve is able to influence the volume of reserves available to the banking system.

IMPORTANT TERMS AND CONCEPTS QUIZ

Choose the best definition for each of the following terms.

1. _____ Run on a bank
2. _____ Barter
3. _____ Unit of account
4. _____ Money
5. _____ Medium of exchange
6. _____ Store of value
7. _____ Commodity money
8. _____ Fiat money
9. _____ M1
10. _____ M2
11. _____ Near moneys
12. _____ Liquidity
13. _____ Fractional reserve banking
14. _____ Deposit insurance
15. _____ Moral hazard
16. _____ FDIC
17. _____ Required reserves
18. _____ Asset
19. _____ Liability
20. _____ Balance sheet
21. _____ Net worth
22. _____ Deposit creation
23. _____ Excess reserves
24. _____ Money multiplier
25. _____ Systemic risk

a. Reserves in excess of the legal minimum
b. Item an individual or firm owns
c. Many depositors concurrently withdrawing cash from their accounts
d. Item used to hold wealth from one point in time to another
e. Ease with which an asset can be converted into cash
f. System where bankers keep reserves equal to only a portion of total deposits
g. Standard unit for quoting prices
h. Value of all assets minus the value of all liabilities
i. Ratio of newly created deposits to new reserves
j. System of exchange where people trade one good for another without using money
k. Sum of coins, paper money, checkable deposits, money market mutual funds, and most savings account balances
l. Accounting statement listing assets on the left-hand side and liabilities and net worth on the right-hand side
m. Standard object used in exchanging goods and services
n. Object, without value as commodity that serves as money by government decree
o. Liquid assets that are close substitutes for money
p. System that guarantees depositors against loss if bank goes bankrupt
q. Process by which banking system turns one dollar of reserves into several dollars of deposits
r. Item an individual or firm owes
s. Sum of coins, paper money, and checkable deposits
t. Object used as a medium of exchange that also has substantial value in nonmonetary uses
u. Minimum amount of reserves a bank must hold
v. Government agency that insures depositors' checking and savings accounts
w. People with insurance are less vigorous in protecting against the insured risk
x. System of money based on electronic bookkeeping entries
y. Risks to the entire system of banks or financial institutions.

BASIC EXERCISES

This exercise is designed to help you understand the multiple creation of bank deposits by working through a specific simplified example.

1. Column 1 of **Table 29-1** is partly filled in for you to show the changes in the balance sheet of Bank A immediately following Janet's cash deposit of $10,000. At this point, bank deposits have increased by $ _____. Assuming the required reserve fraction is 10 percent, fill in the last two rows of column 1, showing the initial changes in required and excess reserves.

Table 29-1

Balance Sheet Changes

	(1) Bank A	(2) Bank A	(3) Bank B	(4) Bank B	(5) Bank C
Assets					
Reserves	$10,000	_____	_____	_____	_____
Loans	0	_____	_____	_____	_____
Liabilities					
Deposits	$10,000	_____	_____	_____	_____
Addendum					
Required reserves	_____	_____	_____	_____	_____
Excess reserves	_____	_____	_____	_____	_____

NOTE: Required reserve ratio is 10 percent.

2. Assume that Bank A responds to Janet's deposit by making as large a loan as it can to Earl, given the required reserve ratio. Now fill in column 2 to represent the changes in Bank A's balance sheet after the loan has been made and Earl has taken the proceeds of the loan in cash.

3. Earl uses the money from the loan to buy a car and the car dealer deposits this cash in Bank B. Fill in column 3 to represent the changes in Bank B's balance sheet following this cash deposit. At this point, total bank deposits have increased by $_____ .

4. Assume now that Bank B also makes as large a loan as possible. Fill in column 4 to represent changes in Bank B's balance sheet after it makes the loan and this latest borrower takes the proceeds in cash.

5. Assume that the proceeds of this loan eventually get deposited in Bank C. Fill in column 5 to represent the changes in the balance sheet of Bank C following the increase in deposits. At this point total bank deposits have increased by $ _____.

6. Fill in the following sequence of increased deposits following the initial increase at Bank A, assuming that each bank makes the largest possible loan.

Increased deposits at Bank A   <u>$10,000</u>

Increased deposits at Bank B   _____

Increased deposits at Bank C   _____

Increased deposits at Bank D   _____

Increased deposits at Bank E   _____

If you have not made any mistakes, you will notice that each increase in deposit is less than the previous increase and can be expressed as $(1.0 - 0.1) \times$ (the previous increase in deposits) or $(1.0 -$ reserve requirement ratio) × (the previous increase in deposits).

Mathematically this is an infinite geometric progression with decreasing increments. If we carried the sum out far enough it would approach a limit given by $10,000 ÷ _____,

or $_____. (You might try testing this result by using a computer to calculate the sum for a very large number of terms.) This specific numerical example illustrates the more general principle that the multiplier for the maximum increase in deposits following an increase in bank reserves is

1 ÷ _____ _____ _____.

SELF-TESTS FOR UNDERSTANDING

TEST A

Circle the most appropriate answer.

1. Money serves all but which one of the following functions?
   a. medium of exchange
   b. hedge against inflation
   c. unit of account
   d. store of value

2. Which of the following is not an example of commodity money?
   a. gold coins
   b. cigarettes
   c. a $10 bill
   d. diamonds

3. Where was paper money first used?
   a. China
   b. Egypt
   c. India
   d. Italy

400

4. Which of the following does not belong in M1?
   a. the coins in your pocket
   b. Jodi's checking account
   c. the cash in the vault at the bank downtown
   d. the traveler's check that Heather has left over from last summer

5. The difference between M2 and M1 includes which of the following? (There may be more than one correct answer.)
   a. checking accounts
   b. money market mutual fund balances
   c. marketable U.S. government debt
   d. savings deposits

6. Liquidity is defined as the
   a. viscosity of financial assets.
   b. ease with which assets can be converted to money.
   c. net worth of a financial institution.
   d. ratio of liabilities to assets.

7. Which of Randy's assets is the most liquid?
   a. the U.S. savings bond his grandparents gave him
   b. his collection of 1950s baseball cards
   c. the $20 bill in his wallet
   d. the 100 shares of Microsoft stock he bought last summer

8. A bank's (or your) net worth is found by
   a. summing up all assets.
   b. adding total assets to total liabilities.
   c. dividing total assets by total liabilities.
   d. subtracting total liabilities from total assets.

9. Which of the following is not an asset for a bank?
   a. excess reserves
   b. holdings of U.S. government securities
   c. checking account balances held by depositors
   d. mortgage loans made by the bank

10. The key item that makes a bank's balance sheet balance is its
    a. holdings of excess reserves.
    b. assets.
    c. required reserves.
    d. net worth.

11. If a bank holds more reserves than required, the difference is
    a. the bank's net worth.
    b. liquidity.
    c. solvency.
    d. excess reserves.

12. Banks could increase profits by
    a. holding more commodity money and less fiat money.
    b. holding fewer excess reserves in order to make more loans.
    c. reducing their liabilities.
    d. substituting M2 for M1.

13. If Damien deposits cash that he used to keep under his mattress into his checking account, the initial deposit will result in
    a. an increase in M1.
    b. a decrease in M2.
    c. an increase in the net worth of the banking system.
    d. no change in M1 or M2.

14. The most important government regulation of banks in terms of limiting the multiple creation of deposits is
    a. bank examinations and audits.
    b. limits on the kinds of assets that banks can buy.
    c. the required reserve ratio.
    d. requirements to disclose the volume of loans to bank officials.

15. If the minimum reserve requirement ratio for all bank deposits is 5 percent, then the maximum multiple creation of deposits by the banking system as a whole following a cash deposit of $2,000 would be
    a. $100 = (0.05) × ($2,000).
    b. $2,100 = (1 + 0.05) × ($2,000).
    c. $2,105 = ($2,000)/(1 − 0.05).
    d. $40,000 = ($2,000)/(0.05).

16. If the reserve requirement ratio is 10 percent instead of 5 percent, then the maximum multiple creation of deposits would be
    a. smaller than in question 15.
    b. larger than in question 15.
    c. the same as in question 15.

17. If banks hold some of every increase in deposits in the form of excess reserves, then the amount of deposits actually created following a cash deposit would be
    a. less than that indicated in question 15.
    b. the same as that indicated in question 15.
    c. more than that indicated in question 15.

18. If the required reserve ratio is 20 percent and Rachel deposits $100 in cash in the First National Bank, the maximum increase in deposits by the banking system as a whole is
    a. 0.
    b. $20.
    c. $100.
    d. $500.

19. If the required reserve ratio is 20 percent and Sharon deposits $100 in the First National Bank by depositing a check from her mother written on the Second National Bank, the maximum increase in deposits by the banking system as a whole is
   a. 0.
   b. $20.
   c. $100.
   d. $500.

20. If a bank's total reserve holdings are $35 million and it has $12 million of excess reserves, then its required reserves are
   a. $12 million.
   b. $23 million.
   c. $35 million.
   d. $47 million.

TEST B

Circle T or F for true or false.

T   F   1. A major advantage of the use of money rather than barter is that money avoids the problems of finding a "double coincidence of wants."

T   F   2. Fiat money in the United States may be redeemed for gold from the U.S. Treasury.

T   F   3. Many assets serve as a store of value but only money is also a medium of exchange.

T   F   4. In periods with high rates of inflation, money is a good store of value.

T   F   5. Banks could increase their profitability by holding higher levels of excess reserves.

T   F   6. The existence of deposit insurance is an important reason for the dramatic decline in the number of bank failures in the United States since the 1930s.

T   F   7. The term moral hazard refers to situations where insurance causes people to be less vigilant in guarding against possible losses.

T   F   8. Multiple deposit creation applies to increases in the money supply but reductions in the money supply can come about only through government taxation.

T   F   9. Required reserves are part of a bank's liabilities, whereas excess reserves are part of a bank's assets.

T   F   10. If a bank's liabilities exceed its assets, the bank is said to have negative net worth.

SUPPLEMENTARY EXERCISES

1. If the required reserve ratio is 20 percent and banks want to hold 10 percent of any increase in deposits in the form of excess reserves and people want to hold $1 more in currency for every $10 increase in deposits, what is the eventual increase in deposits following a $1,000 cash deposit in the First National Bank? What is the eventual increase in the money supply?

2. If M is the required reserve fraction, E is the ratio of excess reserves to deposits, and C is the ratio of currency to deposits, what is the formula that relates the change in deposits to a change in reserves?

403

ECONOMICS IN ACTION

THE REFORM OF DEPOSIT INSURANCE

As described in the text, the establishment of federal deposit insurance had a dramatic effect on the number of bank failures. Some critics argue that experience during the 1980s suggests that we may have had too much of a good thing. Economist Edward J. Kane has been especially critical of the actions of federal government officials, both elected and appointed, concerning deposit insurance. He was one of the first to describe the collapse of the Federal Savings and Loan Insurance Corporation (FSLIC), the deposit insurance agency for S&Ls, as resulting from a combination moral hazard and principal-agent problem.[2]

Moral hazard arose because deposit insurance provided an incentive for some S&Ls to engage in risky behavior. The period of high interest rates in the late 1970s and early 1980s had left these institutions with little or negative net worth. Owners of these institutions saw high-risk but potentially high-return loans as their only salvation. Insurance protected their depositors. Negative net worth meant that their own investment in the S&L had already been wiped out. They literally had nothing to lose by engaging in risky behavior.

Kane also charges that Congress and bank regulators (the agents) failed to act in the best interest of U.S. taxpayers (the principals). Kane charges that at critical points, and with the support and encouragement of key members of Congress, the FSLIC allowed bankrupt institutions to continue in business. Succumbing to lobbying pressures to focus on the original book value of assets rather than current market value allowed officials to pretend that bankrupt institutions were still solvent. The result was that problems were deferred as the cost of appropriate action increased. Opposition to increased federal spending and the impact on the deficit that would accompany the official closing of failed institutions further contributed to delay.

What is an appropriate stance for deposit insurance? There have been a large number of proposals. They include the mandatory use of market prices to value assets; mandatory and higher net worth requirements for financial institutions; automatic rules for closing insolvent institutions that remove the element of discretion on the part of regulators; deposit insurance premiums that vary with the riskiness of a bank's portfolio; and public notice of the results of bank examinations.

A number of observers have also argued that the present deposit insurance limit is so high that depositors have little incentive to concern themselves with the riskiness of a bank's portfolio. If a smaller amount, perhaps the first $25,000 or $50,000 of deposits, were insured and it was clear that deposits above this level had no insurance protection, depositors with large balances, especially businesses, would have a real incentive to pay attention to the riskiness of their bank's assets. According to this view, a bank that was imprudent would (and should) suffer a run on its deposits with little reason to expect that the run would spill over and harm sound banks.

---

[2]*Moral hazard* refers to the tendency of insurance to make people less concerned with the risks associated with their behavior—after all, it's covered by insurance. Principal-agent relationships occur whenever one party, the principal, has to hire others, the agents, to act on the principal's behalf. An example would be stockholders who hire executives to manage corporations. It is often difficult for the principals (stockholders) to monitor the behavior of their agents (executives) to ensure that the agents act to promote the principals' interests and not their (the agents') own.

1. What changes, if any, do you think there should be to the system of deposit insurance? Why? How far should the government go to protect depositors? How does one design a system of deposit insurance that addresses the problem of moral hazard?

   You might want to consult the following:

   Edward J. Kane, *The S&L Insurance Mess: How Did It Happen,* (Washington, D.C.: The Urban Institute Press, 1991).

   Lawrence J. White, *The S&L Debacle,* (New York: Oxford University Press, 1991).

   Gary H. Stern and Ron Feldman, "Too Big to Fail: The Hazards of Bank Bailouts," *The Region,* (Federal Reserve Bank of Minneapolis, December 2003). Available online at http://woodrow.mpls. frb.fed.us/pubs/region/03-12/tbtf.cfm. This article is one of a number of papers on deposit insurance reform at http://woodrow.mpls.frb.fed.us/research/studies/tbtf/.

STUDY QUESTIONS

1. What functions does money share with other assets, and what functions are unique to money?

2. How does fiat money differ from commodity money? In particular, how do they compare with regard to the list of desirable characteristics discussed in the text?

3. Where would you draw the line if asked to come up with a measure of money for the American economy?

4. Rank the following in terms of their liquidity and justify your ranking: a 12-month savings certificate, the balance in your checking account, a corporate bond issued by Intel, some leftover traveler's checks from your most recent trip, a share of stock in DuPont, a $20 bill, and a piece of lakeside vacation property.

5. What is full-bodied money? Is money in the United States today full-bodied? If not, where does its value come from?

6. If the government is going to insure deposits, it seems natural that it be allowed to examine a bank's books and put limits on some types of loans to control its risk. Alternatively, the need for deposit insurance could be eliminated if reserve requirements were set at 100 percent. What do you think would happen to bank service charges if reserve requirements were 100 percent? What other changes might you expect? In particular think about the incentive to create alternatives to bank deposits.

7. How can you tell when something is an asset or a liability?

8. As every banker wants her assets to exceed her liabilities, in what sense does a bank's balance sheet balance?

9. As the government controls the printing press, how can banks create money?

10. In what ways is the deposit creation multiplier, $1/m$, oversimplified? Does adjusting for these complications make the deposit creation multiplier larger or smaller?

ECONOMICS ONLINE

The latest information on the size of M1 and M2 can be found at

http://www.federalreserve.gov/releases/H6

The Federal Reserve Bank of San Francisco hosts an online museum of American currency, the American Currency exhibit, at

http://www.frbsf.org/currency/

Banknotes.com's World Currency Gallery displays pictures of money from around the world.

http://www.banknotes.com/images.htm

Monetary Policy: Conventional and Unconventional

30

Important Terms and Concepts

Monetary policy

Central bank

Central bank independence

Open market operations

Federal funds rate

Discount rate

Reserve requirements

Quantitative easing

Risk of default

Risk premium (or "Spread")

Unconventional monetary policy

Learning Objectives

After completing this chapter, you should be able to:

- distinguish between the concepts "money" and "income."

- explain why older arguments about whether a country's central bank should be independent have been replaced by arguments about how central banks should be accountable to the public.

- draw and explain the logic behind both the supply-of-bank-reserves and the demand-for-bank-reserves schedules.

- analyze the impact of open market operations using the demand-for- and supply-of-bank reserves.

- explain how bond prices and interest rates are related.

- describe the impact of open market operations on bond prices and interest rates.

- explain why the Fed's control of the size of bank deposits is not exact.

- use the expenditure schedule along with the aggregate demand and supply curves to describe how changes in monetary policy affect the economy's macroeconomic equilibrium.

- explain how the impact of higher prices on the demand for bank reserves helps to explain why the aggregate demand curve has a negative slope.

CHAPTER REVIEW

In the preceding chapter we learned how deposits are created by the actions of banks. In this chapter we will see how actions taken by the Federal Reserve System can influence interest rates and the economy's overall macro-economic equilibrium. The emphasis in this chapter is on building models. In subsequent chapters we will use these models to understand policy issues.

(1)   The Federal Reserve System was established in 1914 and is the nation's _____ bank. There are _____ district banks throughout the country, with headquarters in Washington, D.C. The people in charge in Washington are the seven members of the _____ of _____ of the Federal Reserve System. Major decisions about open market operations are made by the FOMC, or the _____ _____ _____ Committee. Decisions about government spending and taxes are the nation's (fiscal/monetary) policy. Policy actions by the Federal Reserve constitute the nation's _____ policy. Older arguments about how much independence a country's central bank should enjoy have been replaced by arguments about how to hold independent central banks accountable to the public.

In normal times, the Fed increases the supply of bank reserves by purchasing Treasury (bills/notes). We saw in the preceding chapter that the multiple creation of bank deposits is limited by the required reserve ratio and by the volume of bank reserves. Reserve requirements help to determine the deposit creation multiplier. The Fed's other two major policy instruments—open market operations and lending to banks—directly affect total bank reserves. We have seen that controlling reserve requirements and the volume of bank reserves do not allow for the precise control of the bank deposits (or the stock of money) because of possible changes

(2) in (excess/required) reserve holdings by banks and in currency holdings by the public. In contrast, the Fed has greater ability to hit specific interest rate targets through the use of open market operations.

A reduction in reserve requirements does not change total bank reserves, but it will initially result in a(n)

(3) (increase/decrease) in noninterest-earning excess reserves. Multiple deposit creation will take place as banks try to put these nonearning excess reserves to work. Banks can add to their reserve holdings by borrowing directly from the Fed. The Fed influences the volume of borrowing by changing the interest rate it charges banks. In the United States, the interest rate for these borrowings is called the _____ _____.

(4)   In normal times, open market operations—the purchase and sale of Treasury _____ —represent the most important and most commonly used instrument of monetary policy. Open market operations affect bank behavior by adding to or subtracting from the amount of bank reserves. The essence of an open market purchase is that the Fed creates bank reserves when it (buys/sells) Treasury bills. The result is a(n) (increase/decrease) in noninterest-earning excess reserves, and the usual multiple deposit creation process is set in motion. An open market sale has exactly opposite effects. Payment to the Fed for Treasury bills means a(n) (reduction/increase) in bank reserves and initiates a process of multiple deposit (creation/destruction).

The impact of open market operations on interest rates can be analyzed by considering the demand and supply for bank reserves. There are many interest rates in a modern economy. Typically, they all rise and fall together. Some borrowers must pay higher interest rates in order to secure credit because they represent a higher risk of nonpayment. This gives rise to risk premiums. Risk premiums are likely to rise sharply in a financial crisis meaning that all borrowers except the U.S. Treasury will face higher borrowing costs. The higher interest rates can, in turn, slow economic activity.

Open market operations are the major determinant of the supply of reserves while the need for banks to hold reserves at least as great as that demanded by the Fed's minimum reserve requirement is the major determinant of the demand for bank reserves. In addition, there is an active inter-bank market for reserves, the market for federal funds, where banks with excess reserves can lend reserves to banks that need to borrow to meet their reserve requirement. The price associated with these transactions is the interest rate borrowing banks pay for the use of excess reserves from other banks. This interest rate is called the _____ _____ rate.   (5) An open market purchase will shift the supply curve of bank reserves to the (left/right) and (increase/lower) the federal funds rate. An open market sale will have exactly opposite effects. Changes in the federal funds rate from either type of open market operation will then influence other interest rates.

What exactly is entailed in an open market purchase? It is easiest to consider a case where the Fed buys Treasury bills from a bank. When it does this, the Fed pays for the Treasury bill by crediting the bank with additional reserves. Initially our selling bank will have more reserves without an increase in deposits or required reserves, will likely to step up its own loan operations, and will be more likely to lend reserves to other banks in the market for federal funds.

When the Fed buys Treasury bills, this action will typically increase the price of Treasury bills. Simple mathematics shows that an increase in the price of Treasury bills will be associated with a(n) (decrease/increase) in   (6) interest rates. When the price of a security paying a fixed number of dollars per year in interest increases, the rate of return on that security, as measured by the ratio of the interest payments to the price of the security, must decline.

The mathematics of the relationship between bond prices and interest rates is explored in more detail in the Supplementary Exercises to this chapter.

When the economy is weak for a long time, the central bank may reduce its interest rate to zero, and yet still not stimulate growth sufficiently. In cases such as these, it might turn to one or more _____   (7) _____ _____. These policies include massive lending to banks and open-market purchases of securities other than Treasury bills. The latter is sometimes called quantitative _____. With an understanding of how open market operations can affect the federal funds rates, we are in a position to see how changes in monetary policy affect aggregate demand. Policy shifts in the (supply/demand)-   (8) of-reserves schedule will change interest rates as we move along the _____-for-reserves schedule. The change in interest rates will affect interest-sensitive categories of demand, especially investment spend-

409

ing. Changes in investment spending lead to a (<u>shift in/movement along</u>) the expenditure schedule. The (<u>shift in/movement along</u>) the expenditure schedule will shift the aggregate (<u>demand/supply</u>) curve through the multiplier process. Overall macroeconomic equilibrium is reestablished at the new intersection of the aggregate demand curve and the aggregate supply curve. The division of effects, as between real output and prices, is determined by the slope of the aggregate _____ curve. This sequence of events is diagrammed at the end of this chapter in the text.[1]

The same reasoning helps us to understand two other important points:

Why the aggregate demand curve has a negative slope and why the multiplier formula $1/(1 - MPC)$ is oversimplified:

Higher prices not only reduce the purchasing power of money fixed assets and affect the international price competitiveness of American goods, but they also increase the demand for bank deposits. Unless the Fed is conducting monetary policy to fix the interest rate on federal funds, which it can do by shifting the supply schedule whenever the demand schedule shifts, the increase in the demand for bank deposits that derives from the higher price level will shift the demand-for-bank reserves schedule to the right, leading to an increase in interest rates and lower investment spending. Thus higher prices can affect aggregate demand through their impact on interest rates and investment as well as their impact on consumption and net exports.

The reduction in investment spending induced by the rise in interest rates is an additional important reason why the multiplier process of the income-expenditure diagram is oversimplified.

Expansionary monetary policy that lowers interest rates and increases investment spending will eventually affect the aggregate supply curve as investment projects are completed and add to the capital stock. We concentrate here on impacts on the aggregate demand curve as they are the most immediate.

---

[1]Expansionary monetary policy that lowers interest rates and increases investment spending will eventually affect the aggregate supply curve as investment projects are completed and added to the capital stock. We concentrate here on impacts on the aggregate demand curve as they are the most immediate.

IMPORTANT TERMS AND CONCEPTS QUIZ

Choose the best definition for each of the following terms.

1. _____ Monetary policy
2. _____ Central bank
3. _____ Quantitative easing
4. _____ Risk of default
5. _____ Open market operations
6. _____ Risk premium
7. _____ Federal funds rate
8. _____ Discount rate
9. _____ Reserve requirement
10. _____ Unconventional monetary policy

a. Interest rate banks pay (get) when they borrow (lend) reserves from each other
b. A bank for banks responsible for the conduct of monetary policy
c. Branch of the U.S. Treasury responsible for minting coins
d. a higher interest rate to compensate the lender for a higher risk borrower
e. Minimum amount of reserves a bank must hold
f. risk that a borrower may not pay in full or on time
g. Actions Fed takes to affect bank reserves, interest rates, or both
h. Open-market purchases of assets other than Treasury bills
i. Interest rate Fed charges on loans to banks
j. Fed's purchase or sale of government securities
k. Unusual forms of central bank lending and unusual forms of open-market operations

BASIC EXERCISES

OPEN MARKET OPERATIONS

1. This exercise is designed to review the mechanics and impact of open market operations.

    a. Use **Figure 30-1** to analyze the impact of an open market purchase. The purchase of a government security (Treasury bill or bond) by the Fed results in a(n) (increase/decrease) in total bank reserves. This change in bank reserves can be represented as a shift of the supply-of-reserves schedule to the _____. (Draw a new supply-of-reserves schedule that represents the result of the open market purchase.) As a result of the open market purchase, interest rates will _____.

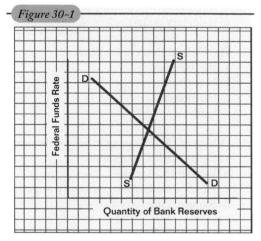

Figure 30-1

411

b. Use **Figure 30-2** to analyze the impact of an open market sale. The sale of a government security (Treasury bill or bond) by the Fed results in a(n) (<u>increase/decrease</u>) in total bank reserves. This change in bank reserves can be represented as a shift of the supply-of-reserves schedule to the _____. (Draw a new supply-of-reserves schedule that represents the result of the open market sale. As a result of the open market purchase, interest rates will _____.

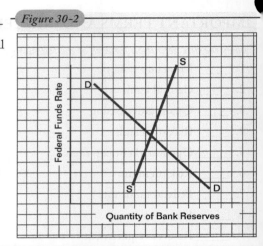

Figure 30-2

SELF-TESTS FOR UNDERSTANDING

TEST A

Circle the most appropriate answer.

1. If Mary says she earns $78,000 a year, she is referring to her
   a. money.
   b. income.
   c. assets.
   d. wealth.

2. The Federal Reserve is responsible for the conduct of
   a. environmental policy.
   b. fiscal policy.
   c. international economic policy.
   d. monetary policy.

3. The Federal Reserve is a bank for
   a. the Treasury.
   b. households.
   c. businesses.
   d. banks.

4. Which of the following is *not* an instrument of conventional monetary policy?
   a. Open market operations
   b. Lending to banks
   c. Antitrust actions to promote competition in banking
   d. Required reserve ratios

5. Who has direct responsibility for open market operations?
   a. the board of governors
   b. the federal open market committee
   c. the president of the United States
   d. the banking committee of the U.S. Senate

6. Open market operations involve the Fed buying and selling
   a. stocks in American companies.
   b. U.S. government securities, like Treasury bills or bonds.
   c. gold.
   d. corporate bonds.

7. Open market operations give the Fed the strongest control over
   a. interest rates on corporate bonds.
   b. the interest rate on 10-year government securities.
   c. the federal funds rate.
   d. mortgage interest rates.

8. An open market sale will shift the supply of bank reserves to
   a. the right.
   b. the left.

9. When making an open market purchase, the Fed gets the money to make the purchase from
   a. the Treasury.
   b. the Bureau of Printing and Engraving.
   c. cash in its vault.
   d. making a computer entry on its own books to credit the reserve account of the bank from which it purchases the security.

10. The impact of an open market purchase on the expenditure schedule reflects its initial impact on
    a. disposable income and consumption.
    b. taxes and government spending.
    c. interest rates and investment spending.
    d. sales and corporate profits.

11. An open market purchase will lead to all but which one of the following?
    a. supply-of-bank reserves schedule shifts to the right
    b. expenditure schedule shifts up
    c. multiplier increases
    d. aggregate demand curve shifts to the right

12. An open market sale will result in all but which one of the following?
    a. decrease in the quantity of bank reserves
    b. increase in interest rates
    c. lower investment spending
    d. higher price level

413

13. The immediate impact of a change in reserve requirements would be on the
    a. total volume of bank reserves.
    b. division of reserves (as between required reserves and excess reserves).
    c. account balances for the U.S. Treasury.
    d. discount rate.

14. The discount rate is the interest rate
    a. used by department stores when holding sales.
    b. the Fed charges banks that borrow reserves.
    c. banks use for their best customers.
    d. earned on checking accounts by depositors with large balances.

15. Which is the most frequently used instrument of conventional monetary policy?
    a. changes in the discount rate
    b. open market operations
    c. changes in reserve requirements
    d. stricter bank examinations

16. Which of the following would fit into the category of unconventional monetary policy known as
    quantitative easing? (There may be more than one correct answer)
    a. the purchase of Treasury bonds
    b. changes in reserve requirements
    c. the purchase of assets other than Treasury securities from banks or other financial institutions
    d. changes in the discount rate

17. Which of the following help to explain why the Fed does not have precise control of the money supply?
    (There may be more than one correct answer.)
    a. Banks may vary the amount of excess reserves they desire to hold.
    b. Open market operations can change the volume of bank reserves.
    c. Individuals and businesses change the amount of currency as opposed to bank deposits they want to
       hold.
    d. Changes in reserve requirements will affect the deposit creation multiplier.

18. The Fed is likely to have most success in hitting its target for the
    a. federal funds rate.
    b. quantity of bank deposits.
    c. level of GDP.
    d. rate of inflation.

19. An increase in interest rates from 8 percent to 9 percent would be associated with _____ in the price of
    existing bonds.
    a. a decline
    b. no change
    c. an increase

20. Changes in interest rates resulting from changes in monetary policy are likely to affect investment spending and initially lead to a shift in the _____. (There may be more than one correct answer.)
    a. expenditure schedule
    b. aggregate supply curve
    c. consumption function
    d. aggregate demand curve

21. Knowing that an increase in the level of prices will increase the demand for bank reserves helps to explain why
    a. the aggregate supply curve has a positive slope.
    b. the aggregate demand curve has a negative slope.
    c. equilibrium occurs at the intersection of the aggregate demand and aggregate supply curves.
    d. the multiplier response to a change in autonomous spending may be greater than 1.0.

TEST B

Circle T or F for true or false.

T F 1. In recent years there has been a movement toward more independent central banks in a number of countries.

T F 2. Most power in the Federal Reserve System is held by the 12 district Federal Reserve banks.

T F 3. Monetary policy decisions by the Federal Reserve are subject to review by the president of the United States before being implemented.

T F 4. An open market purchase by the Fed lowers the rate on federal funds without changing the quantity of bank reserves.

T F 5. An open market sale that increases interest rates will increase bond prices.

T F 6. Changing the discount rate is the most frequently used instrument of monetary policy today.

T F 7. Since bank reserves do not earn interest, the demand for reserves is not affected by changes in interest rates.

T F 8. Higher interest rates would normally lead banks to reduce their holdings of excess reserves.

T F 9. The initial impact of changes in monetary policy on interest-sensitive categories of demand affects GDP and prices as the economy moves along a given aggregate supply curve.

T F 10. The impact of the price level on the demand for bank reserves, and hence interest rates, helps to explain why the aggregate demand curve has a negative slope.

415

SUPPLEMENTARY EXERCISES

1. **An Algebraic Model of the Economy**

   The following algebraic model builds on models from earlier chapters but this time includes explicit expressions for the demand for and supply of bank reserves. For simplicity the model assumes that the price level does not change. That is, it is equivalent to assuming that the aggregate supply curve is horizontal.

   Consider an economy where consumption and investment spending are given by

   $$C = 1{,}550 + 0.6DI$$

   $$I = 2{,}000 - 50R$$

   where R is the interest rate. In this economy, taxes are one-sixth of income and net exports are -150.
   a. If government purchases are 1,500 and R is 8 (that is, 8 percent), what is the equilibrium level of income?
   b. If the Fed lowers the interest rate to 4 percent, what happens to the equilibrium level of income?
   c. The Fed can lower the interest rate by an appropriate increase in bank reserves; that is, an appropriate shift in the supply schedule for bank reserves. But what is appropriate? Assume the demand for bank reserves can be represented by

   $$BRD = 0.02Y - 3R$$

   where the term in Y reflects the impact of nominal GDP on the bank deposits and hence the required reserves of banks.

   Let the supply of bank reserves be represented by

   $$BRS = OMO + 2R$$

   where OMO is the amount of bank reserves supplied by open market operations. If $OMO = 140$, what is the equilibrium level of income? Of R?
   d. What increase in OMO is necessary to reduce the interest rate to 4 and produce the increase in Y you found in question 2?

2. **Bond Prices and Interest Rates**
   a. Consider a bond that pays $60 a year forever. If interest rates are 6 percent, such a bond should sell for $1,000 as ($60 ÷ $1,000) = .06. Assume now that interest rates fall to 4 percent. With interest payments of $60, what bond price offers investors a return of 4 percent? If interest rates rise to 10 percent, what must be the price of the bond paying $60 to offer investors a return of 10 percent?
   b. Bonds that pay only interest and never repay principal are called consols. Most bonds pay interest for a certain number of years and then repay the original borrowing or principal. Bond prices reflect the present value of those interest and principal payments as follows:

   where INT = interest payments

      r = interest rate

      PRIN = principal

      N = maturity, number of years of interest payments (also number of years to principal payment)

   Use a computer or financial calculator to verify that if INT = $60, PRIN = $1,000, N = 10, and r = .06, the present value of interest and principal payments = $1,000.

416

Calculate the present value of interest and principal payments when $r = .04$ and when $r = .10$ while INT, PRIN, and N remain unchanged. These calculations show what would happen to the price of an existing bond if interest rates change. Do your results confirm the negative correlation between bond prices and interest rates discussed in the text?

c. Redo the calculations in question b but for values of $N = 5$ and $N = 30$. Is the sensitivity of bond prices to a change in interest rates the same for all maturities?

3. **Federal Open Market Committee**

The Federal Open Market Committee (FOMC) has 12 voting members: the seven members of the Board of Governors and five of the 12 district bank presidents. The president of the Federal Reserve Bank of New York is always a voting member of the FOMC. The remaining four votes rotate among the other 11 presidents. Presidents of nine banks share three votes. That is, each of these presidents is a voting member of the FOMC once every three years. Two bank presidents are voting members every other year. What banks do these two presidents represent?

ECONOMICS IN ACTION

STRUCTURE AND ACCOUNTABILITY OF THE FEDERAL RESERVE

In October 1993, Congressman Henry Gonzales (D-Texas), Chairman of the House Banking Committee, convened a series of committee hearings to consider issues related to the structure and accountability of the Federal Reserve. Appointment procedures for presidents of the 12 district Federal Reserve Banks and the secrecy surrounding meetings of the Federal Open Market Committee (FOMC) were among the items of special concern to Congressman Gonzales.

With regard to the meetings of the FOMC, Congressman Gonzales proposed that decisions be disclosed within a week and that detailed transcripts and videotapes of each meeting be released within 60 days. He argued that his proposals would promote individual accountability and that "accurate information does not undermine markets. Partial information and leaked information undermine market efficiency."[2]

The FOMC now issues a press release announcing its decisions the same day that it meets. However, Alan Greenspan, chairman of the Board of Governors, and the other Federal Reserve representatives who appeared before the committee argued that videotaping would hinder free debate as individuals, concerned that their remarks might be misinterpreted and "cause unnecessary volatility in financial markets," would self-censor what they said. "Unconventional policy prescriptions and ruminations about the longer-term outlook for economic and financial market developments might never be surfaced . . . for fear of igniting a speculative reaction when the discussion was disclosed."[3]

---

[2] "Greenspan Warns Against Easing Fed's Secrecy," *New York Times*, October 20, 1992.
[3] Testimony by Alan Greenspan, Chairman, Board of Governors of the Federal Reserve System, before the Committee on Banking, Finance, and Urban Affairs, U.S. House of Representatives, October 13, 1993.

417

The president of each district bank is appointed by the district bank's Board of Directors, subject to the approval of the Board of Governors in Washington, D.C. District bank presidents serve as voting members of the FOMC on a rotating basis. Critics of the Federal Reserve argue that, in view of their membership on the FOMC and the importance of monetary policy, district bank presidents should be selected or reviewed by elected officials rather than appointed bodies. Options might include appointment by the president and/or confirmation by the Senate. Again Chairman Greenspan spoke against these changes, arguing that the current system represents a deliberate choice by the Congress to isolate decisions about monetary policy from political pressures. He argued that the Federal Reserve is accountable to the Congress and the public through reporting requirements and the daily scrutiny of the business and financial press. However, he warned that "if accountability is achieved by putting the conduct of monetary policy under the close influence of politicians subject to short-term election-cycle pressures, the resulting policy would likely prove disappointing over time.... The public-private and regional makeup of the Federal Reserve was chosen by Congress, in preference to a unitary public central bank, only after long and careful debate. The system was designed to avoid an excessive concentration of authority in federal hands and to ensure responsiveness to local needs."[4]

1. When and in how much detail should decisions and minutes of the FOMC be released?

2. Is Greenspan right when he argues that the advance announcement of contingent plans limits their effectiveness?

3. Who should select district bank presidents? Should voting membership on the FOMC be restricted to members of the Board of Governors and exclude district bank presidents?

STUDY QUESTIONS

1. What is the difference between money and income?

2. How much independence do you think is desirable for the Fed? Why? How does one ensure accountability?

3. Use a demand and supply diagram to show how open market operations affect the quantity of bank reserves and interest rates.

4. Open market operations are the most used instrument of monetary policy. Reserve requirements are changed only infrequently and the changes in the discount rate tend to be passive rather than active. What do you think explains the heavy reliance on open market operations rather than other instruments of monetary policy?

5. What is the difference between conventional and unconventional monetary policy?

---

[4]Ibid.

6. Why do interest rates and bond prices move inversely to each other?

7. Why can't the Fed control the stock of money to the penny?

8. What are the links by which changes in monetary policy affect spending and thus output, employment, and prices? Use an expenditure diagram and an aggregate demand–aggregate supply diagram to illustrate your answer.

9. "Recognizing that an increase in prices increases the demand for bank reserves helps to explain why the aggregate demand curve has a negative slope." What is the logic behind this statement?

ECONOMICS ONLINE

All 12 district Federal Reserve banks and the Board of Governors are online with their own web pages. You can access a wide variety of reports and lots of data about the economy from these sites.

Atlanta	http://www.frbatlanta.org
Boston	http://www.bos.frb.org
Chicago	http://www.chicagofed.org
Cleveland	http://www.clevelandfed.org/
Dallas	http://www.dallasfed.org
Kansas City	http://www.kc.frb.org
Minneapolis	http://minneapolisfed.org
New York	http://www.ny.frb.org
Philadelphia	http://www.phil.frb.org
Richmond	http://www.rich.frb.org
St. Louis	http://www.stls.frb.org
San Francisco	http://www.frbsf.org
Board of Governors	http://www.federalreserve.gov

The Federal Open Market Committee has its own homepage with links to meeting dates, announcements, and minutes.

http://www.federalreserve.gov/fomc

Laurence Meyer, a former member of the Board of Governors, describes a typical meeting of the Federal Open Market Committee in this speech given as the Gillian Lecture at Willamette University in 1998.

http://www.federalreserve.gov/boarddocs/speeches/1998/199804022.htm

The Federal Reserve Bank of San Francisco maintains an online search engine for Federal Reserve publications from all banks, Fed in Print.

http://www.frbsf.org/publications/fedinprint/index.html

You can access lots of economic data at FRED, an online databank maintained by the Federal Reserve Bank of St. Louis:

http://research.stlouisfed.org/fred2/

The Financial Crisis and the Great Recession

31

Important Terms and Concepts

Bubble

Collateral

Foreclosure

Insolvent

Leverage

Mortgage

Mortgage-backed securities (MBS)

Recapitalization

Securitization

Subprime mortgage

Troubled Asset Relief Program (TARP)

Learning Objectives

After completing this chapter, you should be able to:

- understand both sides of the debate over whether the fiscal stimulus enacted in 2009 worked.

- explain what is meant by an asset price bubble and how such a bubble comes into existence.

- explain what happens to an economy when an asset price bubble bursts.

- understand why the recession of 2007–2009 has been called the worst recession since the Great Depression.

- understand the significance of interest rate spreads and how they contributed to the recession and financial crisis of 2007–2009.

- explain the relationship between the housing bubble and subprime mortgages.

- explain the connection between the bursting of the housing bubble and the financial crisis of 2007–2009.

- understand how the financial crisis of 2007–2009 led to the Great Recession.

CHAPTER REVIEW

The recession of 2007-2009 is the focus of this chapter. There are many lessons that can be drawn from understanding the forces at work in the "Great Recession" and examining the effectiveness of the policy response. The roots of the recession can be traced back to earlier in the decade and America's credit markets. When the

(1) U.S. economy stuttered following a mild recession in 2001, the Federal (Reserve/government) made borrowing (cheaper/more expensive), in an effort to stimulate the economy.

Extremely low interest rates fueled an (increase/decrease) in the demand for housing which added to an

(2) already developing housing market _____. Low returns on assets like Treasury _____ pushed investors into riskier assets, raising their price thus lowering their _____. The gap between interest rates on risky assets and safe assets, interest rate spread, (narrowed/widened).

At the same time low default rates on all sorts of lending fooled lenders into believing the riskier assets were

(3) not so risky after all, leading to an explosion of _____ mortgages, loans made to higher risk borrowers.

Narrowing interest rate spreads led investors, including banks, to make wider use of leverage to boost returns. Leverage refers to the use of borrowed funds to purchase assets. The downside of leverage is that it can magnify losses. Altogether there were four financial market trends bubbling beneath the surface before the housing market bubble burst: the bubble itself, lenient lending standards, compressed risk spreads, and high leverage.

When the bubble burst the crisis came into sharp focus. In 2006 housing prices began to fall, creating a number of problems for the economy. Residential home construction slowed significantly. Consumer wealth fell

(4) leading to a reduction in consumer _____. With $C + I$ on the decline, recession became a real concern.

With the housing market in disarray, borrowers began to default on loan payments and

(5) _____ rose dramatically. Banks suffered losses when the foreclosed properties could not be sold for enough to cover the loan. Since banks had lowered their lending standards in the face of a booming housing market, the losses were magnified. By itself, the subprime mortgage debacle was thought to be too small to cause a serious recession, but, it turned out that there were other issues at play.

(6) During the housing boom mortgage-backed _____ evolved as a tool for financial institutions seeking ever higher returns on investment. Investment banks, acting as securitizers, would buy subprime mortgages from lenders, package them with others from around the country into more diversified mortgage-backed securities (MBS). These MBS would be less risky because they represented a geographically diversified portfolio of mortgages.

(7) Good idea in theory but in practice, when the housing _____ burst, housing prices fell everywhere so the expected gains from diversification evaporated. Additionally, several very large financial institutions were caught holding substantial investments in MBS. In practice, the situation was far more ominous. During the boom, Wall Street created and sold a variety of new financial securities whose value was at least, in part, dependent upon mortgages. These securities were so complex that when the values of mortgage backed

securities fell, investors had no clue what these new securities were worth. The global financial system began to come apart at the seams.

Credit began to dry up as banks began to recognize the danger. Credit is important to each of the four components of aggregate spending: _____, _____, _____   (8) _____ and _____ _____. The fear of recession began to settle on financial institutions and policy makers. Policy makers at the Fed stepped in to try to limit the damage.

The Fed began to move to lower interest rates in order to stimulate (<u>aggregate supply/aggregate demand</u>).   (9) Even while the Federal Funds rate fell, other interest rates rose, making credit even scarcer. Furthermore, banks became very conservative and began to horde excess reserves, tightening down the screws on credit even more. The Fed was pushed to respond in more unconventional ways.

The Fed together with the Treasury mounted a series of unconventional operations to rescue some very large financial firms. In some cases, they engineered mergers between weak companies and strong companies and in other cases they lent enormous sums of money to nonbank financial institutions, like AIG, a very large insurance company. The crowning jewel of the rescue effort may well have been when Federal Reserve Chairman Ben Bernake and Treasury Secretary Henry Paulson persuaded Congress to pass the $700 billion _____ _____ _____ _____ (TARP).   (10)

The original purpose of TARP was to buy up unwanted securities, hold onto them until the recession subsided and then sell them back to the market. Instead, Secretary Paulson used the TARP funds to recapitalize the banks. The recapitalized banks survived and the first step to a long bumpy recovery was taken. The second step vas Congressional passage in February of 2009 of a massive fiscal stimulus package totaling $787 billion.

The financial crisis and the ensuing recession exposed several shortcomings in the structure of the economy: 1. Financial regulation prior to the crisis was too lax; 2. The regulatory structure had not kept up with the evolving financial system; 3. Financial institutions were allowed to operate with far too much _____; 4. Excessive complexity and opacity in securities markets make the financial system   (11) fragile, which is very dangerous to the economy; 5. It was no longer widely agreed than monetary policy was the best approach to stabilizing aggregate demand; 6. The Fed has unconventional policy tools at its disposable when conventional tools are exhausted; and, 7. The _____ _____ is not dead.

IMPORTANT TERMS AND CONCEPTS QUIZ

Choose the appropriate definition for each of the following terms.

1. _____ Bubble
2. _____ Collateral
3. _____ Foreclosure
4. _____ Insolvent
5. _____ Leverage
6. _____ Mortgage
7. _____ Mortgage-backed securities (MBS)
8. _____ Recapitalization
9. _____ Securitization
10. _____ Subprime mortgage
11. _____ Troubled Asset Relief Program (TARP)

a. When the value of a company's liabilities exceeds the value of its assets
b. A program that allowed the Treasury to purchase assets and equity from banks and financial institutions
c. A loan used to buy a house
d. An increase in the price of an asset that goes far beyond what can be justified by improving fundamentals
e. Turning loans into marketable securities
f. Asset or assets that a borrower pledges to guarantee repayment of a loan
g. A security whose value derives from the monthly mortgage payments of many households
h. A mortgage where the borrower fails to meet the traditional standards of prime borrowers.
i. Buying an asset with borrowed funds to supplement owned funds
j. When some investor provides a bank with new equity capital in return for partial ownership
k. Process through which a mortgage lender obtains control of the property after the mortgage goes into default

BASIC EXERCISES

This exercise uses the aggregate demand and aggregate supply model to analyze the impact of the financial crisis on the real economy.

1. Use **Figure 31-1** to show what happens in the real economy when credit markets dry up. Consumer expenditures, business investment spending, government spending and net exports will all (<u>increase/decrease</u>). This will cause the (<u>aggregate demand/aggregate supply</u>) curve to shift to the (<u>right/left</u>). As s result, real GDP will _____.

2. Use Figure 31-1 to show the impact of the $787 billion stimulus package on the real economy. The additional government spending will cause the (<u>aggregate demand/aggregate supply</u>) curve to shift to the (<u>left/right</u>). As a result, real GDP will _____.

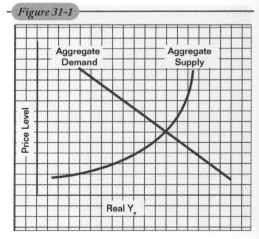

Figure 31-1

424

SELF-TESTS FOR UNDERSTANDING

TEST A

Circle the most appropriate answer.

1. The interest rate that the Federal Reserve most directly affects through the conduct of conventional monetary policy is
   a. the prime rate of interest.
   b. the market rate of interest.
   c. the federal funds rate.
   d. the Treasury bill rate.

2. When the price of a financial asset rises, the yield on that asset
   a. rises.
   b. stays the same.
   c. falls.

3. If asset A and asset B are similar in all respects except that asset B is riskier, we can expect that the return from asset B will be _____ the return from asset A.
   a. lower than
   b. the same as
   c. higher than

4. Which of the following was not a risk factor for the economy prior to the bursting of the housing bubble?
   a. lenient lending standards
   b. compressed risk spreads
   c. high inflation
   d. high leverage

5. Falling home prices which reduces consumer wealth will lead to which of the following:
   a. an increase in aggregate demand
   b. no change in aggregate demand
   c. a decrease in aggregate demand

6. Which of the following is a characteristic of a subprime mortgage?
   a. a borrower whose credit worthiness is subpar
   b. A mortgage interest rate below the prime interest rate
   c. a lender whose portfolio of loans is subpar
   d. all of the above

7. Consider a bank with the following balance sheet:

Assets		Liabilities and Net Worth	
Assets		Liabilities	
Reserves	$2,000,000	Checking deposits	$5,400,000
Loans Outstanding	$4,000,000	**Net Worth**	
Total	$6,000,000	Stockholders' Equity	$600,000
		Total	$6,000,000

This bank is leveraged at a rate of
a. 10 to 1.
b. 1 to 1.
c. 2.7 to 1.
d. Not enough information to tell.

8. In the midst of the 2007-2009 financial crisis and recession, the Fed employed which of the following unconventional policy tools? (There may be more than one correct answer)
a. encouraged or arranged mergers between weak financial institutions and strong financial institutions
b. made loans to nonbank financial institutions
c. gave taxpayers a tax rebate
d. bailed out General Motors

9. Which of the following are considered reasons why the housing bubble brought on a serious recession? (There may be more than one correct answer)
a. Mortgage interest rates fell drastically.
b. A great deal of wealth was destroyed.
c. Confidence was completely shattered.
d. Borrowing became very difficult.

10. Risky securities would include which of the following? (There may be more than one correct answer)
a. junk bonds
b. treasury bills
c. emerging-market debt
d. mortgage-backed securities

11. In the wake of the bursting housing bubble, why was the subprime mortgage explosion of 2003–2006 significant enough to be a major cause of the 2007–2009 recession? (There may be more than one correct answer)
a. The scale of the subprime mortgage market was far larger than most people believed.
b. The mortgage-backed securities that were created from subprime mortgages ended up being concentrated in the hands of only a few investors.
c. It increased the federal budget deficit.
d. It gave impetus to the creation of the TARP fund.

12. In theory, how did the creation of mortgage-backed securities reduce risk? (There may be more than one correct answer)
    a. by lowering interest rates
    b. through government guaranteed rates of return
    c. through geographical diversification
    d. by spreading the risk among thousands of investors all over the world

13. When the housing bubble burst around 2006, which part of the country was affected? (There could be more than one correct answer)
    a. Northeast
    b. West
    c. South
    d. Midwest

14. The federal funds rate refers to which of the following?
    a. the rate of interest paid by the economy's most secure borrowers
    b. the rate of interest paid by the U.S. Treasury
    c. the rate of interest paid by banks borrowing funds overnight from other banks
    d. the interest rate ceiling imposed by the U.S. government on mortgage loans

15. Which of the following would be considered a fundamental value on which housing prices should depend? (There may be more than one correct answer)
    a. household income
    b. mortgage interest rates
    c. balance of trade
    d. labor force participation rates

16. What is the immediate consequence of falling interest rate spreads?
    a. the reward for bearing risk increases
    b. the reward for bearing risk remains unchanged
    c. the opportunity cost of safe investments increases
    d. the reward for bearing risk falls

17. In addition to offering subprime mortgages, what other unwise lending practices came into vogue during the housing boom from 2003 to 2006? (There may be more than one correct answer)
    a. making loans to refinance existing mortgages
    b. making loans with small or even zero down payments
    c. making loans with fixed rates of interest
    d. making loans to families that would be devoting in excess of 33 percent of their household income to their mortgage payment

18. When an investment bank buys up mortgages from lenders, bundles them together and resells them to investors, the investment bank has created _____.
    a. mortgage-backed securities
    b. collateral
    c. subprime mortgages
    d. leverage

427

19. When the financial crisis brought on recession, how did the administration of President Obama respond?
    a. by creating a financial crisis Czar
    b. with massive tax cuts
    c. by declaring war on recession
    d. with a combination of tax rebates and increased expenditures

20. With many financial firms teetering on the precipice of collapse, investors seemed unwilling to bear any risk so they flocked to purchase _____.
    a. gold
    b. Treasury bills
    c. commodities
    d. foreign financial assets

TEST B

Circle T or F for true or false.

T   F   1. The Federal Reserve typically tries to increase the federal funds rate in order to stimulate the economy.

T   F   2. The federal funds rate is the rate of interest the U.S. government has to pay when they borrow.

T   F   3. The difference between the interest rate on risky assets and the interest rates on safe Treasury securities is commonly referred to as the Treasury asset risk premium (TARP).

T   F   4. In financial markets leverage refers to the practice of purchasing financial assets with borrowed funds.

T   F   5. Mortgage-backed securities are financial assets whose value derives from the value of the mortgages that make up the asset.

T   F   6. The Federal Reserve may only make loans to banks.

T   F   7. The financial crisis of 2007–2009 had its roots in events that began as early as 2001.

T   F   8. Riskier securities tend to offer higher yields than securities considered safe.

T   F   9. Leverage is essential to a bank's profitability.

T   F   10. Poor enforcement of financial market regulations was a contributing factor to the financial crisis of 2007–2009 and the subsequent recession.

ECONOMICS IN ACTION

AMERICAN RECOVERY AND REINVESTMENT ACT

As discussed in the chapter, the financial crisis of 2007-2009 and the subsequent recession prompted an array of policy responses from the Federal Reserve and the Bush and Obama administrations. In many ways the policy responses were unprecedented and caused a firestorm of controversy. With a presidential election looming, the American Recovery and Reinvestment Act will move to the front burner in the political discourse.

On February 17, 2009, Congress passed the American Recovery and Reinvestment Act (ARRA) of 2009 at the urging of President Obama, who signed it into law four days later. A direct response to the economic crisis, the Recovery Act has three immediate goals:

- create new jobs and save existing ones

- spur economic activity and invest in long-term growth

- foster unprecedented levels of accountability and transparency in government spending

The Recovery Act intends to achieve those goals by:

- providing $288 billion in tax cuts and benefits for millions of working families and businesses

- increasing federal funds for education and health care as well as entitlement programs (such as extending unemployment benefits) by $224 billion

- making $275 billion available for federal contracts, grants and loans

With a presidential election coming up soon, the debate over the impact of the ARRA will intensify. Already attempts have been made to estimate the impact. The Congressional Budget Office (2010) estimated that the employment increase attributable to the ARRA" was in the range of 500,000 to 900,000 in 2009 and is in the range of 1.3 to 3.3 million for 2010. The Council of Economic Advisors (2010) measured the employment increase due to the Act by the end of the second quarter of 2010, to be an increase in employment of 3.6 million workers. Blinder and Zandi (2010) found that the employment increase due to the ARRA (including both spending and tax cuts) was 2.7 million jobs. Economists Timothy Conley and Bill Dupor estimate that the ARRA created/saved approximately 450,000 state and local government jobs and destroyed/forestalled roughly one million private sector jobs.

1. This chapter and others lay out the economic theory that helps us to think clearly about questions like this, but when economists come up with different estimates of the impact of public policy, how do you decide?

    You might want to consult the following:
    Blinder, A. and M. Zandi (2010), "How the Great Recession Was Brought to an End."
    Congressional Budget Office (2010), "Estimated Impact of the American Recovery and Reinvestment Act on Employment and Economic Output from April 2010 through June 2010," CBO Report, August.
    Council of Economic Advisors (2010), "The Economic Impact of the American Recovery and Reinvestment Act of 2009: Fourth Quarterly Report," July 14.
    The American Recovery and Reinvestment Act: Public Sector Jobs Saved, Private Sector Jobs Forestalled, Timothy Conley and and Bill Dupor, updated May 17, 2011, unpublished paper

STUDY QUESTIONS

1. If you were watching home prices rise during the years 2000–2006, how might you have decided whether or not you were witnessing a "bubble"?

2. What factors do you think bankers normally use to distinguish "prime" borrowers from "subprime" borrowers?

3. Explain why a mortgage-backed security becomes riskier when the values of the underlying houses decline. What, as a result, happens to the price of the mortgage-backed security?

4. Explain how a collapse in home prices might lead to a recession.

5. Explain how a collapse of the economy's credit-granting mechanisms might lead to a recession.

6. Explain the basic idea behind the TARP legislation. Was that idea carried out in practice?

7. **(More difficult)** In March 2008, the Fed helped prevent the bankruptcy of Bear Stearns. However, in September 2008, the Fed and the Treasury let Lehman Brothers go bankrupt. What accounts for the different decisions?

8. What lessons have we learned from the financial crisis experienced in 2007–2009?

9. Can the American Recovery and Reinvestment Act be credited with producing an economic recovery?

ECONOMICS ONLINE

Information on how the $787 billion of the American Recovery and Reinvestment Act was spent can be found at:

www.recovery.gov

Information of the financial market reforms embodied in the Dodd-Frank Act of 2010 can be found at:

http://banking.senate.gov/public/_files/070110_Dodd_Frank_Wall_Street_Reform_comprehensive_summary_Final.pdf

The Debate over Monetary and Fiscal Policy

32

Important Terms and Concepts

Velocity

Equation of exchange

Quantity theory of money

Monetarism

Lags in stabilization policy

Learning Objectives

After completing this chapter, you should be able to:

- compute velocity given data on nominal income and the stock of money.

- describe the determinants of velocity.

- explain the difference between the quantity theory and the equation of exchange.

- describe why the equation of exchange is not a theory of income determination and why monetarists' use of the same equation turns it into a theory of income determination.

- distinguish between lags affecting fiscal policy and those affecting monetary policy.

- explain why the Fed may need to engage in unconventional monetary policy.

- identify the pros and cons from bursting asset bubbles

- explain why the Fed does not have precise control over both M and r.

- explain how and why the slope of the aggregate supply curve helps to determine the effectiveness of stabilization policy.

- explain how long lags might mean that efforts to stabilize the economy could end up destabilizing it.

- summarize the views of advocates and opponents of activist stabilization policy by the government.

CHAPTER REVIEW

This is one of the most important and most difficult of the macroeconomic chapters. While not much new material is introduced, the chapter summarizes and synthesizes many of the concepts presented in preceding chapters concerning the theory of income determination as it discusses a number of thorny issues that policymakers must confront.

Earlier chapters presented an essentially Keynesian model of income determination with its focus on the categories of aggregate demand. The monetarist viewpoint is a modern manifestation of an even older tradition known as the quantity theory of money. The concept of velocity is perhaps the most important tool associated with this approach. Velocity is the average number of times per year that a dollar changes hands to accomplish

(1) transactions associated with GDP. Velocity is measured as nominal _____ divided by the stock

of _____. Alternative measures of money, for example, M_1 and M_2, give rise to alternative measures of velocity, V_1 and V_2.

Related to the concept of velocity is something called the equation of exchange, which is simply another way of defining and calculating velocity. The equation of exchange says:

(2) Money × velocity = _____.

In symbols, it is:

_____ × _____ = _____ × _____.

Statisticians and national income accountants measure the stock of money and nominal GDP. Economists then calculate velocity by dividing nominal GDP by the stock of money. As a result, the equation of exchange is always true.

The quantity theory asserts that there is a close link between changes in nominal GDP and changes in

(3) the stock of _____. This link comes about because the quantity theory assumes that velocity

(does/does not) change very much. If velocity is constant, then a change in the money stock translates directly

into a change in _____ _____. If velocity is 8 and the money stock increases by

$25 billion, then nominal GDP will rise by $ _____ billion.

An analysis of the determinants of velocity as well as the study of historical data suggest that one

(4) (should/should not) expect velocity to be constant. Velocity reflects how much money people hold to make transactions, which in turn reflects such institutional factors as the efficiency of the payments mechanism— the frequency of paychecks and how easy it is to move funds between checking accounts and savings accounts. The amount of money people want to hold, and hence velocity, is also affected by the interest rate as a measure of the opportunity cost of holding money. For example, an increase in expected inflation is likely to

(decrease/increase) nominal interest rates and _____ the amount of money people want to hold.

432

Monetarism, like the quantity theory, starts with the equation of exchange. But rather than assuming that velocity does not change, monetarists try to predict how velocity will change. From a monetarist perspective, determinants of nominal GDP are broken down into implications for the stock of money and implications for _____. After accounting for appropriate changes, simple multiplication can be used to predict (5) nominal GDP. The effectiveness of a monetarist approach depends upon how easy it is to predict changes in velocity.

At first glance it may appear that a Keynesian approach to income determination cannot analyze changes in monetary policy whereas a monetarist approach ignores fiscal policy. Such a conclusion would be oversimplified and misleading. In formal theory the two viewpoints are closer than is commonly recognized. Keynesian theory implies that monetary policy can have important impacts on aggregate demand through its impact on interest rates and investment spending. An expansionary change in monetary policy will lead to a(n) (decline/increase) (6) in interest rates. The change in interest rates will (increase/decrease) investment spending. As we have seen, an increase in investment spending shifts both the expenditure schedule and the aggregate demand curve. Putting all the pieces together we can see that expansionary monetary policy will tend to (increase/decrease) GDP. Restrictive monetary policy would work in exactly the opposite way.

Monetarists are able to analyze the impact of changes in fiscal policy as follows: Expansionary fiscal policy will tend to be associated with (higher/lower) interest rates. As a result, velocity will (increase/decrease) and a (7) monetarist would forecast a (higher/lower) value for nominal GDP. Neither alone nor together are Keynesian and monetarist theories sufficient to determine output and prices as both are theories of the demand side of the economy and ignore the supply side.

The financial crisis of 2007-2009 thrust the Fed into unchartered territory. Conventional (monetary/fiscal) policy had already cut short-term interest rates to practically zero, and the economy still needed stimulus. The Fed found it necessary to turn to _____ monetary policy, consisting primarily of: creating bank (8) (deposits/reserves) by buying assets other than Treasury bills; lending massive amounts to banks and even some non-bank financial institutions; and participating in emergency rescue operations for troubled financial institutions.

The Fed's unconventional actions during the financial crisis spawned a debate that continues today. Part of that debate revolves around the appropriate role of the Fed in combating the fallout from asset price bubbles. The housing bubble that began to burst in 2006 has been identified as a major contributor to the financial crisis of 2007-2009. The Fed remains reticent to intervene to let the air out of asset price bubbles for two reasons: First, identifying an asset price bubble before it bursts is a very tricky business, and second, the Fed may not have any policy instruments that it can apply directly at asset price bubbles.

Stabilization policy affects the economy primarily by shifting the aggregate demand curve. The final result, however, in terms of changes in output and prices, also depends upon the slope of the aggregate supply curve. A flat aggregate supply curve means that shifts in the aggregate demand curve will have large effects on

433

(9) (output/price) with only a small change in _____. On the other hand, shifts of the aggregate demand curve will have big effects on prices without much change in output if the aggregate supply curve is (steep/flat). While some argue that the aggregate supply curve is flat and others that it is steep, an emerging consensus sees the slope of the aggregate supply curve as depending upon the period of analysis. The aggregate supply curve is likely to be flatter in the (long/short) run and steeper in the _____ run.

Some economists favor an activist-oriented approach to stabilization policy with significant latitude for discretionary policy. Others favor less activism and a greater reliance on rules. Beyond views about the slope of the aggregate supply curve, these differences also reflect differing political philosophies and judgments concerning the importance of such factors as the speed of the economy's self-correcting mechanisms, the length of various policy lags, and the accuracy of economic forecasting.

It takes time before someone notices that the economy is not operating as hoped for and before the appropriate part of the government can decide what policy measures should be adopted. Once a particular policy is decided upon, there may not be much impact on output and prices until the buying habits of households and firms adjust to the new policy. Because of lags, policy changes today are likely to have their greatest impact in the future. For policy to be effective, economists must be able to anticipate future events. The more accurate the economic forecasts, the more demanding the standards we can set for stabilization policy.

Some argue that stable government policies are best for private spending while others argue that if stable policies mean instability in the economy that would be even worse for firms and households. The flexibility to (10) use changes in spending, taxes, and monetary policy means that activist policy (does/does not) imply that government spending must take an ever larger proportion of the economic pie.

IMPORTANT TERMS AND CONCEPTS QUIZ

Choose the best definition for each of the following terms.

1. _____ Quantity theory of money
2. _____ Velocity
3. _____ Equation of exchange
4. _____ Monetarism

a. Variables that normally turn down prior to recessions and turn up prior to expansions

b. Mode of analysis that uses the equation of exchange to organize and analyze macroeconomic data

c. Average number of times a dollar is spent in a year

d. Formula that states that nominal GDP equals the product of money stock and velocity

e. Theory of aggregate demand stating that nominal GDP is proportional to the money stock

BASIC EXERCISES

This exercise is designed to give you practice computing and using velocity.

1. **Table 32-1** contains historical data for nominal GDP, M1, and M2.

Table 32-1

GDP, Money, and Velocity

	Nominal GDP ($ billions)	M_1 ($ billions)	M_2 ($ billions)	V_1	V_2
1995	7,397.7	1,138.8	3,569.3	_____	_____
1996	7,816.9	1,103.2	3,729.0	_____	_____
1997	8,304.3	1,075.9	3,924.2	_____	_____
1998	8,747.0	1,084.3	4,207.8	_____	_____
1999	9,268.4	1,110.1	4,516.3	_____	_____
2000	9,817.0	1,106.0	4,790.6	_____	_____
2001	10,128.0	1,133.6	5,190.4	_____	_____
2002	10,487.0	1,198.3	5,621.3	_____	_____
2003	11,004.0	1,255.3	5,928.4	_____	_____
2004	11,728.0	1,328.3	6,230.1	_____	_____

SOURCE:GDP: *Economic Report of the President*, 2005. Tables B-1 and B-69.

a. Use this data to compute V_1, velocity based on M_1; and V_2, velocity based on M_2. Be sure to round your answers for velocity to two decimal places.

b. Assume you are a monetarist working for the Federal Reserve and are asked to predict nominal GDP one year in advance. Even if you knew the money supply, *M*, you would still need an estimate of *V*. One way to estimate velocity is to use data from the previous year. The idea is that, since you can't know velocity for 2000 until you know nominal GDP and M_1 or M_2 for 2000, you might use velocity for 1999 to predict GDP for 2000. **Table 32-2** assumes that the Federal Reserve can control the money supply exactly. Use your numbers for velocity from the previous year to fill in the blank columns in Table 32-2 to see how well velocity and money predict income.

Table 32-2

Money, Velocity, and GDP

	Actual M_1 ($ billions)	V_1 from Previous Year	Estimated Income ($ billions)	Actual Income ($ billions)	Estimated Income ($ billions)	V_2 from Previous Year	Actual M_2 ($ billions)
1996	1,103.2	_____	_____	7,816.9	_____	_____	3,729.0
1997	1,075.9	_____	_____	8,304.3	_____	_____	3,924.2
1998	1,084.3	_____	_____	8,747.0	_____	_____	4,207.8
1999	1,110.1	_____	_____	9,268.4	_____	_____	4,516.3
2000	1,106.0	_____	_____	9,817.0	_____	_____	4,790.6
2001	1,133.6	_____	_____	10,128.0	_____	_____	5,190.4
2002	1,198.3	_____	_____	10,487.0	_____	_____	5,621.3
2003	1,255.3	_____	_____	11,004.0	_____	_____	5,928.4
2004	1,328.3	_____	_____	11,728.0	_____	_____	6,230.1

*Express estimate for Nominal GDP to one decimal point.

435

c. Which years show the largest prediction errors? Why?

2. For this exercise you are asked to assume the role of adviser to the Federal Reserve's Open Market Committee. **Figure 32-1** uses the demand and supply of bank reserves to show the quantity of bank reserves and the rate of interest when the committee last met. Assume that the economy was then at full employment with price stability. The next meeting of the Open Market Committee begins with a report detailing the unexpected increase in the stock of money and interest rates since the last meeting. What to do is not so obvious, however, as suggested by the following arguments offered by two different members of the committee:

Figure 32-1

Demand and Supply of Bank Reserves

A: This report confirms my fear that aggregate demand is expanding too rapidly. The resulting increase in nominal GDP is increasing the demand for money and hence the demand for bank reserves. We risk unnecessary inflation and should move to reduce aggregate demand by an appropriate change in monetary policy.

B: This report confirms my concern that there has been an increase in the demand for bank reserves that is unrelated to GDP. Businesses and individuals have been harmed buying esoteric and risky financial securities. As a result of these losses, there has been a general increase in the demand for safer bank deposits and hence an increase in the demand for bank reserves. If we do not take appropriate action the increase in interest rates since our last meeting will reduce aggregate demand and threaten recession.

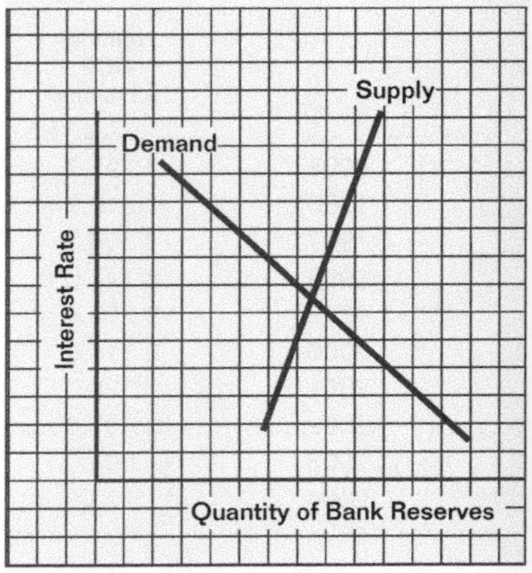

Use Figure 32-1 to illustrate what each speaker is arguing and what actions each is suggesting. Each is arguing for a particular policy to shift the supply-of-reserves schedule. What is that shift and how is it consistent with each speaker's analysis? What is likely to happen if the Fed implements A's desired policy when B's analysis is correct? What is likely to happen if the Fed implements B's desired policy when A's analysis is correct?

SELF-TESTS FOR UNDERSTANDING

TEST A

Circle the most appropriate answer.

1. Velocity is measured by
   a. dividing the money stock by nominal GDP.
   b. computing the percentage change in nominal GDP from year to year.
   c. dividing nominal GDP by the stock of money.
   d. subtracting the rate of inflation from nominal interest rates.

2. The equation of exchange says that
   a. for every buyer there is a seller.
   b. $M \times V$ = nominal GDP.
   c. demand equals supply.
   d. P. T. Barnum was right when he said, "There is a sucker born every minute."

3. According to the equation of exchange, an increase in M may lead to (There may be more than one correct answer.)
   a. an increase in Y (real GDP).
   b. an increase in P.
   c. a reduction in V.
   d. an increase in nominal GDP.

4. According to the quantity theory, an increase in M will lead to a(n) _____. (There may be more than one correct answer.)
   a. increase in Y (real GDP).
   b. increase in P.
   c. reduction in V.
   d. increase in nominal GDP.

5. Between 1996 and 1997 the money supply (M_1) decreased by 3.3 percent and yet nominal GDP rose by 5.8 percent. It must be that velocity
   a. decreased.
   b. was unchanged.
   c. increased.

6. From 2001 to 2002 M_1 increased by 5.7 percent and V_1 declined from 8.93 to 8.75. It must be that nominal GDP increased by _____ 5.7 percent.
   a. less than
   b. exactly
   c. more than

7. The historical record shows
   a. that both V_1 and V_2 have been stable.
   b. continual decrease in V_2.
   c. continual increases in V_1.
   d. that V_2 has shown less variation than V_1.

8. Assume that velocity is 7. If one can be sure that velocity will not change, what increase in M will be required to increase real GDP by $140 billion?
   a. $7 billion
   b. $20 billion
   c. $140 billion
   d. insufficient information

437

9. Because M_2 is _____ than M_1, V_2 should be _____ than V_1.
   a. larger; larger
   b. larger; smaller
   c. smaller; smaller
   d. smaller; larger

10. All but which of the following represent unconventional monetary policies?
    a. creating bank reserves by buying assets other than Treasury bills
    b. changing the discount rate
    c. lending massive amounts to banks and non-banks
    d. participating in emergency rescue operations for troubled financial institutions

11. According to a monetarist analysis of income determination all but which one of the following is likely to increase nominal GDP?
    a. an open market purchase that increases the stock of money
    b. an increase in government spending
    c. a technological change in banking practices that increases velocity
    d. an increase in income taxes

12. A change in interest rates that accompanies an open market purchase is likely to
    a. increase velocity.
    b. have no effect on velocity.
    c. reduce velocity.

13. Which of the following has been expressed by the Fed as a concern which has prevented it from stepping in to fight asset price bubbles? (There may be more than one correct answer.)
    a. asset price bubbles can be very beneficial to the economy
    b. identifying asset price bubbles before they burst is very difficult to do
    c. asset price bubbles are a natural consequence of capitalism and should be allowed to run their course
    d. none of the tools the Fed has available directly target asset price bubbles

14. Which of the following is an example of a lag in policymaking as opposed to a lag in spending by firms and households?
    a. The construction of a new plant, induced by lower interest rates, cannot start for nine months, because it takes that long to prepare architectural drawings and contractors' bids.
    b. Congress takes five months to consider a presidential tax proposal.
    c. Through multiplier impacts, a $3 billion increase in defense spending eventually raises GDP by $5 billion.
    d. Refrigerator sales rise in the month following receipt of a $300 tax rebate.

15. The time it takes to make a change is probably shorter for _____ policy while lags affecting private spending are probably shorter for _____ policy.
    a. fiscal; monetary
    b. monetary; fiscal
    c. fiscal; fiscal
    d. monetary; monetary

438

16. Assume that the stock of money and interest rates are both at levels desired by the Federal Reserve. Following a shift in the demand for money, the Fed can control _____. (There may be more than one correct answer.)
    a. M but not r
    b. r but not M
    c. both M and r

17. Stabilization policy will be effective in combating recession if the aggregate supply curve is _____ and effective in combating inflation if the aggregate supply curve is _____.
    a. flat; steep
    b. steep; flat
    c. flat; flat
    d. steep; steep

18. If the aggregate supply curve is relatively flat, then
    a. velocity will be constant.
    b. both monetary and fiscal policy will have relatively large effects on output without much effect on prices.
    c. a change in interest rates will have little impact on investment.
    d. monetary policy will be effective while fiscal policy will not.

19. All but which of the following are reasons for the existence of a lag in stabilization policy?
    a. delays in data collection
    b. mere size of the US economy
    c. capitalism
    d. the slowness of democracy

20. Active stabilization policy
    a. must increase the size of government.
    b. will only be successful if the size of government declines.
    c. need not imply any tendency toward big government.
    d. will only mean larger and larger government deficits.

TEST B

Circle T or F for true or false.

T F 1. If the stock of money is $1 trillion and nominal GDP is $8 trillion, then velocity is 8.

T F 2. Velocity is determined by how often people are paid and is unaffected by the rate of interest.

T F 3. The quantity theory is not really a theory because velocity, by definition, is equal to the ratio of nominal GDP divided by the money stock.

T F 4. Buying or selling Treasury bills in the open market is the way that the Fed conducts conventional policy.

T F 5. The lag between a change in fiscal policy and its effects on aggregate demand is probably shorter than the lag between a change in monetary policy and its effects on aggregate demand.

T F 6. The lag in adopting an appropriate policy is probably shorter for monetary policy than for fiscal policy.

439

T F 7. Identifying asset price bubbles before they burst is a relatively straightforward exercise.

T F 8. The shape of the aggregate supply curve is likely to be relatively flat in the short run and steeper in the long run.

T F 9. If the aggregate supply curve is steep, then changes in fiscal and monetary policy will have major impacts on prices with little impact on output.

T F 10. Long lags will help make for better stabilization policy because there is more time for a complete analysis of possible actions.

SUPPLEMENTARY EXERCISES

LEADING INDICATORS

Is the stock market a good leading indicator of overall economic conditions? **Figure 32-2** shows stock prices from January 1950 through December 2004 as measured by Standard and Poor's 500 stock price index. Using just Figure 32-3, make an estimate of how many recessions there have been since 1950. Try to date each one approximately. The National Bureau of Economic Research (NBER) is the organization that dates business cycles. Check their web site http://www.nber.org to see how your business cycles compare with theirs. How many

Figure 32-2

Is the Stock Market a Leading Indicator?

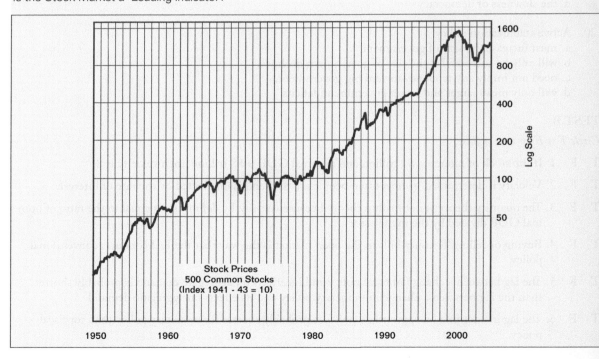

Stock Prices
500 Common Stocks
(Index 1941 - 43 = 10)

recessions does the NBER identify? How many did you identify? How many false indications of recession were there? What about the forecasting record of other leading indicators? What are the stock market and other leading indicators saying about the state of the economy over the next six to twelve months?

In addition to the problem of false turning points, there are two other limitations to a purely mechanical use of leading indicators that you should be aware of:

a. Most large declines in a leading indicator are the result of not one large decline, but rather a series of consecutive small declines. At the same time, each series has so many ups and downs that most small declines are followed by a small increase. One needs some way of separating those small declines that signal the start of a major slump from those that are quickly reversed.

b. A leading indicator that always changes direction a fixed amount of time before the economy does would be extremely useful. However, the length of time between movements in most leading indicators and the economy is quite variable.

ECONOMICS IN ACTION

WHAT TO DO?

What indicators should the Federal Reserve use when formulating monetary policy? General agreement exists that monetary policy should contribute to broad macroeconomic objectives—price stability, full employment, economic growth—although different observers would argue that greater weight should be placed on different objectives, e.g., price stability or full employment. However, the Fed does not control the rate of inflation or the rate of unemployment. A related problem is that observations on different macroeconomic variables are available at different times. Estimates of GDP come only every three months. Unemployment and inflation are measured monthly. Data on M1 and M2 are announced every week while interest rates are available at a moment's notice.

At times the Fed has put more emphasis on interest rates and at others on M1, M2, or bank reserves as indicators of monetary policy. When testifying before Congress in July of 1993, and reporting on growth ranges expected for M1 and M2 for 1994, Alan Greenspan, chairman of the Board of Governors of the Federal Reserve System, made the following argument:

The historical relationships between money and income, and between money and the price level, have largely broken down, depriving the aggregates of much of their usefulness as guides to policy. At least for the time being, M2 has been downgraded as a reliable indicator of financial conditions in the economy, and no single variable has yet been identified to take its place. . . . In the meantime, the process of probing a variety of data to ascertain underlying economic and financial conditions has become even more essential to formulating sound monetary policy. . . . In these circumstances it is especially prudent to focus on longer-term policy guides. One important guidepost is real interest rates, which have a key bearing on longer-run spending decisions and inflation prospects.

Greenspan emphasized what he called the equilibrium real rate of interest:

> . . . specifically the real rate level that, if maintained, would keep the economy at its production potential over time. . . . Real rates, of course, are not directly observable, but must be inferred from nominal interest rates and estimates of inflation expectations. The most important real rates for private spending decisions almost surely are the longer maturities. Moreover, the equilibrium rate structure responds to the ebb and flow of underlying forces affecting spending.

Greenspan concluded:

> While the guides we have for policy may have changed recently, our goals have not. As I have indicated many times to this Committee, the Federal Reserve seeks to foster maximum sustainable economic growth and rising standards of living. And in that endeavor, the most productive function the central bank can perform is to achieve and maintain price stability.

1. What indicators of monetary policy would you favor if you were a member of the Federal Open Market Committee?

2. When is it appropriate to emphasize measures of the stock of money and when is it appropriate to emphasize interest rates?

3. While one can observe nominal interest rates, how does one measure the equilibrium real rate of interest in a way that makes it operational for the conduct of monetary policy?

Source: Testimony by Alan Greenspan, Chairman of the Board of Governors of the Federal Reserve System, before the Subcommittee on Economi Growth and Credit Formation of the Committee on Banking, Finance, and Urban Affairs, U.S. House of Representatives, July 20, 1993.

STUDY QUESTIONS

1. What is the difference between the equation of exchange, the quantity theory, and monetarism?

2. What do you think explains the different historical experience of V_1 and V_2?

3. Why can't one use monetarism to determine nominal GDP, Keynesian analysis to determine real GDP, and then compute the price level by dividing the one by the other?

4. What is the difference between policy lags and expenditure lags? Which are likely to be more important for fiscal policy? For monetary policy?

5. What's wrong with the following? "Long lags make for better policy as they provide more time for determining the best policy."

6. How does unconventional monetary policy differ from conventional monetary policy?

7. Do you think the Fed should intervene and actively try to burst asset price bubbles?

8. Why are concerns about excessive levels of government spending not a legitimate reason to oppose active stabilization policy?

9. Do you favor a more or less activist stabilization policy? Why?

ECONOMICS ONLINE

The Fed's latest release on interest rates and the money supply along with a number of other data series can be found here.

http://www.federalreserve.gov/releases

The Federal Reserve Bank of St. Louis offers electronic access to lots of historical data about the economy at its web site FRED, Federal Reserve Economic Data. FRED will graph data for you.

http://research.stlouisfed.org/fred2

Budget Deficits in the Short and Long Run

33

Important Terms and Concepts

Budget deficit

Budget surplus

National debt

Structural deficit or surplus

Monetizing the deficit

Crowding out

Crowding in

Learning Objectives

After completing this chapter, you should be able to:

- explain how measures to balance the budget may unbalance the economy.

- explain how appropriate fiscal policy depends on the strength of private demand and the conduct of monetary policy.

  explain the implications of changing the mix of monetary and fiscal policy while leaving GDP and prices unchanged.

- explain the difference between the government's budget deficit and the national debt.

- discuss some facts about budget deficits and the national debt: When have budget deficits been largest? What has happened to the national debt as a proportion of GDP?

- describe how the concept of structural deficits or surpluses differs from officially reported deficits or surpluses.

- distinguish between real and fallacious arguments about the burden of the national debt.

- describe the inflationary consequences of a budget deficit and explain why deficits will be more inflationary if they are monetized.

- explain why a debt held by foreigners imposes a larger burden than a debt held by domestic citizens.

- explain why most economists measure the true burden of deficits by their impact on the capital stock.

- evaluate arguments supporting the crowding-out and crowding-in properties of government deficit spending.

CHAPTER REVIEW

By itself this chapter cannot make government deficits larger or smaller, but it can help to increase your understanding of the impacts of both government deficits and the national debt.

(1) The government runs a deficit when its (spending/revenue) exceeds its _____. There is a surplus when _____ is greater than _____. The national debt measures the government's total indebtedness. The national debt will increase if the government budget shows a (deficit/surplus). The national debt will decrease if the government budget shows a(n) _____.

What is appropriate deficit policy? Earlier chapters discussed the use of fiscal and monetary policy to strike an appropriate balance between aggregate demand and aggregate supply in order to choose between inflation and unemployment. Considerations of balanced budgets, per se, were absent from that discussion. The conclusion that budget policy should adapt to the requirements of the economy is shared by many economists. Note that this conclusion implies that appropriate fiscal policy depends upon the stance of monetary policy and the strength of private demand.

Some have advocated a policy of strict budget balance. There is good reason to expect that such a policy would balance the budget at the risk of unbalancing the economy. Consider an economy in an initial equilibrium at full employment with a balanced budget. An autonomous decline in private spending would shift the

(2) expenditure schedule (down/up), resulting in a shift of the aggregate demand schedule to the (right/left). In the absence of any further policy action, the result would be a(n) (decline/increase) in GDP. The change in GDP will also mean a(n) (decline/increase) in tax revenues. The government's budget will move from its initial position of balance to one of (deficit/surplus). At this point, deliberate policy actions to reestablish budget balance would call for either a(n) (decrease/increase) in taxes or a(n) (decrease/increase) in government spending. In either case the result would be an additional shift in the expenditure schedule and aggregate demand curve that would (accentuate/counteract) the original shift that was due to the autonomous decline in private spending.

The fact that tax revenues depend on the state of the economy is important to understanding many complicated issues about the impact of deficits. As seen above, it helps to explain why a policy of budget balancing can unbalance the economy in the face of changes in private spending. It helps to explain why deficits can sometimes be associated with a booming economy and at other times with a sagging economy. It also helps to explain interest in alternative measures of the deficit. The concept of the structural deficit/surplus attempts to control for the effects of the economy on the deficit. It does so by looking at spending and revenues at a speci-

(3) fied high-employment level of income. Changes in tax revenues due to changes in GDP (will/will not) affect the actual deficit or surplus but (will/will not) affect the structural deficit or surplus. For this reason, many analysts prefer to use the structural budget as a measure of the stance of fiscal policy.

Are deficits inflationary? Note that a deficit that arises when the economy slips into recession due to a decline in private spending is likely to be correlated with a reduction, not an increase, in interest rates and the rate of inflation.[1] An increase in the structural deficit—that is, a deliberate (increase/reduction) in spending or

_____ in taxes—would shift the aggregate demand curve to the right and increase both interest   (4)

rates and prices. Exactly how much inflation would occur will depend upon the slope of the aggregate supply

curve, whether the economy is close to or far away from full employment, and the conduct of monetary policy.

Concerns about the impact of the deficit on interest rates may lead a central bank to engage in an open mar-

ket purchase to increase bank reserves. If the central bank acts to increase bank reserves by buying government

securities, one says it has _____ the deficit. Deficit-induced open market purchases would   (5)

reduce interest rates from what they would have been, result in a further expansionary shift in the aggregate de-

mand curve and mean even higher prices. Thus monetization of the deficit could lead to (greater/less) inflation.

While a problem in some countries, monetization of the deficit has not been a problem in the United States.

Many feelings about the burden of the national debt may be as deeply ingrained and just as irrational as

a Victorian's ideas about sex or a football coach's ideas about winning. Many fallacious arguments about the

burden of the debt do, however, contain some elements of truth. Arguments about the burden of future in-

terest payments or the cost of repaying the national debt are not relevant when considering debts held by

domestic citizens but are relevant when considering debts held by _____. To the extent   (6)

that debt is held by domestic citizens, interest payments and debt repayments impose little burden on the na-

tion as a whole; they are only transfers from taxpayers to bondholders, who may even be the same individuals.

However, the impact on incentives from higher taxes to accomplish these transfers should not be ignored. A

 eal burden of the debt would arise from a deficit in a high-employment economy that crowded out private

(consumption/investment) spending and left a smaller capital stock to future generations.

There will continue to be arguments as to whether U.S. deficits have entailed such a burden. Until 1980,

the federal government's deficit had shown its largest increases during periods of _____ and   (7)

_____. Government deficits during periods of slack may actually result in a benefit rather

than a burden if, as a result of increased demand, they lead to (crowding in/crowding out) rather than

_____ _____. Major concerns about deficits during the late 1980s and the early

part of the 21st century were that they occurred during a period of (high/low) employment and that they were

thus likely to have led to crowding _____.

Changes in the mix of fiscal and monetary policy may leave real GDP and the price level unaffected

but there will be important effects on the budget deficit, the composition of output, and economic growth.

Consider an economy at full employment with a government budget that is in balance. A reduction in tax rates

would shift the aggregate demand curve to the (right/left). The impact on aggregate demand could be offset by (8)

a move to (restrictive/expansionary) monetary policy. The reduction in tax rates will mean that the government

is now running a (deficit/surplus). This change in the government budget together with the change in monetary

---

[1]By assumption, this deficit arose as the aggregate demand curve shifts to the left. It is inflationary only in the sense that a move to balance the budget would mean a further shift of the aggregate demand curve to the left and a larger reduction in the rate of inflation.

policy will mean (higher/lower) interest rates and a(n) _____ level of investment spending. Because of the change in investment spending, over time this economy is likely to grow (faster/more slowly) that it would have before the change in the mix of fiscal and monetary policy.

IMPORTANT TERMS AND CONCEPTS QUIZ

Choose the best definition for each of the following terms.

1. _____ Budget deficit
2. _____ Budget surplus
3. _____ National debt
4. _____ Structural budget
5. _____ Monetizing the deficit
6. _____ Crowding out
7. _____ Crowding in

a. Amount by which governmental revenue exceeds spending

b. Ratio of government debt to GDP

c. State of budget under current fiscal policy if the economy was at full employment

d. Amount by which government spending exceeds revenue

e. Increase in private investment spending induced by deficit spending

f. Purchases of government bonds by central bank to finance deficit

g. Contraction of private investment spending induced by deficit spending

h. Federal government's total indebtedness

BASIC EXERCISES

This exercise is designed to show how a rigid policy of balanced budgets may unbalance the economy. To simplify the calculations, the exercise focuses on the income-expenditure diagram.

1. a. Fill in the last column of **Table 33-1** to determine the initial equilibrium level of income. The equilibrium level of income is $_____.

   b. At the initial equilibrium level of income, what is the government's actual deficit or surplus? _____

   c. The high-employment level of income is $10,700. What is the structural deficit/surplus?

      _____

   d. Investment spending now declines by $100 billion. Use **Table 33-2** to compute the new equilibrium level of income. _____

      How has the actual government deficit/surplus changed, if at all? _____

      How has the structural deficit/surplus changed, if at all? _____

   e. The government is contemplating a reduction in spending of $50 billion, an amount that should balance the government's budget if income does not change. Use **Table 33-3** to see if reducing government spending by $50 billion will balance the budget. What is the new equilibrium level of income? Did the reduction in government spending balance the budget? If not, why not?

448

Table 33-1

Income (Output) Y	Taxes T	Disposable Income DI	Consumption Spending C	Investment Spending I	Government Purchases G	Exports X	Imports IM	Total Spending C + I + G + (X − IM)
10,000	1,800	8,200	6,860	1,625	1,900	1,150	1,335	_____
10,100	1,825	8,275	6,920	1,625	1,900	1,150	1,345	_____
10,200	1,850	8,350	6,980	1,625	1,900	1,150	1,355	_____
10,300	1,875	8,425	7,040	1,625	1,900	1,150	1,365	_____
10,400	1,900	8,500	7,100	1,625	1,900	1,150	1,375	_____
10,500	1,925	8,575	7,160	1,625	1,900	1,150	1,385	_____
10,600	1,950	8,650	7,220	1,625	1,900	1,150	1,395	_____
10,700	1,975	8,725	7,280	1,625	1,900	1,150	1,405	_____
10,800	2,000	8,800	7,340	1,625	1,900	1,150	1,415	_____

Table 33-2

Income (Output) Y	Taxes T	Disposable Income DI	Consumption Spending C	Investment Spending I	Government Purchases G	Exports X	Imports IM	Total Spending C + I + G + (X − IM)
10,000	1,800	8,200	6,860	1,525	1,900	1,150	1,335	_____
10,100	1,825	8,275	6,920	1,525	1,900	1,150	1,345	_____
10,200	1,850	8,350	6,980	1,525	1,900	1,150	1,355	_____
10,300	1,875	8,425	7,040	1,525	1,900	1,150	1,365	_____
10,400	1,900	8,500	7,100	1,525	1,900	1,150	1,375	_____
10,500	1,925	8,575	7,160	1,525	1,900	1,150	1,385	_____
10,600	1,950	8,650	7,220	1,525	1,900	1,150	1,395	_____
10,700	1,975	8,725	7,280	1,525	1,900	1,150	1,405	_____
10,800	2,000	8,800	7,340	1,525	1,900	1,150	1,415	_____

Table 33-3

Income (Output) Y	Taxes T	Disposable Income DI	Consumption Spending C	Investment Spending I	Government Purchases G	Exports X	Imports IM	Total Spending C + I + G + (X − IM)
10,000	1,800	8,200	6,860	1,525	1,850	1,150	1,335	_____
10,100	1,825	8,275	6,920	1,525	1,850	1,150	1,345	_____
10,200	1,850	8,350	6,980	1,525	1,850	1,150	1,355	_____
10,300	1,875	8,425	7,040	1,525	1,850	1,150	1,365	_____
10,400	1,900	8,500	7,100	1,525	1,850	1,150	1,375	_____
10,500	1,925	8,575	7,160	1,525	1,850	1,150	1,385	_____
10,600	1,950	8,650	7,220	1,525	1,850	1,150	1,395	_____
10,700	1,975	8,725	7,280	1,525	1,850	1,150	1,405	_____
10,800	2,000	8,800	7,340	1,525	1,850	1,150	1,415	_____

2. This problem is meant to illustrate how the effects of changes in fiscal policy depend upon what happens to monetary policy. The solid lines in **Figure 33-1** show an economy in an initial position of equilibrium at full employment with a balanced budget, low interest rates, and no trade deficit, i.e., exports equal imports. The dashed line shows the same economy following a decrease in personal income taxes. Assume the decrease in taxes is equal to $100 billion at the full-employment level of income.

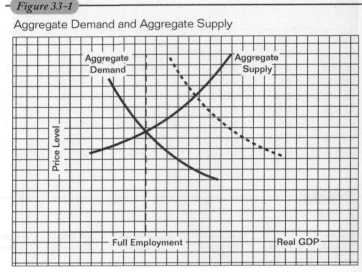

Figure 33-1

Aggregate Demand and Aggregate Supply

   a. Assume the monetary authority wants to avoid the inflation that would be associated with the increase in the structural deficit. Should the monetary authority engage in an open market purchase or sale? Why?

   b. Assume the monetary authority is successful in offsetting the expansionary impact of the increase in the structural deficit. That is, open market operations are successful in shifting the aggregate demand curve back to its initial position. Initially the economy was at full employment with no inflation, a balanced budget, low interest rates, and no trade deficit. Call this outcome Option A. Now the economy is again at full employment with no inflation, but with a structural deficit and high interest rates. Call this outcome Option B. What difference does it make whether the economy is at full employment under Option A or Option B?

SELF-TESTS FOR UNDERSTANDING

TEST A

Circle the most appropriate answer.

1. The federal government deficit is
   a. the excess of tax revenues over transfer payments.
   b. another term for political gridlock.
   c. total indebtedness of the government.
   d. the difference between government spending and the government's revenue for a given year.

2. The federal government runs a surplus when
   a. spending is greater than tax receipts.
   b. interest payments on the national debt are less than 5 percent.
   c. Social Security payments are balanced by Social Security taxes.
   d. revenues exceed spending.

3. The national debt is
   a. equal to the cumulation of past federal government deficits and surpluses.
   b. another term for the federal government's deficit.
   c. what the U.S. government and private businesses owe foreigners.
   d. the excess of spending over revenue for a given year.

4. The structural deficit (surplus) is
   a. equal to interest payments on the national debt.
   b. equal to zero by definition.
   c. defined as the deficit (surplus) the government would run if the economy were at full employment.
   d. the excess of government investment spending over allocations for these projects.

5. At high levels of unemployment, the government's actual deficit will be _____ the structural deficit.
   a. smaller than
   b. the same as
   c. larger than

6. Many observers argue that the structural deficit is a better measure of the stance of fiscal policy than the actual deficit because the
   a. actual deficit can be larger or smaller depending upon the impact of changes in private demand on GDP.
   b. actual deficit does not include the impact of automatic stabilizers.
   c. structural deficit is based on real rather than nominal interest rates.
   d. structural deficit represents what the president proposes rather than what is enacted by Congress.

7. Which mix of fiscal and monetary policy is likely to lead to a higher rate of economic growth? (Assume that either mix of policies achieves the same level of real GDP.)
   a. a small structural deficit and low interest rates
   b. a large structural deficit and high interest rates
   c. Both a and b have the same implications for economic growth.

8. Which of the following is likely to increase the government's structural deficit?
   a. open market purchase
   b. decline in private investment spending
   c. reduction in personal income tax rates
   d. increase in exports from strong economic expansion in Europe

9. Which of the following is likely to increase the government's actual deficit? (There may be more than one correct answer.)
   a. open market purchase
   b. decline in private investment spending
   c. reduction in personal income tax rates
   d. increase in exports from strong economic expansion in Europe

451

10. Until the 1980s, large government deficits had been primarily associated with periods of _____.
    (There may be more than one correct answer.)
    a. high inflation
    b. war
    c. recession
    d. low unemployment

11. An autonomous decline in private spending will lead to all but which one of the following?
    a. a downward shift in the expenditure schedule
    b. a decline in the equilibrium level of GDP
    c. an increase in the government deficit or a reduction in the surplus
    d. a decline in the structural budget deficit or surplus

12. Rigid adherence to budget balancing will
    a. help the economy adjust to shifts in private spending.
    b. have little impact on business cycles.
    c. accentuate swings in GDP from autonomous changes in private spending.
    d. help maintain full employment.

13. The inflationary consequences of a budget deficit are likely to be greatest when
    a. the deficit is the result of a decline in private spending.
    b. the Fed conducts monetary policy to offset the impact of the deficit.
    c. the aggregate supply curve is flat.
    d. there is an increase in the structural deficit at a time of full employment.

14. If the Federal Reserve monetizes a budget deficit, there will be a(n)
    a. smaller inflationary impact.
    b. unchanged inflationary impact.
    c. larger inflationary impact.

15. An increase in the deficit is likely to be correlated with which of the following? (There may be more than one correct answer.)
    a. faster growth in GDP
    b. lower interest rates
    c. a reduction in the rate of inflation
    d. higher interest rates
    e. greater inflation
    f. a slowing of the rate of growth of GDP

16. The macroeconomic impact of a decrease in taxes that increases the structural deficit could be offset by a(n)
    a. equal increase in transfer payments.
    b. open market purchase.
    c. equal increase in government spending.
    d. change in monetary policy that increases interest rates.

452

17. Which of the following is a valid argument about the burden of the national debt for an economy whose debt is held entirely by its own citizens?
    a. Future generations will find interest payments a heavy burden.
    b. When the debt is due, future generations will be burdened with an enormous repayment.
    c. The debt will bankrupt future generations.
    d. If the deficits causing the debt reduced private investment spending, then future generations would be left with a smaller capital stock.

18. "Crowding out" refers to
    a. increased population pressures and arguments for zero population growth.
    b. the effects of government deficits on private investment spending.
    c. what happens at the start of the New York City Marathon.
    d. the impact of higher prices on the multiplier.

19. Crowding out is likely to occur if the _____. (There may be more than one correct answer.)
    a. amount of private savings is unchanged
    b. economy is operating near full employment
    c. rate of unemployment is high
    d. aggregate supply curve is flat

20. Crowding in is more likely to occur when
    a. the economy is operating near full employment.
    b. prices are rising.
    c. the government lowers expenditures.
    d. there is substantial slack in the economy.

TEST B

Circle T or F for true or false.

T F 1. A policy calling for continuous balance in the government's budget will help offset shifts in autonomous private demand.

T F 2. A structural deficit of zero is necessary if the equilibrium level of GDP is to equal the full-employment level of GDP.

T F 3. The "mix" of fiscal and monetary policy is of little importance for the composition of output.

T F 4. When the economy is in a recession, the structural deficit will be smaller than the actual deficit.

T F 5. The inflationary impact of any budget deficit depends on the conduct of monetary policy.

T F 6. Government deficits since 1980 mean that the ratio of national debt to GDP has never been higher than it is today.

T F 7. Interest payments on the national debt, whether to domestic citizens or foreigners, are not really a burden on future generations.

T F 8. A major limitation of the simple crowding-out argument is the assumption that the economy's total pool of savings is fixed.

T F 9. Crowding in is likely to occur when the economy is operating with slack employment, whereas crowding out is likely to occur at full employment.

T   F   10. Government deficits may impose a real burden on future generations if, as a result of crowding out, there is less private investment and a smaller capital stock in the future.

SUPPLEMENTARY EXERCISES

1. **Government Deficits and Interest Rates**

   Between 1957 and 1958, the federal government's budget shifted from a surplus of $2.3 billion to a deficit of $10.3 billion. This was the largest deficit since World War II and in dollar terms was bigger than any deficit during the Great Depression. At the same time, interest rates declined. The rate on three-month Treasury bills declined from an average of 3.267 percent in 1957 to 1.839 percent in 1958. The rate on three- to five-year securities fell from 3.62 percent to 2.90 percent.
   Between 1974 and 1975, the federal government's budget deficit increased from $11.6 billion to $69.4 billion. Interest rates again declined. The rate on three-month Treasury bills declined from 7.886 percent to 5.838 percent, while the rate on three- to five-year securities declined more modestly from 7.81 percent to 7.55 percent.
   Between 1981 and 1982, the federal government deficit increased dramatically from $58.8 billion to $135.5 billion. Again, interest rates declined. The rate on three-month Treasury bills declined from 14.029 percent to 10.686 percent. Interest rates on longer term government securities also declined.
   Between 1991 and 1992, the federal government's deficit went from $210.4 billion to $298 billion, the largest year-to-year increase to date. Interest rates on long-term government bonds declined from 7.86 percent to 7.01 percent while rates on short-term government borrowing declined almost two percentage points from 5.42 percent to 3.45 percent.
   How do you explain the seemingly contradictory results that larger deficits are associated with lower, not higher, interest rates? Do these observations prove that larger deficits will always be associated with lower interest rates?

2. **Repudiate the National Debt?**

   If the national debt is so onerous, we could solve the problem by simply repudiating the debt; that is, we would make no more interest or principal payments on the outstanding debt.
   Imagine that in keeping with democratic principles such a proposition were put to American voters. Who do you think would vote pro and who would vote con? Which side would win? Would the outcome of the vote be different if the debt were held entirely by foreigners? By banks and other financial institutions? (The Treasury publishes data on who holds the national debt in the *Treasury Bulletin*. These data are also published in the annual *Economic Report of the President*. You might want to look at these data and consider what would happen to depositors, shareholders, and pensioners, both current and prospective, if the national debt held by banks, corporations, and pension funds was suddenly worthless.)
   Would repudiating the national debt make it easier or harder to sell government securities in the future?

454

ECONOMICS IN ACTION

HOW SHOULD ONE PROJECT THE STATE OF THE FEDERAL BUDGET?

The Congressional Budget Office (CBO) was established to provide non-partisan, technical assistance to Congress as it wrestles with spending and tax proposals. In addition to background papers that examine the microeconomic implications of various programs, CBO also publishes regular macroeconomic analysis of the overall federal budget.

To help lawmakers, CBO publishes baseline budget projections of deficits and surpluses over a ten-year horizon. These baseline projections draw a lot of attention and play an important role in congressional policy debates. For example, the ten-year budget projections figured prominently in debate over the President Bush's tax cut proposals in the spring of 2001.

While considering the long-run implications of budget proposals is clearly a good thing, the way that CBO projects deficits and surpluses in the baseline budget projections is not above criticism. One should note that the construction of the baseline projections is constrained by law. In particular CBO has been instructed to assume that current laws continue without change. The result is that for many programs, the CBO projections assume that spending only increases to match inflation.

Economists Alan Auerbach and William Gale criticize these ten-year projections, arguing that they are "not always consistent with responsible budgeting practices" and often employ "a series of unrealistic assumption regarding future taxes and spending." While the CBO forecasts may accurately project current law, Auerbach and Gale argue that they are not a good "forecast of what is most likely to occur."

For example, with regard to annual discretionary spending, CBO procedures hold real spending constant at its current level. Auerbach and Gale argue that a more realistic approach would assume that inflation-adjusted spending grows in proportion to either GDP or population. Similarly CBO projections model tax receipts under current law. A number of recent tax cuts are scheduled to expire in the near future. The CBO procedure counts the increased tax revenue following the expiration of the tax cuts while most analysts assume that the tax cuts will be extended in some form. The CBO includes tax revenues under something called the Alternative Minimum Tax (AMT) while most analysts believe that Congress will modify the AMT as it begins to affect large numbers of taxpayers who were not intended to pay the AMT.

In addition Auerbach and Gale argue that a ten-year forecast is inherently arbitrary and policymakers should be concerned about trends over an even longer time horizon. Projections for Social Security and Medicare are relatively benign over the next ten years, as it is not until sometime between 2010 and 2020 that baby boomers will start to retire in significant numbers. Restricting one's view to ten years may obscure significant fiscal problems that lie just beyond the ten-year horizon.

1. What do you think is a good way to project the state of the federal budget?

2. How long a time horizon should be used for projections?

3. How would you project discretionary programs, the funding for which is determined as part of the annual federal budget process? Is projecting current law sufficient or do you think it more realistic to assume that spending is either a constant proportion of GDP or grows in proportion to population?

Sources: William G. Gale and Peter R. Orszag, "The Budget Outlook: Projections and Implications," *The Economists' Voice*: Vol. 1: No. 2, Article 6, 2004. This article is available online at http://www.bepress.com/ev/vol1/iss2/art6

To learn more about the Alternative Minimum Tax see Leonard E. Burman, William G. Gale, and Jeffrey Rohaly, "Unintended Consequences Run Amok—The Individual Alternative Minimum Tax," *Journal of Economic Perspectives, Spring 2003*, and Leonard E. Burman, William G. Gale, Matthew Hall, Jeff Rohaly, and Mohammed Adeel Saleem, "The Individual Alternative Minimum Tax: A Data Update," August 31, 2004, available online at http://www.taxpolicycenter.org/publications/template.cfm?PubID=411051.

STUDY QUESTIONS

1. What is the difference between the government's deficit and its debt? What is the link between the two?

2. What does the historical record show about when the federal government has run large deficits?

3. What does the historical record show about the ratio of federal government debt to GDP?

4. Why are policies to stabilize the deficit likely to destabilize the economy?

5. When is a budget deficit appropriate and why? When is it inappropriate?

6. What is the difference between the structural deficit and the actual deficit? Which is usually larger and why? Which is a more accurate measure of the stance of fiscal policy?

7. Does an increase in the deficit always indicate a move to expansionary fiscal policy? Why?

8. Does an increase in the deficit always lead to higher interest rates and more inflation? Why?

9. Why do economists argue that foreign-held debt imposes more of a burden than government debt held by Americans?

10. What is crowding out and crowding in? When is one more likely than the other and why?

11. Since deficits are a result of fiscal policy decisions, why does the impact of deficits depend upon the conduct of monetary policy?

ECONOMICS ONLINE

Find out more about the magnitude of the national debt and how you can own a part of it from the Bureau of the Public Debt in the U.S. Treasury Department.

http://www.publicdebt.treas.gov/

The Congressional Budget Office posts all of its reports including historical data and periodic projections of the federal government budget on its Web site:

http://www.cbo.gov

The Trade-Off between Inflation and Unemployment

34

Important Terms and Concepts

Demand-side inflation

Supply-side inflation

Phillips curve

Stagflation caused by supply shocks

Self-correcting mechanism

Natural rate of unemployment

Vertical (long-run) Phillips curve

Rational expectations

Indexing

Learning Objectives

After completing this chapter, you should be able to:

- explain how prices can rise following either the rapid growth of aggregate demand or the sluggish growth of aggregate supply.

- explain what the Phillips curve is and what it is not.

- explain why the economy's self-correcting mechanism means that the economy's long-run choices lie along a vertical Phillips curve.

- explain how the accuracy of expectations about inflation can affect the slope of both the aggregate supply curve and the Phillips curve.

- discuss the implications of and evidence for the hypotheses of rational expectations.

- explain how and why one's views on appropriate aggregate demand policy are likely to depend upon one's views on

  ○ the social costs of inflation vs. unemployment.

  ○ the slope of the short-run Phillips curve.

  ○ how quickly inflationary expectations adjust.

  ○ the efficiency of the economy's self-correcting mechanism.

- discuss measures that have been advocated to reduce the natural rate of unemployment.

- discuss the advantages and disadvantages of universal indexing.

CHAPTER REVIEW

This chapter discusses the hard choices that policy makers must make when deciding how to respond to inflation or unemployment. Previous chapters discussed how changes in various tools of fiscal and monetary policy can be used to influence aggregate demand. This chapter uses that material to study the policy implications for fighting unemployment and inflation.

Here, as in many other areas of life, one cannot have one's cake and eat it too. Actions taken to reduce unemployment will often lead to higher rates of inflation, while actions to reduce inflation will often lead to higher rates of unemployment. Economists can help to define the nature of this trade-off, examine the factors that are responsible for it, and clarify the implications of different choices, but they cannot tell anyone which choice to make. In a democratic society, this decision is left to the political process.

Any shift in the aggregate demand or aggregate supply curve, whether induced by policy or not, is likely to affect both prices and output. The nature of the association between changes in prices and changes in output will depend upon which curve shifts. If fluctuations in economic activity are predominantly the result of shifts

(1) in the aggregate demand curve, then higher output will be associated with (higher/lower) levels of prices. The transition to higher prices is a period of inflation. A higher level of output means more employment and a (higher/lower) rate of unemployment. Hence, shifts in the aggregate demand curve imply that inflation and unemployment are (negatively/positively) correlated. That is, if you plotted the rate of unemployment on the horizontal axis and the rate of inflation on the vertical axis, the resulting curve, called the _____ curve would have a (positive/negative) slope.

Data for the 1950s and 1960s are consistent with the view sketched above and seemed to imply that policy makers could choose between inflation and unemployment. In particular, it used to be thought that the Phillips curve implied that policy makers could permanently increase output beyond the level of full employment, or potential output, at the cost of only a small increase in the rate of inflation. Subsequent experience has shown

(2) that this view is (correct/incorrect). The Phillips curve represents the statistical correlation between inflation and unemployment. It ignores the implications of the economy's self-correcting mechanisms.

(3)   As we have seen, output beyond the level of potential output results in a(n) (inflationary/recessionary) gap. The economy's self-correcting mechanism will shift the aggregate supply curve to reestablish long-run equilibrium at the _____ rate of unemployment. The economy's long-run choices lie along a(n) _____ Phillips curve.

In the short run, shifts in the aggregate demand curve will move the economy up or down the short-run Phillips curve, but the economy's self-correcting mechanism implies that this trade-off is only temporary. How long this trade-off lasts depends upon the speed of the economy's self-correcting mechanism. Differing views about the relative costs of inflation and unemployment, the slope of the short-run Phillips curve, and the speed of the economy's self-correcting mechanism are an important part of differences in Keynesian and monetarist policy prescriptions.

460

Changes in money wages are an important determinant of shifts in the aggregate supply curve that lead an inflationary gap to self-destruct. It is the original increase in prices while wages are unchanged that induces firms to expand output. As workers recognize that the purchasing power of their money wages has declined, the subsequent increases in wages to restore real wages will lead to shifts in the aggregate supply curve. Rather than always being a step behind, workers can try to protect their real wages by anticipating the increase in prices. In this case the expectation of higher prices will lead to higher wages and a shift in the aggregate supply curve in anticipation of inflation.[1] Compared with cases where the aggregate supply curve did not shift, a shift in the aggregate demand curve accompanied by an expectations-induced shift in the aggregate supply curve will have a (larger/smaller) impact on output and a(n) _____ impact on prices. The result will be a   (4) (higher/lower) rate of inflation and the slope of the short-run Phillips curve will be (steeper/flatter).

Economists associated with the hypothesis of *rational expectations* have focused special attention on the formation of expectations. While much remains to be learned, these economists argue that errors in predicting inflation should not be systematic. An implication of this view is that, except for random elements, both the aggregate supply curve and the short-run Phillips curve will be vertical. Not only is there no long-run trade-off between inflation and unemployment, but, according to this view, there is also no systematic short-run trade-off.

Others are less convinced that expectations are rational in the sense of no systematic errors. These economists believe that people tend to underpredict inflation when it is rising and overpredict it when it is falling. Long-term contracts also make it difficult to adjust to changing expectations of inflation. These economists argue that policy measures to shift the aggregate demand curve can affect output and employment in the short run. But remember that these short-run impacts will eventually be constrained by the long-run Phillips curve, which is

_____.   (5)

Most economists believe that aggregate demand policy will affect employment and inflation in the short run and will also affect the place where the economy ends up on the long-run Phillips curve. Thus, to fight a recession rather than to wait for the economy's self-correcting mechanism will mean more employment in the short run and is likely to mean more inflation in the long run as compared to a status quo policy that waits on the economy's self-correcting mechanisms. (See Figure 34-9 in the text.) Whether one wants to use aggregate demand policy or wait for natural processes depends on one's assessment of the costs of inflation and unemployment, the slope of the short-run Phillips curve, the quickness with which inflationary expectations adjust, and the efficiency of the economy's self-correcting mechanisms.

A number of policies have been advocated in the hope that they will improve the inflation-unemployment trade-off. Increased efforts at education and job retraining are seen as efforts to reduce frictional unemployment and lower the natural rate of unemployment.

---

[1] The story of workers trying to protect themselves against inflation seems to imply that labor is responsible for inflation. When the economy is booming, workers will be concerned about inflation, but firms will willingly pay higher wages to attract workers in a tight labor market. The real cause of inflation is not workers or firms but rather excessive aggregate demand.

461

A number of individuals have argued that rather than trying to reduce the rate of inflation, we should simply learn to live with it and rely on automatic adjustments of monetary payments to reflect changes in prices, a process known as indexing. Inflation-linked adjustments of tax brackets, Social Security benefits, as well as other

(6)   government transfer programs, and escalator clauses in wage contracts are examples of _____. A number of observers also advocate this mechanism for interest rates.

Indexing does seem to offer some relief from many of the social costs of inflation. As workers, firms, and lenders scramble to protect themselves against anticipated future increases in prices, current prices and inter-

(7)   est rates will (increase/decrease) to reflect the expectation of inflation. If actual inflation turns out to be greater or less than expected, there will be a redistribution of wealth that many feel is essentially arbitrary. Uncertainty over future prices may make individuals and businesses extremely reluctant to enter into long-term contracts. Indexing appears to offer relief from these problems. Labor contracts and other agreements could be written in real rather than nominal terms, and arbitrary redistributions would be avoided because money payments would reflect actual, not expected, inflation. At the same time, there is concern that learning to live with inflation may make the economy (more/less) inflation prone.

IMPORTANT TERMS AND CONCEPTS QUIZ

Choose the best definition for each of the following terms.

1. _____ Phillips curve
2. _____ Self-correcting mechanism
3. _____ Natural rate of unemployment
4. _____ Long-run Phillips curve
5. _____ Demand-side inflation
6. _____ Rational expectations
7. _____ Indexing
8. _____ Supply-side inflation

a. Graph depicting unemployment rate on horizontal axis and inflation rate on vertical axis
b. Vertical line at the natural rate of unemployment
c. Unemployment rate at full employment
d. Vertical line at natural rate of inflation
e. Forecasts that make optimal use of available and relevant data
f. Adjustments of monetary payments whenever a specified price index changes
g. The economy's way of curing inflationary and recessionary gaps
h. Rise in the price level caused by rapid growth of aggregate demand
i. Rise in the price level caused by slow growth of aggregate supply

BASIC EXERCISES

This exercise is designed to illustrate the nature of the inflation-unemployment trade-off that policy makers must face when planning aggregate demand policy.

1. **Figure 34-1** shows an economy with a recessionary gap. Which of the following monetary and fiscal policies could be used to help eliminate this gap?

   ❑ open market (purchase/sale)

   ❑ (increase/decrease) in taxes

   ❑ (increase/decrease) in government transfer payments to individuals

   ❑ (increase/decrease) in government purchases of goods and services

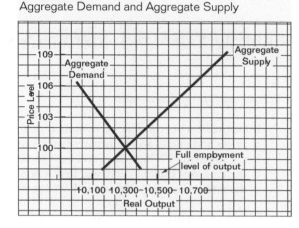

Figure 34-1

Aggregate Demand and Aggregate Supply

2. Assume the full-employment level of income is $10,500 billion. Draw a new aggregate demand curve, representing one or more of the appropriate policies you identified in question 1 that will restore full employment for this economy. Following a shift in the aggregate demand curve, prices will rise to _____.

3. Consider the following statement:

   "The increase in prices that resulted when we restored full employment was a small price to pay for the increased output. Why not try moving even farther along the aggregate supply curve? If we further stimulate the economy to lower unemployment we can increase output to, say, $10,700 billion and prices will only rise to 106. We can thus have a permanent increase in output of $200 billion every year in return for a one-time increase in prices of just under 3 percent. That's a pretty favorable trade-off."
   What is wrong with the reasoning of this argument?

4. **Figure 34-2** shows an economy following an adverse shift in the aggregate supply curve. Equilibrium used to be an output of $10,500 and a price level of 103. Answer the following questions to see how stabilization policy that shifts the aggregate demand curve is constrained in efforts to offset the adverse impact of the shift in the aggregate supply curve.

   a. If there is to be no decline in employment,

   the government will need to implement

   (expansionary/restrictive) policies to shift the

   aggregate demand curve. The government

   could maintain employment, but at the cost of

   an increase in prices to _____.

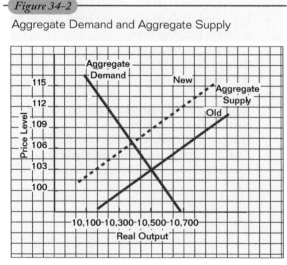

Figure 34-2

Aggregate Demand and Aggregate Supply

463

b. Alternatively, the government could avoid any increase in prices. Such a decision would require (<u>expansionary/restrictive</u>) policies and would result in a new equilibrium level of output of

_____.

SELF-TESTS FOR UNDERSTANDING

TEST A

Circle the most appropriate answer.

1. If fluctuations in economic activity are caused by shifts in the aggregate demand curve, then
   a. prices and output will be negatively correlated.
   b. the short-run Phillips curve will be vertical.
   c. the long-run Phillips curve will have a negative slope.
   d. the rates of inflation and unemployment will tend to be negatively correlated.

2. If fluctuations in economic activity are the result of shifts in the aggregate supply curve, then
   a. prices and output will be positively correlated.
   b. the short-run Phillips curve will have a negative slope.
   c. the long-run Phillips curve will be horizontal.
   d. the rate of inflation and rate of unemployment will tend to be positively correlated.

3. The Phillips curve
   a. is a statistical relationship between unemployment and inflation when economic fluctuations are dominated by changes in the growth of aggregate demand.
   b. is the set of long-term equilibrium relationships between the rate of unemployment and the rate of inflation.
   c. is the third turn at the Indianapolis 500 Speedway.
   d. shows how nominal interest rate changes when expectations of inflation change.

4. The economy's self-correcting mechanisms mean that in the long run the Phillips curve is likely to
   a. have a negative slope.
   b. have a positive slope.
   c. be horizontal.
   d. be vertical.

5. The long-run Phillips curve will be vertical
   a. at the natural rate of inflation.
   b. at the point where real and nominal interest rates are equal.
   c. at the natural rate of unemployment.
   d. wherever the aggregate demand and aggregate supply curves intersect.

6. The positively sloped aggregate supply curve is drawn on the assumption that
   a. the cost of productive inputs remains unchanged in the short run as output changes.
   b. wages are fully indexed.
   c. the Phillips curve is never vertical.
   d. wage and price controls limit the impact of inflation.

7. An increase in wages, due either to inflation that has occurred in the past or inflation that is expected to occur in the future, can be modeled as a(n)
   a. upward shift in the aggregate supply curve.
   b. inward shift in the production possibilities frontier.
   c. downward shift in the aggregate demand curve.
   d. leftward shift in the long-run Phillips curve.

8. An increased emphasis on expectations of future inflation in wage settlements will lead to a ____ aggregate supply curve and a ____ Phillips curve.
   a. flatter; flatter
   b. flatter; steeper
   c. steeper; steeper
   d. steeper; flatter

9. Consider a shift to the right of the aggregate demand curve due to expansionary monetary and fiscal policy. Assume that the adoption of expansionary policies leads to expectations of inflation that induce a simultaneous shift in the aggregate supply curve. The resulting change in output will be _____ if there were no shift in the aggregate supply curve.
   a. smaller than
   b. the same as
   c. larger than

10. Under the same conditions as question 9, the resulting change in prices will be _____ if there were no shift in the aggregate supply curve.
    a. smaller than
    b. the same as
    c. larger than

11. Stabilization policy faces a trade-off between inflation and unemployment in the short run because changes in monetary and fiscal policy have their most immediate impact on the
    a. aggregate supply curve.
    b. Phillips curve.
    c. production possibilities frontier.
    d. aggregate demand curve.

12. Which of the following are necessary for expectations to meet the economist's definition of rational expectations? (There may be more than one correct answer.)
    a. They are based on relevant and available information.
    b. They can only be made by economists and statisticians.
    c. There are no systematic errors.
    d. They are always correct.

13. A strong believer in rational expectations would be surprised by which one of the following occurrences?
    a. An announcement by the Fed that it will increase the rate of growth of the money supply leads to expectations of higher inflation.
    b. Plans to lower taxes give rise to expectations of higher prices.
    c. Plans to fight inflation by restrictive policy succeed in reducing the rate of inflation with no increase in unemployment.
    d. An examination of the record shows that people consistently underestimate the rate of inflation during periods when it is increasing.

14. The hypothesis of rational expectations implies that increases in output beyond the level of potential output can be produced by
    a. expected increases in prices.
    b. unexpected increases in prices only.
    c. any increase in prices whether expected or not.
    d. preannounced increases in the money supply or reductions in taxes.

15. Which of the following is not a feasible alternative for aggregate demand policy following an adverse shift of the supply curve to the left?
    a. Do nothing and initially experience both higher prices and lower output.
    b. Avoid the reduction in output at the cost of even higher prices.
    c. Avoid the increase in prices at the cost of an even greater decline in output.
    d. Avoid both the reduction in output and increase in prices by using fiscal policy to shift the aggregate demand curve and monetary policy to shift the aggregate supply curve.

16. Restrictive monetary and fiscal policy adopted to reduce the rate of inflation will work quicker and have a smaller impact on unemployment when
    a. changes in inflationary expectations take a long time.
    b. the long-run Phillips curve is vertical.
    c. expectations of inflation adjust quickly to the change in macro policy.
    d. the natural rate of unemployment equals the natural rate of inflation.

17. Who is most likely to advocate government action to eliminate a recessionary gap? The economist who believes
    a. the short-run Phillips curve is quite steep.
    b. expectations of inflation will adjust rapidly to lower rates of inflation.
    c. we should pay any price to avoid higher inflation.
    d. the short-run Phillips curve is fairly flat.

18. If job retraining or other measures are successful in reducing the natural rate of unemployment, then the
    a. long-run Phillips curve will shift to the left.
    b. aggregate demand curve will become less steep.
    c. short-run Phillips curve will become vertical.
    d. natural rate of inflation will increase.

19. A general policy of indexing
    a. is an attempt to shift the aggregate supply curve downward and to the right.
    b. would help to balance the federal government's budget.
    c. is an attempt to ease the social cost of inflation.
    d. runs little risk of accelerating the rate of inflation.

20. Which of the following is an example of indexing?
    a. tax penalties on firms that grant excessive wage increases
    b. the adjustment of nominal interest rates in response to expectations of inflation
    c. the average change in prices on the New York Stock Exchange
    d. increases in Social Security checks computed on the basis of changes in the consumer price index

TEST B

Circle T or F for true or false.

T F 1. Inflation occurs only as a result of shifts in the aggregate demand curve.

T F 2. In contrast to expansionary monetary or fiscal policy, an autonomous increase in private spending will increase output without increasing prices.

T F 3. If fluctuations in economic activity are predominantly the result of shifts in the aggregate supply curve, the rate of unemployment and the rate of inflation will tend to be positively correlated.

T F 4. The economy's self-correcting mechanism implies that the only long-run policy choices for the economy lie along a vertical Phillips curve.

T F 5. The natural rate of unemployment is given by the position of the long-run Phillips curve.

T F 6. A belief that the economy's self-correcting mechanism works quickly is an argument in favor of activist demand-management policy.

T F 7. Expectations of inflation that lead to higher wages will be somewhat self-fulfilling as the increase in wages shifts the aggregate supply curve.

T F 8. One can minimize the inflationary effects of fighting a recession by using fiscal policy rather than monetary policy.

T F 9. Following an adverse shift in the aggregate supply curve, aggregate demand policies can stop the rise in prices with no increase in unemployment.

T F 10. The economy's self-correcting mechanism means that, in the face of a recessionary gap, output and prices will eventually be the same with or without expansionary stabilization policy.

ECONOMICS IN ACTION

HOW NATURAL IS THE NATURAL RATE?

The experience of the 1990s has led a number of economists to refine their views of the natural rate of unemployment. Based on estimates from the late 1980s or early 1990s, many would have expected that an unemployment rate of under 5 percent would have been accompanied by significant inflation. Instead, as the rate of unemployment fell from 7.5 percent in 1992 to under 4 percent by late 2000, the rate of inflation decreased rather than increased. For much of 1998, inflation as measured by the CPI was only 1.5 percent. Although inflation rose somewhat in 1999 and 2000, it was still quite low by historical standards, especially when viewed in light of the low rate of unemployment.

What happened? Has the trade-off between unemployment and inflation vanished? As the economy recovers from the 2001 recession, should policy again aim for a rate of unemployment of 4 percent or even lower?

Some argued that while there may still be a trade-off between unemployment and inflation, the "new economy" meant a dramatic decline in the natural rate of unemployment. Advocates of this view argue that new information technologies lowered the natural rate of unemployment as they increased growth in productivity. In addition, increased international competition weakened the resolve of unions while stiffening the spine of management engaged in wage negotiations.

Economist Robert J. Gordon believes that much of the experience of the 1990s was related to good luck, fortuitous events that are unlikely to be as favorable over the long run. According to Gordon, falling food prices, reductions in the rate of increase of the cost of medical care, and cheap imports were an important part of the good inflation news in the 1990s but are not likely to be factors that one can count on continuing forever.

Economist Robert Hall argues that our good fortune reflects well-executed monetary policy. He believes that the best policy for central bankers is "to set clear targets for inflation and stick by them
. . . If the [Federal Reserve] convinces traders in financial markets that inflation will be low and steady, the economy will gravitate toward the lowest possible unemployment rate."

Economists Lawrence Katz and Alan Kreuger have suggested that 4 to 4.5 percent may be as low as one should aim for. They argue that the decline from 7.5 percent to under 4.5 percent was relatively easy as employers could hire from students, spouses, and laid-off workers. Katz and Kreuger point to the increasing proportion of long-term unemployment as the rate of unemployment fell and argue that once the rate of unemployment is at 4 to 4.5 percent, many people who are still unemployed will have a hard time meeting labor force needs as they may have obsolete skills and suffer from physical or mental limitations.

Some, like economist James Stock, argue that while there is a link between inflation and overall economic activity, one needs broader measures than just unemployment. Stock points out that in the late 1990s while the rate of unemployment was low suggesting possible inflationary pressures, other indicators such as plant utilization still showed significant capacity.

1. What has happened to the rate of inflation recently?

2. What do you think the value of the natural rate of unemployment is?

3. If you were responsible for macroeconomic policy, what if anything should policy do to move the economy toward the natural rate of unemployment?

SOURCE: Michael M. Weinstein, "Unemployment's Natural Rate May Have a Mind of Its Own," *New York Times,* April 22, 1999; Stuart Silverstein, "Some Economists Question Link Between Wages and Inflation," *Los Angeles Times,* January 14, 2001.

STUDY QUESTIONS

1. Why does the correlation between inflation and unemployment depend upon the source of macroeconomic fluctuations?

2. Does the Phillips curve offer macroeconomic policymakers a menu of choices between the rate of unemployment and inflation? Why or why not?

3. What is meant by the statement that the economy's self-correcting mechanisms mean that in the long run, the Phillips curve is vertical?

4. What is the natural rate of unemployment?

5. How does the expectation of future inflation and the expectations-related shifts in the aggregate supply curve affect the Phillips curve?

6. How can expectations of inflation be rational if they are never accurate?

7. What sort of policies might reduce the natural rate of unemployment?

8. Should wages and interest rates be fully indexed?

9. Should stabilization policy aim to reduce inflation to zero? Why or why not?

10. Has the natural rate of unemployment changed in recent years? If so, how and why?

ECONOMICS ONLINE

How accurate are expectations of inflation? Are there systematic errors when inflation is rising or falling? You can access two surveys of expectations of inflation online.

The Livingston Survey, begun by Joseph Livingston in 1946, summarizes the inflation forecasts of economists from industry, government, banking, and academia. The Livingston Survey data are available online from the Federal Reserve Bank of Philadelphia:

http://www.phil.frb.org/econ/liv/index.html

The Federal Reserve Bank of St. Louis posts data on inflation expectations from the University of Michigan survey of consumers. Data on consumer inflation expectations is found under the "Business/Fiscal" heading at:

http://research.stlouisfed.org/fred2/categories/98

The U.S. government now issues inflation-indexed bonds. Find out more about inflation-indexed bonds from the Bureau of the Public Debt, U.S. Treasury.

http://www.treasurydirect.gov/instit/annceresult/tipscpi/tipscpi.htm

International Trade and Comparative Advantage

Important Terms and Concepts

Specialization	Tariff	Infant-industry argument
Absolute advantage	Quota	Strategic argument for protection
Comparative advantage	Export subsidy	Dumping
Mercantilism	Trade adjustment assistance	

Learning Objectives

After completing this chapter, you should be able to:

- list the important factors that lead countries to trade with one another.

- explain how voluntary trade, even if it does not increase total production, can be mutually beneficial to the trading partners.

- explain in what ways international and intranational trade are similar and dissimilar.

- distinguish between absolute and comparative advantage.

- explain how absolute advantage and comparative advantage are related to the location and slope of a country's per capita production possibilities frontier.

- explain how trade means that a country's consumption possibilities can exceed its production possibilities.

- compare the advantages and disadvantages of tariffs and quotas.

- analyze the arguments used to advocate trade restrictions.

- explain the role of adjustment assistance in a country favoring free trade.

- explain the fallacy in the "cheap foreign labor" argument.

CHAPTER REVIEW

The material in this chapter discusses the basic economic forces that influence the international division of labor in the production of goods and services and the resulting pattern of international trade. Trade between cities or states within a single country is, in principle, no different than trade between nations. Economists and others spend more time studying international trade rather than intranational trade for several reasons: International trade involves more than one government with a resulting host of political concerns; it usually involves more than one currency; and the mobility of labor and capital between nations is typically more difficult than within nations.

Exchange rates—that is, how much of one country's currency it takes to buy one unit of another country's currency—are an important determinant of international trade and will be discussed in the next chapter. However, the real terms of trade—how many import goods a country can get indirectly through export production rather than through direct domestic production—are the important measure of the benefits of trade, and they are considered here in some detail.

Individual countries can try to meet the consumption needs of their citizens without trade by producing everything their populations need. Alternatively, they can specialize in the production of fewer commodities and trade for commodities they do not produce. Even if there were no differences between countries, special-

(1) izing and trading would still make sense if there were important economies of _____— in production.

An important reason for trade is that differences in climate, oil deposits, minerals, and other natural resources, as well as differences in labor inputs and productive capital, will affect the efficiency with which countries

(2) can produce different goods. It is the law of (<u>absolute/comparative</u>) advantage that then indicates where countries should concentrate their production to maximize the potential gains from trade.

Assume country A can produce 80,000 bushels of wheat if it produces one less car, while country B can produce only 70,000 bushels of wheat. For the same world production of cars, world production of wheat will in-

(3) crease if country (<u>A/B</u>) produced ten fewer cars and country _____ produced ten more cars. (World wheat production would increase by _____ bushels.) In this case country A has a comparative advantage in the production of _____.[1]

Looking only at its own domestic production, the opportunity cost of one more car in country A is

(4) _____ bushels of wheat. Country B can produce one more car by giving up only _____ bushels of wheat. Thus it should not be surprising if country B concentrates on the production of _____ and trades with country A, which concentrates on the production of _____.[2]

---

[1]Note that we have said nothing so far about absolute advantage. For example, if it takes 300 labor hours to produce one car or 70,000 bushels of wheat in country B and 600 labor hours to produce 1 car or 80,000 bushels of wheat in country A, country B has an absolute advantage in the production of both goods while country A still has a comparative advantage in the production of wheat.

[2]Does the law of comparative advantage imply that all countries should specialize in the production of just a few commodities? No, it does not, for several reasons. One important reason is that production possibilities frontiers are likely to be curved rather than straight lines. The implication of the curved

It is also important to realize that comparative advantage is not a static concept. The mix of industries that maximizes a country's comparative advantage is not something that can be determined once for all time. Rather, there will need to be continual adjustments in response to innovations and competition, both domestically and abroad. Countries that try to isolate themselves from foreign competition have usually ended up with stagnating industries and incomes.

As countries concentrate production on those goods in which they have a comparative advantage, equilibrium world prices and trade flows—that is, exports and imports—will be determined at the point where world demand equals world supply, not at the intersection of domestic demand and supply curves. Advanced courses in international trade show how prices derived under conditions of free trade will lead competitive, profit-maximizing firms to exploit the comparative advantage of individual countries and help to achieve an efficient allocation of resources.

Most countries do not have unrestricted free trade. Rather, imports are often restricted by the use of
_____ and _____, and exports are often promoted through the use of export (5)
_____. Tariffs reduce the quantity of imports by raising their _____ while quotas raise the price of imports by restricting _____. Either a tariff or a quota could be used to achieve the same reduction in imports, but the choice between the two has other consequences.

Tariff revenues accrue directly to the _____ while the benefits of higher prices under a (6)
quota are likely to accrue to private producers, both foreign and domestic. (The government might be able to capture some of these profits by auctioning import licenses, but this is not usually done.)

Tariffs still require foreign suppliers to compete among themselves. This competition will favor the survival of (high/low) -cost foreign suppliers. What about domestic firms? They (do/do not) have to pay the tariff, so (7)
high-cost domestic suppliers (can/cannot) continue in business. Quotas are apt to be distributed on almost any grounds except economic efficiency and thus have no automatic mechanism that works in favor of low-cost foreign suppliers.

Why do countries impose tariffs and quotas? Many trade restrictions reflect the successful pleadings of high-cost domestic suppliers. Free trade and the associated reallocation of productive resources in line with the law of comparative advantage would call for the elimination of these firms in their traditional lines of business. It is not surprising that managers and workers resist these changes. If everyone is to benefit from the increased output opportunities offered by free trade, then a program of trade _____ assistance will be neces- (8)
sary to help those most affected by the realignment of productive activities.

Other traditional justifications for trade restrictions include the national _____ argument (9)
and the _____-industries argument. In both cases it is extremely difficult to separate firms with

---

frontier is that the opportunity cost of cars in terms of wheat for country B will rise as B produces more cars. Simultaneously, the opportunity cost of cars in terms of wheat for country A will fall as A concentrates on wheat. In equilibrium, the opportunity cost, or slope of the production possibilities frontier, in both countries will be equal. At this point neither country has an incentive for further specialization. Exactly where this point will occur will be determined by world demand and supply for cars and wheat.

legitimate claims from those looking for a public handout. In recent years some have argued that the threat of trade restrictions should be used in a strategic manner to convince others not to impose restrictions.

Much of the free trade fuss in the United States is concerned about competing with low-cost foreign producers who pay workers lower wages. Concerns about wages need to be joined with measures of productivity. A clear understanding of comparative advantages shows that the standard of living of workers in (the exporting/ (10) the importing/both) country(ies) can rise as a result of specialization and trade. Even countries with high wages can benefit from trade when high wages are associated with high productivity and trade induces adjustments in the structure of worldwide production consistent with the principle of _____ advantage.

IMPORTANT TERMS AND CONCEPTS QUIZ

Choose the most appropriate definition for each of the following terms.

1. _____ Imports
2. _____ Exports
3. _____ Specialization
4. _____ Absolute advantage
5. _____ Comparative advantage
6. _____ Mercantilism
7. _____ Tariff
8. _____ Quota
9. _____ Export subsidy
10. _____ Trade adjustment assistance
11. _____ Infant-industry argument
12. _____ Strategic trade policy
13. _____ Dumping

a. Maximum quantity that can be imported per unit of time
b. Threats to implement protectionist policies designed to promote free trade
c. Selling goods in a foreign market at higher prices than those charged at home
d. Domestically produced goods sold abroad
e. Selling goods in a foreign market at lower prices than those charged at home
f. Tax on imports
g. Decision by a country to emphasize production of particular commodities
h. Provision of special aid to those workers and firms harmed by foreign competition
i. Ability of one country to produce a good less inefficiently (relative to other goods) than another country
j. Foreign-produced goods purchased domestically
k. Tariff protection for new industries, giving them time to mature
l. Payment by the government that enables domestic firms to lower prices to foreign buyers
m. Ability of one country to produce a good using fewer resources than another country requires
n. Doctrine arguing that exports are good while imports are bad

BASIC EXERCISES

This exercise is designed to review the law of comparative advantage.

1. Assume that the hours of labor shown below are the only input necessary to produce calculators and backpacks in Canada and Japan.

	Calculators	Backpacks
Canada	4	5
Japan	2	3

   Which country has an absolute advantage in the production of calculators? _____

   Which country has an absolute advantage in the production of backpacks? _____

2. If labor in Canada is reallocated from the production of calculators to the production of backpacks, how many calculators must be given up in order to produce one more backpack? _____ What about Japan? How many calculators must it give up in order to produce one more backpack? _____ Which country has a comparative advantage in the production of backpacks? _____ Which country has a comparative advantage in the production of calculators? _____ According to the law of comparative advantage, _____ should concentrate on the production of backpacks while _____ concentrates on the production of calculators.

3. Assume each country has 12 million hours of labor input that initially is evenly distributed in both countries between the production of backpacks and calculators: 6 million for each. Fill in the following table of outputs.

	Output of Calculators	Output of Backpacks
Canada	_____	_____
Japan	_____	_____
Total	_____	_____

4. Assume that Canada now reallocates 2.4 million labor hours away from the production of calculators and into backpacks. The change in Canadian calculator output is −_____. The change in Canadian backpack output is +_____.

5. What reallocation of labor in Japan is necessary to be sure that world output of calculators (Japan plus Canada) remains unchanged? _____ labor hours. What are the changes in Japanese output from this reallocation? The change in Japanese calculator output is +_____. The change in Japanese backpack output is −_____.

6. By assumption, the world output of calculators has not changed, but the net change in the world output of backpacks is a(n) (increase/decrease) of _____ backpacks.

7. Questions 3 through 6 showed how specialization according to the law of comparative advantage could increase the output of backpacks without decreasing the output of calculators. This is just one possibility. Adjustments in line with the law of comparative advantage could increase the output of both goods. Suppose Japan had reallocated 1,350,000 labor hours to the production of calculators. Fill in the following table and compare total outputs with your answers to question 3.

Calculators

	Labor Input (millions of hours)	Output
Canada	3.60	_____
Japan	7.35	_____
Total		_____

Backpacks

	Labor Input (millions of hours)	Output
Canada	8.40	_____
Japan	4.65	_____
Total		_____

8. Work through questions 4 and 5 again, but assume this time that the initial reallocation of 2.4 million labor hours in Canada is away from backpacks and to the production of calculators. Calculate the reallocation in Japan necessary to maintain world backpack output. What happens to the total output of calculators? Why?

9. Assume that the production of backpacks in Canada requires 6 hours rather than 5 hours. Work through the original output levels in question 3 and the reallocation of labor in questions 4 and 5 to see what now happens to total output of calculators and backpacks. Does your answer to question 6 differ from your original answer? Why or why not??

SELF-TESTS FOR UNDERSTANDING

TEST A

Circle the most appropriate answer.

1. Even if there were no differences in natural resources, climate, labor skills, etc., nations would still find it advantageous to specialize production and trade
   a. because of differences in absolute advantage.
   b. to take advantage of economies of scale.
   c. to take advantage of differences in national currencies.
   d. when inflation rates differ.

2. International trade is different from intranational trade because of
   a. political issues that arise from different governments.
   b. limitations of the ability of labor and capital to move between countries compared to their ability to move within countries.
   c. the use of different currencies.
   d. all of the above.

3. Economists argue that
   a. efficiency in international trade requires countries to produce those goods in which they have an absolute advantage.
   b. efficiency in international trade requires countries to produce those goods in which they have a comparative advantage.
   c. efficiency in international trade requires countries that have an absolute advantage in the production of all goods to become self-sufficient.
   d. countries with export surpluses will have a comparative advantage in the production of all goods.

4. Using per capita production possibilities frontiers showing the production of clothes on the vertical axis and cars on the horizontal axis, the absolute advantage in the production of clothes would be determined by comparing
   a. the slope of the per capita production possibilities frontiers.
   b. where the per capita production possibilities frontiers cut the horizontal axis.
   c. the area under the per capita production possibilities frontiers.
   d. where the per capita production possibilities frontiers cut the vertical axis.

5. Using per capita production possibilities frontiers described above, the comparative advantage in the production of clothes would be determined by comparing
   a. the slope of the per capita production possibilities frontiers.
   b. where the per capita production possibilities frontiers cut the horizontal axis.
   c. the area under the per capita production possibilities frontiers.
   d. where the per capita production possibilities frontiers cut the vertical axis.

6. Which of the following is an example of comparative advantage?
   a. Wages of textile workers are lower in India than in America.
   b. The slope of the production possibilities frontier between tomatoes and airplanes differs for Mexico and the United States.
   c. American workers must work an average of only 500 hours to purchase a car, while Russian workers must work 4,000 hours.
   d. In recent years, Swedish income per capita has exceeded that of the United States.

7. Specialization and free trade consistent with the law of comparative advantage will enable
   a. increased world production of all traded goods.
   b. increases in the standard of living for workers in both exporting and importing countries.
   c. countries to consume at some point outside their production possibilities frontier.
   d. all of the above.

8. From a worldwide perspective, economic efficiency is enhanced if production and trade is organized according to the law of comparative advantage. Economic efficiency within a single country is enhanced if regional production and trade are organized according to
   a. absolute advantage.
   b. the political power of particular states or regions.
   c. which regions have the highest unemployment.
   d. comparative advantage.

9. If shoes can be produced with two hours of labor input in Italy and three hours of labor input in the United States, then it is correct to say that
   a. Italy has an absolute advantage in the production of shoes.
   b. Italy has a comparative advantage in the production of shoes.
   c. the United States has an absolute advantage in the production of shoes.
   d. the United States has a comparative advantage in the production of shoes.

10. Assuming that shoes are produced as in question 9 and shirts can be produced with four hours of labor in both countries, then it is correct to say that
    a. the United States has a comparative advantage in the production of shirts.
    b. Italy has a comparative advantage in the production of shirts.
    c. Italy has an absolute advantage in the production of shirts.
    d. the United States has an absolute advantage in the production of shirts.

11. Under free trade, world prices for exports and imports would be such that
    a. countries would specialize production along lines of absolute advantage.
    b. all countries would show a slight export surplus.
    c. the quantity supplied by exporters would just equal the quantity demanded by importers.
    d. every country would be self-sufficient in all goods.

12. Which one of the following is not intended to restrict trade?
    a. export subsidies
    b. tariffs
    c. quotas

13. A tariff affects trade by
    a. imposing a tax on imported goods.
    b. limiting the quantity of goods that can be imported.
    c. offering a subsidy to producers who export for foreign sales.
    d. the voluntary actions of foreign manufacturers to limit their exports.

14. A quota affects trade by
    a. imposing a tax on imported goods.
    b. limiting the quantity of goods that can be imported.
    c. offering a subsidy to producers who export for foreign sales.
    d. the voluntary action of foreign manufacturers to limit their exports.

15. Which of the following is an example of a tariff?
    a. Japanese car manufacturers agree to limit exports to the United States.
    b. U.S. law limits the imports of cotton shirts to 20 million.
    c. Television manufacturers outside Great Britain must pay a 10 percent duty on each set they ship to Great Britain.
    d. Foreign bicycle manufacturers receive a rebate of taxes from their own government for each bicycle they export.

16. One economic advantage of tariffs over quotas is that tariffs
    a. typically give preferential treatment to long-term suppliers.
    b. expose high-cost domestic producers to competition.
    c. force foreign suppliers to compete.
    d. help avoid destructive price wars.

17. The imposition of a tariff on steel will lead to all but which one of the following?
    a. a lower volume of steel imports
    b. higher domestic steel prices
    c. reduced domestic demand for steel
    d. a smaller market share for domestic producers

18. The imposition of a quota on steel will lead to all but which one of the following?
    a. a lower volume of steel imports
    b. increased domestic production of steel
    c. lower domestic steel prices
    d. reduced domestic demand for steel

19. A quota that limits the importation of foreign computer chips is likely to be in the interest of all but which of the following? (There may be more than one correct answer.)
    a. domestic chip manufacturers
    b. domestic computer manufacturers
    c. labor employed domestically in the production of computer chips
    d. consumers interested in buying computers

20. Which one of the following is a justification for fewer trade restrictions?
    a. Some industries would be so vital in times of war that we cannot rely on foreign suppliers.
    b. A temporary period of protection is necessary until an industry matures and is able to compete with foreign suppliers.
    c. Competition from foreign suppliers will help keep prices to consumers low.
    d. The threat of trade restrictions may prevent the adoption of restrictions by others.

TEST B

Circle T or F for true or false.

T F 1. A country with an absolute advantage in producing all goods is better off being self-sufficient than engaging in trade.

T F 2. A country with an absolute advantage in the production of all goods should only export commodities.

T F 3. The unequal distribution of natural resources among countries is one important reason why countries trade.

T F 4. Which of two countries has a comparative advantage in the production of wine rather than cloth can be determined by comparing the slopes of the production possibilities frontiers of both countries.

T F 5. It is possible for all countries to simultaneously expand exports and reduce imports.

T F 6. Tariffs act like a tax on imported goods and have no impact on the price of similar goods that are produced by domestic firms.

T F 7. A quota on shirts would reduce the volume of imported shirts by specifying the maximum quantity of shirts that can be imported.

T F 8. The infant-industry argument is used to justify protection for industries that are vital in times of war.

T F 9. Dumping of goods by the United States on Japanese markets would necessarily harm Japanese consumers.

T F 10. If foreign labor is paid less, foreign producers will always be able to undersell American producers.

| Appendix | *Supply, Demand, and Pricing in World Trade*

This exercise is designed to illustrate the material in the Appendix to Chapter 34 and give you practice in understanding how world prices are determined and in analyzing the impact of quotas and tariffs. To simplify the analysis, the question assumes that the world is composed of only two countries, the United States and India.

1. **Figure 35-1** shows the demand and supply for shirts in the United States and India. Prices in India are expressed in terms of American dollars. In the absence of international trade, what are the domestic price and quantity of shirts in India and the United States?

	Price	Quantity
India	_____	_____
United States	_____	_____

2. Assume now that India and the United States are free to trade without restrictions. What is the world price of shirts? _____. At this price what happens to domestic demand, production, exports, and imports?

	Price	Domestic Demand	Domestic Production	Exports	Imports
India	_____	_____	_____	_____	_____
United States	_____	_____	_____	_____	_____

Figure 35-1

Demand and Supply: Shirts

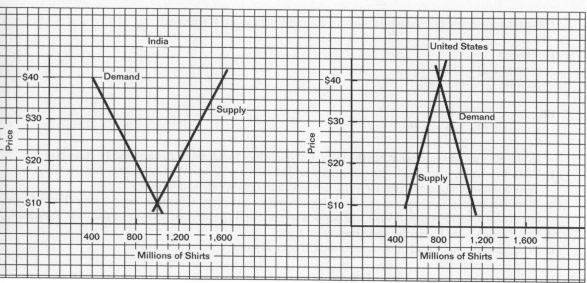

3. Assume that American producers are able to persuade the government to impose a quota limiting shirt imports to 200 million. Following imposition of the quota, what happens to prices, demand, production, and trade?

	Price	Domestic Demand	Domestic Production	Exports	Imports
India	_____	_____	_____	_____	_____
United States	_____	_____	_____	_____	_____

Compared to the free trade equilibrium described in question 2, shirt prices have increased in (India/the United States) and decreased in _____. The production of shirts has increased in _____ and decreased in _____.

4. What tariff would have yielded the same results as the quota of 200 million shirts? _____.

5. Discuss the reasons for choosing between a tariff and a quota.

SUPPLEMENTARY EXERCISES

1. Demand and supply for widgets in Baulmovia and Bilandia are as follows:

   Baulmovia
   Demand: $Q = 156 - 7P$
   Supply: $Q = -44 + 18P$

   Bilandia
   Demand: $Q = 320 - 10P$
   Supply: $Q = -20 + 10P$

   a. In the absence of trade, what are the price and quantity of widgets in Baulmovia? In Bilandia?
   b. With free trade, what is the one common world price for widgets? Which country exports widgets? Which country imports widgets? What is the volume of exports and imports?
   c. Manufacturers in the importing country have convinced the government to impose a tariff on widget imports of $4.50 a widget. What will happen to trade and the price of widgets in the two countries?
   d. What quota would have the same impact on trade?
   e. What factors might lead one to prefer a tariff over a quota?

2. This exercise offers another review of the law of comparative advantage.

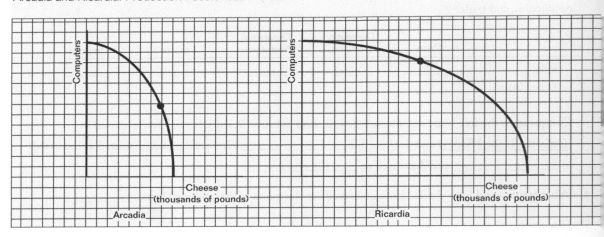

Figure 35-2

Arcadia and Ricardia: Production Possibilities Frontiers

Figure 35-2 shows the production possibilities frontier for Arcadia and Ricardia. For every computer they buy, citizens of each country want to consume 1,000 pounds of cheese. As a result production and consumption in each country takes place at the dot on the frontier. Some have argued that citizens in both countries could consume more of both goods if each country concentrated production on the good in which it has a comparative advantage and traded for the other good.

In order to construct a numerical example, assume that at the dot the slope of the PPF for Arcadia is −2 while the slope of the PPF for Ricardia is −1/2. (Arcadia must give up two computers for an additional 1,000 pounds of cheese, while Ricardia can increase the production of cheese by 2,000 pounds at the cost of only one less computer.)

a. Which country has a comparative advantage in the production of computers? _____

b. Which country has a comparative advantage in the production of cheese? _____

c. Construct a numerical example that shows how what changes in production and what pattern of trade would allow both countries to consume outside their PPF.

3. Cimonoce is a small country that produces wine and cloth. The production possibilities frontier for Cimonoce is

$$W = 324 - C^2$$

where W = millions of barrels of wine and C = millions of bolts of cloth.

a. Use a piece of graph paper. Label the vertical axis "wine" and the horizontal axis "cloth." Draw the production possibilities frontier.

b. Since Cimonoce is a small country, it can export or import cloth or wine without affecting world prices. World prices are such that Cimonoce can export one million barrels of wine for 750,000 bolts of cloth or it can export 750,000 bolts of cloth for one million barrels of wine. The government's chief economist argues that regardless of consumption preferences, Cimonoce should produce 14.4 million bolts of cloth and 10.8 million barrels of wine. Do you agree? Why? (Hint: Consider what a graph of consumption possibilities looks like. For any production combination of wine and cloth, Cimonoce's consumption possibilities are given by a negatively sloped straight line through the production point. The slope of the consumption possibilities line reflects world prices. A movement up the straight line to the left of the production point would imply exporting cloth in order to import and consume more wine. A movement down the straight line to the right would reflect exporting wine in order to import and consume more cloth. Exactly where Cimonoce chooses to consume is a matter of preferences, but its choice is constrained by its consumption possibilities line, which in turn is determined by Cimonoce's production choice and world prices for cloth and wine. Why does the production point 10.8 million barrels of wine and 14.4 million bolts of cloth offer the greatest consumption possibilities?)

ECONOMICS IN ACTION

TRADE IN TEXTILES

Since the end of World War II there has been a conscious effort to lower barriers to international trade. Part of this effort has been driven by the intellectual arguments in favor of the benefits of free trade and part has been driven by a strong feeling that protectionist pressures in the 1930s added to the depth and severity of the Great Depression. Much of the advance to date has come in the form of reduced tariff barriers resulting from complicated, multinational negotiations and treaties.

Sensitive areas where tariff reductions have been more difficult include textiles and clothing along with trade in agricultural products. Other areas of concern include trade in steel, services, and intellectual property like books and movies. With tariffs in many developed countries now eliminated or very low, increasing attention is being paid to nontariff barriers that limit trade. Nontariff barriers include policies like quotas, excessively detailed and time-consuming processing at ports of entry, and the strict adherence to rules and regulations that serve only to protect domestic producers.

Reaching an agreement on freer trade in textiles in the mid-1990s was only possible when it was proposed that changes be made over a 10-year period of adjustment. Thus, a complicated system of tariffs and quotas that had evolved since 1950 was scheduled for elimination at the beginning of 2005. The production of textiles has been important to many developing countries and full implementation of the 1995 Multi-Fibre Agreement was seen as a major concession that would aid economic development. One estimate projected a gain of 27 million jobs in developing countries from the elimination of tariffs and quotas on textiles.

As January 2005 approached, a number of countries were having second thoughts. Developing countries that had secured preferential quota arrangements were now facing international competition. The big new competitor was China, which would be able to export textiles without limit. The rules allowed for "safeguard" tariffs against Chinese textile exports that would permit an additional three years of adjustment. At the end of 2004, there were cries in the United States and Europe to adopt safeguard tariffs to resist an expected surge in textile exports from China.

Other voices argued for restraint, pointing out that the magnitude of expected adjustments in 2005 was due in part to most countries waiting to the last moment to eliminate quotas. While it appears that bulk production of basic clothes may concentrate in Asia, primarily China, India, and Pakistan, there were those who expected production for the fashion industry to concentrate in Turkey and Latin America.

Textile production in Africa was of special concern as it did not appear that African producers had the efficiency of Asian production or the proximity of Turkey and Latin America to markets in Europe and the United States. The economic literature on international trade argues that benefits within a country should be sufficient to provide trade adjustment help to workers in industries that cannot compete following a move to freer trade. The same principle ought to apply internationally, but it is not clear how such help might be organized.

1. What has happened to trade in textiles? Who have been the winners and losers from the elimination of tariffs and quotas? How large is the increase in textile exports from China? What about exports from other countries? Have any countries adopted safeguard tariffs and if so, under what conditions?

Sources: "Textile and China," *The Washington Post*, December 16, 2004; "Textile producers weave a web to restrict China: Less efficient poor nations fear they will lose rich-world trade when the global quota system ends this year," *Financial Times of London*, October 22, 2004. "Textile and Clothing Summary," Global Trade Negotiations Home Page, Center for International Development, Harvard University, May 2004.

Trade data on U.S. imports of textiles and apparel are available online from the Office of Textiles and Apparel, U.S. Department of Commerce, International Trade Administration: http://otexa.ita.doc.gov/mrspoint.htm and from the U.S. Census Bureau: http://www.census.gov/foreign-trade/statistics/index.html. Data on exports and imports from different countries is available from the World Trade Organization at http://www.wto.org/english/res_e/statis_e/its2002_e/its02_bysector_e.htm.

STUDY QUESTIONS

1. Why do countries trade with each other? Why don't they try to be self-sufficient in the production of all goods?

2. What is the difference between absolute advantage and comparative advantage? (Use a per capita production possibilities frontier to illustrate your answer.)

3. Why do economists argue that a country with an absolute advantage in the production of all goods can still gain from trade if it specializes in a manner consistent with the law of comparative advantage? (Consider a two-good, two-country example.)

4. Why isn't it possible for all countries to improve their balance of trade by simultaneously increasing exports and decreasing imports?

5. Why aren't a country's consumption possibilities limited by its production possibilities?

6. It is often asserted that for every tariff there is a corresponding quota in the sense of having the same impact on prices and production. Is this statement correct and if so what difference(s) would one policy make over the other?

7. Since higher prices following the imposition of a tariff or a quota will reduce domestic demand, how can these policies ever be in the interest of domestic producers?

8. How do you evaluate the arguments supporting strategic trade policies?

9. What is the role of trade adjustment assistance and why do many think it a necessary element of a policy that favors free trade?

10. What is the infant-industry argument? Do you believe it is ever a compelling argument? Why or why not?

11. Some industries argue for trade protection on the grounds of national defense. Do you believe this is ever a compelling argument? Why or why not?

12. "In order to increase the consumption possibilities of Americans, the United States should never prohibit dumping by foreign manufacturers." Do you agree? Why or why not?

13. Why isn't it obvious to many economists that the United States should enact tariffs to level the playing field and protect American workers from unfair competition from low-wage foreign workers?

485

ECONOMICS ONLINE

Data on American international trade is reported by several U.S. government offices.

U.S. Census Bureau

http://www.census.gov/ftp/pub/foreign-trade/www

Office of Trade and Economic Analysis, International Trade Administration

http://www.ita.doc.gov/

Data on American international accounts is available online from the Bureau of Economic Analysis, U.S. Department of Commerce

http://www.bea.gov/

Information on international trade from the World Trade Organization can be found through the WTO homepage.

http://www.wto.org

486

The International Monetary System: Order or Disorder?

36

Important Terms and Concepts

Exchange rate

Appreciation

Depreciation

Devaluation

Revaluation

Floating exchange rates

Purchasing-power parity theory

Fixed exchange rates

Balance of payments deficit and surplus

Current account

Capital account

Gold standard

Bretton Woods system

International Monetary Fund (IMF)

"Dirty" or "managed" float

Learning Objectives

After completing this chapter, you should be able to:

- identify the factors that help determine a country's exchange rate under a system of floating exchange rates.

- explain why an appreciation of the dollar against any other currency is simultaneously a depreciation of that currency against the dollar.

- distinguish between long-, medium-, and short-run factors that help determine the demand and supply of currencies.

- use a demand and supply diagram to show how changes in GDP, inflation, or interest rates can lead to appreciation or depreciation of the dollar under a system of floating exchange rates.

- show, on a supply-demand graph, how fixed exchange rates can lead to a balance of payments deficit or surplus.

- explain the difference between the current and capital accounts.

- explain why under a system of floating exchange rates a deficit on the current account will be accompanied by a surplus on the capital account.

- explain why, under the gold standard, countries lost control of their domestic money stock.

- describe the options, other than changing the exchange rate, that were available under the Bretton Woods system to a country wanting to eliminate a balance of payments deficit or surplus.

- explain why, under a system of fixed exchange rates, there was very little risk in speculating against an overvalued currency.

- explain how speculators can reduce the uncertainty exporters and importers face under a system of floating exchange rates.

CHAPTER REVIEW

Meeting: President Richard M. Nixon and H. R. Haldeman, Oval Office, June 23, 1972 (10:04–11:39 a.m.)

Haldeman: Bums is concerned about speculation against the lira.

Nixon: Well, I don't give a (expletive deleted) about the lira . . . There ain't a vote in it.

Source: Statement of Information: Appendix III, *Hearings before the Committee on the Judiciary,* House of Representatives, Ninety-third Congress, Second Session, May–June 1974, page 50.

Even American presidents now pay attention to exchange rates. So should you. Even if you are never president, exchange rates are important for all Americans. Consumers are affected by the price of imports, and jobs for workers can be affected by the price of exports and imports. This chapter discusses exchange rates, that is, the price of one currency in terms of another. The discussion in the text covers the economic factors that determine exchange rates, the implications of attempts by governments to fix exchange rates, and a review of recent history focusing on the evolution of the world's current mixed international monetary system.

Discussions of international monetary arrangements involve a whole new vocabulary of fixed and floating exchange rates, current and capital accounts, appreciating and depreciating currencies, and devaluations and revaluations. It may help you to keep the vocabulary straight if you remember that most of the analysis of international monetary arrangements is merely an application of the supply-demand analysis originally introduced in Chapter 4.

(1) Find out how much it would cost, in American dollars, to buy one Canadian dollar. This figure is the current _____ rate, expressed in American dollars. Many newspapers now publish exchange rates on a daily basis. A student in Canada could do the same thing and get a price for American dollars in terms of Canadian dollar. If you both call on the same day you should both get the same price (ignoring sales commissions).[1] If the American dollar price of one Canadian dollar increases, so that it takes more American dollars to buy one Canadian dollar, we say that the Canadian dollar has _____ relative to the American dollar. When it takes more American dollars to buy a Canadian dollar, it will take (fewer/more) Canadian dollars to buy one American dollar and we would say that the American dollar has _____ relative to the Canadian dollar.

(2) Under a system of floating exchange rates, exchange rates will be determined by market forces of _____ and _____. Consider an example that consists of just two currencies, the Japanese yen and the American dollar. The demand for yen comes from holders of American dollars who are interested in

(a)   Japanese exports, such as cars, cameras, and televisions;

(b)   Japanese physical assets, such as factories, office buildings, and land;

_____

[1]If in the United States, you get a price of 80 cents for one Canadian dollar. The Canadian student would get a price of 1.25 Canadian dollar for one American dollar. If x is the American dollar price of one Canadian, then $1/x$ is the Canadian dollar price of one American dollar.

488

(c) _____ Japanese financial assets, such as stocks and bonds.

The supply of Japanese yen also has three sources: the demand by Japanese for American (<u>exports/imports</u>), American _____ assets, and American _____ assets. (Note that the demand and supply of yen has an interpretation in terms of the demand and supply of dollars. The demand for yen by holders of dollars is simultaneously a(n) _____ of dollars. Understanding this mirror-image aspect of exchange rates should help keep the vocabulary and analysis straight.)

Under a system of floating rates, the equilibrium exchange rate will be at a level where demand equals supply. A change in any factor that affects demand or supply will change the exchange rate. For example, a sudden increase in demand for British wool on the part of Americans would shift the (<u>demand/supply</u>) curve for pounds. (3) The dollar price of pounds will (<u>increase/decrease</u>), a result economists call a(n) (<u>appreciation/depreciation</u>) of the pound in terms of the dollar. Conversely, a sudden increase in demand for California wines on the part of the English would shift the _____ curve of pounds and would mean a(n) (<u>appreciation/depreciation</u>) of the pound in terms of the dollar.

In the long run, the exchange rate between two currencies should be influenced by the prices of traded goods according to the theory of _____ _____ _____. In order that (4) its goods remain competitive on world markets, a country with a very high rate of inflation will see its exchange rate (<u>appreciate/depreciate</u>). In the medium run, a country that experiences an economic boom is likely to find its imports rising, a development that by itself should lead to a(n) _____ of its exchange rate. But if the economic boom means higher interest rates and strong investment opportunities that attract foreign investment, the result may be a(n) _____ of the exchange rate. Exchange rates, especially in the short run, will be affected by the movement of large pools of investment funds that are sensitive to international differences in interest rates. An increase in interest rates should attract funds, (<u>appreciating/depreciating</u>) the exchange rate.

Governments may try to peg the exchange rate. In fact, from the end of World War II until 1973, the world operated on a system of fixed exchange rates, established at the _____ Woods conference. (5) At the time, it was thought that fixed exchange rates were necessary to stimulate the growth of international trade, so countries could reap the benefits of specialization according to the law of comparative advantage. Pegging an exchange rate is very similar to any other sort of price control and is subject to similar problems.

If, say, the Japanese government pegs the exchange rate at too high a level, the supply of Japanese yen will exceed the demand for yen, and Japan will experience a balance of payments (<u>deficit/surplus</u>) If the government (6) pegs the rate too low, then (<u>demand/supply</u>) will exceed _____ and the result will be a balance of payments _____.

It is traditional to measure the demand and supply of currencies as either current or capital transactions. The current account includes private transactions for exports, imports, cross-border payments of interest, dividends, unilateral transfer, and gifts. The capital account includes private payments for financial investments and physical assets. Under a system of floating exchange rates, we know that any current account deficit

(7) must be offset by a capital account _____ as total demand equals total supply. Adjustments in the _____ _____ ensure the equality of the quantity demanded and supplied. Under a system of fixed exchange rates there may be an imbalance in private demand and supply requiring government intervention to maintain the exchange rate.

A government pegging its exchange rate and faced with a balance of payments deficit will need to use its

(8) holdings of international reserves, that is, foreign currencies, in order to (<u>buy/sell</u>) its own currency. A country faced with a balance of payments surplus will need to supply its currency to satisfy the demand of foreigners offering their currencies. As a result, it will find its international reserves (<u>increasing/decreasing</u>).

Under fixed exchange rates, most of the pressure for adjustment is placed on countries experiencing a bal-

(9) ance of payments (<u>deficit/surplus</u>). If nothing else, such a country will eventually run out of international reserves. If a country does not want to change its exchange rate, other adjustment options include monetary and fiscal policies that (<u>increase/decrease</u>) interest rates, (<u>increase/decrease</u>) the rate of inflation, or induce a general (<u>contraction/expansion</u>) in the level of economic activity. Many of these adjustments occurred automatically under the gold standard as a balance of payments deficit led to an outflow of gold and an automatic (<u>increase/reduction</u>) in the stock of money.

A major weakness of the Bretton Woods system of fixed exchange rates was that deficit countries disliked adjusting their domestic economies for balance of payments reasons rather than for domestic political and economic reasons. Another weakness was the special role accorded the U.S. dollar.[2]

In recent years many of the world's major industrialized countries have operated under a mixed system of fixed and floating rates. Some exchange rates are allowed to change on a daily basis in response to market forces. At the same time, many governments intervene by buying or selling currencies, hoping to influence the exchange rate to their advantage. Some have worried that floating exchange rates would be so volatile as to destroy world trade. However, market-determined prices need not be volatile, and importers and exporters can

(10) often relieve the business risk of changes in exchange rate by dealing with _____.

In January 1999, members of the European Union agreed to link their currencies at fixed exchange rates and,

(11) in January 2002 replaced their own currencies with the _____. While the common currency implies a system of fixed exchange rates among the euro countries, remember that there is a floating exchange rate between the euro and other currencies like there is between the dollar and yen.

The International Monetary Fund, or IMF, was established to oversee the fixed exchange rates established as part of the Bretton Woods agreement. Now the IMF provides loans to countries with significant balance of payments problems. These loans usually come with significant restrictions and conditions. Some critics have

---

[2]The United States has run a deficit on its current and capital account in recent years without seeming to be subject to the problems discussed in the text. Rather than the United States government having to buy dollars, foreign governments have been willing to buy dollars. See Economics in Action in the next chapter for additional discussion of this issue.

490

argued that IMF conditions only help to ensure that international investors from rich countries are protected while the contractionary macroeconomic policies bring hardship for local citizens.

IMPORTANT TERMS AND CONCEPTS QUIZ

Choose the best definition for each of the following terms.

1. _____ Exchange rate
2. _____ Appreciation
3. _____ Depreciation
4. _____ Devaluation
5. _____ Revaluation
6. _____ Floating exchange rates
7. _____ Purchasing-power parity theory
8. _____ Fixed exchange rates
9. _____ Balance of payments deficit
10. _____ Balance of payments surplus
11. _____ Current account balance
12. _____ Capital account balance
13. _____ Gold standard
14. _____ Bretton Woods system
15. _____ International Monetary Fund
16. _____ Dirty float

a. Decrease in the amount of foreign currency a unit of domestic currency can buy
b. Price of one currency in terms of another
c. Exchange rates determined in free market by supply and demand
d. Increase in official value of a currency
e. Value of currencies linked to the dollar whose value was linked to gold
f. System where exchange rates change in response to market forces, but with intervention by central banks
g. International agency that extends loans for infrastructure to developing countries
h. Amount by which quantity supplied of a country's currency exceeds quantity demanded
i. Balance of trade involving purchases and sales of financial and real assets
j. International agency that monitors exchange rate policies of member countries
k. Reduction in official value of a currency
l. Balance of trade in goods and services plus cross-border payments for interest, dividends, gifts, and unilateral transfers
m. System where currencies are defined in terms of gold
n. Increase in the amount of foreign currency a unit of domestic currency can buy
o. Exchange rates set by the government
p. Amount by which quantity demanded of a country's currency exceeds quantity supplied
q. Idea that exchange rates adjust to reflect differences in the prices of traded goods

BASIC EXERCISES

1. **Purchasing-Power Parity**

   This exercise is designed to illustrate the theory of purchasing-power parity.
   Assume that the United States and France are the only suppliers of wine on the world market. Consumers of wine are indifferent between French and California wines and buy whichever is cheaper. Initially, the dollar-euro exchange rate is assumed to be $1.20 to the euro and California wine sells for $12 a bottle.

491

Ignoring transportation costs, the initial dollar price of French wines must be $12. Accordingly, we know that the initial franc price of French wine is 10 euros a bottle.

Assume now that inflation in the United States has raised the price of California wine to $15.60 a bottle, while inflation in France has raised the price of French wine to 12 euros. Based on this data, answer each of the following:

a. If the exchange rate is fixed at $1.20 to the euro, what is the new dollar price of French wine?

$_____. What would happen to the sales of French and California wines? If wine is the only good traded between France and the United States, what happens to the U.S. balance of payments?

b. If the dollar-euro exchange rate is free to adjust, what dollar price of a euro is necessary to equalize the dollar (or euro) price of both wines? _____ This change in the dollar price of a euro is a(n) (appreciation/depreciation) of the euro and a(n) _____ of the dollar.

c. Assuming that the change in the price of wine is typical of the change in other prices, who had the higher rate of inflation? _____

d. From questions a and c, it is seen that the purchasing-power parity theory implies that under fixed exchange rates a currency with more inflation will experience a balance of payments (deficit/surplus).

e. From questions b and c, it is seen that the purchasing-power parity theory implies that under floating exchange rates a currency with more inflation will (appreciate/depreciate).

2. **The Risks of Speculation against Fixed Exchange Rates**

Assume that in the fall of 1967 you are treasurer for a large multinational corporation with 10 million British pounds to invest. The fixed official exchange rate vis-à-vis the U.S. dollar has been $2.80. At this exchange rate Britain has been experiencing large and growing deficits in its balance of payments and has been financing this deficit by buying pounds with foreign currencies. Britain's holdings of foreign currencies are running low, and there is a general feeling that Britain will have to devalue the pound. Exactly how large the devaluation will be and exactly when it will occur are uncertain, but given the history of chronic deficits, there is absolutely no chance that the pound will be revalued.

Complete **Table 36-1** to measure the risks of speculating against the pound. (Changing from pounds to dollars and back again will involve transaction costs. Table 36-1 abstracts from these costs, which are apt to be small.)

Table 36-1

Speculation Against the Pound

	(1)	(2)	(3)
Initial holdings of pounds	£10,000,000	£10,000,000	£10,000,000
Current exchange rate	$2.80	$2.80	$2.80
Number of dollars if you sell pounds for dollars	_____	_____	_____
Possible new exchange rate	$2.80*	$2.60	$2.40
Number of pounds following reconversion to pounds after devaluation	_____	_____	_____

*This exchange rate assumes Britain takes other steps and does not devalue the pound.

492

What is the worst outcome?

As the talk of devaluation heats up, what are you apt to do? How will your actions affect the British balance of payments deficit and the pressures for devaluation?

Table 36-2

Dollar–Yen Exchange Rates/Balance of Payments

Event	Shift in Demand Curve for Yen (left, right, no shift)	Shift in Supply Curve for Yen (left, right, no shift)	Floating Rates Appreciation or Depreciation of Yen	Fixed Rates Change in Japanese Balance of Payments*
a. Federal Reserve policy raises interest rates in the United States.				
b. A change in tastes increases American demand for Japanese electronics.				
c. The U.S. economy enters a recession.				
d. Major labor strikes in Japan have resulted in a sudden increase in the (yen) price of Japanese goods.				
e. A terrible typhoon destroys the Japanese rice crop and increases the demand for American rice.				

*Appropriate answers would be deficit, surplus, or no change.

3. **Determination of Exchange Rates**

This exercise is designed to contrast the impact of similar events under systems of fixed and floating exchange rates.

Assume that the world is divided into two countries, the United States and Japan. **Table 36-2** lists a number of events. Fill in the squares in the table to analyze the impact of these events on the dollar–yen exchange rate under a system of floating rates, and the Japanese balance of payments under a system of fixed exchange rates. Assume that each event takes place from an initial equilibrium that under fixed exchange rates entails neither a deficit nor a surplus. **Figure 36-1** illustrates such an equilibrium at an initial exchange rate of 110 yen per dollar.

Figure 36-1

Demand and Supply: Yen

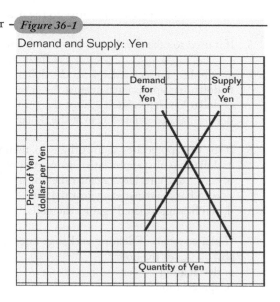

493

SELF-TESTS FOR UNDERSTANDING

TEST A

Circle the most appropriate answer.

1. The exchange rate between the American dollar and the Mexican peso tells us
   a. how much gold each currency is worth.
   b. the dollar price of a peso and the peso price of a dollar.
   c. whether the Mexicans are running a balance of payments deficit.
   d. how many pounds each currency will purchase.

2. If an American can buy a Polish zloty for 40 cents, how many zloty must a Pole spend to buy a dollar?
   a. 0.4 zloty
   b. 4 zloty
   c. 2.5 zloty
   d. 40 zloty

3. If the euro appreciates relative to the British pound, then a euro will buy
   a. fewer pounds than before.
   b. the same number of pounds as before.
   c. more pounds than before.

4. If under a system of floating exchange rates the Mexican peso used to cost 20 cents and now costs 10 cents, one would say that the _____. (There may be more than one correct answer.)
   a. peso has appreciated relative to the dollar
   b. peso has depreciated relative to the dollar
   c. dollar has appreciated relative to the peso
   d. dollar has depreciated relative to the peso

5. If it used to take one euro to buy one dollar and now it takes 0.80 euros, one would say that the _____. (There may be more than one correct answer.)
   a. euro has appreciated against the dollar
   b. dollar has appreciated against the euro
   c. dollar has depreciated against the euro
   d. euro has depreciated against the dollar

6. If the yen appreciates against the euro, then we know that the
   a. dollar has also appreciated against the yen.
   b. euro has appreciated against the dollar.
   c. euro has depreciated against the yen.
   d. yen has appreciated against the dollar.

7. Under a system of floating exchange rates, an increase in the demand for dollars by foreigners will cause a(n) _____ of the dollar.
   a. devaluation
   b. appreciation
   c. revaluation
   d. depreciation

494

8. Which of the following, by itself, would cause an appreciation of the dollar? (There may be more than one correct answer.)
   a. an increase in American GDP
   b. an increase in foreign GDP
   c. a decrease in American interest rates
   d. a decrease in foreign interest rates
   e. an increase in inflation in the United States
   f. an increase in inflation in the rest of the world

9. Which of the following, by itself, would cause a depreciation of the dollar?
   a. a decrease in American GDP
   b. an increase in foreign GDP
   c. an increase in American interest rates
   d. a decrease in foreign interest rates
   e. a decrease in inflation in the United States
   f. a decrease in inflation in the rest of the world

10. Under a system of floating exchange rates, which one of the following conditions will tend to depreciate the Japanese yen relative to the British pound?
    a. an economic boom in Britain
    b. a higher level of inflation in Japan than in Britain
    c. an increase in interest rates in Japan
    d. a sudden increase in British demand for imports from Japan

11. Which of the following would lead to an appreciation of the peso relative to the dollar?
    a. a recession in America
    b. less inflation in America than in Mexico
    c. an increase in Mexican interest rates
    d. a boom in Mexico

12. Purchasing-power parity theory says that
    a. only the volume of exports and imports determines exchange rates; interest rates have nothing to do with exchange rates.
    b. all countries are better off with a system of fixed exchange rates.
    c. adjustment of fixed exchange rates should be symmetrical between deficit and surplus countries.
    d. in the long run, exchange rates adjust to reflect differences in price levels between countries.

13. If inflation in United States is at an annual rate of 2 percent and inflation in Brazil is at 8 percent, then the purchasing-power parity theory suggests that in the long run the dollar price of one Brazilian real will
    a. increase at an annual rate of 8 percent.
    b. decrease at an annual rate of 6 percent.
    c. increase at an annual rate of 6 percent.
    d. increase at an annual rate of 2 percent.

14. In question 13, one would say that the higher rate of inflation in Brazil results in a(n)
    a. depreciation of the real relative to the dollar.
    b. appreciation of the real relative to the dollar.
    c. depreciation of the dollar relative to the real.
    d. cross-subsidy of the real by the dollar.

15. Assume that the real–dollar exchange rate is fixed, that Brazil and the United States are the only two countries in the world, and that inflation rates differ as described in question 13. Which country will have a balance of payments deficit?
    a. the United States
    b. Brazil

16. When accounting for American international transactions, which of the following would be counted in the current account?
    a. Karen and David buy a case of French wine.
    b. Jared buys shares on the Italian stock market.
    c. The Japanese government buys a ten-year U.S. government security.
    d. Northwest Airlines buys an airport hanger in Tokyo.

17. From an initial position of equilibrium under a system of fixed exchange rates, which of the following would lead to a balance of payments deficit? (There may be more than one correct answer.)
    a. a reduction in foreign interest rates
    b. an increase in domestic interest rates
    c. domestic inflation in excess of inflation in the rest of the world
    d. a devaluation by a country's major trading partner

18. If the country of Zenon tries to fix its exchange rate at a level above that determined by demand and supply, it will likely _____. (There may be more than one correct answer.)
    a. run a balance of payments deficit
    b. run a balance of payments surplus
    c. find its exports being priced out of world markets
    d. see reduced interest by foreigners in investing in Zenon

19. Which one of the following policies would not help to eliminate a deficit under a system of fixed exchange rates?
    a. monetary and fiscal policies to raise the level of unemployment
    b. a devaluation of the exchange rate
    c. monetary and fiscal policies that increase the rate of inflation
    d. a change in monetary policy that increases interest rates

20. If it takes 9 cents to buy one Swedish kronor and $0.90 to buy one euro, then how many kronor should it take to buy one euro?
    a. $(0.09 \div 0.90) = .10$
    b. $(0.90 \div 0.09) = 10$
    c. $(1.0 \div 0.09) = 11.111$
    d. $(1.0 \div 0.90) = 1.111$

496

TEST B

Circle T or F for true or false.

T F   1. If one dollar previously cost 120 yen and now costs 100 yen, the dollar has appreciated relative to the yen.

T F   2. A pure system of floating exchange rates requires government intervention—purchases and sales of its own currency—in order to work properly.

T F   3. Under a system of floating exchange rates, a sudden increase in the demand for U.S. exports will lead to appreciation of the dollar relative to other currencies.

T F   4. Under a system of fixed exchange rates, a sudden increase in the demand for imports by Americans would increase the U.S. balance of payments deficit (or reduce the size of the surplus).

T F   5. Purchasing-power parity is a theory of the long-run determination of exchange rates.

T F   6. Under a system of fixed exchange rates, a country that attempts to peg its exchange rate at an artificially low level will end up with a balance of payments surplus.

T F   7. Today, world international monetary relations are based on the gold standard.

T F   8. A major advantage of the gold standard was that countries could control their own domestic money stock.

T F   9. The Bretton Woods gold-exchange system established a system of fixed exchange rates based on the convertibility of dollars into gold.

T F 10. Under the Bretton Woods system of fixed exchange rates, both surplus and deficit countries felt the same pressure to correct any imbalance in their balance of payments.

SUPPLEMENTARY EXERCISE

WORLD TRADE UNDER FIXED AND FLEXIBLE EXCHANGE RATES

Some observers worried that the introduction of a system of floating exchange rates would have adverse effects on the volume of world trade, as exporters and importers would have trouble coping with short-run fluctuations in exchange rates. You might compare the growth in world trade with the growth in world output. The IMF regularly publishes estimates of world output and world trade as part of its World Economic Outlook. Start at http://www.imf.org/external/index.htm. Click on the link for the latest World Economic Outlook and then click on the link for the WEO database. Has trade grown faster than output or have floating exchange rates held back the growth of world trade?

ECONOMICS IN ACTION

HEDGING ONE'S INTERNATIONAL INVESTMENTS

The movement of exchange rates complicates the lives of companies and individual investors who by choice or necessity have to deal with international investments. Imagine that interest rates in Britain offer a better return than in the United States. Do you want to convert your dollars into pounds, invest in Britain, and then convert back to dollars? The higher interest rate may look tempting, but any advantage of higher interest rates in Britain could be completely offset by an adverse movement in the dollar/pound exchange rate. For example, assume that a pound costs $1.75 when you invest to take advantage of a 10 percent interest rate in Britain compared to a 5 percent interest rate in the United States. What happens if at the end of the year, when you go to convert your pounds back into dollars, the pound has depreciated to $1.55 or appreciated to $1.95? As the example shows, changes in exchange rates can have a major impact on international investors and on the dollar value of international earnings of corporations.[3] Economists would say that these changes add to the variability and risk of international investments. If potential returns are sufficiently attractive, there is an incentive to learn how to manage the associated risk.

It is often argued that one should fully hedge international investments. That is, if you make an investment in Britain you should at the same time take other actions that lock in the exchange rate you will use to convert your pounds back into dollars. While such actions mean you would not benefit from an appreciation of the pound, you would also avoid the loss that would accompany a depreciation. The use of futures markets—that is, dealing with speculators in foreign exchange—is one way to lock in a particular exchange rate.

How important is it to hedge one's international investments? Economist Kenneth Froot argues that whether one should hedge international investments depends upon one's time horizon. Using almost 200 years' worth of data on exchange rates between the dollar and the pound along with investment returns in the United States and the United Kingdom, Froot argues that hedging reduced the variance of international investments that were held for short horizons (e.g., one or two years). However, he also found that as one's investment horizon lengthened, there was less need to hedge international investments. How can this be?

Consider the following simple example. Assume that over longer time horizons, exchange rates tend toward levels defined by purchasing-power parity, real interest rates are the same in the United States and Britain, and nominal investment returns reflect any differences in inflation. If inflation is higher in Britain, then nominal interest rates in Britain should be higher than in the United States. Note that nominal interest rates in Britain are measured in terms of pounds while in the United States they are measured in terms of dollars. If exchange rates are determined by purchasing-power parity, the pound will depreciate at a rate that just offsets the difference in nominal interest rates. A U.S. investor would not be disadvantaged by the depreciation in the pound and would receive no benefit from dealing with speculators who would incorporate the difference in rates of inflation into the future exchange rates they offer investors. This view suggests that one should evaluate particular investments

---

[3]Changes in exchange rates are not just an issue for a system of flexible exchange rates. The system of fixed rates under the Bretton Woods agreement included long periods of stable exchange rates marked by sudden and often large adjustments of official exchange rates. If one of those large changes occurred when you had made an international investment, you could be much worse or better off.

in the United States or Britain on their merits and that markets may work to minimize the risks associated with changes in the exchange rates if one is investing for the long term.[4]

How do businesses respond to the ups and downs of the dollar? A story in *The New York Times* talked about how Eastman Kodak and other companies deal with changes in exchange rates. These changes are of growing importance as American companies increase foreign operations. David Fiedler, director of foreign exchange for Kodak, reported that in the short term he uses financial hedges to protect against changes in exchange rates. Over the longer term he views questions of foreign exchange as a "business problem like any other business problem." That is, exchange rate risk is something that should be given careful consideration from the very beginning, when making decisions about markets, suppliers, and production sites. "Before 1988, Mr. Fiedler . . . often had to respond to currency swings within minutes after a phone call about foreign developments startled him from sleep. 'That's a real motivator to think of another way,' he said."

1. If you were to make a personal financial investment in a foreign stock market, in what market would you invest? How do you evaluate the exchange rate risks of your choice?

2. What strategies might business follow, other than financial hedges, to minimize the risks associated with international operations?

Sources: "Companies Learn to Live with Dollar's Volatility," *The New York Times,* August 31, 1992; Kenneth A. Froot, "Currency Hedging over Long Horizons," Working Paper No. 4355, National Bureau of Economic Research, May 1993.

STUDY QUESTIONS

1. If you know the dollar price of a euro, how can you figure out how many euros it takes to buy a dollar?

2. What is the difference between an appreciation and a depreciation of the dollar? Which is better for American tourists? For American exporters?

3. What factors would cause an appreciation of the dollar? What factors would cause depreciation?

4. Is it possible for the dollar to appreciate against the pound and, at the same time, for the pound to appreciate against the dollar? Why?

5. What is meant by purchasing-power parity? How is it possible for exchange rates to vary from levels determined by purchasing-power parity?

6. How did the gold standard work to maintain fixed exchange rates?

7. What was the difference between the gold standard and the Bretton Woods system?

---

[4]Froot's argument is controversial. Measures of the returns one might have received in the past are no guarantee of what one will receive in the future. Even if over the long term one need not worry about movements in exchange rates, an investment that does poorly in either country will have been a mistake.

8. What is a balance of payments deficit? Is it possible to have an overall deficit under a system of floating exchange rates? Fixed exchange rates?

9. What is meant by the current account? The capital account? How are these measures related to a country's balance of payments?

10. Under a system of fixed exchange rates, what policies might a country adopt to eliminate a balance of payments deficit? Surplus?

11. Who bore most of the burden for adjustment under the Bretton Woods system, deficit or surplus countries? Why wasn't the burden of adjustment equal?

12. Under fixed exchange rates, balance of payment deficits reflect an overvalued exchange rate. The overvalued exchange rate increases the price of a country's exports. A devaluation would help to correct the balance of payments deficit by lowering the price of exports, increasing the demand for exports, and increasing employment in export industries. Yet most countries have resisted devaluation even when facing chronic deficits. What do you think explains this reluctance?

13. When would a country prefer a system of fixed exchange rates and when might it prefer a system of floating exchange rates?

14. What steps might exporters and importers take to minimize the risk of currency fluctuations under a system of floating exchange rates?

15. Why is it said that under fixed exchange rates currency speculation was destabilizing, while under floating exchange rates it is likely to be stabilizing?

16. What is meant by the term "dirty" or "managed" float?

17. What is the IMF and how effective have its policies been?

18. What are the advantages/disadvantages for Europe of adopting the euro?

ECONOMICS ONLINE

You can get up-to-the-minute and historical information about exchange rates at a number of web sites.

Current information is available at:

Federal Reserve Bank of New York:

> http://www.newyorkfed.org/markets/fxrates/noon.cfm

Bloomberg:

> http://www.bloomberg.com/markets/currencies/fxc.html

CNN Financial:

http://money.cnn.com/markets/currencies/

The Federal Reserve Bank of St. Louis posts historical daily and monthly data on exchange rates at

http://research.stlouisfed.org/fred2/categories/15

The Oanda exchange rate converter allows you to find the exchange rate between any of 164 currencies back to January 1, 1990.

http://www.oanda.com/converter/classic

Exchange Rates and the Macroeconomy

37

Important Terms and Concepts

Open economy

Exchange rate

Appreciation

Depreciation

International capital flows

Closed economy

Trade deficit

$(X - IM) = (S - I) - (G - T)$

Learning Objectives

After completing this chapter, you should be able to:

- explain how an appreciation or depreciation of the exchange rate affects net exports.

- show how an appreciation or depreciation of the exchange rate affects real GDP and the price of domestically produced goods by shifting the aggregate demand and aggregate supply curves appropriately.

- describe how changes in interest rates affect international capital flows and the exchange rate.

- explain why the reaction of international capital flows to changes in interest rates works to offset the impact of changes in fiscal policy.

- explain why the reaction of international capital flows to changes in interest rates works to enhance the impact of changes in monetary policy.

- explain in what way government deficits and trade deficits are linked.

- explain how a change in the mix of fiscal and monetary policy affects macroeconomic variables such as GDP, real interest rates, prices, the trade deficit, and the exchange rate.

CHAPTER REVIEW

This chapter integrates the discussion of international trade and exchange rates of the preceding two chapters with the earlier discussions of income determination and fiscal and monetary policy.

(1)   An economy that did not trade with any other economy would be called a(n) _____ economy. Today all industrial economies and most developing economies have extensive links with other economies through trade in goods and services and financial assets. Such economies are called _____ economies. These international linkages can affect important macroeconomic outcomes such as GDP and prices. While a complete and rigorous examination of these linkages is the stuff of more advanced courses in economics, we can use the model of income determination that we developed in earlier chapters to shed light on a number of important issues.

We start with a review of factors affecting the demand for exports and imports. As we saw earlier, the demand for exports and imports is influenced by income and prices. A decrease in foreign income will

(2) (decrease/increase) the demand for American exports and is an important reason why economic fluctuations abroad (are/are not) felt in the United States.

Exports and imports are also influenced by changes in the exchange rate, as these changes alter the relative

(3) price of foreign and domestic goods. An appreciation of the dollar makes foreign goods (less/more) expensive. The result is likely to be a(n) (decrease/increase) in American imports and a(n) _____ in American exports. Putting these two effects together shows that an appreciation of the exchange rate will lead to a(n) (decrease/increase) in net exports, $(X - IM)$. Similar reasoning shows that a depreciation of the dollar should lead to a(n) _____ in exports, a(n) _____ in imports, and a(n) _____ in net exports.

A change in net exports that comes from a change in exchange rates is analogous to any other autonomous

(4) change in spending. It shifts the expenditure schedule and leads to a (movement along/shift in) the aggregate demand curve. More precisely, following an appreciation of the dollar, net exports decline, the expenditure schedule shifts (down/up), and the aggregate demand curve shifts to the (left/right). Opposite results follow from a depreciation of the dollar.

A change in exchange rates can also lead to a shift in the aggregate supply curve through its impact on the price of imported intermediate goods. An appreciation of the dollar makes imported inputs (less/more) expen-

(5) sive. This result can be modeled as a(n) (downward/upward) shift in the aggregate supply curve. A depreciation of the dollar makes imported inputs _____ expensive and leads to a(n) _____ shift in the aggregate supply curve.

Once we understand the impact of a change in interest rates on international capital flows and on the exchange rate, we will have all the pieces necessary to examine how fiscal and monetary policy work in an open economy with flexible exchange rates. We saw in the previous chapter that an increase in interest rates is apt

(6) to (decrease/increase) the demand by foreigners for American financial assets. This change in the demand for

504

dollars should lead to a(n) (appreciation/depreciation) of the dollar. Tracing through the impact of this capital-flow-induced change in the exchange rate is the key to understanding how fiscal and monetary policy work in an open economy.

To review, consider a change in fiscal policy. A move to expansionary fiscal policy, say a(n) (decrease/increase) in taxes, would shift the expenditure schedule (up/down) and shift the aggregate demand curve to the (7) (right/left). For a closed economy where interest rates do not change, that would be the end of the story. But, if as is likely, the fiscal stimulus results in higher interest rates, there is more to the story. The impact of higher interest rates on international capital flows will lead to a(n) (appreciation/depreciation) in the exchange rate. This change in the exchange rate will shift the aggregate demand curve to the (left/right) and shift the aggregate supply curve (down/up). The shift in the aggregate demand curve, induced by the change in the exchange rate, works to (enhance/offset) the original expansionary change in fiscal policy. The shift in the aggregate supply curve works to (lower/raise) prices and to (increase/decrease) output. If the shift in the aggregate supply curve induced by the change in exchange rates were large enough, it could offset the impact on output from the exchange-rate-induced shift in the aggregate demand curve. Evidence suggests that for the United States, the shift in the aggregate supply curve is small relative to that of the aggregate demand curve and that, on net, the shifts in the two curves work to (enhance/offset) the impact of expansionary fiscal policy on output.

A move to restrictive monetary policy can be analyzed in the same way. The initial effects will include an increase in interest rates that leads to a(n) (appreciation/depreciation) of the exchange rate. The impact of the (8) change in the exchange rate will (enhance/offset) the original restrictive change in monetary policy.

Income and product definition of GDP can be manipulated to illustrate the important link between government budget deficits and trade deficits.[2]

$$(X - IM) = (S - I) - (G - T).$$

If the government deficit increases, that is, if $(G - T)$ becomes larger, then $(S - I)$ must increase and/or $(X - IM)$ must decrease. For $(S - I)$ to increase either private savings must increase or private investment will need to decrease. A decrease in $(X - IM)$ means that either exports decrease or imports increase, i.e., a larger trade deficit. As we have seen, in a world of flexible exchange rates, any deficit on the current account must be offset by a surplus on the capital account. Thus a trade deficit will be associated with a net capital inflow, that is, increased indebtedness to foreigners. It is changes in income, interest rates, exchange rates, and prices that enforce the link between savings, investment, budget deficits, trade deficits, and international capital flows. During the 1990s the reduction in the federal government deficit did not result in a smaller trade deficit because domestic savings (decreased/increased) and domestic investment _____.

The analysis would also be complete if the Fed conducts monetary policy by fixing interest rates regardless of what happens to fiscal policy.
Remember that on the income side GDP $= Y = DI + T = C + S + T$ while on the product side GDP $= Y = C + I + G + (X - IM)$. Since both expressions equal GDP, we can set $C + S + T = C + I + G + (X - IM)$. Canceling C on both sides of the equal sign and rearranging terms yields the expression above. This expression can also be written as $G + I + X = S + T + IM$. In terms of the circular flow diagram we saw earlier, this formulation says that injections must equal leakages.

Is the American trade deficit a problem? The answer to this question depends upon whether capital inflows are a market response to extravagant spending that result in high interest rates in the United States attracts foreign capital or the result of an autonomous increase in foreign demand for investment in the United States. The former suggests an economy spending beyond its means while the latter suggests a strong economy in which people want to invest. More generally, individuals and firms borrow from "foreigners" all the time. If they use these funds wisely, for example to invest future income, financing the borrowing need not be a special burden. On the other hand, if there is nothing to show for the increased debt, the result may be significant financial problems. There is a legitimate concern about how long large trade deficits and capital inflows can continue. Is there a limit to the willingness of foreigners to accumulate American assets and what happens if and when foreigners no longer want to do so?

A number of suggestions have been made to reduce the American trade deficit. For a number of years, many argued for a change in the mix of fiscal and monetary policy. According to this view, the increase in the American trade deficit during the 1980s was the result of expansionary fiscal policy and tight monetary policy. Reversing these actions, could work in reverse and lower the trade deficit as long as other factors, specifically the difference between domestic savings and investments, did not change. Rapid economic growth abroad would increase American (exports/imports). Protectionism would lower imports, but retaliation by foreign governments could (lower/raise) American exports with little change in net exports. For any of these measures to work, the accounting identity of $(X - IM) = (S - I) - (G - T)$ shows that any reduction in the trade deficit will require a combination of lower budget deficits, higher savings, or lower investment.

IMPORTANT TERMS AND CONCEPTS QUIZ

Choose the best definition for each of the following terms.

1. _____ Net exports
2. _____ Closed economy
3. _____ Open economy
4. _____ Trade deficit
5. _____ International capital flows

a. Balance of payments accounting for exports and imports
b. Graph depicting response of inflation to changes in the exchange rate
c. Economy that trades with other economies
d. Difference between exports and imports
e. Interest-sensitive money flows between countries
f. Economy that does not trade with other economies

BASIC EXERCISES

This exercise is designed to review how the operation of fiscal and monetary policy is affected by interest-sensitive capital flows in an open economy.

1. **Table 37-1** is designed to help you review the impact of changes in the exchange rate on various macroeconomic variables. First, complete the column for an appreciation of the exchange rate. Then

506

complete the column for a depreciation of the exchange rate. Indicate how each variable changes, i.e., increases or decreases, shifts left, right, up or down, as appropriate. Be sure you can explain why each variable shows the change you have indicated. If the change in GDP and the price level seems ambiguous, see if you can resolve the ambiguity by assuming, as in the text, that any shift in the aggregate demand curve is greater than the shift in the aggregate supply curve.

Table 37-1

Impact of Changes in the Exchange Rate

Macroeconomic Variable	Exchange Rate Appreciation	Exchange Rate Depreciation
Exports		
Imports		
Net Exports		
Expenditure Schedule		
Aggregate Demand Curve		
Aggregate Supply Curve		
Real GDP		
Price Level		

2. **Table 37-2** is designed to analyze the impact on GDP and the price level of changes in fiscal and monetary policy. The completed upper portion of the table ignores any impact on exchange rates. Remembering that changes in interest rates are likely to influence the international investment of funds and hence the demand for dollars, complete Table 37-2 to determine whether capital flows offset or enhance these changes in monetary and fiscal policy. You should first determine how the exchange rate is affected and then consider the impact of the change in the exchange rate on GDP and prices. Finally, combine your results from the change in policy and the change in exchange rates to determine the overall impact. **Figure 37-1** may be helpful when completing Table 37-2.

Figure 37-1

Aggregate Demand and Aggregate Supply

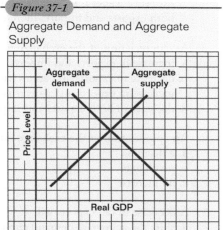

Table 37-2

Fiscal Policy in an Open Economy

	Decrease In G	Decrease In Taxes	Open Market Sale	Open Market Purchase
Aggregate Demand Curve	Left	Right	Left	Right
Real GDP	Down	Up	Down	Up
Price Level	Down	Up	Down	Up
Interest Rate	Down	Up	Up	Down
Exchange Rate				
Real GDP				
Price Level				
Overall Impact				
Real GDP				
Price Level				

3. What general conclusion can you draw about the effectiveness of monetary and fiscal policy in a world of interest-sensitive capital flows and flexible exchange rates?

SELF-TESTS FOR UNDERSTANDING

TEST A

Circle the most appropriate answer.

1. An increase in foreign GDP is likely to lead to
   a. a decrease in our exports.
   b. little if any change in our exports.
   c. an increase in our exports.

2. An appreciation of the exchange rate will make
   a. both exports and imports cheaper.
   b. exports more expensive for foreigners but imports cheaper for domestic citizens.
   c. exports cheaper for foreigners but imports more expensive for domestic citizens.
   d. both exports and imports more expensive.

3. An appreciation of the exchange rate will lead to a(n)
   a. increase in exports and imports.
   b. decrease in exports and an increase in imports.
   c. increase in exports and a decrease in imports.
   d. decrease in both exports and imports.

4. An appreciation of the exchange rate will lead to _____ in net exports.
   a. a decrease
   b. no change
   c. an increase

5. A decrease in net exports will
   a. shift the aggregate demand curve to the left.
   b. have no impact on the aggregate demand curve.
   c. shift the aggregate demand curve to the right.

6. An appreciation of the exchange rate will
   a. shift the aggregate supply curve up.
   b. have no impact on the aggregate supply curve.
   c. shift the aggregate supply curve down.

7. Evidence suggests that when the exchange rate changes, shifts in the aggregate demand curve will _____ shifts in the aggregate supply curve.
   a. be smaller than
   b. just offset
   c. be larger than

8. On balance, an appreciation of the exchange rate should tend to
   a. raise real GDP and raise the price of domestically produced goods.
   b. raise real GDP but lower the price of domestically produced goods.
   c. lower real GDP but raise the price of domestically produced goods.
   d. lower real GDP and lower the price of domestically produced goods.

508

9. A depreciation of the exchange rate tends to
   a. raise real GDP and raise the price of domestically produced goods.
   b. raise real GDP but lower the price of domestically produced goods.
   c. lower real GDP but raise the price of domestically produced goods.
   d. lower real GDP and lower the price of domestically produced goods.

10. Higher foreign interest rates are likely to be followed by an _____. (There may be more than one correct answer.)
    a. inflow of international capital
    b. increase in foreign investments by domestic citizens, i.e., a capital outflow
    c. appreciation of the exchange rate
    d. increase in net exports

11. An increase in domestic interest rates should lead to which one of the following?
    a. capital outflow
    b. appreciation of the dollar
    c. increase in exports
    d. upward shift in the expenditure schedule

12. An appreciation in the dollar vis-à-vis other currencies should lead to all but which one of the following?
    a. a decrease in exports
    b. an increase in imports
    c. a shift of the aggregate demand curve to the right
    d. a downward shift of the aggregate supply curve

13. A move to expansionary fiscal policy will tend to lead to all but which one of the following?
    a. an increase in interest rates
    b. an appreciation of the dollar
    c. a decrease in American imports
    d. an increase in the American trade deficit

14. A move to expansionary monetary policy will tend to lead to all but which one of the following?
    a. a decrease in interest rates
    b. an appreciation of the dollar
    c. an upward shift in the expenditure schedule
    d. an increase in inflationary pressures

15. Taking account of interest-sensitive international capital flows means that in an open economy the impact of fiscal policy is
    a. smaller than in a closed economy.
    b. the same as in a closed economy.
    c. larger than in a closed economy.

16. Taking account of interest-sensitive international capital flows means that in an open economy the impact of monetary policy is
    a. smaller than in a closed economy.
    b. the same as in a closed economy.
    c. larger than in a closed economy.

17. In an open economy that trades with other countries,
    a. $IM - X = (S - I) + (G - T)$.
    b. $X - IM = (S - I) - (G - T)$.
    c. $X - IM = (I - S) - (G - T)$.
    d. $IM - X = (S - I) - (G - T)$.

18. If there is no change in the balance of domestic savings and investment, then any increase in the government deficit must be matched by a(n) _____. (There may be more than one correct answer.)
    a. increase in the trade deficit
    b. reduction in the equilibrium level of output
    c. capital inflow
    d. reduction in interest rates

19. Which one of the following would help to reduce the U.S. trade deficit?
    a. higher government deficits
    b. increased domestic investment
    c. increased domestic savings
    d. a decrease in exports

20. A reduction in the government deficit need not lead to a reduction in the trade deficit if there is an increase in _____. (There may be more than one correct answer.)
    a. private saving
    b. private investment
    c. consumption spending
    d. imports

TEST B

Circle T or F for true or false.

T F 1. International trade means that an economic boom in the United States is likely to lead to recession in the rest of the world.

T F 2. A change in net exports has no multiplier impacts.

T F 3. A shift in the expenditure schedule coming from an autonomous change in domestic investment spending would be expected to have no impact on a country's trade deficit.

T F 4. A depreciation in the exchange rate is inflationary.

T F 5. A depreciation in the exchange rate should help to reduce a country's trade deficit.

T F 6. Under floating exchange rates, a country with a trade deficit will also experience a capital inflow.

T F 7. Interest-sensitive international capital flows make monetary policy less effective.

T F 8. International capital flows are unaffected by changes in fiscal policy.

510

T F 9. Increased protectionism has been shown to be an effective tool for eliminating a trade deficit.

T F 10. The only way to reduce the trade deficit is by reducing the government's budget deficit.

ECONOMICS IN ACTION

WITHER THE DOLLAR?

Writing in *The New York Times* in November 2004, Edmund Andrews described three views of the continuing American trade deficit and the associated increases in American international indebtedness.

There were those, including Federal Reserve chairman Alan Greenspan and prominent members of the Bush administration who saw little to worry about. These observers argued that global financial markets were so much larger than they used to be that large borrowing on the part of the United States should not be a problem. Indeed, some in the Bush administration argued that large borrowing was a sign of American strength and indicated the interest of foreigners in investing in the United States.

Others were not as sanguine and worried about a sudden collapse of the value of dollar as the capacity and willingness of international investors to absorb additional dollar denominated debt could reach a limit and quickly reverse. Economist Kenneth Rogoff worried that a large drop in the dollar would drive up interest rates as foreign investors would demand "higher returns to compensate for higher risks." The result could be a dramatic decline in the dollar and American GDP.

Economist Catherine Mann offered a third viewpoint. While concerned that the magnitude of current deficits, both that of the federal government and the trade deficit, seemed unsustainable, Ms. Mann was more optimistic that adjustment to more sustainable levels would be gradual rather than abrupt. She noted that much of the recent capital inflow had come from Asian central banks buying significant quantities of U.S. government securities. Much of this investment seemed aimed at stabilizing exchange rates to keep Asian exports competitive. Mann described these developments as one of "global co-dependency" and argued that a number of countries had a vested interest in preventing a sharp decline in the dollar. While there could easily be a decline in the dollar, Mann expected it to be an orderly decline and not "a panicky flight by foreign investors."

1. As this edition of the Study Guide was being prepared, the dollar had depreciated significantly against the euro, with the dollar price of a euro increasing from $1.20 in Sept. 2008 to $1.47 in May 2011. There had been similar declines in the value of the dollar against the British pound and the Canadian dollar. What has happened to the international value of the dollar since early 2005? Has the dollar continued to depreciate against European currencies? What about the exchange rate between the dollar and Asian currencies? Has any change in the value of the dollar been gradual or abrupt?

2. As noted in Chapter 36, it must always be true that $X - IM = (S - I) - (G - T)$. The implication of this expression is that any reduction in the trade deficit will require a combination of higher levels of domestic savings relative to domestic private investment or a smaller government deficit. What has happened to the trade deficit, domestic savings, domestic investment, and the deficit/surplus position of the federal government along with states and local governments?

511

The Federal Reserve Bank of St. Louis maintains an extensive online database for many economic time series, including exchange rates. You can access information on exchange rates at http://research.stlouisfed.org/fred2/categories/15 and information on national income accounts at http://research.stlouisfed.org/fred2/categories/18.

Sources: "The Dollar is Down: Is it a Cause for Concern?" Edmund L. Andrews, *The New York Times*, November 16, 2004.

You might also want to look at

- "Managing Exchange Rates: Achievement of Global Re-balancing or Evidence of Global Co-dependency?" Catherine L. Mann, *Business Economics*, July 2004.

- "America's current account deficit is not only sustainable, it is perfectly logical given the world's hunger for investment returns and dollar reserves," Richard Cooper, *The Financial Times*, November 1, 2004.

- "The U.S. deficit problem is not only a domestic issue, but a global concern and neither candidate has the answer," Maurice Obstfeld and Kenneth Rogoff, *The Financial Times*, November 1, 2004.

- "The disappearing dollar: How long can it remain the world's most important reserve currency?, " *The Economist*, December 2, 2004.

- "A Field Guide to the Falling Dollar, " *The New York Times*, December 5, 2004.

STUDY QUESTIONS

1. What is the difference between an open versus a closed economy?

2. How does an appreciation in the exchange rate affect net exports? What about a depreciation? Why?

3. How does a change in the exchange rate affect the aggregate demand curve? The aggregate supply curve? Which effect is likely to be larger?

4. Does an increase in interest rates lead to an appreciation or depreciation of the exchange rate? Why?

5. Consider a move to contractionary fiscal policy that reduces aggregate demand. What is the likely impact on interest rates, international capital flows, the exchange rate, and net exports? Do these changes tend to enhance or offset the original change in fiscal policy?

6. Consider a move to expansionary monetary policy that increases aggregate demand. What is the likely impact on interest rates, international capital flows, the exchange rate, and net exports? Do these changes enhance or offset the original change in monetary policy?

7. What is the link between government deficits and trade deficits? Under what conditions does an increase in the government deficit lead to an increase in the trade deficit?

8. What is your evaluation of the cumulative impact of American trade deficits since 1980?

9. Why isn't increased protectionism a surefire way to reduce the trade deficit?

10. Why didn't the large currency deprecations in Southeast Asia in 1997 and 1998 lead to expansions in output?

ECONOMICS ONLINE

The Organization for Economic Co-operation and Development (OECD) was originally composed of 20 or so European and North American industrialized economies plus Australia, Japan, and New Zealand. With changes in the world economy over the past 20 years, the OECD now describes itself as "30 member countries sharing a commitment to democratic government and the market economy." The OECD monitors economic trends and does comparative analysis of member countries. Its homepage can be found at

http://www.oecd.org

Statistics Netherlands maintains a set of Web links to statistical agencies for a number of countries. These links can be found at

http://www.cbs.nl/en-GB/default.htm?Languageswitch=on

What are current differences in interest rates in different countries? Bloomberg.com posts interest rate data for some of the world's largest economies at

http://www.bloomberg.com/markets/rates/index.html

Answer Key

Chapter 1

Chapter Review

(1) information; value

Important Terms and Concepts Quiz

1. e
2. a
3. d
4. b
5. f

Basic Exercises

1. C
2. G
3. B
4. E
5. A
6. I
7. H
8. J
9. D
10. F

Self-Tests for Understanding

Test A

1. c
2. b
3. d
4. a
5. c
6. a
7. b
8. d
9. c
10. b

Test B

1. F
2. F
3. T
4. T
5. F
6. F
7. F
8. F
9. F
10. F
11. F
12. F
13. F
14. F
15. F
16. F
17. F
18. F

Appendix

Chapter Review

(1) horizontal; vertical; origin

(2) vertical; horizontal; constant; positive; up; negative; no

(3) ray; 45-degree

(4) tangent

(5) contour; production indifference

Important Terms and Concepts Quiz

1. d
2. h
3. g
4. b
5. f
6. c
7. e
8. i

Basic Exercises

1. a. 400
    b. increase; 800
    c. 600
    d. −50
    e. Slope equals vertical change divided by horizontal change or the change in salary divided by the change in the quantity demanded. The change in the number of new Ph.D. economists demanded as salary changes is equal to the reciprocal of the slope: The demand curve implies that a $1,000 increase in salary will reduce the quantity demanded by 20.

2. a. 4
    b. 5

c. above

d. non-economics

Self-Tests for Understanding: Appendix

Test A

1. b
2. b
3. c
4. d
5. a
6. a
7. c; a; b; d
8. A&E; C; B&D; none
9. d slope = vertical change/horizontal change; (16-10)/ (5-8) = 6/-3 = -2
10. c
11. b
12. b
13. b
14. d
15. c
16. a
17. d
18. a slope = 2/5 = 0.4
19. b
20. b

Test B

1. F
2. F
3. T
4. T
5. F
6. T
7. F
8. T
9. T
10. F

Chapter 2

Chapter Review

(1) domestic product; GDP; productivity

(2) inputs; outputs; free; private

(3) open; closed; closed

(4) recessions

(5) factors

(6) labor; 15 cents; service

(7) small

Important Terms and Concepts Quiz

1. h
2. i
3. a
4. f
5. e
6. g
7. d
8. j
9. b

Basic Exercises

1. 1960: 13.7%; 39.6%; 46.7%
   2010: 10.5%; 17.5%; 66.9%

2. 1960: 49.4%; 2.9%; 25.0%; 9.7%; 13.0%
   2009: 19.3%; 25.6%; 33.8%; 7.3%; 14.0%

3. Men: 21.8%; 49.6%; 74.5%; 89.7%; 91.8%; 86.8%; 70%; 22.1%
   Women: 23%; 48.6%; 68.2%; 74.7%; 75.1%; 75.7%; 60.2%; 13.8%

Self-Tests for Understanding

Test A

1. a, d
2. c.
3. b, c
4. d
5. a
6. c
7. a
8. d
9. d
10. c
11. d
12. d
13. b
14. d
15. d

517

16. a

17. c

18. d

19. c

20. a

Test B

1. T

2. F

3. F

4. T

5. T

6. F

7. F

8. F

9. F

10. T

Chapter 3

Chapter Review

(1) scarce

(2) opportunity cost

(3) scarce; specialized; slope

(4) increase; increasing; specialized

(5) inside; inefficient,

(6) will

Important Terms and Concepts Quiz

1. f

2. k

3. m

4. h

5. a

6. g

7. l

8. j

9. e

10. c

11. d

12. i

Basic Exercise

1. 560,000; 40,000; rises; 120,000; continue to rise; specialized

2. Point A is not attainable; point B is attainable; point C is attainable; on and inside; on

3. Point B is inefficient. You should be able to shade a small triangular area above and to the right of point B out to and including a small segment of the PPF.

4. Without additional information about the preferences of the citizens of Adirondack one cannot determine which point on the production possibilities frontier is best for a country.

Self-Tests for Understanding

Test A

1. c

2. c

3. d

4. d

5. a

6. b

7. c

8. b

9. d

10. d

11. b

12. c

13. c

14. a

15. b

16. c

17. c

18. a

19. b

20. d

Test B

1. F

2. F

3. T

4. F

5. F

6. F

7. T

8. T

9. F

10. F

Supplementary Exercises

2. a. 300,000 cars (set T = 0); 1,000 tanks (set C = 0)

    c. Yes, it bows out.

    d. $1/2C^*$, $1/2T^*$ should be on straight line connecting C^* and T^*. Combination is attainable, lies inside frontier; inefficient, not on frontier as frontier bows out.

    e. 6 cars; 30 cars; 120 cars

    f. Opportunity cost = $(0.6)T$ cars; yes, opportunity cost increases as the production of tanks increases.

Chapter 4

Chapter Review

(1) price; negative; more; movement along; shift in

(2) price; positive; more; shift in

(3) demand

(4) $300; 4,000; less; 6,000; 2,000; surplus; reduction; shortage; demanded; supplied; increase

(5) intersection; equilibrium

(6) demand; supply; movement along; supply; demand; demand

(7) maximum; minimum; above

(8) hard; auxiliary restrictions

(9) shortages; decrease

(10) high

Important Terms and Concepts Quiz

1. f
2. e
3. g
4. c
5. m
6. k
7. i
8. q
9. o
10. p
11. n
12. h
13. a
14. j
15. b

Basic Exercises

1. b. 60; 1,100

    c. increased; 70; increased; 1,200; less

    The impact of the change in price following the shift of the demand curve means that the change in the equilibrium quantity will be less than the horizontal shift in the demand curve.

    d. increase; decrease; 75; 1,100; less than

2. a. demand; right; rise; rise

    b. supply; right; fall; rise

    c. supply; left; rise; fall

    d. demand; left; fall; fall

3. a. 100; 100; neither, as ceiling exceeds equilibrium price

    b. 110; 80; shortage

    Price ceilings lead to shortages when they are less than the free market equilibrium price.

    c. 90; 120; surplus

    Price floors lead to surpluses when they are greater than the free market equilibrium price.

    d. 100; 100; neither, as floor is less than equilibrium price

Self-Tests for Understanding

Test A

1. c
2. a
3. d
4. c
5. c
6. b
7. a
8. a
9. d
10. b
11. c
12. a
13. b, d
14. b
15. b
16. c
17. b
18. a
19. d

20. b

Test B

1. F
2. T
3. T
4. F
5. F
6. T
7. T
8. F
9. F
10. F
11. T
12. F
13. T
14. F
15. F

Chapter 5

Chapter Review

(1) marginal; will; decrease; increase

(2) consumer's; price; greater; increase

(3) greater; marginal; more; up; negative; marginal

(4) shift in; utility; inferior; fewer

(5) horizontal; negative

Important Terms and Concepts Quiz

1. d
2. e
3. c
4. h
5. b
6. g
7. a
8. i

Basic Exercises

1. a. 110; 100; 80; 70; 50; 30; 20

   b. 2; 4; 5

   c. consumer's

   d. Col. 3: 20; 30; 20; 0; −40; −100; −170; 2
   Col. 5: 50; 90; 110; 120; 110; 80; 40; 4
   Col. 7: 70; 130; 170; 200; 210; 200; 180; 5

   2; 4; 5; exactly the same

   e. at P = \$90, Q_d = 2, at P = \$60, Q_d = 4, at P = \$40, Q_d = 5

2. a. \$80 (\$270 - \$190)

   b. \$ 135 (\$270 − 3 x \$45)

   c. consumer surplus up by \$15 (\$60 - \$45)

   d. 5

   e. \$155 (\$380 − 5 x \$45)

   f. 6; beyond this point price exceeds marginal utility.

Self-Tests for Understanding

Test A

1. b
2. a
3. d
4. a
5. d
6. c
7. c
8. d
9. c
10. c
11. a
12. b
13. c
14. b
15. b
16. d
17. c
18. d
19. d
20. a, c

Test B

1. F
2. T
3. T
4. F
5. T
6. F
7. T
8. F

520

9. F

10. F

Appendix

Appendix Review

(1) straight; negative; intercept; slope

(2) indifference; indifferent; are; never; negative

(3) in; more; substitution; decreases

(4) budget; indifference; highest; budget line

(5) budget line

Important Terms and Concepts Quiz: Appendix

1. c

2. d

3. a

4. e

Basic Exercise: Appendix

1. a. max hamburgers = 80; max books = 20

   b. 40; 10

   c. 6; 4

   d. At point W, Gloria has so many books that she would give up some for just a few more hamburgers as shown by the slope of the indifference curve. The budget allows Gloria a much better deal—she would get four hamburgers for each book she gives up. Choosing to move along the budget line increases Gloria's total utility as it allows her to move to higher indifference curves.

   e. equals the slope of the budget line

2. a. Z

   Neither is an inferior good as point Z shows an increase in the quantity demanded for both following the increase in income.

   b. Y

Self-Tests for Understanding: Appendix

Test A

1. c

2. c

3. d

4. c

5. b

6. d

7. c

8. b

9. b

10. c

11. d

12. b

13. a

Test B

1. F

2. T

3. F

4. F

5. F

6. T

7. F

8. F

9. T

10. T

Supplementary Exercise: Appendix

2. $F = (Y + 20P_C - 12P_F)/2P_F$

   $C = (Y - 20P_C + 12P_F)/2P_C$

   where P_F = price of food, P_C = price of clothing and Y = income.

   The demand curves come from solving the following two equations for F and C:

   Optimal purchases require that the marginal rate of substitution equals the ratio of market prices, or

   $(F + 12)/(C + 20) = P_C/P_F$

   The budget constraint requires that:

   $F P_F + C P_C = Y$

3. $F = 114$; $C = 43$

4. $F = 84$; $C = 44$

5. $F = 124$; $C = 48$; no

Chapter 6

Chapter Review

(1) elasticity; demand

(2) zero; infinite; changes

(3) elastic; inelastic; unit elastic

(4) will not; 1.0

(5) greater; decrease; increase; less; increase; decrease

(6) cross

521

(7) complements; negative; increase; right

(8) substitutes; positive; decrease; left

(9) shift in

Important Terms and Concepts Quiz

1. f
2. e
3. b
4. g
5. i
6. d
7. h
8. a
9. j

Basic Exercises

1. a. See diagrams below
   b. 1.0
   c. 1.0
   d. 1.0
      Do not be fooled by appearances.
2. a. straight
   b. %Δ price: 10.53%; 11.76%; 13.33%; 15.38%
      %Δ quantity: −18.18%; −15.38%; −13.33%; −11.76%
      elasticity: 1.73; 1.31; 1.00; 0.76; decreases

c. Total Revenue: $600,000; $648,000; $672,000; $672,000; $648,000.

Total revenue increases (decreases) as price declines if the elasticity of demand is greater (less) than 1.0. Total revenue increases (decreases) as price increases if the elasticity of demand is less (greater) than 1.0.

Self-Tests for Understanding

Test A

1. b
2. a
3. c
4. a
5. c
6. b
7. d
8. c
9. a
10. b
11. a
12. b
13. b
14. a
15. c
16. c
17. c

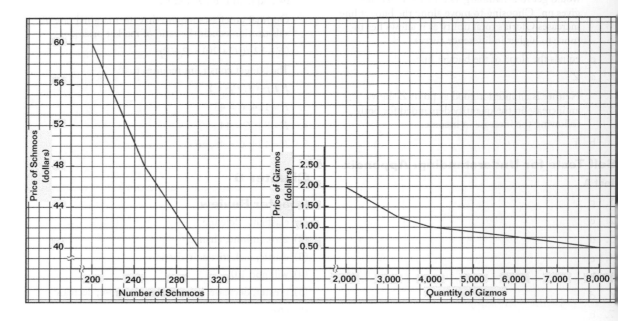

18. b
19. d
20. b

Test B

1. F
2. F
3. T
4. F
5. F
6. T
7. F
8. T
9. F
10. T
11. T
12. F
13. F
14. F

Appendix

Basic Exercises: Appendix

1. Not much; plotting historical data is an inappropriate way to estimate a demand curve.

2. a. 2005: $P = 22$; $Q = 380$

   2006: $P = 23$; $Q = 395$

   2007: $P = 24$; $Q = 410$

   When only the demand curve shifts, the historical data on price and quantity trace out the supply curve. If you connect the three points, you should have a graph of the supply curve. Each point comes from the intersection of the demand curve for the specific year with the unchanging supply curve. In this case, the points of market equilibrium provide no information about the demand curve.

   b. 2005: $P = 22.0$; $Q = 380$

   2006: $P = 20.5$; $Q = 407.5$

   2007: $P = 11.5$; $Q = 472.5$

   With shifts in both demand and supply curves, the points of market equilibrium trace out neither curve. Try drawing the demand and supply curves for each year on the same diagram. As both curves shift, a line connecting the successive points of market equilibrium gives no information about either curve.

Economics in Action

1. a. Elasticity of demand = (3,570/1,997) ÷ (5.50/3.75) = 1.22

   b. While the elasticity of demand is an indicator of the change in total revenue, a profit maximizing firm is interested in profits not revenues. Increased output may entail increased costs. In Mr. Grant's case, changing from first to second run movies dramatically cut the proportion of the ticket price claimed by movie distributors. The cut was so dramatic that net revenue before paying employees, utilities, etc., but after paying the admission tax and after paying the distributors, was unchanged at 61 cents a ticket.

2. a. If total revenue is to remain unchanged the price elasticity of demand would have to equal 1.0.

   b. Data on historical quantities is not a good way to measure demand. The relevant question is what would the demand for air travel in the summer of 1992 have been if fares had not been reduced. It is also relevant to note that some air travelers, those buying their tickets at the last minute, paid full fare and were not eligible for the discounted fares. At the same time it does appear that the fare war was a bonanza for travelers and not so good for airlines. A significant reduction in ticket prices appears to have induced only a modest increase in air travel.

3. The elasticity of demand must be greater than 1.0. Their statements imply that lower prices would increase sales enough to cover not only the lost revenue on existing sales when price declines but also any increase in cost from producing more books.

Chapter 7

Chapter Review

(1) increase; physical; revenue

(2) revenue; price

(3) more; less; reduce; increase

(4) reduce; less; more

(5) increasing; decreasing; constant

(6) short

(7) output; total

(8) long run; lower

(9) is unchanged; less; fall; more; rises

Important Terms and Concepts Quiz

1. k

2. d

3. b

4. h

5. f

6. g

7. i

8. e

9. c

Basic Exercises

1. 100 acres: increasing returns: 0 to 2 workers; decreasing returns: 2 to 4 workers; negative returns: 4 to 6 workers

2. 200 acres: increasing returns: 0 to 2 workers; decreasing returns: 2 to 5 workers; negative returns: 5 to 6 workers.

    300 acres: increasing returns: 0 to 2 workers; decreasing returns: 2 to 6 workers.

    The output-labor curve shifts up as land increases.

3. 100: 1; 3; 2; 1; −1; −2

    200: 2; 4; 3.5; 2.5; 1; −1

    300; 3; 4.5; 3.5; 3; 2; 1

4. Marginal returns to land generally decline.

5. increasing; increasing; constant; increasing; decreasing

    $10,000; $20,000; $17,500; $12,500; $5,000; −$5,000

    Hire 4 workers: (12,000 x $5) − ($8,000 x 4) = $28,000

    Hire 3 workers: (9,500 x $5) − ($8,000 x 3) = $23,500

    Hire 5 workers: (13,000 x $5) − ($8,000 x 5) = $25,000

Self-Tests for Understanding

Test A

1. d

2. c

3. d

4. b

5. d

6. b

7. c

8. c

9. d

10. a

11. b

12. a

13. a

14. d

15. c

16. c

17. b

18. d

19. b

20. d

Test B

1. F

2. T

3. F

4. F

5. T

6. F

7. F

8. F

9. T

10. F

Appendix

Appendix Review

(1) production indifference; more

(2) negative; will; diminishing marginal; do not

(3) straight

(4) lowest; less; more

(5) expansion

Important Terms and Concepts Quiz: Appendix

1. c

2. d

3. a

Basic Exercise: Appendix

1. 200; 2; 100; 3. Total costs are constant along a single budget line. Total costs are greater along higher budget lines.

2. $80

Self-Tests for Understanding: Appendix

Test A

1. d

2. b

3. c

524

4. c

5. c

6. b

7. c

8. d

9. d

Test B

1. F

2. T

3. T

4. F.

5. F

6. F

7. T

Supplementary Exercises

1. See diagram. In order to graph the combinations of labor and machines that will achieve a production level of 500,000 widgets, create a table of possible combinations:

Table of inputs and output
(all units measured in thousands)

Labor	Machines	Widgets
250	1,000	500
500	500	500
750	333	500
1,000	250	500

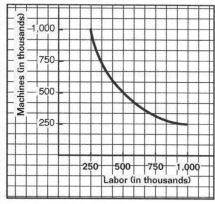

2. The slope of the production indifference curve = $-MPP_L/MPP_M$. The slope of the budget line = $-P_L/P_M$. The cost minimizing level of inputs is determined by finding where these two slopes are equal.

$MPP_L = 1/2 \, (M/L)^{1/2}$

$MPP_M = 1/2 \, (L/M)^{1/2}$

$MPP_L/MPP_M = M/L$; $P_L / P_M = 12/48$; at cost minimizing level of inputs $M/L = 12/48$ or $L = 4M$

When the price of labor hours is 12 and the price of machine hours is 48, the least costly combination of inputs requires that $L = 4M$.

From the production function

$W = L^{1/2} M^{1/2}$

Knowing that for the least-cost combination of inputs $L = 4M$, the equation for output can be rewritten as $500,000 =$
$M^{1/2} (4M)^{1/2}$

$500,000 = (4M^2)^{1/2} = 2M$

$M = 250,000$ machine hours

$L = 1,000,000$ labor hours

3. a. Total output $= 500 \, L^{1/2}$

   b. MPP of labor $= 250/L^{1/2}$; the MPP of labor is the slope of the total product curve.

   c. For this production function, MPP of labor declines continuously, but is never negative.

   d. 1,085,069.45 labor hours; (Find the quantity of labor such that the MRP of labor is equal to the price of labor. $(250/L^{1/2}) \times 50 = 12$.)

   Output $= 520,833.33$ widgets.

4. For this production function, the expansion path is a straight line.

5. Constant: $(2M)^{1/2} (2L)^{1/2} = 2M^{1/2}L^{1/2} = 2W$. A doubling of inputs doubles output.

Chapter 8

Chapter Review

(1) average; marginal

(2) marginal; marginal; profits; revenue; cost

(3) total

(4) marginal; marginal; positive; zero; equals

Important Terms and Concepts Quiz

1. f

2. e

3. a

4. g

5. b

6. h

7. c

525

Basic Exercises

1. a. Total Profits: 1,500; 3,600; 5,200; 6,300; 6,600; 6,100; 5,000; 3,400; 1,300; −1,300; 5 widgets

   b. Marginal Revenue: 3,500; 3,100; 2,700; 2,300; 1,900; 1,500; 1,100; 700; 300; −100

      Marginal Cost: 2,000; 1,000; 1,100; 1,200; 1,600; 2,000; 2,200; 2,300; 2,400; 2,500, 5 widgets. The 5th widget adds 300 to profit: Increasing output to 6 widgets would lower profit by 500.

   c. profit; does not; does not; the difference between average revenue and average cost is greatest when output = 2. expanding output as long as MR > MC increases profits, but expanding output further, even if AR > AC, will reduce total profits.

   d. In the top panel of Fig 8-1, the total cost curve shifts up by $3,000. The total profit curve in the middle panel measures the difference between the two curves in the top panel; following the increase in fixed costs, the total profit curve shifts down by $3,000. In the bottom panel, neither curve shifts. The marginal revenue curve measures the slope of the total revenue curve and the marginal cost curve measures the slope of the total cost curve. Even though the total cost curve shifted up, there is no change in its slope.

2. a. is not; horizontal; vertical; horizontal

   b. $375,000

Self-Tests for Understanding

Test A

1. b
2. c
3. c
4. d
5. b
6. a
7. b
8. d
9. d
10. a
11. c
12. c
13. b
14. c
15. c
16. a

17. b
18. b
19. a
20. d

Test B

1. F
2. F
3. F
4. F
5. T
6. T
7. T
8. F
9. F
10. F

Appendix

1. a. yes

   b. yes; game 2 and game 10

   c. yes; game 3, game 4, game 6, game 7 and game 8

   d. yes; game 5 and game 9

2. a. The marginal profit curve should drop continuously and should equal zero where total profits are maximized not where total profits equal zero.

   b. The marginal cost curve should go through the minimum of the average cost curve. When average cost is falling, the marginal cost curve should be below the average cost curve, and when average cost is rising, the marginal cost curve should be above the average cost curve.

Supplementary Exercises

1. a. $16,000

   b. $AC = 16,000/Q + 120 − 0.4Q + 0.002Q^2$
      $MC = 120 − 0.8Q + 0.006Q^2$

   c. It should.

   d. $MR = 300 − 0.5Q$

   f. $Q = 200$

   g. Find the positive value of Q such that MC = MR; $120 − 0.8Q + 0.006Q^2 = 300 − 0.5Q$; $Q = 200$

   h. When Q = 200, P = $250; TR = $50,000; TC = $40,000; total profits = $10,000

   j. $AC = 20,000/Q + 120 − .04Q + 0.0002Q^2$ No change in profit maximizing level of output as the change in fixed costs does not change either marginal cost or marginal revenue; total profits = $6,000

2. a. Set MC = MR.

Marginal cost: when $P_L = 12$ and $P_M = 48$, the least cost combination of inputs uses four hours of labor input for each hour of machine time. (See Supplementary Exercise 2 in Chapter 7.) To produce one widget, a firm would use two hours of labor with a half-hour of machine time for a total cost of $48. As the production function exhibits constant returns to scale, average and marginal cost are equal at $48 per widget.

$W = 2,500,000 - 25,000\,P_W$

Total Revenue = $100\,W - .00004\,W^2$

MR = $100 - .00008\,W$

To find the profit maximizing level of output set MC = MR.

$48 = 100 - .00008\,W$

$W = 650,000$

$L = 1,300,000$

$M = 325,000$

$P_W = \$74$

b. Output: $W = (200,000)^{1/2}L^{1/2}$

Labor Input: $L = W^2/200,000$

Total (labor) cost = $12W^2/200,000$

Marginal (labor) cost = $24W/200,000$

$= .00012W$

MR = $100 - .00008\,W$

Set MC = MR

$.00012W = 100 - .0008\,W$

$.0002\,W = 100$

$W = 500,000$

$L = 1,250,000$

$P_W = \$80.$

3. We know that profit maximizing firms set MR = MC and MC = MR > 0. If MR > 0, total revenue increases if quantity increases and total revenue decreases if quantity decreases. That is the price elasticity of demand for a profit maximizing firm is > 1.

Chapter 9

Chapter Review

(1) limited

(2) stock; bonds; plowback (or retained earnings)

(3) are not; more; bonds; meet bond payments

(4) falls; loss; increase

(5) are not; riskiness

(6) higher; lower; insurance

(7) random walk

(8) reduce; insurance; derived; fell; recession

(9) borrowed; magnifies

Important Terms and Concepts Quiz

1. k
2. c
3. m
4. g
5. q
6. o
7. n
8. i
9. e
10. b
11. j
12. a
13. d
14. r
15. p
16. f
17. l

Basic Exercises

a.

$t = 1$	74.07407
$t = 2$	68.58711
$t = 3$	63.50658
$t = 4$	58.80239
$t = 5$	54.44666
$t = 6$	50.41357
$t = 7$	46.67923
$t = 8$	43.22151
$t = 9$	40.01992
$t = 10$	37.05548
PV principal	463.1935
sum	1000

b.

$i = .07, P = 1070.236$

$i = .06, P = 1147.202$

$i = .09, P = 935.8234$

$i = .10, P = 877.1087$

c.	Years	*P*
	$t = 1$	1018.868
	$t = 2$	1036.668
	$t = 3$	1053.46
	$t = 4$	1069.302
	$t = 5$	1084.247
	$t = 6$	1098.346
	$t = 7$	1111.648
	$t = 8$	1124.196
	$t = 9$	1136.034
	$t = 10$	1147.202
	$t = 11$	1157.737
	$t = 12$	1167.677
	$t = 13$	1177.054
	$t = 14$	1185.9
	$t = 15$	1194.245
	$t = 16$	1202.118
	$t = 17$	1209.545
	$t = 18$	1216.552
	$t = 19$	1223.162
	$t = 20$	1229.398
	$t = 21$	1235.282
	$t = 22$	1240.832
	$t = 23$	1246.068
	$t = 24$	1251.007
	$t = 25$	1255.667

Self-Tests for Understanding

Test A

1. b
2. b
3. c
4. b
5. a, d
6. d
7. c
8. d
9. a
10. d
11. b
12. c
13. c
14. e
15. c
16. a
17. b
18. b,c
19. d
20. c

Test B

1. T
2. T
3. F
4. T
5. F
6. F
7. F
8. F
9. F
10. F

Supplementary Exercises

1. The prices of bonds for all companies are likely to move together in response to changes in economy-wide interest rates. Stock prices are more heavily influenced by the fortunes and misfortunes of individual companies. As a result, changes in share prices are more likely to differ across companies.

2. The return on the diversified portfolio will be an average of the returns on individual stocks. The diversified portfolio misses the big gainers but minimizes the impact of the worst performers. The portfolio gross return in Table 9-1 is an average. Looking at the returns from Table 9-2, we see that if the individual put all $10,000 into Apple, he or she would have performed better than the portfolio. However, if the individual chose Home Depot, he or she would have received a lower return relative to the portfolio in Table 9-1. By investing in several different stocks, the individual is protected against poor returns (Home Depot and FedEx) for one company.

   The rate of return (gross return as a percentage of the initial share price) for these companies is as follows:

   Apple: $23,353.63, 133.54%

   Best Buy: $10,770.84, 7.71%

   Cisco: $9,904.91, -0.95%

   Exxon Mobil: $12,405.34, 24.05%

FedEx: $8,248.48, -17.52%

General Electric: $10,269.72, 2.70%

Home Depot: $6,932.16, -30.68%

Merck: $13,679.12, 36.79%

Microsoft: $12,059.75, 20.60%

Wal-Mart: $10,480.77, 4.81%

For the portfolio with the shares equally divided between the 10 companies, the investor would have earned a rate of return of 18.1%.

Chapter 10

Chapter Review

(1) Many; Identical; Easy; Perfect; do not; zero

(2) horizontal; marginal

(3) marginal; losses; variable; marginal cost; variable

(4) horizontal; demand; supply

(5) loss; two; better; opportunity; economic; accounting

(6) profits; (shaded rectangle should go from the y axis to the point where marginal cost equals 20, down to the average cost curve and then back to the Y axis); enter; right; fall; $15.00 (minimum long run average cost; see the Basic Exercise); long-run average

Important Terms and Concepts Quiz

1. d
2. f
3. e
4. a
5. g
6. b

Basic Exercise

1. 1,400; $5,544 = $(P - AC)Q$; $5,310; $5,330

2. 1,200; -$4,380 = $(P - AC)Q$; -$4,550; -$4,532; -$10,140 (fixed costs)

3. 0; price does not cover average variable cost.

4. Firm's short-run supply curve is the portion of its marginal cost curve above average variable cost.

5. While under perfect competition marginal revenue equals price, one also needs to consider how a change in output affects costs. That is, the relevant comparison is price with marginal cost.

6. $15.00; 1,300 widgets

Self-Tests for Understanding

Test A

1. b
2. c
3. a
4. d
5. c
6. c
7. b
8. c
9. b
10. b
11. c
12. d
13. d
14. b
15. c
16. c
17. b
18. d
19. c
20. d

Test B

1. F
2. F
3. F
4. F
5. F
6. F
7. F
8. T
9. F
10. F

Supplementary Exercises

1. a. Average Cost = $10,140/Q + 0.00001Q^2 - 0.02Q + 16.3$

   b. Average variable cost = $0.00001Q^2 - 0.02Q + 16.3$

   c. Marginal cost = $.00003Q^2 - .04Q116.3$

3. To find the minimum of either average cost curve sets its derivative equal to zero.

   At min AC, $Q = 1,300$; AC = 15.00; at $Q = 1,300$, MC = 15.00

At min AVC, $Q = 1,000$; AVC = 6.30; at $Q = 1,000$, MC = 6.30

4. Supply = 0 if $P < 6.30$

Supply = $[0.4+(-0.000356 + 0.00012P)^{1/2}] / 0.00006$ if $P \geq 6.30$

Chapter 11

Chapter Review

(1) one; no

(2) natural; barriers; entry

(3) negative; lower; decrease

(4) marginal; marginal; price; is not

(5) average; less; below; above

(6) demand; greater; less; less; will not; higher; lower

(7) price; marginal revenue; less; greater; greater than

(8) down

(9) will not; does not; maker

Important Terms and Concepts Quiz

1. e
2. a
3. g
4. b
5. f
6. d

Basic Exercises

1. a. 14

   b. Marginal revenue: $6,900; $6,500; $6,100; $5,700
      Marginal cost: $5,625; $6,075; $6,525; $6,975
      revenue; cost; 14

   c. 9,100

   d. 30,884

   e. Marginal revenue: same as in b.
      Total cost: $96,816; $103,441; $110,516; $118,041; $126,016
      Marginal cost: $6,625; $7,075; $7,525; $7,975
      13 widgets; $9,300;

   f. $200; If Mario increased his price by $1,000, the quantity sold would not maximize profits.

   g. $17,459

   h. No change in output = 14 widgets; no change in price = $9,100; profits down $13,000 to $17,884. No change in pollution as output is unchanged.

The differences between questions e and h reflect the differences between the effects of a change in marginal and fixed costs. In Question e marginal cost changed as the tax was imposed on each widget produced. In Question h marginal cost is unchanged as the pollution charge is independent of the number of widgets produced.

2. a. Total Revenue: $2,400,000; $3,093,750; $3,675,000; $4,143,750; $4,500,000; $4,743,750; $4,875,000; $4,893,750

      Marginal Revenue: $37; $31; $25; $19; $13; $7; $1

      Price $33; Output 143,750; Profits $806,250

   b. Centerville: Total Revenue: $480,000; $1,125,000; $1,680,000; $2,145,000; $2,520,000; $2,805,000; $3,000,000; $3,105,000

      Marginal Revenue: $43; $37; $31; $25; $19; $13; $7

      Price $30; Quantity 100,000

      Middletown: Total Revenue: $1,920,000; $1,968,750; $1,995,000; $1,998,750; $1,980,000; $1,938,750; $1,875,000; $1,788,750

      Marginal Revenue: $13, $7; $1; –$5; –$11; –$17, –$23

      Price $45; Quantity 43,750

      Profits: $1,031,250

   c. Middletown; Centerville

Self-Tests for Understanding

Test A

1. d
2. c
3. b
4. d
5. c
6. c
7. a
8. c
9. a
10. d
11. c
12. c
13. c
14. b
15. c

530

16. c
17. b
18. c
19. b
20. a

Test B

1. F
2. T
3. F
4. F
5. T
6. F
7. T
8. F
9. F
10. F

Supplementary Exercises

1. a. Total revenue = $11,900Q - 200Q^2$

 Marginal revenue = $11,900 - 400Q$

 Average cost = $225Q + 52,416/Q$

 Marginal cost = $450Q$

 c. $11,900 - 400Q = 450Q$; $850Q = 11,900$; $Q = 14$

 d. Per-unit charge:

 $TC = 52,416 + 225Q^2 + 1,000Q$

 $AC = 225Q + 52,416/Q + 1,000$

 $MC = 450Q + 1,000$

 Fixed charge:

 $TC = 65,416 + 225Q^2$

 $AC = 225Q + 65,416/Q$

 $MC = 450Q$

 Note that the addition of a fixed cost element does not change marginal cost.

2. If a monopolist is originally producing where demand is inelastic, then an increase in market price will increase profits. The increase in price reduces costs as quantity declines and increases revenue as the percentage decline in the quantity sold is more than offset by the percentage increase in price. Thus the initial point could not have been a point of profit maximization. Similar reasoning rules out b, the case of unit elastic demand, as a point of profit maximization: profits increase as the reduction in quantity from an increase in price reduces costs while revenue is unchanged from the assumption of unit elasticity of demand.

Chapter 12

Chapter Review

(1) monopolistic; negative; marginal revenue; marginal cost; zero; entry; average

(2) oligopoly; cartel; price leadership

(3) zero; lower; larger

(4) will; will not; marginal; cost

(5) payoff; strategy; dominant; maximin; Nash; zero-sum; reputation; credible

(6) entry; exit; opportunity cost; capital

Important Terms and Concepts Quiz

1. g
2. m
3. a
4. i
5. c
6. n
7. k
8. e
9. b
10. p
11. h
12. l
13. q
14. j
15. f
16. d

Basic Exercises

1. a. Profit-maximizing level of output = 1,000 meals

 b. Marginal revenue: $2,200; $1,400; $600; –$200

 Marginal cost: $1,000; $1,000; $1,000; $1,000

 Profit-maximizing level of output = 1,000 meals

 MC is less than MR at less than 1,000 meals

 MC exceeds MR at more than 1,000 meals

 See also the Supplementary Exercise to this chapter.

2. a. 1,000; $200; Marginal revenue exceeds marginal cost up to 1,000 sets and is less than marginal cost beyond 1,000 sets.

 b. No change in price or quantity. It is the kink in the demand curve that gives rise to the discontinuity in marginal revenue. Fluctuations of marginal cost within this discontinuity have no

531

impact on the profit maximizing level of output or price.

   c. Marginal cost would have to rise above $150 a set.

   d. Marginal cost would have to fall below $50 a set.

Self-Tests for Understanding

Test A

1. b
2. c
3. a
4. b
5. a
6. b
7. c
8. b
9. d
10. b
11. d
12. c
13. c
14. b
15. c
16. c
17. d
18. c
19. b
20. a

Test B

1. T
2. T
3. F
4. F
5. F
6. T
7. T
8. F
9. T
10. F

Supplementary Exercises

1. Total Revenue $= 25Q - Q^2/100$

   Marginal Revenue $= 25 - Q/50$

   Average Cost $= 10{,}000/Q + 5$

   Marginal Cost $= 5$

Profit-maximizing level of output sets MC = MR:

$25 - Q/50 = 5$; $Q = 1000$

2. TR $= 80Q - 0.005Q^2$

   AR $= 80 - 0.005Q$

   MR $= 80 - 0.01Q$

   AC $= 0.00000015625Q^2 - 0.003125Q + 40.625$

   MC $= 0.00000046875Q^2 - 0.00625Q + 40.625$

   a. Set MR = MC

      $Q = 6{,}000$; $P = 60$; profits $= 135{,}000$

   b. Set MR = 0

      $Q = 8{,}000$; $P = 40$; profits $= 115{,}000$

   c. yes

Chapter 13

Chapter Review

1. less; less
2. increasing; reduction; increase
3. predatory pricing; is not; variable
4. concentration; Herfindahl-Hirshman; little
5. scale; scope; is not; below; above
6. high
7. decline; less; losses
8. reduces;

Important Terms and Concepts Quiz

1. l
2. e
3. k
4. m
5. g
6. f
7. d
8. b
9. c
10. j
11. a
12. i

Basic Exercises

1. a. Q: 60; 90; 120; 150

      AC: 15¢; 11.7¢;10¢;9¢

      MC: 5¢;5¢; 5¢; 5¢

b. $6 million loss at all levels of output.

c. No; fixed costs are never covered.

2. a. 75¢ a pound

b. The admonition to shut down if price drops below average variable cost assumes that the acts of shutting down and restarting are themselves costless. If, in contrast, it is costly to shutdown and then restart production lines, a firm might continue with production for a short period of time even if price is less than average variable cost to avoid the costs of shutting down and restarting. In the case of predatory pricing, a firm would deliberately accept losses for a short period of time, if it gave the firm monopoly power and the ability to earn economic profits in the future sufficient to overcome the losses incurred while driving out rivals. Thus a price below average variable cost might be an indication of predatory pricing, but it might also be a rational response to changing market conditions and by itself is likely to be insufficient evidence of predatory pricing.

3. 80, 90, 90; 3,000; 2,075; 5,750

The Herfindahl-Hirshman Index gives greater weight to large firms because its squares market share.

Self-Tests for Understanding

Test A

1. b, d
2. a, b, d
3. a, d
4. b
5. d
6. c
7. b
8. b
9. b
10. a
11. c
12. d
13. b
14. b
15. d
16. a
17. c
18. c
19. c
20. d

Test B

1. F
2. F
3. F
4. T
5. T
6. F
7. F
8. F
9. F
10. F

Economics in Action

In June 2001, the Justice department's case was dismissed by Judge J. Thomas Marten who said, "There is no doubt that American may be a difficult, vigorous, even brutal competitor, but here, it engaged only in bare, but not brass, knuckle competition." In January 2002, the Justice Department appealed.

The government lost its appeal.

Chapter 14

Chapter Review

(1) are not

(2) selection; planning; distribution

(3) was not; efficient

(4) efficient; decreasing

(5) increase; cost; greater; is not; equals

(6) price; marginal cost; price; price

(7) utility; cost; equals

(8) maximize

(9) input; output

Important Terms and Concepts Quiz

1. c
2. e
3. b
4. d
5. f

Basic Exercise

1. $25; $15
2. $10; more
3. decrease; $3; fewer
4. $18

Self-Tests for Understanding

Test A
1. d
2. b
3. d
4. c
5. d
6. c
7. b
8. c
9. b
10. b
11. c
12. a
13. b
14. c
15. b
16. c

Test B
1. T
2. F
3. F
4. T
5. F
6. F
7. T
8. T
9. F
10. T

Supplementary Exercises
1. a. No
   b. increase; 1; increase; 2; inefficient
   c. Consumers respond to the same set of prices and consume so that marginal utility equals price,
2. a. 120; 1,200; 160; 800; +40; +400. Note that this reallocation of inputs should work to move the ratio of marginal physical products in the production of corn and tomatoes toward equality.
   b. In competitive markets, profit maximizing firms adjust the use of inputs until the ratio of marginal physical products is equal to the ratio of input prices. By adjusting to common prices, the ratio of marginal physical products is equated across alternative uses.

Chapter 15

Chapter Review
(1) opportunity
(2) marginal cost; marginal utility; on
(3) little
(4) externalities; detrimental; beneficial
(5) higher; higher
(6) private; inefficient; much; less
(7) depletability; excludability; public
(8) difficult; rider
(9) zero; zero
(10) does not; less
(11) irreversible
(12) limited

Important Terms and Concepts Quiz
1. q
2. h
3. b
4. i
5. n
6. e
7. d
8. f
9. k
10. p
11. l
12. g
13. m
14. r
15. o
16. s
17. c

Basic Exercise
1. Col. 1: $2,640,000; $11; $2,112,000; $10.56
2. Col. 2: 120; $2,640,000; $11; 100; $2,200,000; $11; cost of producing widgets unchanged; cost per hour of police service up 4.17 percent.
3. Col. 3: 80; $2,640,000; $11; 100; $3,300,000; $16.50; cost of producing widgets unchanged; cost per hour of police service up 50 percent over 10 years.

Self-Tests for Understanding

Test A
1. c
2. c
3. d
4. c

534

5. d (and possibly b)
6. d
7. a
8. c
9. b
10. c
11. d
12. d
13. b
14. c
15. a, b, c, d
16. d
17. b
18. a
19. c
20. b

Test B

1. F
2. F
3. T
4. F
5. F
6. F
7. T
8. T
9. T
10. F

Supplementary Exercises

1. a. See table and diagram below.
   b. Widgets:

      MP(*L*) = 22.61

      AP(*L*) = 45.23

      Recitals:

      MP(*L*) = 50

      AP(*L*) = 50

   c. Widgets:

      MP(*L*) = 25.63

      AP(*L*) = 51.26

      Recitals:

      MP(*L*) = 50

      AP(*L*) = 50

   Productivity of widget
   workers is up 13.3 percent.
   No increase in the productivity of musicians.

   d. Opportunity cost of recitals has risen 13.3 percent
      from 0.45 widgets to 0.51 widgets.
      PPF: Recitals = $50[40{,}000 - W^2/(3600K)]$

   e. Except for when all labor is allocated to playing
      recitals, the new production possibilities frontier
      is outside the original frontier.

Chapter 16

Chapter Review

(1) innovation

(2) invention; innovation; entrepreneurs; small
   entrepreneurial

(3) cost; entry

(4) ratchet

(5) externalities

(6) trading; licensing

(7) higher; lower

Important Terms and Concepts Quiz

1. r
2. g
3. c
4. p
5. i
6. n
7. s
8. a
9. d

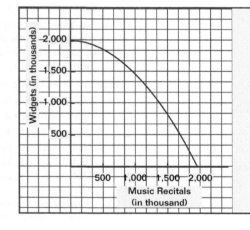

Table of production possibilities
(K = 22,500 and L = 40,000)

	Widgets	Music Recitals
A	1,800,000	0
B	1,558,846	500,000
C	1,272,792	1,000,000
D	900,000	1,500,000
E	0	2,000,000

10. l

11. q

12. o

13. h

14. j

15. b

16. e

17. m

18. f

Basic Exercises

1. $31,000; $51,047; $83,849; $137,393; $224,584

    Note that although the growth rate increases by the same one-half of one percent, the difference in GDP per capita gets bigger and bigger.

2. 2 percent

Self-Tests for Understanding

Test A

1. b

2. c

3. b, d

4. d

5. a,b,c,d

6. b

7. a

8. c

9. b

10. d

11. d

12. a

13. d

14. c

15. d

16. b

17. c

18. b, d

19. b

20. b

Test B

1. F

2. F

3. T

4. T

5. T

6. T

7. F

8. T

9. T

10. T

Chapter 17

Chapter Review

(1) externality; decrease; taxes

(2) controls; inefficient; more

(3) marginal

(4) can never; price

(5) discourage; incentive; encourage; incentive; encouraging

Important Terms and Concepts Quiz

1. c

2. e

3. a

4. d

Basic Exercises

1. a. 15 cents; 10 million

    b. falls; rises; declines; shifts up by 5 cents; no change or falls to zero, i.e., some firms leave industry; declines.

    c. Since the tax is per bag, not per unit of pollution, the pollution control equipment will not reduce a firm's pollution tax.

    d. No. Since the equipment is only 75 percent effective, the total cost of using the equipment (4 cents plus the 1.25 cent emission tax per bag) is greater than the tax of 5 cents per bag.

    e. Less than 3.75 cents; more than 5.33 cents

    f. Price rises and industry output declines as some high-cost firms leave the industry.

2. a. Energy: 18.0; 17.8; 17.7; 17.4; 17.1; 16.7; 16.7; 16.4; 16.0; 15.6; 15.2; 14.4; 14.1; 13.5; 13.2; 12.6; 12.3; 12.2; 12.3; 12.2; 11.9; 11.9; 11.7; 11.6; 11.4; 11.4; 11.3; 10.9; 10.5; 10.2; 10.1; 9.7; 938; 9.6; 9.4; 9.1; 8.8

    b. Energy use rose during the late 1960s as the relative price of energy fell. The rise in energy prices following 1973 led to a significant decline in energy consumption per dollar of GDP. Energy consumption per thousand dollars of GDP has continued to decline throughout the 1980s even as relative energy prices have fallen. Patterns of energy consumption per thousand dollars of GDP up to 1981 could be interpreted as a movement along a demand curve in response to changes in relative price. The introduction of energy conservation practices, e.g., home insulation, energy-efficient machines and cars meant that one would not expect energy consumption to return to earlier levels even as relative energy prices declined. Changes in the structure of the economy, i.e., the increasing importance of services as compared to manufacturing, is also likely to have reduced the demand for energy. Energy prices were lower at the end of 2004 than they were in the early 1980s yet energy use is dramatically lower. In 2005 and 2006, energy use continued to all as energy prices started moving from lows touched in previous years.

Self-Tests for Understanding

Test A

1. b
2. e
3. c
4. b
5. d
6. b
7. a
8. b
9. b
10. b
11. a
12. d
13. c
14. b
15. d
16. b
17. a
18. c
19. c
20. d

Test B

1. F
2. F
3. F
4. F
5. F
6. F
7. F
8. F
9. T
10. T

Supplementary Exercise

1. MC = 15.

   $P = 65 - .025Q$; TR $= 65Q - 0.025Q^2$; MR $= 65 - 0.05Q$.

   Set MC = MR to solve for profit maximizing output: $15 = 65 - .05Q$; $Q = 1,000$; $P = 40$ cents; Profit = 25 cents on each of 1,000 million bags or $250 million.

2. If price rises by 5 cents, quantity demanded will decline to 800 million bags. At price of 45 cents, profit is 25 cents a bag or $200 million. Set MC = MR to determine profit maximizing level of output: $20 = 65 - 0.05Q$; $Q = 900$; $P = 42.5$ cents ; profits 22.5 cents a bag or $202.5 million.

3. Long-run equilibrium price equals minimum average cost = 15 cents. Market quantity = 2,000 million bags; 200 firms producing 10 million bags each.

4. Short run: For representative firm AC $= .4(Q - 10)^2 + 20$.

   TC $= 0.4Q^3 - 8Q^2 + 60Q$.

   MC $= 1.2Q^2 - 16Q + 60$.

   As each firm supplies 1/200 of the market, we can find the short-run profit maximizing position of each firm by setting MC equal to price.

   MC $= 65 - 0.025(Q \times 200)$, or

   $1.2Q^2 - 16Q + 60 = 65 - 5Q$.

   The mathematics of solving this equation for Q are a bit cumbersome. Rounding off, firm output = 9.6 million bags; industry output = 1,920 million bags; and price = 17 cents. Note that price is now less than average cost.

   Long run: Some firms leave in response to short-run losses. Long-run equilibrium occurs where remaining firms produce at minimum average cost.

   Price = 20 cents; market demand = 1,800; each of 180 firms produce 10 million bags.

537

The conditions in this problem—marginal cost for the monopolist equal to the minimum average cost of competitive firms, new firms can operate with the same cost curves, i.e., the long run industry supply curve is horizontal and the same demand curve under either market structure—imply the following: 1) by restricting output, the monopolist creates less pollution than the perfectly competitive industry; 2) the monopolist is unable to pass on the full extent of the pollution tax; and 3) in long-run equilibrium under perfect competition, consumers pay all of the pollution tax.

Economics in Action

1. Simon won the original bet and received a check for $567.07 from Ehrlich. You can read about the bet in John Tierney's article "Betting the Planet," *New York Times Magazine,* December 2, 1990.

   The United States Geological Survey publishes data on mineral prices. You might start with this Web site: http://minerals.usgs.gov/minerals/pubs/metal_prices/

Chapter 18

Chapter Review

(1) direct; indirect; personal income; payroll; corporate

(2) average; marginal; progressive; proportional; regressive; reduce

(3) payroll; regressive; do not; zero; are not

(4) sales; property; federalism

(5) equity; horizontal; vertical; vertical; benefits; benefits

(6) burden; greater; excess burden; does not; smallest

(7) higher; lower; smaller

(8) incidence; shifting

(9) demand; supply; inelastic; workers; firms

Important Terms and Concepts Quiz

1. b
2. p
3. i
4. n
5. r
6. g
7. s
8. v
9. a
10. j
11. u
12. w

13. x
14. k
15. y
16. f
17. m
18. h
19. t
20. o
21. c
22. z
23. d
24. q
25. e
26. l

Basic Exercises

2. $42; 50 million
3. $46; 44 million
4. $4; it is less than increase in tax.
5. All are likely to decline.
7. The first demand curve.
8. $50; 48 million; Figure 18-3; Figure 18-3; consumers

Self-Tests for Understanding

Test A

1. b
2. d
3. c
4. b, c
5. d
6. c
7. c
8. d   As long as the marginal rate exceeds the average rate the average rate will increase whether the marginal rate increases, decreases or remains unchanged.
9. b
10. b
11. b
12. b
13. b
14. b
15. c
16. c
17. c
18. b

538

19. a
20. c
21. a

Test B

1. F
2. T
3. T
4. T
5. T
6. F
7. F
8. T
9. F
10. F

Supplementary Exercise

1. Taxes: 0; $2,000; $4,000; $6,000; $16,000; $46,000
   Average Tax Rate: 0; 0.0667; 0.10; 0.12; 0.16; 0.184
   Marginal Tax Rate: 0; 0.20; 0.20; 0.20; 0.20; 0.20

2. b. Revenue = TQ

   Harris: Revenue =
   $25.608\ T - 2.95\ T^2$

   T = $4.34 maximizes tax revenue; taxes = $55.57 billion

   Grossman: Revenue

   $= 27.5184\ T - 10.91\ T^2$

   T = $1.26 maximizes tax revenue; taxes = $17.35 billion

   c. Harris: ΔQ = -1.475; elasticity = 0.275
   Grossman: ΔQ = −5.455; elasticity = 1.107 When demand is more elastic, every increase in the tax leads to a larger reduction in the quantity demanded. As a result the revenue maximizing tax is lower.

   Harris did not solve for the revenue maximizing tax. Rather he analyzed the impact of $2 increase in cigarette taxes and estimated a net increase in revenue of $28 billion. The straight line approximation to the Harris demand curve for this exercise shows a gross increase in revenue of $37.56 billion following a $2 tax increase.

   d. When the supply curve is infinitely elastic (horizontal), consumers pay all of any increase in taxes. If the supply curve were perfectly inelastic (vertical), then producers would pay all of any increase in taxes and there would be no change in the quantity demanded regardless of the elasticity

of demand. If the supply curve has a positive slope, that is if the elasticity of supply is not infinite or zero, then the incidence of any increase in taxes will be divided between consumers and producers depending upon the elasticities of demand and supply.

Chapter 19

Chapter Review

(1) productivity; revenue
(2) negative; more; positive; higher; below
(3) discounting; fewer; lower
(4) is not; exceed
(5) all; no
(6) most; part; is
(7) higher; equal
(8) increase; increase; more
(9) greater; greater; greater

Important Terms and Concepts Quiz

1. g
2. c
3. l
4. d
5. j
6. m
7. e
8. h
9. a
10. i
11. n
12. f
13. k

Basic ExerciseS

1. Economic profit = Net revenue – opportunity cost of labor – cost of other inputs; Economic profit = $500 – ($10 × 40) – $60 = $500 – $460 = $40.

2. $60; The rent for the sunny plot should reflect the difference in the cost of production as compared to the marginal plot.

3. If the owner of the sunny plot tried charging a rent that exceeded the $60 difference in production costs, Darlene would make a greater profit by growing her flowers on the marginal plot. With a rent of $60 for the sunny plot she would be indifferent about using either plot.

Self-Tests for Understanding
Test A
1. d
2. a
3. c
4. b
5. c
6. c
7. a
8. c
9. d
10. d
11. a
12. b
13. c
14. a
15. c
16. b
17. b
18. b
19. c
20. a

Test B
1. F
2. T
3. T
4. T
5. F
6. T
7. F
8. F
9. T
10. F

Appendix

Important Terms and Concepts Quiz: Appendix
1. a

Basic Exercises: Appendix
1. a. $1,818.18; $2,066.12; $3,884.30; –$115.70
   b.   cost; no
   c. $1,904.76; $2,267.57; $4,172.33; $172.33
   d.   present value of returns; yes
   e.   5 percent: $200; $4,200; $2,200; $110; $2,310.
        10 percent: $400; $4,400; $2,400; $240; $2,640

f.   5 percent: $1,800; $90; $4,390; $190
     10 percent: $1,600; $160; $4,260; –$140

2. The contest sponsors could meet their payments to Mr. Calhoun by investing a smaller sum in 1993 and using both the initial investment along with the interest earnings to make the necessary future payments. Present value calculations show how much must be invested today to fund the future payments. Assuming the first payment was made right away, the sponsors need to invest a sum sufficient to fund 19 future payments of $50,000, or

$$\sum_{t=1}^{19} \frac{\$50,000}{(1+i)^t}$$

If the interest rate was 6.5%, the present value of the 19 future payments was only $557,906. Including the first payment to Mr. Calhoun brings the total cost of $1,000,000 to $607,906. A higher interest rate would mean higher interest earnings and result in a lower present value, while a lower interest rate would mean a higher present value and require a larger initial investment by the contest sponsors.

Supplementary Exercise
If dividends and future stock prices are known for sure, buying that stock should offer investors the risk adjusted market rate of return. If earnings and dividends reflect monopoly profits, the price of the stock will be high while the rate of return will still reflect the risk adjusted market rate of return. The biggest winners (the ones who will earn the highest rate of return), will be those who identified the potential for oil companies to generate higher future dividends before others in the market. These are the individuals who paid a low initial price and who therefore stand to gain the most.

Chapter 20

Chapter Review
(1) leisure; more; decrease; income
(2) more; substitution; increases; offset
(3) greater; revenue; negative
(4) demand; higher
(5) monopolist; monopsonist; lower; higher; two; bilateral
(6) Entrepreneurs, monoploy, reduces
(7) fixed, public, marginal

Important Terms and Concepts Quiz
1. i
2. f
3. h

4. a

5. c

6. e

7. g

8. d

9. j

10. k

Basic Exercises

1. 60; 55; 50; 45; 40; 35; 30; 25; 20; 15

2. $4,800; $4,400; $4,000; $3,600; $3,200; $2,800; $2,400; $2,000; $1,600; $1,200

3. 7; profits = $9,800

4. $2,000; 800; 8; $11,200; if 7 workers, profits also = $11,200 as MRP = wage for eighth worker.

5. a. $3,600

    b. 900 workers

    c. $2,800 and 600 workers, or $2,400 and 700 workers

Self-Tests for Understanding

Test A

1. d

2. a

3. b

4. c

5. b

6. c

7. b

8. a

9. d

10. b

11. c

12. c

13. a

14. c

15. c

16. d

17. d

18. b

19. a

20. c

Test B

1. T

2. T

3. F

4. F

5. F

6. F

7. F

8. F

9. T

10. F

Supplementary Exercises

a. $2,000; 8

b. greater

Total labor cost: $600; $1,600; $3,000; $4,800; $7,000; $9,600; $12,600; $16,000; $19,800; $24,000

Marginal labor cost: $600; $1,000; $1,400; $1,800; $2,200; $2,600; $3,000; $3,400; $3,800; $4,200

d. 6 workers

e. $1,600

f. $13,200 = $80 × 285 − 6 × $1,600.

g. Both wages and employment would increase. Tony would hire 7 workers at $2,200 a month. The "high" minimum wage increases employment because it changes Tony's marginal cost of labor schedule.

h. No. If the union had more than 7 workers, it might want a lower wage to increase employment. If the union had 7 or fewer workers, it might be able to extract a higher wage by bargaining for some of Tony's profits.

Chapter 21

Chapter Review

(1) 22,000; absolute; relative

(2) 50.3%; 3.4%

(3) different; are not; overstate

(4) efficiency

(5) decrease

(6) break-even

(7) negative; small

Important Terms and Concepts Quiz

1. a

2. g

3. e

4. h

5. f

6. c

7. b

Basic Exercises

1. Col 7: 18,600; 23,198; 25,703; 26,361; 26,274; 26,416; 28,303; 29,036; 31,500

3. Col. 4: 4,598; 2,505; 658; -87; 142; 1,887; 733; 2,464
   Col. 5: 1,402; 1,195; 2,342; 5,387; 408; 9,563; 442; 1,361
   Col. 6: 23%; 32%; 78%; 102%; 74%; 84%; 38%; 36%
   The marginal tax rates in column 6 should be equivalent to the slopes of the line segments you graphed in Figure 21-1.

Self-Tests for Understanding

Test A

1. d
2. c
3. b
4. b
5. a
6. c
7. a
8. c
9. b
10. c
11. d
12. c
13. c
14. a
15. a,d
16. c
17. a
18. a Differences in schooling might reflect voluntary decisions or discrimination in access to schooling.
19. d
20. d

Test B

1. T
2. F
3. F
4. F
5. F
6. F
7. F

8. F

9. T

10. F

Appendix

Discrimination by employers; If some employers discriminate against particular workers, other employers should be able to hire these workers at lower wages and thus produce at lower cost than the first set of employers. Discrimination by employees does not give rise to a similar opportunity for a non-discriminator to operate at lower cost.

Supplementary Exercises

1. The graph is a Lorenz curve, named for American economist Max O. Lorenz who developed the graph in 1905 as a way to describe income distribution. If everyone received the same income, then the Lorenz curve for such a country would lie along the 45 degree line. Lorenz argued that the extent to which the line sags below the 45 degree line can be used as a measure of income inequality.

   For the three countries pictured in the graph, the line for Finland lies closest to the 45 degree line while the line for Mexico is furthest away. Plot the Lorenz curve for other countries to see how they compare to these three.

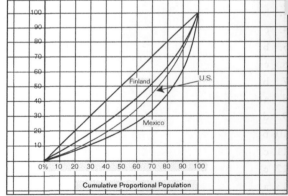

2. There are three interpretations of the word average: 1) the most frequent, measured by the mode, 2) the value that evenly divides a population, measured by the median, and 3) the sum of a variable of interest divided by the size of the population, measured by the arithmetic average or mean .

   The median income of $43,318 tells us that 50% of U.S. households earned more than $43,318 in 2003 and 50% of households earned less. The mean reports the arithmetic average income level. If a small number of households earn extremely high incomes, this will increase the average but leave the median unaffected. Many feel that the median income is a better measure of typical household income. The fact that the U.S. median is below the average implies that a small number of households have very high income levels.

4. Answers will vary.

Chapter 22

Chapter Review

(1) microeconomics; macroeconomics

(2) price; quantity; domestic product

(3) inflation; deflation; recessions; higher; higher; left; decrease; stagflation

(4) money; final; excludes; includes; are not

(5) nominal; real; Real; nominal; real

(6) is not; increase; decreasing; larger; lower

(7) up; depends; risen

(8) inflation; stabilization; recessions; inflation

Important Terms and Concepts Quiz

1. p
2. h
3. i
4. m
5. o
6. q
7. l
8. b
9. n
10. d
11. j
12. g
13. k
14. r
15. c
16. s
17. e
18. f

Basic Exercises

1. a. Panels c and d
   b. Panel b; yes, most notably 1929–1933
   c. Panel a
   d. Panel c

2. a. shift aggregate demand curve to left
   b. shift aggregate demand curve to right
   c. Real GDP will fall as aggregate demand curve is shifted to the left; prices will rise as aggregate demand curve is shifted to the right.

3. a. col (3) : $600; $300; $225; $1,125 col (6): $868; $416; $297; $1,581
   b. 40.5 percent
   c. $620; $320; $247.50; $1,187.50
   d. 5.56 percent
   e. The increase in real GDP is less than the increase in nominal GDP as the increase in nominal GDP includes both the increase in production and the increase in prices. The increase in real GDP is the better measure of the change in output.

Self-Tests for Understanding

Test A

1. b
2. d
3. a
4. c
5. a
6. b
7. a
8. a
9. c
10. d
11. d
12. b
13. a
14. d
15. d
16. b
17. d
18. c
19. c
20. b

Test B

1. F
2. T
3. F
4. T
5. F
6. F

543

7. T

8. T

9. T

10. T

Economics in Action

1. The NBER committee dated the end of the 1990s expansion, or the business cycle peak, as March 2001. The committee dated the end of the recession as November 2001.

Chapter 23

Chapter Review

(1) productivity

(2) more; more; demand; supply; right; increase

(3) is; 200

(4) potential; actual

(5) discouraged; decrease; understate; understate; overstate

(6) frictional; cyclical; structural

(7) frictional; increased; lower

(8) cannot; partial; some

(9) real; the same; as; were unchanged

(10) different; less; more

(11) higher; nominal; real

(12) will; be unchanged; small; large; nominal

Important Terms and Concepts Quiz

1. a

2. t

3. r

4. k

5. c

6. q

7. b

8. v

9. e

10. h

11. j

12. n

13. i

14. d

15. p

16. m

17. o

18. l

19. f

20. s

Basic Exercises

1. a. $250,000; $5,250,000; $4,772,727; $5,750,000; $5,227,273. Borrowers gain at expense of lenders.

    b. $775,000; $5,775,000; $5,250,000; $5,225,000; $4,750,000. Both are treated equally.

    c. $1,000,000; $6,000,000; $5,454,545; $5,000,000; $4,545,455. Lenders gain at expense of borrowers.

2. a. 1.70; −1.81; −2.04; −3.00; −0.52; 5.98; 9.05; 5.11; 6.21; 5.53; 6.57; 1.47; 2.77; 4.39; 1.62; 3.95; 1.48; 1.01; 0.91; 4.64; 2.01; 3.77; 3.93; 1.82; 2.44; 4.00; −0.18; −0.45; −1.99

    c. When actual inflation turns out to be greater than expected, the difference between nominal interest rates that were set at the beginning of the period and the actual rate of inflation may be negative.

3. 1.07; 1.09; 1.03; 1.24; 1.52; 1.52; 1.35; 1.24; 1.16; 1.12; 0.85; 0.84; 0.80; 0.82; 0.89; 0.84; 0.81; 0.77; 0.75; 0.75; 0.78; 0.77; 0.65; 0.70; 0.88; 0.82; 0.75; 0.86; 1.00 After adjusting for inflation unleaded gas prices were highest in 1980 and 1981.

Self-Tests for Understanding

Test A

1. d

2. a

3. c

4. c

5. b, a, d, c

6. a, b, d

7. a

8. c

9. b

10. b

11. a, d

12. c

13. b

14. b

15. c

544

b

b

a

a

c

t B

F

T

F

F

F

F

F

F

F

T

ppendix

portant Terms and Concepts Quiz: ppendix

b

f

d

a Don't forget to multiply by 100.

c

sic Exercises: Appendix

a. 2,500; 400

b. $16,500 = 2,500 \times \$2.36 + 400 \times \$26.50$

c. $110 = (16,500/15,000) \times 100$

e. 10 percent

f. $15,771 ; 5.1 percent

2004 index, using 2005 base, 91.1. 2005 base implies inflation of 9.8 percent. The slightly lower rate of inflation reflects a larger weight on more slowly rising clothing prices when using the 2005 expenditure pattern.

upplementary Exercise

a and b. Insufficient information; for example, the value of the price index for Canada for 2004 shows how 2004 Canadian prices compare to Canadian prices in the base period, 1982–1984,

not how Canadian prices compare to those in other countries.

c. Inflation within a country can be measured by the percentage change in that country's price index. Italy had the most inflation; Germany had the least inflation.

2. 69,905; 119,246; 250,760

Chapter 24

Chapter Review

(1) growth; stabilization

(2) investment (or capital formation); innovation; invention; human

(3) convergence; innovate; imitate; rights

(4) low; are not; decrease

(5) investment

(6) goods; services

(7) cost disease

Important Terms and Concepts

1. h
2. a
3. b
4. e
5. k
6. l
7. d
8. m
9. j
10. i
11. g
12. c
13. n

Basic Exercises

1. a. 24.52
   b. 33.30
   c. No. labor productivity grows more slowly, but it continues to grow.

2. 1.4%: 200.4; 401.6

   2.5%: 343.7; 1,181.4

   2.9%: 438.4; 1,921.9

Test A

1. c

545

2. a

3. b, c

4. a, b, d

5. c

6. a

7. b

8. d

9. c

10. c

11. b

12. a

13. b, c

14. c

15. b

16. a

17. c

18. a, b

19. a

20. a, b, c

Test B

1. F

2. F

3. F

4. T

5. T

6. T

7. F

8. F

9. F

10. F

Supplementary exercise

6.211%; 4.084%; 36 years

Chapter 25

Chapter Review

(1) demand; consumption; investment; government; exports; imports; net exports

(2) before; taxes; transfer

(3) disposable; more; movement along; shift in

(4) *C*; *I*; *G*; *X*; *IM*; less; decrease

(5) increase; larger; more; smaller

Important Terms and Concepts Quiz

1. g

2. d

3. h

4. c

5. k

6. 1

7. b

8. n

9. a

10. i

11. e

12. m

13. j

14. o

Basic Exercises

1. a.   consumption spending; disposable income; .75;.75;.75;.75

    b.   .9; .825; .8; .7875; .78

    c.   No they are not. The MPC is the same at all levels of income. The APC falls as income rises

    d.   See diagram below

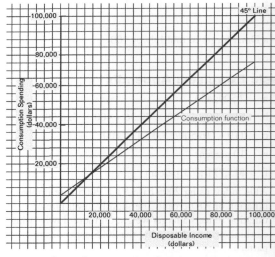

    e.   slope of consumption function

    f.   rays become less steep, that is their slope decreases. For a straight line consumption function with a positive Y intercept the APC w be greater than the MPC although the differenc will get smaller as income increases.

a. $18,000; $78,000; $9,600,000

b. .78; .9

c. $21,750; $74,250; $9,600,000

d. In this example, MPC is the same for the rich and poor. The rich reduce their consumption by the same amount that the poor increase their consumption.

$C = 3,000 + .75\ DI$

a. 0.55/0.50 = 1.1

b. The estimate in a is greater than the slope of the consumption function. It overestimates the MPC because it includes the effect of the shift of the consumption function.

lf-Tests for Understanding

t A

b

b

d

b

b

d

c

a

c

b

c

c

a

d

d

d

c

c

a

b

t B

F

F

F

T

T

T

F

8. T

9. T

10. T

Appendix

Appendix Review

(1) final; produced

(2) exports; imports; produced

(3) income

(4) depreciation

(5) value added

Important Terms and Concepts Quiz: Appendix

1. a

2. b

3. c

Basic Exercises: Appendix

1. a. $2,200

   b. $1,700

   c. $1,700; wages = $1,200; profits $500

   d. $500

   e. $1,200 ($1,700 - $500)

   f. $1,700

   g. $1,700

   h. $1,700

2. a. $1,000; $2,100; $1,600; $4,700

   b. The $200 addition to inventories.

Self-Tests for Understanding: Appendix

Test A

1. c

2. c

3. b

4. c

5. a

6. d

7. d

8. b

9. c

10. d

11. b

12. d

13. c

14. c

15. a

16. d

17. c

18. c

Test B

1. F

2. T

3. F

4. F

5. F

6. T

7. F

8. F

9. F

10. T

Supplementary Exercise

1. MPC = $60/DI^{1/2}$; MPC declines as income rises. Consumption spending rises following redistribution from rich to poor as increase in consumption by poor is greater than decline in consumption by rich.

Chapter 26

Chapter Review

(1) increase; increasing; decrease

(2) equal to

(3) horizontal; vertical

(4) intersection

(5) less; reduce; increase; less; downward; lower; increase; increase; higher

(6) price level

(7) less; recessionary; inflationary

(8) autonomous; induced

(9) MPC

(10) income; MPC

(11) smaller; inflation; trade; income; financial

(12) do not; shift in; horizontal

Important Terms and Concepts Quiz

1. f

2. b

3. g

4. j

5. a

6. i

7. e

8. c

9. k

10. h

11. l

12. d

Basic Exercises

1. e. $10,000

   f. 9,600; 9,800; 10,000; 10,200; 10,400; 10,600; 10,800

   g. Spending would be greater than output, inventories would decline, firms would increase output.

   h. recessionary gap, 250; inflationary gap, $200

2. a. 9,700; 9,900; 10,100; 10,300; 10,500; 10,700; 10,900; equilibrium = 10,500

   b. 5; equilibrium level; GDP; autonomous spending

   c. 0.80

   d. 5 = 1/(1-0.8)

   e. 0.80; yes

3. b. 9,500

   c. 10,500

   d. aggregate demand curve

   e. negative

4. The increase in investment spending shifts the aggregate demand curve to the right. Points on the new aggregate demand curve include $P = 90$, $Y = 11,000$; $P = 100$, $Y = 10,500$; $P = 110$; $Y = 10,000$

Self-Tests for Understanding

Test A

1. c

2. c

3. a, c, d, e, g

4. c

5. d

6. c

7. a

b

c

a

a

c

b

a, b, c

c

b

d

c

a, c, e, g

c

c

b

b

a

st B

T

F

F

T

T

F

T

F

F

F

T

T

T

T

ppendix A

asic Exercise: Appendix A

$C = 340 + 0.8 (Y - T) = -1100 + 0.8 Y$

$C + I + G + (X - IM) = 2000 + 0.8 Y$

$Y = 2,000 + 0.8Y$; $Y(1 - 0.8) = 2000$; $Y = 2000/(1 - (1 - 0.8)) = 10,000$

4. $Y = 2,100 + .8Y = 10,500$; Increase in $Y = 500$; Multiplier = 5 = 500/100

Appendix B

Basic Exercise: Appendix B

1. Total spending: 9,625; 9,812; 10,000; 10,287; 10,375; 10,562; 10,750; equilibrium = 10,000

2. Total spending: 9,750; 9,937; 10,125; 10,312; 10,500; 10,687; 10,875; equilibrium = 10,500

3. multiplier = 500/125 = 4

4. The multiplier is smaller because imports increase with income. The slope of the expenditure schedule = 375/500 = 0.75. Multiplier = 1/(1 − 0.75) = 1/0.25 = 4. Alternatively, MPC = 0.8 and the marginal propensity to import, MPI = 0.05. Multiplier = 1/(1 − MPC − MPI) = 1/(1 − 0.8 − 0.05) = 1/(1 − 0.75) = 1/(0.25) = 4.

Supplementary Exercises

1. a. $Y = C + I + G + (X - IM)$

$Y = 340 + 0.8DI(-1) + 1,500 + 1,750 + (1,200 - 1,350)$

$Y = 0.8Y[(-1) - 1,800] + 3,400$

$Y = 0.8Y(-1) + 2,000$

At equilibrium $Y = Y(-1)$:

$Y = 0.75Y + 2,000$

$0.25Y = 2,000$

$Y = 10,000$

   b. Yes, the economy converges to a new equilibrium value of 10,500. The multiplier is 5 (= 500/100), the same multiplier we get from using the simple multiplier formula.

   c. The effects of changes in government spending and net exports will be similar to results in 1b, that is, the multiplier is 4, so for every dollar change in autonomous spending, equilibrium income will change by four dollars.

   d. If the MPC changes, the slope of the consumption function, and therefore the slope of the expenditure function, will change. If the MPC increases, then the consumption function and the expenditure schedule will be steeper. An increase in the MPC will lead to an increase in the size of the multiplier.

Chapter 27

Chapter Review

(1) increase; movement along; shift in; right

(2) intersection; decrease; increases

(3) inflationary; inward; movement along; higher; lower

(4) recessionary

(5) inflationary; supply; falling; rising

Important Terms and Concepts Quiz

1. f

2. c

3. d

4. b

5. a

6. e

Basic Exercises

1. a. increases; increases; $10,250

   e. 95; $10,125

   f. Inflationary gap; increasing wages and other business costs will shift the aggregate supply curve up; 100 and $10,000

   g. no gaps

   h. recessionary gap; elimination of gap likely to be very slow; 90; $10,250

2. horizontal

   a. no

   b. Output and prices increase as the economy moves along the aggregate supply curve. The increase in prices reduces net exports and the purchasing power of money-fixed assets. The reduction in net exports and the resulting shift in the consumption function means a downward shift in the expenditure schedule (not drawn) that partially offsets the expansionary impact of the original increase in investment spending and reconciles equilibrium in the income-expenditure diagram with that of the aggregate demand-aggregate supply diagram (Y_2, P_2). That is, to complete the analysis one would need to draw a third expenditure schedule between the solid and dashed ones already shown in Figure 27-4. We know from the equilibrium determined in the aggregate demand-aggregate supply diagram that this final expenditure schedule will intersect the 45-degree line at a real GDP level of Y_2.

3. s to left, m, -, -; m, s up, -, +; s to right, m, +, +; m, s down, +, -; s to left, m, -, -; m, s up, -, +

Self-Tests for Understanding

Test A

1. b

2. b

3. a

4. d

5. a

6. c

7. a, b, c, d, e

8. a

9. d

10. c

11. d

12. a

13. c

14. b, d

15. a, b, d

16. c

17. c

18. c

19. d

20. c

Test B

1. T

2. T

3. T

4. T

5. T

6. F

7. T

8. T

9. F

10. F

Supplementary Exercises

1. $C + I + G + (X - IM) = 2,500 + .8Y - 5P$

2. $P = 500 - .04Y$ or $Y = 12,500 - 25P$

3. Solve the ADC and the ASC for the equilibrium levels of Y and P

   $12,500 - 25P = 7,750 + 25P;\ P = 95;\ Y = 10,125;$
   $C = 7,022.5;\ I = 1,500;\ G = 1,800;\ X - IM = -197.5$

$P = 90; Y = 10,000; C = 6,945; I = 1,450; G = 1,800;$
$X - IM = -195$

New expenditure schedule:

$C + I + G + (X - IM) = 2,450 + .8Y - 5P$

New aggregate demand curve:

$P = 490 - .04Y$

Chapter 28

Chapter Review

1) fiscal; expenditure; demand; supply

2) up; 1; 1

3) are not; higher; permanent; less than; investment

4) income; consumption; minus; plus; up; down

5) less; smaller

6) smaller

7) MPC, smaller; smaller; flatter

8) less than

9) increase; decrease; decrease; increase

10) supply; increase

Important Terms and Concepts Quiz

1. c

2. e

3. b

4. d

Basic Exercises

1. Total spending: 9,700; 9,850; 10,000; 10,150; 10,300; 10,450; 10,600; equilibrium = 10,000

2. Total spending: 9,500; 9,650; 9,800; 9,950; 10,100; 10,250; 10,400; equilibrium = 9,500

3. 2.5 = 500/200; in Chapter 26 the multiplier = 5. Multiplier is lower here because income taxes mean that each round of induced spending in the multiplier chain is smaller, hence the change in the equilibrium level of income is less.

4. 300 = 750/2.5

5. 9,500; the multipliers are the same.

Self-Tests for Understanding

Test A

1. c

2. d

3. b

4. c

5. c

6. c

7. c

8. b

9. a

10. d

11. a

12. b

13. a

14. a

15. c

16. b

17. c

18. c

19. c

20. b

Test B

1. F

2. T

3. F

4. F

5. F

6. F

7. F

8. T

9. F

10. F

Appendix A

1. $200; yes $\Delta C = 200 = 0.8 \times 250$

2. Total spending: 9,700; 9,850; 10,000; 10,150; 10,300; 10,450; 10,600; equilibrium = 10,000

3. No. The increase in GDP from the multiplier process increased tax revenues by $125, an amount less than the $250 reduction in taxes that initiated the multiplier process.

4. 11,000; 10,500; variable taxes reduce the slope of the expenditure schedule and hence the value of the multiplier for the economy.

Appendix B

1. $Y = 340 + 0.8 [Y - (-700 + 0.25)Y] + 1,500 + 1,750 - 150$

   $Y = [1 - 0.8 (1 - 0.25)] = 340 + 560 + 1,500 + 1,800 - 200$

$Y = 4,000/ 0.4 = 10,000$

2. No; $Y = 3,990/0.4 = 9,975$, the value of the expenditure multiplier is higher than the value of the tax multiplier.

3. 2.5; 2.5; 2.5; 2.0

4. Simultaneous reduction in G and T reduces Y to 9,950; multipliers = 5;5;5;and 4; with fixed taxes the slope of the expenditure schedule is steeper and multipliers are larger.

Supplementary Exercises

1. Income taxes are an important reason why Okun's multiplier is less than the oversimplified formula.

2. The multiplier for a change in taxes is less than the multiplier for changes in autonomous spending.

Chapter 29

Chapter Review

(1) barter; more difficult

(2) money; commodity; fiat

(3) M1; M2

(4) 1,868.0; 8,853.8

(5) lending; 900; reserve requirement

(6) 1/(reserve requirement)

(7) smaller; excess; smaller

(8) contraction; no

Important Terms and Concepts Quiz

1. c
2. j
3. g
4. m
5. m
6. d
7. t
8. n
9. s
10. k
11. o
12. e
13. f
14. p
15. w
16. v
17. u
18. b
19. r
20. 1
21. h
22. q
23. a
24. i
25. y

Basic Exercises

1. $10,000; col. 1: $1,000; $9,000

2. col. 2: $1,000; $9,000; $10,000; $1,000; 0

3. col. 3: $9,000; 0; $9,000; $900; $8,100; $19,000

4. col. 4: $900; $8,100; $9,000; $900; 0

5. col. 5: $8,100; 0; $8,100; $810; $7,290; $27,100

6. B: $9,000; C: $8,100; D: $7,290; E: $6,561; 0.1; $100,000; required reserve ratio.

Self-Tests for Understanding

Test A

1. b
2. c
3. a
4. c
5. b, d
6. b
7. c
8. d
9. c
10. d
11. d
12. b
13. d
14. c
15. d
16. a
17. a
18. d
19. a
20. b

t B

T
F
T
F
F
T
T
F
F
T

pplementary Exercises

2,500; 1,500

Change in deposits = (change in reserves) $\times$ [1/(M + E + C)]

apter 30

apter Review

central; 12; Board; Governors; Federal Open Market; fiscal; monetary

bills; excess

increase; discount rate

bills; buys; increase; reduction; destruction

federal funds; right; lower

decrease

unconventional monetary policies; easing

supply; demand; shift in; shift in; demand; supply

portant Terms and Concepts Quiz

g
b
h
f
j
d
a
i
e
k

sic Exercises

a. increase; right; decrease

b. decrease; left; increase

Self-Tests for Understanding

Test A

1. b
2. d
3. d
4. c
5. b
6. b
7. c
8. b
9. d
10. c
11. c
12. d
13. b
14. b
15. b
16. a, b
17. a, c
18. a
19. a
20. a, d
21. b

Test B

1. T
2. F
3. F
4. F
5. F
6. F
7. F
8. T
9. T
10. T

Supplementary Exercises

1. a. $Y = 9,200; C = 6,050; I = 1,600; G = 1,500; X - IM = -150$

    b. Y increases to 9,400; $C = 6,250; I = 1,800; G = 1,600; X - IM = -150$

    c. In this model, equilibrium in the income-expenditure diagram depends on the rate of interest. The expenditure schedule is as follows:

$C + I + G + (X - IM)$

$= 1,550 + 0.6(5/6) Y + 2,000 - 50R + 1,500 - 150$

$= 4,900 - 50R + .5Y$

The 45-degree line is $C + I + G + (X - IM) = Y$. Solving these two equations for one expression in Y and R yields

$Y = 9.800 - 100R$

Setting the demand for bank reserves equal to supply of bank reserves yields a second expression in Y and R.

$Y = 50OMO + 250R$.

Once the Fed determines OMO this equation along with the expenditure schedule can be used to find Y and R. When $OMO = 140$, $R = 8$; $Y = 9,000$

d. Now R is treated as known, $R = 4$, and one can use the two equations to solve for OMO and Y. OMO=168; $Y = 9,400$.

2. a. $1,500; $600

   b. $1,220.80; $698.87

Chapter 31

Chapter Review

1. reserve; cheaper
2. increase; bubble; bills; yield
3. subprime
4. spending
5. foreclosures
6. securities
7. bubble
8. consumption; investment; government spending; net exports
9. aggregate demand
10. Troubled Asset Relief Program
11. leverage; business cycle

Important Terms and Concepts Quiz

1. d
2. f
3. k
4. a
5. i
6. c
7. g
8. j
9. e

10. h
11. b

Basic Exercises

a. decrease, aggregate demand, left, decline
b. aggregate demand, right, increase

Self-Tests for Understanding

Test A

1. c
2. c
3. c
4. c
5. c
6. a
7. a
8. a, b
9. b, c, d
10. a, c, d
11. a, b
12. c, d
13. a, b, c, d
14. c
15. a,b
16. d
17. b, d
18. a
19. d
20. b

Test B

1. F
2. F
3. F
4. T
5. T
6. F
7. T
8. T
9. T
10. T

554

apter 32

apter Review

GDP; money

nominal GDP; M; V; P; Y

money; does not; nominal GDP; 200

should not; increase; decrease

velocity

decline; increase; increase

higher; increase; higher

monetary; unconventional; reserves

output; prices; steep; short; long

does not

portant Terms and Concepts Quiz

e

c

d

b

sic Exercises

a. V_1: 6.50; 7.09; 7.72; 8.07; 8.35; 8.88; 8.93; 8.75; 8.77; 8.83

    V_2: 2.07; 2;10; 2;12; 2.08; 2.05; 2.05; 1.95; 1.87; 1.86; 1.88

b.   Estimates based on V_1: 7,166.4; 7,623.8; 8,369.1; 8,954.7; 9,234.2; 10,062.4; 10,705.6; 10,986.3; 11,643.5

    Estimates based on V_2: 7,728.6; 8,226.2; 8,904.4; 9,388.3; 9,831.3; 10,636.2; 10,968.8; 11,060.0; 11,564.0

c.   Errors are highest when velocity changes. The greater variation in V_1 leads to larger prediction errors based on M_1.

Each speaker is arguing that the demand for money has shifted to the right. In both cases the shift is consistent with the reported increase in M and r.

Speaker A is arguing that the shift in the demand for money derives from an autonomous shift in the aggregate demand curve to the right. According to A, it is the increase in nominal GDP that has shifted the demand for money schedule. A shift of the money supply curve to the left, i.e., an open market sale, would increase interest rates even further, inducing an offsetting shift of the aggregate demand curve to the left. With a bit of luck, the policy induced shift of the aggregate demand curve to the left would offset the autonomous shift in the aggregate demand curve to the right, and there would be no inflation.

Speaker B is arguing that there has been an autonomous increase in the demand for money, that is an increase that is unrelated to any change in nominal GDP. If there is no offsetting increase in the supply of money schedule, the rise in interest rates will cause a decline in interest sensitive spending and a shift of the aggregate demand curve to the left increasing unemployment. In this case the appropriate action would be to shift the money supply curve to the right and hold interest rates constant to avoid inducing a shift in the aggregate demand curve.

The appropriate policy response, whether to focus on M or r, depends upon the origins of the shift in the demand for money.

Self-Tests for Understanding

Test A

1. c
2. b
3. a, b, c, d
4. a, b, d
5. c
6. a
7. d
8. d
9. b
10. b
11. d
12. c
13. b, d
14. b
15. b
16. a, b
17. a
18. b
19. c
20. c

Test B

1. T
2. F
3. F
4. T
5. T

6. T

7. F

8. T

9. T

10. F

Supplementary Exercise

NBER identifies a total of 9 recessions between 1950 and 2004. Based on the graph, you most likely found more than nine downturns in the stock market.

Chapter 33

Chapter Review

(1) spending; revenue; revenue; spending; deficit; surplus

(2) down; left; decline; decline; deficit; increase; decrease; accentuate

(3) will; will not

(4) increase; reduction

(5) monetized; greater

(6) foreigners; investment

(7) recession; war; crowding in; crowding out; high; out

(8) right; restrictive; deficit; higher; lower; more slowly

Important Terms and Concepts Quiz

1. d

2. a

3. h

4. c

5. f

6. g

7. e

Basic Exercises

1. a. Total spending: 10,200; 10,250; 10,300; 10,350; 10, 400; 10,450; 10,500; 10,550; 10, 600; equilibrium = 10,400

   b. Budget is balanced

   c. Surplus; 75

   d. Total spending: 10,100; 10,150; 10,200; 10,250; 10, 300; 10,350; 10,400; 10,450; 10, 500; equilibrium = 10,200; actual deficit increases to 50; structural surplus is unchanged at 75

   e. Total spending: 10,050; 10,100; 10,150; 10, 200; 10,250; 10,300; 10,350; 10, 400; 10, 450; equilibrium = 10,100; the reduction in government spending reduces GDP which

reduces tax receipts; deficit declines but not to zero because the decline in GDP reduces taxes

2. a. An open market sale would reduce bank reserv increase interest rates, reduce investment spend and shift the aggregate demand curve to the le offsetting the shift to the right from the reduct in taxes.

   b. Under option B the reduction in taxes will mea more consumption spending, while higher inte rates will reduce private investment spending. a result, option B is likely to be associated with lower rates of economic growth.

Self-Tests for Understanding

Test A

1. d

2. d

3. a

4. c

5. c

6. a

7. a

8. c

9. b, c

10. b, c

11. d

12. c

13. d

14. c

15. a, b, c, d, e, f It all depends on why the deficit increas

16. d

17. d

18. b

19. a, b

20. d

Test B

1. F

2. F

3. F

4. T

5. T

6. F

7. F

8. T

9. T

10. T

Supplementary Exercises

1. It is important to distinguish between deficits during periods of recession and deficits from deliberate increases in G or reductions in T. All of the examples come from periods when the economy was falling into recession.

2. Repudiating the national debt would almost certainly make it more difficult to issue securities to finance deficit spending in the future. Once a nation defaults on its debt, investors are not likely to trust that it will keep its promise to make interest payments on debt in the future. As a result a country will need to pay higher interest rates to attract willing investors in the future.

Chapter 34

Chapter Review

(1) higher; lower; negatively; Phillips; negative

(2) incorrect

(3) inflationary; natural (or full-employment); vertical

(4) smaller; larger; higher; steeper

(5) vertical

(6) indexing

(7) increase; more

Important Terms and Concepts Quiz

1. a
2. g
3. c
4. b
5. g
6. e
7. f
8. i

Basic Exercise

1. purchase; decrease; increase; increase
2. 103
3. The aggregate supply curve will continue to shift up as long as output exceeds the full-employment level of output.
4. a. expansionary; 109
   b. restrictive; 10,167

Self-Tests for Understanding

Test A

1. d
2. d
3. a
4. d
5. c
6. a
7. a
8. c
9. a
10. c
11. d
12. a, c
13. d
14. b
15. d
16. c
17. d
18. a
19. c
20. d

Test B

1. F
2. F
3. T
4. T
5. T
6. F
7. T
8. F
9. F
10. F

Chapter 35

Chapter Review

(1) scale

(2) comparative

(3) A; B; 100,000; wheat

(4) 80,000; 70,000; cars; wheat

(5) tariffs; quotas; subsidies; price; quantity

(6) government

(7) low; do not; can

(8) adjustment

(9) defense; infant

(10) both; comparative

Important Terms and Concept Quiz

1. j
2. d
3. g
4. m
5. i
6. n
7. f
8. a
9. 1
10. h
11. k
12. b
13. e

Basic Exercise

1. Japan; Japan
2. 1.25; 1.5; Canada; Japan; Canada; Japan
3. Calculators: 1,500,000; 3,000,000; 4,500,000
   Backpacks: 1,200,000; 2,000,000; 3,200,000
4. 600,000; 480,000
5. 1,200,000 hours; 600,000 calculators; 400,000 backpacks
6. increase; 80,000
7. Calculators: 900,000; 3,675,000; 4,575,000
   Backpacks: 1,680,000; 1,550,000; 3,230,000

   The output of both calculators and backpacks has increased as compared to the initial situation in Question c.
8. Canadian backpack output would fall to 720,000. Japan would need to reallocate 1,440,000 labor hours. Total calculator output would fall to 4,380,000. This reallocation is not in line with the principle of comparative advantage.
9. There will be no change in total world output. Neither country has a comparative advantage. The opportunity cost of increased calculator or backpack production is the same in both countries.

Self-Tests for Understanding

Test A

1. b
2. d
3. b
4. d
5. a
6. b
7. d
8. d
9. a
10. a
11. c
12. a
13. a
14. b
15. c
16. c
17. d
18. c
19. b, d
20. c

Test B

1. F
2. F
3. T
4. T
5. F
6. F
7. T
8. F
9. F
10. F

Appendix

1. India: $10; 1,000 United States: $40; 800
2. $20; India: 800; 1,200: 400; 0
   United States: 1,000; 600; 0; 400

558

3. India: 15; 900; 1,100; 200; 0

United States: 30; 900; 700; 0; 200

United States; India; United States; India

4. $15

Supplementary Exercises

1. a. Baulmovia: 8,100; Bilandia: 17,150

   b. 12; Baulmovia; Bilandia; 100

   c. Baulmovia: price = 10;

   Bilandia: price = 14.5;

   Trade = 50.

   d. 50

   Tariff revenues accrue to the government. Tariffs do not protect high-cost foreign producers.

2. a. Arcadia

   b. Ricardia

   c. Arcadia should increase the production of computers and export computers to Ricardia which should increase the production of cheese and export cheese to Arcadia. For example

   Change in Production

	Computers	Cheese
Arcadia	+ 4	− 2
Ricardia	− 2	+ 4
World	+ 2	+ 2

   Following the changes in production, both countries will be able to consume outside their PPF. If Arcadia exports up 3 computers for 3,000 pounds of cheese while Ricardia imports 3 computers for 3,000 pounds of cheese, both countries end up with 1 more computer and an additional 1000 pounds of cheese as compared to their pre-trade situation. Try locating these points of production and consumption to illustrate that adjustments of production in line with the law of comparative advantage allows both countries to consume outside their production possibilities frontier.

3. Production of 14.4 million bolts of cloth and 10.8 million barrels of wine allows Cimonoce to choose from the outermost consumption possibilities line. Note that to be on the outermost consumption possibilities line Cimonoce must choose to produce at the point where the slope of the production possibilities frontier equals the ratio of world prices.

Chapter 36

Chapter Review

(1) exchange; appreciated; fewer; depreciated

(2) demand; supply; exports; physical; financial; supply

(3) demand; increase; appreciation; supply; depreciation;

(4) purchasing power parity; depreciate; depreciation; appreciation; appreciating

(5) Bretton

(6) deficit; demand; supply; surplus;

(7) surplus; exchange rate

(8) buy; increasing

(9) deficit; increase; decrease; contraction; reduction

(10) speculators

(11) euro

Important Terms and Concepts Quiz

1. b
2. n
3. a
4. k
5. d
6. c
7. q
8. o
9. h
10. p
11. l
12. i
13. m
14. e
15. j
16. f

Basic Exercises

1. a. $14.40. Sales of French wine would increase. Sales of California wines would decrease. The U.S. balance of payments would show a deficit.

   b. $1.30; appreciation; depreciation

   c. United States (30 percent vs. 20 percent)

   d. deficit

   e. depreciate

2. Col. 1: $28,000,000; £10,000,000

   Col. 2: $28,000,000; £10,769,231

Col. 3: $28,000,000; £11,666,667

If there is no devaluation, you are out only the transactions costs. If the pound is devalued, you stand to make a handsome profit. As the prospect of devaluation increases, there is a greater incentive to sell your pounds before their price falls. Your efforts to sell pounds, along with similar actions by others, will only increase the pressure for devaluation.

On November 18, 1967, the pound was devalued from $2.80 to $2.40.

3. a. left; right; depreciation; deficit
    b. right: no shift; appreciation; surplus
    c. left; no shift; deprecation; deficit
    d. left; right; depreciation; deficit
    e. no shift; right; depreciation; deficit.

Self-Tests for Understanding

Test A

1. b
2. c
3. c
4. b, c
5. a, c
6. c
7. b
8. b, d, f
9. f
10. b
11. c, possibly d
12. d
13. b
14. a
15. b
16. a
17. c, d
18. a, c, d
19. c
20. b

Test B

1. F
2. F
3. T
4. T
5. T
6. T
7. F
8. F
9. T
10. F

Supplementary Exercise

According to data from the IMF, world trade has grown more rapidly than world GDP since 1970, a period dominated by floating exchange rates among the worlds leading industrial countries. Since 1970, world output had grown at an annual rate of 3.7% while world trade has grown at an annual rate of 5.9%.

Chapter 37

Chapter Review

(1) closed; open

(2) decrease; are

(3) less; increase; decrease; decrease; increase; decrease; increase

(4) shift in; down; left

(5) less; downward; more; upward

(6) increase; appreciation

(7) decrease; up; right; appreciation; left; down; offset; lower; increase; offset

(8) appreciation; enhance

(9) decreased; increased

(10) exports; lower

Important Terms and Concepts Quiz

1. d
2. f
3. c
4. a
5. e

Basic Exercises

1. Appreciation: Exports decrease; Imports increase; Net exports decrease; Expenditure Schedule shifts down; Aggregate Demand Curve shifts to the left; Aggregate Supply Curve shifts down; Real GDP decreases; Price level decreases.
    Depreciation: Exports increase; Imports decrease; Net exports increase; Expenditure Schedule shifts up; Aggregate Demand Curve shifts to the right; Aggregate Supply Curve shifts up; Real GDP increases; Price level increases.

560

2. Decrease in *G*: Interest rate decreases; Exchange rate depreciates; GDP and price level up, which work to offset the initial impact of the decrease in *G*.
   Decrease in Taxes: Interest rate increases; Exchange rate appreciates; GDP and price level down, which work to offset the initial impact of the increase in *G*.
   Open Market Sale: Interest rate increases; Exchange rate appreciates; GDP and price level down, which work to enhance the initial impact of the open market sale.
   Open Market Purchase: Interest rate decreases; Exchange rate depreciates; GDP and price level increase, which work to enhance the initial impact of the open market purchase.

3. The impact of monetary policy is enhanced. The impact of fiscal policy is diminished.

Self-Tests for Understanding

Test A

1. c
2. b
3. b
4. a
5. a
6. c
7. c
8. d
9. a
10. b, d
11. b
12. c
13. c
14. b
15. a
16. c
17. b
18. a, c
19. c
20. b, c

Test B

1. F
2. F
3. F
4. T
5. T

6. T
7. F
8. F
9. F
10. F